HBJ ALGEBRA 1

Second Edition

Arthur F. Coxford

Joseph N. Payne

 Harcourt Brace Jovanovich, Publishers

Orlando   San Diego   Chicago   Dallas

ABOUT THE AUTHORS

ARTHUR F. COXFORD
Professor of Mathematics Education
University of Michigan
Ann Arbor, Michigan

JOSEPH N. PAYNE
Professor of Mathematics Education
University of Michigan
Ann Arbor, Michigan

Printed in the United States of America

ISBN 0–15–353640–3

EDITORIAL ADVISORS

Linda Dritsas
Coordinator/Secondary Mathematics
Fresno Unified School District
Fresno, California

Alice Mitchell
Mathematics Supervisor
Campbell Union High School District
San Jose, California

Jo Ann Mosier
Mathematics Teacher
Fairdale High School
Louisville, Kentucky

Marie Sahloff
Chairperson, Department of Mathematics
DeVeaux Junior High School
Toledo, Ohio

David Shaffer
Mathematics Teacher
New Milford High School
New Milford, Connecticut

Richard Wyllie
Chairperson, Department of Mathematics
Downers Grove South High School
Downers Grove, Illinois

The contributions of **Brother Neal Golden, S.C.,** who wrote the *Appendix: Computer Bank*, are gratefully acknowledged.

PICTURE CREDITS

PREFACE

The focus of the HBJ Algebra program is on helping students to become successful within a curriculum that moves in the direction of the *NCTM Standards for School Mathematics*; that is, in a curriculum that emphasizes conceptual understandings, multiple representations and connections, mathematical modeling, and problem solving. The following discussion briefly outlines how this is accomplished in *HBJ Algebra 1, Second Edition*.

PEDAGOGY

Applications are used, where appropriate, to motivate content and to connect mathematical concepts in the lesson to the real world. Problem-solving strategies, such as looking for and using patterns and inductive reasoning, are used to develop generalizations.

READING ALGEBRA

Reading and translating algebra is an ongoing process in the HBJ Algebra program. The **Check Your Understanding** exercises, in particular, address the issues of reading and comprehension.

CONTENT CONNECTIONS

Algebra content is connected on a lesson-by-lesson basis to related topics within the text. Content is also connected to topics in geometry, probability, statistics, and trigonometry throughout the HBJ Algebra program. When appropriate, mathematical topics are connected to other academic subject areas as well as applied fields.

PROBLEM SOLVING

In the HBJ Algebra program, problem-solving strategies are (1) used in lessons to develop concepts, (2) presented as techniques for solving problems, and (3) applied to real-world situations. Provision for maintaining problem-solving strategies is included in the **Maintain** exercises for each lesson, in the **Cumulative Maintenance**, and in the **Non-Routine Problems**.

CLASSWORK/ HOMEWORK EXERCISES

Objectives are stated at the beginning of the exercise set for each lesson in order to inform students of the major goals of the lesson.

Check Your Understanding exercises provide an informal assessment of the student's comprehension of the main concepts and vocabulary of the lesson.

Practice and Apply exercises are carefully sequenced to provide abundant practice with the skills and concepts presented in the lesson.

Maintain exercises review prior-taught skills, concepts, and problem-solving strategies.

Connect and Extend exercises relate the lesson to equivalent representations of the content and apply learned procedures to new problem-solving situations.

Non-Routine Problems allow students to apply their problem-solving skills in unfamiliar and varied situations.

REVIEW CAPSULES	**Review Capsule** exercises review *only* those prior-taught skills and concepts that will be needed in the lesson that immediately follows.
REVIEW AND TESTING	Provision for review and test preparation are provided in the **Maintain** exercises, **Review Capsules**, in-chapter **Review, Chapter Review, Chapter Summary, Chapter Test**, and **Cumulative Maintenance**.
	In addition, the **Focus on College Entrance Tests** are designed to prepare students for the type of problem-solving that appears on college entrance tests.
CALCULATOR TECHNOLOGY	The use of the scientific calculator is integrated within the appropriate lessons. A graphing-calculator component, *Investigating Algebra with the Graphing Calculator*, is described in the Teacher's Edition.
COMPUTER TECHNOLOGY	Computer-related exercises (identified by a computer logo) are included in the Classwork/Homework exercises where appropriate. Each set of these exercises is referenced to the related program that can be found in Part I of the *Computer Bank, Computer Applications*. Additional exercises are also provided in the *Computer Bank*.
	Part II of the *Computer Bank, Investigating Algebra with the Computer*, contains interactive computer activities. The software required for these activities is available for IBM®PC, IBM compatibles, and Apple® (II +, IIe, IIc, or GS) microcomputers.
	Two other software components, the *Computer Test Generator* and the *Expert Algebra Tutor*, are described in the *Teacher's Edition*.
CRITICAL THINKING QUESTIONS	These questions are designed to provoke classroom discussion about mathematical concepts with an emphasis on developing high-order thinking skills. Questions are given in the *Teacher's Edition*.
CRITICAL THINKING EXERCISES	These exercises which address high-order thinking skills are identified as such in the *Teacher's Edition*.

CONTENTS

Chapter **4**: MORE ON SOLVING EQUATIONS 144

Chapter **5**: RELATIONS AND FUNCTIONS 174

Chapter 13: QUADRATIC FUNCTIONS AND EQUATIONS 528

Chapter 14: OTHER APPLICATIONS OF ALGEBRA 578

COMPUTER BANK

Part 1: COMPUTER APPLICATIONS 610

1 Uses of Algebra

The Statue of Liberty is a **symbol** of freedom throughout the world. In this chapter, you will be introduced to symbols that are used to convey ideas in algebra.

What do the symbols shown on this page represent?

1-1   Variables and Expressions

You can use a pattern to show the cost of any number of CD's (compact disks) when you know the cost of one CD.

Number	Total Cost in Dollars
1	10.50×1, or 10.50
2	10.50×2, or 21.00
3	10.50×3, or 31.50
4	10.50×4, or 42.00
$\vdots$	$\vdots$
n	$10.50 \times n$

↑—Variable

↑ Pattern in general terms

The expression that shows the pattern

$$10.50 \times n$$

is an **algebraic expression.** The letter n is a **variable** that represents the number of CD's bought. Algebraic expressions contain <u>at least</u> one variable. They may also contain numbers and operation symbols. Any letter may be used as a variable.

Multiplication in an algebraic expression can be written in other ways.

$10.50 \cdot n$ ↑—Raised dot

$10.50(n)$ ↑ Parentheses

$10.50n$ ↑ Write the number and the variable next to each other.

Learning and understanding the language and vocabulary of algebra is an essential skill for both computation and problem solving. The table below will help you both to read and understand the meaning of some common algebraic expressions.

Algebraic Expression	Meaning
$10m$ Read: "Ten m."	Ten **times** m The **product** of 10 and m Ten **multiplied** by m
$\dfrac{4}{x}$ Read: "Four divided by x."	The **quotient** of 4 and x The **ratio** of 4 and x

Algebraic Expression	Meaning
$r + t$ Read: "r plus t."	t **added** to r The **sum** of r and t r **increased by** t The **total** of r and t
$q - s$ Read: "q minus s."	s **subtracted from** q q **less** s q **decreased by** s

You can write an algebraic expression for a word description.

EXAMPLE 1 Write an algebraic expression for each word description.

Word Description	Algebraic Expression
a. The cost, c, **increased by** the tax, $1.18	$c + 1.18$
b. The cost in cents of s stamps at **25¢ each**	$25 \cdot s$, or $25s$
c. The total weekly earnings, w, **divided by** 37, the number of hours worked	$w \div 37$, or $\frac{w}{37}$

NUMERICAL EXPRESSIONS

Numerical expressions do not contain a variable. Here are some examples of numerical expressions.

$$16 - (12 \div 3) \qquad (3 \cdot 8) - 6 \qquad \frac{18 + 51}{3}$$

To find the value of (**evaluate**) a numerical expression containing parentheses, perform the operations inside parentheses first.

Fraction bars are like parentheses. They indicate that the numerator and denominator of a fraction are each to be treated separately.

EXAMPLE 2 Evaluate each numerical expression.

a. $(3 \cdot 8) - 6 = 24 - 6$
$\qquad\qquad\quad = 18$

b. $16 - (12 \div 3) = 16 - 4$
$\qquad\qquad\qquad\quad = 12$

c. $\frac{18 + 51}{3} = \frac{69}{3}$
$\qquad\quad = 23$

d. $\frac{26 - 11}{5} + 8 = \frac{15}{5} + 8$
$\qquad\qquad\quad = 3 + 8$
$\qquad\qquad\quad = 11$

Objectives: To write algebraic expressions for word descriptions
To evaluate numerical expressions containing parentheses

██████████ **CHECK YOUR UNDERSTANDING**

Name the variable or variables in each expression. If an expression has no variables, write **N**.

1. $6t - 25$

2. $r + q$

3. $5 - s + (s + 1)$

4. $\dfrac{18 + 50}{26}$

5. Write $62p$ in two other ways.

6. Write three word expressions for $t - r$.

7. Which of these is a numerical expression, $t(5 - a)$ or $19 - (6 + 2)$? Why?

8. Write an algebraic expression for the number of hours in d days.

██████████ **PRACTICE AND APPLY**

For Exercises 9–11, use the variable n to express the pattern in general form.

9.
$1 \times 0 = 0$
$2 \times 0 = 0$
$3 \times 0 = 0$
$4 \times 0 = 0$
$\underline{\ ?\ } \times 0 = 0$

10.
$5 \cdot 1 = 5$
$6 \cdot 1 = 6$
$7 \cdot 1 = 7$
$8 \cdot 1 = 8$
$\underline{\ ?\ } \cdot 1 = \underline{\ ?\ }$

11.
$12 \div 1 = 12$
$13 \div 1 = 13$
$14 \div 1 = 14$
$15 \div 1 = 15$
$\underline{\ ?\ } \div 1 = \underline{\ ?\ }$

With each algebraic expression in Exercises 12-17, match the letter of the corresponding phrase in a through l that gives its meaning. More than one answer may be possible.

12. $4n$

13. $\dfrac{n}{4}$

14. $n - 4$

15. $n + 4$

16. $4 - n$

17. $\dfrac{4}{n}$

a. n divided by 4	**b.** n minus 4
c. 4 subtracted from n	**d.** The ratio of n and 4
e. n subtracted from 4	**f.** The product of 4 and n
g. n multiplied by 4	**h.** n decreased by 4
i. 4 divided by n	**j.** 4 more than n
k. 4 added to n	**l.** The sum of 4 and n

Write two word expressions for each algebraic expression.

18. $q - 5$

19. $5 + q$

20. $b - a$

21. $\dfrac{r}{s}$

22. $5q$

23. $n \div t$

24. $16s$

25. $\dfrac{q}{5}$

26. rs

27. $t + n$

Write an algebraic expression for each word description.

28. The sum of the restaurant bill, b, and the tip, t

29. The net income, i, added to the total deductions, d

30. The amount of tax withheld, w, subtracted from the total tax owed, t

31. The total number of days absent, a, subtracted from 180

32. The cost of 2 tickets at d dollars per ticket

33. The cost of renting a boat for h hours at \$4.50 per hour

34. The number of books you can buy for \$25 if each book costs d dollars

35. The number of times at bat, t, divided by 24, the number of hits

Evaluate each numerical expression.

36. $(12 - 8) + 3$

37. $15 + (18 - 7)$

38. $40 - (1 + 10)$

39. $(16 + 23) \div 3$

40. $4 + (64 \div 4)$

41. $21 - (80 \div 16)$

42. $18 - (0 \cdot 150)$

43. $0 \cdot (360 \div 12)$

44. $(7 \cdot 15) + (3 \cdot 15)$

45. $36 - (12 \cdot \frac{1}{3}) - 1$

46. $24 - (4 \div \frac{1}{2})$

47. $28 + (0 \div 4) - (10 \div 2)$

48. $\dfrac{(4 \cdot 2) + (5 \cdot 2)}{6}$

49. $\dfrac{(16 \div 2) - (14 \div 7)}{2}$

50. $\dfrac{(16 + 2) + (13 - 5) - (7 + 9)}{(12 \div 3) + (9 - 6) + (5 - 2)}$

■■■■■■■ MAINTAIN

Write in lowest terms.

51. $\dfrac{8}{12}$

52. $\dfrac{9}{36}$

53. $\dfrac{18}{54}$

54. $\dfrac{45}{60}$

55. $\dfrac{12}{18}$

Multiply. Write your answers in lowest terms.

56. $\frac{1}{2} \times \frac{1}{3}$

57. $\frac{1}{4} \times \frac{4}{5}$

58. $\frac{2}{3} \times \frac{2}{5}$

59. $\frac{3}{8} \times 7$

60. $\frac{5}{6} \times 3\frac{1}{5}$

■■■■■■■ CONNECT AND EXTEND

Copy each table. Then complete the pattern.

61.

4	5	6	7
n	$n + 1$	$n + ?$	?

62.

54	53	52	51
t	$t - 1$	$t - ?$	?

63.

2	4	6	8
r	$2r$	?	?

64.

13	15	17	19
q	$q + ?$	?	?

■■■■■■■ NON-ROUTINE PROBLEM

65. Janine had d dollars on Monday. She spent half of this on Tuesday, half of what was left on Wednesday, and half of what was left on Thursday. How much did she spend on Thursday? (HINT: First try a specific amount for Monday, such as \$8.00.)

4　*Chapter 1*

1-2 Order of Operations

Homeroom 203 is planning a four-day ski trip. Marsha and Bill wrote this expression to represent round-trip transportation costs and lodging expenses.

$$2 \cdot \$18 + 4 \cdot \$35$$

Here is how Bill and Marsha evaluated the expression.

Bill	**Marsha**
$2 \cdot 18 + 4 \cdot 35$	$2 \cdot 18 + 4 \cdot 35$
$36 + 4 \cdot 35$	$36 + 4 \cdot 35$
$40 \cdot 35$	$36 + 140$
$\$1400$ ⟵ **Incorrect**	$\$176$ ⟵ **Correct**

Only one answer can be correct. Mathematicians have agreed to follow the rules for order of operations so that expressions such as $2 \cdot \$18 + 4 \cdot \$35$ will have a **unique** (exactly one) value.

RULES

> ## Order of Operations
>
> **1** Perform operations within parentheses, or in the numerators and denominators of fractions.
>
> **2** Do all multiplications and divisions in order from left to right.
>
> **3** Do all additions and subtractions in order from left to right.

READING/ TRANSLATION

Expression	Meaning	Value
$4 \cdot 7 + 9$	Multiply 4 and 7. Then add 9.	$4 \cdot 7 + 9 = 28 + 9$ $= 37$
$18 - 2 \cdot 5$	Multiply 2 and 5. Then subtract this from 18.	$18 - 2 \cdot 5 = 18 - 10$ $= 8$
$16 + 10 \div 2$	Divide 10 by 2. Then add 16.	$16 + 10 \div 2 = 16 + 5$ $= 21$
$3(5 + 6)$	Add 5 and 6. Then multiply by 3.	$3(5 + 6) = 3 \cdot 11$ $= 33$
$3 \cdot \dfrac{7 - 5}{6 \div 2}$	Subtract 5 from 7. Divide 6 by 2. Multiply by 3.	$3 \cdot \dfrac{7 - 5}{6 \div 2} = 3 \cdot \dfrac{2}{3}$ $= 2$

Parentheses, ( ), and brackets, [ ], are **grouping symbols.** A fraction bar is also a grouping symbol. When an expression contains more than one grouping symbol, perform the operations within the <u>innermost</u> grouping symbols first. Then work towards the outermost grouping symbols. In other words, work from the inside out.

EXAMPLE 1 Evaluate $3 + [5 + 2(8 \div 4)]$.

Solution: $3 + [5 + 2(8 \div 4)] = 3 + [5 + 2(2)]$ ◄——— **Next, evaluate 2(2)**

$$= 3 + [5 + 4]$$
$$= 3 + 9 = \mathbf{12}$$

You follow the same rules to evaluate an algebraic expression for a specific value of the variable.

EXAMPLE 2 Evaluate $\dfrac{x - y}{4}$ for $x = 19$ and $y = 10$.

Solution: Replace x with 19 and y with 10.

$$\frac{x - y}{4} = \frac{19 - 10}{4}$$
$$= \frac{9}{4}, \text{ or } \mathbf{2\tfrac{1}{4}}$$

When the same variable appears more than once in an expression, it must be replaced by the *same number each time.*

CALCULATOR

Scientific calculators follow the rules for order of operations. When expressions have no parentheses, enter the numbers and operations in order from left to right.

12 $\boxed{-}$ 6 $\boxed{\times}$ 2 $\boxed{=}$ $\boxed{\qquad\qquad 0.}$

8 $\boxed{+}$ 15 $\boxed{\div}$ 3 $\boxed{=}$ $\boxed{\qquad\qquad 13.}$

Most scientific calculators have parentheses keys, $\boxed{(}$ and $\boxed{)}$. Enter the parentheses or brackets where they appear in the problem. Remember, however, to press the $\boxed{\times}$ key to indicate "hidden" multiplication, such as $3 \times (18 - 6)$ in $96 - 3(18 - 6)$.

96 $\boxed{-}$ 3 $\boxed{\times}$ $\boxed{(}$ 18 $\boxed{-}$ 6 $\boxed{)}$ $\boxed{=}$ $\boxed{\qquad\qquad 60.}$

Objective: To use the rules for order of operations to evaluate numerical and algebraic expressions

▀▀▀▀▀▀▀ **CHECK YOUR UNDERSTANDING**

1. Give three examples of grouping symbols.

2. Why is it necessary to have rules for order of operations?

3. When an expression contains more than one grouping symbol, which operations are performed first?

4. Which is greater, $75 - 5 \cdot 12 - 7$ or $75 - 5(12 - 7)$? How much greater is it?

For Exercises 5–10, name the operation that should be performed first.

5. $9 + 8 - 5$

6. $18 - 3 + 5$

7. $6 \cdot 8 \div 2$

8. $9 + 11 \div 4$

9. $3 \cdot 8 - 4 \div 2$

10. $15 - (2 \div 2)$

▀▀▀▀▀▀▀ **PRACTICE AND APPLY**

Evaluate. Follow the rules for order of operations and for the use of grouping symbols. Express fractions in lowest terms.

11. $7 \cdot 9 + 6$

12. $8 + 3 \cdot 7$

13. $6 \cdot (3 + 11)$

14. $(6 + 3) \cdot 3$

15. $4 + (2 \cdot 7)$

16. $0 + 7\frac{1}{2} \cdot 0$

17. $8 \cdot 7 + 9 \div 9$

18. $89 \cdot (2 + 6)$

19. $5 \cdot 7 - 12$

20. $15 - 6 \div 2$

21. $5(2 \cdot 10)$

22. $(5 \cdot 2)10$

23. $6 \cdot 15 \cdot 4$

24. $30 - 7 \cdot 0$

25. $7(1 + 8) \div 9$

26. $9 + \dfrac{15 - 14}{3}$

27. $21 - \dfrac{14}{12 - 5}$

28. $20 \cdot 9 + \dfrac{8 - 3}{5}$

29. $540 \div 2 \cdot 6 + \dfrac{6 - 2 \cdot 3}{9}$

30. $1 - \dfrac{4}{2 \cdot 7 + 4}$

31. $\dfrac{13 - 2 \cdot 6}{5 + 2 \cdot 3}$

32. $3 + \dfrac{4(3 - 1)}{8}$

33. $\dfrac{5}{8} + \dfrac{6}{2(7 + 1)}$

34. $\dfrac{2(7 - 3)}{3(4 + 5)}$

35. $2[3 + 2 \cdot (10 - 3)]$

36. $3[15 - (5 + 3)]$

37. $8[29 - (14 - 5)]$

38. $4[24 \div (6 + 2)]$

39. $4[(24 \div 6) + 2]$

40. $2[(11 \cdot 8) \div 4]$

41. $2[11 \cdot (8 \div 4)]$

42. $8 \div [16 - 2(3 + 4)]$

43. $8 \div [(16 - 2)3 + 4]$

For Exercises 44–59, evaluate for the given values of the variables.

44. $50 + 2w$, for $w = 20$

45. $100 - 5q$, for $q = 8$

46. $2(a + b)$, for $a = 4$ and $b = 5$

47. $2p + 2s$, for $p = 4$ and $s = 5$

48. $\dfrac{8x}{x - y}$, for $x = 10$ and $y = 6$

49. $\dfrac{3r}{2s}$, for $r = 10$ and $s = 15$

50. $\frac{3}{4}c + \frac{5}{7}d$, for $c = 12$ and $d = 14$

51. $\frac{5}{6}m - \frac{2}{9}r$, for $m = 12$ and $r = 9$

52. $2.3g + 0.7f$, for $g = 4$ and $f = 8$

53. $5r - 9.2s$, for $r = 2.8$ and $s = 0.6$

54. $2m + m$, for $m = 8$

55. $5z + 6n - 2z$, for $z = 5$ and $n = 15$

56. $3t + 1.5t$, for $t = 10$

57. $(3 + 1.5)t$, for $t = 100$

58. $5s - 4s$, for $s = 1.9$

59. $(5 - 4)s$, for $s = 1.9$

Evaluate for the given values of the variables.

60. $\frac{2(t - 1)}{t}$, for $t = 11$

61. $\frac{a + 2b}{5}$, for $a = 10$ and $b = 2$

62. $\frac{m + m + m}{3m}$, for $m = 0.1$

63. $\frac{m \cdot m \cdot m}{m}$, for $m = 1.5$

Insert parentheses to make each statement true.

64. $1 + 9 \cdot 2 + 7 = 90$

65. $3 + 3 + 3 \cdot 3 = 21$

66. $56 \div 6 - 2 \cdot 1 = 14$

67. $2 \cdot 12 \div 2 + 6 = 3$

■■■■■■■ **MAINTAIN**

68. Give two other ways of writing $5(r + 1)$. (*Pages 1–4*)

69. Write three different word expressions for $27 \div b$. (*Pages 1–4*)

Write an algebraic expression for each word description. (*Pages 1–4*)

70. The cost of t tickets at $5.50 per ticket

71. Five inches more than Bob's height, h

72. John's age, a, decreased by 10

73. The price of the sofa, s, decreased by $55

■■■■■■■ **CONNECT AND EXTEND**

Write an algebraic expression to represent each word description.

74. The cost of a service call for a plumber who charges a base fee of $25 plus $35 per hour for t hours

75. The amount in a savings account if the balance in the account is $475 and $15 is withdrawn per week for w weeks

76. The total cost of p pounds of potatoes at 69¢ per pound and r pounds of chicken at 98¢ per pound

77. The amount in a checking account after z weeks if the present balance is $355 and $35 is added per week

78. If $p - q = 31$, what is the value of $p - q - 10$?

79. If $a + b = 27$, what is the value of $a + b + 19$?

80. If $r - s + 51 = 100$, what is the value of $r - s$?

81. If $t + u - 32 = 46$, what is the value of $t + u$?

1-3 Exponents and Formulas

EXPONENTS

The expression $3^4 = 81$ in the box at the right shows that 81 is the **fourth power of 3.** The raised 4 is called an **exponent.**

The 3 in 3^4 is called the **base.** The exponent indicates how many times the base 3 is used as a factor.

$$\underset{\text{Base}}{\nwarrow}\; 3^{\overset{\text{Exponent}}{4}} = 81 \;\longleftarrow \text{Power}$$

The fourth power of 3 is 81.

READING/ TRANSLATION

Expression	Read	Meaning
4^3	4 cubed	$4 \cdot 4 \cdot 4$, or **64**
5^2	5 squared	$5 \cdot 5$, or **25**
$(\frac{1}{6})^4$	The fourth power of $\frac{1}{6}$	$\frac{1}{6} \cdot \frac{1}{6} \cdot \frac{1}{6} \cdot \frac{1}{6}$, or $\frac{1}{1296}$
a^1	The first power of a	**a**
y^5	The fifth power of y	$y \cdot y \cdot y \cdot y \cdot y$

NOTE: When there are no parentheses, an exponent refers to the base directly to its left. Thus,

$$3c^2 \text{ means } 3 \cdot c \cdot c \quad \text{ and } \quad (3c)^2 \text{ means } 3c \cdot 3c, \text{ or } 9c^2.$$

EXAMPLE 1 Evaluate each expression for $b = 4$.

Solution:

a. $2b^3 = 2 \cdot b \cdot b \cdot b$
$= 2 \cdot \underline{4 \cdot 4 \cdot 4}$
$= 2 \cdot \quad 64$
$= \mathbf{128}$

b. $(2b)^3 = (2b) \cdot (2b) \cdot (2b)$
$= \underline{2 \cdot 4} \cdot \underline{2 \cdot 4} \cdot \underline{2 \cdot 4}$
$= \quad 8 \quad \cdot \quad 8 \quad \cdot \quad 8$
$= \mathbf{512}$

When expressions contain exponents, another step is needed in the order of operations.

RULES

> **Summary: Order of Operations**
> 1. Perform operations within parentheses or grouping symbols.
> 2. Evaluate powers.
> 3. Do multiplications and divisions in order from left to right.
> 4. Do additions and subtractions in order from left to right.

EXAMPLE 2 Evaluate each expression.

a. $9 + 4 \cdot 3^3 = \underline{\ ?\ }$

$$9 + 4 \cdot 3^3 = 9 + 4 \cdot 3 \cdot 3 \cdot 3$$
$$= 9 + 4 \cdot 27 \leftarrow \textbf{Rule 2}$$
$$= 9 + 108 \leftarrow \textbf{Rule 3}$$
$$= 117 \leftarrow \textbf{Rule 4}$$

b. $\frac{1}{5}(8a - b)^2$ for $a = 8$ and $b = 4$

$$\frac{1}{5}(8a - b)^2 = \frac{1}{5}(8 \cdot 3 - 4)^2$$
$$= \frac{1}{5}(24 - 4)^2 \leftarrow \textbf{Rule 1}$$
$$= \frac{1}{5}(20)^2$$
$$= \frac{1}{5}(400) \leftarrow \textbf{Rule 2}$$
$$= 80 \leftarrow \textbf{Rule 3}$$

FORMULAS

Exponents are used in many formulas, especially in those related to area and volume. Formulas use variables to show how quantities are related.

Example 3 uses a formula to find the area enclosed by two squares. A **square** has four equal sides and four right angles.

EXAMPLE 3 Use the formula $A = s^2 - t^2$ to find the total area of the walk surrounding a square garden when $s = 14$ feet and $t = 10$ feet.

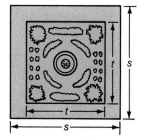

Solution:
$$A = s^2 - t^2$$
$$A = 14^2 - 10^2 \longleftarrow \textbf{Evaluate powers.}$$
$$A = 196 - 100 \longleftarrow \textbf{Now subtract.}$$
$$A = 96$$

The area of the walk is **96 ft²**. (Read: 96 square feet)

NOTE: Area is given in square units. Thus, in Example 3, the area of the garden is

$$10 \text{ ft} \times 10 \text{ ft} = (10 \times 10)\text{ft}^2, \text{ or } 100 \text{ ft}^2.$$

CALCULATOR

Scientific calculators have a y^x or an x^y key that can be used to evaluate powers. For example, to evaluate 9^5, press

$$9 \ \boxed{y^x} \ 5 \ \boxed{=} \qquad \boxed{59049.}$$

On some calculators, the key sequence may be different. Check your calculator manual.

Objective: To evaluate expressions involving formulas

CHECK YOUR UNDERSTANDING

1. Write in words: 6^4

2. In the expression 25^3, what number is the base?

3. In the expression $2^4 = 16$, what is the power?

4. Which has the same meaning as $(3c)^2$, $3 \cdot 3 \cdot c \cdot c$ or $3 \cdot c \cdot c$?

5. Which has the same meaning as $5r^3$, $5 \cdot 5 \cdot 5 \cdot r \cdot r \cdot r$ or $5 \cdot r \cdot r \cdot r$?

6. To evaluate $12 \div 3 + 5 \cdot 2^4$, which operation is performed first?

Write without exponents.

7. 10^2 8. t^4 9. $2a^5$ 10. $(5n)^3$ 11. $(\frac{4}{5})^2$

Write each of the following as an expression using exponents.

12. $4 \cdot 4 \cdot 4$ 13. $\frac{1}{8} \cdot \frac{1}{8} \cdot \frac{1}{8} \cdot \frac{1}{8}$ 14. $s \cdot s \cdot s$ 15. $r \cdot r - s$ 16. $5 + t \cdot t \cdot t$

PRACTICE AND APPLY

Complete.

17. $2^5 = ?$ 18. $3^? = 81$ 19. $?^8 = 1$ 20. $6^3 = ?$

21. $(1.5)^2 = ?$ 22. $(\frac{3}{5})^3 = ?$ 23. $?^2 = 1.21$ 24. $(\frac{2}{3})^? = \frac{16}{81}$

25. $(?)^3 = \frac{27}{125}$ 26. $(0.1)^? = 0.001$ 27. $1^{25} = ?$ 28. $?^5 = 100,000$

Evaluate each expression.

29. $3 + 7^2$ 30. $6(9^2 - 4^3)$ 31. $1^5 + 6^3 - 5^2$

32. $196 \div (7 - 5)^2$ 33. $4 \cdot 7 - 3^2$ 34. $4 \cdot 2^3 - 20$

35. $12(2)^2 \div 24 + 3^2$ 36. $144 - 8 \div 2^3$ 37. $9 \cdot (4)^2 \div 2^2 \cdot 3$

38. $3n^2$ for $n = 5$ 39. $(3n)^2$ for $n = 5$ 40. $3t^3$ for $t = 2$

41. $(3t)^3$ for $t = 2$ 42. $5q^4 - 6$ for $q = 3$ 43. $(5q)^2 - 6$ for $q = 3$

Evaluate for $t = 2$ and $s = 5$.

44. $(t + s)^2$ 45. $(s - t)^3$ 46. $\left(\frac{s}{t}\right)^3$ 47. $\frac{12}{s^2}$

48. $\frac{6^2}{s - t}$ 49. $\frac{12}{t^2}$ 50. $\frac{s - t}{s^3}$ 51. $\frac{12}{4s^2}$

The formula for the area of a square is $A = s^2$. Find A for each value of s.

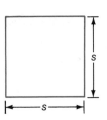

52. 25 in   **53.** 1.3 cm   **54.** $2\frac{1}{2}$ ft   **55.** 7.6 cm

A *cube* is a solid having six equal sides, or faces. The formula for the *surface area* of a cube (sum of the areas of the six sides) is $T = 6s^2$. Find T for each value of s.

56. 3 m   **57.** $\frac{1}{3}$ ft   **58.** $2\frac{1}{2}$ ft   **59.** 0.8 cm

A *trapezoid* has four sides, only two of which are parallel. The formula for the area of a trapezoid is $A = \frac{1}{2}h\,(a + b)$. Find A for each value of a, b and h.

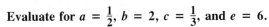

60. $h = 10$ cm, $a = 15$ cm, $b = 8$ cm
61. $h = 2$ cm, $a = 12$ cm, $b = 5$ cm
62. $h = 2$ ft, $a = \frac{3}{4}$ ft, $b = \frac{1}{4}$ ft
63. $h = 4$ in, $b = \frac{1}{4}$ in, $a = \frac{1}{2}$

Evaluate for $a = \frac{1}{2}$, $b = 2$, $c = \frac{1}{3}$, and $e = 6$.

64. $(5b)^2$ **65.** $5b^2$ **66.** $(3a)^2$ **67.** $3e^2$ **68.** a^3

For each of Exercises 69-78:
a. Evaluate each expression for $t = \frac{1}{2}$, $t = 0.25$, and $t = 1$.
b. For which value of t does the expression have the smallest value?

69. t **70.** $2(t + 3)$ **71.** $2 - t$ **72.** $t - t^2$ **73.** $t \div 4$

74. t^3 **75.** $1 \div t$ **76.** $t \div 2$ **77.** $t^3 \div t$ **78.** $\dfrac{1 - t}{5}$

■■■■■ **MAINTAIN**

Solve. (*Pages 5-8*)

79. Does $32 - 16 \div 4$ equal 4 or 28? Explain.

80. Does $\dfrac{48 \div 6 + 2}{9 - 7}$ equal 3 or 5? Explain.

81. Evaluate $\dfrac{5(t + 2)}{t}$ for $t = 9$.

82. Evaluate $\dfrac{7m}{7m}$ for $m = 1.5$.

83. Evaluate $16t \div (4s) + 3 \cdot s \cdot t$ for $t = 9$ and $s = 6$.

84. Evaluate $b \div 3 + a^2$ for $a = 7$ and $b = 12$.

Evaluate *(Pages 1-4)*

85. $(9 - 4) + 7$

86. $(56 - 21) \div 7$

87. $(2 + 8) \cdot 8$

88. $(12 \cdot 4) - (30 \div 6)$

89. $0 \cdot (42 \div 14)$

90. $(19 - 7) \cdot (72 \div 9)$

■■■■■■■ **CONNECT AND EXTEND**

91. If $n(n + 1) = 25$, what is the value of $n(n + 1) - 1$?

92. If $n(n - 1) = 61$, what is the value of $n(n - 1) + 10$?

93. If $a + b = 12$, what is the value of $(a + b)^2$?

94. If $t - r = 29$, what is the value of $(t - r)^2 - 5$?

95. If $(x - y)^2 = 25$, what is the value of $(x - y)^2 + 80$?

96. If $(p + q)^2 = 123$, what is the value of $2(p + q)^2 - 100$?

At a yearly inflation rate of 3.5%, the cost, C of a \$1.00-hamburger in n years is $C = (1.035)^n$. Use a calculator to find the cost of a hamburger for each number of years. Round each answer to the nearest cent.

97. 2 years

98. 5 years

99. 10 years

100. 20 years

■■■■■■■ **NON-ROUTINE PROBLEM**

101. Roberto needs to draw a line that is six inches long, but he does not have a ruler. He does have some sheets of notebook paper that are each $8\frac{1}{2}$ inches wide and 11 inches long. Describe how Roberto can use the notebook paper to measure six inches.

—————— **REVIEW CAPSULE FOR SECTION 1-4** ——————

Write a fraction for each mixed number.

1. $1\frac{1}{2}$

2. $3\frac{1}{5}$

3. $2\frac{1}{2}$

4. $1\frac{2}{3}$

5. $3\frac{3}{4}$

6. $4\frac{5}{6}$

Multiply. Express answers in lowest terms.

7. $6 \times \frac{2}{3}$

8. $\frac{1}{4} \times 8$

9. $\frac{2}{3} \times \frac{3}{4}$

10. $\frac{5}{6} \times \frac{3}{5}$

11. $5 \times 1\frac{2}{5}$

12. $2\frac{1}{4} \times 6$

13. $2\frac{1}{2} \times 1\frac{1}{2}$

14. $5\frac{1}{4} \times 1\frac{1}{7}$

1-4 Patterns and Formulas

WRITING FORMULAS

An essential problem-solving skill in the study of algebra is the ability both to **write formulas** and to **use formulas** to solve problems.

EXAMPLE 1 These data were recorded for a 1927 automobile during an antique auto race.

Problem: **a.** Write a formula that relates d and t.

t: time in hours	0	1	2	3	4
d: distance in miles	0	12	24	36	48

Solution: Look for a pattern.
Pattern: Each value for d is 12 times the value for t.
Formula: $d = 12 \cdot t$, or $d = 12t$.

Problem: **b.** Use $d = 12t$ to find how far the antique car travels in 10.5 hours.

Solution: $d = 12t$ ◄——— **Replace t with 10.5.**

$d = 12(10.5)$

$d = 126$ The car would travel **126** miles.

USING FORMULAS

A **formula** uses variables to state a relationship among numbers. The value of one variable is found by substituting values for the other variables. Then you evaluate the resulting numerical expression.

EXAMPLE 2 In an experiment, a penny was dropped from the roof of a high-rise apartment building. It took $2\frac{1}{2}$ seconds to reach the ground. Use the formula $d = 16t^2$, where d represents distance in feet and t represents the time in seconds, to find the height of the apartment building.

Solution: $d = 16t^2$ ◄——— **Replace t with $\frac{5}{2}$.**

$d = 16(\frac{5}{2})^2$

$d = 100$ The height of the building is **100** feet.

Objectives: To express patterns by writing a formula
To evaluate formulas

▬▬▬ CHECK YOUR UNDERSTANDING

For Exercises 1-4:
a. Tell what the variables represent.
b. Write the meaning of the formula in words.

1. Perimeter of a rectangle:
$P = 2l + 2w$

2. Area of a triangle:
$A = \frac{1}{2}bh$

3. Circumference of a circle: $C = 2\pi r$

4. Area of a parallelogram: $A = bh$

▬▬▬ PRACTICE AND APPLY

Choose the formula that corresponds to the pattern in the table.
Choose a, b, c, or d.

5.

Total score: T	95	85	75	65
Quiz score: q	90	80	70	60

a. $T = q - 5$ **b.** $T = 5q$
c. $T = q + 5$ **d.** $q = T + 5$

6.

Wages: w	$7.50	$15.00	$22.50
Hours: h	1	2	3

a. $w = 7.50h$ **b.** $w + 7.50 = h$
c. $w = \dfrac{7.50}{h}$ **d.** $w = \dfrac{h}{7.50}$

7. The formula $d = 4.9t^2$ relates the distance, d, in meters to the number of seconds, t that an object falls. Use the formula to find how many meters Luke's penny falls in 1.5 seconds.

8. The formula $C = 500 + n$ gives the cost C in cents of printing n tickets for a football game. How much will it cost <u>in dollars</u> to print 1000 tickets?

For Exercises 9-14:
a. Copy and complete each table.
b. Complete the formula that shows the relationship between the variables in the table.

9. Montly Apartment Rent

Months, m	1	2	3	4	5
Rent, R,	$450	$900	$1350	_?_	_?_

Formula: $R = \underline{\ ?\ } \cdot m$, or $R = \underline{\ ?\ }$

10. Average Test Scores

Total score, T	320	340	380	400	500
Average score, a	64	68	76	_?_	_?_

Formula: $a = T \div \underline{\ ?\ }$

Uses of Algebra **15**

11. Number of Bricks Needed for a Wall

Area in square feet: A	40	80	100	400	600
Number: n	280	560	700	?	?

Formula: $n =$ _?_

12. Cost of First-Class Mail

Ounces: n	1	2	3	4	5
Cost in dollars: C	0.25	0.45	0.65	0.85	?

Formula: $C = 0.25 +$ _?_ $\cdot (n - 1)$

13. Ages of Two Brothers

Tom's age: t	7	9	13	19	27
Fred's age: a	16	18	22	?	?

Formula: $a =$ _?_

14. Business Profits in Dollars

Income: i	800	1000	2250	4000	4500
Expenses: a	150	350	450	775	?
Profit: P	650	650	1800	?	2300

Formula: $P =$ _?_

You can use the formula below to estimate the average weight, *w*, of an adult. In this formula, the weight, *w*, is given in pounds and the height *h*, is given in inches.

$$w = 5.5h - 220$$

15. What is the average weight of a person 68 inches tall?

16. What is the average weight of a person 5 feet 6 inches tall?

17. How much above or below average weight is a person who is 6 feet tall and weighs 185 pounds?

18. How much above or below average weight is a person who is 5 feet 7 inches tall and weighs 140 pounds?

The volume, *V*, of a refrigerator car can be found by using the formula, $V = lwh$, where *l*, *w*, and *h* are the length, width, and height of the car. Volume is measured in cubic units, such as cubic feet (ft³), cubic meters (m³), and so on.

19. Find the volume of a refrigerator car when $l = 60$ feet, $w = 10\frac{1}{2}$ feet, and $h = 12$ feet.

20. A box car that carries general freight has the same width and height as the car in Exercise 19, but is 44 feet long. What is the difference in volume between the cars?

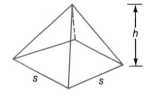

You can use the program on page 611 to compute the unit price for an item given the total purchase price, *p*, and the number of units, *n*.

Use the program to find the unit price given the following values.

21. $p = \$1.35; n = 45$

22. $p = \$6.19; n = 4$

23. $p = \$1.05; n = 50$

24. $p = \$3.79; n = 6$

25. $p = \$6.85; n = 16$

26. $p = \$1.15; n = 40$

■■■■■■■ **MAINTAIN**

The formula for the volume of a pyramid with a square base is $V = \frac{1}{3}s^2h$. Find V for each value of *s* and *h*. (*Pages 9-13*)

27. $s = 4, h = 6$ **28.** $s = 9, h = 13$ **29.** $s = 5.2, h = 15$

Evaluate. (*Pages 5-8*)

30. $4 \cdot 8 + 9$

31. $7 - 12 \div 2 + 6$

32. $3 \cdot 7 - 15 \div 5$

33. $3 + \dfrac{12 - 8}{4}$

34. $34 - \dfrac{6 \cdot 10}{3}$

35. $\dfrac{12 + 4 \cdot 7}{16 \div 2 + 2}$

■■■■■■■ **CONNECT AND EXTEND**

Write a formula to represent the area, *A*, of the shaded portion of each figure.

36.   **37.** 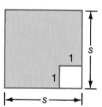   **38.** 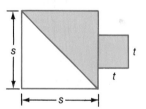   **39.**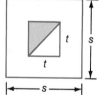

In Exercises 40-43, use the formula

$$p = 100 \left(1 - \frac{s}{g}\right)$$

to find the percent of discount, *p*, on a purchase. In the formula, *g* represents the original price and *s* represents the sale price.

SALE!
10%–33⅓% OFF

40. Original price: $96; Sale Price: $72

41. Original price: $48.96; Sale price: $42.84

Uses of Algebra   **17**

42. In the formula $p = 100\left(1 - \frac{s}{g}\right)$, suppose that $\frac{s}{g} = \frac{1}{2}$. What is the discount on an item that originally cost $45.80?

43. In the formula $p = 100\left(1 - \frac{s}{g}\right)$, suppose that $\frac{s}{g} = 1$. How much will you pay for an item that originally cost $32.75?

44. Write a formula that gives the total area, T.

45. a. Write a formula to find the volume, V.
   b. Find the volume when $l = 8$ centimeters, $w = 4$ centimeters, and $h = 5$ centimeters.

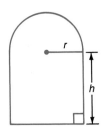

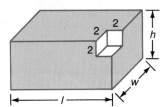

■■■■■■ **NON-ROUTINE PROBLEM**

46. Each of the three boxes shown in the figure at the right contains socks. The socks are either gray, G, or black, B. One box contains two gray socks; one box contains two black socks; and one box contains one gray sock and one black sock. None of the boxes is labeled correctly. From which box can you draw exactly one sock to determine how all three boxes should be labeled?

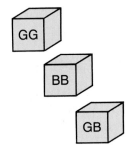

——— **REVIEW CAPSULE FOR SECTION 1-5** ———

Evaluate each expression for the given value of the variable. *(Pages 5-8)*

1. $3(x + 4) - 2$ when $x = 2$

2. $14 - 2(y - 5)$ when $y = 7$

3. $4(k - 5) + 5$ when $k = 5$

4. $12 + 4(t + 1)$ when $t = 9$

5. $2r + (r - 7)$ when $r = 12.5$

6. $21t - 8$ when $t = 0.5$

In Exercises 7-12, find the value of Q when $n = 0, 2, 4, 6,$ and 8. *(Pages 5-8, 9-13)*

7. $Q = 4n + 1$

8. $Q = 7n + 3$

9. $Q = 100n + 1$

10. $Q = \frac{4n + 6}{4n + 3}$

11. $Q = \frac{8n + 12}{2}$

12. $Q = \frac{2n + 1}{2n + 1}$

Write an algebraic expression for each word description. *(Pages 1-4)*

1. The cost of 4 compact discs at d dollars per compact disc

2. The number of miles, m divided by 15, the number of gallons

3. The cost to fill r tanks of air at $2.00 per tank

4. The number of seashells, s, subtracted from 52

Evaluate. Follow the rules for order of operations and for the use of grouping symbols. Express fractions in lowest terms. *(Pages 5–8)*

5. $6(12 \div 3)$

6. $168 \div 14 + \dfrac{8 + (3 \cdot 4)}{5}$

7. $8[3 \cdot 4(18 - 5)]$

Evaluate for the given values of the variables. *(Pages 5-8)*

8. $80 - 8m$, for $m = 10$

9. $(2a + b)$ for $a = 3, b = 5$

10. $\dfrac{m(m \cdot 4)}{3m}$, for $m = 0.5$

Evaluate each expression. *(Pages 9-13)*

11. $5 + 9^2$

12. $13(3)^2 \div (62 - 7^2)$

13. $(6q)^2 - 12$ for $q = 3$

Use the formula $A = \frac{1}{2}h(a + b)$ to find A. *(Pages 14-18)*

14. $h = 10, a = 12, b = 15$

15. $h = 0.6, a = 0.03, b = 0.11$

Historical Digest: Egyptian Algebra

Much of what is known about Egyptian algebra and arithmetic comes from the Rhind papyrus (about 1600 B.C.). The Rhind papyrus is a collection of 85 problems with answers copied by the scribe Ahmes from an older manuscript.

The first part of the collection deals with fractions because the Egyptians found them troublesome. They could work only with fractions having a numerator of 1. Simple algebraic equations are treated in another part. One problem is to find a number such that

"The sum of it and one seventh of it shall together equal 19."

The answer is $16\frac{5}{8}$, but the papyrus give it in this form.

$$16 + \frac{1}{2} + \frac{1}{8}$$

Is the papyrus correct?

Surface Area / Diagrams and Formulas

Landscape gardeners apply strategies such as **drawing a diagram** and **using a geometric formula** to solve problems related to their work.

EXAMPLE 1: Harry works for Creative Landscaping, Inc. One of his assignments is to care for the Luckman family's lawn.

   a. What information does he need to order the required amount of fertilizer for the lawn?

Solution: Since the amount of fertilizer depends on the size of the lawn, Harry needs to know the area of the lawn.

   b. How can Harry find the area?

Solution:

1. To find the area of the lawn, Harry drew and labeled the diagram at the right.

2. Harry used the formula $A = lw$ and a calculator to compute the area.

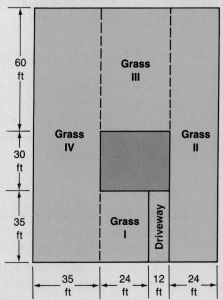

   I. $A = (35)(24) = 840$ square feet
  II. $A = (125)(24) = 3000$ square feet
 III. $A = (60)(36) = 2160$ square feet
 IV. $A = (125)(35) = \underline{4375}$ square feet
          Total area: **10,375 square feet**

Harry knows that Brand A of a fertilizer requires 1 pound of fertilizer for each 250 square feet of grass.

EXAMPLE 2: **a.** How much fertilizer will be needed?

Solution: Since 250 square feet require 1 pound, divide the total area by 250.

10375 ÷ 250 = | 41.5 |

Harry will need **42 pounds** of fertilizer.

b. If Brand A is sold in 20-pound bags at $9.95 per bag and in 40-pound bags at $16.95 per bag, how much will the fertilizer cost?

Solution: One 40-pound bag: $16.95
One 20-pound bag: $ 9.95
Total: **$26.90**

EXERCISES

Suppose Harry could obtain another brand of fertilizer, Brand B, that required 1 pound for each 100 square feet of lawn. Brand B comes in 20-pound bags at $4.99 per bag and in 40-pound bags at $7.99 per bag.

1. What would it cost Harry to use Brand B?

2. Which brand would you suggest that Harry use? Why?

Suppose you decide to paint a room in your house. You will need these facts for your project.

Room dimensions:	15 feet by 12 feet
Ceiling height:	8 feet
Door dimensions:	3 feet by $6\frac{1}{2}$ feet (The 3 doors will not be painted.)
Window dimensions:	3 feet by $3\frac{1}{2}$ feet (There are 2 windows.)

The walls and the ceiling will receive two coats of paint.
One gallon of paint covers 400 square feet on the first coat.
One gallon of paint covers 500 square feet on the second coat.
One gallon of paint costs $10.97 and one quart costs $5.79.

3. How much paint will you need for the first coat? The second coat? How much in all?

4. How much paint will you buy? Choose one of the following.
   i. 2 gallons   **ii.** 3 gallons   **iii.** 2 gallons plus 1 quart
   iv. 2 gallons plus 2 quarts   **v.** 2 gallons plus 3 quarts

5. How much would 3 gallons cost?

6. How much would 2 gallons plus 1 quart cost?

7. Why would you not buy 2 gallons plus 2 quarts or 2 gallons plus 3 quarts?

1-5 Open Sentences

You can use algebraic and numerical expressions together with these symbols to write mathematical sentences.

Symbol	Meaning	Symbol	Meaning
=	Is equal to	≥	Is greater than or equal to
≠	Is <u>not</u> equal to	≤	Is less than or equal to
>	Is greater than	≈	Is approximately equal to
<	Is less than		

This table shows several mathematical sentences.

Sentence	Meaning
$23 \neq 6$	Twenty-three is **not equal to** 6.
$x - 3 = 9$	The quantity $(x-3)$ **equals** 9.
$n > 12$	A number n is **greater than** 12.

**OPEN
SENTENCES**
The sentences, $x - 3 = 9$ and $n > 12$, are *open sentences*. An **open sentence** contains at least one variable. The variable in an open sentence must be replaced by a number from a specified set of numbers before you can tell whether the sentence is true or false.

DEFINITION

> The replacements for the variable that make an open sentence true are the **solutions** or the **solution set** of the sentence.

EXAMPLE 1 Which numbers, 5, 6, or 7, are solutions of $3x + 6 = x + 20$?

Solution: Replace x with 5.   Does $3 \cdot 5 + 6 = 5 + 20$?   No; $21 \neq 25$
Replace x with 6.   Does $3 \cdot 6 + 6 = 6 + 20$?   No; $24 \neq 26$
Replace x with 7.   Does $3 \cdot 7 + 6 = 7 + 20$?   Yes; $27 = 27$

The solution is **7**.

EQUATIONS
In Example 1, the open sentence $3x + 6 = x + 20$ is an **equation.**
Equations are mathematical sentences that contain the symbol, "=."
The set of numbers {5, 6, 7} is the **replacement set** of the variable x.
You use braces, { }, to indicate a set.

INEQUALITIES   Mathematical sentences such as $y^2 + 7 > 9$ and $5\,p \le 20$ are **inequalities.** Inequalities often have more than one solution.

EXAMPLE 2 Which of the numbers $\{1, 2, 3, 4\}$ are solutions of $5t + 2 \ge 12$?

Solution: Replace t with 1.   Is $5 \cdot 1 + 2 \ge 12$?   No; $7 \not\ge 12$.
Replace t with 2.   Is $5 \cdot 2 + 2 \ge 12$?   Yes; $12 = 12$.
Replace t with 3.   Is $5 \cdot 3 + 2 \ge 12$?   Yes; $17 > 12$.
Replace t with 4.   Is $5 \cdot 4 + 2 \ge 12$?   Yes; $22 > 12$.

The solutions are **2, 3,** and **4.**

Open sentences may be true for all numbers, some numbers, or no numbers in the replacement set. An open sentence is true for *some numbers* in the replacement set when there is *at least one number* (one number or more than one number) in the replacement set that makes the sentence true. When no number in the replacement set makes the sentence true, the solution set is the **empty set,** or the **null set.** The symbol for the empty set is **ɸ.**

EXAMPLE 3 Which equations are true for all numbers, for some numbers, or for no numbers when the replacement set is the set of whole numbers?

Whole numbers, $W = \{0, 1, 2, 3, 4, \cdots\}$

└**The three dots mean the numbers continue on and on.**

Equation	Solution
a. $r + 7 = 7 + r$	**a.** True for all numbers in the replacement set. For example, $0 + 7 = 7 + 0$, $10 + 7 = 7 + 10$.
b. $t^2 + 15 = 15 - t^2$	**b.** True only for $t = 0$.
c. $p + 7 = p - 7$	**c.** Not true for any number in the replacement set. Except for zero, the sum of two whole numbers cannot equal their difference. The solution set is ɸ, the empty set.

Objective: To determine the solutions of an open sentence

CHECK YOUR UNDERSTANDING

1. Which sentences have the same meaning?
a. $p > 2.5$ **b.** $p = 2.5$ **c.** $p \approx 2.5$ **d.** $2.5 < p$

2. *Complete:* The set of numbers from which you choose replacements for a variable is called the __?__ .

3. *Complete:* Open sentences contain at least one __?__ .

4. What is the symbol for "is less than or equal to?"

5. What are the "solutions" of an open sentence?

Classify each sentence as true, <u>T</u>, or false, <u>F</u>. When a sentence is false, tell why it is false.

6. $5 \cdot \frac{3}{8} = \frac{8}{3} \cdot 5$

7. $812 + 91 = 91 + 812$

8. $0 \cdot 491 < 0 \cdot 512$

9. $597 - 0 = 597 + 0$

10. $\left(\frac{1}{5} + \frac{1}{3}\right) + \frac{5}{12} > \frac{1}{5} + \left(\frac{1}{3} + \frac{7}{12}\right)$

11. $12\frac{1}{2} \cdot 1 = \frac{25}{2}$

PRACTICE AND APPLY

Classify each sentence as true, <u>T</u>, or false, <u>F</u>. When a sentence is false, tell why it is false.

12. $a + 4 = 4 + a$ when $a = 7$

13. $9 \cdot c^2 = c^2 \cdot 9$ when $c = 0$ or 1 or 2

14. $3\frac{1}{2}n = 3\frac{1}{2}$ when $n = 1$

15. $439 + t = 439$ when $t = 0$

16. $x^2 > 1$ when $x = \frac{3}{4}$

17. $q^3 < q^2$ when $q = \frac{1}{2}$

Solve. For Exercises 18-26, the replacement set is {2, 4, 6, 8, 10}.

18. $x + 2 = 10$

19. $x + 2 < 10$

20. $x + 2 \geq 10$

21. $n \neq 3 + 5$

22. $a^2 > 50$

23. $3x \leq 15$

24. $x < 2$

25. $n^3 - 7 > 6$

26. $x \neq 2 + x$

For Exercises 27-35, the replacement set is {0, 1, 2, 3, 4, 5}.

27. $x + 3 < 15$

28. $x + 2 < 10$

29. $2x^2 + 1 = 19$

30. $10 + x > 30$

31. $x + 3 = x + 4$

32. $x + 1 \leq 5$

33. $3x > 9$

34. $100 - y^2 \neq 96$

35. $25 < 2x + 3x$

For Exercises 36-44, the replacement set is {0, 5, 10, 15, 20}

36. $30 = 2t + 30$

37. $4p + 70 = 150$

38. $50 = 5w$

39. $6.2 + x > 9.8$

40. $2y + 10 < 15$

41. $2a - a \neq 5$

42. $1 + z^2 = z^2$

43. $z^2 - 5 = z$

44. $5a + 1 \leq 1 + 5a$

Which equations are true for all numbers, for some numbers, or for no numbers when the replacement set is the set of whole numbers?

45. $r \cdot 5 = r + 5$ **46.** $t + 3t = 4t$ **47.** $n \cdot n = n$

48. $q^3 + 0 = q^3$ **49.** $21 + s = s + 21$ **50.** $1 + x = 21$

51. $7m = 0$ **52.** $2t + 4 = 2(t + 2)$ **53.** $b \cdot 1 = 1 \cdot b$

▨▨▨▨ MAINTAIN

Write a formula that relates the variables in each table. *(Pages 14-18)*

54.

Hours worked, h	1	2	3	4	5
Total wages, w	5	10	15	20	25

Formula: $w = \underline{\ ?\ }$

55.

Regular price, r	$26	$28	$30	$32
Sale price, s	$19	$21	$23	$25

Formula: $s = \underline{\ ?\ }$

Evaluate. *(Pages 9-13)*

56. $200 - 3 \cdot 4^3$ **57.** $(4 + 6)^2$ **58.** $66 - 4^3$ **59.** $4 \cdot 5 - 3^2$

Evaluate for $x = 5$ and $y = 3$. *(Pages 9-13)*

60. $18 - (x^2 - y^2)$ **61.** $(x - y)^4 - 10$ **62.** $xy + x^2 + y^2$ **63.** $x^3 - y^3 + 2xy$

▨▨▨▨ CONNECT AND EXTEND

Identify each statement as true, <u>T</u>, or false, <u>F</u>. When a statement is false, give an example to explain your answer. The replacement set is the set of whole numbers.

64. For all numbers n, $n < n \cdot n$.

65. For no number x, $3x = 3x + 9$.

66. For some numbers a and b, $a - b = b - a$.

67. For all numbers a and b, $a + b = b + a$.

68. For some number q, $q \cdot q \cdot q < 1$.

69. For no number p, $p - 1 = p$.

70. a. If a represents Alice's age and b represents Bob's age, what does $a = b + 4$ represent?
    b. Give three possible ages for Alice and Bob.

────── **REVIEW CAPSULE FOR SECTION 1-6** ──────

Complete.

1. $\frac{1}{4} = \frac{?}{8}$ **2.** $\frac{5}{?} = \frac{10}{12}$ **3.** $\frac{3}{8} = \frac{?}{40}$ **4.** $\frac{1}{14} = \frac{5}{?}$

5. $3\frac{3}{4} = \frac{?}{4}$ **6.** $5\frac{3}{8} = \frac{?}{8}$ **7.** $8\frac{4}{9} = \frac{?}{9}$ **8.** $7\frac{5}{6} = \frac{?}{6}$

1-6 Rational Numbers

SETS OF NUMBERS

Some sets of numbers can be represented by listing their **elements** or **members.** The three dots mean the numbers continue on without end.

Counting or natural numbers: N $= \{1, 2, 3, 4, \cdots\}$

Whole Numbers: W $= \{0, 1, 2, 3, \cdots\}$

INTEGERS

The set of **integers** consists of the set of whole numbers and their **opposites.** The opposite of a positive integer is a **negative integer.** The opposite of a negative integer is a **positive integer.** For example, $^-2$ (read ''negative 2'') is the opposite of 2, and 3 is the opposite of $^-3$. The integer **0 is its own opposite.**

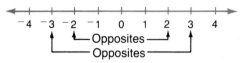

Integers: I $= \{\cdots\ ^-4,\ ^-3,\ ^-2,\ ^-1, 0, 1, 2, 3, 4, \cdots\}$

Not all points on the number line represent integers. Numbers such as $^-1\frac{2}{3}$, $\frac{^-1}{3}$, $\frac{3}{2}$, $2\frac{5}{6}$, and so on, are **rational numbers.**

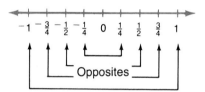

DEFINITION

> A **rational number** is a number that can be expressed in the form $\frac{a}{b}$, where a and b are integers and b is not equal to 0.

There are many ways of writing the same rational number:

Rational Number	Expressed as $\frac{a}{b}$	Some Other Names
4	$\frac{4}{1}$	$\frac{8}{2}, \frac{16}{4}, \frac{100}{25}, \cdots$
0	$\frac{0}{1}$	$\frac{0}{2}, \frac{0}{3}, \frac{0}{500}, \cdots$
0.73	$\frac{73}{100}$	$\frac{365}{500}, \frac{1460}{2000}, \frac{2190}{3000}, \cdots$
$^-5\frac{3}{4}$	$\frac{^-23}{4}$	$\frac{^-46}{8}, \frac{^-69}{12}, ^-5\frac{6}{8}, \cdots$

The set of **rational numbers,** *Q,* is made up of the positive rational numbers, the negative rational numbers, and zero.

You can use rational numbers to represent amounts above and below zero, gains and losses, and so on.

	In Words	Number
Temperature	32° above zero	32°
	10° below zero	⁻10°
Elevation	150 meters above sea level	150
	38 meters below sea level	⁻38
Football	A gain of 10 yards	10
	A loss of 4 yards	⁻4
Money	A deposit of $125	125
	A withdrawal of $63	⁻63

A rational number such as $\frac{1}{3}$ and $\frac{2}{11}$ can be represented by an **infinite repeating decimal**. Infinite means "without end."

$$\frac{1}{3} = 0.333 \cdots = 0.\overline{3} \qquad\qquad \frac{2}{11} = 0.1818 \cdots = 0.\overline{18}$$

The bar indicates the digits that repeat.

EXAMPLE Write a decimal for each rational number: **a.** $\frac{6}{11}$ **b.** $^-3\frac{1}{15}$

Solutions: **a.** $\frac{6}{11}$ ⟶ $11\overline{)6.0000 \cdots}$ with quotient $0.5454 \cdots$

$\frac{6}{11} = 0.5454 \cdots$, or **$0.\overline{54}$**

b. First, write a decimal for $\frac{1}{15}$.

$\frac{1}{15}$ ⟶ $15\overline{)1.000 \cdots}$ with quotient $0.066 \cdots$ ⟵ Note that the repeating pattern starts after the zero.

$3\frac{1}{15} = 3.0\overline{6}$ So $^-3\frac{1}{15} = $ **$^-3.0\overline{6}$.**

Rational numbers such as 0.75 and 1.4 are **terminating decimals.** However, they can be written as infinite repeating decimals.

$$\frac{3}{4} = 0.75 = 0.75000 \cdots \qquad\qquad 1\frac{2}{5} = \frac{7}{5} = 1.4 = 1.4000 \cdots$$

— Zero repeats. —

> Every rational number can be written as an infinite repeating decimal.

Objectives: To identify natural numbers, whole numbers, integers, and rational numbers

To use positive and negative numbers to represent quantities in real-life situations

To express a rational number as a repeating or terminating decimal

▬▬▬▬ **CHECK YOUR UNDERSTANDING**

For Exercises 1– 8 , classify each statement as true, <u>T</u>, or false, <u>F</u>. When a statement is false, tell why it is false.

1. $\frac{1}{3}$ is a natural number.

2. $\frac{1}{3}$ is an integer.

3. $12\frac{5}{6}$ is a rational number.

4. 6.5 is a rational number.

5. The opposite of 5 is ⁻5.

6. The opposite of $-\frac{9}{10}$ is $\frac{9}{10}$.

7. The number 0 is neither positive nor negative.

8. The number 0 is a counting number.

9. Why does the definition of rational number state that $b \neq 0$?

10. Which rational number, $\frac{7}{15}$ or $\frac{7}{20}$, can be written as a terminating decimal?

▬▬▬▬ **PRACTICE AND APPLY**

Write each rational number in the form $\frac{a}{b}$, where a and b are integers and b is not equal to 0.

11. 0.4   **12.** 0.75   **13.** 0.37   **14.** 0.24   **15.** $-6\frac{1}{3}$ **16.** $8\frac{2}{5}$

17. $3\frac{3}{4}$ **18.** $-6\frac{8}{9}$ **19.** 67.25   **20.** ⁻0.01   **21.** 0   **22.** ⁻100

23. 0.001   **24.** $66\frac{2}{3}$ **25.** 1.95   **26.** ⁻1   **27.** 18   **28.** ⁻7

For Exercises 29–44, represent each of the following by a positive or negative rational number.

29. A temperature 6° above zero

30. A temperature 3° below zero

31. An elevation of 462 meters below sea level

32. An elevation of 6070 meters above sea level

33. A deposit of $76.20 in a checking account

34. A withdrawal of $155 from a savings account

35. A weight gain of $2\frac{1}{2}$ pounds

36. A weight loss of 31 pounds

37. A paycheck deduction of $3.15

38. An income tax refund of $73.20

39. A temperature rise of 5.7°

40. A fall in temperature of 3.5°

41. A profit of $750

42. A loss of $315

43. A salary increase of $2.50 per hour

44. Growth of $2\frac{3}{4}$ inches

Write a decimal for each fraction or mixed number. Use a bar to indicate the repeating nonzero digits.

45. $\frac{1}{6}$ **46.** $\frac{5}{9}$ **47.** $\frac{16}{3}$ **48.** $2\frac{1}{2}$ **49.** $7\frac{3}{16}$ **50.** $\frac{8}{25}$

51. $1\frac{3}{8}$ **52.** $4\frac{1}{12}$ **53.** $-\frac{3}{20}$ **54.** $-\frac{6}{7}$ **55.** $-\frac{3}{11}$ **56.** $\frac{5}{13}$

■■■■ **MAINTAIN**

Find the solutions for each open sentence. The replacement set is $\{0, \frac{1}{2}, 1, \frac{3}{2}, 4\}$.
(Pages 22–25)

57. $5q = 0$

58. $8m > 0$

59. $5\frac{1}{2} - t = 1\frac{1}{2}$

60. $2q + 8q = 10q$

61. $t > t^2$

62. $y^3 \le y^2 \cdot y$

■■■■ **CONNECT AND EXTEND**

For Exercises 63–66, complete each statement. Look for the pattern to complete Exercise 66.

63. a. When dividing by 3, there are two possible non-zero remainders. They are __?__.
   b. Therefore, the decimal for $\frac{2}{3}$ can repeat in blocks of no more than __?__ digits.

64. a. When dividing by 7, there are six possible non-zero remainders. They are __?__.
   b. Therefore, the decimal for $\frac{6}{7}$ can repeat in blocks of no more than __?__ digits.

65. a. When dividing by 13, there are __?__ possible nonzero remainders.
   b. Therefore, the decimal for $\frac{1}{13}$ can repeat in blocks of not more than __?__ digits.

66. a. When dividing by a rational number b, there are __?__ possible non-zero remainders.
   b. Therefore, the decimals for $\frac{a}{b}$ can repeat in blocks of no more than __?__ digits.

■■■■ **NON-ROUTINE PROBLEMS**

67. What is the product of these 99 fractions?

$$\frac{1}{2} \cdot \frac{2}{3} \cdot \frac{3}{4} \cdot \frac{4}{5} \cdots \frac{99}{100}$$

68. In Exercise 67, what is the product when the last fraction is $\frac{n-1}{n}$?

1-7 Real Number Properties

You know that rational numbers can be written as repeating or terminating decimals. Numbers that cannot be written as repeating or terminating decimals are called *irrational numbers*. The numbers $\sqrt{2}$ and π are examples of **irrational numbers.** The rational numbers and irrational numbers together form the set of *real numbers*. When you graph real numbers on a number line, you can assume:

1. *Each real number corresponds to exactly one point.*
2. *Each point corresponds to exactly one real number.*

COMPLETENESS PROPERTY

> The **real numbers** are in one-to-one correspondence with the points on a number line.

In algebra, we assume certain basic properties of addition and subtraction of real numbers. For example, the *order* in which you add or multiply two numbers does not change the sum or product.

$18 + 9 = 27$ and $9 + 18 = 27$ $\qquad$ $84 \cdot \frac{1}{12} = 7$ and $\frac{1}{12} \cdot 84 = 7$

These illustrate the **Commutative Properties.**

COMMUTATIVE PROPERTIES

> **Addition** $\qquad\qquad a + b = b + a$
>
> **Multiplication** $\qquad a \cdot b = b \cdot a$

Suppose that you have three numbers to add or multiply. The way in which they are *grouped* does not change the sum or product.

$$(7 + 5) + 9 = 21 \qquad \text{and} \qquad 7 + (5 + 9) = 21$$
$$(8 \cdot \tfrac{1}{2}) \cdot 16 = 64 \qquad \text{and} \qquad 8 \cdot (\tfrac{1}{2} \cdot 16) = 64$$

These illustrate the **Associative Properties.** Remember that in the statements of these properties, a, b, and c represent real numbers.

ASSOCIATIVE PROPERTIES

> **Addition** $\qquad\qquad a + (b + c) = (a + b) + c$
>
> **Multiplication** $\qquad a \cdot (b \cdot c) = (a \cdot b) \cdot c$

The real numbers 0 and 1 have special properties.

When 0 is added to any real number, the sum is identical to the number. This illustrates the *Identity Property for Addition.*

When any real number is multiplied by 1, the product is the real number. This illustrates the *Identity Property for Multiplication.*

IDENTITY PROPERTIES

Addition	$a + 0 = 0 + a = a$	$3.9 + 0 = 0 + 3.9 = 3.9$
Multiplication	$a \cdot 1 = 1 \cdot a = a$	$\frac{5}{6} \cdot 1 = 1 \cdot \frac{5}{6} = \frac{5}{6}$

EXAMPLE 1 Use the properties to find a value of the variable that makes each sentence true. Name the property that gives the reason for each answer.

Sentence	Solution	Reason
a. $172 \cdot \frac{3}{4} = \frac{3}{4} \cdot x$	$x = 172$	Commutative Property for Mult.
b. $3 + z = 3$	$z = 0$	Identity Property for Addition
c. $(12 \cdot 9)10 = 12 (t \cdot 10)$	$t = 9$	Associative Property for Mult.
d. $r + (4 + 18) = 4 + (18 + 11)$	$r = 11$	Commutative and Associative Properties for Addition

MENTAL COMPUTATION   You can use the Commutative and Associative Properties to help you perform mental computations.

EXAMPLE 2 Use the Commutative and Associative Properties to find each answer.

a. $63 + (17 + 95) = (63 + 17) + 95$ ⟵ **By the Associative Property**
$= 80 + 95$
$= 175$

b. $10 \cdot \left(8 \cdot \frac{7}{10}\right) = 10 \left(\frac{7}{10} \cdot 8\right)$ ⟵ **By the Commutative Property**

$= \left(10 \cdot \frac{7}{10}\right) \cdot 8$ ⟵ **By the Associative Property**

$= 7 \cdot 8,$ or **56**

Objectives: To use the Commutative, Associative, and Identity Properties
To use number properties to perform mental computations

▆▆▆▆▆ CHECK YOUR UNDERSTANDING

For Exercises 1–4, first name the property. Then write a numerical expression to illustrate the property.

1. The product of any real number and 1 is the real number.

2. The sum of a real number and 0 is the real number.

3. The way in which three factors are grouped does not affect the product.

4. The order in which you find the sum of two real numbers does not affect the sum.

▆▆▆▆▆ PRACTICE AND APPLY

Name the property illustrated by each statement.

5. $5(6 + m) = (6 + m)5$

6. $29.3 + 0 = 29.3$

7. $(a + b) \cdot 1 = (a + b)$

8. $(10 \cdot 5) \cdot 4 = 10(5 \cdot 4)$

9. $(\frac{1}{3} + 6) + (2 + \frac{4}{3}) = (6 + \frac{1}{3}) + (\frac{4}{3} + 2)$

10. $(8.9 + 7) + w = 8.9 + (7 + 6.2)$

11. $r \cdot \frac{1}{5} \cdot s = \frac{1}{5} \cdot r \cdot s$

12. $9(\frac{1}{3} \cdot \frac{4}{5}) = (9 \cdot \frac{1}{3}) \cdot \frac{4}{5}$

Use number properties to find a value of the variable that makes each statement true. Name the property or properties that give the reason for each choice.

13. $19p = 6(19)$

14. $3(5 \cdot 7) = (3 \cdot 7)h$

15. $3.9m = 3.9$

16. $0 + y = 0.1$

17. $(7 + 9) + x = 7 + (4 + 9)$

18. $2.5 + 18 = 18 + y$

19. $\frac{2}{3}(0.9) = k$

20. $(\frac{2}{3})(\frac{3}{5}y) = (\frac{2}{3} \cdot \frac{3}{5})10$

21. $(t + \frac{1}{3}) + \frac{1}{2} = (\frac{1}{2} + \frac{1}{3}) + \frac{1}{4}$

22. $(9 + 2) + 2 = t + (9 + t)$

Use the Commutative and Associative Properties to find each answer. Use mental computation where possible.

23. $325 + 475 + 150$

24. $(16\frac{5}{8} + 3\frac{1}{6}) + 19\frac{5}{6}$

25. $125(9 \cdot 4)$

26. $18(10 \cdot 1\frac{1}{2})$

27. $(4 \cdot 13)25$

28. $37 + (29 + 3)$

29. $350 + (262 + 50)$

30. $(0.9 + 6.8) + 0.2$

Write a decimal for each rational number. Use a bar to indicate the digits that repeat (*Pages 26-29*)

31. $\frac{3}{5}$ **32.** $\frac{5}{8}$ **33.** $\frac{9}{2}$ **34.** $\frac{-11}{3}$ **35.** $\frac{-15}{32}$ **36.** $\frac{5}{16}$

Find the solutions for each open sentence. The replacement set is {1, 3, 5, 7, 9, 11}. (*Pages 22–25*)

37. $3w \cdot 0 = 0$ **38.** $2q + 1 = 7$ **39.** $\frac{1}{3}f > 10$

40. $11 - p < 8$ **41.** $5h - h \neq 3h$ **42.** $16 < x + 3x$

CONNECT AND EXTEND

43. Does the Associative Property hold for subtraction? Give an example to explain your answer.

44. Does the Commutative Property hold for subtraction? Give an example to explain your answer.

45. Does the Commutative Property hold for division? Give an example to explain your answer.

Let ∗ mean "Cube the first number and square the second number. Then multiply."

46. Find $2 * y$ when $y = 3$.   **47.** Find $3 * v$ when $v = 6$.

48. Find $r * 2$ when $r = 3$.   **49.** Find $2 * r$ when $r = 3$.

50. Find $r * 1$ when $r = 5$.   **51.** Find $1 * r$ when $r = 5$.

52. Compare Exercises 48 and 49 and Exercises 50 and 51. Is ∗ a commutative operation? Explain.

NON-ROUTINE PROBLEM

53. In a bowling alley, bowling pins are set up as shown in the figure at the right. Move exactly three of the pins to form a triangle exactly like the original triangle, but facing the opposite direction.

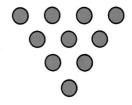

––––– **REVIEW CAPSULE FOR SECTION 1–8** –––––

Evaluate. (*Pages 1–4*)

1. $3 \cdot 10 + 3 \cdot 6$ **2.** $8 \cdot 50 - 8 \cdot 3$ **3.** $11 \cdot 40 - 11 \cdot 7$

4. $16 \cdot \frac{7}{8} + 16 \cdot \frac{3}{4}$ **5.** $\frac{5}{6} \cdot 12 + \frac{5}{6} \cdot 180$ **6.** $1.5 \cdot 3.2 - 1.5 \cdot 2.4$

1-8 Other Real Number Properties

Andy and Joyce usually bicycle 8 miles daily on a path in the park. This week they took a path which is 2.6 miles longer. How far did they bicycle this week?

One Way	Another Way
7(8 + 2.6)	7(8) + 7(2.6)
7(10.6)	56 + 18.2
74.2 miles	74.2 miles

The expressions 7(8 + 2.6) and 7(8) + 7(2.6) are **equivalent** because they have the same value. This illustrates the **Distributive Property** (multiplication over addition).

DISTRIBUTIVE PROPERTY

$$a(b + c) = ab + ac \qquad 9\left(3 + \tfrac{2}{3}\right) = 9 \cdot 3 + 9 \cdot \tfrac{2}{3}$$

$$(a + b)c = ac + bc \qquad (0.5 + 1)\,10 = 0.5(10) + 1(10)$$

MENTAL COMPUTATION

You can use the Distributive Property to help you perform mental computations.

EXAMPLE 1   Use mental computation when you can.

a. $24\left(\tfrac{1}{2} + \tfrac{1}{3}\right) = 24 \cdot \tfrac{1}{2} + 24 \cdot \tfrac{1}{3}$

$\qquad = 12 + 8 = 20$

b. $45(8) = (40 + 5)\,(8)$ ←——— **Express 45 as (40 + 5).**

$\qquad = 40 \cdot 8 + 5 \cdot 8$

$\qquad = 320 + 40 = \mathbf{360}$

c. $\left(7\tfrac{4}{5}\right)10 = \left(7 + \tfrac{4}{5}\right)10$

$\qquad = 7 \cdot 10 + \tfrac{4}{5} \cdot 10$

$\qquad = 70 + 8 = \mathbf{78}$

Multiplication is also distributive with respect to subtraction.

$$a(b - c) = ab - ac \quad \text{and} \quad (b - c)a = ba - ca.$$

The symbol for equality, =, is used to show that two expressions are equivalent. The properties of equality are listed below.

PROPERTIES OF EQUALITY

Reflexive Property: $a = a$		$6.95 = 6.95$
Symmetric Property:	If $a = b$, then $b = a$.	If $8 + 9 = 17$, then $17 = 8 + 9$
Transitive Property:	If $a = b$ and $b = c$, then $a = c$.	If $12 - 7 = 3 + 2$ and $3 + 2 = 5$, then $12 - 7 = 5$

EXAMPLE 2 Which property of equality is illustrated by each statement?

a. If $2(y + 1) = 14$, then $14 = 2(y + 1)$ **Symmetric Property**

b. If $t - 1 = a$ and $a = 9$, then $t - 1 = 9$ **Transitive Property**

EXERCISES: Classwork/Homework

Objectives: To use the Distributive Property
To use the Properties of Equality

CHECK YOUR UNDERSTANDING

For Exercises 1–4, complete each statement.

1. If $x = 3$ and $3 = y$, then $x = y$ is an example of the __?__ property.

2. When two expressions have the same value, they are said to be __?__.

3. To show that two expressions are equivalent, you use the symbol, __?__.

4. If $7 + 2 = 3 + 6$, then $3 + 6 = 7 + 2$ is an example of the __?__ property.

For Exercises 5–16, name the property illustrated by each statement.

5. $7(20 + 4) = 7 \cdot 20 + 7 \cdot 4$

6. $10(6 + \frac{1}{5}) = 10 \cdot 6 + 10 \cdot \frac{1}{5}$

7. Every real number is equal to itself.

8. $(9 + \frac{1}{2})2 = 9 \cdot 2 + \frac{1}{2} \cdot 2$

9. $3(w - 1) = 3 \cdot w - 3 \cdot 1$

10. If $t + 2 = 9$ and $9 = 8 + 1$, then $t + 2 = 8 + 1$.

11. $(9 + 5)x = 9 \cdot x + 5 \cdot x$

12. If $7 + t = 18$ then $18 = 7 + t$.

13. If $56 = 9a$, then $9a = 56$.

14. $k(x - y) = kx - ky$

15. If $10 + s = 21$ and $21 = 18 + 3$, then $10 + s = 18 + 3$.

16. $2(2 + c) = 2 \cdot 2 + 2 \cdot c$

▬▬▬ PRACTICE AND APPLY

Use the Distributive Property to evaluate each expression.

17. $3(10 + 6)$

18. $16(\frac{7}{8} - \frac{3}{4})$

19. $\frac{3}{5}(\frac{5}{4} + \frac{5}{8})$

20. $8(50 - 3)$

21. $9(60 - 2)$

22. $8(200 + 6)$

23. $11(40 + 7)$

24. $\frac{3}{4}(3000 - 8)$

25. $(400 - 6)9$

26. $(800 - 11)5$

27. $\frac{3}{4}(20 + 16)$

28. $\frac{5}{6}(12 + 180)$

29. $18(1000 + 20 + 4)$

30. $25(400 + 10 + 8)$

31. $5(86)$

32. $11(205)$

33. $\frac{1}{4}(102)$

34. $9(1009)$

A frame is $(3 + x)$ units long and 5 units wide.

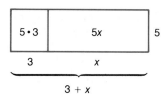

35. Area $= 5(3 + x) = 15 + $ __?__

36. Find the area inside the frame when the replacement set for x is $\{7, 19, 265\}$.

A frame is $(4 + x)$ units long and 6 units wide.

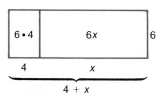

37. Area $= 6(4 + x) = $ __?__ $+$ __?__

38. Find the area inside the frame when the replacement set for x is $\{1.5, 6.2, 9.8\}$

Find the value of the variable that makes each statement true. Name the property that gives the reason for your choice.

39. $12 \cdot x = 12 \cdot 2$

40. $t(\frac{1}{5} + \frac{1}{4}) = 20 \cdot \frac{1}{5} + 20 \cdot \frac{1}{4}$

41. $12 \cdot 15 + 8 \cdot 15 = (12 + 8)x$

42. $x + \frac{3}{4} = 9 + \frac{3}{4}$

43. If $18 - 5 = 13$ and $13 = 7 + 6$, then $18 - 5 = 7 + t$.

44. If $(14 + 19) = 33$ and $33 = 11 \cdot 3$, then $b = 11 \cdot 3$.

Use the Distributive Property to write each expression in the form $a(b + c)$ or $(b + c)a$.

45. $\frac{1}{4} \cdot 24 + \frac{1}{4} \cdot 88$

46. $35 \cdot \frac{1}{7} + 14 \cdot \frac{1}{7}$

47. $10(4) + 10(6)$

48. $2(67) + 8(67)$

49. $86(97) - 86(3)$

50. $21(4) - 6(4)$

51. $2 \cdot x + 2 \cdot y$

52. $5(d + 1) + 3(d + 1)$

53. $xy(3) + xy(7)$

Name the property illustrated by each statement. (*Pages 30–33*)

54. $(a^2 + b^2) + 0 = a^2 + b^2$

55. $(100 + 0.5) + 25 = 25 + (100 + 0.5)$

56. $3(x + 2y) = (x + 2y)3$

57. $(21x^3y^2) \cdot 1 = 21x^3y^2$

58. $(x^2 + y^2) \cdot 1 = (x^2 + y^2)$

59. $(33xy)z = 33(xyz)$

Represent each of the following by a positive or negative rational number. (*Pages 26–29*)

60. Five years from now

61. Five years ago

62. Depositing $120 in an account

63. Losing 1500 feet in altitude

64. Losing 5 points on one problem in a test

65. Finishing a race with a margin of 5 yards over the nearest competitor

Classify each sentence as true, _T_, or false, _F_. If a statement is false, give an example to show why it is false.

66. Division is distributive with respect to division.

67. Division is distributive with respect to multiplication.

68. Division is distributive with respect to subtraction.

69. Subtraction is distributive with respect to addition.

70. Addition is distributive with respect to addition.

71. Multiplication is distributive with respect to subtraction.

When the sum of any two numbers in a set of numbers is a member of the set, then the set of numbers is said to be _closed_ under the operation of addition. For example, the sum of any two natural numbers is a natural number. So the natural numbers are closed under the operation of addition.

72. Is the set of whole numbers closed under addition?

73. Is the set of whole numbers closed under subtraction?

74. Is the set of whole numbers closed under multiplication?

75. Is the set of whole numbers closed under division?

76. Kathy arranged six squares, like the one at the right, to form a geometric figure with each square having at least one side in common with another square. More than one such geometric figure can be formed. What is the perimeter of each possible geometric figure? (Hint: Make drawings of the possibilities.)

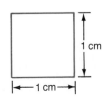

Uses of Algebra **37**

Focus on College Entrance Tests

Accuracy and speed are important in College Entrance tests. If you can recognize situations in which the basic properties for the real numbers can be applied, it is often possible to reduce the amount of time needed to determine a correct answer.

REMEMBER: The fewer the computations, the less possibility there is for error!

EXAMPLE

$$\frac{12(16 - 8) - 8(16 - 8)}{4} = \underline{\ ?\ }$$ **a.** 2   **b.** 4   **c.** 8   **d.** 16

Solution: By the Distributive Property, $12x - 8x = (12 - 8)x = 4x$.

Thus, $\dfrac{12(16 - 8) - 8(16 - 8)}{4} = \dfrac{\overset{1}{\cancel{4}}(16 - 8)}{\underset{1}{\cancel{4}}}$

$= 16 - 8$, or **8**   **Answer: c**

TRY THESE   Choose the best answer. Choose *a, b, c,* or *d.*

1. $\dfrac{6(15 - 3) - 3(15 - 3)}{3} = \underline{\ ?\ }$

   a. 12   **b.** 24   **c.** 45   **d.** 72

2. $\dfrac{4(21 + 3) - 2(21 + 3)}{2} = \underline{\ ?\ }$

   a. 72   **b.** 48   **c.** 24   **d.** 12

3. $\dfrac{3(38 - 14) + 5(38 - 14)}{24} = \underline{\ ?\ }$

   a. 8   **b.** 15   **c.** 18   **d.** 24

4. $\dfrac{6(31 - 29) - 2(31 - 29)}{2} = \underline{\ ?\ }$

   a. 2   **b.** 4   **c.** 6   **d.** 8

5. $3(20 - 5) - 4(20 - 5) + (20 - 5) = \underline{\ ?\ }$

   a. -30 **b.** -15 **c.** 0   **d.** 15

6. $\dfrac{42 + 42 + 42 + 42}{4} = \underline{\ ?\ }$ $\left(\text{Think: } \dfrac{4(42)}{4} = \underline{\ ?\ }\right)$

   a. 4   **b.** $40\frac{1}{2}$ **c.** 42   **d.** 84

7. $(38 + 25) - (38 + 20) = \underline{\ ?\ }$

   a. 83   **b.** 45   **c.** 0   **d.** 5

Chapter Summary

IMPORTANT TERMS

Algebraic expression (p. 1)
Associative Property (p. 30)
Base (p. 9)
Commutative Property (p. 30)
Completeness Property (p. 30)
Distributive Property (p. 34)
Empty set (p. 23)
Equation (p. 22)
Evaluating expressions (p. 2)
Evaluating formulas (p. 14)
Exponent (p. 9)
Formula (p. 10)
Grouping symbols (p. 6)
Identity Property (p. 31)
Inequality (p. 23)
Infinite repeating decimal (p. 27)

Integer (p. 26)
Irrational number (p. 30)
Natural number (p. 26)
Numerical expression (p. 2)
Open sentence (p. 22)
Opposite (p. 26)
Rational number (p. 26)
Real number (p. 30)
Reflexive Property (p. 35)
Replacement set (p. 22)
Solution set (p. 22)
Symmetric Property (p. 35)
Transitive Property (p. 35)
Variable (p. 1)
Whole number (p. 26)

IMPORTANT IDEAS

1. **Order of Operations**
   1 Perform operations within parentheses or grouping symbols.
   2 Evaluate powers.
   3 Do multiplications and divisions in order from left to right.
   4 Do additions and subtractions in order from left to right.

2. When an expression contains more than one grouping symbol, perform the operations within the innermost grouping symbols first. Then work towards the outermost grouping symbols.

3. To write a formula, you look for a pattern and then express that pattern with numbers and variables.

4. To use a formula, you replace the known variables with given values (replacement set) in order to find the unknown variables.

5. The symbol for the empty set is ϕ.

6. Every rational number can be written as an infinite repeating decimal.

7. **Completeness Property:** The real numbers are in one-to-one correspondence with the points on a number line.

8. The following properties are true for all real numbers.
   a. Commutative (See page 30.)
   b. Associative (See page 30.)
   c. Identity (See page 31.)
   d. Distributive (See page 34.)

Chapter Review

Write an algebraic expression for each word description. *(Pages 1–4)*

1. The cost of 3 concert tickets at p dollars per ticket
2. The sum of the cost of parts, q, and the cost of labor, b
3. The amount, a, spent on lunch, divided by 4
4. The price of long-distance calls, d, subtracted from the total telephone bill, c

Evaluate for the given values of the variable. *(Pages 5–8)*

5. $4(3a + c)$, for $a = 4$, and $c = 2$
6. $81 \div 9m$, for $m = 3$
7. $\frac{5(t \cdot t)}{2t}$, for $t = 0.2$

Evaluate each expression. Follow the rules for order of operations and for the use of grouping symbols. Express fractions in lowest terms. *(Pages 5–8, 9–13)*

8. $3(2 \cdot 16)$
9. $12(20 \div 2^2)$
10. $169 \div 13 + \frac{8 - (2 \cdot 1)}{3}$
11. $\frac{9 \cdot 3 + 6}{33 \div (7 - 4)}$
12. $11[7 + 3(4 \cdot 6)]$
13. $(2t^2) + 3^3$, for $t = 3$

Use the formula $A = \frac{1}{2}bh$ to find A. *(Pages 9–13)*

14. $b = 7, h = 12$
15. $b = \frac{3}{4}, h = 2\frac{1}{2}$
16. $b = 3.5, h = 6$

17. The table below shows the cost of imported cheese.
    a. Copy and complete the table.
    b. Complete the formula that shows the relationship between the variables in the table. *(Pages 14–18)*

Ounces, n	2	4	6	8	10
Cost, C	0.75	1.55	2.35	?	?

Formula: $C = n \cdot \underline{\,?\,} - 0.05$

Solve. The replacement set is $\{3, 5, 7, 9\}$. *(Pages 22–25)*

18. $x + 4 = 9$
19. $a^2 < 40$
20. $z + 10 = 10 + z$
21. $4t + 1 > 20$
22. $w \neq 4 + 5$
23. $n^2 - 7 > 9$

Represent each of the following by a positive or negative rational number. *(Pages 26–29)*

24. A weight gain of $3\frac{1}{2}$ pounds
25. A loss of 5 yards on a football play
26. A fall of 7 meters
27. A temperature $30°$ above zero

Write a decimal for each fraction or mixed number. Use a bar to indicate the repeating nonzero digits. (*Pages 26–29*)

28. $\frac{7}{9}$ **29.** $\frac{22}{3}$ **30.** $-\frac{8}{15}$ **31.** $3\frac{5}{13}$ **32.** $\frac{1}{9}$ **33.** $-\frac{6}{11}$

Name the property illustrated by each statement. (*Pages 30–33*)

34. $6(3 + t) = (3 + t)6$ **35.** $27.4 \cdot 1 = 27.4$

36. $(7 + 9.6) + 5 = 7 + (9.6 + 5)$ **37.** $\frac{7}{4} \cdot 19 = 19 \cdot \frac{7}{4}$

38. $365 + 0 = 365$ **39.** $\left(r \cdot \frac{1}{3}\right)p = r\left(\frac{1}{3} \cdot p\right)$

Use the Distributive Property to evaluate each expression. (*Pages 34-37*)

40. $9(2 + 5)$ **41.** $11(207)$ **42.** $8(40 - 2)$

43. $14\left(\frac{5}{6} - \frac{2}{3}\right)$ **44.** $12(70 + 4)$ **45.** $9(2006)$

Name the property illustrated by each statement. (*Pages 34-37*)

46. If $72 = 6b$, then $6b = 72$.   **47.** $36.95 = 36.95$

48. If $7 + r = 13$ and $13 = 5 + 8$, then $7 + r = 5 + 8$.   **49.** If $b(6 - 3) = 9$, then $9 = b(6 - 3)$.

Chapter Test

Write an algebraic expression for each word description.

1. The total coupon value, v, subtracted from the weekly food bill, b
2. The sum of a $1500 loan and the total interest, t
3. The cost of y record albums at $7.55 per album

Evaluate each expression. Express fractions in lowest terms.

4. $(3 + 14) \cdot 8$

5. $(70 \div 10) + (8 - 3)$

6. $\dfrac{9(19 - 15)}{33 + 11 + 7}$

7. $2[8 \cdot (11 - 2) \div 36]$

Evaluate for the given values of the variables.

8. $17p - 3b$, for $p = 8$, $b = 11$

9. $\frac{1}{2}a + \frac{3}{4}c$, for $a = 16$, $c = 4.8$

10. Use $A = \frac{1}{2}h(a + b)$ to find the area of a trapezoid when $b = 6.8$ meters, $a = 3.2$ meters, and $h = 7$ meters.

Find the solutions for each sentence. The replacement set is $\{0, 1, 2\}$.

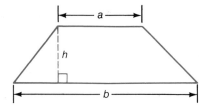

11. $w + 11 = 13$

12. $r + 3 \neq r + 7$

13. $9t > t$

Classify each sentence as true, <u>T</u>, or false, <u>F</u>. When a sentence is false, tell why it is false.

14. Every integer is a rational number.

15. 0.3 is a natural number.

16. The opposite of 2 is $\frac{1}{2}$.

17. $\frac{9}{5}$ is a rational number.

18. Write a positive or negative rational number which represents a bank withdrawal of $105.10

Write a decimal for each fraction or mixed number. Use a bar to indicate the repeating nonzero digits.

19. $\frac{4}{9}$

20. $-\frac{13}{3}$

21. $4\frac{8}{15}$

Use number properties to find a value of the variable that makes each statement true. Name the properties that give the reason for each choice.

22. $15(11 + 4) = (15 \cdot t) + (15 \cdot 4)$

23. $(8 + 9) + a = 8 + (4 + 9)$

24. If $a + 6 = 12$ and $12 = 5 + 7$, then $a + 6 = 5 + 7$.

25. If $r - 5 = 7$, then $7 = r - 5$.

Skills

Find the value of each of the following. (*Pages 1–4, 5–8*)

1. $(7 \cdot 2) - 4$ **2.** $6 + (49 \div 7)$ **3.** $(11 + 7) \div 3$ **4.** $(24 \div 2) \div (8 - 4)$

5. $\dfrac{11 - 9}{7 \cdot 3}$ **6.** $\dfrac{4(6 - 2)}{6 - 6 \div 3}$ **7.** $\dfrac{4 \cdot 4 - 7}{7 + 10 \cdot 2}$ **8.** $4[(5 - 2) \div 3]$

Find B for $n = 4$, $n = 5$, and $n = 6$. (*Pages 9–13*)

9. $B = 3n - 1$ **10.** $B = 8(n - 2)$ **11.** $B = n^2 + 3$ **12.** $B = n^3$

Find the solutions for each open sentence. The replacement set is $\{1, 3, 5, 7, 9\}$. (*Pages 22–25*)

13. $x + 3 = 12$ **14.** $x \neq 6 + 1$ **15.** $10 + x > 14$ **16.** $9x < 7$

Write each rational number in the form $\dfrac{a}{b}$, where a and b are integers and b is not equal to 0. (*Pages 26–29*)

17. 0.3 **18.** $^-0.25$ **19.** $2\frac{1}{3}$ **20.** $^-6\frac{1}{6}$ **21.** $^-38$ **22.** 7.37

Name the property illustrated by each sentence. (*Pages 30–33, 34–37*)

23. $\frac{1}{3} + 0 = \frac{1}{3}$ **24.** $2 \cdot (5 \cdot 7) = (2 \cdot 5) \cdot 7$ **25.** $11 + 4 = 4 + 11$

Use the Distributive Property to evaluate each expression. (*Pages 34–37*)

26. $4(10 + 8)$ **27.** $6(100 + 5)$ **28.** $8(200 + 7)$

Problem Solving and Applications

For Exercises 29 and 30, write an algebraic expression to represent each word description. (*Pages 1–4*)

29. The cost of t gallons of gasoline at $1.15 per gallon

30. The amount spent, a, subtracted from $250

Solve. (*Pages 14–18*)

31. Use the formula $V = lwh$ to find the volume, V, of a rectangular garden pool where $l = 6$ meters, $w = 4$ meters, and $h = \frac{1}{2}$ meter.

32. Use the formula $A = \frac{1}{2}h(b + c)$ to find the area, A, of a car window where $h = 18$ inches, $b = 13$ inches, and $c = 17$ inches.

CHAPTER 2

Operations with Real Numbers

The use of **negative numbers** is not restricted to algebra. As this sign shows, Badwater, California is 280 feet below sea level. This can be represented as -280.

Name other everyday uses of negative numbers.

2-1 Opposites and Order

On the number line below, 3 and ⁻3 (read: negative 3) are on *opposite* sides of 0. Also, 3 and ⁻3 are the *same distance* from 0.

OPPOSITES

The numbers 3 and ⁻3 are **opposites.** That is,

> 3 is the *opposite* of ⁻3.
> ⁻3 is the *opposite* of 3.

These statements can be expressed in symbols by using a dash, −, to represent "the opposite of."

$$3 = -(^-3) \longleftarrow \textbf{Read: "3 is the opposite of negative 3."}$$

$$^-3 = -3 \longleftarrow \textbf{Read: "Negative 3 is the opposite of 3."}$$

Note that negative 3 (written ⁻3) and the opposite of 3 (written −3) name the same number. For convenience, we use the lowered negative sign to mean "negative 3" <u>and</u> the "opposite of 3." So −3 can be read either way.

EXAMPLE 1 Write without parentheses.

a. $-(-5)$ **b.** $-(9.6 - 3.2)$

Solutions: **a.** $-(-5) = 5$ $\longleftarrow$ **Think: The opposite of negative 5 is 5.**

b. $-(9.6 - 3.2) = -(6.4)$ $\longleftarrow$ **Think: The opposite of 6.4 is negative 6.4.**

$$= -6.4$$

You can use algebraic symbols to represent opposites in real-life situations.

EXAMPLE 2 Use algebraic symbols to represent this statement.

The opposite of a loss of 5° in temperature is a gain of 5°.

Solution: $-$ (-5) $=$ 5

So $-(-5) = 5.$

If a is a real number, the opposite of a is written $-a$. However, this does not mean that a is a negative number. For example:

$$\text{If } a = 6, \text{ then } -a = -6.$$
$$\text{If } a = -6, \text{ then } -a = -(-6) = 6.$$

The number 0 is its own opposite.

EXAMPLE 3   Solve: $-x = 7$

Solution: $-x = 7$ ← **Think: The opposite of some number is 7.**

$x = -7$ Thus, the solution is **−7.**

COMPARING NUMBERS   You can also use a number line to compare numbers.

For any two numbers on the number line, the smaller is to the left of the larger.

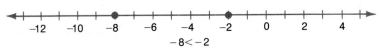

$-8 < -2$

EXAMPLE 4   Use $>$ or $<$ to compare the numbers. Refer to the number line above.

a. $3 \underline{\ ?\ } -9$ b. $-11\frac{1}{2} \underline{\ ?\ } -7$ c. $0.5 \underline{\ ?\ } 0$

Solutions: a. $3 > -9$ ← **3 is to the right of −9.**

b. $-11\frac{1}{2} < -7$ ← **$-11\frac{1}{2}$ is to the left of −7.**

c. $0.5 > 0$ ← **0.5 is to the right of 0.**

EXERCISES: Classwork/Homework

Objectives: To identify the opposite of a number
To compare numbers

CHECK YOUR UNDERSTANDING

1. *Complete:* On a number line, opposites are the same $\underline{\ ?\ }$ from 0, but are on $\underline{\ ?\ }$ sides of 0.

2. What symbol is used to represent "the opposite of"?

3. Write in words: $-(-9)$

4. Write in words: -9

5. What number is its own opposite?

6. If b and c are rational numbers and $b > c$, is b to the right or left of c on the number line?

7. If t is a number greater than 0, will $-t$ be a positive or a negative number?

8. If t is a number less than 0, will $-t$ be a positive or a negative number?

![bar] **PRACTICE AND APPLY**

Write the opposite of each number.

9. 6   **10.** -7 **11.** -9 **12.** 8.73   **13.** $-6\frac{1}{2}$ **14.** 0

15. 9.02   **16.** -6.33 **17.** $-\frac{2}{3}$ **18.** 5   **19.** -9.001 **20.** $-\frac{1}{8}$

Use algebraic symbols to represent each statement.

21. Depositing $27 in a checking account is the opposite of withdrawing $27.

22. The opposite of taking an elevator down 6 floors is taking an elevator up 6 floors.

23. A weight gain of $2\frac{1}{2}$ pounds is the opposite of a weight loss of $2\frac{1}{2}$ pounds.

24. An altitude of 400 meters above sea level is the opposite of a depth of 400 meters below sea level.

25. The opposite of owing $200 is having $200 in savings.

26. A fall of 20° in temperature is the opposite of a rise of 20°.

Write without parentheses.

27. $-(5)$ **28.** $-(-9)$ **29.** $-(3.14)$ **30.** $-(-3.14)$ **31.** $-\frac{5}{6}$

32. $-(-5)$ **33.** $-(9)$ **34.** $-(-0.9)$ **35.** $-(0.9)$ **36.** $-(21 \cdot 0)$

37. $-(3.6 - 2.4)$ **38.** $-(16 + 0)$ **39.** $-(71 \cdot 0)$ **40.** $-(\frac{1}{2} \cdot \frac{3}{4})$ **41.** $-(33 \div 11)$

42. $-(t)$ **43.** $-(-t)$ **44.** $-(r \cdot 0)$ **45.** $-(-m)$ **46.** $-[-(-9)]$

Solve.

47. $-x = 9$ **48.** $-m = -6$ **49.** $-x = 0$ **50.** $-y = 6\frac{1}{2}$

51. $-y = 3.25$ **52.** $-x = -2$ **53.** $-a = -\frac{3}{4}$ **54.** $-a = 1$

Use $<$ and $>$ to compare the numbers. Draw a number line if necessary.

55. $-5 \underline{\ ?\ } 5$ **56.** $-15 \underline{\ ?\ } -5$ **57.** $-8 \underline{\ ?\ } 0.2$ **58.** $-12 \underline{\ ?\ } -15$

59. $7 \underline{\ ?\ } 5$ **60.** $-15 \underline{\ ?\ } -20$ **61.** $0 \underline{\ ?\ } -9$ **62.** $0 \underline{\ ?\ } -8.6$

63. $6\frac{2}{3} \underline{\ ?\ } -6$ **64.** $6.2 \underline{\ ?\ } 6.3$ **65.** $07.4 \underline{\ ?\ } -7.5$ **66.** $-8\frac{2}{5} \underline{\ ?\ } -8\frac{1}{5}$

67. $-(-6) \underline{\ ?\ } 0$ **68.** $0 \underline{\ ?\ } -(-5)$ **69.** $-(-2) \underline{\ ?\ } 3$ **70.** $-(-3) \underline{\ ?\ } 0$

Name the property illustrated by each statement. (*Pages 30–37*)

71. If $23.5 = a$, then $a = 23.5$.

72. $c \cdot 2\frac{1}{8} = 2\frac{1}{8} \cdot c$

73. $p(q + r) = pq + pr$

74. $(a + b)12 = 12a + 12b$

75. $(d^2 - f^2) + 0 = d^2 - f^2$

76. $183p(qr) = (183pq)r$

77. If $a + b = c$ and $c = 18$, then $a + b = 18$.

78. If $f^2 - 5 = g^2$, then $g^2 = f^2 - 5$.

Write an algebraic expression for each word description. (*Pages 1–4*)

79. John's age, a, three years ago

80. The amount earned, a, less taxes, t

81. The cost of 5 tickets at d dollars a ticket

82. The total cost of a book, b, and a magazine, m

83. The amount spent, s, subtracted from the amount earned, e

84. The yearly income, y, divided by 52, the number of weeks in a year

■■■■■ **CONNECT AND EXTEND**

85. If a is a positive real number, is $-a$ positive or negative?

86. If $-a$ is a positive real number, is a positive or negative?

87. If a is a negative real number, is $-a$ positive or negative?

88. If $-a$ is a negative real number is a positive or negative?

89. If $-a$ is a positive real number, is $-(-a)$ positive or negative?

90. If $-a$ is a negative real number, is $-(-a)$ positive or negative?

■■■■■ **NON-ROUTINE PROBLEMS**

91. Alvin had $1.19 in coins. Louise asked him for change for a dollar but he did not have the correct change. What coins did he have?

92. Trace this figure. Then divide the figure into four pieces that have the same size and shape.

————— **REVIEW CAPSULE FOR SECTION 2-2** —————

For Exercises 1–12, tell whether each number is to the right or left of zero on the number line.

1. -1

2. $-(-1)$

3. $\frac{1}{8}$

4. $-2\frac{3}{4}$

5. $-(-\frac{1}{2})$

6. 0.01

7. $-(0.03)$

8. $-(-0.9)$

9. $-\frac{4}{5}$

10. 0.0015

11. $-(-8\frac{6}{7})$

12. $12\frac{2}{5}$

2-2 Addition on the Number Line

You can use number lines to add integers.
Arrows pointing to the right represent positive numbers.
Arrows pointing to the left represent negative numbers.

EXAMPLE 1 In Burlington, Vermont, the temperature was 3°C at two o'clock. An hour later, it had increased 6°C. What was the final temperature?

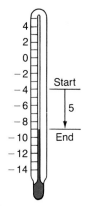

Solution: Draw a number line.

1 Start at 0. Draw an arrow to the right that ends at 3.

2 From 3, draw an arrow that extends 6 units to the right.

3 Read the sum from the coordinate of the point where the second arrow ends.

$$3 + 6 = 9$$

You use a similar procedure to add two negative numbers.

EXAMPLE 2 In Minneapolis, Minnesota, the temperature at 2 A.M. was -4°C. Three hours later, it had decreased another 5°C. What was the temperature at 5 A.M.?

Solution: Start at 0. Draw an arrow 4 units to the left. From -4, draw a second arrow 5 units to the left.

$$-4 + (-5) = -9$$

Example 3 shows how to use a number line to add a positive and a negative number.

EXAMPLE 3 In Dallas, Texas, the temperature was 6°C at 8 P.M. By midnight, it had decreased 8°C. What was the temperature then?

Solution: Start at 0. Draw an arrow 6 units to the right. Then, from 6, draw an arrow 8 units to the left.

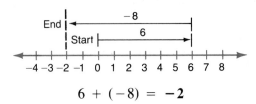

$$6 + (-8) = -2$$

EXERCISES: Classwork/Homework

Objective: To use a number line to add numbers

CHECK YOUR UNDERSTANDING

1. *Complete:* Arrows pointing to the __?__ represent positive integers.

2. *Complete:* Arrows pointing to the __?__ represent negative integers.

For Exercises 3–8, write an addition sentence for each diagram.

3.
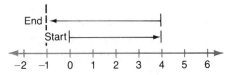

4.
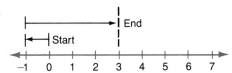

5.
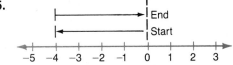

6.

7.
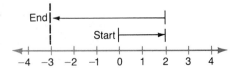

8.
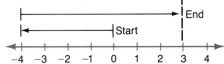

PRACTICE AND APPLY

Use a number line to find each sum.

9. $4 + (-3)$

10. $-6 + 4$

11. $5 + 2$

12. $-4 + (-2)$

13. $4 + 5$

14. $0 + (-4)$

15. $-4 + 0$ **16.** $3 + (-7)$ **17.** $6 + (-7)$

18. $-2 + (-9)$ **19.** $-9 + 8$ **20.** $9 + (-8)$

You already know that the sum of two positive numbers is positive. Use a number line to find these sums.

21. $-1 + (-2)$ **22.** $-7 + (-3)$ **23.** $-6 + (-4)$

24. Was each sum in Exercises 21–23 positive or negative?

25. *Complete:* The sum of two negative numbers is __?__.

Use a number line to find these sums.

26. $-3 + 3$ **27.** $10 + (-10)$ **28.** $1 + (-1)$

29. Was each sum in Exercises 26–28 positive, negative, or equal to zero?

30. *Complete:* The sum of a number and its opposite is __?__.

Use a number line to find these sums.

31. $-9 + 8$ **32.** $-5 + 3$ **33.** $9 + (-8)$ **34.** $5 + (-3)$

35. In Exercises 31 and 32, which number is farther from 0, the positive number or the negative number?

36. In Exercises 31 and 32, is the sum of the numbers positive or negative?

37. In Exercises 33 and 34, which number is farther from 0, the positive number or the negative number?

38. In Exercises 33 and 34, is the sum of the numbers positive or negative?

Write an addition problem for each sentence. Then solve the problem. Use a number line if necessary.

39. An airline pilot recorded these altitude changes. What was the result of the changes?

5:05 P.M.: -700 m
5:15 P.M.: -150 m

40. An elevator went up to the 26th floor. Then it came down 18 floors. At what floor was it then?

41. The low temperature on one night in Ames, Iowa was $-5°C$. During the day, the temperature rose $12°C$. What was the temperature then?

42. A submarine captain kept a log of the depth of the ship. What was the depth after the dive at 12:30 P.M.?

12:00 Noon: Cruising at -25 m
12:30 P.M.: Dive: -15 m

Write without parentheses. (*Pages 45–48*)

43. $-(18.5 - 13.6)$ **44.** $-(\pi \cdot 1)$ **45.** $-(-9)$ **46.** $-(-n)$

Use $>$, $<$, or $=$ to compare the numbers (*Pages 45–48*)

47. $-12 \underline{\ ?\ } -13$

48. $-(-12) \underline{\ ?\ } -13$

49. $-12 \underline{\ ?\ } -(-13)$

50. $-(-12) \underline{\ ?\ } -(-13)$

Find the value of the variable that makes each statement true.
Name the property that gives the reason for each choice. (*Pages 34-37*)

51. If $21 - 6 = 15$ and $r = 8 + 7$,
then $21 - 6 = 8 + 7$.

52. If $34 - 5 = 29$, then
$29 = z - 5$.

53. $x + 144 = 0 + 144$

54. $30(9 - \frac{2}{3}) = 30 \cdot 9 - 30 \cdot t$

Evaluate for the given values of the variables. (*Pages 5–13*)

55. $p^3 - q^2$, for $p = 5$ and $q = 1$

56. $\frac{1}{2}a + \frac{3}{4}b$, for $a = 0.5$ and $b = 18.4$

57. $5(n - r)$, for $n = 7$ and $r = 2$

58. $\frac{n}{3} + \frac{2}{3}n$, for $n = 21$

Use a number line to find each sum.

59. $7 + (-1) + (-3)$ **60.** $-2 + (-3) + (-4)$ **61.** $0 + (-8) + (-5) + 5$

62. $2 + (-2) + 2$ **63.** $1 + (-1) + (-3) + 2$ **64.** $-2 + (-2) + (-2) + 6$

65. You have $1000 in one-dollar bills. How can you arrange the bills in ten stacks, with at least one bill in each stack, so that you can make any whole number of dollars from $1 to $1000 merely by combining one or more stacks?

—————— **REVIEW CAPSULE FOR SECTION 2–3** ——————

Which of the two numbers in each pair is farther from zero on the number line? Write "same" if they are the same distance from zero. (*Pages 45–48*)

1. -3 and -2 **2.** 0.5 and 0.25 **3.** -5 and 5 **4.** $-\frac{1}{4}$ and $\frac{3}{8}$

5. $-4\frac{1}{3}$ and $4\frac{1}{3}$ **6.** 1.1 and -0.999 **7.** $\frac{2}{3}$ and $-\frac{1}{6}$ **8.** -6 and 3.7

2-3 Addition of Real Numbers

In the previous lesson, you used number lines to find sums of positive and negative numbers. Since this is not always convenient, it is also useful to have a rule for addition of real numbers. The rule involves an idea called *absolute value*.

This number line shows that opposites, such as 3 and -3, are the *same distance* from 0. However, 3 and -3 lie in *opposite directions* from 0.

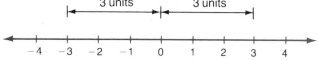

ABSOLUTE VALUE

To indicate distance, but not direction from zero, you use absolute value. The symbol, | |, is used to represent absolute value.

In Words	In Symbols
The absolute value of -3 is 3.	$|-3| = 3$
The absolute value of 3 is 3.	$|3| = 3$

← **Distances are positive numbers.**

DEFINITION

> The **absolute value** of a real number x is the distance of x from 0. It is written $|x|$.

When $x = 0$, $|x| = 0$. For all other real numbers, $|x|$ is a positive number.

Example	Meaning	Solution
$|-5|$	Distance of -5 from 0	$|-5| = 5$
$|8|$	Distance of 8 from 0	$|8| = 8$
$|-3\frac{1}{2}|$	Distance of $-3\frac{1}{2}$ from 0	$|-3\frac{1}{2}| = 3\frac{1}{2}$
$|0|$	Distance of 0 from 0	$|0| = 0$

Since $|x|$ is a positive real number for all real numbers x except 0, $-|x|$ is a negative real number.

EXAMPLE 1 Evaluate: **a.** $|-6| - |3|$ **b.** $-(|-5| + |-1|)$

Solution: **a.** $|-6| - |3| = 6 - 3$ ←——— $|-6| = 6; |3| = 3$
$= 3$

Solution: **b.** $-(|-5| + |-1|) = -(5 + 1)$ ←——— **Do the work inside parentheses first.**

$$= -6$$

In the previous lesson, you used a number line to find the sum of two negative numbers.

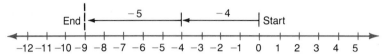

Since both arrows go in the same direction, first add the length of each arrow. The sum will be the opposite of this number.

$$-4 + (-5) = -(|-4| + |-5|), \text{ or } -9$$

ADDING NEGATIVE NUMBERS

> The sum of two negative numbers is the opposite of the sum of their absolute values.

EXAMPLE 2   Add: $-6 + (-5)$

Solution: ☐1 $|-6| + |-5| = 6 + 5$ ←——— **Add the absolute values.**

$$= 11$$

☐2 $-6 + (-5) = -11$ ←——— **Write the opposite of 11.**

This diagram shows how to add a positive and a negative number.

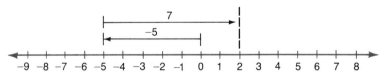

The longer arrow will show whether the sum is positive or negative. To find the sum, you subtract the length of the shorter arrow from the length of the longer arrow. The sum will have the same sign as the longer arrow. This suggests the following.

ADDING: UNLIKE SIGNS

> To find the sum of a positive and a negative number, subtract the smaller from the greater absolute value.
> Then write the result with the same sign as the addend having the greater absolute value.

EXAMPLE 3 Add: **a.** $8 + (-10)$ **b.** $20 + (-8)$

Solution: **a.** $|-10| - |8| = 2$ ←——— **Subtract the smaller from the larger absolute value.**

$8 + (-10) = -2$ ←——— **Since $|-10| > |8|$, the sum is negative.**

Solution: **b.** $20 + (-8)$ ←——— **Subtract the smaller from the larger absolute value.**

$|20| - |-8| = 12$

$20 + (-8) = 12$ ←——— **Since $|20| > |-8|$, the sum is positive.**

EXERCISES: Classwork/Homework

Objectives: To find the absolute value of a real number
To add real numbers

CHECK YOUR UNDERSTANDING

Evaluate.

1. $|-6|$ **2.** $|9|$ **3.** $-|-3\frac{1}{2}|$ **4.** $|5| - |4|$ **5.** $|-2| + |-13|$

Give the sign for each sum. Write $\underline{P}$ for positive and $\underline{N}$ for negative.

6. $-6 + (-3)$ **7.** $6 + (-3)$ **8.** $3 + (-6)$ **9.** $13 + 26$

10. $7 + (-15)$ **11.** $-6 + (-4)$ **12.** $8 + (-9)$ **13.** $-16 + 26$

14. $-9.8 + 10.1$ **15.** $1\frac{1}{2} + (-1\frac{1}{4})$ **16.** $(-\frac{2}{3}) + (-\frac{1}{8})$ **17.** $8.9 + (-9.1)$

PRACTICE AND APPLY

Evaluate.

18. $|-4| + |3|$ **19.** $|-9| + |-3|$ **20.** $|-12| - |12|$ **21.** $|-100| - |-50|$

22. $|9| + |-12|$ **23.** $|-235| + |16|$ **24.** $|0.2| + |-0.37|$ **25.** $|-\frac{5}{8}| + |\frac{1}{2}|$

Use $>$, $=$, or $<$ to compare the numbers.

26. $|0| \underline{\ ?\ } |-11|$ **27.** $|-2| \underline{\ ?\ } -|2|$ **28.** $|-\frac{1}{2}| \underline{\ ?\ } |\frac{1}{3}|$ **29.** $|-1| \underline{\ ?\ } |1|$

30. $|2| - |-1| \underline{\ ?\ } 0$ **31.** $|-3| - |-3| \underline{\ ?\ } 0$ **32.** $|9| + |-12| \underline{\ ?\ } 0$

For Exercises 33-56, add.

33. $-3 + 6$ **34.** $(-3) + (-6)$ **35.** $3 + (-6)$ **36.** $9 + (-6)$

37. $2 + (-5)$ **38.** $-3 + 7$ **39.** $-4 + (-9)$ **40.** $8 + (-3)$

41. $9 + 0$ **42.** $-9 + 8$ **43.** $7 + (-8)$ **44.** $0 + (-9)$

45. $8 + (-7)$ **46.** $294 + (-29)$ **47.** $-374 + 216$ **48.** $-178 + (-203)$

49. $(-3.7) + 8.6$ **50.** $-4.0 + 0.7$ **51.** $-1.6 + (-6.0)$ **52.** $-6.0 + 7.2$

53. $2\frac{3}{4} + (-1\frac{1}{2})$ **54.** $-\frac{3}{5} + (-\frac{2}{3})$ **55.** $-9\frac{1}{3} + 8\frac{5}{6}$ **56.** $-7 + 4\frac{1}{2}$

For Exercises 57–64:
a. Use positive and negative numbers to represent each word description.
b. Answer the question.

57. An elevator on the 21st floor goes down 8 floors. Then it goes up 4 floors and the door opens. On what floor is the elevator now?

58. On three successive plays, a football team lost 4 yards, gained 5 yards, and gained 7 yards. What was the team's net gain in the three plays?

59. The temperature at 9 A.M. was 3°C. At noon, the temperature had risen 7°. By 5 P.M., it had fallen 6°. What was the temperature at 5 P.M.?

60. The stock of HCJ Corporation opened in the morning at $52 per share. Two hours later, it lost $4. By closing time, it gained $2. What was its value at closing?

61. A plane was flying at an altitude of 12,000 meters. Then it dropped 3000 meters and rose 780 meters. What was the plane's new altitude?

62. Joann has $250 in her checking account. She wrote checks for $75 and $40 and made a deposit of $110. What was her new balance?

63. A submarine is cruising at a depth of 40 meters below the ocean's surface. The submarine then descends 15 meters and rises 18 meters. What is the submarine's new depth?

64. A company's loss during its first year of operation was $15,890. During its second and third years, it had profits of $5750 and $30,765. Find the net profit or loss over the three years.

████ **MAINTAIN**

Write an addition sentence for each diagram. (*Pages 49-52*)

65.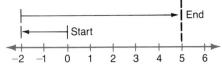

66.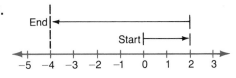

67.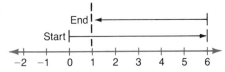

68.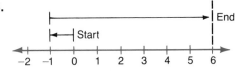

Write without parentheses. (*Pages 45–48*)

69. $-(-7)$ **70.** $-(9.6 - 3.8)$ **71.** $-(21 \cdot 0)$ **72.** $-(-t)$

Use $>$ and $<$ to compare the numbers. (*Pages 45–48*)

73. $0 \underline{\ ?\ } -2$ **74.** $-(-1) \underline{\ ?\ } -1$ **75.** $-\frac{2}{3} \underline{\ ?\ } -\frac{1}{3}$ **76.** $-8\frac{1}{3} \underline{\ ?\ } -7\frac{1}{5}$

Evaluate. (*Pages 9–13*)

77. $8^2 - 5$ **78.** $10^2 - 9^2$ **79.** $5^4 \div 5^2$ **80.** $6(6^2 - 6)$

81. $(10 - 7)^2$ **82.** $(4 + 6)^3$ **83.** $3^3 \cdot 5$ **84.** $\dfrac{2 \cdot 6^2 - 2^2 \cdot 6}{2 \cdot 6}$

████ CONNECT AND EXTEND

Classify each statement as true, <u>T</u>, or false, <u>F</u>. When a statement is false, tell why it is false.

85. For any number x, $|x| = x$.

86. For any number y, $|y| = |-y|$.

87. For any numbers x and y where $x < y$, $|x| < |y|$.

88. For any number x, $-(-x) = x$.

In Exercises 89–90, complete each argument.

89. Prove: $-14 + 8 = -6$

  Argument: Since $-14 = [-6 + (-8)]$, then $-14 + 8 = [-6 + (-8)] + 8$.

      Then $-14 + 8 = -6 + [(-8) + 8]$ Why?

      So $-14 + 8 = -6 + 0$ Why?

      Therefore, $-14 + 8 = -6$ Why?

90. Prove: $-11 + 17 = 6$

  Argument: Since $17 = 11 + 6$, then $-11 + 17 = -11 + (11 + 6)$

      Then $-11 + 17 = (-11 + 11) + 6$ Why?

      So $-11 + 17 = 0 + 6$ Why?

      Therefore, $-11 + 17 = 6$ Why?

—— **REVIEW CAPSULE FOR SECTION 2-4** ——

Subtract.

1. $6.2 - 0.8$ **2.** $12.3 - 8.5$ **3.** $10.47 - 3.64$ **4.** $14 - 10.7$

Subtract. Write your answers in lowest terms.

5. $\frac{9}{10} - \frac{2}{10}$ **6.** $15 - \frac{5}{8}$ **7.** $\frac{3}{12} - \frac{1}{4}$ **8.** $\frac{3}{5} - \frac{1}{2}$

9. $3\frac{1}{6} - \frac{2}{3}$ **10.** $6\frac{1}{2} - 3\frac{7}{8}$ **11.** $3\frac{1}{8} - 2\frac{5}{6}$ **12.** $13\frac{5}{8} - 6\frac{11}{12}$

2-4 Subtraction of Real Numbers

Another name for opposite is **additive inverse.**

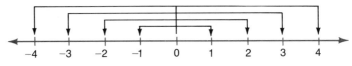

-3 is the additive inverse of 3.

2 is the additive inverse of -2.

The number 0 is its own additive inverse.

The sum of a number and its additive inverse is zero.

ADDITIVE INVERSE PROPERTY

For any real number, a, there is a real number $-a$ such that

$$a + (-a) = 0.$$

$$3 + (-3) = 0$$
$$8.9 + (-8.9) = 0$$
$$-\frac{2}{3} + \frac{3}{3} = 0$$

PATTERNS

Look for patterns to see the relationship between adding and subtracting real numbers.

Subtraction

$$10 - 3 = 7$$

Addition

$$10 + (-3) = 7$$

◄——— For both, the answer is 7.

└——Additive inverse——┘

$$17 - 6.1 = 10.9$$

$$17 + (-6.1) = 10.9$$

◄——— For both, the answer is 10.9.

└——Additive inverse——┘

This suggests that subtracting a number is equivalent to adding its additive inverse.

DEFINITION

Subtraction of Real Numbers

To subtract a number b from a number a, add the additive inverse of b to a. That is,

$$a - b = a + (-b)$$

$$11 - 9 = 11 + (-9)$$
$$= 2$$

$$-6 - (-5) = -6 + 5$$
$$= -1$$

EXAMPLE 1 Subtract: $3 - 7$

Solution: Write the subtraction problem as an addition problem.

$3 - 7 = 3 + (-7)$ ◀— **Add −7, the additive inverse of 7.**

$\quad\quad\quad = -4$

You can use addition to check your answers.

EXAMPLE 2 Subtract: $-5.1 - (-8.2)$

Solution: $-5.1 - (-8.2) = -5.1 + 8.2$ ◀— **Add 8.2, the additive inverse of −8.2.**

$\quad\quad\quad\quad\quad\quad\quad\quad = \mathbf{3.1}$

Check: Does $3.1 + (-8.2) = -5.1$? Yes ✓

Example 3 shows how to add or subtract three or more numbers.

EXAMPLE 3 Evaluate: **a.** $-7 + 5 - 8$ **b.** $14 - 7 - (-22)$

Solution: **a.** $-7 + 5 - 8 = 5 - 7 - 8$ ◀— **By the Commutative Property**

$\quad\quad\quad\quad\quad\quad\quad\quad = 5 + [(-7) + (-8)]$ ◀— **Use the Associative Property to group the negative addends.**

$\quad\quad\quad\quad\quad\quad\quad\quad = 5 + \quad\quad (-15)$

$\quad\quad\quad\quad\quad\quad\quad\quad = \mathbf{-10}$

Solution: **b.** $14 - 7 - (-22) = 14 - 7 + 22$ ◀— **The opposite of −22 is 22.**

$\quad\quad\quad\quad\quad\quad\quad\quad\quad\quad = \underline{14 + 22} + (-7)$ ◀— **Group the positive addends.**

$\quad\quad\quad\quad\quad\quad\quad\quad\quad\quad = \quad 36 \quad + (-7)$

$\quad\quad\quad\quad\quad\quad\quad\quad\quad\quad = \mathbf{29}$

CALCULATOR To use a calculator to subtract, use the change of sign key, $\boxed{^{+/-}}$, after a negative number. For example, to subtract $-7.84 - (-2.99)$, enter:

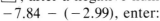

The display will show

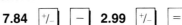

Objective: To subtract real numbers

CHECK YOUR UNDERSTANDING

1. What is another name for the opposite of a number?

2. What is the sum of a real number and its additive inverse?

Write an addition problem for each subtraction problem.

3. $6 - 3$ 4. $0 - 9$ 5. $-10 - 5$ 6. $-9 - 15$

7. $-5 - (-2)$ 8. $-5 - (-10)$ 9. $8 - (-4)$ 10. $20 - (-7)$

11. $0 - (-6)$ 12. $0 - (-8)$ 13. $-5.4 - (-2.1)$ 14. $2.9 - (-8.3)$

PRACTICE AND APPLY

Subtract.

15. $5 - 11$ 16. $6 - 8$ 17. $-4 - 5$ 18. $-5 - 1$

19. $-6 - 2$ 20. $-6 - 4$ 21. $4 - (-6)$ 22. $-6 - (-4)$

23. $-4 - 6$ 24. $-8 - 3$ 25. $-4 - 8$ 26. $-8 - 4$

27. $16 - (-15)$ 28. $24 - (-12)$ 29. $15 - 15$ 30. $9 - 9$

31. $-9 - 10$ 32. $-10 - 10$ 33. $-2.4 - 9.4$ 34. $-54 - 14$

35. $-7.8 - 0$ 36. $0 - 7.8$ 37. $\frac{1}{2} - (-\frac{1}{2})$ 38. $\frac{5}{3} - (-\frac{2}{3})$

39. $-54 - (-14)$ 40. $-64 - (-74)$ 41. $12.3 - 6.7$ 42. $6.7 - 12.3$

43. $12.3 - (-6.7)$ 44. $-6.7 - (-12.3)$ 45. $-12.3 - (-6.7)$ 46. $-6.7 - 12.3$

Evaluate.

47. $7 + (-6) + 3$ 48. $5 + (-10) + (-13)$ 49. $4 - 3 + 6$

50. $-5 - 9 + 5$ 51. $-6 + (-12) + (-10)$ 52. $-10 - 12 - 3$

53. $-9 + (-12) + (-10)$ 54. $-8 - 16 - (-12)$ 55. $-20 + 6 - 11$

56. $14 - 21 - (-14)$ 57. $10 - 3 - (-8)$ 58. $-3 - (-1) - (-5)$

Write the problem that each calculator sequence represents.

59. 10.18   3.9

60. 2.69 — 5.88 =

61. 9.9 +/- — 10.58 +/- =

62. 30.9 — 7.75 =

63. The temperature six hours ago was $-1°C$. It is now $11°C$. How much did the temperature change in the last six hours?

64. The actual temperature is $20°F$. The wind chill temperature is $-15°$. How much colder than the actual temperature is the wind chill?

65. The lowest temperature ever recorded in West Virginia was $-37°F$. The lowest temperature recorded in Wyoming was $-63°F$. Find the difference between the two temperatures.

66. The highest point in Texas, Guadalupe Peak, is 2667 meters above sea level. The greatest known depth of the Atlantic Ocean (in the Puerto Rico trench) is 8648 meters below sea level. Find the difference between the points.

▬▬▬ MAINTAIN

Evaluate. (*Pages 53–57*)

67. $|9| + |-8|$

68. $-|\frac{1}{2}| + |-\frac{1}{2}|$

69. $-6 + |-6|$

70. $|-12| - |9|$

Add. (*Pages 49–52, 53–57*)

71. $-35 + 20$

72. $-5.9 + (-6.1)$

73. $21 + (-50)$

74. $-8\frac{1}{2} + 4\frac{3}{4}$

Use the Distributive Property to evaluate each expression. (*Pages 34–37*)

75. $20(6 + 0.5)$

76. $(\frac{5}{6} + \frac{1}{2}) 12$

77. $18(\frac{2}{3} - \frac{1}{6})$

78. $(3 - 1.25)4$

79. $(306)9$

80. $11(198)$

81. $\frac{3}{4}(128)$

82. $(1018)6$

▬▬▬ CONNECT AND EXTEND

Classify each of the following as true, _T_, or false, _F_. When an equation is false, tell why it is false. The replacement set is the set of real numbers.

83. $-6 + (-2) = 4$

84. $-\frac{2}{3} - (-\frac{2}{3}) = \frac{1}{3}$

85. $-4 - (-2) = 2 - (-4)$

86. $0 = 0.24 - (-0.24)$

87. $8 - (-8) = 0$

88. $6 - 2 = 6 + (-2)$

89. $|8 - 2| = |2 - 8|$

90. $|8 - 2| = |8| - |2|$

91. $|2 - 8| = |2| - |8|$

92. $-3 + (-3) = -6$

93. $a - b = a + (-b)$

94. $|a - b| = |b - a|$

──── REVIEW CAPSULE FOR SECTION 2–5 ────

Evaluate for the given variable. (*Pages 5–8*)

1. a. $6x$, for $x = 3$
   b. $2x + 4x$, for $x = 3$

2. a. $3a$, for $a = 5$
   b. $7a - 4a$, for $a = 5$

3. a. $2b$, for $b = 7$
   b. $b + b$, for $b = 7$

4. a. $12t$, for $t = 2$
   b. $9t + 3t$, for $t = 2$

5. a. $6s$, for $s = 4$
   b. $10s - 4s$, for $s = 4$

6. a. $15y$, for $y = 1$
   b. $10y + 5y$, for $y = 1$

Complete. (*Pages 34–37*)

7. $7(-3 + 5) = 7(2) = \underline{\quad?\quad}$

8. $5(9 + 6) = 5(?) = \underline{\quad?\quad}$

9. $4(-2 + 9) = 4(?) = \underline{\quad?\quad}$

10. $-9(8 - 2) = -9(?) = \underline{\quad?\quad}$

11. $x(8 + 3) = x(?) = \underline{\quad?\quad}$

12. $m(-1 + 4) = m(?) = \underline{\quad?\quad}$

Decoding / Tables/Working Backwards

Decoding is the process of translating **ciphertext** (secret code) information to **plaintext** (English) information. The reverse process, writing plaintext information in ciphertext, is called **encoding.**

One way to set up a secret code is to use the American Standard Code for Information Interchange **(ASCII)** shown at the right and a formula. The ASCII is a standard code used with computers.

EXAMPLE 1: Use the key (formula) $C = A - 3$ to encode this message.

SEND MONEY ◄── **Plaintext**

Solution:

1 Write the ASCII value for each character.

S	E	N	D	space	M	O	N	E	Y
↓	↓	↓	↓	↓	↓	↓	↓	↓	↓
83	69	78	68	32	77	79	78	69	89

2 Use the formula to translate the ASCII characters to ciphertext characters.

A: 83 69 78 68 32 77 79 78 69 89

A − 3: 80 66 75 65 29 74 76 75 66 86

└─ **Ciphertext** ─┘

Character	ASCII Decimal Value
A	65
B	66
C	67
D	68
E	69
F	70
G	71
H	72
I	73
J	74
K	75
L	76
M	77
N	78
O	79
P	80
Q	81
R	82
S	83
T	84
U	85
V	86
W	87
X	88
Y	89
Z	90
space	32
$	36
,	44
0	48
1	49
2	50
3	51
4	52
5	53
6	54
7	55
8	56
9	57

To decode a message, you **work backward** from the *C* values in the formula to obtain the *A* values.

To <u>encode</u> when the key is $C = A - 3$, <u>subtract</u> 3 from each ASCII *A*-value.

To <u>decode</u> when the key is $C = A - 3$, <u>add</u> 3 to each ciphertext *C*-value.

EXAMPLE 2: Decode the message.
Encoding key: $C = 2A - 3$

129	167	175	61	103	85	93
93	93	61	163	141	127	161
135	163	61	127	131	151	135

Solution: Work <u>backwards</u>. Since the key is $C = 2A - 3$, first <u>add</u> 3 to each ciphertext value. Then <u>divide</u> by 2.

1 Add 3.

132	170	178	64	106	88	96
96	96	64	166	144	130	164
138	166	64	130	134	154	138

2 Divide by 2.

66	85	89	32	53	44	48
48	48	32	83	72	65	82
69	83	32	65	67	77	69

3 Refer to the table of ASCII values. Work backward from these values to obtain the plaintext.

BUY 5,000 SHARES ACME ← **Decoded Message**

EXERCISES

Decode each message. Use the key given for each message.

1. $C = A + 7$

94	80	83	83	39	72	89
89	80	93	76	39	85	76
94	39	96	86	89	82	39
77	89	80	75	72	96	

2. $C = A - 12$

71	57	64	64	20	53	
64	64	20	58	67	70	
57	61	59	66	20	71	
72	67	55	63			

3. $C = 2A + 3$

139	141	163	161	169	149	171
67	75	103	109	99	91	99
99	99	67	149	159	67	133
137	137	161	173	159	171	67
101	99	99	107	105		

4. $C = 3A - 2$

217	232	256	205	247	250	94
148	94	229	217	226	226	217
235	232	94	202	235	226	226
193	244	247	94	217	232	94
196	244	217	250	217	247	214
94	238	235	253	232	202	247

2-5 Combining Like Terms

A **term** is a real number, a variable, or the product of real numbers and variables. Each of these is a *term*.

$$3x^2 \qquad \frac{1}{2}xy^3 \qquad \frac{4}{5}x^2 \qquad 7mn \qquad \frac{a}{2b} \qquad 2x \qquad 8$$

LIKE TERMS

$3x^2$ and $\frac{4}{5}x^2$ are *like terms*. **Like terms** have the same variables. In like terms, corresponding variables have the same exponents.

Terms	Like Terms	Reason
$3z$ and $5z$	Yes	Same variable, z, with same exponent, 1
$2y^2$ and $-3x^2$	No	Different variables
$3m^2n$ and $5mn$	No	Different exponents for m
9 and $4y$	No	The number 9 has no variable

Like terms differ only in their *coefficients*. The **coefficient,** or **numerical coefficient,** is the numerical part of the term.

Term	Numerical Coefficient
$-7y$	-7
$16m^2n^2$	16
$1 \cdot q$ or q	1

Note carefully the last expression in the table.

$$q = 1 \cdot q = 1q$$

Similarly,

$$-q = -1 \cdot q = -1q$$

To **combine like terms** means to **add or subtract the like terms.**

To add or subtract like terms, you apply the Distributive Property. Then you add or subtract the numerical coefficients.

EXAMPLE 1   Combine like terms: $8x + x$

Solution: $8x + x = 8x + 1x$
$\qquad\qquad\quad = (8 + 1)x \quad \longleftarrow$ **By the Distributive Property**
$\qquad\qquad\quad = \mathbf{9x}$

EXAMPLE 2 Combine like terms: $-3m - 7m$

Solution: $-3m - 7m = (-3 - 7)m$ ⟵ $-3m - 7m = -3m + (-7m)$

$\qquad\qquad\qquad = -10m$

When you combine like terms, you are **simplifying an algebraic expression.**

EXAMPLE 3 Simplify: $5t + 3r + 9t - 10r - 8$

Solution: Use the Commutative and Associative Properties to group like terms.

$$5t + 3r + 9t - 10r - 8 = (5t + 9t) + (3r - 10r) - 8$$
$$= \quad 14t \quad + \quad (-7r) \quad - 8$$
$$= 14t - 7r - 8$$

When you simplify an algebraic expression, the original expression and the simplified one are equivalent. **Equivalent algebraic expressions** name the same number for all replacements of the variable.

SUBSTITUTION PROPERTY

If two expressions are equivalent, you can always replace one with the other in a given expression.

EXERCISES: Classwork/Homework

Objective: To combine like terms

CHECK YOUR UNDERSTANDING

Identify each pair of terms as *like terms* or *unlike terms*. Give a reason for each answer.

1. $2x$ and $3x$

2. $9m$ and $6r$

3. $\frac{1}{2}y$ and $2y^2$

4. $-6m$ and $8m^2$

5. $4xy$ and $7xy$

6. $3a$ and $-11a$

State the numerical coefficient of each term.

7. $2a$

8. $-\frac{1}{2}x^2$

9. $-0.05t$

10. $\frac{2}{3}r^3$

11. t

12. y

Complete each problem.

13. $12x + 8x = (?)x$
$\qquad = \underline{\ ?\ }x$

14. $7t - 5t = (?)t$
$\qquad = \underline{\ ?\ }t$

Combine like terms.

15. $8x + 2x$

16. $7y + 13y$

17. $15m + 6.2m$

18. $5a^2 + 7a^2$

19. $8mn + 6mn$

20. $3ab + 11ab$

21. $9x + x$

22. $15y + y$

23. $4m^2 + m^2$

24. $3ab + ab$

25. $m + 19m$

26. $a + 9a$

27. $4y + (-12y)$

28. $m + (-16m)$

29. $-4.1y + (-2.3y)$

30. $-0.4x + (-0.6x)$

31. $-16t + (-t)$

32. $(-15x) + (-1x)$

33. $7m - 6m$

34. $9t - 3t$

35. $12x - 9x$

36. $8a - 5a$

37. $4x - 1x$

38. $9m - 1m$

39. $-3a - 4a$

40. $-7b - 5b$

41. $-5m - (-8m)$

42. $-3t - (-2t)$

43. $-6r - (-1r)$

44. $-30q - (-1q)$

Simplify.

45. $3a + 2a + 4$

46. $8x + 3x + 9$

47. $15y + 6y + 3$

48. $4m + 7m - 5$

49. $6 + 2x + 4x$

50. $15 + 9y - 4y$

51. $5x + 7x - 6y$

52. $4y - y + 8$

53. $5x - x - 15$

54. $4a - b - 7b$

55. $2m + 7m - 8m$

56. $4a + 7a - 9a$

57. $7x - x + 3y + 57$

58. $12x - 3y + x + 2y$

59. $15xy - 2xy - 7xy + x$

60. $8rt + 3rt + t - 3t$

61. $4\frac{1}{2}xy + 7\frac{1}{3}xy + 2\frac{1}{4}xy$

62. $19m - m - 3n + 2n$

63. $4.75r + 1.62r + r$

64. $2.7m - 1.9m + m$

65. $4.87 + 6.52q + q$

For each of Exercises 66–69, find the sum of the areas of the figures.

66. Rectangle: $A = (\text{length} \cdot \text{width})$

67. Parallelogram: $A = (\text{base} \cdot \text{height})$

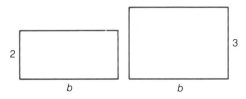

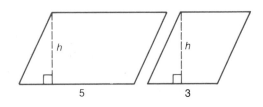

68. Triangle $A = \frac{1}{2}(\text{base} \cdot \text{height})$

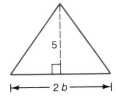

69. Rectangle: $A = (\text{length} \cdot \text{width})$

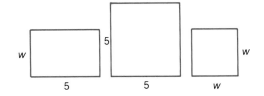

For Exercises 70–73, write a formula for the area of each shaded region. Simplify the result. Use the formulas for the area of a rectangle and of a triangle (see Exercises 68 and 69 above).

70.

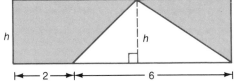

71.

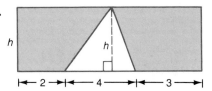

72.

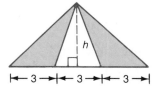

73.

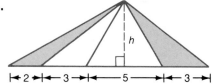

■■■■■■ **MAINTAIN**

Subtract. (*Pages 58–61*)

74. $-3 - (-2)$

75. $0 - (-50)$

76. $18 - (-7)$

77. $-0.9 - (-1.7)$

78. $-0.8 - (-2.7)$

79. $-3\frac{3}{4} - (-1\frac{3}{4})$

80. $5\frac{1}{2} - (-7\frac{3}{4})$

81. $0.24 - 0.93$

82. $0.53 - 0.87$

For Exercises 83–86:
 a. Use positive and negative numbers to represent each description.
 b. Solve the problem. (*Pages 53–57*)

83. A hot-air balloon rose 342 yards, dropped 58 yards, and then rose 32 yards. What was its final altitude?

84. The temperature is 12°C. A high pressure system changes it by -8°C. If the temperature changes again by another 3°C, what is the final reading?

85. An airplane on a search mission flies north from its base for 86 miles. Then it flies south for 59 miles, then north for 38 miles, and finally south for 158 miles. How far south of its base is the plane?

86. On the first sale of the day, Groggin Electric lost $3.52. On the next sale, there was a profit of $2.75. Then there were profits of $2.99 and $1.08 followed by losses of $3.01 and $2.76. Is the the total result a profit or a loss?

Evaluate each expression when $x = 3$, $z = -4$, and $t = -2$. (*Pages 5–8, 9–13*)

87. $-3x + 2z + 4$

88. $(2x + z) \div t$

89. $4(x + t)$

90. $(3x)^2 t$

91. $(x - z)^2$

92. $(xzt) \div (-6)$

■■■■■■■ **CONNECT AND EXTEND**

Simplify.

93. $3(x + 7y) + 5(x + 7y) + 9(x + 7y)$

94. $5(x + y) + 7(x + y) + 8(x + y)$

95. $5(2x + 8y) + 9(2x + 8y) + 5(2x + 8y)$

96. $6(x^2 + y^2) + 7(x^2 + y^2)$

97. $(x^2 + y^2) + 3(x^2 + y^2)$

98. $5(a + b) + (a + b) + 8(a + b)$

Complete.

99. $ax + bx = (\underline{?} + \underline{?})x$

100. $mx - my = (\underline{?} - \underline{?})m$

101. $cr - dr = (\underline{?} - \underline{?})r$

102. $7r + 6r = (\underline{?} + \underline{?})r$

103. $a(x + y) + b(x + y) = (\underline{?} + \underline{?})(x + y)$

104. $c(x + y) - d(x + y) = (\underline{?} - \underline{?})(x + y)$

■■■■■■■ **NON-ROUTINE PROBLEM**

105. The figure at the right can be formed by using 16 toothpicks. Move exactly two of the toothpicks to form exactly four squares of the same size. Each of the four squares must touch at least one other square.

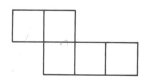

———— **REVIEW CAPSULE FOR SECTION 2-6** ————

Multiply.

1. 0.7×0.8

2. 5.6×8.2

3. 4.059×1000

4. 0.056×34.9

Multiply. Write your answers in lowest terms.

5. $\frac{1}{4} \times \frac{4}{5}$

6. $\frac{2}{3} \times \frac{2}{5}$

7. $\frac{3}{8} \times 7$

8. $4\frac{3}{10} \times 8\frac{5}{16}$

Write without parentheses. (*Pages 45–48*)

1. $-(-1.5)$ **2.** $-(600)$ **3.** $-(16 + 21)$ **4.** $-(9.2 - 5.6)$

Use > or < to compare the numbers. (*Pages 45–48*)

5. $-0.2 \underline{\ ?\ } 0.2$ **6.** $-1 \underline{\ ?\ } -2$ **7.** $-3\frac{1}{4} \underline{\ ?\ } -2\frac{3}{4}$ **8.** $-14 \underline{\ ?\ } -13\frac{7}{8}$

Use a number line to find each sum. (*Pages 49–52*)

9. $5 + (-4)$ **10.** $-6 + 4$ **11.** $-7 + (-2)$

Evaluate. (*Pages 53–57*)

12. $|5| + |-13|$ **13.** $|-\sqrt{13}|$ **14.** $|4| + |-3|$ **15.** $-|1.6| + |1.6|$

Add or subtract as indicated. (*Pages 53–57, 58–61*)

16. $-5 + 2$ **17.** $(4 - 10) - 5$ **18.** $[5 + 4] + [(-7) + 3]$
19. $7 + (-12)$ **20.** $10 - 26 - 8$ **21.** $-2.3 - 0.16 - 0.05$

Simplify. (*Pages 64–68*)

22. $5 + 2a + 6a$ **23.** $7x - x - 3.2x$ **24.** $\frac{3}{4}x - \frac{1}{3}y - \frac{1}{2}x + \frac{2}{5}y$

Historical Digest: Negative Numbers

Did you think negative numbers were a little strange the first time you saw them? You are not alone!

- Thousands of years ago, the Chinese used black number rods for negative numbers and red number rods for positive numbers.
- The ancient Greeks said that a problem such as "What added to 5 gives 4?" was absurd.
- In 600 A.D., the Hindus represented -7 as $\overset{\circ}{7}$.
- In 1225, the Italian mathematician Leonardo Fibonacci first tried to describe a number such as -3 as being a debt of 3.

Find out how negative numbers are represented in business today.

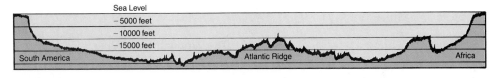

2-6 Multiplication of Real Numbers

The New York Stock Exchange reported that Amtok Oil lost 5 points the previous day of trading.

Amtok Oil: -5 ← **Loss**

If the loss continued 4 days in a row, you would write:

$4 \cdot (-5) = -20$ ← **Total loss for 4 days**

PATTERNS
Look at the pattern in Table 1. In the table, the first factor, 4, remains the same. The second factor decreases by 1 at each step. Recall that factors are the quantities being multiplied.

If the pattern continues, what are the missing products?

$$4 \cdot 4 = 16 \qquad\qquad 4 \cdot (-1) = -4$$
$$4 \cdot 3 = 12 \qquad\qquad 4 \cdot (-2) = -8$$
$$4 \cdot 2 = 8 \qquad\qquad 4 \cdot (-3) = \quad ?$$
$$4 \cdot 1 = 4 \qquad\qquad 4 \cdot (-4) = \quad ?$$
$$4 \cdot 0 = 0$$

Table 1

The table suggests that the product of a positive number and a negative number is a negative number.

Since multiplication of real numbers is commutative,
$$4 \cdot (-2) = -2 \cdot 4 = -8$$

UNLIKE SIGNS

> The product of a positive number and a negative number is a negative number.
>
> $1.2 \cdot (-6) = -7.2$
> $-86 \cdot 7 = -602$

EXAMPLE 1 Multiply: $-21 \cdot 92$

Solution: $-21 \cdot 92 = -(\ ? \ )$ ←——— **The product is negative.**
$$= -1932$$

You know that the product of two positive numbers is positive. Now look at the pattern in Table 2. In the table, the first factor, -4, remains the same. The second factor decreases by 1 at each step.

If the pattern continues, what are the missing products?

$$
\begin{array}{ll}
-4 \cdot 3 = -12 & \qquad -4 \cdot (-1) = 4 \\
-4 \cdot 2 = -8 & \qquad -4 \cdot (-2) = 8 \\
-4 \cdot 1 = -4 & \qquad -4 \cdot (-3) = ? \\
-4 \cdot 0 = 0 & \qquad -4 \cdot (-4) = ?
\end{array}
$$

Table 2

This suggests the following.

LIKE SIGNS

> The product of two numbers having the same sign is a positive number.
>
> $(-20)(-13.9) = 278$
> $-\dfrac{1}{3} \cdot (-15) = 5$

EXAMPLE 2 Multiply: $-18 \cdot \left(-\dfrac{2}{3}\right)$

Solution:
$$
-18 \cdot \left(-\dfrac{2}{3}\right) = (\,?\,) \quad \longleftarrow \text{ The product is positive.}
$$
$$
= \dfrac{\overset{6}{\cancel{18}}}{1} \cdot \dfrac{2}{\underset{1}{\cancel{3}}}
$$
$$
= 12
$$

You already know that the product of a real number and zero is zero.

PROPERTY OF ZERO

> For any real number a, $a \cdot 0 = 0 \cdot a = 0$.

To multiply three or more numbers, group the numbers in pairs.

EXAMPLE 3 Simplify: $(-5)\,(6)\,(-1)\,(1.8)$

Solution: $(-5)(6)(-1)(1.8) = [(-5)(6)][(-1)(1.8)] \longleftarrow$ **By the Associative Property**
$$
= -30\,(-1.8) \longleftarrow (-5)(6) = -30; (-1)(1.8) = -1.8
$$
$$
= 54
$$

Operations with Real Numbers **71**

EXERCISES: Classwork/Homework

Objective: To multiply real numbers

■■■■■ **CHECK YOUR UNDERSTANDING**

Copy and complete.

1. The product of two positive numbers is a __?__ number.

2. The product of a positive number and a negative number is a __?__ number.

3. The product of two negative numbers is a __?__ number.

4. The product of a negative number and a positive number is a __?__ number.

Write each sum as a multiplication problem.

5. $4 + 4 + 4 + 4 + 4 + 4$

6. $-7 + (-7) + (-7) + (-7) + (-7)$

7. $-45 + (-45) + (-45) + (-45)$

8. $-26 + (-26) + (-26)$

In Exercises 9–12, state whether each product is positive or negative.

9. $4 \cdot (-6)$

10. $-3 \cdot 9$

11. $-8 \cdot (-9)$

12. $-6 \cdot (-1)$

■■■■■ **PRACTICE AND APPLY**

Multiply.

13. $6 \times (-3)$

14. -5×2

15. $2 \times (-5)$

16. $5(-2)$

17. $2(5)$

18. $7(0)$

19. $-4 \cdot 3$

20. $4 \cdot (-3)$

21. $-\frac{3}{4} \cdot \frac{2}{3}$

22. $(-4)(-3)$

23. $4(-7)$

24. $(-2.5)(-0.1)$

25. $(-5)(-5)$

26. $6 \cdot 3$

27. $-6 \cdot 3$

28. $8 \cdot (-\frac{1}{4})$

29. $12 \cdot 6$

30. $12 \cdot (-6)$

31. $(-1)(5)$

32. $8(-2.5)$

33. $\frac{2}{3}(-12)$

34. $8.1(0)$

35. $-5(2.4)$

36. $-7.2(\frac{1}{4})$

37. $-1 \cdot (-1)$

38. $-\frac{2}{3} \cdot (-\frac{3}{2})$

39. $-0.5 \cdot (-12)$

40. $(1)(-1)(1)$

41. $2(-4)(5)(-1)$

42. $(-5)(6)(2)(-2)$

43. $\frac{1}{2}(-8)(5)$

44. $(-0.1)(10)(10)$

45. $(-0.1)(0.1)(0.1)$

46. $(-2\frac{1}{2})(\frac{2}{5})(1)$

47. $(4)(0)(-9)$

48. $(3\frac{1}{2})(\frac{1}{2})(-2)$

49. $(\frac{2}{3})(\frac{2}{3})(\frac{2}{3})$

50. $(\frac{7}{5})(-\frac{7}{5})(2)(-2)$

51. $(\frac{8}{7})(-1)(\frac{7}{8})(5)$

52. $5(4)(-2)$

53. $-5(4)(-2)$

54. $-6(-5)(-4)$

55. $-2(-2)(-2)$

56. $(-3)^2$

57. $(-4)^2$

58. $(-1)^2$

59. $(1)^2$

60. $(-1)^3$

Replace the __?__ with $<, =, >$, to make true statements.

61. $2(-3) \underline{\ ?\ } -3(2)$

62. $-6(-1) \underline{\ ?\ } -1(6)$

63. $-0.34(-6) \underline{\ ?\ } -0.17(-3)$

64. $-\frac{3}{2}(\frac{1}{2}) \underline{\ ?\ } -\frac{1}{2}(\frac{3}{2})$

65. $-6(0) \underline{\ ?\ } 0(6)$

66. $|4 \cdot 5| \underline{\ ?\ } |4| \cdot |5|$

67. $|-0.34 \cdot -2| \underline{\ ?\ } |-0.34| \cdot |-2|$

68. $|0 \cdot 1| \underline{\ ?\ } |0| \cdot |1|$

69. $|0.2 \cdot 0.1| \underline{\ ?\ } |-0.2| \cdot |0.1|$

70. $|\frac{2}{3} \cdot \frac{1}{2}| \underline{\ ?\ } |\frac{2}{3}| \cdot |\frac{1}{2}|$

Evaluate each expression for $x = -3$, $y = -2$, and $p = 0$.

71. $2x$

72. $3y$

73. $-2x$

74. $-7y$

75. $5pxy$

76. $3x + y$

77. $2y + p$

78. x^2y^2

Use the sign change key, $\boxed{\text{+/-}}$, on a calculator to multiply.

79. $-456(-67)$

80. $459(-238)$

81. $760(-32)(-1)$

82. $-79(-570)(-1)$

▬▬▬ MAINTAIN

Combine like terms. (*Pages 64–68*)

83. $5x + 9 + 2x - 3$

84. $3x + 2y + 2x + 3y$

85. $y - 6y - 5 + 2y + 3$

86. $2b - 4b - 2 + 3b$

87. $x^2 + 2x + 3x + 2x^2$

88. $x^2 - 3x - x^2 + 5x$

Subtract. (*Pages 58–61*)

89. $-10 - 12$

90. $-10 - (-12)$

91. $-12 - 10$

92. $-12 - (-10)$

93. $-4 - (-15)$

94. $-15 - 4$

95. $4 - 15$

96. $-15 - (-4)$

Tell whether each equation is true for all numbers, some numbers, or no numbers, when the replacement set is the set of rational numbers. (*Pages 22–25*)

97. $5t - t = 4t$

98. $t^3 \cdot 0 = t^3$

99. $d \cdot (-1) = (-1) \cdot d$

▬▬▬ CONNECT AND EXTEND

Let p be any positive number, let n be any negative number, and let z be zero. Write <u>positive</u>, <u>negative</u>, or <u>zero</u> for the value of each expression. If the value cannot be determined, write <u>cannot be determined</u>.

100. $p + z$

101. $n + z$

102. $n + p$

103. $p + (-p)$

104. $-n + n$

105. $p - n$

106. $z - p$

107. $z - n$

108. np

109. nz

110. $n(-p)$

111. $-np$

2-7 Comparing Averages: Mean/Median/Mode

Large amounts of data are often gathered to study the average size of something: earnings, testing scores, hours of sleep, and so on. In such situations, you often need to find a single number called a **measure of central tendency,** to summarize the data or to compare different sets of data. The *mean, median,* and *mode* are three measures of central tendency.

DEFINITIONS

> The **mean** of a set of data is the sum of all the values divided by the number of values.
>
> The **median** of a set of data is the middle value. When there is an even number of values, the median is the mean of the two middle values.
>
> The **mode** of a set of data is the value that occurs most often. A set of data can have more than one mode or no mode.

EXAMPLE Salaries for the fourteen employees of Camcorporation are shown in the table.

President	$250,000
Vice-President	100,000
Comptroller	50,000
Production-line	
Workers (8)	20,000
Secretaries (2)	19,000
Janitor	14,000

Problem: **a.** Find the mean salary.

Solution: Use multiplication and addition to find the total for salaries.

Mean: $\dfrac{\text{Sum of values}}{\text{Number of values}}$

Mean: $\dfrac{250,000 + 100,000 + 50,000 + 8(20,000) + 2(19,000) + 14,000}{14}$

Mean: $\dfrac{612,000}{14} = \$43,714$ ◄——— **Rounded to the nearest dollar**

Problem: **b.** Find the median salary.

Solution: To find the median, *arrange the data in order from highest to lowest* (or from lowest to highest). Since there are 14 values, find the mean of the 7th and 8th values.

Median: **$20,000** ◄——— **The 7th and 8th values are the same.**

Problem: **c.** Find the mode of the salaries.

Solution: More employees make $20,000 than any other salary.

Mode: **$20,000**

COMPARING AVERAGES   In the Example, the median and the mode best represent the "average" salary of the employees because they are closer to more values than the mean. In this case, the mean is higher than most values because it is affected by the two high salaries. In most cases, the median is the average that best summarizes a set of data.

EXERCISES: Classwork/Homework

Objective: To find the mean, median and mode of a set of data

CHECK YOUR UNDERSTANDING

Find the mean, median, and mode for each set of data. When necessary, round your answer to the nearest whole number.

1. 42   45   41   38
    40   42   32   40

2. 85   86   89   89   70
    74   88   85   100   85

3. *Complete:* A number that represents a set of data is called a _?_ .

4. *Complete:* In a set of data, the value that occurs most often is the _?_ .

5. *Complete:* The middle value (or the mean of the middle values) in a set of data is called the _?_ .

6. *Complete:* In a set of data, the value that considers the order of the values is the _?_ .

7. *Complete:* The average that is most affected by very large or very small values is the _?_ .

8. Which measure of central tendency will always be one of the values in a set of data? Why?

PRACTICE AND APPLY

A store manager recorded the number of customers entering the store from 9 A.M. to 6 P.M. on an average day. Use this information for Exercises 9–13.

9. Over what 5-hour period does the store have the greatest number of customers?

10. During what hour does the mode occur?

Hours	Customers
9:00–10:00	10
10:00–11:00	21
11:00–12:00	25
12:00–1:00	27
1:00–2:00	30
2:00–3:00	40
3:00–4:00	35
4:00–5:00	45
5:00–6:00	53

Operations with Real Numbers   **75**

11. Suppose that the manager decides to hire part-time help from 4:00 P.M. to 6:00 P.M. Why is this a reasonable decision?

12. What is the mean number of customers per hour coming into the store? Round your answer to the nearest whole number.

13. Is the answer to Exercise 12 helpful to the manager in deciding when to hire part-time help? Explain.

The table at the right shows yearly salaries for six persons who work at the Torvale Car Rental Agency. Use this table for Exercises 14–18.

14. What is the mean yearly salary?

15. Is the mean yearly salary greater or less than most of the salaries?

16. What is the median yearly salary?

17. Are most of the salaries closer to the mean yearly salary or the median yearly salary?

18. Which average—the mean yearly salary or the median yearly salary—best represents most of the yearly salaries?

Yearly Salaries	
Manager	$40,000
Assistant	$25,000
Clerk	$12,500
Clerk	$12,000
Clerk	$11,500
Clerk	$10,000

This table shows the number of centimeters of rain that fell in Barrow, Alaska in a recent year. Refer to the table for Exercises 19–22.

19. What is the mean monthly rainfall (nearest whole number)?

20. What is the median monthly rainfall?

21. What is the mode for this data?

22. Meteorologists use the mean to give average monthly rainfall. Why is the mean considered the best average in this case?

Rainfall in Barrow			
Jan.	0.5 cm	July	2 cm
Feb.	0.5 cm	Aug.	3 cm
March	0.5 cm	Sept.	2 cm
April	0.5 cm	Oct.	2 cm
May	0.5 cm	Nov.	1 cm
June	1 cm	Dec.	0.5 cm

23. Which measure of central tendency would you use to compare color choices for automobiles? Why?

24. Which measure of central tendency would you use to compare the costs of a head of lettuce over five consecutive weeks? Why?

25. Suppose you are a production line-worker at Camcorporation in the Example on page 74. Would you quote the mean or the median salary to convince your employer that you should receive a raise? Explain.

■■■■■■■ **MAINTAIN**

Multiply. (*Pages 70–73*)

26. $(-5)(-6)(10)$

27. $(-5)(-6)(-10)$

28. $(-0.4)(125)(-8)$

29. $(-3)(14)(-2)$

30. $(-0.5)(100)(4)$

31. $(-6)(-4)(-3)$

Combine like terms. (*Pages 64–68*)

32. $4st^2 - 9st^2$

33. $-1.8xy + 3 - 4.6xy$

34. $9t^2 - 9t^2 + 12$

Evaluate each numerical expression. (*Pages 5–8*)

35. $19 + 5 \div 5 \cdot 4$

36. $14 + 3 \cdot 12$

37. $33 \div 3 \div 3 - 11$

38. $4 - 18 \div 2$

39. $14 \div 2 \cdot 3 - 5$

40. $3 \cdot 4 \cdot 2 \div 6$

■■■■■■■ **CONNECT AND EXTEND**

41. The mean of eight numbers is 24. What is the sum of the numbers?

42. Suppose that 5 points are added to each value in a set of data. How will this affect the mean, median, and mode of the original set of data?

43. Suppose that each value in a set of numerical data is multiplied by 5. How will this affect the mean, median, and mode of the original set of data?

44. Find the mean of ten numbers if the mean of the first four numbers is 10 and the mean of the next six numbers is 16.

─────── **REVIEW CAPSULE FOR SECTION 2–8** ───────

Round each number to the nearest tenth.

1. 1.59

2. 0.42

3. 0.005

4. 21.35

5. 157.09

6. 7.03

7. 14.94

8. 76.13

9. 1.006

10. 0.019

2-8 Division of Real Numbers

Cora is hang gliding. The glider drops 35 yards in 5 minutes.

EXAMPLE 1 What was the glider's altitude change per minute?

Think: Since the altitude decreases, the answer will be negative.

Solution: $-35 \div 5 = -7$

The altitude change was **−7 yards** per minute.

You already know that multiplication and division are related. Use this fact and the results of Example 1 to find the pattern for dividing positive and negative numbers.

Multiplication	**Division**
Since $5 \times 3 = 15$,	$15 \div 3 = 5$, and $15 \div 5 = 3$.
Since $-5 \times 3 = -15$,	$-15 \div 3 = -5$, and $-15 \div -5 = 3$.
Since $5 \times -3 = -15$,	$-15 \div 5 = -3$, and $-15 \div -3 = 5$.

Thus, the pattern for dividing positive and negative numbers is the same as the pattern for multiplying them.

DIVIDING REAL NUMBERS

> The quotient of a positive number and a negative number is a negative number.
>
> $-32 \div 16 = -2$
> $65 \div (-13) = -5$
>
> The quotient of two numbers having the same sign is a positive number.
>
> $-32 \div (-16) = 2$
> $-65 \div (-13) = 5$

EXAMPLE 2 Divide: **a.** $-18 \div 6$ **b.** $16 \div -4$ **c.** $-20 \div -5$

Solution: **a.** $-18 \div 6 = -3$ ⟵ negative ÷ positive = negative

b. $16 \div -4 = -4$ ⟵ positive ÷ negative = negative

c. $-20 \div (-5) = 4$ ⟵ negative ÷ negative = positive

RECIPROCALS   Two numbers whose product is one are **reciprocals** or **multiplicative inverses** of each other.

$$\text{The reciprocal of } 3 \text{ is } \tfrac{1}{3} \text{ because } 3 \cdot \tfrac{1}{3} = 1.$$

$$\text{The reciprocal of } -\tfrac{5}{8} \text{ is } -\tfrac{8}{5} \text{ because } -\tfrac{5}{8} \cdot \left(-\tfrac{8}{5}\right) = 1.$$

$$\text{The reciprocal of } \tfrac{1}{6} \text{ is } 6 \text{ because } \tfrac{1}{6} \cdot 6 = 1.$$

The number zero has no reciprocal, because the product of zero and any real number is 0, not 1.

MULTIPLICA-TIVE INVERSE PROPERTY

For any real number a, $a \ne 0$, there is exactly one number $\frac{1}{a}$ such that

$$a \cdot \frac{1}{a} = 1.$$

$$12 \cdot \tfrac{1}{12} = 1$$

$$-\tfrac{5}{6} \cdot (-\tfrac{6}{5}) = 1$$

$$\tfrac{1}{8} \cdot 8 = 1$$

You can also divide by multiplying by the reciprocal of the divisor.

EXAMPLE 3   Divide: **a.** $24 \div (-6)$ **b.** $-24 \div \left(-\tfrac{5}{6}\right)$

Solution: **a.** $24 \div (-6) = 24 \times -\tfrac{1}{6}$
— Reciprocals —
$$= -4$$

b. $-24 \div \left(-\tfrac{5}{6}\right) = -24 \times -\tfrac{6}{5}$
— Reciprocals —
$$= \tfrac{144}{5}, \text{ or } 28\tfrac{4}{5}$$

Finding an arithmetic mean or **average** involves division. Recall that the arithmetic mean of a set of values is the sum of the values divided by the number of values.

EXAMPLE 4   A city's low temperatures for one week are shown below. Find the mean low temperature for the week to the nearest tenth.

S	M	T	W	T	F	S
$-2.5°$C	$-3.8°$C	$4.2°$C	$2.9°$C	$-2.8°$C	$-1.4°$C	$-3.2°$C

Solution: **1** Add the negative temperatures.
$$-2.5 + (-3.8) + (-2.8) + (-1.4) + (-3.2) = -13.7$$
2 Add the positive temperatures: $4.2 + 2.9 = 7.1$

3 Find the sum of the positive and negative temperatures. Then divided by 7, the number of temperatures.

$$\text{Mean} = \frac{-13.7 + 7.1}{7} = \frac{-6.6}{7} \approx -0.9$$

The mean low temperature is about **−0.9°C.**

EXERCISES: Classwork/Homework

Objective: To divide real numbers

Tell whether the quotient is positive or negative.

1. $-6 \div 2$ **2.** $-6 \div (-2)$ **3.** $6 \div (-2)$ **4.** $6 \div 2$

For Exercises 5–11, use the factors in Column A to find the quotient in Column B.

Column A	Column B
5. $108(91) = 9828$	$9828 \div 91 = \underline{\ ?\ }$
6. $-7(35) = -245$	$-245 \div 35 = \underline{\ ?\ }$
7. $-63(-24) = 1512$	$1512 \div (-24) = \underline{\ ?\ }$
8. $24(-15) = -360$	$-360 \div (-15) = \underline{\ ?\ }$
9. $-17(18) = -306$	$-306 \div 18 = \underline{\ ?\ }$
10. $(-21)(-39) = 819$	$819 \div -39 = \underline{\ ?\ }$
11. $399(-6) = -2394$	$-2394 \div -6 = \underline{\ ?\ }$

▬▬▬▬ PRACTICE AND APPLY

Divide.

12. $-20 \div 5$ **13.** $-20 \div (-5)$ **14.** $20 \div 5$

15. $0 \div 5$ **16.** $0 \div (-5)$ **17.** $100 \div (-2)$

18. $-9 \div 9$ **19.** $6 \div 6$ **20.** $4 \div (-4)$

21. $48 \div (-8)$ **22.** $-56 \div (-1)$ **23.** $-12 \div \frac{1}{3}$

24. $0 \div (-24)$ **25.** $\frac{-5}{8} \div \frac{3}{2}$ **26.** $\frac{-3}{7} \div \left(\frac{-8}{21}\right)$

27. $-2.56 \div (-0.8)$ **28.** $\frac{7}{10} \div 14$ **29.** $12 \div \left(\frac{-2}{3}\right)$

30. $\frac{785}{-100}$ **31.** $\frac{-3.2}{-1000}$ **32.** $-6\frac{2}{3} \div 3\frac{3}{4}$

Find the next number in each sequence by dividing.

33. $-40, -20, -10, \underline{\quad?\quad}$ **34.** $40, -20, 10, \underline{\quad?\quad}$ **35.** $96, -24, 6, \underline{\quad?\quad}$

36. $-512, 64, -8, \underline{\quad?\quad}$ **37.** $-200, -2, -0.02, \underline{\quad?\quad}$ **38.** $-1, 0.1, -0.01, \underline{\quad?\quad}$

39. The Union Filter Corporation reported the following profit, shown as a positive amount, and loss, shown as a negative amount, for the last six months of a year. Find the mean (average) profit or loss for the 6 months.

July	August	September	October	November	December
$55,800	$12,500	−$10,900	−$7,700	$16,700	−$20,800

40. A town's low temperatures for one week are recorded below. Find the mean low temperature for the week. Round your answer to the nearest tenth.

S	M	T	W	T	F	S
$-1.1°$	$-0.6°$	$0.3°$	$-1.2°$	$-2.3°$	$-0.7°$	$-0.4°$

41. At the end of a year, the national inflation rate was 9.8%. The table below shows the change in rate for each of the first seven months of the following year. Find the mean change for these seven months.

J	F	M	A	M	J	J
-0.3%	-0.2%	$+0.8\%$	$+1.2\%$	-0.6%	$+0.5\%$	$+1.4\%$

42. The following table shows the change (in feet per second) in the average speed of a moving car over a five-minute interval. Find the mean change in the average speed between 9:01 and 9:06.

Time Interval	9:01–9:02	9:02–9:03	9:03–9:04	9:04–9:05	9:05–9:06
Change in Speed	$+1.4$	-0.4	$+0.3$	-0.1	$+0.8$

Simplify. If you use a calculator, remember to use the sign change key.

43. $(3)(-5) \div (\frac{-24}{8})$

44. $(-3)(-4)(-(\frac{-9}{-3}))$

45. $\dfrac{(-51) \div (-17)}{-(3 \div \frac{-1}{3})}$

46. $\dfrac{(-4 \div 2) \div [(-3)(-4)(-2)]}{-6 \div (-8) \div (-2)}$

47. $\dfrac{(-1)^2 - (-2)^3 + (-3)^2 - (-4)^2}{(-5)^2 - (-3)^2 + (-1)^3 - (-2)^2}$

Evaluate each expression for $x = -10$, $y = -15$, and $q = 0$.

48. $\dfrac{x + y}{-5}$

49. $\dfrac{x - y}{-5}$

50. $\dfrac{y + q}{15}$

51. $\dfrac{2x + q}{4}$

52. $\dfrac{3y}{5}$

53. $\dfrac{x^2 + y}{-5}$

54. $\dfrac{y^2 + q^2}{x}$

55. $\dfrac{x^2y^2q^2}{x}$

Find the mean, median, and mode for each set of numbers. (*Pages 74–77*)

56. 8, 8, 13, 14, 9 **57.** 9, 9, 9, 9, 9, 9 **58.** 3.4, 1.7, 8.3, 5.3, 6.8

For Exercises 59–61, replace the _?_ with >, <, or = to make a true statement. (*Pages 70–73*)

59. $(-6)9 \underline{\ ?\ } -6(8)$ **60.** $(-10)(1) \underline{\ ?\ } (-10)(-1)$ **61.** $25(-4) \underline{\ ?\ } (-25)(-4)$

62. The distance, d, in which a driver can stop a car on dry pavement is given by formula:

$$d = 0.4s + 0.02s^2$$

where s is the speed of the car in kilometers per hour. Use the formula to find the distance it will take a car to stop when it is traveling at 80 kilometers per hour. (*Pages 14–18*)

63. The number of points, p, that a hockey team has accumulated is given by the formula:

$$p = 2x + y$$

where x = the number of wins and y = the number of ties. Find the number of points that the Rangers have if they played 65 games, won 45, and lost 8. (*Pages 14–18*)

CONNECT AND EXTEND

Find the value of x that makes each statement true.

64. $480 \div x = -8$ **65.** $-360 \div x = -6$ **66.** $-248 \div x = -8$

67. $-0.09 \div x = -3$ **68.** $-3.6 \div -x = 4$ **69.** $459 \div -x = -9$

NON-ROUTINE PROBLEM

70. Suppose that you earn $100 every minute. How long will it take you to earn a billion dollars?

a. Which answer is closest?

   i. one year   **ii.** 10 years
   iii. 20 years   **iv.** 100 years

b. Use a calculator to find the exact answer. Compare the answer with your estimate.

—— **REVIEW CAPSULE FOR SECTION 2-9** ——

Write a fraction for each mixed number.

1. $6\frac{1}{2}$ **2.** $7\frac{3}{4}$ **3.** $-6\frac{1}{4}$ **4.** $-9\frac{3}{4}$ **5.** $1\frac{1}{10}$ **6.** $-3\frac{5}{8}$

2-9 Preparing to Solve Equations

The rules for addition, subtraction, multiplication, and division of real numbers are useful in evaluating algebraic expressions.

EXAMPLE 1 Evaluate $y^2 - xy + 3$ for $y = -2$ and $x = 3$.

Solution: $y^2 - xy + 3 = (-2)(-2) - (3)(-2) + 3$ ⟵ **Replace y with −2 and x with 3.**

$= 4 - (-6) + 3$ ⟵ **4 − (−6) = 4 + 6**

$= 4 + 6 + 3 = 13$

Examples 2, 3, and 4 will help you to sharpen the skills needed to solve equations. Example 2 shows you how to find the product of a number and an algebraic term having a numerical coefficient.

EXAMPLE 2 Multiply: **a.** $-\frac{1}{2} \cdot 2x$ **b.** $-\frac{3}{4} \cdot (-\frac{4}{3}x)$

Solutions: Use the Associative Property to group the numbers.

a. The product will be negative. **b.** The product will be positive.

$$-\frac{1}{2} \cdot 2x = -\left(\frac{1}{2} \cdot 2\right)x$$ ⟵ **By the Associative Property** ⟶ $$-\frac{3}{4} \cdot \left(-\frac{4}{3}x\right) = \left(\frac{\overset{1}{\cancel{3}}}{\cancel{4}} \cdot \frac{\overset{1}{\cancel{4}}}{\cancel{3}}\right)x$$

$$= -1 \cdot x = -x$$ $$= 1 \cdot x = x$$

In Example 3, you use the fact that the product of a number and its reciprocal (multiplicative inverse) is 1.

EXAMPLE 3 By what number would you multiply each expression to obtain y? Show that your answer is correct.

a. $-\frac{1}{4}y$ **b.** $-y$ ⟵ **−y = −1 · y**

Solutions: Multiply by the reciprocal of the numerical coefficient

a. Reciprocal of $-\frac{1}{4}$: **−4** **b.** Reciprocal of -1: **−1**

$$-4 \cdot \left(-\frac{1}{4}y\right) = \left[-4 \cdot \left(-\frac{1}{4}\right)\right] \cdot y$$ $$-1 \cdot (-1 \cdot y) = \left(-1 \cdot (-1)\right) \cdot y$$

$$= 1 \cdot y = y$$ $$= 1 \cdot y = y$$

In Example 4, you use the Additive Inverse Property which states that the sum of a number and its additive inverse is zero.

EXAMPLE 4 What number would you add to each expression to obtain x? Show that your answer is correct.

    a. $x + 9$ **b.** $x + (-6)$

Solutions: Add the additive inverse of 9 and of -6.

a. Additive inverse of 9: -9

$$x + 9 + (-9) = x + [9 + (-9)]$$
$$= x + 0$$
$$= x$$

b. Additive inverse of (-6): **6**

$$x + (-6) + 6 = x + (-6 + 6)$$
$$= x + 0$$
$$= x$$

EXERCISES: Classwork/Homework

Objective: To practice the skills needed to solve equations

CHECK YOUR UNDERSTANDING

In Exercises 1–10, match each expression with an equivalent expression in the box at the right.

$$
\begin{array}{c}
0 \\
1 \\
-1 \\
t \\
-t
\end{array}
$$

1. $-\frac{1}{3}(-3)$ **2.** $15 + (-15)$ **3.** $1 \cdot t$

4. $(-1) \cdot t$ **5.** $-4 + t + 4$ **6.** $\frac{4}{5} \times \frac{5}{4}$

7. $\left(-\frac{1}{8}\right) \cdot 8t$ **8.** $t + (-1) + 1$ **9.** $(-1)(-t)$ **10.** $(-t)\left(\frac{1}{t}\right)(0)$

PRACTICE AND APPLY

Evaluate each expression for $x = -15$, $y = -10$, and $q = 0$.

11. $x + y$ **12.** $y + q$ **13.** $2x$ **14.** $3y$ **15.** xy

16. qy **17.** x^2 **18.** y^2 **19.** $x^2 + y^2$ **20.** $q^2 + y^2$

21. q^3 **22.** $x^2 + q^2$ **23.** $q \cdot x \cdot y$ **24.** x^2y **25.** $y - x$

26. $x - y$ **27.** $x - y + q$ **28.** $q - y$ **29.** $\dfrac{y}{x}$ **30.** $\dfrac{q}{y}$

Multiply.

31. $\frac{1}{3} \cdot 3y$ **32.** $\frac{1}{4} \cdot 4y$ **33.** $-\frac{1}{5} \cdot 5y$ **34.** $-\frac{1}{6} \cdot 6y$ **35.** $\frac{2}{3} \cdot \frac{3}{2}y$

36. $-\frac{2}{5} \cdot \frac{5}{2}y$ **37.** $-\frac{5}{7} \cdot \frac{7}{5}y$ **38.** $-\frac{5}{7} \cdot 7a$ **39.** $\frac{3}{5} \cdot (-5a)$ **40.** $-1 \cdot (-1a)$

41. $\frac{2}{3} \cdot (-3y)$ **42.** $\frac{5}{6} \cdot (-18b)$ **43.** $-1 \cdot \frac{4}{5}c$ **44.** $\frac{3}{5}(-25p)$ **45.** $-\frac{3}{5}(-25p)$

By what number would you multiply each expression to obtain y? In Exercises 46–61, show that your answer is correct.

46. $\frac{3}{5} y$　　　　　**47.** $\frac{9}{7} y$　　　　　**48.** $-7y$　　　　　**49.** $-8y$

50. $-\frac{1}{5} y$　　　　**51.** $-\frac{2}{3} y$　　　　**52.** $-\frac{2}{5} y$　　　　**53.** $-\frac{9}{10} y$

54. $-1y$　　　　　**55.** $-y$　　　　　**56.** y　　　　　**57.** $1y$

58. $3\frac{1}{4} y$　　　　**59.** $-7\frac{1}{4} y$　　　　**60.** $-8\frac{1}{2} y$　　　　**61.** $\frac{y}{2}$

What number would you add to each expression to obtain x?
In Exercises 62–85, show that your answer is correct.

62. $x + 10$　　　　**63.** $x + 1$　　　　**64.** $x + (-5)$　　　　**65.** $x + (-9)$

66. $x + (-10)$　　　**67.** $x + (-4)$　　　**68.** $-6 + x$　　　　**69.** $-12 + x$

70. $16 + x$　　　　**71.** $21 + x$　　　　**72.** $x + (12 - 4)$　　**73.** $x + (-9 + 3)$

74. $(-12 + 5) + x$　**75.** $(-3 - 1) + x$　**76.** $(-9 - 17) + x$　**77.** $x + (8 - 13)$

Example:　$x - 1 = x + (-1)$　　　Opposite of (-1): 1　　　Therefore, add **1.**

78. $x - 7$　　　　　**79.** $x - 15$　　　　**80.** $x - 2$　　　　**81.** $x - 23$

82. $x - 19$　　　　**83.** $x - \frac{1}{5}$　　　　**84.** $x - (-1)$　　　　**85.** $x - (-2)$

Evaluate each expression for $x = -20$, $y = -10$, and $q = -1$.

86. $2x + 3y$　　　　**87.** $2x - y$　　　　**88.** $x - 2y$　　　　**89.** $2x + 3q$

90. $q - 2y$　　　　**91.** $q - 3x$　　　　**92.** $3xy$　　　　　**93.** $-5q^2x^2y$

■■■■■ **MAINTAIN**

Divide. (*Pages 78–82*)

94. $96 \div (-12)$　　**95.** $-89 \div (-1)$　　**96.** $-1 \div (-1)$　　**97.** $-2\frac{1}{8} \div 2\frac{1}{8}$

98. $-5.44 \div 4$　　**99.** $\frac{-1001}{-1001}$　　**100.** $\frac{720}{-9}$　　**101.** $\frac{-336}{16}$

Find the mean, median, and mode. (*Pages 74–77*)

102.　**Heights of World's Ten Highest Dams**

325 m	317 m	285 m	272 m	265 m
265 m	242 m	237 m	235 m	233 m

103.　**Number of Peas Found in 27 Pods**

4, 5, 6, 3, 1, 6, 4, 4, 4,
3, 5, 6, 3, 4, 3, 4, 2, 1,
4, 5, 4, 5, 4, 3, 5, 4, 6

Evaluate each expression. (*Pages 9–13*)

104. $18(3)^2 \div 2^3 + 8$　　　　**105.** $1^5 + 4^3 - 2^4$　　　　**106.** $9 \cdot (4)^3 \div 2^3 - 3^2$

Operations with Real Numbers　**85**

Focus on College Entrance Tests

A **number sequence** is a succession of numbers that follow a fixed pattern. Each number in the sequence is related to the preceding number according to a definite plan. **Identifying that plan** is the key step in determining other numbers in each sequence.

Write the next two numbers in each sequence.

   a. $-5, 10, -20, 40, -80, \cdots$

   b. $5, 2, 5, 4, 5, 6, 5, \cdots$

Solution: **a. Think:** $-5 \cdot (-2) = 10 \quad 10 \cdot (-2) = -20 \quad -20 \cdot (-2) = 40$

     Rule: Multiply the preceding number by (-2).

     Next two numbers: **160, -320**

     b. Think: 5, 2, 5, 4, 5, 6, 5
                +2   +2

     Rule: Add 2 to every other term. Otherwise write 5.

     Next two numbers: **8, 5**

Write the next four numbers in each sequence.

1. $1, 5, 9, 13, 17, \cdots$

2. $400, 373, 346, 319, 292, \cdots$

3. $7\frac{3}{4}, 7\frac{5}{8}, 7\frac{1}{2}, 7\frac{3}{8}, 7\frac{1}{4}, \cdots$

4. $0.1, 0.4, 1.6, 6.4, 25.6, \cdots$

5. $-2, -4, -8, -16, -32, \cdots$

6. $-26, -20, -14, -8, -2, \cdots$

7. $2.52, 3.02, 3.52, 4.02, \cdots$

8. $-3, 3, -3, 3, -3, \cdots$

9. $5, 6, 8, 11, 15, \cdots$

10. $0, 3, 8, 15, 24, \cdots$

11. $9, 9, 18, 18, 27, 27, \cdots$

12. $2, 5, 15, 18, 54, \cdots$

13. $100, 81, 64, 49, 36, \cdots$

14. $4, 16, 5, 25, 6, \cdots$

15. $1, \frac{1}{4}, \frac{1}{9}, \frac{1}{16}, \frac{1}{25}, \cdots$

16. $3, 7, 23, 87, 343, \cdots$

Chapter Summary

IMPORTANT TERMS

Absolute value (p. 53)
Additive inverse (p. 58)
Equivalent expressions (p. 65)
Like terms (p. 64)
Mean (p. 74)
Median (p. 74)

Mode (p. 74)
Multiplicative inverse (p. 79)
Numerical coefficient (p. 64)
Opposites (p. 45)
Reciprocal (p. 79)
Term (p. 64)

IMPORTANT IDEAS

1. For any two real numbers, the smaller is to the left of the larger on the number line.

2. The sum of two negative numbers is the opposite of the sum of their absolute values.

3. To find the sum of a positive and a negative number, subtract the smaller from the greater absolute value. Then write the result with the same sign as the addend having the greater absolute value.

4. **Additive Inverse Property:** For any real number, a, there is a real number $-a$ such that $a + (-a) = 0$.

5. **Subtracting Real Numbers:** To subtract a number b from a number a, add the additive inverse of b to a. That is, $a - b = a + (-b)$.

6. **Substitution Property:** If two expressions are equivalent, you can always replace one with the other in a given expression.

7. **Multiplication**
   a. **Unlike Signs:** The product of a positive number and a negative number is a negative number.
   b. **Like Signs:** The product of two numbers having the same sign is a positive number.

8. **Multiplicative Property of Zero:** For any real number a, $a \cdot 0 = 0 \cdot a = 0$.

9. The **mean** of a set of data is the sum of all the values divided by the number of values.

10. The **median** of a set of data is the middle value. When there is an even number of values, the median is the mean of the two middle values.

11. The **mode** of a set of data is the value that occurs most often. A set of data can have more than one mode or no mode.

12. **Dividing Real Numbers:** The quotient of a positive number and a negative number is a positive number. The quotient of two numbers having the same sign is a positive number.

13. **Multiplicative Inverse Property:** See page 79.

Write the opposite of each number (*Pages 45–48*)

1. 4   **2.** -12 **3.** 16.4   **4.** $-\sqrt{7}$ **5.** $-\pi$ **6.** $-8\frac{1}{3}$

Write without parentheses. (*Pages 45–48*)

7. $-(9.3 + 7.4)$ **8.** $-(87.0)$ **9.** $-(-t)$ **10.** $-(9.1 - 3.2)$

Use > or < to compare the numbers. (*Pages 45–48*)

11. $-(-4)$ _?_ 1   **12.** 10 _?_ -14 **13.** -3 _?_ 7   **14.** $-\sqrt{3}$ _?_ 1

Use a number line to find each sum. (*Pages 49–52*)

15. $7 + (-3)$ **16.** $-4 + 5$ **17.** $-8 + (-1)$

Evaluate. (*Pages 53–57*)

18. $|36,000|$ **19.** $|4.21| - |2.33|$ **20.** $|-4| + |12|$ **21.** $|-246| + |30|$

Add. (*Pages 53–57*)

22. $(-11) + 4$ **23.** $8 + 7$ **24.** $(-1.3) + (-2.9)$ **25.** $0 + (-1\frac{3}{4})$

Use positive and negative numbers to represent each word description. Then answer the question. (*Pages 53–57*)

26. A jet ski was traveling at a speed of 25 miles per hour. It then slowed down by 7 miles per hour and sped up 3 miles per hour. What was its new speed?

27. The temperature at 7 P.M. was 5°C. By 5 A.M. it had dropped 7°C. What was the new temperature at 5 A.M.?

Subtract. (*Pages 58–61*)

28. $15 - 21$ **29.** $-3 - 7$ **30.** $-6.8 - (-8.1)$ **31.** $\frac{7}{9} - (-\frac{1}{9})$

Solve. (*Pages 58–61*)

32. The actual temperature is 17°F. The wind chill temperature is -7°F. How much colder than the actual temperature is the wind child temperature?

33. The actual temperature is 24°F. The wind chill temperature is -11°F. How much colder than the actual temperature is the wind chill temperature?

Combine like terms. (*Pages 64–68*)

34. $9m - 17m$ **35.** $3g + 10g$ **36.** $-25rt - (3rt)$ **37.** $15ac + (-4ac)$

38. $7x + 8x + 10$ **39.** $14m - 3m - 4$ **40.** $31n + 5mn - 3n$ **41.** $42x - 36 + 72x$

Multiply. (*Pages 70–73*)

42. $(-0.2)(3.1)$ **43.** $(6)(-4)$ **44.** $(-19)(-1)(2)$ **45.** $-1\frac{1}{2} \cdot (-\frac{2}{3})$

A weight lifter recorded how much weight he could bench press each day for one week. Use the information in the table at the right for Exercises 46–49.
(*Pages 74–77*)

Day	Weight
Mon.	220 lb
Tues.	225 lb
Wed.	230 lb
Thurs.	230 lb
Fri.	240 lb
Sat.	245 lb
Sun.	250 lb

46. To the nearest pound, what was the mean weight lifted?

47. Is the mean weight greater or less than most of the weights?

48. What is the median weight?   **49.** What is the mode for these weights?

Divide. (*Pages 78–82*)

50. $-14 \div 14$ **51.** $117 \div (-9)$ **52.** $\frac{-7.38}{-100}$ **53.** $(-\frac{2}{3} \div -\frac{1}{2})$

54. The following table shows the amount of gain and loss in the price of a stock over a five-day period. Find the mean change over the five days. (*Pages 78–82*)

M	T	W	T	F
$-\frac{1}{8}$	$+\frac{5}{8}$	$-\frac{11}{4}$	$+\frac{3}{4}$	$-\frac{5}{8}$

Evaluate each expression for $x = 7$, $y = -9$ and $z = \frac{1}{2}$. (*Pages 83–85*)

55. $x + y$ **56.** $y^2 + xz$ **57.** $(x - y)z$ **58.** $yz - x^2$ **59.** $y^2 + y$

Multiply. (*Pages 83–85*)

60. $-7 \cdot \frac{4}{7}t$ **61.** $-2 \cdot \frac{2}{3}c$ **62.** $\frac{1}{3} \cdot (-3m)$ **63.** $\frac{1}{2} \cdot (-14x^2)$ **64.** $-\frac{3}{4} \cdot 14p$

By what number would you multiply each expression to obtain y? (*Pages 83–85*)

65. $14y$ **66.** $-\frac{1}{7}y$ **67.** $3\frac{1}{4}y$ **68.** $-6\frac{5}{8}y$ **69.** $\frac{-y}{11}$

What number would you add to each expression to obtain x? (*Pages 83–85*)

70. $x + 11$ **71.** $x - 7$ **72.** $-6 + x$ **73.** $12 + x$ **74.** $(-1 + 9) + x$

Evaluate.

1. $-(-526.36)$ 2. $|-(-3.1)|$ 3. $-|-\pi|$ 4. $|-304|$

Use > or < to compare the numbers.

5. $|-9|$ __?__ $-|9|$ 6. 0.13 __?__ -0.14 7. $-|21|$ __?__ $|11|$

Perform the indicated operations.

8. $(-4) + 7$ 9. $(-5.4) + (-8.3)$ 10. $-15 \div (-\frac{5}{6})$

11. $-3 - (-12)$ 12. $(-\frac{3}{4})(-\frac{11}{2}) - 1$ 13. $(-3.2) \div (-1.6)$

14. Randy has $194 in his checking account. He wrote a check for $167 and made a deposit of $312. What was his new balance?

15. The temperature was 14°C at noon. By 3 P.M. it had dropped to -1°C. How much did the temperature change during that time?

Combine like terms.

16. $25rs - (-4rs) + 6$

17. $3\frac{1}{3}gt - \frac{1}{3}g + \frac{1}{3}gt - 2$

Find the mean, median, and mode for each set of data. When necessary, round your answer to the nearest whole number.

18. 60   56   57   61
    56   58   59   60

19. 21   20   19   21
    21   19   20   18

20. A town's low temperatures for one week are recorded below. Find the mean low temperature for the week.

S	M	T	W	T	F	S
$-1.3°$	$-0.4°$	$0.2°$	$-1.1°$	$-2.1°$	$-0.8°$	$0.6°$

Evaluate each expression for $t = 19$, $m = 7$, and $n = -1$.

21. $t - mn$

22. $m + (tn - m)$

23. Multiply: $(-\frac{14}{15})(-105r)$

24. By what number would you multiply $-\frac{7}{8}y$ to obtain y?

25. What number would you add to $(-9 - 12) + x$ to obtain x?

Skills

Solve. (*Pages 45–48*)

1. $-x = 5$ **2.** $-m = 0$ **3.** $-a = -\frac{1}{3}$ **4.** $-y = \pi$ **5.** $-t = 3.72$

Perform the indicated operations. (*Pages 53–61, 70–73, 78–82*)

6. $8 + (-11)$ **7.** $8.4 + (-0.2)$ **8.** $\frac{8}{3} - \left(-\frac{1}{3}\right)$ **9.** $-2 - (-7)$

10. $3\frac{1}{5}(-\frac{1}{8})$ **11.** $(-9)(7)(-2)$ **12.** $-54 \div \left(-\frac{9}{10}\right)$ **13.** $-7.2 \div 3.6$

Simplify. (*Pages 64–68*)

14. $6s - (-5s) + 10$ **15.** $24x - (-x)$ **16.** $3bc + 9bc - 7b$

17. $14x - 5y - (-7x) + 6y$ **18.** $24c - 16d - (-4d) + 6c$

Evaluate each expression for $x = 9$, $y = -3$, and $z = 0$. (*Pages 70–73*)

19. zy **20.** y^2 **21.** $x^2 + y^2$ **22.** $x - y$ **23.** $x \cdot y \cdot z$

Multiply. (*Pages 70–73*)

24. $\frac{1}{4}(12x)$ **25.** $-1(-3x)$ **26.** $\frac{3}{8}(-16y)$ **27.** $(-g)(-3)$ **28.** $\frac{5}{2}(-\frac{2}{5}a)$

29. Find the mean, median, and mode of the data at the right.
(*Pages 74–77*)

Number of Long Distance Calls

9	11	6	10
8	3	10	7

Problem Solving and Applications

30. On four successive plays, a football team lost 4 yards, lost 2 yards, gained 5 yards, and gained 3 yards. What was the team's net gain? (*Pages 53–57*)

31. The actual temperature is 15°F. The wind chill temperature is $-20°F$. How much colder than the actual temperature is the wind chill temperature? (*Pages 58–61*)

32. The table below shows a corporation's profit $(+)$ and loss $(-)$ over a six month period. Find the average profit or loss over the six months. (*Pages 78–82*)

January	February	March	April	May	June
$-\$28,500$	$-\$18,300$	$-\$7,700$	$\$12,500$	$\$14,300$	$\$22,900$

Part 1 **Choose the best answer. Choose *a*, *b*, *c*, or *d*.**

1. Which algebraic expression represents this word expression?
   The total number of miles driven, m, decreased by 13

   a. $m + 13$ **b.** $13m$ **c.** $m - 13$ **d.** $\frac{m}{13}$

2. Evaluate: $(24 - 16) \div (10 - 8)$
   a. 4   **b.** 2   **c.** 6   **d.** 1

3. Evaluate $3(t + 2b)$ for $t = 10$ and $b = 6$.
   a. 42   **b.** 54   **c.** 78   **d.** 66

4. Which has the same meaning as $6 \cdot t \cdot t \cdot t \cdot t$?
   a. $6 - 4t$ **b.** $6t^4$ **c.** $6^4 \cdot t$ **d.** $6 + t^4$

5. Find the value of $(4x)^3$ for $x = 2$.
   a. 32   **b.** 512   **c.** 64   **d.** 24

6. What is the value of I in the formula $I = PRT$ when $P = \$500$,
   $R = 0.06$ and $T = \frac{1}{2}$?
   a. $15   **b.** $150   **c.** $60   **d.** $30

7. What are the solutions of $x + 3 < 9$ when the replacement set is
   $\{0, 3, 6, 9, 12\}$?
   a. 0, 3, 6   **b.** 0   **c.** 0, 3   **d.** 0, 3, 6, 9

8. Which property is illustrated by the statement $a(b + c) = ab + ac$?
   a. Symmetric   **b.** Associative   **c.** Distributive   **d.** Identity

9. Solve: $-x = -8$
   a. -8 **b.** 0   **c.** 8   **d.** $\frac{1}{8}$

10. Find the sum: $-17 + (-14)$
    a. -31 **b.** -3 **c.** 31   **d.** 3

11. Evaluate: $|-12| + (-4) - |7|$
    a. -23 **b.** 15   **c.** 9   **d.** 1

12. Which number is the additive inverse of 4.2?
    a. 2.4   **b.** $|4.2|$ **c.** -4.2 **d.** $|-4.2|$

13. Subtract: $-42 - (-7)$
    a. -35 **b.** 35   **c.** 49   **d.** -49

14. Simplify: $4x + 6x - 3$

    a. $10x - 3$ **b.** $10x^2 - 3$ **c.** $-3 + 10$ **d.** $10x$

15. Multiply: $-\frac{1}{2}(-4)(-8)(2)$

    a. 16 **b.** -32 **c.** 32 **d.** -16

16. Combine like terms: $-x + 2y + 4x - 6y$

    a. $4y - 3x$ **b.** $-3x - 4y$ **c.** $3x - 4y$ **d.** $5x - 4y$

17. What is the mean of the numbers 32, 16, 48, 36, and 18?

    a. 30 **b.** 20 **c.** 32 **d.** 25

18. Which number is the median of $-3, 6, 0, -8, -11, 7, 13$?

    a. -5 **b.** 0 **c.** $-\frac{5}{7}$ **d.** 6

19. Evaluate $a^2 \cdot ab + 4$ for $a = -3$ and $b = -1$.

    a. 16 **b.** 31 **c.** -8 **d.** -10

20. Divide: $\left(-\frac{3}{9}\right) \div \left(-\frac{1}{3}\right)$

    a. -1 **b.** 0 **c.** 3 **d.** 1

21. By what number would you multiply $-\frac{3}{11}t$ to obtain t?

    a. $-\frac{11}{3}$ **b.** $-\frac{3}{11}$ **c.** $\frac{11}{3}$ **d.** -1

Part 2   Solve each problem.

22. A square deck is 12 feet long and 12 feet wide. Use the formula $A = s^2$ to find the area, A, of the deck.

23. The low temperature in Boston one night was $-8°C$. During the day, the temperature rose $17°C$. What was the temperature then?

24. The average temperature on Friday was $10°C$. The average temperature on Saturday was $-3°C$. Find the difference between these two average temperatures.

25. Juan carried the football seven times during Saturday's game. His total yardage on each run was 5, 2, -4, -1, 10, 3, and -8. Find his average number of yards gained or lost for the game.

26. During one week, Ted worked the following number of hours: 8, $6\frac{1}{2}$, 11, 9, and $5\frac{1}{2}$. Find the average number of hours he worked each day.

27. An elevator went up to the 29th floor. Then it came down 14 floors before going up again 17 floors. At what floor was it then?

28. During one month, Hollis lost a total of 24 pounds. The next month he gained 9 pounds. How much did he lose during the two-month period?

29. Use the formula $V = lwh$ to find the volume, V, of a box where $l = 1.2$ meters, $w = 0.5$ meters, and $h = 2$ meters.

3 Solving Equations

The concept of **ratio** plays an important role in design. For example, the glide ability of a hang glider is related to the ratio of the wing spread and the area of the wing.

3-1   Solving Equations: Addition Property

Recall that an equation is a mathematical sentence that uses "=."
To solve equations, think of a balance scale.

To keep the balance scale level, what is added to one side of the scale must also be added to the other side.

If you add 4 to each side of an equation, the result is an equivalent equation.

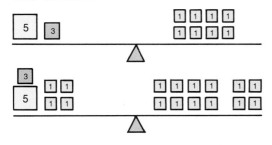

$$5 + 3 = 8$$

$$5 + 3 + 4 = 8 + 4$$
$$8 + 4 = 8 + 4$$

This suggests the following property for equations.

EQUATION ADDITION PROPERTY

Adding the same number to each side of an equation results in an equivalent equation.

$$y + 1 = 2$$
$$y + 1 + (-1) = 2 + (-1)$$
$$y = 1$$

Equivalent equations have the same solutions for the same replacement set. To solve an equation, you get the variable alone on one side of the equation.

EXAMPLE 1   Solve and check: $y + 21 = 8$

Solution: **Think:** What must be added to $y + 21$ to get y?

$$y + 21 = 8 \qquad \longleftarrow \text{ Add } (-21) \text{ to each side.}$$
$$y + 21 + (-21) = 8 + (-21) \qquad \longleftarrow \text{ Solve for } y.$$
$$y + \qquad 0 \qquad = \qquad -13$$
$$y = -13 \qquad \longleftarrow \text{ The coefficient of } y \text{ is 1.}$$

Check: $y + 21 = 8 \qquad \longleftarrow \text{ Replace } y \text{ with } -13.$
$$-13 + 21 \stackrel{?}{=} 8$$
$$8 \stackrel{?}{=} 8 \quad \text{Yes } \checkmark \qquad \text{The solution is } -13.$$

Always check to be sure that the solution of the final equivalent equation also satisfies the original equation.

EXAMPLE 2 Solve and check: $x - 3\frac{1}{2} = 8$

Solution: **Think:** $x - 3\frac{1}{2} = x + (-3\frac{1}{2})$ So add $3\frac{1}{2}$, the additive inverse of $-3\frac{1}{2}$, to each side of the equation.

$$x - 3\frac{1}{2} = 8 \qquad \longleftarrow \qquad \text{Add } 3\frac{1}{2} \text{ to each side.}$$
$$x - 3\frac{1}{2} + 3\frac{1}{2} = 8 + 3\frac{1}{2}$$
$$x = 11\frac{1}{2} \qquad \longleftarrow \qquad \text{The coefficient of } x \text{ is 1.}$$

Check: $\quad x - 3\frac{1}{2} = 8 \qquad \longleftarrow \qquad \text{Replace } x \text{ with } 11\frac{1}{2}.$
$$11\frac{1}{2} - 3\frac{1}{2} \stackrel{?}{=} 8$$
$$8 \stackrel{?}{=} 8 \quad \text{Yes } \checkmark \quad \text{The solution is } \mathbf{11\frac{1}{2}.}$$

Some equations can be solved more easily by writing them in an equivalent form. For example,

$$y + (-5) = 6 \text{ is equivalent to } y - 5 = 6.$$
$$s - (-8) = 19 \text{ is equivalent to } s + 8 = 19.$$

EXAMPLE 3 Solve and check: $0.4 = t - (-0.25)$

Solution: **Think:** $t - (-0.25)$ is equivalent to $t + 0.25$.

$$0.4 = t + 0.25 \qquad \longleftarrow \qquad \text{Add } (-0.25) \text{ to each side.}$$
$$0.4 + (-0.25) = t + 0.25 + (-0.25)$$
$$0.15 = t \qquad \longleftarrow \qquad 0.15 = t \text{ is equivalent to } t = 0.15.$$
$$t = 0.15$$

Check: $0.4 = t - (0.25) \qquad \longleftarrow \qquad \text{Replace } t \text{ with 0.15.}$
$$0.4 \stackrel{?}{=} 0.15 - (-0.25) \qquad \longleftarrow \qquad 0.15 - (-0.25) = 0.15 + 0.25$$
$$0.4 \stackrel{?}{=} 0.4 \quad \text{Yes } \checkmark \quad \text{The solution is } \mathbf{0.15.}$$

Unless otherwise stated, throughout this text, the replacement set for the variable in an equation is the set of real numbers.

EXERCISES: Classwork/Homework

Objective: To use the addition property for equations to solve equations

For each equation in Exercises 1–10, choose an equivalent equation from the box at the right.

1. $r + (-6) = 15$

2. $r - (-6) = 15$

3. $-(-6) + r = 15$

4. $-7 = r$

5. $r = 7$

6. $15 = r - (-6)$

7. $(-6) + r = -15$

8. $-6 + r = 15$

9. $15 = r + (-6)$

10. $15 = -(-6) + r$

A. $r + 6 = 15$
B. $r = -7$
C. $r + (-6) = -15$
D. $r - 6 = 15$
E. $r + 6 = -15$
F. $7 = r$

In each of Exercises 11–16, what number would you add to each side of the equation to obtain x?

11. $x + 2 = 11$

12. $6 + x = 13$

13. $x - 6 = 14$

14. $4.5 = 2.1 + x$

15. $x - (-9) = 8$

16. $-13 = x - (-8)$

■■■■■■ PRACTICE AND APPLY

Solve and check each equation.

17. $x + 7 = 13$

18. $m + 3\frac{1}{2} = 7$

19. $8 + n = 5$

20. $y - 6 = 14$

21. $x - 6\frac{1}{4} = 12\frac{1}{2}$

22. $y - 4 = 13$

23. $5.4 + n = -0.6$

24. $-4 + y = 13$

25. $-3 + y = -12$

26. $25 = x + 6$

27. $2 + x = -1$

28. $0.2 + t = 1.3$

29. $-8 + z = 30$

30. $v - (-5) = 10$

31. $m - (-3) = 1$

32. $-8 + t = -13$

33. $-12 + z = 1$

34. $-15 + a = 0$

35. $r - (-4.6) = 8.1$

36. $s + 4.5 = 7.9$

37. $z - 1.6 = 2$

38. $a + 4.22 = 7$

39. $3.35 + x = 5$

40. $8.91 + x = 11.09$

41. $z - \frac{1}{4} = 1\frac{3}{4}$

42. $t + \frac{3}{5} = \frac{9}{10}$

43. $\frac{1}{4} = \frac{3}{4} + c$

44. $1 + r = 7\frac{1}{2}$

45. $\frac{7}{8} = q + \frac{3}{8}$

46. $y + 5 = 8\frac{1}{4}$

Solve.

47. If $s + 9 = 11$, find the value of $7s$.

48. If $t + 8 = 11$, find the value of $\frac{1}{3}t$.

49. If $r - 1.5 = 3.5$, find the value of $r + 1$.

50. If $t - 6 = 21$, find the value of $\frac{1}{9}t$.

51. If $z - 1\frac{1}{4} = 5\frac{1}{2}$, find the value of $4z - 18$.

52. If $r - \frac{1}{5} = \frac{1}{4}$, find the value of $5r$.

53. If $2.8 + m = 3.7$, find the value of $1 - m$.

54. If $0.2 + p = 9$, find the value of $7p$.

By what number would you multiply each expression to obtain y? (*Pages 83–85*)

55. $7y$ **56.** $\frac{y}{2}$ **57.** $\frac{3}{4}y$ **58.** $-\frac{y}{2}$ **59.** $-\frac{3}{4}y$ **60.** $-y$

Evaluate. If you use a calculator, use the sign change key. (*Pages 78–82*)

61. $\dfrac{-2765 + 273}{89}$ **62.** $\dfrac{16(-336)}{12(-35) + 14(6)}$ **63.** $\dfrac{7(-12) - 7(22)}{3(5)(-7) + (7)(13)}$

Solve. (*Pages 45–48*)

64. $-s = 9$ **65.** $-q = -13.8$ **66.** $-c = -1$ **67.** $-m = 0$

For each of Exercises 68–69, first write an equation for the problem. Use the equation to answer the question.

68. Amy had a bank balance of x dollars. She made a deposit of $125 and wrote a check for $35. Then the balance was $276. Find x.

69. Gregg drove his car from Townville to Capitol City. He called the distance d. He reads from the odometer that he has driven 125 miles at a point where a sign tells him he is 160 miles from Capitol City. What is d?

70. To solve $x + b = c$ for x, what should you add to each side of the equation?

71. To solve $y - d = f$ for y, what should you add to each side of the equation?

72. For which non-zero values of y is $y^{495} + y^{496} = 0$? Explain.

73. Complete the pattern in the sequence.

Sequence: 5   13   21   29   37

Pattern: 5 $\overbrace{\quad}$ $\overbrace{\quad}$ $\overbrace{\quad}$ $\overbrace{\quad}$
          $5 + 1{\cdot}8$ $5 + ?$ $5 + ?$ $5 + ?$

REVIEW CAPSULE FOR SECTION 3–2

Rewrite each mixed number as an improper fraction.

1. $8\frac{1}{3}$ **2.** $-6\frac{2}{5}$ **3.** $2\frac{8}{9}$ **4.** $3\frac{3}{4}$ **5.** $-1\frac{1}{2}$

In Exercises 6–10, write the multiplicative inverse. (*Pages 78–82*)

6. $-\frac{2}{3}$ **7.** 5 **8.** $7\frac{1}{8}$ **9.** $-2\frac{1}{2}$ **10.** -1

3-2 Solving Equations: Multiplication Property

The following table illustrates an important property of equations. Recall that equivalent equations have the same solutions.

Multiply each side of x = −4 by	Equations equivalent to x = −4	Does the solution of the new equation equal −4?
3	$3x = -12$	Yes
$\frac{1}{2}$	$\frac{1}{2}x = -2$	Yes
-9	$-9x = 36$	Yes

The table suggests this property.

MULTIPLICA-TION PROPERTY

> Multiplying each side of an equation by the same *nonzero* number results in an equivalent equation.
>
> $2x = 12$
> $(\frac{1}{2} \cdot 2)x = \frac{1}{2} \cdot 12$
> $x = 6$

EXAMPLE 1 Solve and check: $\frac{3}{5}x = 21$

Solution: **Think:** By what number must $\frac{3}{5}x$ be multiplied to get x?

$\frac{3}{5}x = 21$ ⟵——— **Multiply each side by $\frac{5}{3}$.**

$\frac{5}{3} \cdot \frac{3}{5}x = \frac{5}{3} \cdot 21$ ⟵——— **Solve for x.**

$\overset{1}{\underset{1}{\frac{5}{3}}} \cdot \overset{1}{\underset{1}{\frac{3}{5}}}x = 35$

$x = 35$

Check: $\frac{3}{5}x = 21$ ⟵——— **Replace x with 35.**

$\frac{3}{5}(35) \overset{?}{=} 21$

$21 \overset{?}{=} 21$ Yes ✓   The solution is **35.**

An expression such as $\frac{k}{9}$ means the same as $\frac{1}{9} \cdot k$. Thus, the numerical coefficient of $\frac{k}{9}$ is $\frac{1}{9}$.

EXAMPLE 2 Solve and check: $\frac{k}{9} = -62$

Solution: **Think:** By what number must $\frac{k}{9}$ be multiplied to get k?

$$\frac{k}{9} = -62 \quad \longleftarrow \quad \textbf{Multiply each side by 9.}$$

$$9 \cdot \frac{k}{9} = \mathbf{9} \cdot (-62)$$

$$(9 \cdot \frac{1}{9})k = -558$$

$$k = -558$$

Check: $\quad \frac{k}{9} = -62 \quad \longleftarrow \quad \textbf{Replace } k \textbf{ with } -558.$

$$-\frac{558}{9} \stackrel{?}{=} -62$$

$$-62 \stackrel{?}{=} -62 \quad \text{Yes} \checkmark \quad \text{The solution is } \mathbf{-558.}$$

When the numerical coefficient of the variable is a mixed number, rewrite the mixed number as an improper fraction.

EXAMPLE 3 Solve and check: $3\frac{1}{2}t = 1\frac{1}{6}$

Solution: $\quad 3\frac{1}{2}t = 1\frac{1}{6} \quad \longleftarrow \quad \textbf{Rewrite } 3\frac{1}{2} \textbf{ as } \frac{7}{2} \textbf{ and } 1\frac{1}{6} \textbf{ as } \frac{7}{6}.$

$$\frac{7}{2}t = \frac{7}{6} \quad \longleftarrow \quad \textbf{Multiply each side by } \frac{2}{7}.$$

$$(\frac{2}{7} \cdot \frac{7}{2})t = \frac{2}{7} \times \frac{7}{6} \quad \longleftarrow \quad \frac{\overset{1}{\cancel{2}}}{\cancel{7}} \times \frac{\cancel{7}}{\cancel{6}} = \frac{1}{3}$$

$$t = \frac{1}{3}$$

Check: $\quad 3\frac{1}{2}t = 1\frac{1}{6}$

$$\frac{7}{2}(\frac{1}{3}) \stackrel{?}{=} \frac{7}{6}$$

$$\frac{7}{6} = \frac{7}{6} \quad \text{Yes} \checkmark \quad \text{The solution is } \frac{1}{3}.$$

Example 4 shows that multiplying both sides of the equation $52 = -13p$ by $-\frac{1}{13}$ is equivalent to dividing each side by -13. Thus, there are two ways to solve the equation.

EXAMPLE 4 Solve and check: $52 = -13p$

	Method 1	Method 2
Solutions:	$52 = -13p$ ← Multiply each side by $-\frac{1}{13}$.	$52 = -13p$ ← Divide each side by -13.

$$-\frac{1}{13} \cdot 52 = -\frac{1}{13} \cdot (-13p)$$

$$\frac{52}{-13} = \frac{-13p}{-13}$$

$$-4 = p, \text{ or}$$

$$-4 = p, \text{ or}$$

$$p = -4$$

$$p = -4$$

The check is left for you. The solution is -4.

In general, dividing both sides of an equation by the same nonzero number results in an equivalent equation.

EXERCISES: Classwork/Homework

Objective: To use the multiplication property for equations to solve equations

CHECK YOUR UNDERSTANDING

In Exercises 1–8, by what number must each side of the equation be multiplied in order to get t alone on one side?

1. $3t = 12$ **2.** $-3t = 1.2$ **3.** $-\frac{4}{5}t = 6$ **4.** $1\frac{2}{3}t = 20$

5. $\frac{t}{5} = 6$ **6.** $-\frac{t}{10} = 1$ **7.** $-t = 8$ **8.** $2.1 = -t$

In Exercises 9–12, by what number must each side of the equation be divided in order to get s alone on one side?

9. $3s = 21$ **10.** $-8s = 148$ **11.** $-1 = 5s$ **12.** $-36 = 4s$

PRACTICE AND APPLY

Solve and check each equation.

13. $3x = 21$ **14.** $-8x = 148$ **15.** $2z = -8$ **16.** $\frac{n}{3} = 2$

17. $24 = -12b$ **18.** $-52 = 13t$ **19.** $\frac{z}{6} = 10$ **20.** $5\frac{1}{6}p = -62$

21. $\frac{2}{3}n = 12$ **22.** $\frac{5}{6}n = 15$ **23.** $-9 = \frac{5}{4}v$ **24.** $12 = -\frac{3}{2}n$

25. $\frac{-y}{2} = 1$ **26.** $\frac{y}{0.5} = 1$ **27.** $\frac{2}{3} = \frac{y}{6}$ **28.** $-30 = \frac{5n}{3}$

29. $-y = 6$ **30.** $-2.3s = 4.6$ **31.** $-0.25t = 8$ **32.** $5y = 0$

33. $-2\frac{1}{6} = 8\frac{2}{3}m$ **34.** $-\frac{1}{8} = -x$ **35.** $-\frac{1}{8} = 4n$ **36.** $-r = \frac{1}{4}$

37. $1 = -\frac{2}{3}n$ **38.** $-\frac{2}{9}x = -\frac{4}{3}$ **39.** $\frac{4}{5} = -\frac{2}{15}t$ **40.** $-\frac{1}{4}x = 0$

In Exercises 41–44, write an equation for each problem. Then use the equation to solve the problem.

41. The length of a rectangle is 17 centimeters and its width is x centimeters. Its area is 102 square centimeters. Find x.

42. An auditorium has t rows with 40 seats in each row. There are 480 seats in all. Find t.

43. The stock person at a grocery store filled the front row of the bottom layer of a shelf with 12 cans. If there are 84 cans in all in the bottom layer and n rows, what is n?

44. In Exercise 43, if there are 336 cans in all on the shelf arranged in t layers, what is t?

MAINTAIN

What number would you add to each expression to obtain x? (*Pages 83–85*)

45. $x + 4$ **46.** $x + (-3)$ **47.** $13 + x$ **48.** $-8 + x$

Solve and check each equation. (*Pages 95–98*)

49. $a - 9 = 17$ **50.** $-15 = d - 24$ **51.** $-9.8 = q - 5.5$

52. $-19 + g = 49$ **53.** $y + 13.7 = 8.6$ **54.** $-27 = q + 35$

Use algebraic symbols to represent each sentence. (*Pages 45–48*)

55. The opposite of a loss of $120 is a profit of $120.

56. A rise of $3\frac{1}{2}$ per share of stock is the opposite of a loss of $3\frac{1}{2}$ per share.

CONNECT AND EXTEND

57. If $3t = 6$, then $6t = \underline{\ ?\ }$.

58. If $8s = 4$, then $4s = \underline{\ ?\ }$.

59. If $\frac{n}{3} = 8$, then $\frac{n}{6} = \underline{\ ?\ }$.

60. If $\frac{p}{4} = \frac{2}{3}$, then $\frac{p}{2} = \underline{\ ?\ }$.

61. If $2a + b = 10$, then $4a + 2b = \underline{\ ?\ }$.

62. If $2x + 3 = 15$, then $8x + 12 = \underline{\ ?\ }$.

3-3 Solving Equations: Ratio and Proportion

Walt Chambers is making a broccoli and rice casserole. The recipe uses 2 cups of rice for every 6 servings of casserole.

RATIO

You can use this *ratio* to compare the number of cups of rice to the number of servings of casserole.

2:6   Read: "2 is to 6."

A **ratio** is a comparison of two numbers by division. Ratios can be expressed in several ways.

30:100 $\frac{30}{100}$, or $\frac{3}{10}$ 0.30, or 0.3   30%

An equation such as $\frac{40}{100} = \frac{2}{5}$ is a *proportion*.

DEFINITION

> A **proportion** is an equation that states that two ratios are equal.

STRATEGY

Writing a proportion is a useful strategy for solving many kinds of problems.

EXAMPLE 1 Walt Chambers wants to make 10 servings of the broccoli and rice casserole. How many cups of rice will he need?

Solution:

1 **Find:** Number of cups of rice needed for 10 servings
   Given: The recipe uses 2 cups of rice for every 6 servings.

2 Write two ratios. Let x represent the number of cups of rice needed for 10 servings.

Known Ratio		Unknown Ratio	
$\frac{2}{6}$	← Cups of rice ← Servings	$\frac{x}{10}$	← Cups of rice ← Servings

Write a proportion. $\frac{2}{6} = \frac{x}{10}$

3 Solve the proportion. $(10)\frac{2}{6} = (10)\frac{x}{10}$ ← **Multiply each side by 10.**

Walt will need $3\frac{1}{3}$ **cups** of rice. $\frac{20}{6} = x$, or $3\frac{1}{3} = x$

MEANS AND EXTREMES

Proportions are so useful in problem solving that a special property is often used to solve them.

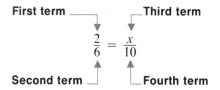

First term → 2, Third term → x, Second term → 6, Fourth term → 10

$$\frac{2}{6} = \frac{x}{10}$$

The first and fourth terms are called the **extremes.**

The second and third terms are called the **means.**

PROPERTY OF PROPORTIONS

> In a proportion, the product of the means equals the product of the extremes. That is,
>
> **if $\frac{a}{b} = \frac{c}{d}$ ($b \neq 0$, $d \neq 0$), then $ad = bc$.**
>
> Also, **if $ad = bc$, then $\frac{a}{b} = \frac{c}{d}$ ($b \neq 0$, $d \neq 0$).**

Example 2 illustrates the use of this property.

EXAMPLE 2 A car travels 320 kilometers on 40 liters of gas. How far can it travel on 75 liters?

Solution: [1] **Find:** The number of kilometers on 75 liters
Given: 320 kilometers on 40 liters

[2] Let x represent the number of kilometers on 75 liters of gas.

Known Ratio		Unknown Ratio	
320	← Kilometers	x	← Kilometers
40	← Liters	75	← Liters

$\frac{320}{40} = \frac{x}{75}$ ← **Write a proportion.**

[3] $(320)(75) = 40x$ ← **Property of Proportions**

$24{,}000 = 40x$ ← **320 [×] 75 [=] 24000.**

$\frac{24{,}000}{40} = x$

$600 = x$

The car can travel **600 kilometers.**

In Examples 1 and 2, the check is left for you.

Objectives: To solve proportions

To use the strategy of writing a proportion to solve word problems

▬▬▬ **CHECK YOUR UNDERSTANDING**

Complete.

1. A __?__ is a comparison of two numbers by division.

2. A proportion is an equation that states that two ratios are __?__

3. If the ratio of blue paint to white paint in a mixture is 1 to 3, then for every gallon of blue paint used, __?__ gallons of white paint are used.

4. If the ratio of nutmeg to cinnamon in a recipe is 2:3, then __?__ teaspoons of cinnamon are used for every 2 teaspoons of nutmeg.

In Exercises 5–8, write the equation that results when you use the Property of Proportions.

5. $\frac{5}{8} = \frac{x}{10}$

6. $\frac{7}{x} = \frac{3}{6}$

7. $\frac{x}{5} = \frac{8}{15}$

8. $\frac{2}{9} = \frac{12}{x}$

▬▬▬ **PRACTICE AND APPLY**

Write each ratio as a fraction, a decimal, and a percent.

9. 3:20

10. 3:5

11. 16:20

12. 14:56

13. 8:80

Solve each proportion.

14. $\frac{3}{x} = \frac{9}{15}$

15. $\frac{x}{4} = \frac{4}{16}$

16. $\frac{18}{30} = \frac{x}{5}$

17. $\frac{x}{9} = \frac{24}{54}$

18. $\frac{7}{8} = \frac{x}{40}$

19. $\frac{9}{2} = \frac{63}{x}$

20. $\frac{11}{x} = \frac{132}{24}$

21. $\frac{x}{13} = \frac{10}{65}$

22. $\frac{5}{13} = \frac{x}{65}$

23. $\frac{21}{5} = \frac{x}{2.5}$

24. $\frac{29}{7} = \frac{x}{1.75}$

25. $\frac{17}{2} = \frac{8.5}{x}$

In Exercises 26–29:

a. **Use a variable to represent the unknown.**

b. **Write a proportion that can be used to solve the problem.**

26. A train traveled 90 miles in $1\frac{1}{2}$ hours. How many miles will it travel in 6 hours going at the same rate?

27. Fifty feet of copper wire weigh 2 pounds. How much will 325 feet of the same wire weigh?

28. The distance between two cities is 1500 kilometers. Find how far apart they are on a map with a scale that reads: "1 cm represents 500 km."

29. In a mixture of concrete, the ratio of sand to cement is 1:4. How many bags of cement are needed to mix with 100 bags of sand?

Solve each problem.

30. A recipe for a two-pound cake calls for $1\frac{1}{2}$ cups of butter. How many cups of butter will be needed for a five-pound cake?

31. A nurse, checking the heartbeat of a patient, counted 19 beats in 15 seconds. What would be the patient's heartbeat for 60 seconds?

32. On a map, 1.5 centimeters represents 60 kilometers. What distance does 6 centimeters represent?

33. A car travels 110 kilometers in 3 hours. How far will it travel in 5 hours at the same rate?

34. In a certain city, 0.7 centimeters of rain fell in 3 hours. How many centimeters of rain would fall in 9 hours at the same rate?

35. Wallpaper to cover 55 square feet costs $16. How much will it cost to buy wallpaper to cover a wall with an area of 330 square feet?

36. A pitcher allowed 10 earned runs in 15 innings. At this rate, how many runs would the pitcher allow in 9 innings? (The answer is called **earned run average, or ERA.**)

37. A 747-jumbo jet has a cruising speed of 595 miles per hour. How long will it take to travel at this rate from the east to the west coast, a distance of about 3300 miles?

■■■■■■ **MAINTAIN**

Solve and check each equation. *(Pages 95–102)*

38. $3s = 24$

39. $\frac{x}{4} = -8$

40. $-\frac{1}{2}y = 4$

41. $-16 = 1\frac{1}{3}m$

42. $x + 12 = 15$

43. $q - (-5) = 1$

44. $t - 1\frac{1}{2} = 3\frac{1}{4}$

45. $-6 = 3 + n$

Add. *(Pages 53–57)*

46. $-5 + 6$

47. $8 + (-12)$

48. $9 + (-7)$

49. $-14 + (-12)$

■■■■■■ **CONNECT AND EXTEND**

50. If $a = 2b$, find $a:b$.
(HINT: Let $a = 1$ and $b = 2$)

51. If $r = 3s$, find $s:r$.

52. If $2p = 3t$, find $p:t$.

53. If $\frac{5}{x} = \frac{3}{y}$, find $y:x$.

■■■■■■ **NON-ROUTINE PROBLEMS**

54. Complete the pattern.

F ⅃ ⅂ T ___?___ ⅃ N ___?___ ___?___

55. What number gives the same result when multiplied by 6 as it does when 6 is added to it?

Write a percent for each decimal or fraction.

1. 0.1   **2.** $\frac{3}{4}$ **3.** $\frac{2}{3}$ **4.** 0.45   **5.** $\frac{5}{6}$ **6.** 1.05

3-4   Solving Percent Equations

PERCENT

Percent means **per hundred** or **hundredths.**

$$17\% = \frac{17}{100} = 0.17 \qquad\qquad 5\% = \frac{5}{100} = 0.05$$

$$0.6\% = \frac{0.6}{100} = \frac{6}{1000} = 0.006 \qquad 228\% = \frac{228}{100} = 2.28$$

There are three types of percent problems. Each type involves three numbers. When two of the numbers are known, you can write an equation and solve it to find the unknown number.

Finding a Percent of a Number	Finding a Number Given its Percent	Finding What Percent a Number is of Another
What number is 75% of 900?	72 is 9% of what number?	What percent is 15 of 10?
Unknown = 0.75 · 900	72 = 0.09 · Unknown	Unknown = 15 · 10

Example 1 shows how to solve two types of percent problems. Example 2b shows how to solve the third type.

EXAMPLE 1   **a.** What number is 75% of 900?   **b.** 72 is 9% of what number?

Solutions: **a.** Let y = the number.   **b.** Let a = the number.

What number is 75% of 900?   72 is 9% of what number?

$$y = 0.75 \cdot 900$$

$$y = 675$$

$$72 = 0.09 \cdot a$$

$$\frac{72}{0.09} = \frac{0.09a}{0.09}$$

$$800 = a$$

So **675** is 75% of 900.   So 72 is 9% of **800.**

Example 2 shows how to find the percent of increase. The percent of decrease is found in a similar manner.

EXAMPLE 2 In 1978, the cost for the first 3 ounces of first-class mail was 15¢. In 1988, the cost rose to 25¢. Find the percent of increase.

Solution: 1 First find the amount of increase.
Amount of increase:
$$25¢ - 15¢ = 10¢$$

2 Find the percent of increase.
Let s = the percent of increase.
What percent of 15¢ is 10¢?

$$s \cdot 15 = 10, \text{ or}$$
$$15s = 10$$
$$s = \frac{10}{15} = \frac{2}{3} \longleftarrow \textbf{Write a percent for } \frac{2}{3}.$$
$$s = 66\frac{2}{3}\%$$

Check: Does $66\frac{2}{3}\%$ of 15 = 10? Yes. ✓ The percent of increase is $66\frac{2}{3}\%$.

CALCULATOR

A calculator with a percent key, $\boxed{\%}$, allows you to solve the three types of percent problems.

What number is 12% of 65?   **65** $\boxed{\times}$ **12** $\boxed{\%}$ $\boxed{7.8}$

36 is 30% of what number?   **36** $\boxed{\div}$ **30** $\boxed{\%}$ $\boxed{120}$

What percent of 32 is 8?   **8** $\boxed{\div}$ **32** $\boxed{\%}$ $\boxed{25}$

EXERCISES: Classwork/Homework

Objective: To solve percent problems

CHECK YOUR UNDERSTANDING

Choose from the box at the right a fraction and a decimal equal to each percent.

$\frac{18}{100}$	$\frac{1.8}{100}$	$\frac{80}{100}$	$\frac{8}{100}$
$\frac{800}{100}$	$\frac{180}{100}$	$\frac{0.8}{100}$	$\frac{8.5}{100}$
0.85	0.18	0.8	1.8
0.008	0.085	0.08	8

1. 8%   **2.** 18%   **3.** 8.5%

4. 80%   **5.** 800%   **6.** 180%

Choose the correct equation.

7. What percent of 10 is 4?
    a. $n \cdot 10 = 4$
    b. $n \cdot 4 = 10$
    c. $n = 10 \cdot 4$

8. What number is 25% of 16?
    a. $t \cdot 25 = 16$
    b. $t = 0.25 \cdot 16$
    c. $t \cdot 16 = 25$

9. 15 is 12% of what number?
    a. $15 \cdot x = 0.12$
    b. $15 = 0.12 \cdot x$
    c. $15 \cdot 0.12 = x$

10. What percent of 60 is 24?
    a. $s \cdot 24 = 60$
    b. $s = 60 \cdot 24$
    c. $s \cdot 60 = 24$

■■■■■■ PRACTICE AND APPLY

Solve.

11. 35% of 28 is what number?

12. 40% of 25 is what number?

13. What percent of 92 is 69?

14. What percent of 65 is 39?

15. 15 is 20% of what number?

16. 21 is 30% of what number?

17. 125% of what number is 45?

18. 3 is what percent of 3000?

19. $37\frac{1}{2}\%$ of 2400 is what number?

20. 3% of what number is 1.86?

21. What percent of 35 is 28?

22. 2.5% of 400 is what number?

23. The price of a new car is $6500. Mrs Gomez made a down payment of 15% of the price of the car when she bought it. How much was the down payment?

24. Mr. Garvey bought a suit for $180 and paid $10.80 as a sales tax. What percent of the cost was the sales tax?

25. An advertisement claims that each serving of a brand of oatmeal contains 4 grams of protein. This is 6% of a person's daily recommended need. How many grams of protein make up a person's daily recommended need?

26. Jennifer bought a coat at a "20% off" sale and saved $35. What was the original price of the coat?

27. How much silver is in 12.5 kilograms of an alloy (mixture) which is 8% silver?

28. A worker who earns $6.50 per hour receives a raise of $0.52 per hour. What is the percent of increase in the worker's wages?

29. The population of a village decreased from 21,000 to 16,000. Find the percent of decrease to the nearest whole percent.

30. The price of a calculator decreased from $40 to $12 over a 9-year period. Find the percent of decrease.

31. The list price on a camera is $60 but it is on sale for $44.40. What is the rate (percent) of discount?

32. A business executive received a salary increase of 15%. This brought his salary to $27,600. What was the salary before the raise?

33. After the price of a pound of meat was increased 12%, the new price was $1.68. What was the price per pound before the increase?

34. After Kenneth Sims lost 20% of his real estate investment, he had $12,500 left. How much did he invest originally?

35. Shirley bought some stock valued at $62.50 per share and sold it for $67.50 per share. Find the percent of profit.

T1^LN ALNT/1   0   0   U   1401   0   0   1   1403
T2^LN ALNT/2   0   0   U   1400   0   0   1   1401
T3^LN ALNT/3   0   0   U   0   931   0   1   1
T4^LN ALNT/4   0   0   U   0   873   0   1   1
C1^LN AUDC/1   0   0   U   1916   0   0   2   1919
C3^LN AUDC/3   0   0   U   0   1623   0   2   1   1
C4^LN AUDC/4   0   0   U   0   1528   0   2   1   1
T1^LN ADOT/1   0   0   U   0   24   0   0   1
T1^LN BLNT/1   0   0   U   2142   0   0   4   2144
T2^LN BLNT/2   0   0   U   2141   0   0   4   2142
T3^LN BLNT/3   0   0   U   0   1571   0   4   1   1
T4^LN BLNT/4   0   0   U   0   1344   0   4   1   1
C1^LN BUDC/1   0   0   U   3051   0   0   6   3054
C3^LN BUDC/3   0   0   U   0   2407   0   6   1   2

◼◼◼◼ **MAINTAIN**

Solve each problem. (*Pages 103–107*)

36. A car traveled 104 miles in 2 hours. How many hours will it take to travel 260 miles going at the same rate?

37. On a map, 2 centimeters represent 250 kilometers. What distance does 5 centimeters represent?

38. A 20-acre field yields 610 bushels of corn. How much would a 25-acre field yield under similar conditions?

39. A truck travels 480 kilometers on 75 liters of gasoline. How many kilometers will it travel on 92.5 liters going at the same rate?

◼◼◼◼ **CONNECT AND EXTEND**

Solve.

40. A store owner is trying to sell a $450 stereo. First the owner raises the price by 20%. Then the owner advertises a "20% off" sale on the new price. What is the final price of the stereo?

41. One store owner raised the price of a $100 guitar by 10% and then decreased the new price by 10%. A second store owner first decreased the price of a $100 guitar by 10% and then increased the new price by 10%. Compare the final prices of the two guitars.

3-5 Probability Ratio and Prediction

A coin is tossed by a referee at the start of a football game. The visiting team captain will call heads or tails.

THEORETICAL PROBABILITY

Since the result of the coin toss is uncertain, you can use this ratio to determine the *theoretical,* or calculated, *probability* that the coin will land "heads up."

$$\textbf{Probability} = \frac{\text{Number of successful ways}}{\text{Number of possible ways}}$$

EXAMPLE 1 **a.** Suppose the visiting team captain calls heads.
What is the probability that the coin also lands "heads" up?

Solution: Let P(H) represent the probability of landing "heads up."

$$P(H) = \frac{1 \text{ head}}{1 \text{ head } + 1 \text{ tail}} \quad \longleftarrow \quad \textbf{There is only one way to land "heads."}$$
$$\longleftarrow \quad \textbf{There are 2 ways for the coin to land.}$$

$$= \tfrac{1}{2}, \text{ or } \textbf{50\%}$$

b. Suppose the visiting team captain calls tails.
What is the probability that the coin also lands "tails" up?

Solution: $$P(T) = \frac{1 \text{ tail}}{1 \text{ head } + 1 \text{ tail}}$$

$$= \tfrac{1}{2}, \text{ or } \textbf{50\%}$$

In Example 1, notice that the sum of the probabilities is one.

$$P(H) + P(T) = \tfrac{1}{2} + \tfrac{1}{2} = 1$$

Probability is a ratio between 0 and 1 which tells how likely it is that a certain event will happen.

EXPERIMENTAL PROBABILITY

Experimental probability, or actual probability, is based on collected data.

EXAMPLE 2 For one season, a football coach kept this record of the outcome of the coin toss at the beginning of each game. Use the table to find the experimental probability of tossing a tail.

Game Number	1	2	3	4	5	6	7	8	9	10	11	Totals
Number of Heads	0	0	1	1	1	0	0	0	1	0	1	5
Number of Tails	1	1	0	0	0	1	1	1	0	1	0	6

Solution: Experimental probability of tossing a tail: $\frac{6}{11} = 0.55$ ◄——— Rounded

Since the experimental probability of tossing a tail is $\frac{6}{11}$, you would expect the coin toss to turn up tails in 6 out of every 11 tosses.

EXAMPLE 3 By testing the stitching on a sample from a shipment of 24,000 footballs, a technician found that 2 out of every 100 were defective. Predict the number of defective footballs in a shipment of 24,000.

Solution: [1] Find the experimental probability that a football is defective.

Experimental probability: $\frac{2}{100} = \frac{1}{50}$, or 2%

[2] Find 2% of 24,000.

2% of 24,000 = 24,000 × 0.02 = 480

Predicted number: About **480** defective footballs

EXERCISES: Classwork/Homework

Objective: To calculate theoretical and experimental probabilities

CHECK YOUR UNDERSTANDING

1. What ratio do you use to calculate a probability?

2. What is the difference between experimental and theoretical probability?

For Exercises 3–6, suppose that you toss a nickel once. Find each theoretical probability.

3. What is the probability that it lands "heads up"?

4. What is the probability that it lands "tails up"?

5. What is the probability that it lands "heads up or tails up"?

6. What is the probability that it lands on an edge and stays that way?

■■■■■■■ **PRACTICE AND APPLY**

7. How many sides, or faces, does a die have?

8. You can toss a die once. What are the numbers that can turn up on the top face?

For Exercises 9–15, you toss a die once. What is the theoretical probability that each number or numbers will turn up?

9. 1   **10.** 7   **11.** 1 or 6   **12.** 1, 2, or 3   **13.** 6

14. 1, 2, 3, 4, 5, or 6   **15.** 1, 3, 5, or 6

The table at the right shows the result of 42 tosses of a die. Refer to the table to write the experimental probability of tossing each number in Exercises 16–21.

Number on Top Face	1	2	3	4	5	6
Number of Times	8	5	9	7	6	7

Write each probability as a ratio and as a percent. Round to the nearest whole-number percent.

16. 1   **17.** 2   **18.** 3   **19.** 4   **20.** 5   **21.** 6

The letters of the word AMERICAN are written on separate cards and placed in a hat. After shuffling the cards, one is drawn without looking. Since there are 8 cards in all, the theoretical probability of drawing a C or an N is

$\frac{2}{8}$, or $\frac{1}{4}$.

22. What is the theoretical probability of drawing an A?

23. What is the theoretical probability of drawing an R?

24. What is the theoretical probability of drawing a vowel?

25. What is the theoretical probability of not drawing a vowel?

26. What is the theoretical probability of drawing a consonant or a vowel?

27. What is the theoretical probability of not drawing a consonant or a vowel?

28. In a shipment of 800 typewriters, the probability that any one typewriter is defective is 2%. Predict the probable number of defective typewriters in the shipment.

29. A sample of 800 toasters contain 40 that are defective. Find the probable number of defective toasters in a shipment of 36,000.

30. A shipment of 12,000 calculators will be returned to the supplier if more than 3% are found to be defective. A sample of 500 showed that 21 were defective. Will the shipment be returned to the supplier?

━━━ **MAINTAIN**

Solve. (*Pages 107–110*)

31. What percent of 125 is 36?

32. What is 36% of 56?

33. 9 is 60% of what number?

34. What percent of 480 is 160?

Solve for *n*. (*Pages 103–107*)

35. $\dfrac{3.0}{4.5} = \dfrac{n}{18}$

36. $\dfrac{n}{1.5} = \dfrac{5}{7.5}$

37. $\dfrac{20}{n} = \dfrac{60}{120}$

38. $\dfrac{4}{5} = \dfrac{28}{n}$

━━━ **CONNECT AND EXTEND**

Leslie tosses a quarter and a nickel.

39. List all possible ways the two coins can land. (HINT: There are 4 ways in all).

40. What is the probability that both coins land "heads up"?

41. What is the probability that the quarter lands "heads up" and the nickel lands "tails up"?

42. What is the probability that one coin lands "heads up" and the other lands "tails up"?

Fred tosses a pair of dice.

43. Use the strategy of making a table to show all the possible ways the dice can land. (HINT: there are 36 ways in all).

44. What is the probability that the sum of the top faces is 8?

45. What is the probability that the sum of the top faces is 12?

46. What is the probability that the sum of the top faces is less than 13?

47. What is the probability that the sum of the top faces is a number greater than 12?

48. What is the probability that the sum of the top faces is 7, 8, or 9?

━━━ **NON-ROUTINE PROBLEMS**

49. There are 12 dollars in one dozen. How many dimes are there in one dozen?

50. If five days ago was the day after Saturday, what was the day before yesterday?

Solve and check each equation. (*Pages 95–98*)

1. $x + 9 = 16$ 2. $11.4 + t = 4.5$ 3. $y - 7.3 = 2$ 4. $\frac{1}{3} = \frac{2}{3} + a$

(*Pages 99–102*)

5. $7x = 14$ 6. $-3.1n = 12.4$ 7. $17t = 68$ 8. $\frac{4}{5} = -\frac{5}{2}r$

Solve each proportion. (*Pages 103–106*)

9. $\frac{2}{x} = \frac{6}{8}$ 10. $\frac{9}{4} = \frac{72}{x}$ 11. $\frac{7}{11} = \frac{x}{33}$ 12. $\frac{43}{5} = \frac{x}{1.5}$

13. A scuba diver uses 220 pounds of compressed air in 10 minutes. How much air will he have used in 25 minutes?

Solve. (*Pages 107–110*)

14. 25% of 32 is what number?   15. What percent of 88 is 66?

16. Tiffany bought a surfboard on sale for 30% off and saved $42. What was the original price of the surfboard?

For Exercises 17–20, you toss a die once. What is the theoretical probability that each number or numbers will turn up? (*Pages 111–114*)

17. 3   18. 2 or 4   19. 1, 2, or 5   20. 8

Historical Digest: Decimal Fractions

Until about four hundred years ago, there was no standard way to write a fraction such as $2\frac{3}{4}$ as a decimal. All of the following methods had been used to write the decimal 2.75.

$2\ ^{⓪}7\ ^{①}\ 5\ ^{②}$	2, 7′ 5″	2$\underline{|75}$
2|75	$2^{75}_{\ (1)\ (2)}$	2|75
2(75	2.7 5	2:75

Even today, different countries represent this number in various ways.

United States: 2.75   **England:** 2·75   **Continental Europe**: 2,75

The decimal system is based on tens and tenths. Why do you think the number 10 was chosen rather than another number such as 5 or 12?

Statistics / Circle Graphs

Graphic artists create the art used in advertising, publications, packaging, television, statistical reports, and so on. A knowledge of proportion, percent, and geometry is essential for artists who prepare graphs for advertising and for statistical reports.

EXAMPLE: The table at the right shows how many non-farm workers were employed in four major occupations in Capital County. Make a circle graph to show the data.

Occupation	Number
Industry	4,575
Services	19,825
Government	9,550
Other	825

Solution: Because you can make errors when entering data in a calculator, it is a good idea to **estimate before solving.** Here is an example.

Estimate the total: $5000 + 20,000 + 10,000 + 1,000 = 36,000$

Estimate the percent for industry: $5000 \div 36,000 \approx \frac{1}{7}$, or about **14%**

1 Find what percent of the total each occupation is. Round percents to the nearest half.

Total: 4575 $+$ 19825 $+$ 9550 $+$ 825 $=$ | $34775.$ |

Industry: 4575 $\div$ 34775 $\%$ | 13.156002 | → **13.0%**

Services: 19825 $\div$ 34775 $\%$ | 57.009345 | → **57.0%**

Government: 9550 $\div$ 34775 $\%$ | 27.462257 | → **27.5%**

Other: 825 $\div$ 34775 $\%$ | 2.3723939 | → **2.5%**

2 For each occupation, find the number of angle degrees in the circle graph. There are 360° in a circle. Round to the nearest whole degree.

Industry: 360 $\times$ 13 $\%$ | 46.8 | → **47°**

Services: 360 $\times$ 57 $\%$ | 205.2 | → **205°**

Government: 360 ⌷×⌷ 27.5 ⌷%⌷   ⌷ 99. ⌷ → 99°

Other: 360 ⌷×⌷ 2.5 ⌷%⌷   ⌷ 9. ⌷ → 9°

3 Use a protractor to draw the circle graph. Figures 1 and 2 show how to measure an angle of 47° followed by an angle of 99°. Figure 3 shows the completed graph.

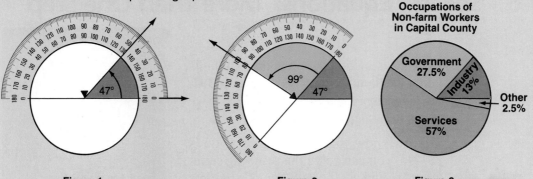

| Figure 1 | Figure 2 | Figure 3 |

Occupations of Non-farm Workers in Capital County

Government 27.5% · Industry 13% · Other 2.5% · Services 57%

EXERCISES For Exercises 1–2, draw circle graphs to show the given data.

1.

How Time is Spent in Football Practice		Principal Crops (number of acres)	
Warm-up	12 minutes	Hay	164,000
Team Drills	15 minutes	Citrus	38,300
Special Drills	23 minutes	Cotton	416,800
Scrimmage	40 minutes	Grain	211,000
Team Meeting	10 minutes	Vegetables	80,000

For Exercises 3–6, refer to the circle graph at the right.

3. Estimate what percent of her time Jill spends sleeping.

4. Estimate what percent of her time Jill spends in school.

5. Estimate what percent of her time Jill spends in sports and recreation.

6. Estimate the number of hours per week Jill spends on homework.

How Jill Spends Her Time Each Week

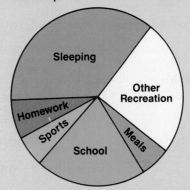

Sleeping · Other Recreation · Homework · Sports · Meals · School

Solve and check. (*Pages 95–102*)

1. $-0.3 = s + 0.7$ **2.** $-4 = d - 8$ **3.** $x - 5 = -9$

4. $-5q = -115$ **5.** $-t = 18$ **6.** $\frac{y}{3} = -15$

3-6 Solving Equations: More Than One Step

The cost in dollars of taking students on a weekend trip to Washington, D.C. is given by

$$220n + 750 = C.$$

If you know that the total cost, C, is $7790, you can solve the resulting equation to find n, the number of students who went on the trip.

To solve equations involving more than one operation, use the Addition Property for equations first. Then use the Multiplication Property.

EXAMPLE 1 Solve $220n + 750 = 7790$ to find how many students went on the trip to Washington, D.C. Check your answer.

Solution:

$$220n + 750 = 7790 \longleftarrow \textbf{Add (}-\textbf{750) to each side.}$$
$$220n + 750 + (-750) = 7790 + (-750)$$
$$220n = 7040 \longleftarrow \textbf{Multiply each side by } \frac{1}{220}.$$
$$\frac{1}{220} \cdot 220n = \frac{1}{220} \cdot 7040$$
$$n = 32$$

Check:

$$220n + 750 = 7790 \longleftarrow \textbf{Replace } n \textbf{ with 32.}$$
$$220(32) + 750 \stackrel{?}{=} 7790$$
$$7040 + 750 \stackrel{?}{=} 7790$$
$$7790 \stackrel{?}{=} 7790 \text{ Yes } \checkmark$$

There were **32** students on this trip to Washington, D.C.

Always check your answer in the original equation.

EXAMPLE 2 Solve and check: $-7 + \frac{3n}{5} = 14$

Solution: $-7 + \frac{3n}{5} = 14$ ◄——— **Add 7 to each side.**

$7 + (-7) + \frac{3n}{5} = 7 + 14$

$\frac{3n}{5} = 21$ ◄——— **Since $\frac{3n}{5} = \frac{3}{5}n$, multiply each side by $\frac{5}{3}$.**

$\frac{5}{3} \cdot \frac{3}{5}n = \frac{5}{3} \cdot 21$

$n = 35$

Check: $-7 + \frac{3n}{5} = 14$ ◄——— **Replace n with 35.**

$-7 + \frac{3(35)}{5} \overset{?}{=} 14$

$-7 + 21 \overset{?}{=} 14$

$14 \overset{?}{=} 14$ Yes ✓ The solution is **35**.

EXERCISES: Classwork/Homework

Objective: To solve equations having more than one operation

CHECK YOUR UNDERSTANDING

What number would you add to each side of the equation to get the term with the variable alone on one side?

1. $4n + 7 = 19$ **2.** $20 + 1.2x = 0$ **3.** $8x - 5 = 11$ **4.** $3t - 7 = 8$
5. $-12 + r = 10$ **6.** $13 = 6x - 17$ **7.** $10 - 7x = 3$ **8.** $6\frac{1}{2} - 5x = 11\frac{1}{2}$

Write the equivalent equation you would use as the first step in solving each equation.

9. $3t + 2 = 5$ **10.** $12 = -2y + 8$ **11.** $15 = 7b - 1$
12. $\frac{a}{4} + 7 = -5$ **13.** $5 = -\frac{1}{3}y + 9$ **14.** $-3.5 = 6x - 0.5$

PRACTICE AND APPLY

Solve and check each equation.

15. $5n + 3 = 33$ **16.** $2n + 3 = 7$ **17.** $5n - 3 = 17$
18. $3t + 17 = 5$ **19.** $4a + 17 = 53$ **20.** $2n + 5 = 17$
21. $3n - 4 = 17$ **22.** $3n - 17 = 4$ **23.** $2a + 15 = 3$
24. $8a - 7 = 41$ **25.** $9a - 1 = 80$ **26.** $2b + 3 = 21$

27. $5 - 3a = 32$

28. $5 - 2y = 15$

29. $7 = 6x + 19$

30. $4 = 30 - 6t$

31. $-5 = 32 - 3b$

32. $5x + 37 = 17$

33. $9a - 8 = 73$

34. $15 - \frac{5}{4}v = 23$

35. $\frac{1}{2}y + 11 = 5$

36. $8n + 22 = 70$

37. $1.2t + 3.4 = -1.0$

38. $-0.6n + 11 = 17$

39. $2.1 = 4.3 - 1.1w$

40. $7.0 = 2.2 - 0.8n$

41. $0 = 0.6n - 3.6$

42. $0 = \frac{7}{10}n - 35$

43. $\frac{5}{6}n + 34 = 9$

44. $\frac{6}{8}n + 12 = 84$

45. $\frac{9}{10}x - 17 = 19$

46. $\frac{16}{15}x + 78 = 14$

47. $\frac{3}{4}x - 3 = 18$

48. $\frac{7}{8}t - 8 = 34$

49. $\frac{2}{3}t - 13 = 57$

50. $\frac{5}{12}t - 12 = 48$

51. $28 = \frac{17}{32}n - 23$

52. $6 = 26 + \frac{2}{5}n$

53. $15 = \frac{3}{10}n - 15$

54. $18 = -\frac{9}{32}n - 26$

55. $53 + \frac{3}{5}x = 26$

56. $49 + \frac{3}{5}x = 16$

 You can use the program on page 612 to solve any equation in the form
$Ax + B = C$.

Use the program to solve the following equations.

57. $4c - 3 = 45$

58. $-23 = \frac{2}{3}n - 5$

59. $0.6x - 4.4 = 7$

■■■■■■ MAINTAIN

A family has three teenagers. Their names are Linda, Gina, and Richard. To decide who will take the garbage out, one name is picked at random from a hat. Find each probability. (*Pages 111–114*)

60. Richard's name is chosen

61. Gina's or Linda's name is chosen

62. Gina's name is not chosen

63. One of the teenager's names is chosen

64. The sales tax on a purchase of $24 was $1.20. What was the rate of sales tax?

65. A store advertised lamps at 20% off. What was the original price of a lamp that was marked $11.60 off?

(*Pages 108–110*)

66. In a survey regarding an election, 8% of the 4800 people surveyed expressed no opinion. How many people expressed no opinion?

67. Clarence bought some stock at $4.50 per share and sold it for $9.90 per share. What was his percent of profit?

Find the mean, median, and mode for each set of numbers. (*Pages 74–77*)

68. $8\frac{1}{2}, 8\frac{1}{2}, 9, 7$

69. $9, 9, 8, 6, 3$

70. $4.1, 2.3, 9.7, 2.3, 2.3, 6.3$

71. $3, 1, 3, 2, 3, 3, 1, 2$

72. $6, 4, 5, 5$

73. $12, 37, 62, 37, 43$

In Exercises 74–76, complete each argument.

74. Prove: $(a + b) + (-b) = a$

   Argument: $(a + b) + (-b) = a + [b + (-b)]$ Why?
   $(a + b) + (-b) = a + 0$ Why?
   $(a + b) + (-b) = a$ Why?

75. Prove: $-(-a) = a$

   Argument: $a + (-a) = 0$ Why?
   $-a + a = 0$ Why?
   $-a + [-(-a)] = 0$ Why?
   $-(-a) = a$ Why?

76. Prove: If $a = b$, then $a + c = b + c$ and $c + a = c + b$

   Argument: $a + c = a + c$ Why?
   $a = b$ Why?
   $a + c = b + c$ Why?
   $a + c = c + a; b + c = c + b$ Why?
   $c + a = c + b$ Why?

77. Trace the figure at the right. Number the dots on the triangle 1–9 so that the sums of the four numbers shown on each side of the triangle are equal. No number may be used more than once.

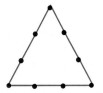

78. A pet store owner wanted to separate his fish so that the same number of fish were in each tank. When he separated the fish by twos, by threes, by fours, by fives, or by sixes, there was always one fish left over. What is the least number of fish the pet owner could have had?

79. Two books, Math I and Math II, are placed side by side on a bookshelf so that Math I is to the left of Math II. Each book cover is $\frac{1}{8}$ inch thick, and the pages, not counting the covers, are 2 inches thick. What is the distance from the first page of Math I to the last page of Math II?

─────── **REVIEW CAPSULE FOR SECTION 3–7** ───────

Combine like terms. (*Pages 64–68*)

1. $6xy + 38xy$

4. $5x + 3x + 9x^2$

2. $9y^2 - 7y^2$

5. $12t - (-t)$

3. $5a + 10b - (-2a)$

6. $23t^2 + t^2 + (-18t^2)$

3-7 Using Formulas: Geometry

Many problems that relate to geometry can be solved by writing an equation for a formula. For example,

the sum of the measures of the angles of a triangle is 180°.

That is,

$$A + B + C = 180°$$

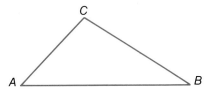

where A, B, and C represent the degree measures of the angles.

EXAMPLE   Find the measure of each angle.

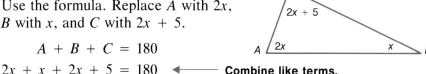

Solution: Use the formula. Replace A with $2x$, B with x, and C with $2x + 5$.

$$A + B + C = 180$$
$$2x + x + 2x + 5 = 180 \quad \longleftarrow \quad \textbf{Combine like terms.}$$
$$5x + 5 = 180$$
$$5x = 175$$
$$x = 35 \quad \longleftarrow \quad \textbf{Find 2x and 2x + 5.}$$
$$2x = 2(35) = 70$$
$$2x + 5 = 2(35) + 5 = 75$$

Check: Does the sum of the measures of the angles equal 180?

$35 + 70 + 75 = 180$? **Yes** ✓

Thus, the angle measures are **35°, 70°,** and **75°.**

EXERCISES: Classwork/Homework

Objective: To solve problems involving geometric formulas

CHECK YOUR UNDERSTANDING

For Exercises 1–4, the degree measure of two angles of a triangle are given. Find the measure of the third angle.

1. 20°, 113°   **2.** 60°, 60°   **3.** 90°, 25°   **4.** 117°, 35°

For Exercises 5–8, refer to figure *ABCD* at the right.

5. What is the sum of the measures of the angles in Triangle I?

6. What is the sum of the measures of the angles in Triangle II?

7. What is the sum of the measures of the angles in *ABCD*?

8. What is the sum of the measures of the angles of a square?

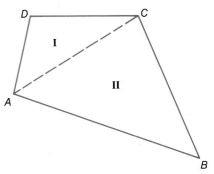

PRACTICE AND APPLY

Find the measure of each angle in the triangle.

9. Acute Triangle

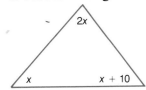

10. Obtuse Triangle

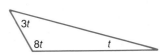

11. Right Triangle

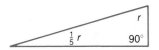

12. Isosceles Triangle

13. Equilateral Triangle

14. Isosceles Right Triangle

The sum of the measures of the angles of a quadrilateral (closed *polygon* having four sides) *is 360°.* That is,

$$A + B + C + D = 360°,$$

where *A*, *B*, *C*, and *D* represent the degree measures of the angles of the quadrilateral. For Exercises 15–20, refer to this formula to find the measure of each angle of the given quadrilateral.

15. Rectangle

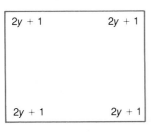

16. Square

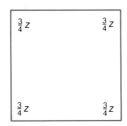

17. Parallelogram

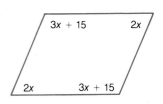

Solving Equations **123**

18. Rhombus

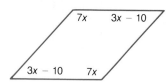

19. Trapezoid

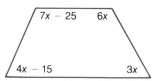

20. Quadrilateral

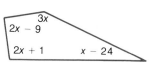

Solve each problem.

21. The measures of the angles of a triangle can be represented by a, $2a + 30$, and $a + 10$. Find the measure of each angle of the triangle.

22. The measure of one angle of a triangle is 70°. The measure of each of the other angles can be represented by $5x$. Find the measures of the two angles.

23. The measure of one angle of a triangle can be represented by $10p$. The measure of each of the other two angles is 15 more than the first angle. Find the measure of each angle.

24. The sum of the measures of two angles is 90°. The measure of one of these angles is $2r$; the measure of the other angle is $2r - 18$. Find the measure of each of these angles.

25. The sum of two angles is 90°. The measures of the angles can be represented by x and $(x + 28)$. Find the measure of each angle.

26. The sum of two angles is 90°. The measures of the angles can be represented by t and $(t - 12)$. Find the measure of each angle.

27. The sum of two angles is 180°. Their measures can be represented by y and $(y + 36)$. Find the measure of each angle.

28. The sum of two angles is 180°. Their measures can be represented by w and $(3w + 18)$. Find the measure of each angle.

29. The measures of the angles of a parallelogram can be represented by x, x, $3x$, and $3x$. Find the measure of each angle of the parallelogram.

30. The sum of the measures of two angles is 180°. The measure of one angle is $5x$. The measure of the other angle is twice the first. Find the measure of each angle.

31. The sum of the measures of two angles is 90°. The measure of one angle is $4q$. The measure of the second angle is three times the first. Find the measure of each angle.

32. The sum of the measures of two angles is 180°. The measure of one angle is $7t$. The measure of the second angle is 2 more than the first. Find the measure of each angle.

▬▬▬▬ **MAINTAIN**

Solve and check. (*Pages 118–121*)

33. $2 - 6t = -34$

34. $\frac{2}{3}m + 7 = 29$

35. $\frac{3}{4}x - 4 = 17$

36. $6q - 15 = 15$

37. $-32 = 24r - 20$

38. $\frac{1}{5}y - 3 = -4$

The letters of the word MATHEMATICS are written on cards and placed in a hat. One card is drawn at random. Find each probability. (*Pages 111–114*)

39. Drawing a C?
40. Drawing an H?
41. Drawing a P?
42. Not drawing a P?
43. Drawing a T?
44. Not drawing a T?

Multiply. (*Pages 83–85*)

45. $-\frac{1}{3}(27x)$
46. $\frac{4}{5}(-35r)$
47. $-\frac{2}{3}(-\frac{3}{2}y)$
48. $-\frac{5}{6}(-24xy)$
49. $\frac{12}{16}(-\frac{4}{6}a)$
50. $-\frac{15}{8}(\frac{16}{5}t)$
51. $-\frac{4}{11}(-22ab)$
52. $\frac{4}{15}(-30r)$
53. $-\frac{1}{3}(\frac{9}{10}bc)$
54. $-\frac{5}{7}(\frac{7}{5}p)$

CONNECT AND EXTEND

Two angles are *complementary* if the sum of their measures is 90. Find the measure of the complement of each angle.

55. 60
56. x
57. $5t$
58. $2x - 30$

Two angles are *supplementary* if the sum of their measures is 180. Find the measure of the supplement of each angle.

59. 95
60. p
61. $3y$
62. $2t + 16$

NON-ROUTINE PROBLEM

63. The figure at the right shows three different views of a cube.

   a. What shape is shown on that side of the cube which is opposite the side showing a circle?

   b. What shape is shown on that side of the cube which is opposite the side showing a triangle?

REVIEW CAPSULE FOR SECTION 3–8

Write an algebraic expression for each word description. (*Pages 1–4*)

1. The sum of the restaurant bill, b, and the amount of tax, t

2. The gross income, g, decreased by the deductions, d

3. The number of days present, p, subtracted from 365

4. The cost of t pounds at a cost of $1.65 per pound

3-8 Translation: Words to Symbols

Translating word expressions to algebraic expressions is an essential skill in solving word problems. This table shows that the *same* algebraic symbol of operation can be used to translate *more than one* word expression.

	Word Expression	Algebraic Expression
ADDITION EXPRESSIONS	The **sum** of a number, t, and -3	$t + (-3)$
	$z°$ **plus** $1.9°$	$z + 1.9$
	Add $7\frac{1}{2}$ to k.	$k + 7\frac{1}{2}$
	$50 **more than** d dollars	$d + 50$
	$-\frac{7}{8}$ **increased by** n	$-\frac{7}{8} + n$
	Increase the quantity $2t + 4$ by 6.	$(2t + 4) + 6$
	The **total** of 16 and $-r$	$16 + (-r)$
SUBTRACTION EXPRESSIONS	x **minus** $2\frac{3}{8}$	$x - 2\frac{3}{8}$
	The **difference of** $60 and b	$60 - b$
	The **difference between** $60 and b	$60 - b$
	Subtract 7.8 from n.	$n - 7.8$
	The quantity $3t - 9$ **decreased by** -8	$(3t - 9) - (-8)$
	a **diminished by** -1	$a - (-1)$
	$y°$ **less** $5°$	$y - 5$
	$y°$ **less than** $5°$	$5 - y$
MULTIPLICATION EXPRESSIONS	1.7 **times** z	$1.7z$
	b **multiplied by** $\frac{2}{3}$	$\frac{2}{3}b$, or $\frac{2b}{3}$
	The **product of** 5 and the quantity $2a - 9$	$5(2a - 9)$
	Twice m centimeters	$2m$
	Triple the width, w	$3w$
DIVISION EXPRESSIONS	The cost, c, **divided by** 12	$c \div 12$, or $\frac{c}{12}$
	The **quotient of** the quantity $2a - 9$ and 15	$\frac{2a - 9}{15}$
	The **quotient of** 15 and y	$15 \div y$, or $\frac{15}{y}$

Recall that terms enclosed in parentheses are treated as one quantity. Thus, $5(a + b)$ can be read "5 times the quantity a plus b".

Note also how these two expressions differ.

$y°$ less $5°$ **is not the same as** $y°$ less than $5°$.

$y - 5$ **is not the same as** $5 - y$.

To translate a word expression, follow this procedure.

PROCEDURE

> **To represent a word expression by algebraic symbols:**
> 1 Choose a variable. Tell what it represents.
> 2 Identify the key word or words that indicate which operation to use.
> 3 Represent the word expression by symbols.

EXAMPLE Use algebraic symbols to represent each word expression.

a. 1.5 seconds more than Amy's record time.

b. The amount of a car loan divided by 36 payments.

Solutions: **a.** 1 Let t = Amy's record time   **b.** 1 Let a = amount of loan
2 1.5 seconds more than t 2 a divided by 36
3   $t + 15$ 3 $a \div 36$

EXERCISES: Homework/Classwork

Objective: To represent word expressions by algebraic symbols

CHECK YOUR UNDERSTANDING

Choose from the box at the right the algebraic expression that represents each word expression. More than one answer may be possible in some cases.

1. The product of y and (-6)	**2.** 6 diminished by y	
3. Subtract 6 from y	**4.** y increased by 6	
5. Six times y	**6.** The quotient of y and (-6)	
7. Subtract y from 6	**8.** y more than 6	
9. 6 less than y	**10.** 6 less y	

$y + 6$	$6 + y$
$y - 6$	$6 - y$
$-6y$	$6y$
$\dfrac{y}{-6}$	$\dfrac{-6}{y}$
$y \div 6$	$6 \div y$

Represent each word expression by an algebraic expression.

11. The difference of 25 and n

12. The total of x and $-6\frac{1}{4}$

13. y decreased by 19.3

14. $\frac{1}{2}$ plus $(-a)$

15. $-18\frac{2}{3}$ minus $(-r)$

16. t less than (-100)

17. The sum of x and $(-x)$

18. a increased by $\frac{5}{8}$

19. -2 subtracted from m

20. Subtract (-30) from m

21. 12 decreased by $|y|$

22. q more than $(2q + 3)$

23. q more than the quantity $(2q + 3)$

24. -0.5 less r

25. r less (-0.5)

26. The quotient of 9 and x

27. The quantity $(q + 7)$ multiplied by 7

28. The product of (-2) and the quantity $(q - 8)$

29. Twice p

30. $(-t)$ divided by 212

31. The quantity $(z^2 - 4x)$ multiplied by 9

32. -1 times p

33. The product of r and $\frac{1}{12}$

34. The quotient of t and (-3)

For Exercises 35–46, first choose a variable and tell what it represents. Then write an algebraic expression for each word expression.

35. Five centimeters more than the width of a rectangle

36. The number of hours worked less $\frac{1}{2}$ hour

37. One-third the perimeter of the base of the Great Pyramid in Egypt

38. The quotient of the distance traveled and the rate, 50 miles per hour

39. The cost of a new car less the depreciation, $1200

40. The distance traveled divided by the time, 3 hours

41. Twice the air distance from San Francisco to Chicago

42. Fifteen pounds more than the average weight

43. The quotient of $1200 and five times the round trip fare

44. Twenty-five kilometers more than twice the distance traveled

45. Five hundred less than the quotient of the number of pages in a telephone directory and 9

46. Four times the perimeter of a parking lot less 16

47. A car travels 6 hours at an average rate of k kilometers per hour. Represent the distance traveled.

48. A plane travels t hours at an average rate of 320 miles per hour. Represent the distance traveled.

49. The Nolan family repays a debt of $1200 in equal monthly payments over *m* months. Represent the amount of each monthly payment.

50. The Martinez family spent a total of $1500 for a vacation that lasted *d* days. Represent the average cost per day.

51. Last year, Glenda paid $3500 in gasoline and maintenance costs for her car. She used the car to travel *m* miles. Represent the average cost per mile.

52. Richard had a total of 23 hits in *k* times at bat. Represent his batting average.
(HINT: Batting average = Number of hits ÷ Times at bat)

━━━━━ **MAINTAIN**

Find the measure of each angle of the triangle. (*Pages 122–125*)

53.
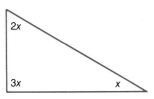

54.
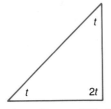

55.

Solve and check each equation. (*Pages 118–121*)

56. $-6x - 14 = 10$

57. $18 = 4n + 2$

58. $10 - 6x = 64$

59. $\frac{t}{3} - 6 = 2$

60. $\frac{c}{-6} + 18 = 20$

61. $6 - \frac{p}{4} = 7$

The table on the right shows the average daily temperature for fifteen days. (*Pages 74–77*)

62. Find the mean, median, and mode.

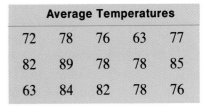

Average Temperatures				
72	78	76	63	77
82	89	78	78	85
63	84	82	78	76

━━━━━ **CONNECT AND EXTEND**

Write the value of each amount of money in cents.

63. $(x + 4)$ nickels

64. $(k + 3)$ dimes

65. *r* nickels plus $(r + 1)$ dimes

66. $30p$ quarters plus $6p$ dimes

67. $\frac{1}{2}y$ nickels plus *y* quarters

68. $\frac{1}{2}t$ dimes plus $3t$ quarters

━━━━━ **REVIEW CAPSULE FOR SECTION 3-9** ━━━━━

Solve and check each equation. (*Pages 64–68, 118–121*)

1. $24 + 3 = 9d - 2d - 1$

2. $3x - 5x + 4 = -8$

3. $12 - 3x - x = 48$

4. $6r + 9 - r = 36$

5. $55 = 8t - 1 - t$

6. $-42 - y - 5y = 0$

3-9 Writing an Equation

The following Guide for Problem Solving will help you to solve the variety of problems that will be presented in this text.

GUIDE FOR PROBLEM SOLVING

1. **Understand the problem.**
   • Note key words and phrases.
   • Identify what is given and what you are asked to find.

2. **Develop a plan.** Use one of these strategies.
   • Write an equation.   • Draw a diagram.
   • Look for patterns.   • Guess and check.
   • Make a model.   • Make tables and graphs.
   • Work backwards to a   • Solve a simpler but
     solution.   related problem.

3. **Carry out the plan:** Solve the problem.

4. **Look back.**
   • Check the results with the conditions in the problem.
   • Ask: "Is the answer reasonable?"

WRITE AN EQUATION

To use the strategy of writing an equation, it is helpful to **identify the conditions** in the problem. Condition 1 tells how to represent one unknown in terms of the other. Condition 2 tells what quantities are equal or unequal.

EXAMPLE 1 A marathon had 448 more local participants than visiting runners. (Condition 1). The total number in the race was 3640. (Condition 2). Find the number of local runners and of visiting runners.

Solution:

1 **Find:** The number of local runners and visiting runners
  Given. There are 448 more local runners ⟵ **Condition 1**
  than visiting runners.
  There are 3640 runners in all. ⟵ **Condition 2**

Represent the unknowns: Let r = number of visiting runners.
          Then $r + 448$ = number of local runners.

2 Write an equation to "connect" Condition 1 and Condition 2.

Think: $\underline{\text{Number of Visiting Runners}} + \underline{\text{Number of Local Runners}} = 3640$

Translate: $r + r + 448 = 3640$

3 Solve the equation.

$$r + r + 448 = 3640 \quad \longleftarrow \quad \text{Combine like terms.}$$
$$2r + 448 = 3640 \quad \longleftarrow \quad \text{Add } (-448) \text{ to each side.}$$
$$2r = 3192 \quad \longleftarrow \quad \text{Multiply each side by } \frac{1}{2}.$$
$$r = 1596 \quad \longleftarrow \quad \text{Don't forget to find } r + 448.$$

$$r + 448 = 1596 + 448 = 2044$$

4 Check: **Condition 1** Does $2044 = 1596 + 448$? Yes ✓
Condition 2 Does $1596 + 2044 = 3640$? Yes ✓

There were **1596** visiting racers and **2044** local racers.

Sometimes Condition 2 is given in the first statement of the problem.

EXAMPLE 2 The total number of apartments in two buildings is 348 (Condition 2). The Fairview apartment building has 12 less than three times the number of apartments in the Tulip Vista building (Condition 1). How many apartments are there in Fairview?

Solution:

1 **Find:** The number of apartments in Fairview
Given: Fairview has 12 less than three times the number of apartments in Tulip Vista.
The total number of apartments in both buildings is 348.

Let a represent the number of apartments in Tulip Vista.
Then $3a - 12 = $ the number of apartments at Fairview.

2 **Think:** <u>Number at Tulip Vista</u> + <u>Number at Fairview</u> = 348
Translate: $\qquad a \qquad + \qquad 3a - 12 \qquad = 348$

3 $4a - 12 = 348$
$\quad\quad 4a = 360$
$\quad\quad\, a = 90 \quad \longleftarrow \quad$ **Don't forget to find 3a − 12.**
$3a - 12 = 258$

4 Check: **Condition 1** Does $258 = 3 \cdot 90 - 12$? Yes ✓
Condition 2 Does $90 + 258 = 348$? Yes ✓

Fairview has **258** apartments.

Solving Equations **131**

Objective: To apply the strategy of writing an equation to solving problems

▰▰▰▰ **CHECK YOUR UNDERSTANDING**

With each sentence in Exercises 1–6, match the corresponding item in a–f.

1. The larger number is 1 more than twice the smaller.

2. The smaller of two numbers is 1 less than the larger.

3. The smaller of two numbers is 8 less than twice the larger.

4. One number is twice another.

5. One number is 9 more than 3 times a second number.

6. One number is 3 less than 9 times another.

a. Let h = first number.
   Then $2h$ = second number.

b. Let q = larger number.
   Then $q - 1$ = smaller number.

c. Let p = smaller number.
   Then $3p + 9$ = larger number.

d. Let t = smaller number.
   Then $2t + 1$ = larger number.

e. Let a = larger number.
   Then $2a - 8$ = smaller number.

f. Let w = first number.
   Then $9w - 3$ = second number.

For Exercises 7–10, refer to this problem.
Nora earns \$15 more per week than her twin brother, Nat. Together, they earn \$375 per week. What is Nora's weekly salary?

7. What two unknowns will you represent to solve the problem?

8. Which sentence tells you how to represent the salaries?

9. What sentence tells you about equal quantities?

10. What symbol will you use to represent the word "together"?

▰▰▰▰ **PRACTICE AND APPLY**

In some problems, one condition is <u>underscored once</u>. Use this condition to represent the unknowns. A second condition is <u>underscored twice</u>. Use both conditions to write an equation for the problem, and solve each problem.

11. <u>One number is 5 times another.</u> <u><u>The sum of the numbers is 72.</u></u> Find the numbers.

12. <u>One number is 5 more than a second number.</u> <u><u>The sum of the numbers is 115.</u></u> Find the numbers.

13. <u>One number is 4 less than another.</u> <u><u>The sum of the numbers is 20.</u></u> Find the numbers.

14. <u><u>The sum of two numbers is 21.</u></u> <u>One number is 3 less than the other.</u> Find the numbers.

15. <u>One number is $\frac{2}{3}$ of another.</u> <u><u>The sum of the numbers is 50.</u></u> What are the numbers?

16. <u>A number is 7 more than five times another number.</u> <u><u>The sum of the numbers is 55.</u></u> Find the numbers.

17. The smaller of two numbers is 10 less than the larger. The sum of the numbers is 76. What are the numbers?

18. The larger of two numbers is 12 more than the smaller. The sum of the numbers is 36. What are the numbers?

19. The sum of three numbers is 64. The second number is 3 more than the first. The third is 11 less than twice the first. Find the numbers.

20. The second of two numbers is 16 less than 3 times the first. The sum of the two numbers is 64. What are the numbers?

21. Together, Bob and Dan earned $52. Bob earned 3 times as much as Dan. How much did each boy earn?

22. Louisa is $\frac{3}{4}$ as tall as Carla. The difference between their heights is 0.4 meters. How tall is each girl?

23. A coat costs $35.50 more than a dress. The total cost of both items is $161.30. How much does each cost?

24. A house and lot sold for $140,000. The house costs 1.5 times as much as the lot. How much does each cost?

25. The number of persons entering the A–Z Store at 10 A.M. one day was 235 more than at 10 A.M. the next day. The total for both days was 885. How many persons entered the store at 10 A.M. on each day?

26. Together, Carol and Dick own 152 shares of stock in Sierra Engineering Corporation. Carol owns 4 less than twice the number of shares that Dick owns. How many shares of stock does each person own?

27. The Harris family's telephone bill for October was $63.80. The cost of long distance calls was $41.96 more than the cost for local calls. Find the cost for long-distance calls.

The following terms are used in Exercises 28–33.

The price of merchandise before it is offered to consumers at a reduced price is called the **list price** or **regular price.**

The amount that an item is reduced is called the **discount.**

The reduced price is called the **sale price.**

28. The rate of discount at a sale is 20%. Jim bought a lamp on sale for $40. Find the list price and the discount. (HINT: Let p = the list price. Then $0.20p$ = the amount of discount and $p - 0.20p = \underline{\ ?\ }$.)

29. At a kitchen appliance sale, the Gomez family bought a refrigerator that was on sale at a 10% discount. The sale price was $594. Find the list price and the amount of discount on the refrigerator.

30. A camera is on sale for $90.40. The rate of discount is 20%. Find the list price and the amount of discount.

31. An 8–track tape is on sale for $5.10. The rate of discount is 25%. Find the list price and the amount of discount.

32. A clock radio is on sale at a discount rate of 35%. The sale price is $45.50. Find the list price and the amount of discount.

33. The sale price of a television set is $360. The discount rate is 40%. Find the list price and the amount of discount.

▬▬▬▬ **MAINTAIN**

Represent each word expression by an algebraic expression. (*Pages 126–129*)

34. The quotient of -9 and r

35. The difference between $d and $125

36. $29 less $y

37. $29 less than $y

38. The product of $18\frac{1}{2}$ and xy

39. $1\frac{2}{3}$ more than z

40. The number of students, s, increased by 45

41. The product of r and 6.5

Solve. (*Pages 122–125*)

42. The measure of one angle of a triangle is 90°. The measure of each of the other two angles is $x°$. Find the measure of the equal angles.

43. The measures of the angles of a triangle can be represented by m, $3m$, and $8m$. Find the measure of each angle.

Combine like terms. (*Pages 64–68*)

44. $21k + 7 + 34k$

45. $24a + 7 - 15a$

46. $11r - 5r - 18r$

47. $-t^2 - 3t - t$

48. $0.8r^2 - 12.6r + 6.3r^2$

49. $-xy + 19y^2 + 8xy$

▬▬▬▬ **CONNECT AND EXTEND**

Solve.

50. Dick's bank contains an equal number of nickels, dimes and quarters. The total value is $10.00. How many of each kind of coin are there?

51. Elaine has only dimes and quarters in her purse. The total value is $2.50. There are 3 more quarters than dimes. How many quarters are there?

52. A piece of string, 60 centimeters long, is cut into 3 pieces. One piece is 2 centimeters longer than the shortest piece and 2 centimeters shorter than the longest piece. How long is each piece?

53. Gina has $2 more than three times the amount that Fred has. When Gina gave Fred $5, Fred then had one-half as much as Gina. How much did Gina have at first?

Focus on College Entrance Tests

Careful attention to **key words** is an aid to logical reasoning in drawing conclusions.

EXAMPLE Assume that the given statement is true. Write <u>True</u>, <u>False</u>, <u>Possible</u>, or <u>Can't tell</u> for each given conclusion. Give a reason for each answer.

Statement: Fairview Stadium has <u>at least</u> 5 gates.

Conclusions	**Analysis**
a. Fairview Stadium has <u>exactly</u> 3 gates.	**a. False.** "<u>At least</u> 5" means that the smallest possible number of gates is 5.
b. Fairview Stadium has <u>exactly</u> 5 gates.	**b. Possible.** See the reason for conclusion **a.**
c. Millard Stadium has <u>at most</u> 7 gates.	**c. Can't tell.** No information is given about Millard Stadium.
d. Fairview Stadium has <u>at most</u> 9 gates.	**d. Possible.** See the reason for conclusion **a.**
e. Fairview Stadium has 5 <u>or more</u> gates.	**e. True.** "<u>At least</u> 5 gates" means 5 gates, or 6 gates, or 7 gates, and so on.

TRY THESE

Assume that each given statement is true. Write <u>True</u>, <u>False</u>, <u>Possible</u>, or <u>Can't tell</u> for the conclusions that follow each statement. Explain each answer.

1. **Statement:** Fred spent $15 <u>at most</u> for the calculator.

   Conclusions: a. Fred spent <u>exactly</u> $13.75 for the calculator.
   b. Fred spent <u>at least</u> $20 for the calculator.
   c. Fred spent <u>more than</u> $8 for the calculator.
   d. Alice spent $4.50 <u>more than</u> Fred for a calculator.

2. **Statement:** Kristin saves <u>at least</u> $10 per week.

   Conclusions: a. In 4 weeks, Kristin has saved <u>at least</u> $40.
   b. Kristin saved <u>less than</u> $520 last year.
   c. Kristin saved <u>at least</u> $520 last year.
   d. In 4 weeks, Kristin saved <u>exactly</u> $50.

3. **Statement:** <u>Between</u> 30 and 40 students belong to the math club this year.

   Conclusions:
   a. <u>Exactly</u> 35 students belong to the math club this year.
   b. <u>More than</u> 35 students belong to the math club this year.
   c. Last year, <u>exactly</u> 35 students belonged to the math club.
   d. <u>Fewer than</u> 45 students belong to the math club this year.

4. **Statement:** The Sandlot Hitters played <u>more than</u> 20 games last season.

   Conclusions:
   a. The Sandlot Hitters had a <u>winning season</u> last year.
   b. The Sandlot Hitters played <u>at most</u> 20 games last season.
   c. The Sandlot Hitters played <u>exactly</u> 21 games last season.
   d. The Sandlot Hitters played <u>between</u> 21 and 28 games last season.

5. **Statement:** <u>Exactly 5 out of every 7 students</u> in Stevens Junior High received a grade of C or better on the test. There are 490 students at Stevens Junior High.

   Conclusions:
   a. Of the 490 students, <u>more than</u> 350 received a grade of C on the test.
   b. <u>Exactly</u> 2 out of every 7 students received a grade lower than C on the test.
   c. Of the 490 students, <u>exactly</u> 140 received a grade lower than C on the test.
   d. Of the 490 students, <u>more than</u> 349 and <u>fewer than</u> 351 received a grade of C or better on the test.

6. **Statement:** Of 2500 people interviewed, <u>fewer than</u> 25% were under the age of 19.

   Conclusions:
   a. Of the 2500 people interviewed, exactly 625 were 19 years old.
   b. Of the 2500 people interviewed, more than 75% were 19 years old or older.
   c. Of the 2500 people interviewed, 500 were between the ages of 12 and 18.
   d. Of the 2500 people interviewed, more than 1900 were over the age of 30.

Chapter Summary

IMPORTANT TERMS

Equivalent equations (p. 95)
Experimental probability (p. 111)
Extremes (p. 104)
Means (p. 104)
Percent (p. 107)

Probability (p. 111)
Proportion (p. 103)
Ratio (p. 103)
Theoretical probability (p. 111)

IMPORTANT IDEAS

1. **Equation Addition Property:** Adding the same number to each side of an equation results in an equivalent equation.

2. The replacement set of the variable in an equation is the set of real numbers, unless it is otherwise stated.

3. **Multiplication Property for Equations:** Multiplying each side of an equation by the same nonzero number results in an equivalent equation.

4. In general, dividing both sides of an equation by the same nonzero number results in an equivalent equation.

5. **Property of Proportions:** In a proportion, the product of the means equals the product of the extremes. That is,

   if $\frac{a}{b} = \frac{c}{d}$ ($b \neq 0$, $d \neq 0$), then $ad = bc$.
   Also, if $ad = bc$, then $\frac{a}{b} = \frac{c}{d}$ ($b \neq 0$, $d \neq 0$).

6. To solve equations involving more than one operation, use the Addition Property for equations first. Then use the Multiplication Property.

7. **To represent a word expression by algebraic symbols:**
   [1] Choose a variable. Tell what it represents.
   [2] Identify the key word or words that indicate which operation to use.
   [3] Represent the word expression by symbols.

8. **Guide for Problem Solving:**
   1. Understand the problem. Note key words and phrases. Identify what is given and what you are asked to find.
   2. Develop a plan. Use one of the strategies. See page 130.
   3. Carry out the plan. Solve the problem.
   4. Look back. Check the results with the conditions in the problem. Ask: "Is the answer reasonable?"

9. **Identifying Conditions:** Condition 1 tells how to represent one unknown in terms of the other. Condition 2 tells what quantities are equal or unequal.

Chapter Review

Solve and check each equation. (*Pages 95–102*)

1. $x + 10 = 13$

2. $-6 + p = 1$

3. $-12 - r = 7$

4. $-3c = 18$

5. $\frac{3}{5}t = 21$

6. $-2.9 + t = 11.3$

7. $-\frac{y}{8} = 1\frac{1}{16}$

8. $r - \frac{1}{5} = 4\frac{4}{5}$

9. $7.5x = 1.5$

Solve each proportion. (*Pages 103–106*)

10. $\frac{17}{1.5} = \frac{y}{1.8}$

11. $\frac{35}{84} = \frac{12}{x}$

12. $\frac{6.5}{13} = \frac{x}{4}$

13. $\frac{12}{8} = \frac{17}{x}$

14. In a mixture of green paint, the ratio of blue paint to yellow paint is 4:3. How many gallons of blue paint should be mixed with 2 gallons of yellow paint to produce this shade of green?

15. In a certain city, 0.6 meters of snow fell in 3 hours. How many meters of snow would fall in 8 hours at the same rate?

Solve. (*Pages 107–110*)

16. What percent of 38 is 57?

17. 25% of 68 is what number?

18. 3.5% of what number is 7?

19. What percent of 75 is 1.5?

20. The price of a home computer is $1800. Missy made a down payment of 20% when she bought it. How much was the down payment?

21. A baseball team won 15 games. That was $62\frac{1}{2}$% of the games played. How many games did the team play?

22. A dealer bought an antique vase for $375 and sold it for $450. What was the percent of increase?

23. The monthly rent for a stereo system rose from $18.50 to $21.75. Find the percent of increase, to the nearest whole percent.

The letters of the word **CALIFORNIA** are written on cards and placed in a hat. One card is drawn at random. Find each probability. (*Pages 111–114*)

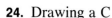

24. Drawing a C

25. Drawing an I

26. Drawing an R

27. Not drawing an L

28. In a shipment of 700 flashlights, the probability that any one flashlight is defective is 3%. Predict the probable number of defective flashlights in the shipment.

Solve and check each equation. (*Pages 118–121*)

29. $11 - \frac{4}{5}m = 3$

30. $3x - 8 = 19$

31. $0.4t - 1.3 = 0.3$

32. $4 = 28 - 8t$

33. $\frac{3}{4}t - 7 = 25$

34. $5x + 6 = -4$

In Exercises 35–37 find the measure of each angle of the triangles. Use the formula A + B + C = 180°. (*Pages 122–125*)

35. Right Triangle

36. Acute Triangle

37. Obtuse Triangle

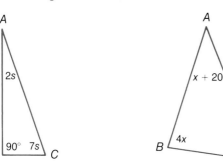
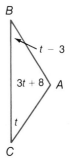

38. The measure of one angle of a triangle is 78°. The measure of each of the other angles can be represented by $6x$. Find the measures of the two angles.

39. The measures of the angles of a triangle can be represented by t, $3t + 4$, and $2t - 16$. Find the measure of each angle of the triangle.

Represent each word expression by an algebraic expression. (*Pages 126–129*)

40. p divided by -7

41. 6.4 less w

42. 5 increased by $2z$

43. $(-c)$ multiplied by $\frac{1}{3}$

44. $2a$ subtracted from -9

45. The quotient of $-x$ and 2

46. The product of -6 and $(x - 3)$

47. -7 more than the quantity $(6a + c)$

Write an equation to solve each problem. Then solve the problem. (*Pages 130–134*)

48. Together, Samantha and Jill earned $95. Jill earned $4 less than twice what Samantha did. How much did each earn?

49. The sum of two numbers is 75. The larger number is 7 more than 3 times the smaller. Find the numbers.

Chapter Test

Solve and check each equation.

1. $x + 4 = 17$

2. $x - 3\frac{1}{4} = 11$

3. $9k = -72$

4. $-6t = 54$

5. $14w + 6 = 13$

6. $7a + 11a = 9$

7. $1.5c + 3 = 7.5$

8. $6 = 3 - (f + 7)$

9. $6b - 4b + 3 = 11$

Solve each proportion.

10. $\dfrac{1.8}{y} = \dfrac{1.5}{7}$

11. $\dfrac{21}{x} = \dfrac{35}{84}$

12. $\dfrac{2.5}{1} = \dfrac{0.5}{n}$

Solve.

13. A machine can fill 96 jars of peanut butter in 2 minutes. At this rate, how many jars can it fill in 60 minutes?

14. Miranda bought a skirt at a "30% off" sale. The original price was $42. How much did she save?

15. The letters of the word FOOTBALL are written on cards and placed in a hat. One card is drawn at random. What is the probability that the card is an L?

16. A sample of 500 toy trucks contains 35 that are defective. Find the probable number of defective toy trucks in a shipment of 25,000.

17. Find the measure of each angle of the triangle shown at the right. Use the formula $A + B + C = 180°$, where A, B, and C represent the measures of the angles of the triangle.

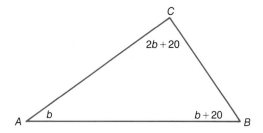

Represent each word expression by an algebraic expression.

18. Twice n less 58

19. y decreased by 1.5

Solve.

20. The number of tickets printed, less 76, is 424. Find the number of tickets printed.

Additional Practice

Skills

Solve and check each equation. (*Pages 95–102, 118–121*)

1. $t - (-7) = 21$

2. $y + \frac{1}{2} = 3\frac{1}{4}$

3. $2.2m = -8.8$

4. $-\frac{5}{9} = \frac{f}{6}$

5. $3 = -\frac{2}{11}u + 9$

6. $1.7w - 0.44 = 5$

Solve each proportion. (*Pages 103–106*)

7. $\frac{14}{91} = \frac{63}{x}$

8. $\frac{5}{n} = \frac{4}{n-1}$

9. $\frac{10}{y+3} = \frac{4}{y-1}$

Solve. (*Pages 107–110*)

10. 8% of 175 is what number?

11. What percent of 120 is 45?

12. 27% of 200 is what number?

13. 32% of what number is 32?

Problem Solving and Applications

A bag contains 4 white, 2 blue, and 3 green marbles. One marble is drawn without looking. (*Pages 111–114*)

14. What is the theoretical probability of drawing a white marble?

15. What is the theoretical probability of drawing a marble that is not green?

In Exercises 16–18, find the measure of each angle. Use the formula $A + B + C = 180°$. (*Pages 122–125*)

16. Acute Triangle

17. Isosceles Triangle

18. Isosceles Right Triangle

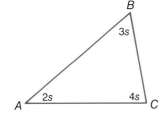

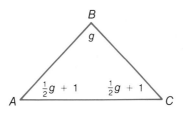

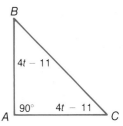

Solve. (*Pages 130–134*)

19. Jean and Emily have 110 old coins in their combined collections. Jean has 25 less than twice the number of coins that Emily has. How many coins does each girl have?

20. The sale price of a book is $9.72. The rate of discount is 25%. Find the list price and the amount of discount.

Cumulative Maintenance: Chapters 1-3

Part 1

Choose the best answer. Choose _a_, _b_, _c_, or _d_.

1. Evaluate: $2 + [7 + 3 (12 \div 4)]$

   a. 32   **b.** 18   **c.** 10   **d.** 21

2. Find the sum: $-23 + (-42)$

   a. 65   **b.** -19 **c.** 19   **d.** -65

3. Multiply: $-\frac{3}{4}(-16)(2)$

   a. -24 **b.** 6   **c.** 24   **d.** -6

4. By what number would you multiply $-\frac{2}{5}b$ to obtain b?

   a. $\frac{5}{2}$ **b.** $-\frac{5}{2}$ **c.** $\frac{2}{5}$ **d.** $-\frac{2}{5}$

5. Evaluate $\frac{-4(a - b^2)}{a}$ for $a = -2$ and $b = 3$.

   a. -22 **b.** -14 **c.** -5 **d.** 22

6. Find the value of $(-2y)^3$ for $y = 0$.

   a. -8 **b.** 8   **c.** -6 **d.** 0

7. What are the solutions of $d - 3 > 6$ when the replacement set is $\{3, 5, 7, 9, 12, 15\}$?

   a. $\{12, 15\}$ **b.** $\{3, 5, 7\}$ **c.** $\{9, 12, 15\}$ **d.** $\{3, 5, 7, 9\}$

8. Add. $|-4.3| + |-2.7|$

   a. 1.6   **b.** 7   **c.** -7 **d.** -1.6

9. Simplify: $-3y + 7y - 6$

   a. $6 - 4y$ **b.** $10y - 6$ **c.** $4y - 6$ **d.** $4y$

10. Which decimal represents the rational number $\frac{7}{11}$?

   a. $0.\overline{63}$ **b.** $0.\overline{636}$ **c.** 0.6   **d.** 0.63

11. Which property involves the order of numbers?

   a. distributive   **b.** symmetric   **c.** associative   **d.** commutative

12. What is the mode of the numbers 0, 0, 9, -3, 6, -3, 0, 4, 2?

   a. -3 **b.** 0   **c.** 2   **d.** 9

13. What number is 50% of 200?

   a. 50   **b.** 400   **c.** 100   **d.** 150

14. What is the theoretical probability of a 6 turning up on one toss of a die?

   a. 6   **b.** $\frac{1}{6}$ **c.** $\frac{1}{2}$ **d.** 1

15. What is the solution of the equation $-\frac{4}{7}y = -8$?

   a. $-\frac{32}{7}$ **b.** -14 **c.** $\frac{32}{7}$ **d.** 14

16. Combine like terms: $-4ab + 2cd - cd + 3ab$

   a. $cd + ab$ **b.** $ab - cd$ **c.** $-cd - ab$ **d.** $-ab + cd$

17. Solve the proportion $\frac{15}{x} = \frac{3}{9}$

   a. $x = 45$ **b.** $x = 5$ **c.** $x = \frac{1}{3}$ **d.** $x = 3$

18. Solve: $150n + 600 = 1500$

   a. $n = 750$ **b.** $n = 10$ **c.** $n = 6$ **d.** $n = 60$

19. What is the solution of the equation $-4 + \frac{2x}{5} = -6$?

   a. -5 **b.** 5 **c.** -25 **d.** 25

20. Which algebraic expression represents this word expression: The product of a number, n, and -2?

   a. $-2 + n$ **b.** $\frac{-2}{n}$ **c.** -2^n **d.** $-2n$

21. For which of the numbers -3, 0, and 3 is $|y|$ positive?

   a. -3 and 3 **b.** -3, 0, and 3 **c.** 0 **d.** 3

Part 2

22. Jean wants to know the average price of a house in her hometown. Which average, the mean or the median, would best represent the price?

23. Frank bought 6 cans of tuna fish for $9.24. The next week he bought 5 more cans. How much did the 5 cans cost?

24. The sum of the measures of two angles is $180°$. The measure of one angle is $6x$. The measure of the other angle is one half the first. Find the measure of each angle.

25. A sample of 600 electric can openers contain 15 that are defective. Find the probable number of defective openers in a shipment of 2000.

26. A rectangular garden is 14 ft long and 10 ft wide. Find the perimeter using the formula $P = 2l + 2w$.

27. A water pump can pump 12 gallons of water in $1\frac{1}{2}$ minutes. How many gallons can it pump in 1 day?

28. Carmen saved $300 less than her sister for a vacation. Together, they saved a total of $2500. How much did they each save?

29. Susan's monthly rent for her apartment rose from $550 to $583. Find the percent of increase.

30. After the price of a new car increased by 4%, the new price was $11,960. What was the price before the increase?

31. A number is 11 more than three times another number. The sum of the numbers is 39. What are the numbers?

More on Solving Equations

In nature, **patterns** can be found in the waves made by drops of rain in a pool. In mathematics, **identifying patterns** is one **strategy** that is useful in problem-solving.

4-1 Drawing a Diagram: Perimeter

PERIMETER

The **perimeter,** P, of a geometric figure such as a triangle is the distance around it. To find this distance, add the lengths of the sides.

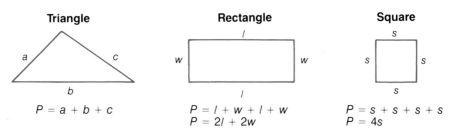

Triangle

$P = a + b + c$

Rectangle

$P = l + w + l + w$
$P = 2l + 2w$

Square

$P = s + s + s + s$
$P = 4s$

Most problems require the use of more than one strategy. The example below requires the use of two strategies: **drawing a diagram** and **writing an equation.**

EXAMPLE

The length of a tennis court for singles is 3 feet shorter than three times the width (Condition 1). The perimeter is 210 feet (Condition 2). Find the dimensions (length and width) of the court.

Solution:

[1] **Find:** The length and width of the court
Given: Length is 3 feet less than 3 times the width. (Condition 1)
Perimeter is 210 feet. (Condition 2)

Represent the unknowns.
Let w = the width.
Then $3w - 3$ = the length.
Draw and label a rectangle.

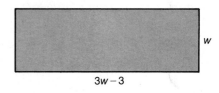

$3w - 3$

[2] Write an equation to "connect" Condition 1 and Condition 2.

Think: <u>Twice the length</u> <u>plus</u> <u>twice the width</u> <u>equals</u> 210.
Translate: $2(3w - 3)$ $+$ $2w$ $=$ 210

[3] **Solve.** $6w - 6$ $+$ $2w$ $=$ 210
$8w - 6 = 210$
$8w = 216$
$w = 27$ ⟵ **Don't forget to find the length.**

Since the length is $3w - 3$, replace w with 27.
$$3w - 3 = 3(27) - 3$$
$$= 78 \longleftarrow \text{Length}$$

4 **Check:** **Condition 1** Does $78 = 3(27) - 3$? $78 = 81 - 3$ Yes ✓

Condition 2 Does $2(78) + 2(27) = 210$? $156 + 54 = 210$ Yes ✓

The width is **27 feet** and the length is **78 feet**.

EXERCISES: Homework/Classwork

Objective: To use the strategies of drawing a diagram and writing an equation to solve problems involving perimeter

CHECK YOUR UNDERSTANDING

Find the length of each side of each figure.

1.

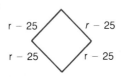

Perimeter: 36 meters

2.

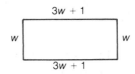

Perimeter: 374 feet

3.

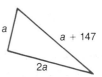

Perimeter: 623 meters

For Exercises 4–6, represent the unknowns. Then write an equation you could use to solve the problem.

4. Find: The length of each side of a square   Given: Perimeter is 64 yards.

5. Find: Dimensions of a rectangular garden
Given: Length is 10 feet more than the width. Perimeter: 120 feet

6. Find: Lengths of the sides of a triangle
Given: One side is 2 feet longer than the shortest side, another side is 4 feet longer than the shortest side. Perimeter: 51 feet

PRACTICE AND APPLY

In some problems, one condition is <u>underscored once</u>. Use this condition to represent the unknowns. A second condition is <u>underscored twice</u>. Use both conditions to write an equation for the problem. Then solve the problem.

7. <u>The length of a rectangle is 8 inches more than twice its width.</u> <u><u>The perimeter is 112 inches.</u></u> Find the length and width of the rectangle.

8. <u>The length of a rectangle is 7 times its width.</u> <u><u>The perimeter of the rectangle is 64 centimeters.</u></u> Find the dimensions of the rectangle.

9. The base of the rectangular building in which spacecraft are assembled at the Kennedy Space Center in Florida has a perimeter of 2256 feet. The length is 180 feet less than the width. Find the dimensions of the base.

10. The longest side of a triangle is twice the length of the shortest side. The third side is four inches shorter than the longest side. Find the lengths of the sides of the triangle if the perimeter is 96 inches.

11. An artist is making a rectangular wooden frame for a painting. The perimeter is 250 centimeters and the length is 1.5 times the width. Find the width and length of the frame.

12. The width of a badminton court is 8 yards less than its length. The perimeter is $42\frac{2}{3}$ yards. Find the dimensions of the court.

An *isosceles triangle* has two equal sides, called *legs*. Use these facts for Exercises 13–14.

13. The third side of an isosceles triangle is 9 centimeters longer than each of the equal sides. The perimeter is 27 centimeters. Find the length of each side.

14. Each of the equal sides of an isosceles triangle is 2 feet more than three times the third side. The perimeter is 32 feet. Find the length of each side of the triangle.

15. A triangular 458-mile course for a boat race is marked by three buoys. The distance between the first and second buoys is 2 miles more than the distance between the second and third buoys. The distance between the first and third buoys is 168 miles. How far is it from the first to the second buoy?

16. A plane travels 1971 kilometers along a triangular route formed by three cities, Malone, Stockton and Cooper. The distance from Malone to Stockton is 299 kilometers more than the distance from Stockton to Cooper and the distance from Malone to Cooper is 674 kilometers. How far is it from Malone to Stockton?

17. Surveyors working on a freeway placed stakes at points A, B, and C such that the distance from A to C equals the distance from B to C. The distance from A to B is 1.6 times the distance from A to C. The perimeter of the triangle is 1929.6 meters. Find all three distances.

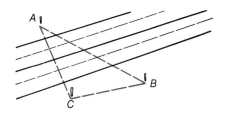

For Exercises 18–20, use this fact.
The sum of the measures of a triangle is 180°.

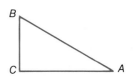

18. In triangle *ABC*, the measure of angle *B* is twice the measure of angle *A* and the measure of angle *C* is three times the measure of angle *A*. Find the measure of each angle.

19. In isosceles triangle *ABC*, angles *A* and *B* are equal in measure and each of these angles is 20° more than three times the measure of angle *C*. Find the measure of each angle.

20. In triangle *ABC*, angle *B* is 8° more than twice the measure of angle *A*, and angle *C* is 12° less than the measure of angle *A*. Find the measure of each angle.

▬▬▬ **MAINTAIN**

Solve. (*Pages 130–134*)

21. Twice the cost of a pair of skis decreased by $60 equals $225. Find the cost of the skis.

22. Three times the number of words Dot types per minute increased by 14 is 194. How many words does Dot type per minute?

Use $>$, $=$, **or** $<$ **to compare the numbers.** (*Pages 49–52*)

23. $|-7|$ ___?___ $|7|$

24. $|-3| - |6|$ ___?___ 0

25. $|-6.2| - |-6.2|$ ___?___ 0

26. $|0|$ ___?___ $|5|$

27. $|-\frac{1}{3}|$ ___?___ $|\frac{1}{2}|$

28. $|-4| + |6|$ ___?___ -2

▬▬▬ **CONNECT AND EXTEND**

29. The length of a rectangle is twice its width. When the length is increased by 4 inches and the width is decreased by 1 inch, a new rectangle is formed. The perimeter of the new rectangle is 198 inches. Find the length and width of the original rectangle.

30. The length of a rectangle is 3 centimeters less than twice its width. If the length is decreased by 2 centimeters and the width is decreased by 1 centimeter, the perimeter will be 24 centimeters. Find the dimensions of the original rectangle.

▬▬▬ **NON-ROUTINE PROBLEMS**

31. Use these numbers and the operations of multiplication and division only to write an expression equal to $17\frac{1}{2}$.

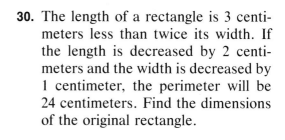

| 1 | 2 | 3 | 4 | 5 | 6 | 7 | 8 |

32. Use these numbers as bases and exponents to write an expression that equals 0. More than one answer might be possible.

| 2 | 3 | 4 | 5 | 32 |

4-2   Solving Equations: Variable on Both Sides

In the following equation, $4x - 6 = x + 9$, terms with the variable, x, appear on both sides of the equation. Use the Addition Property for equations to write an equivalent equation having all the variables on one side. Then combine like terms and solve.

EXAMPLE 1 Solve and check: $4x - 6 = x + 9$

Solution:
$$4x - 6 = x + 9 \quad \longleftarrow \quad \textbf{Add } (-x) \textbf{ to each side.}$$
$$4x - 6 + (-x) = x + 9 + (-x) \quad \longleftarrow \quad \textbf{Group and combine}$$
$$[4x + (-x)] - 6 = [x + (-x)] + 9 \quad \quad \textbf{like terms.}$$
$$3x - 6 = 9$$
$$3x - 6 + 6 = 9 + 6 \quad \longleftarrow \quad \textbf{By the Addition Property}$$
$$\textbf{for equations}$$
$$3x = 15$$
$$\tfrac{1}{3}(3x) = \tfrac{1}{3}(15)$$
$$\quad \longleftarrow \quad \textbf{By the Multiplication}$$
$$x = 5 \quad \quad \textbf{Property}$$
$$\textbf{for equations}$$

Check:
$$4x - 6 = x + 9$$
$$4(5) - 6 \stackrel{?}{=} 5 + 9$$
$$14 \stackrel{?}{=} 14 \text{ Yes } \checkmark \quad \text{The solution is } \mathbf{5}.$$

To solve equations such as $3(x - 1) = 5(x - 3)$, first use the Distributive Property to remove the grouping symbols.

EXAMPLE 2 Solve: $3(x - 1) = 5(x - 3)$

Solution:
$$3(x - 1) = 5(x - 3) \quad \longleftarrow \quad \textbf{Use the Distributive Property.}$$
$$3x - 3 = 5x - 15$$

Method 1: Add $(-5x)$ to each side.

$$-5x + 3x - 3 = -5x + 5x - 15$$
$$-2x - 3 = -15$$
$$-2x - 3 + 3 = -15 + 3$$
$$-2x = -12$$
$$-\tfrac{1}{2}(-2x) = -\tfrac{1}{2}(-12)$$
$$x = 6$$

Method 2: Add $-3x$ to each side.

$$-3x + 3x - 3 = -3x + 5x - 15$$
$$-3 = 2x + 15$$
$$-3 + 15 = 2x - 15 + 15$$
$$12 = 2x$$
$$\tfrac{1}{2}(12) = \tfrac{1}{2}(2x)$$
$$6 = x$$

More on Solving Equations   **149**

Check: $3(x - 1) = 5(x - 3)$ ← Replace x with 6.

$$3(6 - 1) \overset{?}{=} 5(6 - 3)$$
$$3(5) \overset{?}{=} 5(3)$$
$$15 \overset{?}{=} 15 \text{ Yes } \checkmark \quad \text{The solution is } \mathbf{6}.$$

EMPTY SET   When an equation has no solution for the given replacement set, the solution is the **empty set,** or ϕ.

EXAMPLE 3 Solve and check: $-4(3x - 20) = -1 - 12x$.

Solution: $-4(3x - 20) = -1 - 12x$ ← **By the Distributive Property.**

$-12x + 80 = -1 - 12x$ ← **Add 12x to each side.**

$12x - 12x + 80 = 12x - 1 - 12x$

$80 \neq -1$ The solution is the **empty set,** or ϕ.

EXERCISES: Classwork/Homework

Objective: To solve equations that have the variable on both sides

CHECK YOUR UNDERSTANDING

What would you add to each side of the equation in order to get the variable terms on the left side of the equation?

1. $2x + 8 = x + 9$ **2.** $4z + 7 = z - 2$ **3.** $-4y - 7 = -9y + 8$

4. $2x + 5 = -3x + 25$ **5.** $7a - 9 = 3a - 1$ **6.** $-3t + 5 = -4t - 7$

What would you add to each side of the equation in order to get the variable terms on the right side of the equation?

7. $5 - 2t = 3t$ **8.** $-r + 6 = 2r$ **9.** $100 - 9d = 41d$

10. $1 - 9m = 6m - 14$ **11.** $-5m + 6 = 7m - 6$ **12.** $2y + 1 = 3y - 2$

PRACTICE AND APPLY

For Exercises 13–42, solve and check.

13. $5x = 2x + 12$ **14.** $7x = 3x + 24$ **15.** $4y + 12 = 7y$

16. $7y + 8 = 11y$ **17.** $5a - 9 = 2a$ **18.** $9y - 42 = 3y$

19. $12x + 15 = 7x$ **20.** $6y + 32 = 2y$ **21.** $7x + 4 = 9x + 24 - 2x$

22. $3y + 9 = 3y + 15$ **23.** $4a + 1 = 7a - 17$ **24.** $2b - 5 = 8b + 1$

25. $-3r - 8 = -5r + 12$

26. $-6x - 7 = -5x + 3$

27. $t - 7 = 3\frac{1}{2} + 2t$

28. $\frac{1}{2}y + 6 = y - 4$

29. $0.7a + 0.3a = 2a - 4$

30. $q + 7q = -12q + 10$

31. $4(x + 2) = 3x$

32. $7y = -2(y + 9)$

33. $-4(x + 2) = -6x + 2$

34. $5(m - 5) = 3(m + 1)$

35. $2x + 3(x - 9) = 2(x + 3)$

36. $3y + 5(y + 3) = 5y$

37. $-5(y - 9) = -(3 + 5y)$

38. $6 - (8 - 4n) = 2(2n + 1)$

39. $36 - 2(c - 28) = -4(2c + 52)$

40. $2(x - 3) + 3(x - 2) = 8$

41. $2(2n + 1) - 3(n - 5) = 0$

42. $1.3 + 9.4n - 9.03n = 3.52$

████████ **MAINTAIN**

Solve.

43. Each of the equal sides of an isosceles triangle is 5 feet more than the third side. The perimeter is 31 feet. Find the length of each side of the triangle. (*Pages 145–148*)

44. The length of a poster is 6 inches more than the width. The perimeter is 56 inches. Find the dimensions of the poster. (*Pages 145–148*)

45. A television is selling for $560. This is $20 more than twice the cost. What is the cost? (*Pages 130–134*)

46. When Jared's savings are added to five times his savings amount, the sum is $4800. How much has Jared saved? (*Pages 130–134*)

Evaluate. (*Pages 53–61*)

47. $7 + (-32) + 16$

48. $-3 - 15 - (-9)$

49. $-5 + (-29) + 4$

50. $-43 - 18 + (-4)$

51. $6 - 22 + 18$

52. $4 + (-3) + (-16)$

████████ **CONNECT AND EXTEND**

For Exercises 53–56, *a* represents an even integer and *b* represents an odd integer. Solve for *x*. Identify *x* as an even or an odd integer.

53. $2a + 2x = x + b$

54. $4x - a = 3\frac{1}{2}x - 3b$

55. $3a - 2(x + b) = 0$

56. $x + a + b = 2x + 3a - 6b$

——— **REVIEW CAPSULE FOR SECTION 4-3** ———

Write an algebraic expression for each word expression. (*Pages 126–129*)

1. 9 years more than y

2. 12 years less than s

3. 5 less than a number, p

4. A number, n, increased by 3

5. The sum of Jack's age, a, and 3

6. Subtract 15 from an integer, g

More on Solving Equations   **151**

Solving a Simpler Problem

Traffic managers are concerned with the efficient use of highways and streets to facilitate the movement of vehicles and pedestrians. Some traffic-related problems can be solved by applying the strategy of **solving a simpler but related problem.** The solution may involve other strategies such as *drawing a diagram*, *making a table*, and *identifying patterns*.

EXAMPLE

To improve the flow of pedestrian traffic, Fair Fairgrounds will build separate walkways to connect every two of its 12 tents. How many walkways will be needed?

Plan: Simplify the problem. Determine how many walkways will be needed to connect 2 tents, 3 tents, 4 tents, and so on.
Draw a diagram to show the solution of each simpler problem.

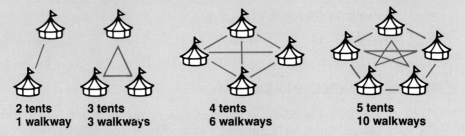

| 2 tents | 3 tents | 4 tents | 5 tents |
| 1 walkway | 3 walkways | 6 walkways | 10 walkways |

Make a table. List the data in the table.

Number of tents	2	3	4	5
Number of walkways	1	3 = 1 + 2 3 − 1 ⬆	6 = 1 + 2 + 3 4 − 1 ⬆	10 = 1 + 2 + 3 + 4 5 − 1 ⬆

Look for a **pattern:**   For n tents, the number of walks needed is
$$1 + 2 + 3 + 4 + \ldots + (n - 1).$$

Solve: Therefore, the number of walks needed for 12 tents is
$$1 + 2 + 3 + 4 + 5 + 6 + 7 + 8 + 9 + 10 + 11, \text{ or } \mathbf{66}.$$

EXERCISES

1. A **diagonal** of a polygon is a segment that joins two vertices that are not next to each other. How many diagonals are there in a polygon of 10 sides?

4 sides   **5 sides**   **6 sides**   Only 3 of the diagonals are shown

2. There are 12 teams in a league. Each team plays every other team once. How many games are played in all?

3. There are 7 pegs on a board. No three pegs are in a straight line. How many elastic bands are needed to join each peg to each other peg using one elastic for each joining?

4. How many triangles are there in this figure?

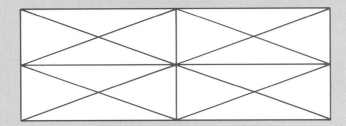

HINT: Find the number of triangles in one section of the figure as shown at the right. Multiply this by 4. Then look for longer diagonals to help you identify the remaining triangles.

5. How many rectangles are there in the figure below?

6. How many different pairs of whole numbers have a sum of 64?

4-3 Guess and Check/Making a Table

**GUESS AND
CHECK**

A useful strategy in problem solving is to make an intelligent guess. Then you check to see whether the guess is correct.

EXAMPLE 1 Chris, Mike, and Dave play on the Wheelchair Whiz basketball team. The numbers on their jerseys are consecutive odd integers. (Condition 1). The sum of the numbers is 27 (Condition 2). Find the numbers.

Method 1: Guess and check

Think: Consecutive integers: $\cdots -2, -1, 0, 1, 2, 3, \cdots$

Consecutive odd integers: $\cdots -3, -1, 1, 3, 5, \cdots$

Guess	Sum	Does it check?
3, 5, 7	15	No. Too small.
9, 11, 13	33	No. Too large.
7, 9, 11	27	This is it!

The numbers are **7, 9,** and **11.**
Is there another way to solve the problem?

Method 2: Write an equation.

Think: Consecutive odd integers differ by 2.

  1 Let t = the smallest odd integer.
  Then $t + 2$ = the next odd integer. ← **Use Condition 1 to represent the unknowns.**
  And $t + 4$ = the largest odd integer.

  2 Write an equation to "connect" Condition 1 and Condition 2.

Think: $\underset{\text{Integer}}{\text{First Odd}} + \underset{\text{Integer}}{\text{Second Odd}} + \underset{\text{Integer}}{\text{Third Odd}} = 27$

Translate: $t \quad + \quad (t + 2) \quad + \quad (t + 4) \quad = 27$

$\boxed{3}$ $3t + 6 = 27$

$3t = 21$

$t = 7$ ⟵ **Don't forget to find $t + 2$ and $t + 4$.**

$t + 2 = 9$

$t + 4 = 11$ **The check is left for you.**

The numbers are **7, 9,** and **11.**

MAKING A TABLE

In problems involving age, you often have to represent a person's age, the person's age a number of years ago, and the person's age a number of years from now. Make a table to show the information.

	Age Now	Age 4 Years Ago	Age 7 Years From Now
Kiyo	15	$15 - 4$, or 11	$15 + 7$, or 22
Gordon	a	$a - 4$	$a + 7$
Rosa	$3t$	$3t - 4$	$3t + 7$

EXAMPLE 2 An electrician has worked 5 times as many years as her apprentice (Condition 1). Four years from now, the electrician will have worked 3 times as many years as the apprentice (Condition 2). How many years has each person worked?

Solution: $\boxed{1}$ Make a table to show the information.

	Years Worked	Years Worked 4 Years From Now
Apprentice	a	$a + 4$
Electrician	$5a$	$5a + 4$

$\boxed{2}$ **Think:** $\dfrac{\text{Electrician's Total Time}}{\text{In 4 Years}} = 3\left(\dfrac{\text{Apprentice's Total Time}}{\text{In 4 Years}}\right)$

Translate: $5a + 4 = 3(a + 4)$

$\boxed{3}$ **Solve:** $5a + 4 = 3a + 12$ ⟵ $3(a + 4) = 3 \cdot a + 3 \cdot 4$

$2a + 4 = 12$

$2a = 8$

$a = 4$ ⟵ **Years worked by apprentice**

$5a = 20$ ⟵ **Years worked by electrician**

$\boxed{4}$ **Check:** Has the electrician worked 5 times as many years as the apprentice? **Yes** ✓

In 4 years, will the electrician have worked 3 times as many years as the apprentice? **Yes** ✓

Objective: To use the strategy of guess and check to solve problems
To use the strategy of making a table to solve problems

▬▬▬ **CHECK YOUR UNDERSTANDING**

Beginning with the given even integer, write the next four larger consecutive even integers.

1. 12   **2.** 100   **3.** -12 **4.** -66 **5.** q **6.** $b + 4$

Beginning with the given odd integer, write the next four larger consecutive odd integers.

7. 9   **8.** 1   **9.** -21 **10.** -101 **11.** k **12.** $k + 10$

13. Charles is x years old. Represent his age 9 years from now.

14. Jill is t years old. Represent her age 5 years ago.

15. Edson is $5t$ years old. Represent his age 12 years ago.

16. Lynn is $(30 - q)$ years old now. Represent her age 15 years from now.

▬▬▬ **PRACTICE AND APPLY**

Solve. In some problems, Condition 1 is <u>underscored once</u>. Condition 2 is <u>underscored twice</u>.

17. <u>The sum of two consecutive even integers</u> is $\underline{\underline{-26}}$. What are the integers?

18. The sum of two consecutive integers is 279. Find the integers.

19. Three consecutive odd integers have a sum of -105. Find the integers.

20. Find <u>three consecutive even integers</u> <u>whose sum is 0</u>.

21. <u>Skip is now three times as old as Paul.</u> <u><u>In 5 years, Skip will be twice as old as Paul will be then.</u></u> How old is each now?

22. Carla is now twice as old as Jennifer. Seven years ago, the sum of their ages was 16. How old is each girl now?

23. <u>The age of two sisters can be represented as consecutive odd integers.</u> <u><u>Twelve years ago, the sum of their ages was 8.</u></u> How old is each now?

24. <u>One teacher has four times as many years experience as a second.</u> <u><u>Six years from now, the first teacher will have twice as many years experience as the second.</u></u> How many years of experience does the first teacher have?

25. Find four consecutive integers such that the sum of the second and fourth is 132.

26. Find three consecutive odd integers where the sum of the two largest is 7 less than three times the smallest.

27. A woman is now 40 years old and her daughter is 14. In how many years will the mother be exactly twice as old as her daughter?

28. Sandra Klee was 25 years old when her son was born. Her present age is 7 years less than three times her son's present age. How old is she now?

29. If $2n + 1$ is an odd integer, what is the preceding integer?

30. If n is an integer, is $2n + 1$ even or odd?

━━━━ MAINTAIN

Solve and check. (*Pages 149–151*)

31. $-8q - 27 = -17q$

32. $4r - 1 = 7(r + 2)$

33. $z = 57 - 2z$

34. $3 - d = 7d + 27$

35. $3(30 + f) = 4(f + 19)$

36. $3t = 2(t - 8)$

Solve. (*Pages 145–148*)

37. The lengths of the sides of a triangle can be represented by consecutive even integers. The perimeter of the triangle is 42. Find the length of the longest side.

38. A plane flies a triangular route formed by 3 cities. The length of the route is 8562 kilometers. If the lengths of the sides can be represented by consecutive integers, what is the length of the shortest side?

Combine like terms. (*Pages 64–68*)

39. $4x - 9x$

40. $34m - 21m$

41. $-32y + (-18y)$

42. $6t + (-11t)$

43. $-8b - 6.3b$

44. $-7b + 9b$

━━━━ CONNECT AND EXTEND

45. Each birthday, you are one year older. Is the percent of increase in your age each year more than, less than, or the same as the year before? Use your present age to explain your answer.

46. Think of your age and the age of one of your parents. As you both grow older each year, does the ratio of your age to that person's age increase, decrease, or remain the same? Explain your answer.

47. Two years ago, Clint was 7 times as old as Patrick. Two years from now, Clint will be 5 times as old as Patrick's age then. What is Clint's present age?

48. The third of four consecutive odd integers equals the sum of the fourth and twice the second. What are the integers?

━━━━ NON-ROUTINE PROBLEMS

49. What is the smallest number of coins that a cashier needs in order to make change for a purchase of less than one dollar?

50. At a banquet, four people are to be seated on one side of the head table. In how many different ways can these four people be seated?

Solve each problem. (*Pages 145–148*)

1. The length of a rectangular stadium is three times the width. The perimeter of the stadium is 160 meters. Find the dimensions of the stadium.

2. The longest side of a triangle is twice the length of the shortest side. The third side is 12 inches shorter than the longest side. Find the lengths of the sides of the triangle if the perimeter is 78 inches.

Solve and check. (*Pages 149–151*)

3. $18 - t = 5t + 6$

4. $9g + 7 = 2g$

5. $4(7 - n) - 3(5n - 6) = -11$

6. $4(2n + 1) = 2(3n - 1)$

7. $4(0.5x - 3) = 9 + 2x$

8. $6 - \frac{1}{2}r = 1\frac{1}{2}r + 18$

Solve. (*Pages 154–157*)

9. Three consecutive odd integers have a sum of 57. What are the integers?

10. John is now four times older than his son, Ethan. Six years ago, the sum of their ages was 18. How old are John and Ethan now?

*Historical Digest: **Problem Solving***

George Polya (1887–1985), a noted professor at Stanford University in California, is best known for his work in problem solving. He wrote a book, *How to Solve It*, in which he outlined a four-step method for problem solving.

Here is one of Polya's famous problems. See if you can solve it!

A traveller, stopping at an inn, discovered that the innkeeper was an old friend. The innkeeper told the traveller that he had three children. The product of their ages was 72 and the sum of their ages was the same as the number of rooms at the inn. The traveller knew the number in the inn but he told the innkeeper that he needed more information to find the ages of the children. The innkeeper told the traveller that the oldest loves to ride horses. What are the ages of the children?

4-4 Solving for a Variable

Problems in science and business often involve solving an equation for one variable in terms of the others. The procedures for solving are illustrated in the table below. To solve for x in the equation

$$x + a = b,$$

you find x in terms of a and b. Compare the solutions of the given equations in the table with those of the general equations.

Given Equation	General Equation
Solve for x. $x + 7 = 12$ $x + 7 + (-7) = 12 + (-7)$ $x = 5$ **Check:** $x + 7 \overset{?}{=} 12$ $5 + 7 \overset{?}{=} 12$ $12 \overset{?}{=} 12$ **Yes** ✓ The solution is **5**.	Solve for x. $x + a = b$ $x + a + (-a) = b + (-a)$ $x = b + (-a)$ **Check:** $x + a \overset{?}{=} b$ $b + (-a) + a \overset{?}{=} b$ $b \overset{?}{=} b$ **Yes** ✓ The solution is $b + (-a)$, or $\boldsymbol{b - a}$.
Solve for w. $38 = 16 + 2w$ $-16 + 38 = -16 + 16 + 2w$ $22 = 2w$ $\frac{1}{2}(22) = \frac{1}{2}(2w)$ $w = 11$ **Check:** $38 = 16 + 2w$ $38 \overset{?}{=} 16 + 2(11)$ $38 \overset{?}{=} 38$ **Yes** ✓ The solution is **11**.	Solve for w. $p = 2 + 2w$ $p - 2 = 2w$ $\frac{1}{2}(p - 2) = \frac{1}{2}(2w)$ $\frac{p - 2}{2} = w$ **Check:** $p = 2 + 2w$ $p \overset{?}{=} 2\left(\frac{p - 2}{2}\right)$ $p \overset{?}{=} 2 + p - 2$ $p \overset{?}{=} p$ **Yes** ✓ The solution is $\dfrac{p + 2}{2}$.
Solve for t. $-12 = -3t$ $4 = t$ The solution is **4**. The check is left for you.	Solve for t. $d = rt$ $\dfrac{d}{r} = t$ The solution is $\dfrac{d}{r}$. The check is left for you.

Objective: To solve an equation or formula for one variable in terms of the other variables

▬▬▬▬ **CHECK YOUR UNDERSTANDING**

Solve the first equation in each pair. Then use the same procedure to solve the second equation for x. Check each solution.

1. $\frac{x}{6} = 24$; $\frac{x}{a} = b$

2. $5x + 4 = 10$; $ax + b = c$

3. $\frac{3x}{5} = 2$; $\frac{ax}{b} = c$

4. $x + 6 = 8 + \frac{1}{4}$; $x + a = b + c$

5. $5x + 4 = 10$; $5x + a = b$

6. $-2x = 16$; $-ax = b$

7. $3(x + 4) = 8$; $3(x + a) = b$

8. $-x + 4 = -5$; $-x + a = b$

9. $-2x + 6 = 0$; $-2x + a = b$

10. $3x + 5 = -7$; $3x + a = -b$

▬▬▬▬ **PRACTICE AND APPLY**

Solve each formula for the variable indicated.

11. Formula for the circumference of a circle: $C = \pi d$ Solve for d.

12. Formula for the area of a parallelogram: $A = bh$ Solve for b.

13. Formula for the area of a triangle: $A = \frac{1}{2}bh$ Solve for h.

14. Formula for the perimeter of a rectangle: $P = 2l + 2w$ Solve for w.

15. Distance/rate/time formula: $d = rt$ Solve for r.

16. Simple interest formula: $i = prt$ Solve for t.

17. Simple interest formula: $i = prt$ Solve for r.

18. Formula for the volume of a rectangular box: $V = lwh$ Solve for h.

19. Formula for calculating a Celsius temperature from Fahrenheit: $C = \frac{5}{9}(F - 32)$ Solve for F.

20. Formula for the sum of the measures of the angles of a triangle: $a + b + c = 180°$ Solve for b.

Solve each formula for the unknown variable. Then substitute the given values to find the required length.

21. $C = \pi d$

$C = 22.6\pi$; $d = \underline{\ ?\ }$

22. $P = a + b + c$

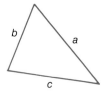

$P = 29.9$; $a = 11.4$;
$b = 7.9$; $c = \underline{\ ?\ }$

23. $P = 2l + 2w$

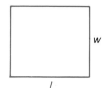

$P = 84$; $w = 20$;
$l = \underline{\ ?\ }$

Solve each formula for the unknown variable. Then find the required length.

24. $A = bh$

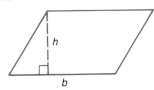

$A = 36.34$ square units;
$h = 4.6$; $b = $ __?__

25. $A = lw$

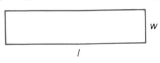

$A = 36.4$ square units;
$l = 13$; $w = $ __?__

26. $A = \frac{1}{2}bh$

$A = 72$ square units;
$b = 9$; $h = $ __?__

27. Alicia deposited an amount of money in the bank at 7% yearly interest. At the end of the year, she received $665 in interest. Use the formula $i = prt$ to find the amount deposited.

28. The perimeter of a rectangle is 20.2 feet. The width is 4.3 feet. Which key sequence would you use to find the length?

a. 20.2 [−] 2 [×] 4.3 [=] [÷] 2

b. 20.2 [−] 2 [×] 4.3 [=]

29. The formula $C = \frac{A}{46}$ gives the number of circuits, C, required for wiring each 46 square meters of floor area. Solve the formula for A to find how many square meters of floor area can be wired by using 5 circuits.

30. The dollar cost for fares of the Stop and Dash Cab Company is given by the formula $C = 2.50 + (n - 1)0.75$ where n is the number of miles traveled. Solve the formula for n to find how many miles were traveled when the fare was $7.75.

Solve each equation for n. Check each solution.

31. $2n + a = b$

32. $2n + 5a = 8a$

33. $6a + 2b = 2n$

34. $2n - a = b$

35. $3a + n = 5b$

36. $2n - b = 5a$

37. $n + a = b + c$

38. $2a + 2n = b + c$

39. $-n = -4b$

40. $-n + a = b$

41. $an = b + c$

42. $an + ac = b$

━━━━ **MAINTAIN**

43. Find four consecutive integers whose sum is -130. (*Pages 154–157*)

44. Find four consecutive odd integers whose sum is 0. (*Pages 154–157*)

45. Anna is now four times as old as her brother Ramon. In 4 years, Anna's age will be twice Ramon's age then. How old is each now?

46. Lydia is 20 years older than Karen. Sixteen years ago, Lydia was 3 times as old as Karen was then. How old are Lydia and Karen now?

Solve and check. (*Pages 149–151*)

47. $5t + 12 = 3t - 6$

48. $5 + 2x = 2(x - 3) + x$

49. $-4(d - 2) - 14 = 36 + 2d$

50. $8p - 2(2p - 1) = 6(p + 2)$

Divide. (*Pages 78–82*)

51. $400 \div 8$

52. $-24 \div (-6)$

53. $-4\frac{2}{3} \div \frac{9}{10}$

54. $6\frac{1}{5} \div (-\frac{8}{25})$

55. $\frac{-7}{10} \div 14$

56. $\frac{5}{11} \div (\frac{-7}{33})$

57. $15 \div (-\frac{2}{3})$

58. $-\frac{174}{6}$

■■■■ CONNECT AND EXTEND

Solve each equation for the variable indicated. Check each solution.

59. $a(b + n) = c$, for b

60. $\frac{n}{a} = b + n$, for a

61. $(a + b)n = c$, for a

62. $b(n - a) = c$, for n

63. $A = \frac{1}{2}h(b + b')$, for b

64. $A = p(l + rt)$, for r

■■■■ NON-ROUTINE PROBLEM

65. Find how many ways the word PROBLEM can be read from left to right in the diagram. Each letter in the word must be connected to the next letter by a marked line.

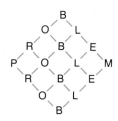

—— REVIEW CAPSULE FOR SECTION 4-5 ——

Choose the formula that corresponds to the pattern in the table.
(*Pages 14–18*)

1.

Distance: d	50	100	150	200
Time: $\quad t$	1	2	3	4

a. $t + 50 = d$ **b.** $d = \frac{t}{50}$

c. $d = \frac{50}{t}$ **d.** $d = 50t$

2.

Distance: d	160	180	200	220
Rate: $\quad r$	40	45	50	55

a. $d = r + 120$ **b.** $d = 4r$

c. $d = \frac{r}{4}$ **d.** $d = r + 4$

4-5 Organizing Data: Distance/Rate/Time

Ron jogs 2 miles from his home to baseball practice. It takes him 20 minutes. To find his average speed, divide the distance by the time.

Rate $= 2 \div \frac{1}{3}$ ◄———— **20 min** $= \frac{1}{3}h$

There are several ways to express the relationship between the distance, d, the rate, r, and the time, t.

$$d = rt \qquad r = \frac{d}{t} \qquad t = \frac{d}{r}$$

MAKING DIAGRAMS/ TABLES

In solving distance/rate/time problems, it is helpful to organize the given information in a table. This will help you to represent the unknowns (Condition 1). Drawing a diagram will help you to write the equation (Condition 2).

EXAMPLE 1 Two cars 525 miles apart start at the same time and travel toward each other. One car travels at a rate of 55 mph (miles per hour); the other travels 50 mph. In how many hours will the cars meet?

Solution: 1 Organize the data in a table. Represent the unknowns. Let t = the number of hours each car travels.

	Rate r	Time t	Distance $d = rt$
Car A	55	t	$55t$
Car B	50	t	$55t$

2 Draw a diagram. Use it and the table to write an equation.

Car A ——► ◄—— Car B

◄———— 525 miles ————►

Think: $\dfrac{\text{Distance for}}{\text{Car A}}$ $+$ $\dfrac{\text{Distance for}}{\text{Car B}}$ $=$ $\dfrac{\text{Total}}{\text{Distance}}$

Translate: $55t$ $+$ $50t$ $=$ 525

3 Solve the equation.

$$105t = 525$$
$$t = 5$$

4 **Check:** Does the total distance covered equal 525 miles?

$$55(5) + 50(5) \overset{?}{=} 525 \text{ Yes } \checkmark$$

The cars will meet in **5** hours.

In Example 2, the motion is in opposite directions.

EXAMPLE 2 Marsha and her brother Don left home by car at the same time, traveling in opposite directions. Don's rate was 6 mph less than Marsha's rate. After 10 hours, they were 940 miles apart. Find the speed at which each person traveled.

Solution: [1] Make a table.
Represent the unknowns.
Let r = Marsha's rate.
Then $r - 6$ = Don's rate.

	Rate r	Time t	Distance $d = rt$
Marsha	r	10 h	$10r$
Don	$r - 6$	10 h	$10(r - 6)$

[2] Draw a diagram. Use the diagram and the table to write an equation.

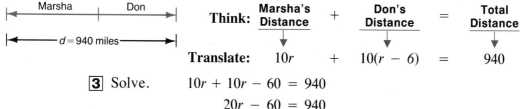

Think: Marsha's Distance + Don's Distance = Total Distance

Translate: $10r$ + $10(r - 6)$ = 940

[3] Solve.
$$10r + 10r - 60 = 940$$
$$20r - 60 = 940$$
$$20r = 1000$$
$$r = 50 \longleftarrow \textbf{Don't forget to find } r - 6.$$
$$r - 6 = 44$$

[4] **Check:** Is Don's rate 6 mph less than Marsha's?
$44 = 50 - 6$? Yes ✓
After 10 hours, were they 940 miles apart?
$50(10) + 44(10) = 940$? Yes ✓

Marsha's rate is **50 mph** and Don's rate is **44 mph**.

EXERCISES: Classwork/Homework

Objective: To solve distance/rate/time problems

CHECK YOUR UNDERSTANDING

1. Solve the formula $d = rt$ for r.

2. Solve the formula $d = rt$ for t.

For Exercises 3–6, use the given information to complete the table.

3. Two hikers start toward each other at the same time from different towns. They meet in 6 hours. The rate of one hiker is twice the rate of the other.

	r	t	d = rt
Hiker A	?	?	?
Hiker B	?	?	?

4. Susan and Joann leave from the same place driving in opposite directions, but Joann leaves 3 hours later than Susan. Susan's average rate of speed is 45 mph and Joann's average rate is 50 mph.

	r	t	d = rt
Susan	?	?	?
Joann	?	?	?

5. A passenger train and a freight train start at the same time from stations which are 648 kilometers apart. The rate of the passenger train is twice the rate of the freight train. They pass each other in 3 hours.

	r	t	d = rt
Passenger	?	?	?
Freight	?	?	?

6. Jack and Harry started on bicycles at the same time from two different places and rode toward each other. Jack traveled at 8 mph and Harry traveled at 10 mph. They met in 5 hours.

	r	t	d = rt
Jack	?	?	?
Harry	?	?	?

PRACTICE AND APPLY

7. Two automobiles start at the same time at the same place and travel in opposite directions. One travels at the rate of 53 mph and the other at the rate of 55 mph. In how many hours will they be 321 miles apart?

8. Two cyclists start from the same place at the same time. One rides at the rate of 10 mph and the other at 9 mph. They travel in opposite directions. In how many hours will they be 47.5 miles apart?

9. One car traveling 50 mph left a certain place 1 hour later than another car traveling in the same direction at the rate of 45 mph. In how many hours will the faster car overtake the other?

10. Frank and Bob start from home in their cars and travel in opposite directions. Frank's rate of speed is twice Bob's. In 4 hours they are 480 kilometers apart. Find each rate.

11. A passenger train leaves the station at 9 A.M. and travels at an average speed of 30 mph. Two hours later, an express train leaves the station on a parallel track and travels at an average rate of 50 miles per hour. At what time will the express overtake the passenger train?

More on Solving Equations **165**

12. A train traveling at an average rate of 60 mph takes 2 hours less time to go from Tray to Peterton than a motorist driving at an average rate of 45 miles per hour. How far is it from Tray to Peterton?

13. Two jets leave Pittsburg at the same time, one flying due north at 540 mph and one flying due south at 630 mph. After how many hours will the jets be 2340 miles apart?

14. It takes Phyllis 15 minutes to drive from home to school when there is heavy traffic. When there is little traffic, Phyllis increases her speed by 10 mph and makes the trip in 12 minutes. How far does Phyllis live from the school?

15. A cyclist had been traveling 24 km/h for 8 hours when he was overtaken by a motorist who left the same starting point 5 hours after the cyclist. Find the motorist's speed.

16. Dick jogs from his house to school at a rate of 9 kilometers per hour. On the return trip from school, he jogs at a rate of 6 kilometers per hour. The round trip takes 1 hour 15 minutes. How far is the school from Dick's house?

17. Lisa left home in a car that was traveling at the rate of 48 kilometers per hour. She walked home at the rate of 6 kilometers per hour. The round trip took 1.5 hours. How far did Lisa ride?

■■■■■ **MAINTAIN**

Solve each formula for the variable indicated. *(Pages 159–162)*

18. Simple interest formula: $i = prt$. Solve for p.

19. Formula for the area of a triangle: $A = \frac{1}{2}bh$. Solve for b.

20. Formula for the perimeter of a rectangle: $P = 2l + 2w$. Solve for w.

21. Formula for the sale price, after a discount, d: $s = p - d$. Solve for p.

Solve. *(Pages 154–157)*

22. The amount of overtime pay earned by three teenagers can be represented as consecutive even integers. If the total overtime pay for the three amounted to $90, how much did each receive in overtime pay?

23. Rosa is now 28 years old and Clare is 8 years old. In how many years will Rosa be twice as old as Clare?

Focus on College Entrance Tests

It is not always necessary to solve an equation for the variable in order to answer a question about the variable.

If $2n - 6 = 1$, what is the value of $n - 3$?

    a. $3\frac{1}{2}$ **b.** 2 **c.** $\frac{1}{2}$ **d.** -1

Think: By the distributive postulate, $2(n - 3) = 2n - 6$.
Thus, $2n - 6 = 2(n - 3)$. Solve for $n - 3$.

Solution: $2(n - 3) = 1$
$$n - 3 = \tfrac{1}{2} \quad \textbf{Answer: c}$$

TRY THESE   Choose the best answer. Choose *a, b, c,* or *d.*

1. If $2x + 4 = 6$, what is the value of $x + 2$?

    a. 1   **b.** 3   **c.** 6   **d.** 12

2. If $3y - 3 = 2$, what is the value of $y - 1$?

    a. -1 **b.** $\frac{2}{3}$ **c.** $1\frac{2}{3}$ **d.** 2

3. If $4n - 12 = -8$, what is the value of $n - 3$?

    a. 2   **b.** 1   **c.** -2 **d.** -8

4. If $6c + 8 = 3$, what is the value of $3c + 4$?

    a. -1 **b.** $-\frac{5}{6}$ **c.** $1\frac{1}{2}$ **d.** 3

5. If $9p - 6 = -1$, what is the value of $3p - 2$?

    a. 1   **b.** $\frac{1}{3}$ **c.** $-\frac{1}{3}$ **d.** -4

6. If $4p - 4 = \frac{1}{2}$, what is the value of $p - 1$?

    a. $\frac{1}{8}$ **b.** $\frac{1}{4}$ **c.** $1\frac{1}{8}$ **d.** 2

7. If $\frac{1}{3}x + \frac{1}{3} = 1$, what is the value of $x + 1$?

    a. $\frac{1}{3}$ **b.** $\frac{2}{3}$ **c.** 2   **d.** 3

8. If $\frac{n}{4} = 3$, what is the value of $\frac{n}{3}$?

    a. $\frac{1}{4}$ **b.** $\frac{3}{4}$ **c.** 4   **d.** 12

9. If $\frac{y}{6} = 4$, what is the value of $\frac{y}{4}$?

    a. $\frac{1}{6}$ **b.** $\frac{2}{3}$ **c.** $\frac{3}{2}$ **d.** 6

Chapter Summary

IMPORTANT TERMS

Empty set (p. 150)
Perimeter (p. 145)

IMPORTANT IDEAS

1. When terms with a variable occur on both sides of an equation, use the Addition Property for equations to get the terms on the same side. Then combine like terms and solve.
2. **Distance Formula:** distance = rate · time, or $d = rt$
3. **Solving Distance/Rate/Time Problems:**
   [1] Organize the information in a table. Use this information to represent the unknowns (Condition 1).
   [2] Draw a diagram to represent the information. Use the diagram and the table to write an equation for the problem (Condition 2).
   [3] Solve the equation.
   [4] Check your answer with the conditions of the problem. Answer the question.

Chapter Review

Solve each problem. (***Pages 145–148***)

1. The width of a swimming pool is 20 meters less than its length. The perimeter is 160 meters. Find the length and width of the pool.
2. In triangle ABC, angles A and B have the same measure. The sum of the measures of angles B and C is 110°. How many degrees are there in each of the three angles?
3. The Dudley's are adding a rectangular patio on to the back of their house. The perimeter of the patio is 70 feet and the length is 2.5 times the width. Find the length and width of the patio.
4. The lengths of the sides of a triangle can be represented by three consecutive even integers. The perimeter of the triangle is 90 feet. Find the lengths of the sides of the triangle.

Solve and check. (***Pages 149–151***)

5. $2x + 5 = 2(x - 1)$
6. $8t = 3t + 15$

7. $3(n + 2) - 16 = 8n$

8. $5(r - 4) - 3(10 - r) = -26$

9. $4x - 1 = 3(2 + x)$

10. $4 - (6 - 5n) = 2(n + 5)$

Solve. (*Pages 154–157*)

11. The sum of two consecutive odd integers is -16. What are the integers?

12. Find three consecutive even integers whose sum is 252.

13. Joe's present age is three times Greg's present age. Five years ago, the sum of their ages was 14. What is each boy's present age?

14. Don Paschal was 50 years old when his granddaughter was born. Now he is two years more than four times his granddaughter's age. How old is his granddaughter now?

Solve each equation for *n*. Check each solution. (*Pages 159–162*)

15. $s = \dfrac{n}{t}$

16. $a - n = 2b$

17. $3p = r - n$

18. $3h = 2n + g$

19. $an + 2b = 4 - c$

20. $-n = x - y$

Solve the formula for the variable indicated. (*Pages 159–162*)

21. Formula for the volume of a rectangular box: $V = lwh$. Solve for w.

22. Formula for the perimeter of a rectangle: $P = 2l + 2w$. Solve for l.

Solve. (*Pages 159–162*)

23. Albert deposited an amount of money in the bank at 6% interest. At the end of the year, he received $270 in interest. Use the formula $i = prt$ to find the amount he deposited.

24. A city park has the shape of a triangle. One side of the park is 160 meters long and another side is 145 meters long. The perimeter of the park is 512 meters. Use the formula $P = a + b + c$ to find the length of the third side of the park.

Solve. (*Pages 163–166*)

25. Two brothers leave Boston at the same time, headed in the same direction. One brother drives 80 kilometers per hour and the other drives 85 kilometers per hour. In how many hours will the brothers be 15 kilometers apart?

26. Two runners going in opposite directions pass each other along a straight trail. The speed of the faster runner is $1\frac{1}{4}$ times that of the slower runner. In one hour they are 18 kilometers apart. Find the rate of each runner.

Solve and check.

1. $7x = 21 - 3x$

2. $2(3y + 1) = -2(y - 5)$

3. $8 - d = 3d + 12$

4. $-2(t - 5) = 2(3t + 1)$

5. $3(3 - a) - 1 = a + 8$

6. $5b - 8 = 6b + 16$

Solve each equation for c. Check each solution.

7. $2c - a = b$

8. $\frac{c}{p} = k$

9. $c - x - y = 2x$

10. $ac + ab = d$

Solve.

11. The lengths of the sides of a triangle can be represented by three consecutive odd integers. The perimeter of the triangle is 123 feet. Find the length of the sides of the triangle.

12. The length of a trampoline is 80 centimeters longer than its width. Its perimeter is 1440 centimeters. Find the length and width.

13. The sum of three consecutive odd integers is 171. What are the integers?

14. Robert is 12 years older than Jay. Seven years ago, Robert was twice as old as Jay was then. How old are Robert and Jay now?

15. Two buses leave the same place at the same time, one headed north and one south. One travels at an average rate of 60 kilometers per hour and the other at an average rate of 70 kilometers per hour. In how many hours will they be 325 kilometers apart?

Skills

Solve and check. (*Pages 149–151*)

1. $9a - 4 = 5a$

2. $5 - 3n = 2n + 15$

3. $2x - 3 = 3(x - 2)$

4. $4(a + 2) = 6(a - 3)$

5. $2(\frac{1}{2}y + 7) = 8y$

6. $2(x + 1) - 3(2x - 2) = 4$

7. $0.3x + 4.2x - 4 = 1.5x + 11$

8. $-a + 4a = -5a - 80$

Solve each equation for *n*. (*Pages 159–162*)

9. $a = nb$

10. $y - n = 4h$

11. $3n + c = d$

12. $n + a = 2h$

13. $na - b = y$

14. $3n + n - 2 = 4c$

Solve each formula for the variable indicated. (*Pages 159–162*)

15. Formula for the area of a parallelogram: $A = bh$
Solve for h.

16. Formula for the perimeter of a triangle: $P = a + b + c$
Solve for c.

Problem Solving and Applications

17. In triangle *ABC*, the measure of angle *B* is three times the measure of angle *A*, and the measure of angle *C* is five times the measure of angle *A*. Find the measure of each angle. (*Pages 145–148*)

18. The width of a rug is 2 meters less than the length. The perimeter of the rug is 28 meters. Find the length and width of the rug. (*Pages 145–148*)

19. The sum of two consecutive integers is 49. Find the integers. (*Pages 154–157*)

20. The sum of two consecutive odd integers is -32. Find the integers. (*Pages 154–157*)

21. Frank leaves home at 8 A.M. and drives at a speed of 40 miles per hour. His sister leaves home at 9:30 A.M. driving in the same direction at a speed of 46 miles per hour. At what time will Frank's sister overtake him? (*Pages 163–166*)

22. Mr. Sanchez is 25 years older than his son. In 15 years he will be twice as old as his son. Find their present ages. (*Pages 154–157*)

23. One car traveling 45 kilometers an hour left a certain place 2 hours after another car traveling in the same direction at the rate of 35 miles an hour. In how many hours will the faster car overtake the other? (*Pages 163–166*)

Part 1

Choose the best answer. Choose *a*, *b*, *c*, or *d*.

1. Find the value of $-(-4x)^2$ for $x = \frac{1}{2}$.
   - **a.** 4
   - **b.** -4
   - **c.** -1
   - **d.** 1

2. Evaluate: $|7.23| - |9.46|$
   - **a.** 2.23
   - **b.** 16.69
   - **c.** -16.69
   - **d.** -2.23

3. What are the solutions of $w + 4 \leq -3$ when the replacement set is $\{-10, -7, -1, 0, 7\}$?
   - **a.** $-1, -7, -10$
   - **b.** $0, -1$
   - **c.** $-10, -7$
   - **d.** -10

4. Solve the equation $4x + 2 = x - 1$
   - **a.** $x = \frac{1}{3}$
   - **b.** $x = 1$
   - **c.** $x = -\frac{3}{5}$
   - **d.** $x = -1$

5. Solve the proportion $\frac{1.4}{2.8} = \frac{x}{8.4}$.
   - **a.** $x = 4.2$
   - **b.** $x = 2.8$
   - **c.** $x = 2$
   - **d.** $x = 4.1$

6. Evaluate $x^2b + b^2x - x^2b^2$ for $x = -2$ and $b = 3$.
   - **a.** -6
   - **b.** -42
   - **c.** 30
   - **d.** 66

7. By what number would you multiply $\frac{2}{3}t$ to obtain $-t$?
   - **a.** $-\frac{2}{3}$
   - **b.** $-\frac{3}{2}$
   - **c.** $\frac{2}{3}$
   - **d.** $\frac{3}{2}$

8. Divide: $\left(\frac{-a}{b}\right) \div \left(\frac{2b}{a}\right)$
   - **a.** $-\frac{a^2}{2b^2}$
   - **b.** -2
   - **c.** $-\frac{a^2}{b^2}$
   - **d.** $\frac{a^2}{2b^2}$

9. Which decimal represents the rational number $\frac{5}{6}$?
   - **a.** $0.\overline{83}$
   - **b.** 0.833
   - **c.** $0.8\overline{3}$
   - **d.** 0.8

10. Which property is illustrated by the statement $n + (d + f) = (n + d) + f$?
    - **a.** reflexive
    - **b.** associative
    - **c.** identity
    - **d.** commutative

11. If the number k is negative, which symbol represents its opposite?
    - **a.** $+k$
    - **b.** $-k$
    - **c.** $-|k|$
    - **d.** $-(k)^2$

12. Solve the equation $5(a - 4) = 3a + 6$.
    - **a.** $a = -13$
    - **b.** $a = 7$
    - **c.** $a = 3\frac{1}{4}$
    - **d.** $a = 13$

13. Which number is the median of $4, 7, -6, 3, -2, 0, -11, 1, 5$?
    - **a.** -2
    - **b.** 1
    - **c.** 0
    - **d.** 3

14. Solve: $4 + \frac{2}{3}x = \frac{1}{3}x + 2$
    - **a.** $x = -6$
    - **b.** $x = -\frac{2}{3}$
    - **c.** $x = -118$
    - **d.** $x = 6$

15. If $\frac{a}{c} = \frac{b}{d}$, which of the following equations is true?

    a. $ab = cd$ **b.** $a + d = b + c$ **c.** $ad = cb$ **d.** $a + b = c + d$

16. 12 is 15% of what number?

    a. 0.8   **b.** 80   **c.** 1.25   **d.** 90

17. What is the probability that Friday follows Thursday?

    a. $\frac{1}{7}$ **b.** 0   **c.** $\frac{1}{5}$ **d.** 1

18. Solve the formula $F = \frac{9C + 160}{5}$ for C.

    a. $C = \frac{5F - 160}{9}$ **b.** $C = \frac{5}{9}(F - 31)$ **c.** $C = \frac{1}{9}(F - 32)$ **d.** $C = 5F - 32$

19. Which expression is not positive if $k < 0$?

    a. $|k|$ **b.** $-k$ **c.** k^2 **d.** $k + k$

20. Solve the equation $x + x + 0.25x = 1800$

    a. 900   **b.** 4500   **c.** 4050   **d.** 800

21. Evaluate $-a(b + c) + a(b + c)$ for $a = -1$, $b = 2$, and $c = -3$.

    a. 0   **b.** -1 **c.** 2   **d.** -3

22. If $2n - 1$ represents an odd integer, which expression represents the next consecutive odd integer?

    a. $2n - 2$ **b.** $2n$ **c.** $2n + 1$ **d.** $2(n + 1)$

23. Simplify: $3(xy + 2) - 4xy + 5 - xy$

    a. $2xy + 11$ **b.** $xy + 5$ **c.** $-2xy + 11$ **d.** 11

Part 2

24. A used car dealer bought a car for $800 and then sold it at a 35% profit. What was the selling price of the car?

25. Find three consecutive integers such that the sum of the second and third is 87.

26. The plan for a new house contained two angles, one of which was two thirds the measure of the other. If the sum of the measures of the two angles is 150°, find the measure of each angle.

27. Bob has worked for 9 more years than his younger brother. Six years from now he will have twice as much experience as his brother. How many years has Bob's brother worked now?

28. Ann marked the boundaries of her rectangular garden and knew that the width was 12 feet less than the length. If the perimeter is 84 feet, find the dimensions of the garden.

29. Two race car drivers both drive for 6 hours each. One driver averages 135 mph and the other averages 147 mph. How much farther did the second driver travel?

5 Relations and Functions

A **coordinate model** was used to plan this card design. Since each seat in a stadium can be located by an ordered pair (row letter, seat number), the occupant of each seat can be directed to hold up a light card or a dark card to create the design.

5-1 Graphing Ordered Pairs

A flat surface, such as a chalkboard, can be thought of as representing a **plane.** To locate, or **graph,** points on a plane, you use two number lines that are **perpendicular** to each other. (That is, they meet at a 90° angle.) The horizontal number line is called the **x axis;** the vertical number line is called the **y axis.**

ORDERED PAIR

To graph a point *P* in a plane, you use an **ordered pair** of numbers (*x*, *y*). The first number, *x*, shows distance to the right or left of the *y* axis. The second number, *y*, shows distance above or below the *x* axis. In the figure at the right, *P*(2, 3) is 2 units to the right of the *y* axis and 3 units above the *x* axis. The axes cross at the **origin,** which is represented by the ordered pair (0, 0).

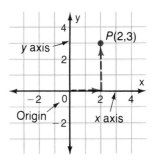

EXAMPLE 1 Graph each point: **a.** *R*(−6, −2)   **b.** *S*(6, −1)   **c.** *T*(−5, 5)

Solutions: **a.** For *R*(−6, −2): Start at the origin. Move 6 units to the left, then 2 units down.

b. For *S*(6, −1): Start at the origin. Move 6 units to the right, then 1 unit down.

c. For *T*(−5, 5): Start at the origin. Move 5 units to the left, then 5 units up.

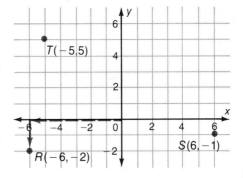

COORDINATE PLANE

The numbers of an ordered pair are the **coordinates** of a point. The first number, or **x coordinate,** is the **abscissa;** the second number, or **y coordinate,** is the **ordinate.** Because the plane associates number pairs or coordinates with points, it is called the **coordinate plane.** The axes separate the coordinate plane into four regions or **quadrants.** *The axes are not in any quadrant.*

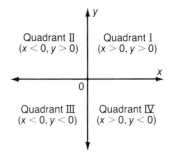

EXAMPLE 2 Name the quadrant or axis on which each point lies.

      a. $S(-1, -2)$ **b.** $P(6, -5)$ **c.** $V(0, -4)$ **d.** $T(5, 0)$

Solutions: Graph the points.

        a. S is in **Quadrant III.**

        b. P is in **Quadrant IV.**

        c. V is on the **y axis.**

        d. T is on the **x axis.**

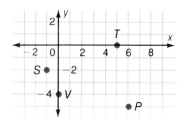

EXERCISES: Classwork/Homework

    Objective: To graph ordered pairs in the coordinate plane

CHECK YOUR UNDERSTANDING

    For Exercises 1–6, name the quadrant, or quadrants, of the coordinate plane described.

1. The first coordinate is positive.
    2. The second coordinate is negative.

3. The first coordinate is negative.
    4. The second coordinate is positive.

5. Both coordinates are positive.
    6. Both coordinates are negative.

7. On which axis is the first coordinate of every point always zero?
    8. On which axis is the second coordinate of every point always zero?

9. Which point in the coordinate plane has zero for both coordinates?

PRACTICE AND APPLY

10. Graph these points on the same pair of coordinate axes.

    a. $A(-3, 4)$ **b.** $B(5, 2)$ **c.** $C(4, -3)$ **d.** $D(-5, -4)$

    e. $F(-4, 0)$ **f.** $G(0, 5)$ **g.** $H(0, -3)$ **h.** $I(-4, -4)$

11. Name the quadrant or axis on which each point in Exercise 10 lies.

12. Name the coordinates for each point graphed at the right.

13. Name the ordinate of every point on the x axis.

14. Name the abscissa of every point on the y axis.

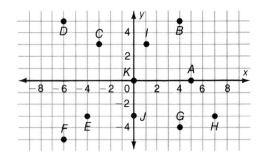

Name the quadrant or axis on which each point lies.

15. $(-3, -2)$ **16.** $(4, -1)$ **17.** $(-5, 6)$ **18.** $(2, 5)$

19. $(3, 0)$ **20.** $(0, -\pi)$ **21.** $(0, 0)$ **22.** $(-1, 4)$

23. $P(x, y)$ when $x > 0$ and $y > 0$ **24.** $Q(x, y)$ when $x < 0$ and $y < 0$

25. $R(x, y)$ when $x > 9$ and $y < 0$ **26.** $T(x, y)$ when $x < 0$ and $y > 0$

27. Plot each set of points A–E. Connect the points of each set in order. The result should be a familiar picture.

A: $\{(-2, 6), (1, 6), (4, 5), (6, 4), (7, 2), (7, 0), (6, -2\frac{1}{4}), (5, -4), (5, -9),$
$(2, -9), (3, -4), (3, -3), (1, -3), (-2, -2\frac{1}{4}), (-3, -2), (-4, -4),$
$(-5, -9), (-8, -9), (-6, -3), (-6, 1) (-9, 1), (-8\frac{1}{2}, 2\frac{1}{4}), (-11, 3),$
$(-12, 4), (-13, 6), (-12, 8), (-10, 10), (-9, 9), (-11, 7), (-11, 5),$
$(-10, 5), (-8, 7), (-5, 7), (-4, 8), (-3, 8), (-2, 7), (-2, 6), (-2, 5),$
$(-3, 3), (-4, 1), (-5, 0), (-6, 2), (-6, 3\frac{1}{2})\}$

B: $\{(7, 2), (8, 0), (9, -2), (10, -3), (11, -3)\}$

C: $\{(6, -2\frac{1}{4}), (6, -9), (5, -9)\}$

D: $\{(-2, -2\frac{1}{4}), (-3, -4), (-4, -9), (-5, -9)\}$

E: $\{(-7, 5)\}$

A fly walks along a certain path in the coordinate plane. List the coordinates, $P(x, y)$, of three points in its path. For Exercises 28–34, draw a graph of the path and describe the graph.

Example: The fly walks along points with an ordinate of 2.

Solution: Choose some points on the path. $\longrightarrow$ $(5, 2)$; $(0, 2)$; $(-7\frac{1}{2}, 2)$

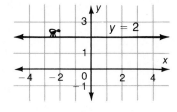

       $\longleftarrow$ **Graph the points. Connect them with a line.**

Description: **A horizontal line 2 units above the x axis.**

28. The fly walks along points with an abscissa of 3.

29. The fly walks along points with an ordinate of -4.

30. The fly walks along points with an ordinate of 0.

31. The fly walks along points with an abscissa of 0.

32. The fly walks along points whose x coordinates are positive and whose y coordinates are 5.

33. The fly walks along points whose x and y coordinates are opposites. (HINT: See the figure at the right.)

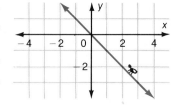

34. The fly walks along points whose distance from the origin is 6.

35. Describe the graph of the set of all points that have the same ordinate.

36. Describe the graph of the set of all points that have the same abscissa.

37. What is the graph of the set of all points that have negative abscissas?

> Each of Exercises 38–43 lists three vertices of a rectangle. Graph the vertices. Then sketch the rectangle and give the coordinate of the fourth vertex.

38. $(-3, -3), (-7, -5), (-7, -3)$

39. $(-7, 3), (-4, 3), (-7, 5)$

40. $(6, 8), (7, 2), (7, 8)$

41. $(0, 3\frac{1}{2}), (6, -4), (6, 3\frac{1}{2})$

42. $(-6, 1), (-1, 5), (-6, 5)$

43. $(-5, -1), (-8, -4), (-6, -6)$

■■■■■ **MAINTAIN**

> Solve each problem. (*Pages 163–166*)

44. Two cars traveling in opposite directions along a highway pass each other at 1 P.M. One car is traveling at 55 mph and the other is traveling at 45 mph. At what time will the cars be 250 miles apart?

45. A bus took three hours to make a round trip between Apopka and Lindenhurst. If the bus traveled at an average speed of 50 mph in one direction and 40 mph in the other direction, how far is Apopka from Lindenhurst?

> Solve each formula for the variable indicated. (*Pages 159–162*)

46. Formula for perimeter of a triangle: $P = a + b + c$. Solve for b.

47. Formula for simple interest: $i = prt$. Solve for t.

> Solve and check. (*Pages 95–102*)

48. $-4.3 + x = 7.9$ **49.** $-15c = 60$ **50.** $-1 + c = -1$ **51.** $-\frac{1}{2}x = 18$

Each of Exercises 52–57 lists three vertices of a parallelogram. Graph the vertices. Then locate three points, each of which could be the fourth vertex. Give the coordinates of all three points.

52. $(-3, -3), (-7, -5), (-7, -3)$ **53.** $(-7, 3), (-4, 3), (-7, 5)$

54. $(6, 8), (7, 2), (7, 8)$ **55.** $(3, 4), (2, 7), (3, 7)$

56. $(-6, 1), (-1, 5), (-6, 5)$ **57.** $(-6, 8), (-8, 5), (-1, 6)$

NON-ROUTINE PROBLEM

58. Copy the coordinate axes shown at the right. Graph the ordered pairs in set **A** in the order listed and join each point to the next.

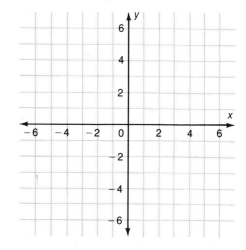

A: $\{(0, 6), (\frac{1}{2}, 5\frac{1}{2}), (\frac{1}{2}, 4), (1\frac{1}{2}, 4\frac{1}{2}),$
$(2, 4), (\frac{1}{2}, 3), (\frac{1}{2}, 2), (1\frac{1}{2}, 1\frac{1}{2}), (2\frac{1}{2}, 2),$
$(2\frac{1}{2}, 3\frac{1}{2}), (3\frac{1}{4}, 4), (3\frac{1}{4}, 2\frac{1}{2}), (4\frac{1}{4}, 3\frac{1}{4}),$
$(5, 3), (5, 2\frac{1}{4}), (4, 1\frac{1}{2}), (5, 1), (4, \frac{1}{2}),$
$(3, 1), (2, \frac{1}{2}), (2, 0)\}$

Now graph the points in sets **B, C,** and **D,** to obtain a reflection of the first graph. Use the same axes.

B: $\{0, 6), (-\frac{1}{2}, 5\frac{1}{2}), (-\frac{1}{2}, 4), \cdots, (-2, 0)\}$
C: $\{(0, -6), (\frac{1}{2}, -5\frac{1}{2}), (\frac{1}{2}, -4), \cdots, (2, 0)\}$
D: $\{(0, -6), (-\frac{1}{2}, -5\frac{1}{2}), (-\frac{1}{2}, -4), \cdots, (-2, 0)\}$

REVIEW CAPSULE FOR SECTION 5-2

Complete the formula that shows the relationship between the variables in the table. (*Pages 14–18*)

1.

Regular price: p	$19	$23	$27	$31	$35
Sale price: s	$13	$17	$21	$25	$29

Formula: $s = p - \underline{\ ?\ }$

2.

Number of gallons: g	1	2	3	4	5
Cost per gallon: c	$1.06	$2.12	$3.18	$4.24	$5.30

Formula: $c = \underline{\ ?\ }$

5-2　Relations and Functions

At his parttime job, Jim Noble is paid $6.00 per hour. The equation **e = 6h** shows the relation between his earnings, *e*, and the number of hours worked, *h*.

This relation can be shown in several ways.

TIME CARD	*Jim Noble*
Monday	*3 Hours*
Tuesday	
Wednesday	*2 Hours*
Thursday	
Friday	*4 Hours*
TOTAL	*9 Hours*

RELATION

Kind of Description	Description
1. Words	**1.** Multiply 6 and the number of hours.
2. Equation	**2.** $e = 6h$
3. Table of ordered pairs	**3.** (see table below)
4. Graph	**4.** (see graph below)

h	0	1	2	3	4	5	6
e	0	6	12	18	24	30	36

Some relations cannot be described by an equation. For this reason, we use ordered pairs to define a *relation*.

DEFINITION

> A **relation** is a set of ordered pairs.

EXAMPLE 1 List the ordered pairs of this relation and graph the relation.

Station	1	2	3	4	5	6	7	8
Fare	$3.50	$3.50	$3.50	$5.00	$5.00	$7.10	$7.10	$7.10

Solution: ①
Associate each station with a fare.

{(1, 3.50), (2, 3.50), (3, 3.50), (4, 5.00), (5, 5.00), (6, 7.10), (7, 7.10), (8, 7.10)}

②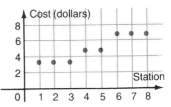

DOMAIN AND RANGE

For the ordered pairs of a relation, the set of all first coordinates is the **domain** of the relation. The set of all second coordinates of the ordered pairs is the **range** of the relation. The letter D is often used to represent the domain; R is used to represent the range.

EXAMPLE 2 Give the domain and range of the relation described in Example 1.

Solution: {(1, 3.50), (2, 3.50), (3, 3.50), (4, 5.00) ◄——— Relation
(5, 5.00), (6, 7.10), (7, 7.10), (8, 7.10)}

D = {1, 2, 3, 4, 5, 6, 7, 8} ◄——— **Domain: Set of all first coordinates of each ordered pair**

R = {3.50, 5.00, 7.10} ◄——— **Range: Set of all second coordinates of each ordered pair**

You can find the domain and range of a relation from its graph.

EXAMPLE 3 The graph at the right defines a relation. Express the relation as a set of ordered pairs. Then give the domain and range of the relation.

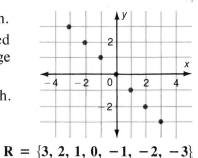

Solution: Read the ordered pairs from the graph.

{(−3, 3), (−2, 2), (−1, 1), (0, 0),
(1, −1), (2, −2), (3, −3)}

D = {−3, −2, −1, 0, 1, 2, 3}   **R = {3, 2, 1, 0, −1, −2, −3}**

A *function* is a special kind of relation.

DEFINITION

> A **function** is a relation for which no two ordered pairs have the same first element.

Relation	Ordered Pairs with the Same First Elements	Is the Relation a Function?
{(0, 0, (1, 11), (2, 22), (3, 33), (4, 44)}	None	**Yes**
{(1, 7), (1, 14), (1, 21)	(1, 7), (1, 14), (1, 21)	**No**
{(10, 20), (11, 30), (12, 40), (10, 50)}	(10, 20), (10, 50)	**No**
{(−2, −2), (−1, −2), (0, −2), (3, −2)}	None	**Yes**

VERTICAL LINE TEST

The graph of a relation shows whether it is a function. If a vertical line can be drawn through two or more points of the graph, the points have the same x coordinate, so the relation is *not* a function. This is called the **Vertical Line Test.**

EXAMPLE 4 Use the graphs to tell whether each relation is a function.

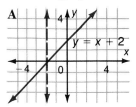 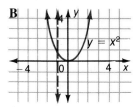 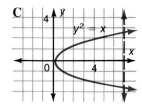

Solutions: **A** and **B** are functions.
C is not a function because a vertical line will intersect its graph in more than one point.

EXERCISES: Classwork/Homework

Objective: To identify the domain and range of a relation
To identify functions

CHECK YOUR UNDERSTANDING

Complete each statement.

1. A relation is a set of __?__ .

2. A function is a special kind of __?__ .

3. In a function, no two ordered pairs have the same __?__ .

4. The set of all second coordinates of the ordered pairs of a relation is the __?__

5. The set of all first coordinates of the ordered pairs of a relation is the __?__ .

6. When a vertical line can be drawn through two or more points of a graph, the points have the same __?__ coordinate.

PRACTICE AND APPLY

Give the domain and range for each relation.

7. $\{(0, 1), (2, 3), (4, 5), (6, 7)\}$

8. $\{(-1, 1), (-2, 2), (-3, 3), (-4, 4)\}$

9. $\{(0, -2), (1, -2), (2, -2), (3, -2)\}$

10. $\{(\frac{1}{2}, \frac{1}{4}), (\frac{3}{2}, \frac{1}{8}), (2, \frac{7}{2})\}$

11. The graph at the right defines a relation. Define this relation by listing the ordered pairs that are the coordinates of the points.

12. The relation in Exercise 11 cannot be defined easily by a simple sentence, but it can be defined easily by a table. Construct such a table for this relation.

13. Give the domain and range of the relation in Exercise 11.

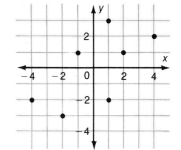

In Exercises 14–16, write the set of ordered pairs for each relation. Then give the domain and range for each relation.

14 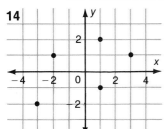   **15.** 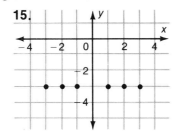   **16.**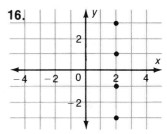

Write a relation for the given domain and range. Write all the possible ordered pairs for the relation.

17. Domain: {1, 2, 3}; range: {4}   **18.** Domain: {−5, 0}; range: {0, 5}

19. Domain: {−6}; range: {−2, 0, 5}   **20.** Domain: {−2, −1, 0}; range: {3, 5}

Write *Yes* or *No* to tell whether the relation is also a function.

21.   **22.**   **23.**   **24.**   **25.**

Determine whether each relation in Exercises 26–30 is also a function. When a relation is not a function, state why it is not.

26. {(−1, 1), (−2, 4), (−3, 9), (−4, 16), (−5, 25)}

27. {(3, −2), (3, −1), (3, 0), (3, 1), (3, 2)}

28. {(1, 5¢), (2, 10¢), (3, 10¢), (4, 15¢), (5, 20¢, (6, 20¢)}

29. {(−5, 5), (−1, 1), (2, −2), (4, −4)}

30. {(5, 8), (5, 9), (6, 10), (6, 11), (7, 12), (7, 13)}

In Exercises 31–36, write the ordered pairs for each relation. Then give the domain and range of the relation.

31.

Time *(t)*	8 A.M.	9 A.M.	10 A.M.	11 A.M.	12 noon
Temperature *(T)*	4°	8°	8°	10°	11°

32.

Year *(y)*	1976	1978	1980	1982	1984 (est.)
Population *(P)*	11,000	12,000	13,000	15,000	16,000

33. $N = \frac{A}{30}$, a formula for finding the number of rolls of wallpaper needed to cover a rectangular wall, where A is the area of the wall and the replacement set for A is {150, 180, 210}

34. $s = 16t^2$, the formula for the distance, s, a freely falling object falls in t seconds, where the replacement set for t is {4, 6, 8, 10}

35. $A = 6s^2$, the formula for the surface area, A, of a cube, where the replacement set for s is {5, 10, 15, 20}

36. $V = \frac{4}{3}\pi r^3$, the formula for the volume, V, of a sphere, where r is the length of the radius and the replacement set for r is {1, 2, 3, 5}. Use 3.14 for π and round each value for V to the nearest whole number.

37. Which of the relations in Exercises 31–36 are functions?

■■■■■■ MAINTAIN

Solve and check. *(Pages 118–121)*

38. $4x - 5 = 7$ **39.** $3z + 2 = 17$ **40.** $6 - 4b = 2$ **41.** $\frac{2}{5}z = 42$

42. $36 - 2b = 32$ **43.** $6c + 4 = -20$ **44.** $4 - 8c = 44$ **45.** $-7 = 11 + 2m$

Solve. *(Pages 163–166)*

46. Joanne and Nancy jog from the same place in the same direction. Nancy jogs at the rate of 4 mph and Joanne, leaving 1 hour later, jogs at the rate of 6 mph. In how many hours will Joanne overtake Nancy?

47. A car and a passenger train start at the same time from stations which are 500 miles apart. The rate of the passenger train is twenty mph less than the rate of the car. They pass each other in five hours. Find the rate at which each one travels.

48. A brand of soup sells at 3 cans for $2.25 or at 80¢ per can.

a. Complete the table below to show the cost of *n* cans if *n* < 10.

When *n* is	0	1	2	3	4	5	6	7	8	9
Cost is	0	80¢	$1.60	$2.25	?	?	?	?	?	?

b. Give the domain and range of this relation.

49. The charge to park a car at a parking garage is $2.50 for the first hour and $1.25 for each additional hour or portion of an hour.

a. Complete the table to show the cost of parking a car for *h* hours when $0 \le h \le 8$.

When *h* is	0	1	2	3	4	5	6	7	8
Cost is	?	?	?	?	?	?	?	?	?

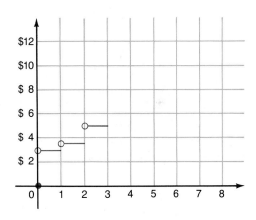

b. *Complete:* When the number of hours is 5 or less, then the cost is any one of the numbers _?_ .

c. Part of the graph is shown at the right. Complete the graph for values of *h* from *h* = 0 to *h* = 8.

For Exercises 50–51, write true, <u>T</u>, or false, <u>F</u>, for each statement. Give a reason for each answer.

50. Every function is a relation.

51. Every relation is a function.

52. Copy the figure at the right. Then find the greatest number of boxes that can be shaded without shading more than 2 boxes in a straight line of 5 boxes.

——— **REVIEW CAPSULE FOR SECTION 5-3** ———

Evaluate each expression for the given values of the variables. (*Pages 5–8*)

1. $3x + y$ for $x = 7$ and $y = 9$

2. $y + 7x$ for $y = -10$ and $x = 5$

3. $y - 2x$ for $y = 9.5$ and $x = -3$

4. $3x + 4y$ for $x = 7$ and $y = -1$

5-3 Graphing Linear Equations

An equation such as **$5x - 9 = 11$** is an equation in one variable, x. It has *one solution*, 4, because $5 \cdot 4 - 9 = 11$ and this is the only value of x for which $5x - 9 = 11$. An equation such as

$$y - 2x = 3$$

has two variables, x and y. The solution of this equation is the *set of ordered pairs (x, y)* for which $y - 2x = 3$. For example, the ordered pairs $(0, 3)$, $(-\frac{3}{2}, 0)$, and $(2, 7)$ are some of the solutions of $y - 2x = 3$.

Check:

$y - 2x = 3$	$y - 2x = 3$	$y - 2x = 3$
$3 - 2(0) \overset{?}{=} 3$	$0 - 2(-\frac{3}{2}) \overset{?}{=} 3$	$7 - 2(2) \overset{?}{=} 3$
$3 \overset{?}{=} 3$ Yes ✔	$3 \overset{?}{=} 3$ Yes ✔	$3 \overset{?}{=} 3$ Yes ✔

To solve an equation such as $y - 2x = 3$, you find *all* its solutions for the given replacement set. When the domain for x is the set of real numbers, there is an infinite number of ordered pairs that are solutions. In such cases, you usually show the solution set as a graph.

EXAMPLE 1 Graph the equation $y - 2x = 3$.

Solution: ① Solve the equation for y. ⟶ $y = 2x + 3$

② Make a table. First, choose values for x. To find y, substitute these values in $y = 2x + 3$.

Replace x with -3.	Replace x with 0.	Replace x with 1.
$y = 2x + 3$	$y = 2x + 3$	$y = 2x + 3$
$y = 2(-3) + 3$	$y = 2(0) + 3$	$y = 2(1) + 3$
$y = -6 + 3$	$y = 0 + 3$	$y = 2 + 3$
$y = -3$	$y = 3$	$y = 5$

x	-3	0	1
y	-3	3	5

③ Graph the points.

Since x can be any real number, draw a line containing the points.

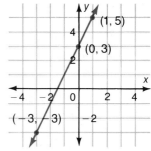

CALCULATOR

You can use a calculator to compute y values. For example, to find the value for $y = -5x - 15$ when $x = -6$, replace x with -6.

$$y = -5x - 15 \longrightarrow y = -5(-6) - 15$$

5 $\boxed{+/-}$ $\boxed{\times}$ **6** $\boxed{+/-}$ $\boxed{-}$ **15** $\boxed{=}$ $\boxed{15.}$

So $y = 15$ when $x = -6$.

LINEAR EQUATION

An equation whose graph is a straight line is a **linear equation.** Since two points determine a straight line, you need to plot only two points to graph a linear equation. However, it is useful to plot a third point as a check.

EXAMPLE 2 Graph each of the following in the coordinate plane.

a. $x = 2$ **b.** $y = -3$

Solutions: **a.** All ordered pairs with an x coordinate of 2 are solutions of the equation. Thus, the graph is a vertical line.

b. All ordered pairs with a y coordinate of -3 are solutions of the equation. Thus, the graph is a horizontal line.

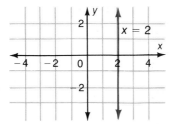
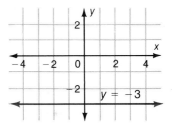

Unless stated otherwise, assume that the domain for each variable in a linear equation is the set of real numbers.

Here is another way to describe a linear equation.

DEFINITION

An equation that can be written in the form
$$Ax + By = C$$
where A, B, and C are real numbers and A and B are not both zero, is a **linear equation in two variables.**

Thus, equations such as $3x - 2y = -6$ and $y - 5 = 0$ are linear equations; equations such as $x^2 + y = 9$ and $xy = 4$ are not.

A function whose ordered pairs satisfy a linear equation is a **linear function.** Thus, the equation $y - 2x = 3$ defines a linear function.

Relations and Functions **187**

Objective: To graph linear equations

CHECK YOUR UNDERSTANDING

Complete the tables.

1. $y = 2x$

x	0	2	4	6
y	0	4	?	?

2. $y = 4x$

x	0	1	2	3	4
y	?	?	?	?	?

3. $y = 3x$

x	0	−1	−2	−3
y	0	−3	?	?

4. $y = -2x + 3$

x	−3	−1	0	1	3
y	9	?	?	?	?

5. $y = 2x + 4$

x	−3	−1	0	1
y	−2	2	?	?

6. $y = -2x + 4$

x	−3	−1	0	1
y	10	?	?	?

Determine whether the given ordered pair of numbers is a solution of the given sentence. Answer <u>Yes</u> or <u>No</u>.

7. $x + y = 5$; $(0, 3)$

8. $x - 3y = 16$; $(16, 0)$

9. $y - x = 10$; $\left(-\frac{1}{2}, 9\frac{1}{2}\right)$

10. $y - x = 0$; $(2.6, 2.6)$

11. $4x + 3y = -12$; $(3, 0)$

12. $2x + y = 10$; $(-5, 0)$

13. $y = 7x$; $(0, 0)$

14. $y - 7x = 0$; $\left(\frac{1}{7}, -1\right)$

15. $y - 8 = 0$; $(3, 8)$

State whether each equation is linear. Answer <u>Yes</u> or <u>No</u>.

16. $3x + 7y = 19$

17. $y = 4x^2 - 7$

18. $7x^2 - 5xy + 9y^2 = 15$

19. $y = 3x$

20. $y - 8x = 0$

21. $\frac{y}{3} = 2x + 1$

State whether the graph of each equation is a straight line. Answer <u>Yes</u> or <u>No</u>.

22. $y + 1 = 5$

23. $2x - y = 8$

24. $y = \frac{4}{3}x - 1$

25. $y = 2x^2 - 1$

26. $xy = 1$

27. $x - y = 0$

PRACTICE AND APPLY

Graph each linear equation in the coordinate plane.

28. $y = 4x - 3$

29. $y = -3x$

30. $y = -2x - 4$

31. $y = x - 5$

32. $y = 5 - x$

33. $x + y = 10$

34. $y = \frac{1}{2}x$

35. $y = \frac{1}{3}x$

36. $y = -\frac{1}{4}x$

37. $2x + y = 4$

38. $3x + y = 6$

39. $2x + 3y = 6$

40. $2x - y = 4$

41. $3x - 2y = 0$

42. $y = -4$

43. $y = -9$

44. $x = 3$

45. $x = 6\frac{1}{2}$

Equations of the form $By = C$ where $b \neq 0$ define *constant functions*.

In Exercises 46–49, complete the table of values for each constant function. Then graph each function.

46. $y = 3$

x	−2	0	2
y	?	?	?

47. $y + 5 = 0$

x	−1	0	3
y	?	?	?

48. $y = 0$

x	−4	0	4
y	?	?	?

49. $2y - 3 = 0$

x	−3	0	6
y	?	?	?

Refer to the graphs in Exercises 46–49 to complete these statements.

50. The graph of a constant function is the __?__ axis or a line parallel to the __?__ axis.

51. The domain of a constant function is __?__ .

52. The range of a constant function is __?__ .

Complete the table for each relation. Then graph the relation.

53. $x = 3$

x	?	?	?
y	−3	0	4

54. $x - 8 = 0$

x	?	?	?
y	−3	0	4

55. $x = 0$

x	?	?	?
y	−5	0	5

56. $\frac{2}{3}x = -6$

x	?	?	?
y	−2	0	2

Refer to the tables and graphs in Exercises 53–56 to complete these statements.

57. The graph of each relation in Exercises 53–56 is the __?__ axis, or a line parallel to the __?__ axis.

58. The range of each relation in Exercises 53–56 is __?__ .

59. An equation of the form $Ax = C$, $A \neq 0$, defines a __?__ (relation or function).

60. A relation of the form $Ax = C$, $A \neq 0$ does *not* define a function because __?__ .

▰▰▰▰▰ **MAINTAIN**

Give the domain and range for each relation. (*Pages 180–185*)

61. $\{(-1, 6), (0, 6), (1, 6), (2, 6)\}$

62. $\{(0, 14), (1, 12), (2, 10), (3, 8), (4, 6)\}$

Determine whether each relation is a function. When a relation is not a function, state why it is not. (*Pages 180–185*)

63. $\{(-2, 0), (0, 0), (2, 0), (4, 0), (6, 0)\}$

64. $\{(-1, 0), (0, -1), (0, 1), (1, 0)\}$

Complete these statements about a point (x, y) in the coordinate plane. (*Pages 175–179*)

65. If the x coordinate is 0, then the point lies on the __?__ axis.

66. All points whose y coordinates are 2 lie on a __?__ (horizontal, vertical) line.

Solve. (*Pages 103–107*)

67. In many ancient Greek temples, the ratio of the length to the width is 5:3. What would be the length of a temple that has a width of 18 meters?

68. A printing press runs 750 copies in 6 minutes. How long will it take to run 300,000 copies at the same rate?

■■■■ CONNECT AND EXTEND

For each equation, write the coordinates of the points $(0, y)$ and $(x, 0)$.

69. $y = 2x - 6$

70. $9y - 26 = 2x$

71. $2x + 3y = 6$

72. $3x + y = 4$

73. $y = -2x$ $(0, 0)$,

74. $3(2x - 4) = 2(y - 5)$

In Exercises 75–79, graph each function. Tell whether each function is a linear function. Give the domain and range of each function.

75. The function pairs each positive real number with the number 1, the number 0 with 0, and each negative real number with the number -1.

76. The function pairs each positive real number with the number 0, and each negative real number x with itself.

77. The function pairs each nonnegative real number x with itself, and each negative real number x with the opposite of x.

78. The function pairs each real number x with its absolute value, $|x|$.

79. The function pairs each real number with $-|x|$.

■■■■ NON-ROUTINE PROBLEM

80. A large block of cheese is 16 centimeters long, 8 centimeters wide, and $7\frac{1}{2}$ centimeters high. What is the greatest number of blocks 5 centimeters long, 3 centimeters wide, and $2\frac{1}{2}$ centimeters high that can be cut from the large block?

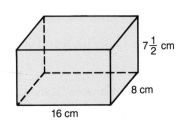

1. Graph these points on the same coordinate axes. (*Pages 175–179*)

   a. $A(10, 0)$ **b.** $B(12, -5)$ **c.** $C(4, -9)$ **d.** $D(-4, -9)$ **e.** $E(-9, 0)$

   f. $F(-9, 4)$ **g.** $G(4, 9)$ **h.** $H(0, 9)$ **i.** $I(0, 10)$ **j.** $J(12, 5)$

2. Name the quadrant or axis on which each point in Exercises 1 lies. (*Pages 175–179*)

3. Name the abscissa and the ordinate for each point in Exercise 1. (*Pages 175–179*)

   Give the domain and range for each relation. (*Pages 180–185*)

4. $\{(1, 12°), (2, 14°), (3, 8°), (4, 4°), (5, 6°), (6, -2°)\}$

5. $\{(1, \$10), (2, \$15), (3, \$25), (4, \$40), (5, \$60), (6, \$85)\}$

6. $\{(1, \pi), (2, \frac{3\pi}{2}), (2, 2\pi), (3, \frac{5\pi}{2}), (4, 3\pi)\}$

7. Write <u>Yes</u> or <u>No</u> to indicate whether each relation in Exercises 4–6 is also a function. (*Pages 180–185*)

   Graph each linear equation in the coordinate plane. (*Pages 186–190*)

8. $y = 2x$ 9. $y = -3x - 7$ 10. $y = -3$ 11. $x = 2$

Historical Digest: Coordinate Systems

René Descartes, a French philosopher and mathematician, came up with the idea of using pairs of numbers to describe the location of points on a plane. He worked on this idea about the same time the Pilgrims were settling in America.

Descartes developed a new branch of mathematics called analytic geometry. He showed how to solve problems involving circles, triangles, and other figures. When you graphed a line earlier in this chapter, you were learning some analytic geometry. Oddly enough, this great mathematical discovery was almost hidden in the appendix of one of Descartes' books on philosophy.

If you look for a street on a city map using an index such as "C-3," you are using a coordinate system. How would you use a coordinate system to locate a person working in office 213 on the 12th floor of an office building?

Statistics / Predicting

Jeanine Curren is the manager of an automobile parts supply house. She must be able to predict the arrival time for a shipment of parts sent to a customer by train.

Jeanine used records of past deliveries to construct the table below. In the table, *x* is the delivery distance in miles and *y* is the delivery time in days.

x	210	290	350	480	490	730	780	850	920	1010
y	5	7	6	11	8	11	12	8	15	12

EXAMPLE: Find the predicted delivery time for a shipment to a customer located 600 rail miles away.

Solution:

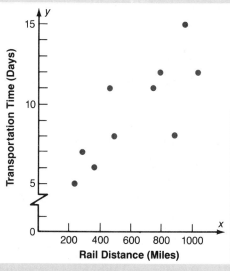

1 Graph the ordered pairs (*x*, *y*) in the table. This is a **scatter plot.**

2 Separate the data into three nearly equal groups with an odd number of ordered pairs in the first and third groups.

First Group		Second Group		Third Group	
x	**y**	**x**	**y**	**x**	**y**
210	5	480	11	850	8
290	7	490	8	920	15
350	6	730	11	1010	12
		780	12		

3 Find the median for the *x* and *y* values in the first and third groups. (For a review of median, see pages 74–75.) Since there is an odd number of values in each group, the **median** is the middle value.

		x	y
Medians:	*First group*	290	6
	Third group	920	12

4 Graph the median points (290, 6) and (920, 12). Draw the line passing through the two points. This is the **median line of fit.**

5 To predict the delivery time, locate 600 on the x axis. Draw a vertical line to the median line of fit. Then draw a horizontal line to the y axis. Read the value on the y axis.

The y value (delivery time) is about 9.

Thus, Jeanine can predict that the delivery time will be **at least 9 days.**

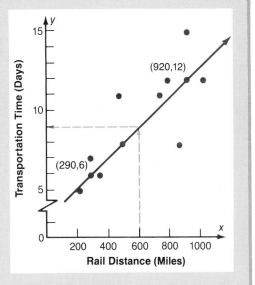

EXERCISES

For each exercise:
a. **Construct a scatter plot.**
b. **Determine the median points.**
c. **Graph the median line of fit.**
d. **Find the predicted value.**

1.

Pages	x	10	20	20	30	40	50	60	100	110	120
Hours to Type	y	6	8	12	16	18	21	32	46	60	58

Find the predicted number of hours needed to type 70 pages.

2.

Tons of Crunchola	x	100	150	170	180	220	240	300	350	400	500
Total Cost (thousands of dollars)	y	65	70	65	85	115	125	140	190	200	200

Find the predicted total cost for 200 tons of crunchola.

3.

Height in Inches	x	62	64	65	66	67	67	69	71	72	74
Weight in Pounds	y	105	115	115	135	140	150	165	170	180	180

Find the predicted weight for a person whose height is 68 inches.

4.

Number of Push-ups	x	15	20	22	25	27	27	32	35	40	42
Number of Chin-ups	y	3	5	4	6	6	9	8	9	11	10

Find the predicted number of chin-ups done by a person who can do 30 push ups.

5-4   Using Graphs to Estimate

Graphs of functions can be useful in estimating answers. For example, to determine the distance of an approaching thunderstorm

1 Count the number of seconds between a flash of lightning and the resulting sound of thunder.

2 Use this number to read the distance from a graph that shows the distance sound travels in air as a function of time.

EXAMPLE   For every 5 seconds, sound travels about 1 mile. That is, $s = \frac{1}{5}t$ when s is the distance in miles and t is the time in seconds.

Questions	Solutions

a. Write three ordered pairs for this function. Note that t cannot be negative.

a.

t	0	3	5
s	0	$\frac{3}{5}$	1

b. Use the ordered pairs to graph the function. (Note the scale on each axis.)

b.

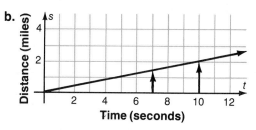

c. Use the graph to estimate the distance to an approaching thunderstorm when a person counts 10 seconds between the lightning and the thunder.

c. Read from the graph. For $t = 10$, s is about **2 miles.**

d. Use the graph to estimate the distance when $t = 7.5$ seconds.

d. For $t = 7.5$, s is about **1.5 miles.**

Objective: To use the graph of a linear equation to estimate the answers to problems

CHECK YOUR UNDERSTANDING

The graph at the right shows the simple interest earned on money in savings for one year at 5%. That is,

$$i = 0.05p$$

where i is the simple interest and p is the principal. Use the graph for Exercises 1–6.

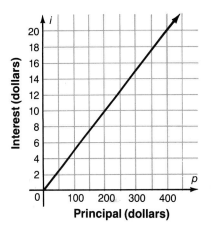

1. Estimate i when $p = \$200$.
2. Estimate i when $p = \$400$.
3. Estimate i when $p = \$150$.
4. Estimate i when $p = \$350$.
5. Estimate p when $i = \$6$
6. Estimate p when $i = \$16$.

PRACTICE AND APPLY

Sound travels in water at a rate of about 1.5 kilometers per second. That is, $s = 1.5t$, where t is the time in seconds and s is the distance in kilometers.

Use this function in Exercises 7–11.

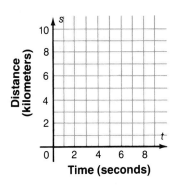

7. Write three ordered pairs for this function. Let $t = 0$, 4, and 6.

8. Use the ordered pairs in Exercise 7 to graph the function.

9. A ship using sonar finds that it takes sound waves 0.5 second to reach the bottom of a lake. Use the graph in Exercise 8 to estimate the depth of the lake at this point.

10. A ship using sonar finds that it takes sound waves 7 seconds to reach a point at the bottom of a body of water. Use the graph in Exercise 8 to estimate the depth at this point.

11. Use the graph in Exercise 8 to estimate how long it would take sound waves to reach a point 4 kilometers below the surface of the ocean.

The function $d = 0.2r$ represents the distance, d, in meters covered by a car traveling at a rate of r kilometers per hour during the average driver's reaction time of $\frac{3}{4}$ second. *Reaction time* is the length of time between the moment a driver decides to stop the car and the moment the brakes are applied.

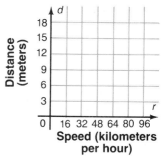

12. Write three ordered pairs for this function. Let $r = $ 16, 48, and 80.

13. Use the ordered pairs in Exercise 12 to graph the function.

Use the graph in Exercise 13 to estimate how many meters a car traveling at each rate will cover during a reaction time of $\frac{3}{4}$ second.

14. 32 kilometers per hour   15. 64 kilometers per hour   16. 88 kilometers per hour

The basic fee for renting a floor polisher is $5 plus an additional $2.50 for each hour of rental. Use this information for Exercises 17–23.

17. Complete the table.

Number of Hours (h)	2	4	6
Cost (C)	?	?	?

18. Use the ordered pairs in Exercise 17 to graph the function.

Use the graph in Exercise 18 to estimate the rental cost for each number of hours.

19. 3 hours   20. 5 hours   21. $4\frac{1}{2}$ hours   22. $5\frac{1}{4}$ hours

23. Write an equation that describes the cost of rental, C, as a function of the number of hours, h.

A plane at an altitude of 22,000 feet begins to climb at the rate of 50 feet per second. Use this information for Exercises 24–30.

24. Complete the table.

Time, t, in seconds	2	4	6
Altitude, A, in feet	?	?	?

25. Use the ordered pairs in Exercise 24 to graph the function.

Use the graph in Exercise 25 to estimate the altitude of the plane for each time, t.

26. $t = 3$ seconds   27. $t = 5$ seconds   28. $t = 2.5$ seconds   29. $t = 8$ seconds

30. Write an equation that describes the altitude, A, of the plane as a function of the time, t, in seconds.

Graph each linear equation in the coordinate plane. (*Pages 186–190*)

31. $y = 2x + 1$ **32.** $x + y = 5$ **33.** $x = -5$ **34.** $2x + y = 6$

Determine whether each relation in Exercises 35–38 is also a function. When a relation is not a function, state why it is not. (*Pages 180–185*)

35. $\{(5, 9), (23, 3), (8, 2)\}$ **36.** $\{(3, 16), (0, 10), (5, 25)\}$

37. $\{(2, 0), (0, -2), (-2, 0), (0, 2)\}$ **38.** $\{(2, -2), (-2, 2), (1, -1), (-1, 1)\}$

Solve. (*Pages 108–110*)

39. 72 is 60% of what number?   **40.** $33\frac{1}{3}\%$ of 96 is what number?

41. 12 is what percent of 80?   **42.** 480 is what percent of 375?

CONNECT AND EXTEND

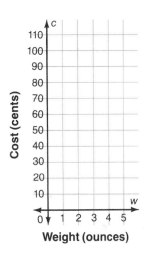

The cost of first class mail is a function of weight. In 1988, the cost for any weight up to, and including, 1 ounce rose to 25¢. Each additional ounce or fraction thereof costs 20¢. For example, 1.6 ounces cost 45¢ and 3.2 ounces cost 85¢.

Use this information for Exercises 43–45.

43. Complete the table.

Weight	1.4 oz	2.7 oz	5.8 oz
Cost	?	?	?

44. This rate holds for 11 ounces and less. Thus, the domain of this function is all possible weights of mail less than or equal to 11 ounces. List the 11 numbers in the range of this function.

45. Graph this function for weights up to, and including, 5 ounces.

NON-ROUTINE PROBLEM

46. The figure at the right shows three squares inside one another. The small square has sides which are 7 centimeters in length, the middle square has sides which are 9 centimeters in length, and the large square has sides which are 12 centimeters in length. Find the area of the shaded portion of the figure.

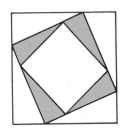

Relations and Functions   **197**

5-5 Graphing Absolute Value Relations

On a number line, the graph of $|x| = 3$ consists of two points whose coordinates are 3 and -3.

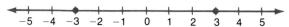

On the coordinate plane, however, the graph of $|x| = 3$ consists of two parallel lines.

EXAMPLE 1 Graph $|x| = 3$ on the coordinate plane.

Solution: **1** Write the equation with "or."
$|x| = 3$ means $x = 3$ <u>or</u> $x = -3$.

2 Draw the graphs of $x = 3$ and $x = -3$ on the coordinate plane.

The graph consists of two parallel lines, one three units to the right of the y axis, and the other three units to its left.

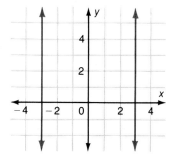

To graph absolute value relations on the coordinate plane, make a table using both positive and negative values of x.

EXAMPLE 2 Graph $y = |x|$.

Solution: **1** Make a table.

x	-5	-3	-1	0	1	3	5
y	5	3	1	0	1	3	5

2 Graph the points in the coordinate plane. Join the points.

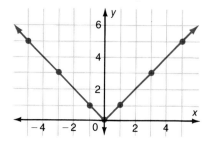

The graph consists of two rays with their initial point at the origin.

Objective: To graph absolute value relations on the coordinate plane

▬▬▬▬ **CHECK YOUR UNDERSTANDING**

1. In the equation $y = |3x|$, $y = 6$. What are the possible values for x?

2. In the equation $y = |-2x|$, let $y = 8$. What are the possible values for x?

Complete each table.

3. $y = |2x|$

x	−2	−1	0	1	2
y	?	?	?	?	?

4. $y = -|x|$

x	−2	−1	0	1	2
y	?	?	?	?	?

▬▬▬▬ **PRACTICE AND APPLY**

Graph each equation on the coordinate plane.

5. $|x| = 2$ 6. $|x| = 5$ 7. $|y| = 3$ 8. $|y| = 1$

9. $y = |2x|$ 10. $y = |5x|$ 11. $y = -|x|$ 12. $y = -|2x|$

13. $y = |x| - 4$ 14. $y = |2x| - 5$ 15. $y = |-3x| + 7$ 16. $x = |2y| - 4$

17. $x = |y|$ 18. $x = |-2y|$ 19. $x = -|2y| - 6$ 20. $x = |-4y| + 3$

21. $x = -|3y|$ 22. $x + |y| = 4$ 23. $x - |y| = 6$ 24. $y + |x| = 10$

▬▬▬▬ **MAINTAIN**

The function $w = \dfrac{d}{5}$ represents the width, w, in feet of an image on a screen when the projector is d feet from the screen. Use this function in Exercises 25–27. (*Pages 194–197*)

25. Write three ordered pairs for this function. Let $d = 5$, 15, and 25.

26. Use the ordered pairs in Exercise 25 to graph the function.

27. A projector is 10 feet from the screen. Use the graph in Exercise 25 to estimate the width of the image at this distance.

Solve. (*Pages 130–134*)

28. One number is twice another number. The sum of the numbers is 18. Find the numbers.

29. Together, Donna and Patricia earn $72. Patricia earns 5 times as much as Donna. How much did each earn?

▬▬▬▬ **CONNECT AND EXTEND**

Graph each inequality in the coordinate plane.

30. $|x| \le 1$ 31. $|x| \ge 4$ 32. $|y| \ge 4$ 33. $y \ge |x|$

34. $y \le |x|$ 35. $y \ge |x - 3|$ 36. $y \le |x + 3|$ 37. $|y| \le |x| + 3$

Focus on College Entrance Tests

Many problems involving the **comparison of two quantities** can be solved by logical reasoning. Little or no computation with paper and pencil may be necessary.

Refer to these instructions for the Example and Exercises.

Each problem consists of two quantities, one in Column I and one in Column II. Compare the two quantities.

- Write **A** if the quantity in Column I is greater.
- Write **B** if the quantity in Column II is greater.
- Write **C** if the two quantities are equal.
- Write **D** if there is not enough information to determine how the two quantities are related.

EXAMPLE

Column I	Column II
$1800 \times 9 \times 32$	$18 \times 32 \times 900$

Solution: Since 32 appears in both products, compare (1800×9) and (18×900).

Since $(1800 \times 9) = 18 \times 100 \times 9$ and $(18 \times 900) = 18 \times 9 \times 100$, the products are equal.

Answer: **C**

TRY THESE

	Column I	Column II
1.	$5 \times 600 \times 3$	$500 \times 7 \times 3$
2.	$0.25 \times 800 \times 9$	$9 \times 25 \times 8$
3.	6% of 1010	1% of 606
4.	$\dfrac{(19)(7)(6)}{(32)(4)}$	$\dfrac{(2)(20)(42)}{(16)(8)}$
5.	$\dfrac{8}{8 - 7.9}$	$\dfrac{8}{8 - 7.99}$
6.	$(4)(6)(8)(2^5)$	$(2)(6)(16)(5^2)$

Chapter Summary

IMPORTANT TERMS

Abscissa (p. 175)
Coordinate plane (p. 175)
Coordinates (p. 175)
Domain, D (p. 181)
Function (p. 181)
Graph (p. 175)
Linear equation (p. 187)
Linear function (p. 187)
Ordered pair (p. 175)
Ordinate (p. 175)
Origin (p. 175)

Perpendicular (p. 175)
Plane (p. 175)
Quadrant (p. 175)
Range, R (p. 181)
Relation (p. 180)
Vertical Line Test (p. 182)
x axis (p. 175)
x coordinate (p. 175)
y axis (p. 175)
y coordinate (p. 175)

IMPORTANT IDEAS

1. In an ordered pair, the first number, x, shows distance to the right or left of the vertical axis. The second number, y, shows distance above or below the horizontal axis.

2. It is necessary to plot only two points to graph a linear equation. However, a third point should be plotted as a check.

3. A sentence involving absolute value can be written as a compound sentence. For example, $|y| = 8$ means $y = 8$ or $y = -8$.

Chapter Review

1. Graph these points on the same pair of coordinate axes. (*Pages 175–179*)

   a. $Q(3, -7)$ **b.** $R(-3, 7)$ **c.** $S(0, -2)$ **d.** $T(6, -5)$ **e.** $U(-6, -6)$

   f. $V(7, 5)$ **g.** $W(6\frac{1}{2}, 0)$ **h.** $X(-2, -5)$ **i.** $Y(-1, 4)$ **j.** $Z(3\frac{1}{2}, -5)$

2. Describe the graph of the set of all points with an abscissa of -2. (*Pages 175–179*)

3. The coordinates of three vertices of a square are $(2, 3)$, $(-5, -4)$, and $(2, -4)$. Graph the vertices, sketch the square, and give the coordinates of the fourth vertex. (*Pages 175–179*)

Give the domain and range for each relation. (*Pages 180–185*)

4. $\{(1, 2), (1, 4), (2, 6), (2, 8), (3, 10), (3, 12)\}$

5. $\{(-2, 1), (-1, \frac{1}{2}), (0, 0), (1, -\frac{1}{2}), (2, -1)\}$

6. $\{(-2, 4), (-1, 1), (0, 0), (1, 1), (2, 4)\}$

7. Write <u>Yes</u> or <u>No</u> to indicate whether each relation in Exercises 4–6 is also a function.

Graph each linear equation in the coordinate plane. (*Pages 186–190*)

8. $y = 3x - 1$ **9.** $y = -4x$ **10.** $4x + 2y = -4$ **11.** $3x + 9 = 0$

The yearly property taxes on private homes in one city are set at 2% of the value of the property. The relationship between the amount of the tax, *t*, and the property value, *p*, is expressed by the function $t = 0.02p$. Use this information to complete the table in Exercise 16. (*Pages 194–197*)

12.

Property Value (*p*)	$40,000	$60,000	$80,000
Amount of Tax (*t*)	?	?	?

13. Use the ordered pairs in the table in Exercise 12 to graph the function.

14. Use the graph from Exercise 13 to estimate the amount of tax when the property value is $50,000.

Graph each equation on the coordinate plane. (*Pages 198–199*)

15. $|y| = 6$ **16.** $y = -|4x|$ **17.** $y = |-2x| + 2$ **18.** $|x| - |y| = 2$

Chapter Test

1. Graph these points on the same coordinate axes.
   a. $A(4, -3)$ **b.** $B(-3, 4)$ **c.** $C(0, -2)$ **d.** $D(-5, -5)$

Give the domain and range of each relation. Then state whether each relation is a function.

2. $\{(0, 0), (1, 1), (2, 2), (3, 2), (4, 3), (5, 3)\}$

3. $\{(5, 0), (0, -5), (-3, 4), (-3, -4), (-5, 0), (0, 5)\}$

Graph each linear equation in the coordinate plane.

4. $y = \frac{1}{2}x$ **5.** $y = x + 4$ **6.** $y = -2x - 1$

The cost, *c*, of running a classified ad in a newspaper is $3 plus 50 cents for each line of print, *l*, required. Use this information for Exercises 7–8.

7. Write three ordered pairs for this function. Let *l* equal 4, 8, and 12. Graph the function.

8. Use the graph in Exercise 7 to estimate the cost for a fourteen-line ad.

Graph each absolute value equation in the coordinate plane.

9. $y = |-3x|$ **10.** $y = |5 - x|$

Skills

Graph these points on the same pair of coordinate axes. (*Pages 175–179*)

1. $A(3, -5)$ **2.** $B(0, 6)$ **3.** $C(-1, -1)$ **4.** $D(6, 7)$ **5.** $E(-2, 2)$

Name the quadrant or axis on which each point lies. (*Pages 175–179*)

6. $(-4, 2)$ **7.** $(8, 0)$ **8.** $(4, -2)$ **9.** $(1, 1)$ **10.** $(0, -3)$

11. $(-9, 0)$ **12.** $(0, 0)$ **13.** $(0, 7)$ **14.** $(-9, -2)$ **15.** $(7, -7)$

Give the domain and range for each relation. Then tell if each relation is a function. (*Pages 180–185*)

16. $\{(-13, 0), (-12, 5), (0, 13), (0, -13), (5, 12), (12, 5)\}$

17. $\{(-2, 2), (-1, 3), (0, 0), (1, -3), (2, -2)\}$

18. $\{(-4, 5), (-2, 3), (0, 2), (2, 3), (4, 5)\}$

19. $\{(-2, 1), (4, 1), (0, 9), (-2, 3)\}$

Graph each linear equation in the coordinate plane. (*Pages 186–190*)

20. $y = -3x$ **21.** $y + 3x = -6$ **22.** $x = 6$ **23.** $y - 2x = 4$

Graph each equation in the coordinate plane. (*Pages 198–199*)

24. $y = |-4x|$ **25.** $|2y + 1| = 3$ **26.** $|x| + |y| = 4$

Problem Solving and Applications

The cost, c, of running a classified ad in a newspaper is $3 plus 50 cents for each line of print, l, required.

Use this information for Exercises 27–28 (*Pages 194–197*)

27. Write three ordered pairs for this function. Let l equal 4, 8, and 12. Graph the function.

28. Use the graph in Exercise 15 to estimate the cost for a fourteen-line ad.

The cost, c, of renting a moving van is $20 per day plus an additional $0.25 for each mile, m, the van is used.

Use this information for Exercises 29–30. (*Pages 194–197*)

29. Write three ordered pairs for this function. Let m equal 4, 12, and 20. Graph the function.

30. Use the graph in Exercise 27 to estimate the cost for traveling 10 miles.

Part 1

Choose the best answer. Choose *a, b, c,* or *d.*

1. Which numbers are opposites?

   a. $\frac{2}{3}, \frac{3}{2}$ **b.** $-\frac{1}{2}, \frac{1}{2}$ **c.** $-\frac{4}{5}, \frac{5}{4}$ **d.** 4.2, 2.4

2. If $-x < 0$, which sentence is true?

   a. $x = 0$ **b.** $x = -2$ **c.** $x > 0$ **d.** $|x| < 0$

3. In which quadrant does the point $(-3, 7)$ lie?

   a. I   **b.** II   **c.** III   **d.** IV

4. Solve the formula $C = 2\pi r$ for r.

   a. $r = C - 2\pi$ **b.** $r = \frac{2C}{\pi}$ **c.** $r = \frac{C}{2\pi}$ **d.** $r = \frac{\pi C}{2}$

5. Which of the following numbers cannot be written as a repeating or terminating decimal?

   a. $\frac{4}{5}$ **b.** π **c.** $\left|\frac{1}{2}\right|$ **d.** $\frac{2}{3}$

6. Find the value of $(6^6 \div 6^4) + (2^7 \div 2^5)$.

   a. $1\frac{1}{2}$ **b.** 36   **c.** 40   **d.** 3

7. Simplify: $9b - 11b + 3b - (-b) + 8b$

   a. $10b$ **b.** $14b$ **c.** $8b$ **d.** $27b$

8. What are the solutions of $2t + 1 < 0$ when the replacement set is $\{-3, -2, -1, 0, 1, 2, 3\}$?

   a. 0, 1, 2, 3   **b.** 0, −1, −2, −3   **c.** 1, 2, 3   **d.** −1, −2, −3

9. Solve: $-\frac{5}{7}x + 3 = -12$

   a. 21   **b.** $10\frac{5}{7}$ **c.** −21   **d.** $16\frac{4}{5}$

10. What percent of 40 is 5?

    a. 1.25%   **b.** 0.125%   **c.** 12.5%   **d.** 125%

11. What is the theoretical probability that a quarter will land "heads up" in one toss?

    a. 1   **b.** $\frac{1}{2}$ **c.** $\frac{1}{4}$ **d.** 0

12. What is the domain of the relation $\{(2,10), (3,20), (4,30), (5,40), (6,50)\}$?

    a. $\{10,20,30,40,50\}$ **b.** $\{2, 4, 6\}$ **c.** $\{2, 3, 4, 5, 6\}$ **d.** $\{3, 5\}$

13. Which ordered pair is a solution of the equation $2x - y = 6$?

    a. $(0, -6)$ **b.** $(0, 6)$ **c.** $(1, 4)$ **d.** $(6, -6)$

14. Which equation has a graph that is a straight line?

    a. $y = |x|$ **b.** $y = x^2$ **c.** $y = 2x + 1$ **d.** $y = |x| + 1$

15. Which point is not on the line $2x + 3y = 12$?

    a. $(0, 4)$ **b.** $(6, 0)$ **c.** $(3, 2)$ **d.** $(2, 3)$

16. Evaluate: $\dfrac{p^2 + 2p - p^3}{4}$ for $p = -1$.

    a. $-\dfrac{1}{2}$ **b.** 0 **c.** $\dfrac{1}{2}$ **d.** 1

17. Solve the equation $4y - 6 = 2(y + 1) - 3$.

    a. $y = 2\frac{1}{2}$ **b.** $y = 3\frac{1}{2}$ **c.** $y = 1\frac{1}{2}$ **d.** $y = -2\frac{1}{2}$

18. Which of the following pairs is a function?

    a. $\{(0,1), (1,2), (2,3)\}$ **b.** $\{(0,1), (1,0), (0,2)\}$
    c. $\{(1,0), (0,1), (2,1), (1,2)\}$ **d.** $\{(2,3), (3,2), (3,0), (2,1)\}$

19. Which equation is not a constant function?

    a. $4y - 8 = 0$ **b.** $y + 2 = 0$ **c.** $y = -1$ **d.** $x = 3$

20. The graph of which equation passes through the origin?

    a. $y = 2x - 3$ **b.** $-2x + 3 = y$ **c.** $x + y = 0$ **d.** $x + y = 1$

21. If $2n$ represents an even integer for any integer n, which expression represents an odd integer?

    a. $2n + 2$ **b.** $2n - 1$ **c.** $2n^2$ **d.** n

Part 2

22. Lisa told her mother that the amount of money she spent each month for gasoline was a function of the number of gallons she bought. If gasoline costs $0.95 per gallon, write a formula for the function relating cost, C, and gallons, G.

23. Two freight trains pass each other in Florida on parallel tracks. One train is traveling at a rate $1\frac{1}{2}$ times that of the slower train. After 5 hours they are 150 miles apart. Find the rate of speed of each train.

24. The length of a rectangular foundation for a new house is $2\frac{1}{4}$ times its width. The perimeter of the foundation is 156 feet. Find the length and width of the foundation.

25. Juan charges $0.35 per square foot of house space to make changes in the blueprints for a new house. Make a table to show his charges for houses containing 1800 ft^2, 2300 ft^2, and 2900 ft^2.

26. Use the ordered pairs from the table in Exercise 25 to graph the function. Assume the graph is linear.

27. Use the graph in Exercise 26 to estimate the charge for a house containing 3200 ft^2.

Lines: Slopes and Equations

The **direct variation** formula

$$K = \frac{R^3}{T^2}$$

says that for any planet in the solar system, the cube of its average distance from the sun divided by the square of its time for one revolution around the sun is a constant.

6-1 Slope of a Line

6% GRADE
11 MILES

Road signs along a highway warn truck drivers of the grade or steepness of a road. A certain road rises a vertical distance of 100 feet over a horizontal distance of 400 feet. You can use a ratio to express the steepness.

$$\text{steepness} = \frac{\text{rise}}{\text{run}} = \frac{\text{vertical change}}{\text{horizontal change}} = \frac{100}{400} = \frac{1}{4}.$$

The measure of steepness is a ratio called *slope*. A **ratio** is the quotient of two numbers, such as $\frac{2}{5}$.

DEFINITION

> The **slope** of a line is the ratio of the vertical change to the horizontal change between any two points on the line. That is,
>
> $$\text{slope} = \frac{\text{vertical change}}{\text{horizontal change}}, \text{(horizontal change} \neq 0).$$

EXAMPLE 1 Find the slope of each line graphed at the right below.

Solutions:

Line	Vertical Change	Horizontal Change	Slope $= \dfrac{\text{Vertical Change}}{\text{Horizontal Change}}$
A	5	2	$\frac{5}{2}$
B	4	4	$\frac{4}{4}$, or **1**
C	9	-3	$\frac{9}{-3}$, or -3
D	2	7	$\frac{2}{7}$

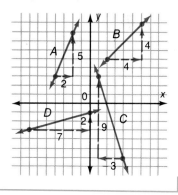

When you know the coordinates of any two points on a line, you can determine the slope of a line. First, you find the difference between the *y* coordinates, or the vertical change, and the difference between the *x* coordinates, or the horizontal change. Then you write the ratio of these differences.

EXAMPLE 2 Find the slope of the line containing the points (1, 3) and (6, 7)

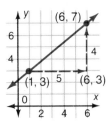

Solution: Subtract the *y* coordinates first. Then subtract the *x* coordinates.

$7 - 3 = 4$ ← **Vertical change: difference of y coordinates**

$6 - 1 = 5$ ← **Horizontal change: difference of x coordinates**

$\text{slope} = \frac{4}{5}$ ← **Slope** $= \dfrac{\text{vertical change}}{\text{horizontal change}}$

No matter which two points on a line are chosen, the ratio of the vertical change to the horizontal change is everywhere the same. Thus, for a given line, the slope is a constant.

Let $P_1(x_1, y_1)$ and $P_2(x_2, y_2)$ be any two points on the line graphed at the right.
Determine the slope of the line.

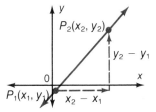

$y_2 - y_1$ ← **Vertical change**

$x_2 - x_1$ ← **Horizontal change**

$\text{slope} = \dfrac{y_2 - y_1}{x_2 - x_1}$ ← **Slope** $= \dfrac{\text{vertical change}}{\text{horizontal change}}$

The letter *m* is customarily used to denote slope.

DEFINITION

> For any two points in a line, $P_1(x_1, y_1)$ and $P_2(x_2, y_2)$,
>
> **slope** $= m = \dfrac{\text{vertical change}}{\text{horizontal change}} = \dfrac{y_2 - y_1}{x_2 - x_1}, (x_2 - x_1 \neq 0).$

EXAMPLE 3 Find the slope of the line containing the points $P_1(-4, 3)$ and $P_2(1, -3)$.

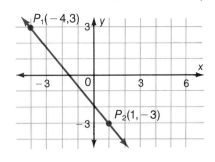

Solution: $m = \dfrac{y_2 - y_1}{x_2 - x_1}$

$$m = \dfrac{\overset{y_2 - y_1}{\overbrace{-3 - (3)}}}{\underset{x_2 - x_1}{\underbrace{1 - (-4)}}}$$

$$m = \frac{-3 + (-3)}{1 + 4}$$

$$= \frac{-6}{5}, \text{ or } -\frac{6}{5} \quad \longleftarrow \quad \text{Slope of the line through } (-4, 3) \text{ and } (1, -3)$$

Lines with positive slope rise from left to right.
Lines with negative slope fall from left to right.

Thus, the line in Example 3 falls from left to right.

EXAMPLE 4 Find the slope of the lines containing each pair of points.

     a. $S(-1, -3)$ and $T(2, -3)$ **b.** $P(4, 5)$ and $N(4, 9)$

Solutions: **a.** $m = \dfrac{y_2 - y_1}{x_2 - x_1}$ **b.** $m = \dfrac{y_2 - y_1}{x_2 - x_1}$

$$m = \frac{-3 - (-3)}{2 - (-1)} \qquad\qquad m = \frac{9 - 5}{4 - 4} \quad\longleftarrow \quad \begin{array}{l}\textbf{Cannot divide}\\ \textbf{by 0}\end{array}$$

$$m = \frac{0}{2 + 1} = \mathbf{0} \qquad\qquad \text{The slope of the line is } \textbf{undefined.}$$

Example 4 suggests the following.

> The slope of any horizontal line is **0**.
>
> The slope of a vertical line is **undefined.**

EXERCISES

Objective: To find the slope of a line

CHECK YOUR UNDERSTANDING

Complete.

1. The measure of steepness of a line is a ratio called __?__ .

2. For any given line, the __?__ is the same ratio, no matter which two points are chosen.

3. The letter __?__ is customarily used to denote slope.

4. The slope of a line in which the horizontal change is __?__ is undefined.

5. Lines with positive slopes __?__ from left to right.

6. Lines with negative slopes __?__ from left to right.

Classify the slope of each line as *positive*, *negative*, or *equal to zero*. If the slope of a line is undefined, write <u>ND</u>.

7.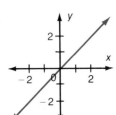

8.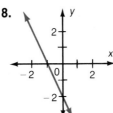

9.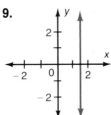

10.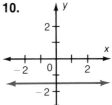

PRACTICE AND APPLY

Find the slope of each line from its graph.

11.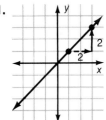

12.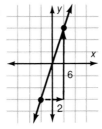

13.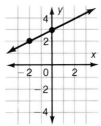

14.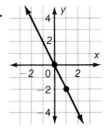

15.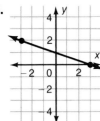

16.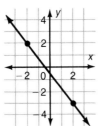

17.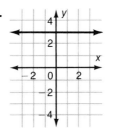

18.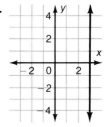

Find the slope of the line containing the given points.

19. $R(3, 2)$; $N(6, 8)$

20. $S(7, 1)$; $T(5, 9)$

21. $A(-4, 3)$; $B(-8, 6)$

22. $H(2,6)$; $T(-2, -3)$

23. $J(3, -5)$; $K(-4, 9)$

24. $P(0, 4)$; $S(-6, 4)$

Find the slope, if it exists, of each side of the given figure.

25. Triangle

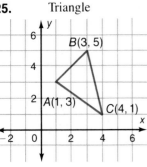

26. Rectangle

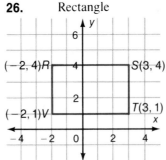

27. Parallelogram

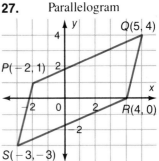

210 *Chapter 6*

Determine whether the given points lie on the same line. (HINT: The slope is the same for all pairs of points on a line.)

28. $(-5, 11)$, $(0, 8)$, $(5, 5)$

29. $(0, 1)$, $(4, -2)$, $(6, -4)$

30. $(6, 3)$, $(3, 2)$, $(0, 0)$

31. $(4, 1)$, $(-1, 7)$, $(3, 3)$

32. Find y so that the line containing $(2, y)$ and $(-3, 4)$ has a slope of 2.

33. Find y so that the line containing $(5, 1)$ and $(6, y)$ has a slope of -3.

34. Find the slope of a line passing through $(a, 0)$ and $(0, a)$.

35. Find the slope of a line containing the origin and $P(40,000, -20,000)$.

36. Let $P_1(x_1, y_1)$ and $P_2(x_2, y_2)$ be any two points on the line graphed at the right. Write a formula for m, the slope of the line.

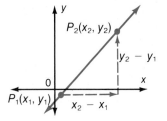

37. Suppose that the line in Exercise 36 is horizontal. How will y_1 and y_2 be related?

38. Suppose that the line in Exercise 36 is vertical. How will x_1 and x_2 be related?

▬▬▬▬▬ MAINTAIN

The speed of a passenger train traveling from Houston to Dallas is 50 mph. Use this information for Exercises 39–41. (*Pages 194–197*)

Number of hours, h	1	2	3	4
Distance traveled, d	?	?	?	?

39. Complete the table.

40. Use the ordered pairs in the table above to graph the function. Assume that the graph is linear.

41. Use the graph in Exercise 40 to estimate the distance the train traveled in 3.5 hours.

Solve. (*Pages 145–148*)

42. In triangle ABC, angle B is twice the measure of angle A, and angle C is $20°$ less than the measure of angle A. Find the measure of each angle.

43. The length of a rectangular field is 5 meters more than twice its width. The perimeter is 100 yards. Find the dimensions of the rectangle.

▬▬▬▬▬ CONNECT AND EXTEND

44. Graph the points $A(-2,1)$, $B(-2, -4)$, and $C(3,1)$ on a coordinate plane. Connect the points to form a right triangle. Use the definition of slope to show that the point $P(1, -1)$ lies on one side of the triangle.

45. Graph the points $A(-2,1)$, $B(4,1)$, $C(4, -5)$, and $D(-2, -5)$ on a coordinate plane. Connect the points to form a square. Show that the point $E(1, -2)$ lies both on the diagonal that connects A and C and on the diagonal that connects B and D.

Lines: Slopes and Equations   **211**

Solve each equation for *y*. (Pages 159–162)

1. $3x - y = 4$ **2.** $2y = 5(x + 1)$ **3.** $4x - 3y = 0$ **4.** $2x + 3y = 7$

5. $x - 2y = 7$ **6.** $y - 4x = 3$ **7.** $2y = -3(x - 2)$ **8.** $2x + y = 12$

6-2 Slope-Intercept Form of a Line

The graphs of each of these linear functions show that when the *x* coordinates differ by 1, the *y* coordinates differ by 3.

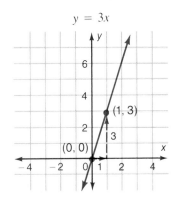

$y = 3x$

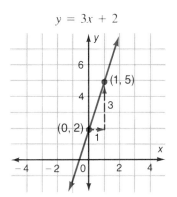

$y = 3x + 2$

Since, for each linear function,

$$\text{slope} = \frac{\text{vertical change}}{\text{horizontal change}} = \frac{3}{1} = 3,$$

it appears that in the equations $y = 3x$ and $y = 3x + 2$ the "**3**" represents the slope of the line.

More generally, if a line *l* is the graph of an equation of the form

$$y = mx + b,$$

m represents the slope of the line. In the equation $y = mx + b$, note that the coefficient of *y* is 1.

EXAMPLE 1 Find the slope of the line defined by the equation $2x + y = 18$.

Solution: Solve for *y* in order to write the equation in the form $y = mx + b$.

$2x + y = 18$

$y = -2x + 18$ ⟵———— **Compare with *y* = *mx* + *b*.**

$y = mx + b$ Therefore, $m = -2$.

Y INTERCEPT The y coordinate at which a line crosses the y axis is called the **y intercept.** Since $x = 0$ for any point on the y axis, you can find the y intercept of a linear function by replacing x with 0 in its equation.

$$y = mx + b \quad \longleftarrow \quad \textbf{Replace x with 0.}$$
$$y = m(0) + b$$
$$y = b \quad \longleftarrow \quad \textbf{y intercept}$$

SLOPE-INTERCEPT FORM

> The equation **$y = mx + b$** is called the **slope-intercept form** of the linear equation.
> Its graph is a straight line with **slope m** and **y intercept b.**

EXAMPLE 2 Find the slope and y intercept of the graph of $5x + y = 6$.

Solution: Rewrite the equation in the form $y = mx + b$.

$$y = -5x + 6 \quad \longleftarrow \quad m = -5; b = 6 \quad \text{Slope: } -5 \quad y \text{ intercept: } 6$$

You can use the slope and y intercept of a line to draw its graph.

EXAMPLE 3 Graph the line with slope -2 and y intercept 3.

Solution: **1** The y intercept is 3. Therefore, graph the point $P(0, 3)$.

2 Since the slope is -2,

$$\frac{\text{vertical change}}{\text{horizontal change}} = -2 = \frac{-2}{1}.$$

Start at P. Move 1 unit to the right and 2 units down. Label the point Q.

3 Connect points P and Q with a straight line.

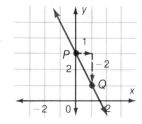

NOTE: In Example 3, you could also start at point P, move 2 units down and then 1 unit to the right. You would arrive at the same point, Q.

You can also write the slope as $-2 = \frac{2}{-1}$. The graph would be the same.

EXAMPLE 4 Use the slope and *y* intercept of $2x - 3y = 9$ to draw its graph.

Solution: ☐1 $2x - 3y = 9$ ←———— **Solve for y.**

$-3y = -2x + 9$

$y = \frac{2}{3}x - 3$ ←———— **Compare with y = mx + b.**

Slope: $\frac{2}{3}$ *y* intercept: -3

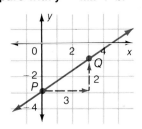

☐2 The *y* intercept is -3. There-fore, graph the point $P(0, -3)$.

Since $m = \frac{2}{3}$, start at *P*. Move 3 units to the right and 2 units up. Label point *Q*.

☐3 Connect points *P* and *Q* with a straight line.

EXERCISES: Classwork/Homework

Objective: To graph a line using the slope-intercept form of its equation

CHECK YOUR UNDERSTANDING

Complete.

1. In the equation $y = mx + b$, *m* represents the ? of the line.

2. The *y* coordinate at which a line crosses the *y* axis is called the ? .

3. In the equation $y = mx + b$, *b* represents the ? of the line.

4. You can find the *y* intercept of a linear function by replacing *x* with ? .

5. The equation $y = mx + b$ is called the ? form of a linear equation.

6. The graph of $y = mx + b$ is a ? .

Write the slope and *y* intercept of the graph of each equation.

7. $y = 2x + 5$ 8. $y = 6x - 7$ 9. $y = 3x + 2$ 10. $y = 4x$

11. $y = \frac{2}{3}x + \frac{1}{2}$ 12. $y = -\frac{1}{2}x - 5$ 13. $y = 3$ 14. $y + 8 = 0$

PRACTICE AND APPLY

First write each equation in the form $y = mx + b$. Then give the slope and *y* intercept of its graph.

15. $2x + y = 4$ 16. $3x + y = 8$ 17. $5x + y = -3$

18. $y - 4x = 1$ 19. $y - 2x = -4$ 20. $2y = 6x - 2$

21. $-2y = 4x + 5$ 22. $6 + 2y = 8x$ 23. $9 - 3y = 3x$

24. $4x - 2y = 12$ 25. $2y + 8 = 0$ 26. $2y - 4x + 6 = 0$

Graph the line whose slope and y intercept are given.

27. $m = 9, b = 6$ **28.** $m = -8, b = -2$ **29.** $m = 3, b = 1$

30. $m = \frac{1}{2}, b = 1$ **31.** $m = -\frac{2}{3}, b = 0$ **32.** $m = \frac{1}{4}, b = -2$

33. $m = 0, b = -2$ **34.** $m = 0, b = 5$ **35.** $m = -\frac{2}{5}, b = -1$

Use the slope and y intercept to graph each line.

36. $y = 3x - 2$ **37.** $y = -6x$ **38.** $y = 5x - 6$

39. $-2x + y = 4$ **40.** $y = -\frac{2}{3}x - 6$ **41.** $3x = y + 6$

42. $y - 3x = 1$ **43.** $4y = 5x + 12$ **44.** $2x - y = 3$

Use this property from geometry to tell whether each pair of lines in Exercises 45–50 is parallel.

> **Parallel lines have the same slope.**

45. $2x + y = 1$ **46.** $x - 3y = 4$ **47.** $3x - 2y = 2$
  $6x + 3y = 4$ $6y + 2x = 8$ $6x = 4y - 9$

48. $2y = 4x - 5$ **49.** $3y + 10 = 2x$ **50.** $y + 6 = 0$
  $3y - 6x = 7$ $2y - 3x = 0$ $y - 2 = 0$

51. What is the slope of all lines parallel to $y = -\frac{3}{4}x$?

52. What is the equation of a line whose slope is -2 and y intercept is 0?

53. What is the equation of a line whose slope is $-\frac{1}{3}$ and whose y intercept is 5?

54. What is the equation of a line whose slope is $-\frac{5}{6}$ and whose y intercept is -3?

▬▬▬▬ **MAINTAIN**

Find the slope of the line containing the given points. (*Pages 207–211*)

55. $A(1,2); B(4, 6)$ **56.** $C(-3,2); D(4, -5)$ **57.** $E(4, -1); F(-4, -5)$

Graph each equation on the coordinate plane. (*Pages 198–199*)

58. $|x| = 1$ **59.** $y = |x| - 5$ **60.** $x = -|2y| + 2$ **61.** $y + |x| = 12$

Solve and check. (*Pages 149–151*)

62. $4x = 2x + 14$ **63.** $7a - 8 = 3a$ **64.** $2p - 6 = 3p + 4$

65. $6y + 12 = 3y$ **66.** $5b - 8 = 3b + 2$ **67.** $-3c + 4 = c - 12$

▬▬▬▬ **CONNECT AND EXTEND**

68. Write the general form of the equation $Ax + By = C$ in the form $y = mx + b$.

69. Use your answer to Exercise 68 to represent the slope m of the line $Ax + By = C$ in terms of A and B.

6-3   Using Slope to Write a Linear Equation

When you know the slope and y intercept of a line, you can write the equation of the line. Write it in the form $y = mx + b$.

EXAMPLE 1 The slope of a line is 2 and its y intercept is 5. Write the equation of the line.

Solution: $y = mx + b$ ◄────── **Replace m with 2 and b with 5.** $y = 2x + 5$

You can also determine the equation of a line when you know its slope and the coordinates of a point on the line.

EXAMPLE 2 A line with slope -3 passes through the point $Q(2, -4)$. Determine the equation of the line.

Solution: **1** In $y = mx + b$, replace m with -3. $y = -3x + b$

2 Since $Q(2, -4)$ is on the line, replace x with 2 and y with -4. Solve for b.

$-4 = -3(2) + b$
$-4 = -6 + b$
$2 = b$ ◄─────── **y intercept**

3 Write the equation of the line with $m = -3$ and $b = 2$.

$y = -3x + 2$

The equation of a line can also be determined from its graph.

EXAMPLE 3 Determine the equation of the line shown in the graph.

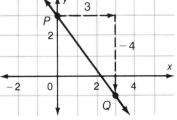

Solution: **1** Read the y intercept from the graph: $b = 3$

2 To find the slope, choose two convenient points on the graph.
$P(0, 3)$; $Q(3, -1)$

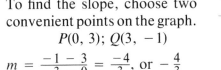

$$m = \frac{-1 - 3}{3 - 0} = \frac{-4}{3}, \text{ or } -\frac{4}{3}$$

3 Write the equation as in Example 1. $y = -\frac{4}{3}x + 3$

EXERCISES

Objective: To write the equation of a line, given its slope and the coordinates of a point on the line

CHECK YOUR UNDERSTANDING

Complete.

1. For an equation in the form $y = mx + b$, m represents the __?__.

2. For an equation in the form $y = mx + b$, b represents the __?__.

For Exercises 3–8, an equation and a point on its graph are given. Determine the y intercept, b.

3. $y = 2x + b; A(3, 1)$ **4.** $y = -x + b; C(-2, 4)$ **5.** $y = -3x + b; F(6, -2)$

6. $y = \frac{1}{2}x + b; R(-1, 6)$ **7.** $y = -\frac{3}{4}x + b; T(4, -7)$ **8.** $y = \frac{1}{4}x + b; U(-8, -10)$

PRACTICE AND APPLY

In Exercises 9–14, the slope and the y intercept of a line are given. Write the equation of the line in the form $y = mx + b$.

9. slope: 3; y intercept: 4   **10.** slope: 2; y intercept: 1

11. slope: $\frac{1}{2}$; y intercept: -3 **12.** slope: $\frac{2}{3}$; y intercept: -2

13. slope: -4; y intercept: $\frac{2}{3}$ **14.** slope: $-\frac{3}{8}$; y intercept: $-\frac{1}{2}$

In Exercises 15–29, one point on a line and the slope of the line are given. Write the equation of the line in the form $y = mx + b$.

15. $P(0, 2); m = 4$ **16.** $Q(-1, 2); m = 3$ **17.** $R(4, 6); m = \frac{1}{2}$

18. $A(-3, 1); m = -2$ **19.** $B(0, -3); m = -\frac{1}{4}$ **20.** $C(1, -1); m = -1$

21. $D(2, 3); m = 2$ **22.** $G(0, 4); m = 3$ **23.** $P(4, 5); m = -3$

24. $T(0, 0); m = 1$ **25.** $H(-2, 1); m = 1$ **26.** $S(0, 0); m = -1$

27. $N(-1, 1); m = \frac{1}{2}$ **28.** $Q(\frac{1}{2}, 3); m = -\frac{2}{3}$ **29.** $V(-3, 4); m = -\frac{1}{3}$

For Exercises 30–35, determine the equation of each line from its graph.

30.

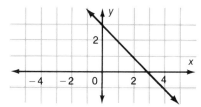

31.

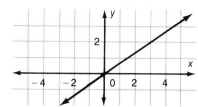

Lines: Slopes and Equations   **217**

32.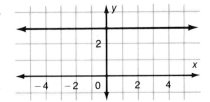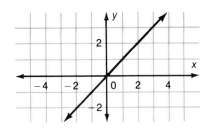

33.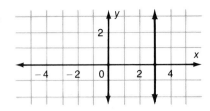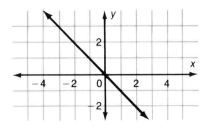

34.

35.

In Exercises 36–41, determine the equation of each line. Write the equation in the form $y = mx + b$.

36. The line has -2 as its y intercept and is parallel to the line defined by the equation $3y = x - 9$.

37. The line has 3 as its y intercept and is parallel to the line defined by the equation $3x - y + 6 = 0$.

38. The line passes through the point $(2, 3)$ and is parallel to the line defined by the equation $2y - 3x = 4$.

39. The line passes through the point $(2, 1)$ and is parallel to the line defined by the equation $2x - y = 8$.

40. The line has the same slope as the graph of $y + 3x = 7$ and the same y intercept as the graph of the equation $y - 4x = 9$.

41. The line has the same slope as the graph of $y + 4x = -8$ and the same y intercept as the graph of the equation $2y - 6x = 10$.

 You can use the program on page 613 to write the equation of a line in the slope-intercept form, given the slope and the coordinates of a point on a line.

Use the program to find the equation of the following lines.

42. Slope: 3; Point $(1, 5)$

43. Slope: -5; Point $(-2, 0)$

44. Slope: -2; Point $(-1, 4)$

45. Slope: $\frac{1}{2}$; Point $(0, -3)$

MAINTAIN

Use the slope and y intercept to graph each line. (*Pages 212–215*)

46. $y = x - 2$　　　**47.** $y = -4x$　　　**48.** $3x = y - 5$　　　**49.** $y + 2x = 3$

Find the slope of the line containing the given points. (*Pages 207–211*)

50. $A(2, 2)$; $B(4, 7)$　　　**51.** $D(-2, 1)$; $E(-6, 3)$　　　**52.** $L(-15, -4)$; $M(-5, -8)$

Solve each problem. (*Pages 154–157*)

53. A lawyer has worked 3 times as many years as his aide. Six years from now, the lawyer will have worked twice as many years as his aide. How many years has each worked?

54. Diane is now twice as old as Karen. Five years ago, the sum of their ages was 26. How old is each now?

■■■■■■ **CONNECT AND EXTEND**

When two lines are perpendicular (meet at a 90°-angle), their slopes are negative reciprocals of each other.

Example: Determine the slope of a line perpendicular to $y = 2x + 9$.

Solution: Slope of $y = 2x + 9$: 2

Negative reciprocal of 2: $-\frac{1}{2}$ ⟵ $2(-\frac{1}{2}) = -1$

Slope of line perpendicular to $y = 2x + 9$: $-\frac{1}{2}$

In Exercises 55–58, write the equation of each line. Write the equation in the form $y = mx + b$.

55. The line has 4 as its y intercept and is perpendicular to the line defined by the equation $y = 2x - 3$.

56. The line passes through $(2, 3)$ and is perpendicular to the line defined by the equation $y + 4x = 5$.

57. The line passes through the point $(-1, 4)$ and is perpendicular to the line defined by $3y - 2x = 9$.

58. The line passes through $(3, -2)$ and is perpendicular to the line defined by $4y + 3x = 7$.

59. Show that the equation of a line with x intercept a and y intercept b is $\frac{x}{a} + \frac{y}{b} = 1$, $a \neq 0$, $b \neq 0$.

60. Show that the y intercept of the line with slope m and passing through a given point (x_1, y_1) is $y_1 - mx_1$.

■■■■■■ **NON-ROUTINE PROBLEM**

61. At 12:00, the two hands of a clock coincide with one another. How many times a day do the two hands coincide?

———— **REVIEW CAPSULE FOR SECTION 6-4** ————

Determine whether the given ordered pair of numbers is a solution of the given sentence. Answer <u>Yes</u> or <u>No</u>. (*Pages 188–192*)

1. $x + y = 5$; $(0,5)$
2. $x - 3y = 5$; $(2,1)$
3. $y - x = 9$; $(0,9)$
4. $2x + y = 8$; $(1,6)$
5. $y = 6x$; $(2,10)$
6. $y - 2x = 0$; $(2, -3)$

Statistics / Tables and Graphs

Statisticians use tables, charts, and graphs to organize and display data. One way to organize data is to use a **frequency table.**

EXAMPLE: The highway mileage rating in miles per gallon for forty compact cars are listed at the left below.

a. Make a frequency table for the data.

Solution: Organize the data in intervals of 5 units.

Mileage Ratings (miles per gallon)
24 35 27 23 26 23 28 29
35 33 34 24 24 35 34 42
18 26 26 26 24 33 28 26
35 26 21 28 33 33 32 36
24 34 42 32 28 22 22 40

FREQUENCY TABLE

Interval	Midpoint	Tally	Frequency
15–19	17	|	1
20–24	22	ⱦ⫿⫿⫿ ⱦ⫿⫿⫿	10
25–29	27	ⱦ⫿⫿⫿ ⱦ⫿⫿⫿ ||	12
30–34	32	ⱦ⫿⫿⫿ ||||	9
35–39	37	ⱦ⫿⫿⫿	5
40–44	42	|||	3

b. Use the midpoints of the intervals to compute the approximate mean of the data. In statistics, $\bar{x}$ (read: x bar) is used to represent the mean.

Solution: $\bar{x} \approx \dfrac{1(17) + 10(22) + 12(27) + 9(32) + 5(37) + 3(42)}{40}$

17 [+] 220 [+] 324 [+] 288 [+]

185 [+] 126 [÷] 40 [=] ▭ 29.▯

The mean, $\bar{x}$, is about **29.**

c. Use the frequency table to draw a **histogram** for the data.

Solution: The horizontal axis shows the mileage data.
The vertical axis shows the frequencies.
The interval midpoint is the center of each bar.

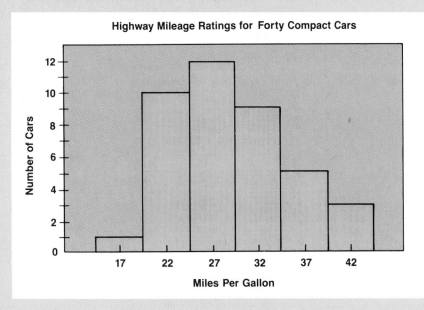

EXERCISES

For Exercises 1–2, make a frequency table using the suggested
interval width. Then draw a histogram for the data.

1. **Quiz Scores of
Thirty Students**

5	7	3	3	9	6
5	4	6	8	5	1
8	6	5	1	9	8
3	4	10	7	2	5
3	4	5	6	8	6

Interval width: 1

2. **Number of Runs Scored
by 50 Hitters**

19	16	26	18	22	28	17	20	22	23
16	18	19	25	29	12	8	23	22	20
18	17	29	23	18	12	11	20	17	12
23	18	10	15	18	19	22	6	11	14
19	17	14	20	18	16	17	19	20	22

Interval width: 3

3. Compute the approximate mean of the data in Exercise 2 by
using the midpoints of the intervals as values.

4. On Monday's test, the mean of 18
girls' scores was 70. The mean of 18
boys' scores was 75. What was the
mean for the entire class?

5. On Friday's test, the mean of 16 girls'
scores was 80 and the mean of 16
boys' scores was 72. What was the
mean for the entire class?

6-4   Using Two Points to Write a Linear Equation

When you know two points on a line, you can use these points to determine the equation of the line by finding the slope and y intercept.

EXAMPLE 1   Determine the equation of the line passing through the points $Q(-3, 7)$ and $R(2, -9)$.

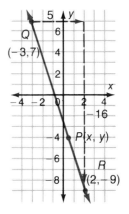

Solution:

[1] Use the given points to find m.
$$m = \frac{-9 - 7}{2 - (-3)} = \frac{-16}{5}, \text{ or } -\frac{16}{5}$$

[2] In $y = mx + b$, replace m with $-\frac{16}{5}$.
$$y = -\frac{16}{5}x + b$$

[3] Since $R(2, -9)$ is on the line, replace x with 2 and y with -9.
$$-9 = -\frac{16}{5}(2) + b$$
$$-9 = -\frac{32}{5} + b$$
$$-\frac{13}{5} = b$$

[4] Write the equation with $m = -\frac{16}{5}$ and $b = -\frac{13}{5}$.
$$y = -\frac{16}{5}x - \frac{13}{5}$$

By multiplying each side of $y = -\frac{16}{5}x - \frac{13}{5}$ by -5, the equation can be written as
$$-5y = 16x + 13, \text{ or } 16x + 5y = -13 \quad \longleftarrow \quad \textbf{General form}$$

GENERAL FORM

A linear equation written in the form
$$Ax + By = C$$
is said to be expressed in **general form.** Recall that the coefficients A, B, and C are real numbers and A and B cannot both equal zero. When writing a linear equation in general form, the coefficient, A, is usually expressed as a positive real number.

MAKING A MODEL

Sometimes a graph can provide a model for a problem. This problem-solving stategy is illustrated in Example 2.

222   *Chapter 6*

EXAMPLE 2 Scientists have found that the number of chirps a cricket makes per minute is related to the temperature. The graph at the right shows that when a cricket chirps 20 times in one minute, the temperature is 42°F. When a cricket chirps 80 times in 1 minute, the temperature is 57°F.

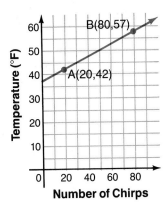

Problem: **a.** Determine the equation of the line passing through $A(20,42)$ and $B(80,57)$.

Solution:

$\boxed{1}$ Use the given points to find m.

$$m = \frac{57 - 42}{80 - 20} = \frac{15}{60}, \text{ or } \frac{1}{4}$$

$\boxed{2}$ In $y = mx + b$, replace m with $\frac{1}{4}$.

$$y = \tfrac{1}{4}x + b$$

$\boxed{3}$ Since $A(20,42)$ is on the line, replace x with 20 and y with 42.

$$42 = \tfrac{1}{4}(20) + b$$
$$42 = 5 + b$$
$$37 = b$$

$\boxed{4}$ Write the equation with $m = \frac{1}{4}$ and $b = 37$.

$$y = \tfrac{1}{4}x + 37$$

Problem: **b.** Use the equation of the line to predict the temperature when a cricket chirps 120 times in one minute.

Solution: In $y = \frac{1}{4}x + 37$, replace x with 120.

$$y = \tfrac{1}{4}(120) + 37$$
$$y = 30 + 37$$
$$y = 67$$

The temperature is **67°F.**

Objective: To write the equation of a line, given the coordinates of two points on the line

CHECK YOUR UNDERSTANDING

In Exercises 1–4, the slope and the y intercept of a line are given. Write the equation of the line in the form $y = mx + b$.

1. slope: -4; y intercept: 3
2. slope: 2; y intercept: -1
3. slope: $\frac{2}{3}$; y intercept: 0
4. slope: $-\frac{1}{2}$; y intercept: -5

Write each linear equation in general form.

5. $y = 2x - 10$
6. $y = -4x - 5$
7. $3y = 4x + 7$
8. $y = \frac{3}{4}x - \frac{11}{4}$
9. $3x = \frac{1}{3}y + 2$
10. $y = -\frac{2}{5}x - \frac{12}{5}$

PRACTICE AND APPLY

Determine the equation of the line passing through the given points. Write the equation in the form $y = mx + b$.

11. $R(1, 1)$; $S(2, 3)$
12. $T(0, 0)$; $V(-3, 4)$
13. $A(0, 1)$; $B(-1, 1)$
14. $D(0, 0)$; $E(-1, -2)$
15. $F(3, 4)$; $N(-2, 5)$
16. $E(5, -1)$; $H(3, -2)$
17. $K(-3, -4)$; $P(-5, -6)$
18. $R(2, 3)$; $S(-1, 5)$
19. $T(4, -3)$; $N(6, 0)$
20. $C(2, 2)$; $N(3, 7)$
21. $T(1, -4)$; $A(3, -6)$
22. $V(0, 4)$; $Y(4, 0)$

Determine the equation of the line passing through the given points. Write the equation in general form.

23. $P(1, 4)$; $S(3, 9)$
24. $T(1, 0)$; $M(3, -6)$
25. $W(-3, -1)$; $Z(9, 7)$
26. $M(0, -1)$; $V(6, 8)$
27. $Z(1, -6)$; $B(6, 0)$
28. $Q(-2, -5)$; $R(-1, -2)$
29. $V(-3, 11)$; $C(6, 5)$
30. $D(0, 0)$; $F(-3, 5)$
31. $D(0, 3)$; $C(-4, -8)$

In Exercises 32–37, use the given slope and one point to write an equation of a line. Then determine whether the other point lies on that line.

32. 6; $(2, 3)$; $(6, 9)$
33. $\frac{1}{2}$; $(4, 2)$; $(-2, -1)$
34. $-\frac{3}{5}$; $(-5, 7)$; $(0, 4)$
35. -4; $(2, 6)$; $(-1, 13)$
36. 2; $(-1, -2)$; $(2, 4)$
37. -3; $(-2, 2)$; $(1, 6)$

For Exercises 38–39, refer to the equation of the line in Example 2.

38. Predict the temperature if a cricket chirps 48 times in 1 minute.

39. On a certain night, the temperature is 80°F. How many times will a cricket chirp in 1 minute?

The graph at the right shows the linear relationship between degrees Celsius and degrees Fahrenheit. The freezing point of water is 0°C and 32°F. The boiling point of water is 100°C and 212°F.

Refer to this graph for Exercises 40–42.

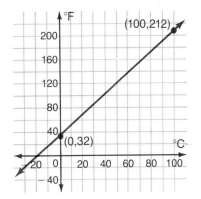

40. Determine the equation of the line that describes the relationship between degrees Celsius and degrees Fahrenheit. HINT: $F = mC + b$

41. At about 6000 feet above sea level, water will boil at 94°C. How many degrees Fahrenheit (to the nearest whole degree) is this? Use the equation from Exercise 40.

42. The highest surface temperature on the ocean is 30°C. How many degrees Fahrenheit is this?

███████ **MAINTAIN**

In Exercises 43–45, one point on a line and the slope of the line are given. Write the equation of the line in the form $y = mx + b$. (*Pages 216–219*)

43. $P(-1, 1)$; $m = -1$ **44.** $R(0, -2)$; $m = 2$ **45.** $T(3, -3)$; $m = -\frac{2}{3}$

Use the slope and y intercept to graph each line. (*Pages 212–215*)

46. $y = 3x - 3$ **47.** $y = -5x$ **48.** $4x - y = 1$ **49.** $2x + y = 1$

Solve each equation for the variable indicated. (*Pages 159–162*)

50. $m = st$ for s **51.** $mr + c = d$ for r **52.** $A = x + y + z$ for x

███████ **CONNECT AND EXTEND**

In each of Exercises 53–56, the coordinates of the vertices of a triangle are given. Write the equations of the lines forming the sides of each triangle. Write the equations in general form.

53. $A(2, 4)$; $B(6, 2)$; $C(3, -1)$ **54.** $D(6, 6)$; $E(8, 4)$; $F(1, 2)$

55. $F(3, 2)$; $G(-2, 3)$; $H(1, -2)$ **56.** $X(-3, 4)$; $Y(-2, -1)$; $Z(1, 1)$

57. Show that if $P(x_1, y_1)$ and $Q(x_2, y_2)$ are different points on the graph of the equation $y = 4x - 2$, then $\dfrac{y_2 - y_1}{x_2 - x_1} = 4$.

Find the slope of the line containing the given points. (*Pages 207–211*)

1. $(5, -1); (8, 2)$ **2.** $(0, 0); (-1, 1)$ **3.** $(-8, 6); (3, -9)$ **4.** $(-5, 9); (3, 9)$

Write each equation in the form $y = mx + b$. Then give the slope and y intercept of its graph. (*Pages 212–215*)

5. $3x + y = 5$ **6.** $3x - 2y = 8$ **7.** $y + 8 = 0$ **8.** $-5y = 3x$

9. Use the slope and y intercept of $2x + y = 8$ to draw its graph. (*Pages 212–215*)

One point on a line and the slope of the line are given. Write the equation of the line in the form $y = mx + b$. (*Pages 216–219*)

10. $A(2, 3); m = 1$ **11.** $P(0, -1); m = -2$ **12.** $C(0, \frac{1}{2}); m = -\frac{2}{3}$

Determine the equation of the line passing through the given points. Write the equation in the form $y = mx + b$. (*Pages 222–225*)

13. $A(4, 4); B(-4, -4)$ **14.** $P(1, 2); Q(0, -1)$ **15.** $C(2, 1); D(-3, 0)$

Determine the equation of the line passing through the given points. Write the equation in general form. (*Pages 222–225*)

16. $M(0, 4); N(4, 2)$ **17.** $S(2, -2); T(-2, 10)$ **18.** $F(1, -1); G(-3, 0)$

Historical Digest: Lewis Carroll

Charles Dodgson, a mathematics instructor at Cambridge University in England, wrote books on many scientific subjects. He also wrote *Alice's Adventures in Wonderland* and *Through the Looking Glass* as Lewis Carroll. It is said that Queen Victoria once asked Carroll for a copy of one of his books. When she received *The Elements of Determinants (With their Applications to Simultaneous Linear Equations)*, she was quite surprised!

Lewis Carroll had many other interests including photography and what he called "pillow problems." Some of these problems were called "doublets." The object was to change one word into another by changing only one letter at a time.

Problem: Change HEAD to TAIL.

   HEAD   HEAL   TEAL   TELL   TALL   TAIL

Can you change EYE to LID?

Solve and check each equation. (*Pages 99–102*)

1. $10 = 2x$　　　　**2.** $-4 = 8x$　　　　**3.** $12 = -3x$

4. $-3y = 18$　　　　**5.** $-2y = -6$　　　　**6.** $8x = 40$

6-5 Direct Variation

$T = 8h$

$T = 10h + 12$

In the ad for yard work, doubling the number of hours, h, doubles the total cost, T.

The equation $T = 8h$ expresses direct variation because only multiplication by a constant is involved.

	Direct Variation $T = 8h$	Not Direct Variation $T = 10h + 12$
Let h = 3.	$T = 24$	$T = 42$
Let h = 6.	$T = 48$	$T = 72$
Let h = 12.	$T = 96$	$T = 132$
	T is doubled when h is doubled	T is not doubled when h is doubled.

Direct variation is a special case of the linear function $y = mx + b$, with $b = 0$. Thus, the graph of a linear function expressing direct variation will always pass through the origin.

The equation $y = kx$ expresses **direct variation between x and y.** That is, y is said to vary directly as x, and k is called the **constant of variation.** Note that k is the slope of the graph of $y = kx$.

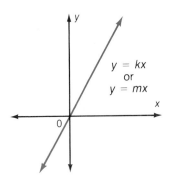

$y = kx$
or
$y = mx$

EXAMPLE 1 **a.** If y varies directly as x, and $y = 8$ when $x = 3$, find k.

b. Write the equation that expresses the variation.

Solution:　**a.** $y = kx$ ◀——— **y varies directly as x.**

$8 = k(3)$ ◀——— **When y = 8, x = 3.**

$\frac{8}{3} = k$ ◀——— **Constant of variation**

b. $y = \frac{8}{3}x$ ◀——— **Write the equation with k = $\frac{8}{3}$.**

After you have found the equation that expresses the direct variation, you can find ordered pairs (x, y) that satisfy the equation.

EXAMPLE 2 If y varies directly as x, and $y = 21$ when $x = 1\frac{1}{2}$, find y when $x = 9$.

Solution:　　　　$y = kx$ ◀——— **Replace x with $\frac{3}{2}$.**

$21 = k(\frac{3}{2})$ ◀——— **Multiply each side by $\frac{2}{3}$.**

$21(\frac{2}{3}) = k(\frac{3}{2})(\frac{2}{3})$

$14 = k$ ◀——— **Constant of variation**

Thus, $y = 14x$. ◀——— **Find y when x = 9.**

$y = 14(9) = \mathbf{126}$

CALCULATOR

Use a calculator to determine whether the set of ordered pairs is an example of direct variation. If so, write an equation that expresses the variation.

x	-3	1.5	2.5	7.5
y	-16.5	8.25	13.75	41.25

First find the quotient, $\frac{y}{x}$, in the first ordered pair. Use $\boxed{\text{STO}}$ to store k in memory.

16.5 $\boxed{^{+}/_{-}}$ $\boxed{\div}$ **3** $\boxed{^{+}/_{-}}$ $\boxed{=}$ $\boxed{\text{STO}}$ [5.5] ◀——— $\frac{y}{x} = k$

To test (1.5, 8.25), multiply 1.5 and the value for k. Use $\boxed{\text{RCL}}$ to recall k.

1.5 $\boxed{\times}$ $\boxed{\text{RCL}}$ $\boxed{=}$ [8.25]

You can test the value of k for each remaining ordered pair. If each ordered pair checks, the relation is an example of direct variation. Since $k = 5.5$ the equation that expresses the variation is $y = \mathbf{5.5x}$.

Objective: To write an equation expressing direct variation and find ordered pairs that satisfy the equation

▬▬▬▬ **CHECK YOUR UNDERSTANDING**

Complete.

1. The equation $y = kx$ expresses __?__ variation between x and y.

2. In $y = kx$, k is called the __?__ of variation.

3. The slope of the graph of $y = kx$ is __?__ .

4. The graph of $y = kx$ will always pass through the __?__ .

Determine whether each set of ordered pairs (x, y) is an example of direct variation. Answer <u>Yes</u> or <u>No</u>.

5.

x	1	2	3	4
y	3	6	9	12

6.

x	−1	−2	−3	−4
y	−7	−14	−21	−28

Determine whether each equation is an example of direct variation. Answer <u>Yes</u> or <u>No</u>.

7. $x = 4y$ 8. $x + y = 6$ 9. $y = 6x$ 10. $x - y = 4$

If y varies directly as x, find the constant of variation, k, for the given values of x and y.

11. $x = 3, y = 2$ 12. $x = -1, y = 4$ 13. $x = 5, y = -2$ 14. $x = -\frac{1}{2}, y = -1$

▬▬▬▬ **PRACTICE AND APPLY**

In Exercises 15–16, determine whether the relation between the variables is that of direct variation. Explain your answer.

15. P is the perimeter of a square and s is the length of one side.

16. John earns \$3.25 an hour mowing lawns. The amount that he earns in cents is A. The number of hours that he works is n.

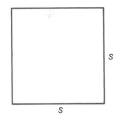

In Exercises 17–19, refer to the table below.

17. Does each number for y equal a constant times the corresponding number for x? Does y vary directly as x? Explain.

x	0	1	2	3	4	5	6
y	0	$2\frac{1}{2}$	5	$7\frac{1}{2}$	10	$12\frac{1}{2}$	15

18. Write an equation that shows the relation between x and y.
$(y = \underline{\ ?\ })$

19. When x is 4, y is 10. When x is 8, y is $\underline{\ ?\ }$. If you double the value of x, is the corresponding value of y doubled? If you choose any value of x and double it, the corresponding value of y is $\underline{\ ?\ }$.

Determine whether each equation is an example of direct variation. Answer <u>Yes</u> or <u>No</u>.

20. $x = 12y$

21. $5x = y$

22. $y = \frac{1}{8}x$

23. $y + 3x = 0$

24. $xy + 4 = y$

25. $y = \frac{x}{4}$

26. $\frac{x}{y} = 7$

27. $y = \frac{18}{x}$

Express each relationship as an equation. Use k as the constant of variation.

28. y varies directly as x.

29. p varies directly as q.

30. r varies directly as s.

31. s varies directly as t.

In Exercises 32–43, assume that y varies directly as x.

32. If $x = 2$ when $y = 3$, find k.

33. If $x = 5$ when $y = 2$, find k.

34. If $x = -3$ when $y = 6$, find k.

35. If $x = 1$ when $y = -4$, find k.

36. If $x = \frac{1}{2}$ when $y = \frac{2}{3}$, find k.

37. If $x = -2$ when $y = -8$, find k.

38. If $y = 9$ when $x = 3$, find k. Then find y when x is 1.

39. If $y = 10$ when $x = 2$, find k. Then find y when x is -2.

40. If $y = 6$ when $x = 4$, find y when x is 10.

41. If $y = -2$ when $x = -1$, find y when x is 5.

42. If $x = -3$ when $y = -2$, find x when y is -4.

43. If $x = 4$ when $y = -3$, find x when y is 0.

In Exercises 44–46, refer to the figure at the right. The figure shows the graph of $y = kx$ for various values of k.

44. As k increases from $\frac{1}{5}$ to 9, what happens to the graph of $y = kx$?

45. As k increases from $-2\frac{1}{2}$ to $-\frac{1}{3}$, what happens to the graph of $y = kx$?

46. Why does the graph of an equation expressing direct variation always pass through the origin?

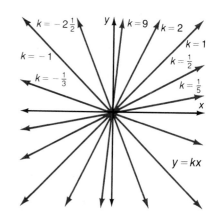

In Exercises 47–48, use the fact that $C = \pi d$ expresses the relation between the circumference of a circle and the length of a diameter.

47. Does C vary directly as d? Explain.

48. When d is 10, C is 10π. When d is 20, C is __?__. If you take one circle and draw another circle that has a diameter twice that of the first, its circumference is __?__ the circumference of the first circle.

MAINTAIN

Determine the equation of the line passing through the given points. Write the equation in general form. (*Pages 222–225*)

49. $D(0,0)$; $E(-2, -5)$ **50.** $P(2,0)$; $Q(5,3)$ **51.** $C(-1, -3)$; $D(3,4)$

Determine the equation of each line. Write the equation in the form $y = mx + b$. (*Pages 216–219*)

52. The line has -1 as its y intercept and is parallel to the line defined by the equation $y - x = -2$.

53. The line passes through the point $(2,6)$ and is parallel to the line defined by $2y - 6x = 4$.

Solve each problem. (*Pages 163–166*)

54. Two trains start at the same time at the same place and travel in opposite directions. One travels at the rate of 46 mph and the other at the rate of 58 mph. In how many hours will they be 364 miles apart?

55. Two planes leave at 10 A.M. from cities which are 2400 miles apart. In 2 hours they meet. The first plane travels 90 mph faster than the second plane. Find the rate at which each plane travels.

CONNECT AND EXTEND

In Exercises 56–59, assume that y equals a negative number times x.

56. As x increases, does y increase or decrease?

57. As x decreases, does y increase or decrease?

58. *Complete:* When any number for x is doubled, the corresponding number for y is __?__.

59. *Complete:* When any number for x is multiplied by n, the corresponding number for y is __?__.

NON-ROUTINE PROBLEMS

60. Robert has $15 more than Marlene. Marlene has $10 more than Albert. Together, they have a total of $56. How much does Robert have?

61. A building has 6 doors. Find the number of ways a person can enter the building by one door and leave by another door.

6-6 Using Direct Variation

You can use direct variation to solve word problems.

EXAMPLE The length of an official flag of the United States varies directly with its width, and the constant of variation is fixed by Federal law. If an official flag is 3 meters wide and 5.7 meters long, what should be the length of an official flag that is 1.5 meters wide?

Solution: Let l = the length of the flag and let w = the width.

Then $l = kw.$ ⟵ **Replace *l* with 5.7 and *w* with 3.**

$5.7 = k(3)$

$1.9 = k$ ⟵ **Use *k* to write the direct linear variation**

Thus, $l = 1.9w.$

$l = 1.9(1.5)$

$l = 2.85$ The length should be **2.85 meters.**

In the Exercises that follow, assume that all variations are linear.

EXERCISES: Classwork/Homework

Objective: To solve problems involving direct variation

CHECK YOUR UNDERSTANDING

1. The labor costs, c, for an automobile repair job vary directly as the number of hours, h, a mechanic works on the car. Labor costs for 3 hours amount to $87. Find the constant of variation, k.

2. The estimated cost, e, of building a house varies directly as the number of square feet of floor space, f. One thousand two hundred square feet cost $60,000. Write the equation that expresses the variation.

Solve each problem.

3. The amount of pay, A, that Sue earns varies directly with the number of hours, h, that she works. Last week, she earned $108.75 for 25 hours of work. How much pay will she earn for 120 hours of work? Assume that the pay rate remains the same.

4. The speed of the blade tips of a windmill varies directly with the speed of the wind. In a 20 mile-per-hour wind, the speed of the blade tips of a windmill near Sandusky, Ohio is 180 miles per hour. Find the speed of the blade tips in a 5 mile-per-hour wind.

5. The gas consumption of a car varies directly as the distance traveled. If a certain car uses 20 liters of gas to travel 200 kilometers, how many liters of gasoline will be used on a trip of 700 kilometers?

6. The amount of stretch, S, in a spring varies directly as the weight attached, w. A certain spring stretches 5 inches when a weight of 15 pounds is attached. Find the weight needed for a stretch of $7\frac{1}{2}$ inches.

7. The distance between two towns on a map varies directly with the actual distance between the towns. If $2\frac{1}{2}$ inches on the map represent 150 miles, what is the actual distance represented by 7 inches on the map?

8. The number of calories in a container of milk varies directly with the amount of milk in the container. If a 10-ounce glass of milk contains 180 calories, how many calories are there in a 14-ounce glass?

9. The toll, T, on a bridge varies directly with the number of axles on a vehicle. On a certain bridge, the toll for a 4-axle truck is $3.00. What will be the toll for a 6-axle truck?

10. The weight of an object on the moon varies directly as its weight on earth. An object with a weight of 14.4 pounds on the moon will have a weight of 90 pounds on earth. If an object has a weight of 120 pounds on earth, find its weight on the moon.

11. The amount of time, T, that it takes to read an article varies directly with the length of the article. Ted takes 3 minutes to read an article of 315 words. How many minutes will it take him to read an article of 945 words if he reads at the same rate?

12. The cost, c, of cleaning a carpet varies directly with the area, A, of the carpet. The cost of cleaning a 9-foot by 12-foot carpet is $21.60. At the same rate per square foot, how much will it cost to clean a carpet 18 feet long by 10 feet wide?

Lines: Slopes and Equations   **233**

13. The weight, w, of a steer being raised for food varies directly with the number of pounds of fodder, f, consumed. It takes 96 pounds of fodder to produce a 6-pound roast of beef. How many pounds of fodder does it take to produce 15 pounds of beef?

14. The amount of antifreeze required to prevent freezing at $-25°C$ varies directly with the capacity of the cooling system. A 20-liter cooling system requires 6.2 liters of antifreeze. How much antifreeze is needed in a 25-liter system?

MAINTAIN

15. A basketball team won 24 games. This was 60% of all the games they played. How many games did the team play? (*Pages 108–110*)

16. The sum of the measure of two angles is 180°. Their measures can be represented by x and $(2x + 15)$. Find the measure of each angle. (*Pages 122–125*)

Determine the equation of the line passing through the given points. Write the equation in the form $y = mx + b$. (*Pages 222–225*)

17. $A(0, 1)$; $B(1, 5)$
18. $C(2, -1)$; $D(1, 0)$
19. $F(-2, 4)$; $G(0, 0)$
20. $R(2, 3)$; $S(-2, -3)$
21. $P(0, 6)$; $T(3, 8)$
22. $J(5, -3)$; $K(-2, 4)$

Solve each problem. (*Pages 154–157*)

23. The sum of three consecutive integers is 141. Find the integers.

24. Three consecutive odd integers have a sum of 267. What are the integers?

CONNECT AND EXTEND

25. Given two ordered pairs (x_1, y_1) and (x_2, y_2) of a direct variation defined by $y = kx$ in which $x_1 \neq 0$ and $x_2 \neq 0$, show that $\frac{y_1}{x_1} = \frac{y_2}{x_2}$.

NON-ROUTINE PROBLEM

26. Meg spent $\frac{1}{4}$ of the quarters she had saved. She gave her brother $\frac{3}{4}$ of the rest. Then she had 3 quarters left. How many quarters had she saved?

Focus on College Entrance Tests

Sometimes a sequence is a succession of geometric figures. Look for what changes and what remains the same. This will help you to identify the pattern.

EXAMPLE   What is the next figure?

Think: The figures are in pairs.
The pairs have the same shape.
The second figure of each
pair is upside down.

Next figure: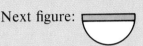

TRY THESE

Identify the pattern. Then draw the next figure in each sequence.

1.
2.
3.
4.
5.
6.
7.
8.
9.
10.
11.
12.

Chapter Summary

IMPORTANT TERMS

Constant of variation (p. 227)
Direct variation (p. 227)
General form of a linear
 equation (p. 222)
Ratio (p. 207)

Slope (p. 207)
Slope-intercept form of a
 linear equation (p. 213)
y intercept (p. 213)

IMPORTANT IDEAS

1. For any two points on a line, $P_1(x_1, y_1)$ and $P_2(x_2, y_2)$,

$$\text{slope} = m = \frac{\text{vertical change}}{\text{horizontal change}} = \frac{y_2 - y_1}{x_2 - x_1}, (x_2 - x_1 \neq 0)$$

2. Lines with positive slope rise from left to right.

 Lines with negative slope fall from left to right.

 The slope of a horizontal line is 0.

 A vertical line has no slope.

3. The graph of an equation of the form $y = mx + b$ is a straight line with slope m and y intercept b.

4. Parallel lines have the same slope.

5. You can write the equation of a line if you know

 a. the slope and the y intercept,

 b. the slope and the coordinates of one point on the line, or

 c. the coordinates of two points on the line.

Chapter Review

Find the slope of the line containing the given points. (*Pages 207–211*)

1. $(-7, 16); (1, 0)$ **2.** $(8, 2); (4, -1)$ **3.** $(-3, 2); (0, 2)$

Write each equation in the form $y = mx + b$. Then give the slope and y intercept of its graph. (*Pages 212–215*)

4. $3y = 2x - 9$ **5.** $x + y = 0$ **6.** $4x - 2y = 8$

Use the slope and y intercept to graph each line (*Pages 212–215*)

7. $y = x + 2$ **8.** $y = 2x + 1$ **9.** $x + 2y = -4$

10. $3y - 9 = x$ **11.** $4x + 6 = y$ **12.** $x - 2y = 11$

The slope and the _y_ intercept of a line are given. Write the equation of the line in the form _y_ = _mx_ + _b_. (_Pages 216–219_)

13. slope: -3; _y_ intercept: 4   **14.** slope: 5; _y_ intercept: 0

15. slope: $-\frac{1}{2}$; _y_ intercept: $-\frac{3}{4}$ **16.** slope: $\frac{5}{8}$; _y_ intercept: 8

One point on a line and the slope of the line are given. Write the equation of the line in the form _y_ = _mx_ + _b_. (_Pages 216–219_)

17. $B(1, 4)$; $m = 2$ **18.** $P(-2, 3)$; $m = \frac{1}{4}$ **19.** $Y(-4, -4)$; $m = -1$

20. $D(5, 0)$; $m = 6$ **21.** $Q(3, -3)$; $m = \frac{3}{2}$ **22.** $G(-4, -4)$; $m = 4$

Determine the equation of the line passing through the given points. Write the equation in the form _y_ = _mx_ + _b_. (_Pages 222–225_)

23. $M(0, 2)$; $N(3, 11)$ **24.** $P(2, 0)$; $Q(-4, 3)$ **25.** $X(0, 0)$; $Y(-3, 15)$

26. $A(1, 2)$; $B(-1, -4)$ **27.** $F(2, -3)$; $G(-2, 5)$ **28.** $J(3, 0)$; $K(-6, -12)$

Determine the equation of the line passing through the given points. Write the equation in general form. (_Pages 222–225_)

29. $C(3, 5)$; $D(5, 3)$ **30.** $X(0, -4)$; $Y(1, -2)$ **31.** $H(4, -1)$; $I(-6, 3)$

Determine whether each equation is an example of direct variation. Answer <u>Yes</u> or <u>No</u>. (_Pages 227–231_)

32. $x = 4y$ **33.** $x = 2y + 7$ **34.** $y = x$ **35.** $xy = -8$

36. If _y_ varies directly as _x_, and $y = 4\frac{1}{2}$ when $x = -2$, find _y_ when $x = 8$.

37. On a scale drawing, 3 centimeters represent 90 meters. How many meters will 5 centimeters represent? (_Pages 232–234_)

38. The cost of silver varies directly as its weight. If 4 ounces of silver cost $56, how much will 7 ounces cost? (_Pages 232–234_)

39. The length of a steel beam shown on a blueprint varies directly with its actual length. On the blueprint, 5 centimeters represent 1 meter. If the length of the beam on the blueprint is 21.5 centimeters, what is the actual length of the steel beam? (_Pages 232–234_)

Find the slope of the line containing the given points.

1. $(7, -4); (-5, -4)$ **2.** $(0, -4); (-2, -5)$ **3.** $(3, -2); (-4, 7)$

Write each equation in the form $y = mx + b$. Then give the slope and y intercept of its graph.

4. $x - y = 2$ **5.** $3x + 4y = 4$ **6.** $2y = 4x - 6$

Graph each linear equation in the coordinate plane.

7. $y = x + 4$ **8.** $y = -2x - 1$

One point on a line and the slope of the line are given. Write the equation of the line in the form $y = mx + b$.

9. $A(0, 3); m = -1$ **10.** $P(1, -2); m = \frac{1}{3}$ **11.** $F(-6, 5); m = 3$

Determine the equation of the line passing through the given points. Write the equation in the form $y = mx + b$.

12. $A(3, 5); B(5, 3)$ **13.** $X(0, -4); Y(1, -2)$ **14.** $M(4, -1); N(-6, 3)$

Determine whether each equation is an example of direct variation. Answer <u>Yes</u> or <u>No</u>.

15. $3y = x$ **16.** $x - y = 8$ **17.** $xy = 7$

18. If y varies directly as x, and $y = 12$ when $x = 3$, find y when $x = 5$.

19. The actual distance between cities varies directly with the distance shown on a map. On the map, 3 centimeters represent 8 kilometers. If the distance between two cities on the map is 18 centimeters, what is the actual distance between the cities?

20. The weight of steel cable varies directly with its length. How heavy is a 150-meter roll of cable, if the weight of a 2-meter section is 0.8 kilograms?

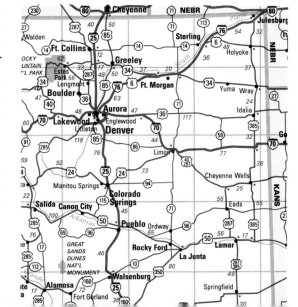

Skills

Find the slope of the line containing the given points. (*Pages 207–211*)

1. $(2, 6); (-4, -6)$ **2.** $(3, -4); (5, -4)$ **3.** $(0, -4); (4, -6)$

Write each equation in the form $y = mx + b$. Then give the slope and y-intercept of its graph. (*Pages 212–215*)

4. $4x + y + 3 = 0$ **5.** $5 - y = 2x$ **6.** $3y - 6 = 2x$

One point on a line and the slope of the line are given. Write the equation of the line in the form $y = mx + b$. (*Pages 216–219*)

7. $A(3, 4); m = 4$ **8.** $B(0, -6); m = -2$ **9.** $C(-2, -4); m = 1$

Determine the equation of the line passing through the given points. Write the equation in the form $y = mx + b$. (*Pages 222–225*)

10. $A(-2, 0); D(0, 4)$ **11.** $C(0, 0); B(2, -3)$ **12.** $M(0, 5); N(-1, -4)$

Determine the equation of the line passing through the given points. Write the equation in general form. (*Pages 222–225*)

13. $S(6, -2); T(0, 3)$ **14.** $F(-4, -1); G(4, -2)$ **15.** $V(0, -3); W(12, 0)$

In Exercises 16–18, assume that y varies directly as x. (*Pages 227–231*)

16. If $y = -3$ when $x = 1$, find y when $x = 4$.

17. If $y = 4$ when $x = 2$, find y when $x = 6$.

18. If $x = -3$ when $y = 12$, find x when $y = 1$.

Problem Solving and Applications

Solve each problem. (*Pages 232–234*)

19. The actual distance between cities varies directly with the distance shown on a map. On the map, 2 centimeters represent 5 kilometers. If the distance between two cities on the map is 14 centimeters, what is the actual distance between the cities?

20. The gas consumption of a car varies directly as the distance traveled. If a certain car uses 25 liters of gas to travel 325 kilometers, how many liters of gasoline will be used on a trip of 585 miles?

Part 1

Choose the best answer. Choose a, b, c, or d.

1. Which point is not a solution of the equation $y = 3x - 5$?

   a. $(2, 0)$ **b.** $(1, -2)$ **c.** $(-1, -8)$ **d.** $(0, -5)$

2. Find the value of $2xy - 4xy^2$ for $x = 2$ and $y = -3$.

   a. 60 **b.** -84 **c.** 84 **d.** -60

3. Which equation has a graph that is a straight line?

   a. $x = 0$ **b.** $|x| = 7$ **c.** $2x + 3y = \frac{1}{2}$ **d.** $y = x^2 + 3$

4. Solve for w: $P = 2l + 2w$

   a. $w = \frac{P}{2} - 21$ **b.** $w = \frac{2l - P}{2}$ **c.** $w = 2P - 1$ **d.** $w = \frac{P - 21}{2}$

5. Which property of equality is illustrated by this statement: If $a = b$ and $b = c$, then $a = c$?

   a. transitive   **b.** distributive   **c.** symmetric   **d.** reflexive

6. Which number is the additive inverse of 4.25?

   a. -5.24 **b.** -4.25 **c.** 0.425 **d.** -425

7. Solve: $-\frac{2}{3}(\frac{3}{2}x) = 0$

   a. $x = 1$ **b.** $x = -1$ **c.** $x = 0$ **d.** $x = \frac{3}{2}$

8. What number would you add to $4x + 3$ to obtain $4x$?

   a. -3 **b.** 3 **c.** $\frac{1}{4}$ **d.** $-\frac{3}{4}$

9. Solve the equation $-\frac{k}{6} = 1\frac{5}{12}$.

   a. $3\frac{1}{2}$ **b.** $8\frac{1}{2}$ **c.** $-3\frac{1}{2}$ **d.** $-8\frac{1}{2}$

10. Solve the equation $\frac{1}{2}n + 2n = 3(n - 1)$.

    a. $n = 6$ **b.** $n = -6$ **c.** $n = 1$ **d.** $n = 4$

11. What is the range of the function $\{(-1,4), (2,-1), (0,3), (-2,2)\}$?

    a. $\{-1,2,0,-2\}$ **b.** $\{(-1,4), (-2,2)\}$ **c.** $\{4,-1,3,2\}$ **d.** $\{-1,0,2\}$

12. If y varies directly as x, and $y = 12$ when $x = 8$, what is the value of the constant of variation k?

    a. $\frac{2}{3}$ **b.** $2\frac{1}{2}$ **c.** 2 **d.** $1\frac{1}{2}$

13. What is the equation of a line with slope -2 and which passes through the point $(3, -1)$?

    a. $y = -2x - 1$ **b.** $y = -2x + 5$ **c.** $y = -2x + 3$ **d.** $y = 5x - 2$

14. What percent of 250 is 100?

    a. 50%   **b.** 60%   **c.** 40%   **d.** 70%

15. Which expression is equal to x?

    a. $\frac{3}{2}\left(-\frac{2}{3}x\right)$ **b.** $-\frac{3}{2}x + \frac{3}{2}$ **c.** $-\frac{3}{2}x - \frac{3}{2}$ **d.** $-\frac{3}{2}\left(-\frac{2}{3}x\right)$

16. Which line passes through the points $(2, 2)$ and $(-2, -2)$?

    a. $y = 2x - 2$ **b.** $y = 2x + 2$ **c.** $y = -x$ **d.** $y = x$

17. If y varies directly as x, and $y = 18$ when $x = 3\frac{1}{2}$, find y when $x = 14$.

    a. 675   **b.** 72   **c.** 36   **d.** 105

18. What is the slope of any horizontal line?

    a. 1   **b.** undefined   **c.** 0   **d.** -1

19. What is the equation of a line with -3 as its y intercept and parallel to the line $y = \frac{2}{3}x + 3$?

    a. $y = -3x + \frac{2}{3}$ **b.** $y = -\frac{2}{3}x + 3$ **c.** $y = \frac{2}{3}x - 3$ **d.** $y = \frac{3}{2}x - 3$

20. Evaluate $\dfrac{n - 1 + n^2}{n + 1 - n^2}$ for $n = -1$.

    a. 1   **b.** -1 **c.** 0   **d.** $\frac{1}{2}$

21. Which equation is a constant function?

    a. $3y - 9 = 0$ **b.** $y^2 - \frac{3}{4} = 0$ **c.** $2x + 3y = \frac{3}{5}$ **d.** $x = -7$

Part 2

22. Carl worked as a mason for three times as many years as his helper Joe. In 7 years, Carl will have twice as much experience as Joe. How many years of experience do Carl and Joe have now?

23. Ann invested her savings in stocks and mutual funds. She tried to maintain a ratio of $3 dollars in stocks for every $2 in mutual funds. If she decided to invest $1800 in mutual funds, how much should she invest in stocks?

24. A car leaves a city at 1 p.m. and travels at a constant rate of 50 miles per hour. Two hours later, another car leaves from the same place and travels over the same route at 60 miles per hour. How long will it take the second car to catch the first car?

25. Kim works in a studio that makes hand-painted toys. Kim's pay varies directly with the number of toys she paints. Last week, she earned $250 by painting 40 toys. How much will she earn by painting 45 toys?

26. The sum of three consecutive odd integers is -45. What are the three integers?

27. Jennifer wants to increase the sales of her greeting cards by 12% next year to $56,000. What are her sales this year?

CHAPTER 5

7 Systems of Sentences

The use of **systems of sentences** is a valuable problem-solving tool for solving problems that involve more than one variable. Such problems may deal with money, mixtures, and distance/rate/time.

7-1 Graphing Systems of Equations

Two or more equations such as

$$x + y = 10 \quad \text{and} \quad x - y = 2$$

form a **system of linear equations** or a system of **simultaneous linear equations.** To solve such a system, you find the ordered pair that makes both equations true. To solve a system of linear equations graphically, graph each equation on the same set of coordinate axes. For two lines that intersect at a point, the coordinates of that point are the **solution** of the system.

EXAMPLE 1 Solve by graphing: $\begin{cases} x + y = 10 \\ x - y = 2 \end{cases}$

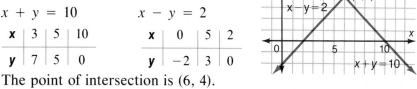

Solution: $x + y = 10$ $x - y = 2$

x	3	5	10
y	7	5	0

x	0	5	2
y	-2	3	0

The point of intersection is (6, 4).

Check: $x + y \overset{?}{=} 10$ $x - y \overset{?}{=} 2$ ⟵ **Check in both equations.**

$6 + 4 \overset{?}{=} 10$ $6 - 4 \overset{?}{=} 2$

$10 \overset{?}{=} 10$ Yes ✔ $2 \overset{?}{=} 2$ Yes ✔   **Solution set:** $\{(6, 4)\}$

The figures below show how the graphs of two linear equations can be related.

Two Intersecting Lines

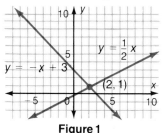

Figure 1

Two Parallel Lines

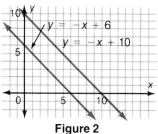

Figure 2

Same Line

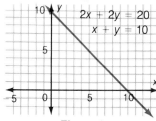

Figure 3

The graphs are *intersecting lines.* Thus, the system has **one solution,** the ordered pair (2, 1).

The graphs are *parallel lines.* (**Parallel lines** are lines that lie in the same plane but have no points in common.) Thus, the system has **no solutions.**

The graphs are the *same line.* (The lines **coincide** or are **coincident.**) **Every point on the line is a solution;** there are an **infinite number of solutions.**

Intersecting lines have *different slopes* and the *same, or different, y intercepts*. (See Figure 1.) Parallel lines have the *same slope* and *different y intercepts*. (See Figure 2.) Coincident lines have the *same slope* and the *same y intercept*. (See Figure 3.)

Thus, to determine whether a system of linear equations has one, none, or an infinite number of solutions, examine the slope and y intercept of each line.

EXAMPLE 2   Determine the number of solutions for each system.

a. $\begin{cases} y = \frac{1}{3}x + 7 \\ y = 2x - 5 \end{cases}$
b. $\begin{cases} y + x = 5 \\ 3x = 15 - 3y \end{cases}$
c. $\begin{cases} y = 2x - 5 \\ y = 2x + 10 \end{cases}$

Solutions: a. The slopes, $\frac{1}{3}$ and 2, are different. The y intercepts, 7 and -5, are different. Thus, the graphs are intersecting lines and there is **one solution.**

b. Write each equation in the form $y = mx + b$.

$\begin{cases} y = -x + 5 \\ y = -x + 5 \end{cases}$ ⟵ **Same equation**

Since the slopes are the same and the y intercepts are the same, the graphs coincide. Every point on the graph is a solution and there are an **infinite number of solutions.**

c. The slopes, 2 and 2, are the same. The y intercepts, -5 and 10, are different. Thus, the graphs are parallel lines, and there are **no solutions.**

This table summarizes how to determine the number of solutions for a system of two linear equations.

Graphs of the Equations		Number of Solutions	Graph of the System
Slopes	y intercepts		
Different	Same or different	One	Two intersecting lines
Same	Different	None	Two parallel lines
Same	Same	Infinitely many	Same line

A system of equations having no solutions is called an **inconsistent system.** Systems that have solutions are called **consistent systems.**

EXERCISES: Classwork/Homework

Objective: To solve systems of equations by graphing

Complete.

1. When the graphs of two linear equations in a system of equations are the same line, the system has __?__ solutions.

2. When the graphs of two linear equations in a system of equations are __?__ lines, the system has one solution.

3. When the graphs of two linear equations in a system of equations are __?__ lines, the system has no solutions.

4. When the linear equations in a system of equations have different slopes and different y intercepts, the system has __?__ solution.

Complete the tables for each exercise. Give the point of intersection of each pair of equations.

5. $x + y = 5$

x	0	1	2	3	4
y	?	?	?	?	?

$x - y = 3$

x	0	1	2	3	4
y	?	?	?	?	?

6. $2x - y = 7$

x	-1	0	1	2	3	4
y	?	?	?	?	?	?

$x + 2y = 6$

x	-1	0	1	2	3	4
y	?	?	?	?	?	?

Determine whether the ordered pair (3, 7) is a solution of each system.

7. $\begin{cases} x + y = 4 \\ x - y = 10 \end{cases}$

8. $\begin{cases} y - x = 4 \\ y + x = 10 \end{cases}$

9. $\begin{cases} x + y = -4 \\ x - y = -10 \end{cases}$

Determine whether each system graphed below has one solution, an infinite number of solutions, or no solution.

10.
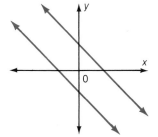

11.
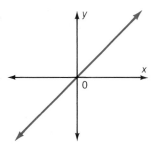

12.
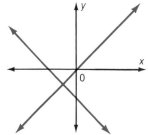

Determine the number of solutions for each system.

13. $\begin{cases} y = 3x + 7 \\ y = 2x - 5 \end{cases}$

14. $\begin{cases} y = 5x + 1 \\ y = 5x - 3 \end{cases}$

15. $\begin{cases} 2y = 8 - 7x \\ 4y = 16 - 14x \end{cases}$

Read the solution set of each system of equations from its graph. Check by substituting in both equations.

16. $\begin{cases} x + y = 10 \\ x - y = 4 \end{cases}$

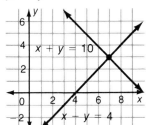

17. $\begin{cases} 2x - y = 3 \\ 4x + y = 9 \end{cases}$

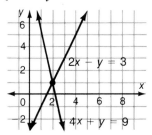

18. $\begin{cases} x + 2y = 4 \\ 2x - y = 8 \end{cases}$

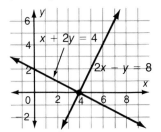

19. $\begin{cases} 2x + y = 3 \\ x - 3y = 5 \end{cases}$

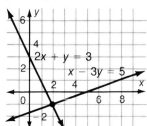

20. $\begin{cases} x + y = 6 \\ x = 5 \end{cases}$

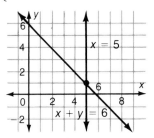

21. $\begin{cases} x = -3 \\ y = 2 \end{cases}$

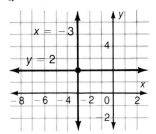

Solve each system by graphing. Check your solutions.

22. $\begin{cases} x + y = 6 \\ x - y = 4 \end{cases}$

23. $\begin{cases} x - y = 5 \\ x + y = 7 \end{cases}$

24. $\begin{cases} x + y = 4 \\ y - x = 2 \end{cases}$

25. $\begin{cases} x - y = 9 \\ 2x + y = 6 \end{cases}$

26. $\begin{cases} x + y = 2 \\ 2y - x = 10 \end{cases}$

27. $\begin{cases} 3x + y = 6 \\ x - 2y = 2 \end{cases}$

28. $\begin{cases} 2x - y = 10 \\ x + 2y = -5 \end{cases}$

29. $\begin{cases} 3x + y = 3 \\ x - 4y = 1 \end{cases}$

30. $\begin{cases} x - 5y = -14 \\ 3x + y = 6 \end{cases}$

31. $\begin{cases} 3x + 2y = 4 \\ 2x - 3y = 7 \end{cases}$

32. $\begin{cases} y = -x + 5 \\ y = \frac{1}{3}x + 1 \end{cases}$

33. $\begin{cases} x + 4y = -5 \\ 3x + y = -4 \end{cases}$

For Exercises 34–51, write *one*, *none*, or *infinitely many* to describe the number of solutions for each system.

34. $\begin{cases} y = -3x + 7 \\ y = -3x + 5 \end{cases}$

35. $\begin{cases} y = 3x + 7 \\ y = -3x + 5 \end{cases}$

36. $\begin{cases} y = 7 - 3x \\ 2y + 6x = 14 \end{cases}$

37. $\begin{cases} y = -x + 10 \\ y = -x + 4 \end{cases}$

38. $\begin{cases} y = x + 10 \\ y = x - 1 \end{cases}$

39. $\begin{cases} y = -x \\ y = -x + 1 \end{cases}$

40. $\begin{cases} 4x + 4y = 7 \\ x + y = \frac{7}{4} \end{cases}$

41. $\begin{cases} y = -2x + 2 \\ y = -2x \end{cases}$

42. $\begin{cases} y = 2x - 8 \\ y = 2x + 10 \end{cases}$

43. $\begin{cases} y = 5 \\ y = -1 \end{cases}$

44. $\begin{cases} y - 9 = 0 \\ y + 1 = 0 \end{cases}$

45. $\begin{cases} y - 3x = 0 \\ 5y - 15x = 0 \end{cases}$

46. $\begin{cases} x + y = 9 \\ x - y = 9 \end{cases}$

47. $\begin{cases} y = 2x - 8 \\ 2x - y = 10 \end{cases}$

48. $\begin{cases} y = -4x + 5 \\ 8x + 2y = 10 \end{cases}$

49. $\begin{cases} x = y + 5 \\ 2x - 2y = 7 \end{cases}$

50. $\begin{cases} y = 4x - 2 \\ x - 4y = 2 \end{cases}$

51. $\begin{cases} 2\frac{1}{2}x - 4 = 3y \\ 6y + 8 = 5x \end{cases}$

The Q Street Flea Market charges $1 per hour to rent a display area. Residents of Q Street pay no base fee. Town residents, not from Q Street, pay a base fee of $2.00. Out-of-town residents pay a base fee of $5.00.

Use this information and the figure at the right in Exercises 52–54.

52. On the same set of coordinate axes, draw graphs showing the rental fees for residents of Q Street, town residents, and out-of-town residents for 1 to 12 hours.

53. How are the slopes of the graphs related?

54. Use the graphs to determine how much more it costs an out-of-town person than a Q Street resident to rent a display area for 8 hours.

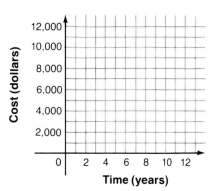

Suppose that the cost of using solar energy to heat a home involves an initial cost of $10,000 with an average yearly cost of $200 for every year after the first. Suppose also that heating with oil involves an initial cost of $4000 with an average yearly cost of $800 for every year after the first.

Use this information and the figure at the right in Exercises 55–58.

55. On the same coordinate axes, draw graphs showing yearly costs for heating with solar energy and oil for 12 years.

56. Which graph has the greater slope?

57. For how many years does it cost less to heat with oil than with solar energy? (Include the initial costs.)

58. How many years does it take for the costs to be equal? (Include the initial costs.)

Solve each problem. *(Pages 232–234)*

59. On a scale drawing, 2 centimeters represent 30 meters. How many meters will 7 centimeters represent?

60. Operating costs for driving a car 10,000 miles per year total $3500. At the same rate, how much will it cost to drive the car 15,204 miles?

In Exercises 61–63, write the set of ordered pairs for each relation. Then give the domain and range for each relation. *(Pages 180–185)*

61.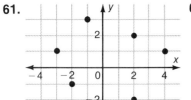

62.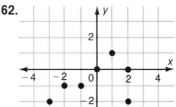

63.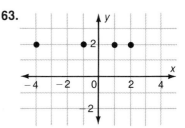

■■■■ **CONNECT AND EXTEND**

A supermarket offers two plans for renting a floor polisher. Under Plan A, the charge is $5 per hour. Under Plan B, there is a basic fee of $6 and an additional charge of $2 per hour.

Use this information in Exercises 64–68.

64. On the same set of coordinate axes, draw a graph showing rental costs under each plan for 0 to 6 hours.

65. When will the costs for both plans be the same?

66. When will it cost less to use Plan A?   **67.** When will it cost less to use Plan B?

68. For which plan do costs increase the fastest for $t > 2$?

Write *one*, *none*, or *infinitely many* to describe the number of solutions for each system.

69. $\begin{cases} Ax + By = C \\ Ax + By = D, C \neq D \end{cases}$

70. $\begin{cases} Ax + By = C \\ NAx + NBy = NC, N \neq 0 \end{cases}$

71. $\begin{cases} Ax + By = C \\ Ax - By = C, B \neq 0 \end{cases}$

■■■■ **NON-ROUTINE PROBLEMS**

72. Draw a circle. Then divide the interior of the circle into seven regions, drawing just 3 straight lines.

73. Find the greatest four-digit number that is divisible by 1, 2, 3, and 4.

Solve each equation for *x* in terms of *y*. (*Pages 159–162*)

1. $2x + 4y = 6$ **2.** $-x + 3y = 7$ **3.** $3x + 5y = 9$ **4.** $2y - x = 1$

5. $y = 3 - x$ **6.** $y = \frac{1}{3}x$ **7.** $y - x = -3$ **8.** $-12x = 7y$

7-2   Substitution Method

One way of solving a system of two linear equations is the **substitution method.** First you solve one of the equations for one of the variables. Then you substitute the value of this variable in the other equation.

EXAMPLE   Solve by the substitution method: $\begin{cases} -x + 2y = 4 & \mathbf{1} \\ 5x - 3y = 1 & \mathbf{2} \end{cases}$

Solution: Since the *x* term in Equation **1** has a coefficient of -1, it will probably be simpler to solve this equation for *x*.

$-x + 2y = 4$ **1**

$\qquad -x = 4 - 2y$ ⟵ ——— **Multiply each side by (-1).**

$\qquad\quad x = 2y - 4$

$\qquad 5x - 3y = 1$ **2** ⟵ ——— **Replace x with (2y − 4).**

$5(2y - 4) - 3y = 1$ ⟵ ——— **Solve for y.**

$10y - 20 - 3y = 1$

$\qquad\qquad\quad 7y = 21$

$\qquad\qquad\quad\ y = 3$ **3** ⟵ ——— **Replace y with 3 in Equation 1.**

$\qquad -x + 2y = 4$ **1**

$\qquad -x + 2(3) = 4$

$\qquad\qquad\quad x = 2$ **4**

Check: $-x + 2y \overset{?}{=} 4$ $5x - 3y \overset{?}{=} 1$

$\qquad -2 + 2(3) \overset{?}{=} 4$ $5(2) - 3(3) \overset{?}{=} 1$

$\qquad\quad -2 + 6 \overset{?}{=} 4$ $10 - 9 \overset{?}{=} 1$

$\qquad\qquad\quad 4 \overset{?}{=} 4$ Yes ✔ $1 \overset{?}{=} 1$ Yes ✔ **Solution set:** $\{(2, 3)\}$

EQUIVALENT SYSTEMS   It is most convenient to use the substitution method when the coefficient of one of the variables is 1 or -1. In solving a system of equations by the substitution method, you find an *equivalent system* from which you can read the solution directly. **Equivalent systems** have the same solution set.

Thus, in the Example,

the system $\begin{cases} -x + 2y = 4 \\ 5x - 3y = 1 \end{cases}$ is equivalent to the system $\begin{cases} x = 2 \\ y = 3 \end{cases}$.

The following summarizes the steps for solving a system of two linear equations by the substitution method.

SUMMARY

To solve a system of two linear equations by the substitution method:

1. Solve one equation for one of the variables.
2. Substitute the resulting expression in the other equation.
3. Solve the resulting equation.
4. Find the values of the variables.
5. Check the solution in both equations of the system.

EXERCISES: Classwork/Homework

Objective: To solve systems of equations using the substitution method

CHECK YOUR UNDERSTANDING

1. In the substitution method, first you solve one of the equations of the system for one variable in terms of the second variable. What is the next step in solving the system?

2. These systems of equations are equivalent.

$\begin{cases} x = 4 \\ 2x + y = 10 \end{cases}$ $\begin{cases} 2y - 3x = -8 \\ y = 2 \end{cases}$

What is the solution set of the two systems?

Evaluate each expression.

3. $2x - 5y$ for $x = y - 2$

4. $5x + 3y$ for $y = x + 3$

5. $2c + 3d$ for $c = d + 1$

6. $8a - b$ for $b = 2a - 5$

Determine the solution set of each system.

7. $\begin{cases} 3x + y = 5 \\ x = 1 \end{cases}$

8. $\begin{cases} b = 4 \\ a - b = 7 \end{cases}$

9. $\begin{cases} 2p - q = 2 \\ p = -1 \end{cases}$

10. $\begin{cases} 3x - 2y = 7 \\ -y = 1 \end{cases}$

11. $\begin{cases} p + 2r = -1 \\ p = 5 \end{cases}$

12. $\begin{cases} s - t = -5 \\ -t = 3 \end{cases}$

For Exercises 13–33, use the substitution method to solve each system.

13. $\begin{cases} x = y + 4 \\ 2x - 5y = 2 \end{cases}$

14. $\begin{cases} y = 3 - x \\ 5x + 3y = -1 \end{cases}$

15. $\begin{cases} x = 8y \\ x - 4y = 12 \end{cases}$

16. $\begin{cases} 5x - y = 1 \\ 3x + 2y = 13 \end{cases}$

17. $\begin{cases} 5a = b \\ a = 10b + 5 \end{cases}$

18. $\begin{cases} r = 5 - s \\ 2r + 7s = 0 \end{cases}$

19. $\begin{cases} 3x + y = 7 \\ x - y = 1 \end{cases}$

20. $\begin{cases} 4x - y = 7 \\ 5x - 8y = 2 \end{cases}$

21. $\begin{cases} r + s = 3 \\ r - s = 1 \end{cases}$

22. $\begin{cases} 2a + b = 5 \\ 8a - b = 45 \end{cases}$

23. $\begin{cases} p - 3q = 0 \\ 2p - 5q = 4 \end{cases}$

24. $\begin{cases} 5c - 3d + 1 = 0 \\ -c + 3d + 7 = 0 \end{cases}$

25. $\begin{cases} y = 8 - x \\ 4x - 3y = -3 \end{cases}$

26. $\begin{cases} 3x + 2y = 16 \\ 7x + y = 19 \end{cases}$

27. $\begin{cases} c + 2d = 4 \\ 3c - 4d = 7 \end{cases}$

28. $\begin{cases} 2r + s = 11 \\ r - s = 2 \end{cases}$

29. $\begin{cases} 4x - 2y = 3 \\ 3x - y = 4 \end{cases}$

30. $\begin{cases} 5a - b = -9 \\ 4a + 3b = -11 \end{cases}$

31. $\begin{cases} 4a + b - 8 = 0 \\ 5a + 3b - 3 = 0 \end{cases}$

32. $\begin{cases} 2u - r + 2 = 0 \\ 6u + 12r - 1 = 0 \end{cases}$

33. $\begin{cases} 4s + 3t - 1 = 0 \\ 8s + 6t - 2 = 0 \end{cases}$

Solve each problem. (*Pages 232–234*)

34. The distance, d, a bicycle travels varies directly as the number of revolutions, n, made by the wheels. Jason's bicycle travels 21 feet when the wheels make 3 revolutions. How many feet will it travel when the wheels make 10 revolutions?

35. A furniture salesperson makes a commission of $600 on sales of $12,000. At the same rate, how much could the salesperson expect to make on a sale of $15,000?

Determine whether each relation is also a function. When a relation is not a function, state why it is not. (*Pages 180–185*)

36. $\{(4, 0), (0, 2), (0, -1)\}$

37. $\{(-3, 1), (-2, -1), (-1, 1), (0, -1)\}$

38. $\{(0.1, 2), (0.2, 3), (0.3, 4)\}$

39. $\{(1, 1), (-1, 1), (-1, -1), (1, -1)\}$

Solve each system. Solve for x and y in terms of the other variables.

40. $\begin{cases} 6x - 4y = 2d \\ x - y + d = 0 \end{cases}$

41. $\begin{cases} 3x = y + h \\ 5x = 3y + 7h \end{cases}$

42. $\begin{cases} 5x - 3y = -2a \\ 2x + 5y = 24a \end{cases}$

43. $\begin{cases} 8x - 3y = -2c \\ x - y - c = 0 \end{cases}$

44. $\begin{cases} 2y = x + b \\ 3y = 2x - 6b \end{cases}$

45. $\begin{cases} 8x - 4y = -4a \\ 4x + 2y = 14a \end{cases}$

7-3 Addition Method

When you add the left sides of the two equations of a system and then add the right sides, the resulting **sum equation** will have the same solution set as the original system. For example, for

$$\begin{cases} x = 5 \\ y = 2 \end{cases}$$

the sum equation is $x + y = 7$.

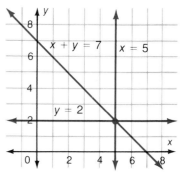

LINEAR COMBINATION

The equation $x + y = 7$ is a **linear combination** of the equations $x = 5$ and $y = 2$.

The graph shows that the ordered pair (5, 2) is a solution of each original equation and of the linear combination. Thus, any of the systems shown below are equivalent to the original system.

$$\begin{cases} x = 5 \\ y = 2 \end{cases} \qquad \begin{cases} x = 5 \\ x + y = 7 \end{cases} \qquad \begin{cases} y = 2 \\ x + y = 7 \end{cases} \longleftarrow \text{ Equivalent systems}$$

Example 1 shows how to use the **addition method** to solve systems of linear equations. The addition method is useful when the coefficients of either the x terms or of the y terms are additive inverses.

EXAMPLE 1 Solve by the addition method: $\begin{cases} 3x + y = 10 & 1 \\ 2x - y = 5 & 2 \end{cases}$

Solution: Since the coefficients of the y terms are additive inverses, adding the corresponding sides of the equations will eliminate the y terms.

$$\begin{array}{ll} 3x + y = 10 & 1 \\ \underline{2x - y = \ \ 5} & 2 \\ 5x \quad\ \ = 15 & \\ \qquad x = 3 & 3 \end{array} \longleftarrow \begin{array}{l} \textbf{Substitute } x = 3 \textbf{ in Equation 1} \\ \textbf{or in Equation 2.} \end{array}$$

$$\begin{array}{ll} 3x + y = 10 & 1 \\ 3(3) + y = 10 & \\ \qquad y = 1 & 1 \end{array}$$

Check:

$$\begin{array}{cc} 3x + y \overset{?}{=} 10 & 2x - y \overset{?}{=} 5 \\ 3(3) + 1 \overset{?}{=} 10 & 2(3) - 1 \overset{?}{=} 5 \\ 9 + 1 \overset{?}{=} 10 & 6 - 1 \overset{?}{=} 5 \\ 10 \overset{?}{=} 10 \quad \text{Yes} \ \checkmark & 5 \overset{?}{=} 5 \quad \text{Yes} \ \checkmark \quad \textbf{Solution set: } \{(3, 1)\} \end{array}$$

The variables in equations are not always x and y.

EXAMPLE 2 Solve by the addition method: $\begin{cases} p + q = 4 & 1 \\ -p + q = 7 & 2 \end{cases}$

Solution:

$$p + q = 4 \qquad 1$$
$$\underline{-p + q = 7} \qquad 2 \qquad \longleftarrow \text{ Add to eliminate } p.$$
$$2q = 11$$
$$q = 5\tfrac{1}{2} \qquad 3 \qquad \longleftarrow \begin{array}{l}\text{Substitute in Equation 1} \\ \text{or Equation 2.}\end{array}$$
$$p + q = 4 \qquad 1$$
$$p + 5\tfrac{1}{2} = 4$$
$$p = -1\tfrac{1}{2} \qquad 4$$

Solution set: $\{(-1\tfrac{1}{2}, 5\tfrac{1}{2})\}$ The check is left for you.

NOTE: It is customary to give the solution(s) of the system in the alphabetical order of the variables involved. In Example 2, the variables used were p and q. Thus, the solution is given as $(-1\tfrac{1}{2}, 5\tfrac{1}{2})$.

The following summarizes the steps for solving a system of two linear equations by the addition method.

SUMMARY

To solve a system of two linear equations by the addition method:

1. Add to eliminate one of the variables. Solve the resulting equation.

2. Substitute the known value of one variable in one of the original equations of the system. Solve for the other variable.

3. Check the solution in both equations of the system.

EXERCISES: Classwork/Homework

Objective: To solve systems of equations by the addition method

CHECK YOUR UNDERSTANDING

Determine which variable in each system would be easier to eliminate by the addition method.

1. $\begin{cases} x + 2y = 3 \\ -x + y = -2 \end{cases}$ **2.** $\begin{cases} 2x - 3y = -2 \\ x + 3y = 4 \end{cases}$ **3.** $\begin{cases} -2x + 3y = 7 \\ 2x - 5y = -3 \end{cases}$ **4.** $\begin{cases} x + 4y = 7 \\ 2x - 4y = -3 \end{cases}$

Write the sum equation for each system.

5. $\begin{cases} x = -2 \\ y = 3 \end{cases}$
6. $\begin{cases} x + y = 7 \\ x - y = 2 \end{cases}$
7. $\begin{cases} p + q = \frac{1}{2} \\ -p + q = -\frac{3}{2} \end{cases}$
8. $\begin{cases} -r + s = 6 \\ r + s = 2 \end{cases}$

▮▮▮▮▮▮ PRACTICE AND APPLY

Use the addition method to solve each system.

9. $\begin{cases} x - y = 4 \\ x + y = 2 \end{cases}$
10. $\begin{cases} 2x + y = 7 \\ 3x - y = 3 \end{cases}$
11. $\begin{cases} y - 4x = 8 \\ y + 4x = 0 \end{cases}$

12. $\begin{cases} a + 5b = 10 \\ -a + 4b = 8 \end{cases}$
13. $\begin{cases} y = 3x + 6 \\ 2y = -3x + 3 \end{cases}$
14. $\begin{cases} 3y = -7x + 7 \\ 2y = 7x - 7 \end{cases}$

15. $\begin{cases} 2t + 3n = 9 \\ 5t - 3n = 5 \end{cases}$
16. $\begin{cases} -7c - 8d = 8 \\ 7c - 8d = 8 \end{cases}$
17. $\begin{cases} y = 2x - 4 \\ y = -2x + 3 \end{cases}$

18. $\begin{cases} c + d = 12 \\ -d = 8 \end{cases}$
19. $\begin{cases} x - y = 8 \\ y = 7 \end{cases}$
20. $\begin{cases} x - y = 2\frac{1}{2} \\ y = 4 \end{cases}$

21. $\begin{cases} x - 2y = 2\frac{1}{2} \\ x + 2y = 3 \end{cases}$
22. $\begin{cases} x + 3y = 9 \\ -x + 2y = 6 \end{cases}$
23. $\begin{cases} 2x - 3y = 8 \\ 2x + 3y = 4 \end{cases}$

24. $\begin{cases} 7x + 3y = 19 \\ 4x - 3y = 3 \end{cases}$
25. $\begin{cases} -6x + 3y = 5 \\ 6x - 5y = 7 \end{cases}$
26. $\begin{cases} 7a + 6b = 0 \\ 15a - 6b = 0 \end{cases}$

27. $\begin{cases} \frac{1}{2}x + y = 9 \\ \frac{3}{4}x - y = 0 \end{cases}$
28. $\begin{cases} 0.4x + y = 1.2 \\ 0.6x - y = 3.9 \end{cases}$
29. $\begin{cases} \frac{3}{4}x - \frac{1}{2}y = 4 \\ \frac{1}{4}x + \frac{1}{2}y = 2\frac{1}{2} \end{cases}$

30. $\begin{cases} 0.1x - 0.01y = 0.1 \\ 0.3x + 0.01y = 0.3 \end{cases}$
31. $\begin{cases} 5\frac{1}{2}x - y = 8 \\ 3\frac{1}{2}x + y = 1 \end{cases}$
32. $\begin{cases} a - b = -1 \\ -a - b = 1 \end{cases}$

33. $\begin{cases} t - w = -1 \\ t + w = 1 \end{cases}$
34. $\begin{cases} 7\frac{2}{3}x - 3y = 29 \\ 1\frac{2}{3}x + 3y = -11 \end{cases}$
35. $\begin{cases} 0.6x - 0.02y = -2.6 \\ -0.6x + 0.13y = -2.9 \end{cases}$

▮▮▮▮▮▮ MAINTAIN

Use the substitution method to solve each system.
(Pages 249–251)

36. $\begin{cases} y = x - 4 \\ 2x - 5y = 2 \end{cases}$
37. $\begin{cases} y = -x + 2 \\ 2x - y = 1 \end{cases}$
38. $\begin{cases} x - y = 4 \\ 2x - 3y = -2 \end{cases}$

39. $\begin{cases} x - y = 3 \\ 5x + y = -13 \end{cases}$
40. $\begin{cases} x - 2y = -2 \\ 2x - 3y = 2 \end{cases}$
41. $\begin{cases} 2x + y = 5 \\ 8x - y = 45 \end{cases}$

Read the solution set of each system of equations from its graph. Check by substituting in both equations. (*Pages 243–248*)

42. $\begin{cases} 3x + y = -7 \\ y = \frac{1}{2}x \end{cases}$

43. $\begin{cases} y = -x \\ x - 4y = -5 \end{cases}$

44. $\begin{cases} x = -1\frac{1}{2} \\ y = 2 \end{cases}$

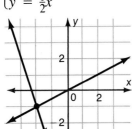

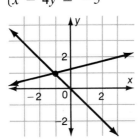

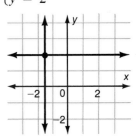

Graph each linear equation in the coordinate plane. (*Pages 186–190*)

45. $x + y = 2$　　　**46.** $x - 2y = 0$　　　**47.** $y = 2x + 3$　　　**48.** $x = -5$

▥ CONNECT AND EXTEND

In Exercises 49–51, solve each system for x and y.

49. $\begin{cases} x + y = c + d \\ x - y = c - d \end{cases}$

50. $\begin{cases} x + y = a \\ x - y = b \end{cases}$

51. $\begin{cases} 3x + 2y = 3a \\ -3x + y = -3 \end{cases}$

52. This system has no solutions.

$$\begin{cases} x - 2y = 5 \\ -x + 2y = 7 \end{cases}$$

Explain what happens when you try to solve the system by using the addition method.

53. This system has an infinite number of solutions.

$$\begin{cases} -2x + y = 3 \\ 2x - y = -3 \end{cases}$$

Explain what happens when you try to solve the system by using the addition method.

▥ NON-ROUTINE PROBLEMS

54. Three bananas were given to two mothers who were with their daughters. Each person had a banana to eat. How is this possible?

55. Frank had 3 piles of leaves in the front yard and 2 piles in the back yard. If he put them all together, how many piles would he have?

———— **REVIEW CAPSULE FOR SECTION 7–4** ————

Multiply. (*Pages 149–151*)

1. $2(3x - 2y)$　　　**2.** $-3(6a + b)$　　　**3.** $-1(2w - 2s)$　　　**4.** $-1(r + 3t)$

5. $-1(-v + 7q)$　　　**6.** $-1(7q - 9)$　　　**7.** $-\frac{1}{2}(4r - 6p)$　　　**8.** $-9(\frac{1}{9}s - t)$

7-4 Using Multiplication with the Addition Method

Adding the corresponding sides of the two equations in a linear system *does not always eliminate* one of the variables. To obtain a sum equation having a single variable in such cases, multiply each side of one or both equations of the system by a number or numbers, so that, after multiplying, the coefficients of one of the variables will be additive inverses.

EXAMPLE 1 Solve: $\begin{cases} 3x + y = 10 & \quad 1 \\ 2x + y = 15 & \quad 2 \end{cases}$

Solution: Multiply each side of Equation **1** by -1.

$$\begin{array}{rl} -3x - y = -10 & \quad 1 \\ \underline{2x + y = \quad 15} & \quad 2 \\ -x \quad = \quad 5 & \end{array}$$

← **Now the coefficients of the *y* terms are additive inverses.**

$$x = -5 \qquad 3$$

← **Substitute *x* = −5 in Equation 1 or in Equation 2.**

$$2x + y = 15 \qquad 2$$
$$2(-5) + y = 15$$
$$y = 25 \qquad 4$$

← **The check is left for you.**

Solution set: $\{(-5, 25)\}$

Sometimes it is necessary to multiply Equation **1** by one number and to multiply Equation **2** by another number.

EXAMPLE 2 Solve: $\begin{cases} 2x + 3y = -1 & \quad 1 \\ 5x - 2y = -12 & \quad 2 \end{cases}$

Solution: Multiply each side of Equation **1** by 2 and multiply each side of Equation **2** by 3. Then *the y terms will be additive inverses* of each other.

$$\begin{array}{rl} 4x + 6y = -2 & \quad 1 \\ \underline{15x - 6y = -36} & \quad 2 \\ 19x \quad = -38 & \end{array}$$

← **2(2x + 3y) = 2(−1)**
← **3(5x − 2y) = 3(−12)**

$$x = -2 \qquad 3$$

← **Substitute *x* = −2 in Equation 1.**

$$2x + 3y = -1 \qquad 1$$
$$2(-2) + 3y = -1$$
$$3y = 3$$
$$y = 1 \qquad 4 \longleftarrow \quad \textbf{The check is left for you.}$$

Solution set: $\{(-2, 1)\}$

The following summarizes the steps.

SUMMARY

> **To solve a system of two linear equations using multiplication with addition:**
>
> **1** Multiply each side of one of the equations by a number, and, if necessary, multiply each side of the second equation by another number. Choose the two numbers so that, after multiplying, the coefficients of one of the variables will be additive inverses of each other.
>
> **2** Use the addition method to solve the new system.
>
> **3** Check the solution set in both equations of the system.

EXERCISES: Classwork/Homework

Objective: To solve systems of equations using multiplication with the addition method

■■■■■■■ CHECK YOUR UNDERSTANDING

Determine the number by which you could multiply *one* equation in each pair in order to eliminate one of the variables.

1. $\begin{cases} 5x + 2y = 14 & 1 \\ 4x - y = 6 & 2 \end{cases}$
2. $\begin{cases} 2p + 3q = 1 & 1 \\ 3p - q = 18 & 2 \end{cases}$
3. $\begin{cases} 9a - 3b = 3 & 1 \\ a + 5b = 11 & 2 \end{cases}$

Determine the number by which each of the equations in <u>a</u> has been multiplied in order to obtain the corresponding equation in <u>b</u>.

	a	b		a	b

4. $\begin{cases} 3x - 2y = -4 & 1 \\ -5x + 3y = -1 & 2 \end{cases}$ $\begin{cases} 15x - 10y = -20 & 1 \\ -15x + 9y = -3 & 2 \end{cases}$
5. $\begin{cases} 3x - 2y = -9 & 1 \\ 3x - 5y = -10 & 2 \end{cases}$ $\begin{cases} 15x - 10y = -45 & 1 \\ -6x + 10y = 20 & 2 \end{cases}$

6. $\begin{cases} 3r + 7t = 22 & 1 \\ 2r - 8t = 2 & 2 \end{cases}$ $\begin{cases} 6r + 14t = 44 & 1 \\ -6r + 24t = -6 & 2 \end{cases}$
7. $\begin{cases} 5p + 3q = 17 & 1 \\ 4p - 5q = 21 & 2 \end{cases}$ $\begin{cases} 25p + 15q = 85 & 1 \\ 12p - 15q = 63 & 2 \end{cases}$

Solve each system.

8. $\begin{cases} 3x + y = 9 \\ 2x + y = 1 \end{cases}$

9. $\begin{cases} 3x + y = 10 \\ 2x + y = 7 \end{cases}$

10. $\begin{cases} 5r - s = -23 \\ 3r - s = -15 \end{cases}$

11. $\begin{cases} 2a + 3b = -5 \\ 5a + 3b = 1 \end{cases}$

12. $\begin{cases} 3x + 2y = -7 \\ 5x - 2y = -1 \end{cases}$

13. $\begin{cases} x + 3y = 14 \\ x - 2y = -1 \end{cases}$

14. $\begin{cases} 2t + 3v = 6 \\ 2t - 5v = 22 \end{cases}$

15. $\begin{cases} 2x + 3y = 8 \\ 3x + y = 5 \end{cases}$

16. $\begin{cases} 2x + y = 3 \\ 7x - 4y = 18 \end{cases}$

17. $\begin{cases} 5x + y = 15 \\ 3x + 2y = 9 \end{cases}$

18. $\begin{cases} 7r - 5t = -2 \\ -8r - t = 9 \end{cases}$

19. $\begin{cases} 4p - 2q = 20 \\ p + 5q = -17 \end{cases}$

20. $\begin{cases} 2a + 5b = 18 \\ -5a + b = -18 \end{cases}$

21. $\begin{cases} 2u + 2z = 8 \\ 5u - 3z = 4 \end{cases}$

22. $\begin{cases} 4a + 3b = -2 \\ 8a - 2b = 12 \end{cases}$

23. $\begin{cases} 2x - 5y = 7 \\ 3x - 2y = -17 \end{cases}$

24. $\begin{cases} 9c + 7d = 14 \\ -6c - d = -2 \end{cases}$

25. $\begin{cases} 4r + 3s = 7 \\ 4r + 4s = 12 \end{cases}$

26. $\begin{cases} 4x - 3y - 5 = 0 \\ -2x + 9y + 1 = 0 \end{cases}$

27. $\begin{cases} 5a - 2b - 11 = 0 \\ 3a + 5b - 19 = 0 \end{cases}$

28. $\begin{cases} 6n - 2k + 3 = 0 \\ 2n + 4k - 5 = 0 \end{cases}$

29. $\begin{cases} 9x - 2y = 2\frac{1}{2} \\ 5x - 6y = -3\frac{1}{2} \end{cases}$

30. $\begin{cases} 3x + 5y = 4\frac{1}{2} \\ -9x - 2y = -7 \end{cases}$

31. $\begin{cases} 8x + 6y = 10 \\ -4x + 3y = -1 \end{cases}$

32. $\begin{cases} 5x + 4y = -\frac{1}{3} \\ 7x + 2y = \frac{4}{3} \end{cases}$

33. $\begin{cases} 2x - 3y = 9.4 \\ -5x + 9y = -12.4 \end{cases}$

34. $\begin{cases} x + 3y = 17.3 \\ 2x - 7y = -36.9 \end{cases}$

35. $\begin{cases} 2r - 7t = 8 \\ 4r - 9t = 19 \end{cases}$

36. $\begin{cases} 4c - 6d = 8 \\ -9c - 6d = -96 \end{cases}$

37. $\begin{cases} 2w - 3q = 8 \\ 3w - 7q = 7 \end{cases}$

What values of r and s will eliminate the y term?

38. $r(-2x + y - 5) + s(x + 3y - 1) = 0$

39. $r(2x + 3y - 3) + s(3x - 5y + 2) = 0$

40. $r(3x + 4y - 10) + s(2x - y + 8) = 0$

41. $r(3x + 2y - 2) + s(2x + 3y + 2) = 0$

You can use the program on page 614 to solve systems of two linear equations in two variables.

Use the program to solve the following systems.

42. $\begin{cases} 3x = 2y + 8 \\ 5y = 4x - 6 \end{cases}$

43. $\begin{cases} y = 5x + 1 \\ x - 2y + 6 = 0 \end{cases}$

44. $\begin{cases} x = y + 6 \\ 4y + 4x = 15 \end{cases}$

Use the substitution method to solve each system. (*Pages 249–251*)

45. $\begin{cases} x - y = 4 \\ 2x - 3y = -2 \end{cases}$

46. $\begin{cases} x - y = 3 \\ 5x + y = -15 \end{cases}$

47. $\begin{cases} 2x + y = 1 \\ 5x + 2y = 4 \end{cases}$

Sound travels in air at a rate of about 350 meters per second. That is, $d = 350t$, where t is the time in seconds and d is the distance in meters. Use this function in Exercises 48–49. (*Pages 194–197*)

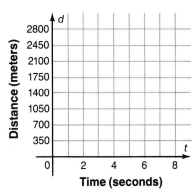

48. Write three ordered pairs for this function. Let $t = 0$, 3, and 6.

49. Use the ordered pairs in Exercise 48 to graph the function.

Use the graph in Exercise 49 to estimate the distance sound would travel for each time, t.

50. $t = 2$ seconds   **51.** $t = 7$ seconds   **52.** $t = 4.5$ seconds   **53.** $t = 8$ seconds

■■■■■■ **CONNECT AND EXTEND**

Solve each system.

54. $\begin{cases} 2x + 1.5y = -1 \\ 0.5x + 2y = 3 \end{cases}$ **55.** $\begin{cases} x - 2.3 = -5y \\ 2x - 2 = 3y \end{cases}$ **56.** $\begin{cases} 2a - 1.5b = 10 \\ 0.3a - 0.05b = 0.8 \end{cases}$

57. $\begin{cases} 2x - 3y = 0.1 \\ 3x - 3 = -5y \end{cases}$ **58.** $\begin{cases} 1.25s + 8.25t = 107.5 \\ 2.5s - t = 0.8 \end{cases}$ **59.** $\begin{cases} 10x + 5y = 3.5 \\ 3y - 0.6 = 3x \end{cases}$

60. Solve the system: $\begin{cases} -3x - y + 10\frac{1}{2} = 0 \\ 6x - 2y - 7 = 0 \end{cases}$

61. Show that for all real numbers f and g, the solution of the system in Exercise 60 is also a solution of
$$f(-3x - y + 10\tfrac{1}{2}) + g(6x - 2y - 7) = 0.$$

——— **REVIEW CAPSULE FOR SECTION 7–5** ———

Choose a variable to represent one unknown and tell what it represents. Then represent the second unknown in terms of the variable. (*Pages 130–134*)

1. Jo invested $2,100 more than Hal.

2. Emily is one-half as old as Roger.

3. Jim has three times as many shirts as he has pants.

4. Suzanne had four more dollars than Joe had.

5. The bookcase is twice as high as it is wide.

6. Cindy owns three fewer pairs of shoes than her mother does.

7. Jose won one more than twice as many games as Rick.

8. The swimming pool is two-thirds as wide as it is long.

Statistics / Making Diagrams

One important task of **statisticians** is to display data so that it can be interpreted more easily. For example, the median and the mode can often be read directly from a **stem-leaf plot**.

The Bright Light Bulb Company conducts tests on the light bulbs it manufactures. Thirty-five sample light bulbs are tested to find the number of hours each one lasts before burning out. The results of one test are shown at the right.

Lifetime of Thirty-six Light Bulbs (to the nearest hour)					
52	81	50	62	71	70
59	53	65	75	76	92
93	77	95	68	83	73
53	88	80	74	57	87
68	73	61	71	66	89
71	79	66	65	88	85

EXAMPLE: Construct a stem-leaf plot for the data in the table.

Solution:

1 Since the smallest entry is 50 and the largest is 95, the **stems** can be the ten's digits, 5 through 9.

Write the stems vertically. Draw a vertical line to the right.

```
5 | 2, 9, 3, 3, 0, 7          ←  5 | 2 represents
6 | 8, 5, 1, 6, 2, 8, 5, 6        the entry 52.
7 | 1, 7, 3, 9, 5, 4, 1, 1, 6, 0, 3
8 | 1, 8, 0, 3, 8, 7, 9, 5
9 | 3, 5, 2
```

The **leaves** are the one's digits of the 36 entries. Write each one's digit to the right of its ten's digit stem.

```
5 | 0, 2, 3, 3, 7, 9
6 | 1, 2, 5, 5, 6, 6, 8, 8
7 | 0, 1, 1, 1, 3, 3, 4, 5, 6, 7, 9
8 | 0, 1, 3, 5, 7, 8, 8, 9
9 | 2, 3, 5
```

2 Rewrite the leaves for each stem in increasing order from left to right. This is an **ordered stem-leaf plot**.

EXERCISES For Exercises 1–2, draw a stem-leaf plot for the given data.

1. **Number of Students on Fifteen School Buses**

40	36	35	28	40
32	35	32	27	25
27	31	40	31	33

2. **Number of Points Scored in Eighteen Basketball Games**

70	57	49	80	74	77
66	52	84	63	76	83
72	64	74	76	66	59

For Exercises 3–6, use the ordered stem-leaf plot in the Example.

3. Find the median of the data.
   (HINT: The mean of the 18th and 19th leaves is $\frac{1+3}{2}$, or 2.)

4. Find the mode of the data.

5. The mean of the data is 72.7 hours.
   a. Which statement would you use if you were in charge of the company's advertising?
   Lasts Up to 95 Hours, or *Lasts an Average of 70 Hours*
   b. Give a reason for your choice.

6. You purchase a Bright Light bulb.
   a. Is it more likely to last 75 hours or 90 hours?
   b. Could it last 105 hours? 45 hours? Explain.

BRIGHT LIGHT
Bulbs

Last Up to 95 Hours

BRIGHT LIGHT
Bulbs

Last an Average
of 70 Hours

A *two-sided stem-leaf plot* can be used to compare two sets of data. The leaves of the second set of data are written to the left of the stems, and they are read from right to left.

Two local movie theaters have both shown the same movie for the past 15 days. The diagram at the right shows each theater's daily attendance for that movie. The *stems* are the hundred's and ten's digits. The *leaves* are the one's digits.

Theater A		Theater B
4, 3, 0	15	
4, 2	16	9
5	17	2, 3, 3, 5, 6, 7
8, 1	18	1, 2, 5, 5, 5, 9
7, 6, 6, 0	19	6, 7
5, 4, 0	20	

0 | 20 represents
the number 200.

7. Find the median and mode for the attendance at Theater A.

8. Find the median and mode for the attendance at Theater B.

9. Which theater had the greater median? the greater mode?

10. Which theater do you think had the greater mean attendance? Find the mean attendance for each theater. Was your guess correct?

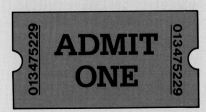

013475229 ADMIT ONE 013475229

Solve each system by graphing. (*Pages 243–248*)

1. $\begin{cases} 2x - y = 8 \\ x + y = 4 \end{cases}$ **2.** $\begin{cases} x + y = 9 \\ x - y = 5 \end{cases}$ **3.** $\begin{cases} 3x = 9 \\ x + y = -1 \end{cases}$

Write *one*, *none*, or *infinitely many* to describe the number of solutions for each system. (*Pages 243–248*)

4. $\begin{cases} y = 3x - 1 \\ y = 5x \end{cases}$ **5.** $\begin{cases} y = 4x - 1 \\ 8x = 2y + 2 \end{cases}$ **6.** $\begin{cases} x = 2y - 4 \\ y = x + 7 \end{cases}$

Use the substitution method to solve each system. (*Pages 249–251*)

7. $\begin{cases} x + y = 10 \\ 3x - 2y = 5 \end{cases}$ **8.** $\begin{cases} 2r + t = 0 \\ 4r - 3t = -10 \end{cases}$ **9.** $\begin{cases} p - 2q = 1 \\ 2p + q = 12 \end{cases}$

10. $\begin{cases} p - 2n = 3 \\ 2p + n = 1 \end{cases}$ **11.** $\begin{cases} 3c + 2d = 0 \\ 2c - d = 7 \end{cases}$ **12.** $\begin{cases} 3a + b - 1 = 0 \\ 2a - 6b - 4 = 0 \end{cases}$

Use the addition method to solve each system. (*Pages 252–255*)

13. $\begin{cases} x + 2y = -4 \\ -x + y = 1 \end{cases}$ **14.** $\begin{cases} 2a - 7b = 41 \\ a + 7b = -32 \end{cases}$ **15.** $\begin{cases} 0.6x + 0.5y = 0 \\ 0.2x - 0.5y = 0.4 \end{cases}$

In Exercises 16–18, use multiplication with the addition method to solve each system (*Pages 256–259*)

16. $\begin{cases} 2x + y = 7 \\ -x + y = 4 \end{cases}$ **17.** $\begin{cases} 4r - 7s = 18 \\ r + 3s = -5 \end{cases}$ **18.** $\begin{cases} 4x + 3y = -2 \\ 3x + 2y = 1 \end{cases}$

Historical Digest: **Ada Lovelace**

Ada Lovelace (1815–1852) was a British mathematician and the first computer programmer. A friend of hers, Charles Babbage, had an idea for a computer that would solve equations. He called this computer the **analytical engine.** Ada Lovelace wrote an explanation of how Babbage's engine could be programmed to solve problems.

The program language developed in 1979 for the U.S. Defense Department was named **Ada** in her honor.

7-5 Using Two Variables to Solve Problems

You can use systems of equations to solve word problems. First, you use Condition 1 to represent the unknowns by two variables. You also use this condition to write one equation of the system. You use Condition 2 to write the second equation for the system.

EXAMPLE   Joe has 6 fewer EE bonds than Art (Condition 1). Twice the number Art has is 5 more than three times the number Joe has (Condition 2). How many EE bonds does each have?

Solution:

1 **Find:** The number of EE bonds Joe and Art each have

Given: Joe has 6 fewer EE bonds than Art. (Condition 1)
Twice the number Art has is 5 more than three times the number Joe has. (Condition 2)

Represent the unknowns: Let x = the number Art has.
Let y = the number Joe has.

2 Write a system of equations to "connect" the conditions.

$$\begin{cases} x - y = 6 & \quad 1 \quad \longleftarrow \quad \text{Condition 1} \\ 2x = 3y + 5 & \quad 2 \quad \longleftarrow \quad \text{Condition 2} \end{cases}$$

3 Solve. Multiply Equation **1** by -3. Write Equation **2** as $2x - 3y = 5$.

$$\begin{array}{rl} -3x + 3y = -18 & \quad 1 \\ \underline{2x - 3y = 5} & \quad 2 \\ -x = -13 & \end{array}$$

$x = 13$ $\longleftarrow$ **Don't forget to find y.**

$x - y = 6$ $\longleftarrow$ **Replace x with 13 in Equation 1.**

$13 - y = 6$

$-y = -7$, so $y = 7$

4 **Check: Condition 1** Does Joe have 6 fewer bonds than Art?
$13 - 7 = 6$?   Yes ✔

Condition 2 Does twice the number Art has equal 5 more than three times the number Joe has? $2 \cdot 13 = 3 \cdot 7 + 5$?   Yes ✔

Art has **13** EE bonds and Joe has **7.**

To solve word problems using a system of equations in two variables:

 1 Use Condition 1 and two variables to represent the unknowns. Write an equation in two variables that expresses Condition 1.

 2 Write a second equation in two variables that expresses Condition 2.

 3 Solve the system of equations.

 4 Check your solution in the original condition of the problem. Answer the question.

EXERCISES: Classwork/Homework

Objective: To solve word problems using systems of equations

CHECK YOUR UNDERSTANDING

Choose two variables to represent the unknowns. Then write an equation to express Condition 1.

1. The sum of two numbers is 16.

2. Two angles have a sum of 90°.

3. The difference between the heights of two boys is 4 centimeters.

4. A service station operator sells twice as much regular as premium gas.

5. A cup of cooked macaroni contains 105 calories more than an ounce of cheese.

6. Amy sold a total of 870 adult and student tickets for the senior class play.

7. The length of a rectangle is twice the width.

8. The perimeter of a rectangular picture frame is 246 centimeters.

PRACTICE AND APPLY

Solve each problem. In some problems, Condition 1 is <u>underscored once</u>. Condition 2 is <u>underscored twice</u>.

9. <u>The sum of two numbers is 52.</u> <u><u>The difference of the same two numbers is 20.</u></u> Find the numbers.

10. <u>One number is 5 more than a second number.</u> <u><u>The sum of the numbers is 115.</u></u> What are the numbers?

11. <u>The width of a rectangle is 6 inches less than the length.</u> <u><u>The perimeter is 72 inches.</u></u> Find the length and the width.

12. The length of a rectangle is 4 feet more than the width. The perimeter is 40 feet. Find the length and width.

13. The distance from St. Louis to Chicago is 111 miles more than the distance from Chicago to Minneapolis. The sum of the two distances is 697 miles. Find the distance from St. Louis to Chicago.

14. The distance by air from New York to London is 545 kilometers more than twice the distance from London to Moscow. The sum of the two distances is 8105 kilometers. Find the distance from New York to London.

15. Two sides of a triangle are equal. Each of the two equal sides is 5 inches more than the third side. The perimeter is 35 inches. Find the length of each side.

16. Each of the two equal sides of a triangle is 1.2 centimeters longer than the third side. The perimeter is 17.4 centimeters. Find the length of each side.

17. Two angles are **supplementary;** that is, the sum of their measures is 180°. The measure of one angle is 30° more than twice the other. What is the measure of each angle?

18. Two angles are **complementary;** that is, the sum of their measures is 90°. The measure of one angle is twice the measure of the other. What is the measure of each angle?

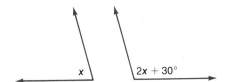

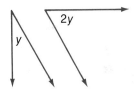

19. Seven times the sum of two numbers is 28. When the second number is multiplied by 3 and added to the first number, the sum equals the second number. Find each number.

20. An oak tree is 20 years older than a pine tree. In eight years, the oak tree will be 3 times as old as the pine tree will be then. Find the present age of each tree.

━━━ **MAINTAIN**

Solve each problem. (*Pages 130–134*)

21. Janet bought skis and ski boots for $175. The boots cost $23 more than the skis. What was the price of the skis?

22. The sale price of a typewriter is $230. The discount rate is 20%. Find the list price and the amount of discount.

7-6   Using Two Variables: Digit Problems

Systems of equations in two variables are particularly useful in solving problems related to numbers and their digits. Suppose that you are asked to represent a two-digit number.

Example: 85

Tens digit: 8

Units digit: 5

Number: $10 \cdot 8 + 5$, or 85

Sum of digits: $8 + 5$

In General: $10t + u$

Tens digit: t

Units digit: u

Number: $10t + u$

Sum of digits: $t + u$

When solving digit problems, be careful to distinguish between representing the *sum of the digits* and representing *the number*.

EXAMPLE   The sum of the digits of a two-digit number is 6 (Condition 1). The number is six times the units digit (Condition 2). Find the number.

Solution: **1** **Find:**   A two-digit number
Given: The sum of the digits is 6.
        The number is 6 times the units digit.

Let t = the tens digit.   Let u = the units digit.
Then $10t + u$ = the number

2 $t + u = 6$ 1 ◀——— **Condition 1**
     $10t + u = 6u$ 2 ◀——— **Condition 2**

3 Combine like terms in Equation **2**.
     $10t - 5u = 0$ 2

To eliminate the variable u, multiply Equation **1** by 5.

$$5t + 5u = 30 \quad 1$$
$$\underline{10t - 5u = 0} \quad 2$$
$$15t = 30$$

$t = 2$ ◀——— **Don't forget to find u.**
$t + u = 6$ ◀——— **Replace t with 2 in Equation 1.**
$2 + u = 6$
$u = 4$ ◀——— **Don't forget to find the number.**

Number: $10t + u = 10 \cdot 2 + 4 = 24$

$\boxed{4}$ **Check:** **Condition 1** Is the sum of the digits equal to 6?

$2 + 4 = 6$? Yes ✔

Condition 2 Is the number six times the units digit?

$24 = 6 \cdot 4$? Yes ✔ The number is **24**.

To represent a three-digit number, let h represent the hundreds digit, t represent the tens digit and u represent the units digit. Then the number is

$$100h + 10t + u. \quad \longleftarrow \quad \textbf{Three-digit number}$$

EXERCISES: Classwork/Homework

Objective: To solve digit problems using systems of equations

CHECK YOUR UNDERSTANDING

1. In the number 72, what is the tens digit? What is the units digit?

2. A two-digit number can be represented as $10t + u$. Why is it incorrect to represent the number as tu?

Write an equation for each sentence. Let t represent the tens digit and let u represent the units digit.

3. The sum of the digits of a two-digit number is 8.

4. A two-digit number is 4 times its units digit.

5. A two-digit number is 9 more than the sum of its digits.

6. The tens digit of a two-digit number is 2 more than the units digit.

7. A two-digit number is twice its units digit.

8. The sum of the digits of a two-digit number is 15.

9. The tens digit of a two-digit number is 5 less than the units digit.

10. The units digit of a two-digit number is 4 more than the tens digit.

For each problem let t represent the tens digit and let u represent the units digit. Write the system of equations you would use to solve the problem.

11. The sum of the digits of a two-digit number is 12. The number is 12 times the tens digit.

12. The sum of the digits of a two-digit number is 9. The number is 6 times the units digit.

13. The units digit of a two-digit number is twice the tens digit. The number is 6 more than 5 times the units digit.

14. The tens digit of a two-digit number is 2 more than the units digit. The number is 5 more than 7 times the tens digit.

Write a system of equations in two variables for each problem. Then solve the problem. For some problems, Condition 1 is <u>underscored once</u>. Condition 2 is <u>underscored twice</u>.

15. <u>The sum of the digits of a two-digit number is 12.</u> <u><u>The number is 12 times the tens digit.</u></u> Find the number.

16. <u>The sum of the digits of a two-digit number is 10.</u> <u><u>The tens digit is 4 more than the units digit.</u></u> Find the number.

17. <u>The units digit of a two-digit number is twice the tens digit.</u> <u><u>The difference between the digits is 4.</u></u> Find the number.

18. The units digit of a two-digit number is 2 less than the tens digit. The number is 2 more than 6 times the sum of the digits. Find the number.

19. The units digit of a two-digit number is 11 less than twice the tens digit. The number is 6 less than 7 times the sum of the digits of the number. Find the number.

20. The tens digit of a two-digit number is 14 less than twice the units digit. The number is 3 less than 4 times the sum of the digits of the number. Find the number.

21. <u>The sum of the digits of a two-digit number is 9.</u> <u><u>The number is 27 more than the original number with its digits reversed.</u></u> Find the number. (HINT: The number with its digits reversed is $10u + t$.)

22. A two-digit number is 5 times the <u>sum of its digits.</u> <u><u>When 9 is added to the number, the result is the original number with its digits reversed.</u></u> Find the number.

23. <u>The sum of the digits of a two-digit number is 11.</u> <u><u>When 45 is added to the number, the result is the original number with its digits reversed.</u></u> Find the number.

24. When 63 is subtracted from a two-digit number, the result is the original number with its digits reversed. The tens digit of the original number exceeds 4 times the units digit by 1. Find the number.

25. A two-digit number is 5 times the sum of its digits. The digits from left to right name consecutive integers. Find the number.

26. A two-digit number is 6 more than 4 times the sum of its digits. The digits from left to right are consecutive even integers. Find the number.

Solve each problem.

27. Keith is 8 years younger than Sean. In 4 years, Keith will be $\frac{2}{3}$ as old as Sean is then. Find their present ages. (*Pages 154–157*)

28. Maria earns $1120 a month. She spends $56 per month on entertainment. What percent of her monthly income is spent on entertainment? (*Pages 107–110*)

Graph these points on the same pair of coordinate axes. (*Pages 175–179*)

29. $A(4, 2)$ **30.** $B(-2, -3)$ **31.** $C(0, 3)$ **32.** $D(-1, 5)$

███████ **CONNECT AND EXTEND**

33. Represent the difference between any two-digit number and the number with its digits reversed.

34. Represent the sum of any two-digit number and the number with its digits reversed.

35. Use your answer to Exercise 33 to show that the difference between any two-digit number and the number with the digits reversed is divisible by 9.

36. Use your answer to Exercise 34 to show that the sum of a two-digit number and the number with its digits reversed is divisible by 11.

37. Show that the difference between a three-digit number and the number with its digits reversed is divisible by 99.

38. Show that the difference between a four-digit number and the number with its digits reversed is divisible by 9.

███████ **NON-ROUTINE PROBLEM**

39. A 5-digit number contains the digits shown at the right. Use the clues below to find the number.

1 2 3

4 5

  Clue 1: The number is less than 40,000.
  Clue 2: The 4 is next to the 2.
  Clue 3: The 2 is not next to the 1 or 3.
  Clue 4: The 5 is not next to the 1 or 3.
  Clue 5: The 4 is next to the 3 or 5.

———— **REVIEW CAPSULE FOR SECTION 7-7** ————

Write an algebraic expression to represent the value of each word expression. (*Pages 126–129*)

Example: The number of cents in n dimes   Solution: $10 \cdot n$,   or $10n$

1. The number of cents in k nickels.

2. The number of cents in t quarters

3. The number of dollars in b half-dollars

4. The number of dollars in k $5.00-raffle tickets

5. The number of cents in q quarters and d dimes

6. The number of cents in d dimes and n nickels

7. The number of dollars in r raffle tickets at $2.50 each and t tickets at $5.00 each

8. The number of dollars in b $100-bonds and q $1000-bonds

7-7 Organizing Data: Mixture Problems

MAKING A TABLE

The strategy of making a table to organize the data is useful in solving mixture problems.

EXAMPLE 1 An auditorium seats 2500 people. How many balcony tickets must be sold for $4.50 each and how many orchestra tickets must be sold for $5.25 each in order to receive total receipts of $12,675 each time the auditorium is full?

Solution:

1 **Find:** The number of balcony tickets and orchestra tickets that must be sold

Given: The auditorium seats 2500 persons. The cost of a balcony ticket is $4.50 and the cost of an orchestra ticket is $5.25. The total receipts are $12,675.

Represent the unknowns: x = balcony tickets, y = orchestra tickets.

2 Make a table to organize the data.

	Number (Condition 1)	Price per Ticket	Total Sales (Condition 2)
Balcony tickets	x	$4.50	$4.50x$
Orchestra tickets	y	$5.25	$5.25y$
TOTAL	2500		$12,675

Use this data and Conditions 1 and 2 to write a system of equations.

$\begin{cases} x + y = 2500 \\ 4.50x + 5.25y = 12,675 \end{cases}$
 1 ◄——— **Number of tickets sold**
 2 ◄——— **Total sales**

3 Solve the system. The substitution method is used below.

$x + y = 2500$ 1 ◄——— **Solve for x in terms of y.**
   $x = 2500 - y$

   $4.50x + 5.25y = 12,675$ 2 ◄——— **Replace x with (2500 − y).**
 $4.50(2500 - y) + 5.25y = 12,675$
 $11,250 - 4.50y + 5.25y = 12,675$
    $11,250 + 0.75y = 12,675$
       $0.75y = 1425$
         $y = 1900$ ◄——— **Don't forget to find x.**

$$x + y = 2500 \quad \longleftarrow \quad \textbf{Replace y with 1900.}$$
$$x + 1900 = 2500$$
$$x = 600$$

4 This check is left for you. They must sell **600 balcony** and **1900 orchestra** seats.

Percents are often used to express the strength of a solution or the amount of a specific ingredient in a solution or mixture.

EXAMPLE 2 A soil analysis of a lawn determines that 50 pounds of fertilizer containing 20% nitrogen is needed. How can this mixture be made from two different fertilizers, one containing 15% nitrogen and the other containing 24% nitrogen?

Solution: **1** **Find:** The amount of two types of fertilizer used
Given: Fertilizer with 15% nitrogen and fertilizer with 24% nitrogen are mixed to make 50 pounds having 20% nitrogen.

Represent the unknowns: x = Fertilizer A, y = Fertilizer B

2

	Number of Pounds (Condition 1)	Percent of Nitrogen	Amount of Nitrogen (Condition 2)
Fertilizer A	x	15%	$0.15x$
Fertilizer B	y	24%	$0.24y$
Mixture	50	20%	$0.20(50)$

$$\begin{cases} x + y = 50 & \quad 1 \quad \longleftarrow \quad \textbf{Condition 1} \\ 0.15x + 0.24y = 10 & \quad 2 \quad \longleftarrow \quad \textbf{Condition 2} \end{cases}$$

3 The addition method is used below to solve the system. To eliminate the decimals, multiply each side of Equation **2** by 100.

$$\begin{array}{rl} 15x + 24y = & 1000 \quad 2 \\ -15x - 15y & -750 \quad 1 \quad \longleftarrow \quad \textbf{-15(x + y) = -15(50)} \\ \hline 9y = & 250 \end{array}$$

$$y = 27.7 \text{ or } 28 \quad \longleftarrow \quad \textbf{Rounded to the nearest pound}$$
$$x + y = 50 \quad \longleftarrow \quad \textbf{Now find x.}$$
$$x + 28 = 50$$
$$x = 22$$

4 The check is left for you. About **22 pounds** of Fertilizer A and **28 pounds** of Fertilizer B are needed.

Objective: To solve mixture problems using systems of equations

▰▰▰▰▰▰ **CHECK YOUR UNDERSTANDING**

For Exercises 1–4, read the problem and complete the table. Then write the system of equations you would use to solve each problem.

1. Eugene has 12 coins in dimes and quarters. The total value of the coins is $1.95. How many coins of each kind does he have?

	Number of Coins	Value of Each	Total Value
Dimes	x	$0.10	$0.10x$
Quarters	y	?	?
TOTAL	?		?

2. The Ciara family invested a sum of money, part at a yearly interest rate of 7.5% and part at a yearly interest rate of 9.6%. The total investment of $15,500 earned $1425 in one year. How much did the family invest at each rate?

	Amount Invested	Interest Rate	Interest
Lower rate	x	7.5%, or 0.075	$0.075x$
Higher rate	y	9.6%, or ?	?
TOTAL	?		?

3. A 12% salt solution is mixed with a 20% salt solution. How many kilograms of each solution are needed to obtain 24 kilograms of a 15% salt solution?

	Number of Kilograms	Percent of Salt	Amount of Salt
Solution A	x	12%	?
Solution B	y	?	?
Mixture	24	?	?

4. Cashews that sell for $6.50 per kilogram are mixed with almonds that sell for $8.00 per kilogram to make a 100-kilogram mixture. The mixture will sell for $7.40 per kilogram. How many kilograms of each type must be used?

	Number of Kilograms	Value per Kilogram	Total Value
Cashews	x	$6.50	$6.50x$
Almonds	y	$8.00	?
Mixture	?	$7.40	?

5. Melissa has 45 coins in dimes and quarters. The total value of the coins is $7.65. How many coins of each kind does she have?

6. José puts quarters and nickels aside for paying tolls. He has a total of 18 coins with a total value of $2.90. How many quarters does he have?

7. Dick Arico invested $5000, part at a yearly rate of 7% and part at a yearly rate of 9%. The total interest earned for one year was $368. How much did he invest at each rate?

8. Partners in a business agreed to take out two loans totaling $35,000. The yearly interest rates were 12% and 15% and the total yearly interest was $4650. Find the amount of each loan.

10. Rachel makes a bank deposit of $595 with 96 five- and ten-dollar bills. How many of each kind of bill did she deposit?

12. A store had a sale on two models of calculators. One model sold for $22.75 and another model for $15.95. Thirty-one calculators were sold. The total amount of sales, not including tax, was $576.05. How many of each model were sold?

14. A baker mixes cookies worth $0.95 per pound with cookies worth $1.70 per pound. How many of each kind must be used to produce a 45-pound mixture that sells for $1.25 per pound?

16. A 4% salt solution is mixed with an 8% salt solution. How many grams of each solution are needed to obtain 400 grams of a 5% solution?

9. Five full-fare bus tickets and one half-fare ticket cost $90.75. Four full-fare tickets and two half-fare tickets cost $82.50. How much does a full-fare ticket cost?

11. Maria paid $7.65 for some 15¢ stamps and some 25¢ stamps. She bought 37 stamps in all. How many of each kind did she buy?

13. A door-to-door salesperson sells dictionaries at $15 each and almanacs at $6.50 each. Sales over three days amounted to 36 books sold with total sales amounting to $361.50. How many of each kind of book were sold?

15. How many kilograms of cashews selling at $6.00 per kilogram must be mixed with 20 kilograms of peanuts selling at $3.25 per kilogram to produce a mixture worth $4.50 per kilogram?

17. A 25% silver alloy is to be melted with a 55% silver alloy. How many grams of each must be used to obtain 30 grams of a 32% silver alloy?

Systems of Sentences **273**

Solve each problem.

18. A seed company sells one-ounce packets of a mixture of marigold seeds. Pretty Face marigolds sell at 50¢ per ounce and Golden Face marigolds sell at 40¢ per ounce. The mixture will sell at 45¢ per packet. How many ounces of each kind of seed must be used?

19. Solution A, which is 10% iodine, is mixed with Solution B, which is 18% iodine, to obtain 320 grams of a solution that is 15% iodine. How many grams of Solution A and how many grams of Solution B are needed for the 15%-solution?

20. A chemist has one solution that is 40% acid and a second solution that is 15% acid. How many grams of each should be used to obtain 40 grams of a solution that is 25% acid?

21. Pecans priced at $5.85 per kilogram are mixed with almonds priced at $4.93 per kilogram to make a 40-kilogram mixture that is to sell at $5.62 per kilogram. How many kilograms of each kind of nut must be used?

22. A solution contains 8 grams of acid and 32 grams of water. How many grams of water must be evaporated to obtain a solution that is 40% acid?

23. A tank contains 100 liters of a solution of acid and water. The solution is 20% acid. How much water must be evaporated to obtain a solution that is 50% acid?

24. A lending library charges a fixed amount for the first day that a book is overdue and an additional charge for each day thereafter. Raoul paid $0.75 for one book that was 7 days overdue and $1.95 for a book that was 19 days overdue. Find the fixed charge and the charge for each additional day.

25. Bob West loaned $7800 to a bank customer for one year, part at 10% and the rest at 12%. If the rates of interest were interchanged, the interest for one year would have been $24 more. Find the amount he loaned at each rate.

████████ **MAINTAIN**

Solve each problem. *(Pages 263–269)*

26. The length of a rectangular desk is 11 inches less than twice the width. The perimeter of the desk is 206 centimeters. Find the length and and the width.

27. Karl's age is now 2 years more than twice his brother's. In 5 years, Karl's age will equal three times his brother's age now. How old is each boy now?

Graph each linear equation in the coordinate plane. *(Pages 186–190)*

28. $y = x + 3$ 29. $y = -3x + 2$ 30. $2x + y = -4$ 31. $y = 6 - x$

Focus on College Entrance Tests

Logical reasoning can help you to solve problems more efficiently. Sometimes it will enable you to solve problems using **mental computation** only. The ability to identify efficient strategies to solve problems is an important test-taking skill.

EXAMPLE 1   If $14 - r \cdot t = 52$, evaluate $14 - r \cdot t - 9$.

Solution: Since $14 - r \cdot t = 52$, $14 - r \cdot t - 9 = 52 - 9$
$$= \mathbf{43}$$

EXAMPLE 2   If $9 - d + f = 111$, evaluate $8(9 - d + f)$.

Solution: Since $9 - d + f = 111$, $8(9 - d + f) = 8 \cdot 111$
$$= \mathbf{888}$$

TRY THESE

1. If $15y + 8x = 53$, evaluate $15y + 8x + 21$.

2. If $p + 8q = 84$, evaluate $p + 8q + 91$.

3. If $14 - r \cdot t = 21$, evaluate $(14 - r \cdot t) \div 3$.

4. If $(p + q) \div 3 = 12$, evaluate $[(p + q) \div 3] \div 4$.

5. If $a + 6b = 2.4$, evaluate $2(a + 6b)$.

6. If $b - 4c = 0.5$, evaluate $4(b - 4c)$.

7. If $21 + x \cdot y = 288$, evaluate $\frac{1}{4}(21 + x \cdot y)$.

8. If $y^2 - k = 624$, evaluate $\frac{1}{2}(y^2 - k)$.

9. If $p + 8q = 84$, evaluate $(p + 8q) \div 12 + 13$.

10. If $x \div y - 8 = 30$, evaluate $(x \div y - 8) \div 5 + 50$

11. If $8t - u = 22$, evaluate $\frac{1}{2}(8t - u) - 9$.

12. If $x \div y - 8 = 12$, evaluate $\frac{1}{4}(x \div y - 8) - 2$.

13. If $x \div y - 8 = 1$, evaluate $x \div y - 9$.

14. If $14 - r \cdot t = 1$, evaluate $13 - r \cdot t$.

Chapter Summary

IMPORTANT TERMS

Consistent system (p. 244)
Equivalent systems (p. 249)
Inconsistent system (p. 244)

Simultaneous linear equations (p. 243)
System of linear equations (p. 243)

IMPORTANT IDEAS

1. **In a system of two linear equations:**

   If the slopes of the lines for the two equations are different, the system has one solution.

   If the slopes are the same and the y intercepts are different, the system has no solutions.

   If the slopes are the same and the y intercepts are the same, the system has an infinite number of solutions.

2. **Steps in Solving a System of Two Linear Equations by the Substitution Method**

   ☐1 Solve one equation for one of the variables.

   ☐2 Substitute the resulting expression in the other equation.

   ☐3 Solve the resulting equation.

   ☐4 Find the values of the variables.

   ☐5 Check the solution in both equations of the system.

3. **Steps in Solving a System of Two Linear Equations by the Addition Method**

   ☐1 Add to eliminate one of the variables. Solve the resulting equation.

   ☐2 Substitute the known value of one variable in one of the original equations of the system. Solve for the other variable.

   ☐3 Check the solution in both equations of the system.

4. **Steps in Solving a System of Two Linear Equations Using Multiplication with the Addition Method** (See page 257.)

5. **Steps in Solving Word Problems Using Systems of Equations in Two Variables**

   ☐1 Use Condition 1 and two variables to represent the unknowns. Write an equation in two variables that expresses Condition 1.

   ☐2 Write a second equation in two variables that expresses Condition 2.

   ☐3 Solve the system of equations.

   ☐4 Check your solution in the original conditions of the problem. Answer the question.

6. A two-digit number may be expressed as $10t + u$, where t represents the tens digit and u the units digit.

Solve each system by graphing. (*Pages 243–248*)

1. $\begin{cases} x - y = 2 \\ 2x + y = 4 \end{cases}$

2. $\begin{cases} y = 3x - 4 \\ y = -2x + 1 \end{cases}$

3. $\begin{cases} 2x + y = -3 \\ 3x + 4y = 3 \end{cases}$

Write *one*, *none*, or *infinitely many* to describe the number of solutions for each system. (*Pages 243–248*)

4. $\begin{cases} y = 2x - 5 \\ y = -x - 5 \end{cases}$

5. $\begin{cases} 2y - x = 6 \\ 2x + 6 = 4y \end{cases}$

6. $\begin{cases} 2x + y = 1 \\ 3y = 3 - 6x \end{cases}$

Use the substitution method to solve each system. (*Pages 249–251*)

7. $\begin{cases} y - 2x = 3 \\ y + 3x = 8 \end{cases}$

8. $\begin{cases} c + 2d = 0 \\ 4x - 7d = 15 \end{cases}$

9. $\begin{cases} 2r - 3s - 1 = 0 \\ r + 6s - 3 = 0 \end{cases}$

Use the addition method to solve each system. (*Pages 252–255*)

10. $\begin{cases} x + y = 4 \\ 3x - y = -6 \end{cases}$

11. $\begin{cases} 2x - 3y = -2 \\ -2x + 5y = 2 \end{cases}$

12. $\begin{cases} \frac{2}{3}x - 2y = 5 \\ \frac{1}{3}x + 2y = 1 \end{cases}$

Use multiplication with the addition method to solve each system. (*Pages 256–259*)

13. $\begin{cases} 2x + 3y = 8 \\ 7x + 3y = -2 \end{cases}$

14. $\begin{cases} 2p - 3q = 2 \\ -6p + 4q = 9 \end{cases}$

15. $\begin{cases} 3a + 5b = -19 \\ 5a - 7b = 45 \end{cases}$

Solve each problem. (*Pages 263–265*)

16. The sum of two numbers is 22. Four times the greater number is equal to seven times the smaller number. Find the two numbers.

17. Eighty-five more student tickets than adult tickets were sold for a concert. The total number sold was 343. How many tickets of each type were sold?

Solve each problem. (*Pages 270–274*)

18. The Lawn and Garden Shop sold 40 bags of lawn seed one week for a total of $263. Large bags of lawn seed sell for $8.50 each and smaller bags for $5.75 each. How many bags of each size were sold that week?

19. Solution A, which is 5% sugar, is mixed with Solution B which is 10% sugar to obtain 10 liters of a solution that is 8% sugar. How many liters of Solution A and how many liters of Solution B are needed for the 8% solution?

Chapter Test

1. Solve this system by graphing: $\begin{cases} 2x - y = 8 \\ x + y = 1 \end{cases}$

2. Use the substitution method to solve: $\begin{cases} 3a - b = -6 \\ 6a + 2b = 0 \end{cases}$

Use the addition method to solve.

3. $\begin{cases} -2x + y = -4 \\ 5x - y = -1 \end{cases}$

4. $\begin{cases} -3x + 2y = -3 \\ 5x - 3y = 5 \end{cases}$

Use any method to solve each system.

5. $\begin{cases} 4x + y = 10 \\ y = -x + 1 \end{cases}$

6. $\begin{cases} 3m + 2n = -8 \\ 5m - 8 = 2n \end{cases}$

Solve each problem.

7. Tony worked 6 hours more than Carl last week. Together, the two boys worked a total of 58 hours. How many hours did each of them work?

8. The sum of the digits of a two-digit number is 9. The value of the number is 6 times the value of its units digit. Find the number.

9. A restaurant owner bought 24 new tables, some large and some smaller. The large tables cost $145 each, while the smaller ones cost $120 each. The total cost of the tables was $3080. How many tables of each size did he buy?

10. A mixture of birdseed contains sunflower seeds worth $1.30 per kilogram and other seeds worth $0.90 per kilogram. How many kilograms of each kind must be used to produce 100 kilograms of a mixture that sells for $1.00 per kilogram?

Additional Practice

Skills

Solve each system by graphing. (*Pages 243–248*)

1. $\begin{cases} x + y = 5 \\ 2x - y = 4 \end{cases}$

2. $\begin{cases} y = -2 \\ 4x - y = 6 \end{cases}$

3. $\begin{cases} x - 2y = 8 \\ 2x + y = 6 \end{cases}$

Use the substitution method to solve each system. (*Pages 249–251*)

4. $\begin{cases} x - 5y = 20 \\ 3x + 7y = -6 \end{cases}$

5. $\begin{cases} 7x - y = 14 \\ 2x + 5y = 41 \end{cases}$

6. $\begin{cases} 3x - 4y = 43 \\ x + y = -9 \end{cases}$

Use the addition method to solve each system. (*Pages 252–255*)

7. $\begin{cases} x - y = 14 \\ 3x + y = 6 \end{cases}$

8. $\begin{cases} 2x - y = -2 \\ -2x + 3y = 0 \end{cases}$

9. $\begin{cases} 5x - 4y = 0 \\ -x + 4y = 2 \end{cases}$

Use multiplication with the addition method to solve each system. (*Pages 256–259*)

10. $\begin{cases} 4x - y = 3 \\ 3x + 2y = 5 \end{cases}$

11. $\begin{cases} 3x + 5y = 7 \\ -x + 3y = 0 \end{cases}$

12. $\begin{cases} 3x + 4y = 5 \\ 2x + 3y = 5 \end{cases}$

Problem Solving and Applications

A $550 refrigerator costs $85 per year to operate. A $650 refrigerator costs $60 per year to operate. Use this information for Exercises 13 and 14.

13. On the same set of coordinate axes, draw graphs showing the total cost after each of the first 10 years for each refrigerator. (Include the initial cost of each.) (*Pages 243–248*)

14. Use the graph to determine after which year the total costs for each refrigerator are the same. (*Pages 243–248*)

15. The length of a rectangle is 8 centimeters more than its width. The perimeter is 68 centimeters. Find the length and width of the rectangle. (*Pages 263–265*)

16. A two-digit number is 7 times the sum of its digits. The number is 36 more than the number obtained when its digits are reversed. Find the number. (*Pages 266–269*)

17. Thomas has 56 coins in dimes and quarters. The total value of the coins is $8.00. How many coins of each kind does he have? (*Pages 270–274*)

18. Sandra borrowed $10,000, part at a 12% yearly interest rate and the rest at 14%. She paid $1270 in interest for a year. Find the amount of each loan. (*Pages 270–274*)

Part 1

Choose the best answer. Choose *a*, *b*, *c*, or *d*.

1. What is the *y* intercept of the line $2y + 6x = -8$?

   a. -4 **b.** -3 **c.** 3   **d.** 4

2. If *y* varies directly as *x*, and $y = 6.5$ when $x = -1.4$, find *y* when $x = 4.2$.

   a. 3.5   **b.** -19.5 **c.** -3.5 **d.** 19.5

3. If two equations represent parallel lines, how many solutions does the system of equations have?

   a. 1   **b.** 0   **c.** 2   **d.** infinite number

4. Which property of equality is illustrated by this statement: If $a = b$, then $b = a$?

   a. reflexive   **b.** commutative   **c.** symmetric   **d.** transitive

5. Solve the system: $\begin{cases} 3x - y = 12 \\ 2x + y = 3 \end{cases}$

   a. $(3\frac{3}{5}, -1\frac{1}{5})$ **b.** $(-3, 3)$ **c.** $(3, -3)$ **d.** $(-6, 0)$

6. The graph of which equation does not pass through the origin?

   a. $x + y = 1$ **b.** $x = y$ **c.** $x + y = 0$ **d.** $y = -x$

7. Solve: $4(3 - y) = 6y - 3$

   a. $y = 4\frac{1}{2}$ **b.** $y = 1\frac{1}{2}$ **c.** $y = \frac{9}{10}$ **d.** $y = 7\frac{1}{2}$

8. Simplify: $-4(xy^2 + 3) - 2(x + xy^2) + 3xy^2$

   a. $-3xy^2 - 2x - 12$ **b.** $-9xy^2 + 2x - 12$
   c. $-3xy^2 + 2x - 12$ **d.** $3xy^2 - 2x - 12$

9. What is the mean of the numbers $1, -1, 0, 1, -1, 0, 1, -1, 1, -1$?

   a. 1   **b.** 0   **c.** -1 **d.** $\frac{1}{10}$

10. What is the theoretical probability of a 4 turning up on one toss of a die?

    a. $\frac{4}{6}$ **b.** 0   **c.** $\frac{5}{6}$ **d.** $\frac{1}{6}$

11. Solve the system: $\begin{cases} x = -3y \\ 2x + y = 15 \end{cases}$

    a. $(-3, 9)$ **b.** $(9, -3)$ **c.** $(0, 0)$ **d.** $(9, 3)$

12. What is the domain of the function $\{(2, -4), (3, -3), (7, 0), (-1, 5)\}$?

    a. $\{2, 3, 7, -1\}$ **b.** $\{-4, -3, 0, 5\}$
    c. $\{-4, 3, 7, 5\}$ **d.** $\{2, -4, 3, -3, 7, 0, -1, 5\}$

13. What is the equation of a line with slope 4 and which passes through the point (2, 9)?

    a. $y = 4x + 1$ **b.** $y = x + 4$ **c.** $y = 4x - 1$ **d.** $y + 4x = 1$

14. Which word describes the number of solutions for the system?

$$\begin{cases} 3x + 4y = 7 \\ 2x - 3y = 5 \end{cases}$$

    a. none   **b.** many   **c.** infinite   **d.** one

15. Solve the system: $\begin{cases} x + y = 0 \\ 3x + y = 0 \end{cases}$

    a. (1, 0)   **b.** (0, 0)   **c.** $(-1, -1)$ **d.** $(0, -1)$

16. Find the value of $|x| + 2x^2 - |x + 2|$ for $x = -3$.

    a. 22   **b.** 20   **c.** 14   **d.** -16

Part 2

Solve each problem.

17. The amount of time it takes Joyce to type a report varies directly with the number of pages. Joyce takes 30 minutes to type 4 pages. How many hours will it take her to type a report that is 62 pages long?

18. Two trucks 300 miles apart start at the same time and travel toward each other. One truck travels at a rate of 60 mph; the other travels at a rate of 40 mph. In how many hours will the trucks meet?

19. A building and its contents are sold for $750,000. The building is worth 15 times as much as its contents. Find the value of each.

20. The sum of two unknown numbers is -10. Four times the larger number is negative three times the smaller number. Find each of the numbers.

21. The sum of the digits of a two-digit number is 12. The number is six times the units digit. Find the number.

22. Ted bought a new suit for $20 less than the sale price of $160. The sale price was 25% off the original price. What was the total discount Ted received?

23. The length of a rectangle is 4 centimeters less than three times its width. If the length is increased by 8 centimeters and the width is decreased by 2 centimeters, the perimeter will be 100 centimeters. Find the dimensions of the original rectangle.

24. During a cool summer, a hardware store had a sale on two models of electric fans. One model sold for $37.50 and the other for $42.75. In all, 26 fans were sold. The total amount of sales, not including tax, was $1011.75. How many fans of each model were sold?

8 Inequalities

Dot's average after bowling three games was 98. What is the lowest score she must get in the fourth game to raise her average to 100?

Problems such as these that involve maximum and minimum values can often be represented by writing **inequalities.**

8-1 Solving Inequalities: Addition Property

Compare the solution sets and graphs for each pair of inequalities in the table below. The replacement set is $\{-1, 0, 1, 2, 3, 4, 5, 6, 7, 8\}$.

Inequalities	Solution Set	Graph
$x < 4$ $x + 7 < 4 + 7$ or $x + 7 < 11$	$\{-1, 0, 1, 2, 3\}$	(number line: -2 0 2 4 6 8)
$x > 4$ $x + 7 > 4 + 7$ or $x + 7 > 11$	$\{5, 6, 7, 8\}$	(number line: -2 0 2 4 6 8)

In the table, $x < 4$ is *equivalent* to $x + 7 < 11$, and
$$x > 4 \text{ is } \textit{equivalent} \text{ to } x + 7 > 11,$$

as each pair has the *same solution set*. This suggests an addition property for inequalities similar to the addition property for equations.

ADDITION PROPERTY FOR INEQUALITIES

> Adding the same number to each side of an inequality results in an equivalent inequality.
>
> $x + 4 > 10$
> $x + 4 + (-4) > 10 + (-4)$
> $x > 6$

In solving inequalities, assume that the replacement set is the set of real numbers unless you are told otherwise.

EXAMPLE 1 Solve and graph: $x + 5 > 8$

Solution: **1** **Think:** What must be added to $x + 5$ to get x?

$$x + 5 > 8 \quad \longleftarrow \quad \text{Add } (-5) \text{ to each side.}$$
$$x + \underline{5 + (-5)} > \underline{8 + (-5)} \quad \longleftarrow \quad \text{Solve for x.}$$
$$x + \quad 0 \quad > \quad 3$$
$$x > 3$$

2 Graph the inequality.   (number line: -2 0 2 4 6)

Solution set: {all real numbers greater than 3}

Note that the open circle around the point 3 on the number line indicates that 3 is *not* a solution.

EXAMPLE 2 Solve and graph: $3x - 1 \le 2x + 3$

Solution: ☐1 $3x - 1 \le 2x + 3$ ⟵   **Add ($-2x$) to each side.**

$$-2x + 3x - 1 \le -2x + 2x + 3$$
$$x - 1 \le 3$$ ⟵   **Add 1 to each side.**
$$x - 1 + 1 \le 3 + 1$$
$$x \le 4$$

☐2 Graph the inequality.

Solution set: {all real numbers less than or equal to 4}

You can check an inequality by substituting two or more of its solutions in the original inequality. Here is a check for Example 2, using the solutions $x = 0$ and $x = -5$.

Check: $3x - 1 \le 2x + 3$ ⟵ **Replace x with 0.** $3x - 1 \le 2x + 3$ ⟵ **Replace x with (-5).**

$$3(0) - 1 \overset{?}{\le} 2(0) + 3 \qquad\qquad 3(-5) - 1 \overset{?}{\le} 2(-5) + 3$$

$$-1 \le 3 \quad \text{Yes} ✔ \qquad\qquad\qquad -16 \le 7 \quad \text{Yes} ✔$$

EXERCISES: Classwork/Homework

Objective: To solve inequalities using the Addition Property for Inequalities

CHECK YOUR UNDERSTANDING

Complete each statement. Use > or <.

1. Since $18 > 12$, $18 + (-5)$ __?__ $12 + (-5)$.
2. Since $21 < 30$, $21 + 15$ __?__ $30 + 15$.
3. Since $-8 > -10$, $-8 + 2$ __?__ $-10 + 2$.
4. Since $-21 < -18$, $-21 + (-5)$ __?__ $-18 + (-5)$.
5. If $z + 3 > 5$, then $z + 3 + (-3)$ __?__ $5 + (-3)$, or z __?__ 2.
6. If $t - 8 < 2$, then $t - 8 + 8$ __?__ $2 + 8$, or t __?__ 10.
7. If $q - 21 > -106$, then $q - 21 + 21$ __?__ $-106 + 21$, or q __?__ -85.
8. If $r + 9 < 0$, then $r + 9 + (-9)$ __?__ $0 + (-9)$, or r __?__ -9.

For each of Exercises 9–16, what number would you add to each side of the inequality to obtain x?

9. $x + 5 > 9$ **10.** $x - 4 < 6$ **11.** $x - 7 < 3$ **12.** $x + 9 > 12$

13. $x - 1.5 \leq 3.2$ **14.** $4.8 \leq x + 0.6$ **15.** $1\frac{1}{2} > x - 2\frac{1}{2}$ **16.** $x + \frac{1}{3} > -\frac{1}{6}$

 **PRACTICE AND APPLY**

Solve and graph each inequality.

17. $t + 4 > 1$ **18.** $n + 3 < 4$ **19.** $y - 5 > 7$

20. $x + 7 > 16$ **21.** $r + 9 < 16$ **22.** $x - 15 > -22$

23. $r - 1.5 < 3.5$ **24.** $m + 0.1 < 2.1$ **25.** $-5\frac{1}{2} > c + 1\frac{1}{2}$

26. $q + \frac{1}{4} > 3$ **27.** $z - 8 > 8$ **28.** $19 < y + 14$

29. $x + 2 < 8$ **30.** $6d + 1 \leq 5d - 3$ **31.** $x - 3 \geq 5$

32. $6x + 2 \geq 14 + 5x$ **33.** $3.5r - 10 \geq 2.5r + 9$ **34.** $\frac{1}{3}t - 1 < 1\frac{1}{3}t - 1$

35. $3n - 2(n - 1) \geq 0$ **36.** $4t - 3(t + 6) > -5$

37. $3(2z - 1) + 8 < 5z$ **38.** $7 + 4(2y) \leq 7y - 5$

39. $1 + 2(y - 1) \geq 3y$ **40.** $6(r - \frac{1}{2}) \geq 5(r + \frac{3}{5})$

41. $5q + 2(9 - 2q) \leq 0$ **42.** $0 \leq 4(1 - 7n) + 29n$

43. $-2(4x - 8) > -3(3x + 5)$ **44.** $-5(1 - 5x) > -12(1 - 2x)$

45. $9x + 1 \leq 4(2x + \frac{1}{4})$ **46.** $3(7y - \frac{1}{3}) \geq 20y - 1$

 **MAINTAIN**

Solve each problem. (*Pages 266–274*)

47. A total of 4500 tickets were sold for a concert. Total receipts amounted to \$34,200. Tickets sold for \$6.50 and \$8.00. How many of each type of ticket were sold?

48. A chemist has one solution that is 35% acid and a second solution that is 20% acid. How many grams of each should be used to obtain 60 grams of a solution that is 25% acid?

49. The sum of the digits of a two-digit number is 9. The number is 5 less than 10 times the units digit. Find the number.

50. The tens digit of a two-digit number is 2 more than the units digit. The number is 14 more than 9 times the tens digit. Find the number.

For Exercises 51–56, find the slope of the line containing the given points. (*Pages 207–211*)

51. $L(2,2)$; $M(6,10)$ **52.** $R(-4,0)$; $S(2,6)$ **53.** $A(1,9)$; $B(-3,1)$

54. $H(4,6)$; $T(-1,-2)$ **55.** $V(-1,5)$; $W(7,5)$ **56.** $D(8,-7)$; $E(8,9)$

■■■■■■ CONNECT AND EXTEND

Complete each statement. In each statement, the variables represent real numbers.

57. If $x > y$, then $x + z$ __?__ $y + z$. (Addition Property for Inequalities)

58. If $x < y$, then $x + z$ __?__ $y + z$. (Addition Property for Inequalities)

59. If $x < y$ and $y < z$, then $x <$ __?__ . (Transitive Property for Inequalities)

60. If $z > y$ and $y > x$, then $z >$ __?__ . (Transitive Property for Inequalities)

61. If $a - 3 < 0$, which is greater, a or 3?

62. If $a + 5 > 0$, which is greater, a or -5?

63. If $b < 0$, which is greater, $b + 3$ or b?

64. If $b < 0$, which is greater, $b + 3$ or 3?

65. The reflexive property of equality states that $a = a$. Is there a similar reflexive property for $>$ and $<$?

66. Show by using examples that if $a > b$ and $c > d$, then it is not always true that $a - c > b - d$.

■■■■■■ NON-ROUTINE PROBLEMS

67. The odometer on a car showed 15951 miles. This number is called a **palindrome** since the same number results when you reverse the digits. Two hours later the odometer showed the next successive palindrome. How many miles had the car traveled in 2 hours?

68. At a club meeting, each person present shakes hands with each other person exactly one time. There are a total of 28 handshakes. Find the number of people at the meeting.

——— **REVIEW CAPSULE FOR SECTION 8–2** ———

For Exercises 1–6, find the solution for each open sentence. The replacement set is $\{-2, -1, 0, 1, 2\}$. (*Pages 22–25*)

1. $2x < 4$ **2.** $3x \geq 3$ **3.** $x^2 \leq 5$

4. $3x - 1 > 2$ **5.** $5x + 2 > 2$ **6.** $2x - 3 < 0$

8-2 Solving Inequalities: Multiplication Properties

The table below shows that *multiplying each* side of an inequality by the *same positive number* does not change the order of the inequality.

Multiplying each side by a negative number, however, reverses the order of the inequality.

Inequality	Multiply by 1.	Multiply by 3.	Multiply by −1.	Multiply by −3.
$3 < 7$	$3 < 7$	$9 < 21$	$-3 > -7$	$-9 > -21$
$-3 < 2$	$-3 < 2$	$-9 < 6$	$3 > -2$	$9 > -6$
$4 > -6$	$4 > -6$	$12 > -18$	$-4 < 6$	$-12 < 18$

The table suggests the following.

MULTIPLICATION PROPERTIES FOR INEQUALITIES

1. For all real numbers, a, b, and c,
   if $a > b$ and $c > 0$, then $ac > bc$.

$$3x > 12$$
$$\tfrac{1}{3}(3x) > \tfrac{1}{3}(12)$$
$$x > 4$$

2. For all real numbers, a, b, and c,
   if $a > b$ and $c < 0$, then $ac < bc$.

$$-\tfrac{1}{2}t > 5$$
$$(-2)(-\tfrac{1}{2}t) < (-2)5$$
$$t < -10$$

EXAMPLE 1 Solve and graph: $-\tfrac{1}{2}x > 1$

Solution: **Think:** By what number must $-\tfrac{1}{2}x$ be multiplied to get x?

$$-\tfrac{1}{2}x > 1 \quad \longleftarrow \quad \text{Multiply each side by } (-2).$$
$$\text{Change} > \text{to} <.$$

$$(-2)\left(-\tfrac{1}{2}x\right) < (-2)(1)$$
$$x < -2$$

Solution set: {all real numbers less than −2}

In Example 2, both the addition and multiplication properties of inequalities are used. As when solving equations, it is usually easier to apply the addition property first.

EXAMPLE 2 Solve: $5 - 4x \leq 17$

Solution:
$$5 - 4x \leq 17 \qquad \longleftarrow \text{Add } (-5) \text{ to each side.}$$
$$-4x \leq 12 \qquad \longleftarrow \begin{array}{l}\textbf{Multiply each side by } \left(-\frac{1}{4}\right). \\ \textbf{Change} \leq \textbf{to} \geq.\end{array}$$
$$-\tfrac{1}{4}(-4x) \geq -\tfrac{1}{4}(12)$$
$$x \geq -3$$

Solution set: {all real numbers greater than or equal to -3}

In Examples 1 and 2, the check is left for you.

CALCULATOR

You can use a scientific calculator to check an inequality. Here is a check for Example 2 using the solution $x = -2$.

Check: $5 - 4x \leq 17$ ⬅ Replace x with -2.

5 − 4 × 2 +/− =   [13]

Is $13 \leq 17$? Yes ✔

EXERCISES: Classwork/Homework

Objective: To solve inequalities using the Multiplication Properties of Inequalities

CHECK YOUR UNDERSTANDING

Complete each statement.

1. Since $12 > 3$, $\frac{1}{3}(12)$ __?__ $\frac{1}{3}(3)$.

2. Since $16 > 12$, $(-\frac{1}{4})(16)$ __?__ $(-\frac{1}{4})(12)$.

3. Since $-1 < 5$, $10(-1)$ __?__ $10(5)$.

4. Since $-8 < -4$, $(-\frac{1}{8})(-8)$ __?__ $(-\frac{1}{8})(-4)$.

5. Since $\frac{1}{5} < 10$, $(-5)(\frac{1}{5})$ __?__ $(-5)(10)$.

6. Since $-\frac{1}{4} > -\frac{3}{4}$, $(-4)(-\frac{1}{4})$ __?__ $(-4)(-\frac{3}{4})$.

7. If $2x > 9$, then $\frac{1}{2}(2x)$ __?__ $\frac{1}{2}(9)$, or x __?__ $\frac{9}{2}$.

8. If $-\frac{1}{3}t < 27$, then $(-3)(-\frac{1}{3}t)$ __?__ $(-3)(27)$, or t __?__ -81.

9. If $-6p < 1.5$, then $(-\frac{1}{6})(-6p)$ __?__ $(-\frac{1}{6})(1.5)$, or p __?__ -0.25.

Solve and graph each inequality.

10. $2x < 8$
11. $5z > 45$
12. $7q > 14$
13. $-4z > 8$
14. $-4d < 8$
15. $-4n > 12$
16. $-6x \leq 0$
17. $-9y \geq 0$
18. $-9t \leq -36$
19. $-10w \geq -20$
20. $\frac{1}{3}z > 2$
21. $-\frac{2}{3}r > 6$
22. $2a + 2\frac{1}{2} > 10\frac{1}{2}$
23. $2c - 5 \geq 10$
24. $3h + 7 \leq 16$
25. $16 < 3x + 4$
26. $7y < 20 - 3y$
27. $5 + 2p < 17$

Solve each inequality.

28. $2t + 3 > 4t - 7$
29. $3y + 9 > -2$
30. $-2x + 5 > 10$
31. $-3a - 4a > -21$
32. $8r - 3r + 1 \leq 29$
33. $5 - 6x \leq 17$
34. $4(5a + 7) \leq 13$
35. $8t \leq 5(2t + 4)$
36. $-3m + 6(m - 4) > 9$
37. $8z - 2(2z + 3) > 0$
38. $-2y - 5 \geq 10y \leq -\frac{15}{2}$
39. $4 - 3p \geq 16 + p$
40. $-2x - 5 < -x + 10$
41. $12x + 3 < 3x - 9$
42. $-4x + 2 < x + 9$
43. $3(x + 2) < -x + 4$
44. $-7(-3x + 4) < 0$
45. $3(x + 2) \geq -2(x + 1)$
46. $3(y + 2) + 8 < 10 - (2 - y)$
47. $-3(2m - 8) < 2(m + 14)$
48. $15x - 2(x - 4) > 3$
49. $-2(n - 3) < 6n - 7(n - 4)$
50. $3(k - 4) - 3 \geq 2k + 1$
51. $5s \leq 10 + 2(3s - 4)$
52. $4 - 5(r - 2) \leq -2(-9 + 2r)$
53. $-3(t + 1) - 5(t + 2) \geq 0$
54. $3z + 7 \geq 8z - 2(5z - 2)$
55. $2(2r + 5) + 1 \leq 5 - 2(3 - r)$
56. $1 - (4d - 1) > 2(d - 3)$
57. $k - 3(2k + 1) < 5(1 + k) + 2$

You can use the program on page 615 to solve any inequality in the form $ax + b < c$.

Use the program to solve the following inequalities.

58. $6 + 4x < 12$
59. $254 < 24x + 123$
60. $82 - 9x < 233$

In Exercises 61–66, first write each equation in the form $y = mx + b$. Then give the slope and y intercept. (*Pages 212–215*)

61. $3x + y = 8$
62. $y - 2x = -4$
63. $-2y = 4x + 6$
64. $y - x = 9$
65. $10 + 2y = 6x$
66. $18 - 6y = 0$

67. Brian invested $2000, part at a yearly interest rate of 8.5% and part at a yearly interest rate of 9.2%. The total interest earned in one year was $180.50. Find the amount invested at each rate.

68. A baker mixes cookies worth $0.75 per pound with cookies worth $1.85 per pound. How many of each kind must be used to produce a 50-pound mixture that sells for $1.63 per pound?

▬▬▬ CONNECT AND EXTEND

Complete each statement. In each statement, *x*, *y*, and *z* represent real numbers. (Exercises 69–72 express the Multiplication Property for Inequalities in generalized form.)

69. If $x > y$ and z is positive ($z > 0$), then xz __?__ yz.

70. If $x < y$ and z is positive ($z > 0$), then xz __?__ yz.

71. If $x > y$ and z is negative ($z < 0$), then xz __?__ yz.

72. If $x < y$ and z is negative ($z < 0$), then xz __?__ yz.

In Exercises 73–82, classify each statement as true, T, or false, F. When a statement is false, give an example that shows why it is false. In these Exercises, *x* and *y* represent real numbers where $x > y$.

73. $y < x$ **74.** $x > 0$ **75.** $y^2 > 0$ **76.** $y^2 > y$ **77.** $xy > 0$

78. $x + y > y$ **79.** $y^2 > x$ **80.** $y^2 < xy$ **81.** $xy < x^2$ **82.** $x^3 < x^2$

▬▬▬ NON-ROUTINE PROBLEMS

83. There are four children in a family. The sum of the squares of the ages of the three youngest children equals the square of the age of the oldest child. What are the ages of the four children?

84. The figure below shows how two squares can be formed by drawing just 7 lines. Show how two squares can be formed by drawing 6 lines.

────── REVIEW CAPSULE FOR SECTION 8–3 ──────

Find the mean for each set of numbers. (*Pages 74–77*)

1. 85, 98, 84, 88, 95

2. 22, 26, 18, 35, 21, 34

3. 130, 145, 152, 124, 148, 135

4. 2, 4, 8, 7, 5, 3, 2, 1, 6, 5

8-3 Conditions and Inequalities

Being able to identify conditions will help you to solve word problems involving inequalities.

EXAMPLE 1 At The Sound Store, the cost of a compact disc player is $10 more than twice the cost of a VCR (Condition 1). Ellen plans to spend less than $640 for both items (Condition 2). What is the greatest amount she can spend for the VCR?

Solution: **1** **Find:** The greatest amount Ellen can spend for the VCR

Given: The cost of the compact disc player is $10 more than twice the cost of the VCR. ◄— **Condition 1**
She plans to spend less than $640 for both items. ◄— **Condition 2**

Represent the unknowns.

Let p = the cost of the VCR.
Let $2p + 10$ = the cost of the compact disc player.

2 Write an inequality to "connect" Condition 1 and Condition 2.

Think: Cost of VCR + Cost of Player   is less than $640.

Translate: p + $2p + 10$ $<$ 640

3 Solve the inequality.

$p + 2p + 10 < 640$ ◄——— **Combine like terms.**
$3p + 10 < 640$ ◄——— **Add −10 to both sides.**
$3p < 630$ ◄——— **Multiply each side by $\frac{1}{3}$.**
$p < 210$

Since $p < 210$, the greatest amount Ellen can spend is **$209.99.**

4 **Check:** Amount for VCR: $209.99
Amount for compact disc player: $2(\$209.99) + 10 = \$429.98$
Is $\$209.99 + \$429.98 < \$640$? Yes ✔

Inequalities **291**

MEAN

Recall that the **mean** of two or more scores is the sum of the scores divided by the number of scores.

EXAMPLE 2 Tom's scores on four tests were 87, 92, 88, and 86. He wants his mean score on five tests to be greater than 90. Find the lowest score Tom can get on the fifth test.

Solution:

1. **Find:** The lowest score Tom can get on the fifth test

   Given: Scores on four tests: 87, 92, 88, 86
   Mean score for five tests to be greater than 90

   Let x = Tom's score on the fifth test.

2. **Think:** The mean of the five tests must be greater than 90.

   Translate: $\dfrac{87 + 92 + 88 + 86 + x}{5}$ $>$ 90

3. $\dfrac{87 + 92 + 88 + 86 + x}{5} > 90$ ◄——— **Multiply each side by 5.**

   $5\left(\dfrac{87 + 92 + 88 + 86 + x}{5}\right) > 5(90)$

   $87 + 92 + 88 + 86 + x > 450$

   $353 + x > 450$

   $x > 97$

4. **Check:** Will a score of 98 give Tom an average greater than 90?

   Is $\dfrac{87 + 92 + 88 + 86 + 98}{5} > 90$? $\dfrac{451}{5} > 90$?   Yes ✔

   Will a score of 97 give Tom an average greater than 90?

   Is $\dfrac{87 + 92 + 88 + 86 + 97}{5} > 90$? $\dfrac{450}{5} > 90$?   No

   Tom's next score must be **greater than 97.**

EXERCISES: Classwork/Homework

Objective: To solve word problems involving inequalities

CHECK YOUR UNDERSTANDING

For Exercises 1–4, choose a variable to represent the unknown. Then write an inequality for each sentence.

1. The cost of a bicycle is greater than $100.

2. The distance decreased by 30 miles is less than 400 miles.

3. The sum of the cost of a ticket and $2.75 is less than $20.

4. The quotient of the cost for dinner and 4 is greater than $7.

For Exercises 5–8, write an inequality for each sentence.

5. The mean of 48, 52, 71, and x is less than 60.

6. The mean of 82, 83, 84, and y is greater than 84.

7. The mean of 120, 132, 160, 118, and b is greater than 130.

8. The mean of 24, 26, 35, 41, and p is less than 35.

PRACTICE AND APPLY

For Exercises 9–23, solve each problem. For some problems, Condition 1 is underscored once. Condition 2 is underscored twice.

9. Larry plans to spend no more than $140 for a jacket and a sweater. Suppose that the cost of a jacket is $10 less than twice the cost of a sweater. What is the greatest amount that Larry can spend for the sweater?

10. Beth and Sara estimate that they should spend less than $600 each month for rent and food and that the amount budgeted for rent should be $30 more than twice the amount budgeted for food. What is the greatest amount budgeted for food?

11. Rosa's scores on three quizzes were 78, 81, and 93. She wants her mean score on four quizzes to be greater than 85. Find the lowest score Rosa can get on the fourth quiz.

12. Peter's grades on four tests were 68, 82, 78, and 80. He wants his mean score on five tests to be greater than 80. Find the lowest score he can get on the fifth test.

13. Ada had a sum of money in a savings account. After she deposited an additional $130, there was more than $750 in the account. What is the least amount that could have been in the account originally?

14. A drama club agreed to buy more than 250 tickets for a theater party. The number of orchestra seats they bought was 80 fewer than the number of balcony tickets. What was the least number of balcony tickets bought?

15. Bob's scores for three games of bowling were 76, 103, and 121. He wants his mean score for four games of bowling to be greater than 100. Find the lowest score he can get on the fourth game.

16. The sum of two consecutive positive integers is less than or equal to 10. Find the integers.

17. The sum of two consecutive positive integers is less than 50. Find the pair with the greatest sum.

18. The sum of two consecutive odd integers is greater than 55. Find the pair with the smallest sum.

19. The sum of two consecutive even integers is less than 100. Find the pair with the greatest sum.

20. Philip is paid $225 a week plus a $15 commission on each piece of photographic equipment that he sells. How many pieces of equipment must he sell in order to make at least $400 per week? (HINT: "At least $400 means greater than or equal to $400.)

21. A gain of 2 pounds would put a certain amateur boxer in the welterweight class. What is the least amount the boxer must weigh now if the minimum welterweight class weight is 140 pounds?

22. The product of 3 and any number from a set of numbers is greater than 12. Find the set of numbers.

23. The product of 4 and any number from a set of numbers is increased by 7. The result is less than 19. Find the set of numbers.

■■■■■ MAINTAIN

24. A family's phone bill for December was $32.50 more than the phone bill for November. Phone service for the two months cost a total of $89.30. How much was the December bill? (*Pages 130–134*)

25. Two trains 700 kilometers apart start at the same time and travel toward each other. One travels at a rate of 80 kilometers per hour and the other at a rate of 95 kilometers per hour. In how many hours will they meet? (*Pages 163–166*)

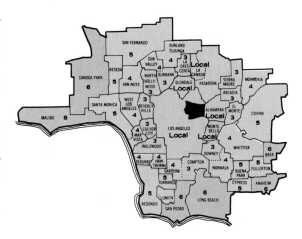

Use the slope and *y* intercept to graph each line. (*Pages 212–215*)

26. $y = 2x + 3$

27. $y = -3x$

28. $y = \frac{1}{2}x - 2$

29. $y - x = 4$

30. $-4x + y = 10$

31. $y = -5x + 3$

■■■■■ CONNECT AND EXTEND

Solve each problem.

32. The sum of two consecutive even integers is greater than 98 decreased by twice the larger integer. Find the least possible values for the integers.

33. Find the greatest possible values for three consecutive integers if the sum of the two smaller integers is less than 32 decreased by half the largest integer.

8-4 Combined Inequalities

COMPOUND SENTENCES

A sentence such as

$$x \geq 5 \quad \longleftarrow \quad \textbf{Read: "x is greater than or equal to 5."}$$

combines an inequality with an equation. Because $x \geq 5$ can be written as two simple sentences with the connective <u>or</u>, it is called a **compound sentence**. A compound sentence with <u>or</u> is a **disjunction**.

DISJUNCTION

$$x \geq 5 \textbf{ means } x = 5 \quad \underline{\textbf{or}} \quad x > 5.$$

The solution set of $x \geq 5$ is the set that makes $x = 5$ true <u>or</u> the set that makes $x > 5$ true. This means that the solution set of $x \geq 5$ is the *union* of the solution sets of $x = 5$ and $x > 5$.

In general, the **union of two sets A and B** (in symbols: $A \cup B$) is the set that contains all the elements in set A <u>or</u> in set B.

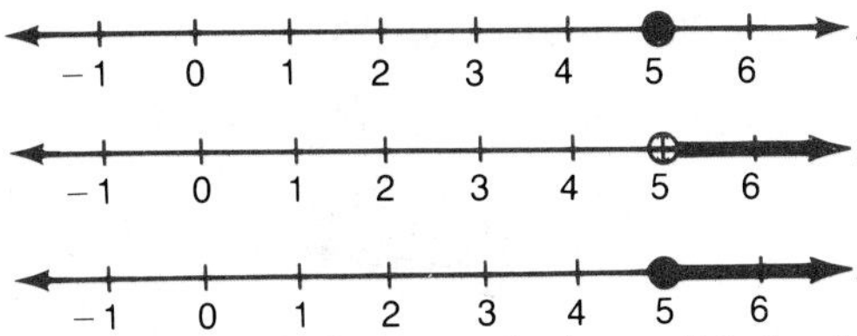

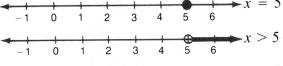

In the graph for $x \geq 5$, the solid dot indicates that the graph includes $x = 5$.

EXAMPLE 1 Solve and graph: $2x \geq -6$

Solution: Write the inequality with <u>or</u>. Then solve for x.

$$2x \geq -6 \quad \text{means} \quad 2x = -6 \quad \underline{\text{or}} \quad 2x > -6$$
$$x = -3 \quad \underline{\text{or}} \quad x > -3$$

<!-- number line graph from -5 to 4 with solid dot at -3 -->

Solution set: {all real numbers greater than or equal to -3}

A sentence such as

$$-6 < x < 2$$

combines two inequalities. Because the sentence can be written as two simple sentences with the connective <u>and</u>, it is also a compound sentence.

CONJUNCTION   A compound sentence with <u>and</u> is a **conjunction.**

$$-6 < x < 2 \quad \text{means} \quad -6 < x \quad \underline{\text{and}} \quad x < 2.$$

The solution set of $-6 < x < 2$ is the set that makes both $-6 < x$ true <u>and</u> $x < 2$ true. Thus, the solution of a compound <u>and</u> sentence is the *intersection of two sets.*

In general, the **intersection of two sets A and B** (in symbols: $A \cap B$) is the set that contains the elements belonging to <u>both</u> sets A <u>and</u> B.

$-6 < x$

$x < 2$

$-6 < x$ <u>and</u> $x < 2$ That is, $-6 < x < 2$.

EXAMPLE 2 Solve and graph: $-9 < 2x - 1 < 5$

Solution: Write the inequality with <u>and</u>. Then solve for x.

$$-9 < 2x - 1 < 5 \quad \text{means} \quad -9 < 2x - 1 \quad \text{and} \quad 2x - 1 < 5$$
$$-8 < 2x \qquad\qquad 2x < 6$$
$$-4 < x \qquad \text{and} \qquad x < 3$$

Solution set: {all real numbers greater than -4 and less than 3}

EXERCISES: Classwork/Homework

Objective: To solve linear inequalities and graph them on a number line

CHECK YOUR UNDERSTANDING

Complete.

1. A compound sentence with <u>or</u> is a __?__ .

2. A compound sentence with <u>and</u> is a __?__ .

3. Set A contains the elements 0, 1, 2, and 3. Set B contains the element 4. The union of sets A and B contains the elements __?__ .

4. Set C contains the elements 3, 4, 5, and 6. Set D contains the elements 1, 2, 3, and 4. The intersection of sets C and D contains the elements __?__ .

Match each graph in Exercises 5–10 with one of the compound sentences given in a–f.

5.

```
  ←——+———+———⊕———●———+———+———+——→
    -3  -2  -1   0   1   2   3
```

a. $-2 \le x$ <u>and</u> $x < 1$

6.

```
  ←——+———+———+———●———+———+———⊕——→
    -3  -2  -1   0   1   2   3
```

b. $x < -3$ <u>or</u> $x > 3$

7.

```
  ←——+———+———+———●———+———●———+——→
    -3  -2  -1   0   1   2   3
```

c. $x < -1$ <u>or</u> $x \ge 0$

8.

```
  ←——+———●———+———⊕———+———+———+——→
    -3  -2  -1   0   1   2   3
```

d. $0 \le x$ <u>and</u> $x \le 2$

9.

```
  ←——⊕———+———+———+———+———⊕———+——→
    -3  -2  -1   0   1   2   3
```

e. $0 \le x$ <u>and</u> $x < 3$

10.

```
  ←——+———⊕———+———⊕———+———+———+——→
    -3  -2  -1   0   1   2   3
```

f. $x < -2$ <u>or</u> $x > 0$

■■■■ **PRACTICE AND APPLY**

Write each compound sentence as two simple sentences joined by <u>or</u> or <u>and</u>.

11. $3x - 1 \le 11$ **12.** $\frac{1}{3}m \ge 4$ **13.** $3 < y < 8$

14. $-1 < a < 0$ **15.** $t - \frac{1}{2} \ge 3\frac{1}{2}$ **16.** $-5 < 2x < 10$

17. $-3 < x + 2 < -1$ **18.** $-2 < -\frac{1}{2}x < -1$ **19.** $-9 < 3k < 15$

Graph the solution set of each compound sentence.

20. $x > 2$ <u>or</u> < -2 **21.** $-2 < x$ <u>and</u> $x < 2$ **22.** $w > -3$ <u>and</u> $w < 4$

23. $a > 3$ <u>and</u> $a < 5$ **24.** $y < 4$ <u>or</u> $-y < 4$ **25.** $y \ge 1$ <u>or</u> $y > 0$

26. $t < -1$ <u>or</u> $t < -3$ **27.** $t \le -1$ <u>or</u> $t \le -3$ **28.** $a < 2$ <u>or</u> $a < -1$

For Exercises 29–46, solve and graph each inequality.

29. $3x \ge 21$ **30.** $-5x < 20$ **31.** $-5 < 2x < 10$

32. $-9 < -2x - 3 < -1$ **33.** $-2 < -\frac{1}{2}x \le -1$ **34.** $\frac{1}{3}m \le -4$

35. $-3 < t \le 6$ **36.** $-2 \le x \le 8$ **37.** $2y + 1 \le 7$

38. $-\frac{1}{2} \le w < \frac{3}{2}$ **39.** $2c + 1 \ge 6$ **40.** $3(p + 2) \le 6$

41. $-(x - 2) \ge 3$ **42.** $-14 \le 4x - 2 \le -6$ **43.** $-19 \le 5m - 4 < -4$

44. $9 \le 2a + 5 < 15$ **45.** $1 \le 3m - 2 \le 16$ **46.** $3 < 2x - 1 < 8$

47. The weight of each boy on a football team is more than 130 pounds and less than 205 pounds. If x represents the weight of any player, then __?__ $< x <$ __?__ is true.

48. In one high school wrestling weight class, wrestlers may weigh more than 167 pounds but no more than 185 pounds. Represent this weight class as an inequality, where w is the weight of any wrestler.

Olympic boxers compete in classes based on mass (weight) expressed in kilograms. In a particular class, a boxer's mass must be greater than the maximum of the next lighter class and no more than the maximum limit for the particular class.

Use this information in Exercises 49–52 to express each class as an inequality where y represents the mass of a boxer in kilograms.

49. Light heavyweight: 76–81

50. Welterweight: 64–67

51. Lightweight: 58–60

52. Bantamweight: 52–54

53. Stocks are sold only in integral numbers of dollars and eighths of a dollar. The inequality $51\frac{1}{8} < x < 52\frac{3}{4}$ indicates that a stock sold on a particular day above $51\frac{1}{8}$ and below $52\frac{3}{4}$. What is the solution set for the inequality?

Solve each inequality. Graph the solution set.

54. $3x - 7 < 28$ <u>and</u> $9x - 4 > x + 4$

55. $5 + 2y < -1$ <u>or</u> $-3 + 2y \geq 3$

56. $3 - 4a \leq 5$ <u>or</u> $2a - 3 \leq 7$

57. $3n - 9 > -3$ <u>and</u> $-9n > -27$

58. $-4 \geq 2y + 8$ <u>and</u> $3y + 10 \geq 7$

59. $3 + 4x < 3x - 2$ <u>and</u> $2 + x \geq -6$

60. $6y - 9 \leq 17y + 13$ <u>and</u> $3(y - 4) \leq 2(3y - 9)$

61. $3 - 2n > n$ <u>or</u> $2n < 6 + 8$

MAINTAIN

Solve. (*Pages 291–294*)

62. Tony's scores for three games of bowling were 120, 132, and 105. He wants his mean score for four games of bowling to be greater than 120. Find the lowest score he can get on the fourth game.

63. At a certain store, the cost of a pair of tennis shoes is $10 more than twice the cost of a sweatshirt. Lateesha plans to spend less than $70 for both items. What is the greatest amount she can spend on the sweatshirt?

In Exercises 64–69, one point on a line and the slope of the line are given. Write the equation of the line in the form $y = mx + b$. (*Pages 216–219*)

64. $A(1,5)$; $m = 2$

65. $B(0,9)$; $m = 1$

66. $C(-2,1)$; $m = -4$

67. $D(0,0)$; $m = -2$

68. $E(2,4)$; $m = -\frac{1}{2}$

69. $F(-4,0)$; $m = \frac{1}{4}$

Solve and graph each inequality. (*Pages 283–286*)

1. $n + 7 < 10$
2. $-5.8 > x - 3.3$
3. $3g + 4 \leq 2g - 1$
4. $6(a - 1) > 5a - 9$
5. $2(2 - c) + 3c \geq 0$
6. $2(1\frac{1}{2} - 4p) < 3(1 - 3p)$

Solve and graph each inequality. (*Pages 287–290*)

7. $-4h > 12$
8. $6r - 3 \geq -9$
9. $13 + 8s > 3(5s + 2)$

Solve each inequality. (*Pages 287–290*)

10. $t - 2(3t + 1) \leq 5(4 + t) + 8$
11. $2(t + 3) + 8 > 7 - (t - 4)$

Solve each problem. (*Pages 291–294*)

12. Cindy's grades on three tests were 85, 92, 75. What is the lowest grade she can get on the next test in order to have an average greater than 85?

13. One integer is four times as great as a second integer. Their sum is less than 75. What is the greatest possible value of each of the two integers?

Solve and graph each inequality on a number line. (*Pages 295–298*)

14. $2n \geq 6$
15. $-9 < 3x < 6$
16. $2(y - 3) \geq -10$

---

*Historical Digest: **Solving Systems***

The earliest evidence on solving problems that involve systems of inequalities dealt with the work of the French mathematician Jean-Baptiste-Joseph Fourier (1768–1830). The **Simplex Method** developed in the 1940's by George Dantzig, a professor at Stanford University, greatly reduced the number of computations necessary to find solutions to these systems. The length of time needed to solve systems was dramatically reduced by the development of the **MARK I** computer in 1944 by a team of scientists at Harvard University led by Howard Aiken. The silicon chip, developed in the mid 1960's, followed by the invention of the large-scale integrated circuit in the mid 1970's made the solution of systems trivial.

This one-chip computer is smaller than a paper clip.

Guess and Check / Hidden Conditions

On first reading, some problems appear not to have enough information to be solved. Identifying a "hidden" condition in these problems can help you solve them.

EXAMPLE: Sue bought 11 pounds of mixed nuts for gifts. She bought some two-pound boxes and some one-pound boxes, but not more than four boxes of each size. How many of each size box did she buy?

Solution:

1. Represent the unknowns.

   Let x = the number of two-pound boxes.
   Let y = the number of one-pound boxes.

2. Write an equation.

   Think: Weight of two-pound boxes + Weight of one-pound boxes equals 11.

   Translate: $2x$ + y = 11

3. Since there is one equation in two variables, use guess and check.

   Think: x and y must be less than or equal to 4.
   "Hidden" condition; x and y are whole numbers.

   Guess 1: Let $x = 1$ and $y = 1$.
   Check 1: $2x + y = 2(1) + 1 = 3$ ◄——— Too small. Try larger values.

   Guess 2: Let $x = 3$ and $y = 4$.
   Check 2: $2x + y = 2(3) + 4 = 10$ ◄——— Still too small.

   Guess 3: Let $x = 4$ and $y = 3$.
   Check 3: $2x + y = 2(4) + 3 = 11$

   So Sue bought **4 two-pound boxes** and **3 one-pound boxes**.

EXERCISES

1. Carlos bought some 22¢-stamps and some 17¢-stamps for $1.44. There were fewer than 6 stamps of each kind. How many of each did he buy?

2. Amy bought used books for $4.95. She paid 50¢ each for some books and 35¢ each for others. She bought fewer than 8 books at each price. How many did she buy for 50¢?

3. A football team scored 37 points in a game by making seven-point touchdowns and three-point field goals. They completed fewer than 5 of each type of score. How many of each type did the team complete?

4. Steve made 22 ounces of dried fruit mix. He used 8-ounce packages of dried apricots and 3-ounce packages of dried apples, but not more than three packages of each kind. How many of each kind did Steve use?

5. Phil used ten- and three-pound weights to put together a total weight of 58 pounds. He used fewer than 7 of each kind of weight. How many of each kind of weight did he use?

6. Albert had $2.60 in nickels and quarters. He had fewer than 10 of each kind of coin. Find the number of each kind of coin he had.

7. Dorothy got paid $53 for her two after school jobs. One job pays $5.50 per hour and the other job pays $4.00 per hour. She worked fewer than 8 hours at each job. How many hours did she work at each job?

8. Ellen bought some goldfish and angelfish for her fishtanks for $15.94. The goldfish cost $1.99 each and the angelfish cost $3.99 each. She did not buy more than four of each type of fish. How many of each fish did she buy?

9. A basketball player scored 20 points in a game by making two-point goals and three-point goals. How many of each kind did the player score? (HINT: More than one answer is possible.)

10. Adult tickets to a school play sell for 75¢ each and student tickets for 50¢ each. Gary sold $5.75 worth of tickets in all. How many of each kind did he sell? (HINT: More than one answer is possible.)

8-5 Open Sentences and Absolute Value

EQUATIONS   Sentences involving absolute value can also be written as compound sentences. Consider an equation such as $|x| = 3$.

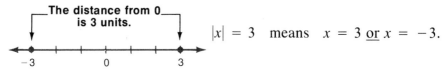

The distance from 0 is 3 units.

$|x| = 3$ means $x = 3$ <u>or</u> $x = -3$.

Thus, to solve an equation involving absolute value, write it as two simpler equations with the connective <u>or</u>. Then solve these equations.

EXAMPLE 1   Solve: $|2x + 6| = 14$

Solution: $|2x + 6| = 14$ means $2x + 6 = 14$ <u>or</u> $2x + 6 = -14$

$$2x = 8 \qquad\qquad 2x = -20$$
$$x = 4 \quad \underline{or} \quad x = -10$$

Check: $|2x + 6| = 14$ ←— **Replace x with 4.** $|2x + 6| = 14$ ←— **Replace x with −10.**

$$|2(4) + 6| \overset{?}{=} 14 \qquad\qquad |2(-10) + 6| \overset{?}{=} 14$$
$$14 \overset{?}{=} 14 \quad \text{Yes} ✔ \qquad\qquad 14 \overset{?}{=} 14 \quad \text{Yes} ✔$$

Solution set: {−10, 4}

Combine like terms *within* the absolute value symbols as a first step in solving equations involving absolute value.

EXAMPLE 2   Solve: $|2k + k| - 12 = 5$

Solution: $|2k + k| - 12 = 5$ ←——— **Combine like terms.**

$|3k| - 12 = 5$ ←——— **Add 12 to each side.**

$|3k| = 17$ ←——— **Write with "or."**

$|3k| = 17$ means $3k = 17$ <u>or</u> $3k = -17$

$$k = \tfrac{17}{3} \quad \underline{or} \quad k = -\tfrac{17}{3} \quad\text{←——— } \textbf{The check is left for you.}$$

Solution set: $\left\{ -\tfrac{17}{3}, \tfrac{17}{3} \right\}$

INEQUALITIES Consider an inequality such as $|x| < 3$. On a number line, the distance from x to 0 must be less than 3 units.

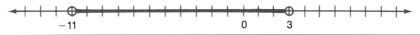

As the graph shows, $|x| < 3$ can be written as $-3 < x < 3$.

The compound sentence $-3 < x < 3$ means $x > -3$ <u>and</u> $x < 3$.

EXAMPLE 3 Solve and graph: $|x + 4| < 7$

Solution: Write $|x + 4| < 7$ as $-7 < x + 4 < 7$.

$$-7 < x + 4 < 7 \text{ means } x + 4 > -7 \quad \underline{\text{and}} \quad x + 4 < 7$$
$$x > -11 \quad \underline{\text{and}} \quad x < 3$$

Solution set: {all real numbers greater than -11 and less than 3}

Now consider an inequality such as $|x| > 3$. On a number line, the distance from x to 0 must be greater than 3.

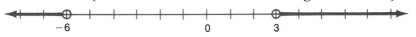

Thus, $|x| > 3$ means $x < -3$ <u>or</u> $x > 3$.

EXAMPLE 4 Solve and graph: $|2x + 3| > 9$

$$|2x + 3| > 9 \text{ means } 2x + 3 < -9 \quad \underline{\text{or}} \quad 2x + 3 > 9$$
$$2x < -12 \qquad\qquad 2x > 6$$
$$x < -6 \quad \underline{\text{or}} \qquad\quad x > 3$$

Solution set: {all real numbers less than -6 or greater than 3}

EXERCISES: Classwork/Homework

Objectives: To solve equations involving absolute value
To solve and graph inequalities involving absolute value

CHECK YOUR UNDERSTANDING

Write each open sentence as a compound sentence using <u>or</u> or <u>and</u>.

1. $|x| = 5$ **2.** $|t + 1| = 5$ **3.** $|2m| = 4$ **4.** $|5y - 10| = 5$

5. $|s| < 3$ **6.** $|p - 4| < 6$ **7.** $|3n| > 12$ **8.** $|2k - 9| > 1$

Match each open sentence in Exercises 9–14 with one of the graphs in a–f.

9. $|x| = 2$

10. $|x - 1| = 2$

11. $|3x| = 3$

12. $|x| > 1$

13. $|x| \leq 2$

14. $|x + 1| < 2$

a.
$$-3 \quad -2 \quad -1 \quad 0 \quad 1 \quad 2 \quad 3$$

b.
$$-3 \quad -2 \quad -1 \quad 0 \quad 1 \quad 2 \quad 3$$

c.
$$-3 \quad -2 \quad -1 \quad 0 \quad 1 \quad 2 \quad 3$$

d.
$$-3 \quad -2 \quad -1 \quad 0 \quad 1 \quad 2 \quad 3$$

e.
$$-3 \quad -2 \quad -1 \quad 0 \quad 1 \quad 2 \quad 3$$

f.
$$-3 \quad -2 \quad -1 \quad 0 \quad 1 \quad 2 \quad 3$$

▌▌▌▌▌▌▌ **PRACTICE AND APPLY**

Solve and check each equation.

15. $|a + 3| = 2$

16. $\left|\frac{1}{2}k\right| = 6$

17. $|5y| = 10$

18. $|3k - 6| = 2$

19. $|2y + 6| = 0$

20. $12 = |3 - x|$

21. $\left|\frac{1}{5}(2 - k)\right| = 3$

22. $|y + y + y| = \frac{1}{3}$

23. $|t + 1| = 9$

24. $\left|\frac{1}{4}(5t - 2)\right| = 6$

25. $|3d - 2| = \frac{1}{2}$

26. $|4k + 6 + 2k| = 5$

27. $15 = |w + 2|$

28. $\left|\frac{2}{3}y\right| = \frac{1}{12}$

29. $|n| + 6 = 2$

30. $|3m + 6| = 4$

31. $|-3m| = 14$

32. $6 - 2 = |x| + 3$

Solve and graph each inequality.

33. $|x| < 5$

34. $|y| > 3$

35. $|n - 2| < 3$

36. $|y + 4| > 6$

37. $|m + 3| > 4$

38. $|r - 1| < 3$

39. $|2x - 1| < 9$

40. $|3y - 2| > 8$

41. $|2n - 6| < 4$

42. $|6 - 3k| < 2$

43. $|3t| > 12$

44. $|b + b| > 10$

45. $|3c - 7| \geq 2$

46. $|2a + 3| \leq 1$

47. $|n| + 3 \leq 5$

48. $|4x + 3| - 2 > 4$

You can use the program on page 616 to solve any equation in the form $|Ax + B| = C$.

Use the program to solve the following absolute value equations.

49. $|x + 1| = 5$

50. $|x + 3| - 7 = 0$

51. $|15 + 5x| = 55$

▌▌▌▌▌▌▌ **MAINTAIN**

Determine the equation of a line passing through the given points.
Write the equation in the form $y = mx + b$. (Pages 222–225)

52. $A(4,2)$; $B(8,1)$

53. $C(2,2)$; $D(5,0)$

54. $E(-2,8)$; $F(4,6)$

55. $G(0,0)$; $H(2,2)$

56. $I(-1,-1)$; $J(-3,1)$

57. $K(3,0)$; $L(0, -6)$

304   *Chapter 8*

Solve each problem. (*Pages 291–294*)

58. Together, Jeff and Erica sold more than 300 tickets for the school play. Jeff sold 10 more than 3 times the number of tickets Erica sold. Find the least number of tickets Erica could have sold.

59. Michelle's grades on three tests were 86, 72, and 90. She wants her mean score on four tests to be greater than 85. Find the lowest score she can get on the fourth test.

▬▬▬▬ **CONNECT AND EXTEND**

Solve.

60. $|x + 2| = x + 2$

61. $|x + 2| < x + 2$

62. $|x + 2| > x + 2$

63. $|-2x| = -2x$

64. $1 < |x| < 4$

65. $5 < |x| < 8$

▬▬▬▬ **NON-ROUTINE PROBLEMS**

66. Sarah doubled the amount in her checking account during the month of January. On the last day of the month, she withdrew $16. Each month after that, she repeated this procedure. However, after withdrawing $16 on the 30th of April, Sarah had no money left in her account. How much did Sarah have in her account at the beginning of January?

67. The owner of the Centerville Bike Shop sold two different bicycles for $99 each. The owner made a 10% profit on the sale of one bike, but took a 10% loss on the sale of the other bike. On the two sales, did the owner make a profit, take a loss, or break even? Explain.

68. Arrange eight 8's in an addition problem so that the sum is 1000.

─────── **REVIEW CAPSULE FOR SECTION 8–6** ───────

Solve each system by graphing. Check your solutions. (*Pages 243–248*)

1. $\begin{cases} x = 4 \\ y = -1 \end{cases}$

2. $\begin{cases} y = 2x \\ y = 3x - 3 \end{cases}$

3. $\begin{cases} x + y = -4 \\ x - y = 6 \end{cases}$

4. $\begin{cases} y + 2x + 6 = 0 \\ y - 2x = 0 \end{cases}$

Determine whether the given point is a solution of the given system. Answer *Yes* or *No*. (*Pages 243–248*)

5. $\begin{cases} a + 2b = 1 \\ 3a + b = 8 \end{cases}; (3, -1)$

6. $\begin{cases} 3p + 5q = 9 \\ 9p + 2q = -12 \end{cases}; (-2, 3)$

7. $\begin{cases} -5s + 3v = 25 \\ 4s + 2v = 2 \end{cases}; (-2, -5)$

8-6 Graphing Linear Inequalities

HALF-PLANES The graph of a linear equation separates the coordinate plane into three sets of points:

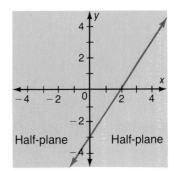

the points in the two **half-planes** and the points on the line.

Thus, every point on the coordinate plane is either in one of the half-planes or on the line.

The equation of the line graphed at the right is $y = \frac{3}{2}x - 3$. Thus, the coordinates of every point in the plane make one of these sentences true.

$$y = \tfrac{3}{2}x - 3; \quad y > \tfrac{3}{2}x - 3; \quad y < \tfrac{3}{2}x - 3$$

The graph of an inequality that uses $>$ or $<$ *does not include* the graph of the related equation. To show this, the graph of the related equation is dashed.

EXAMPLE 1 Graph $y > 2x - 1$.

Solution:

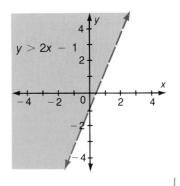

  1 Draw the graph of $y = 2x - 1$ as a **dashed** line.

  2 To identify the half-plane for which $y > 2x - 1$, test a point in each half-plane.

      Try (0, 1).   Try (3, 0).

      $1 > 2(0) - 1$? $0 > 2(3) - 1$?

      $1 > -1$? Yes ✔ $0 > 5$? No

  3 Shade the half-plane containing (0, 1).

OPEN HALF-PLANE Since the graph of $y > 2x - 1$ *does not include* the graph of the related equation, the graph is an **open half-plane.**

The graph of an inequality that uses $\geq$ or $\leq$ *includes* the graph of the related equation. To show this, the graph of the related equation is a solid line. This line is the **edge** or **boundary** of the half-plane.

EXAMPLE 2 Graph $3x - 4y \leq 12$.

Solution:

1. Draw the graph of $3x - 4y = 12$ as a **solid** line.
2. To identify the half-plane for which $3x - 4y < 12$, test a point in each half-plane.

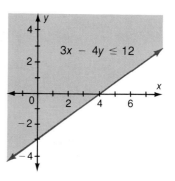

Try (0, 0).	Try (3, −2).
$3(0) - 4(0) < 12$?	$3(3) - 4(-2) < 12$?
$0 < 12$? Yes ✔	$9 + 8 < 12$? No

3. Shade the half-plane containing (0, 0).

CLOSED HALF-PLANE   Since the graph of $3x - 4y \leq 12$ includes the edge or boundary of the half-plane, the graph is a **closed half-plane**.

EXERCISES: Classwork/Homework

Objective: To graph linear inequalities on the coordinate plane

CHECK YOUR UNDERSTANDING

1. The graph of a linear equation separates the coordinate plane into the points in the two __?__ and the points on the __?__.

2. When the graph of an inequality does not include the graph of the related equation, the graph is an __?__ half-plane.

3. The graph of an inequality that uses __?__ or __?__ includes the graph of the related equation.

4. The graph of an inequality that uses __?__ or __?__ does not include the graph of the related equation.

Determine which of the given points, if any, belong to the graph of the given inequality.

5. $y < 3x - 2$; (0, 0); (−5, −7)
6. $y \geq 3x - 2$; (−1, −1); (9, 0)
7. $y > -2x + 1$; (1, −6); (−2, 1)
8. $y \leq -2x + 1$; (2, −2); (−2, 2)

PRACTICE AND APPLY

For Exercises 9–36, graph each inequality in the coordinate plane.

9. $y > x - 3$
10. $y < x + 3$
11. $y > 3x - 4$
12. $y < 2x + 4$
13. $y > -3x$
14. $y < -4x$
15. $y < -2x - 4$
16. $y > -4x + 5$
17. $x + y > 4$
18. $x - y > 2$
19. $2x + 3y > 6$
20. $4x - y < 5$

21. $y > 0 \cdot x + 4$　**22.** $y < 0 \cdot x - 5$　**23.** $y < -4$　**24.** $y > -5$

25. $x < 8$　**26.** $x > -6$　**27.** $x < -4$　**28.** $x > 6$

29. $y \geq -4$　**30.** $y \geq 2x - 5$　**31.** $y \leq 3x - 9$　**32.** $y \geq 2$

33. $y \leq -5$　**34.** $x + y \geq 4$　**35.** $2x - y \leq -6$　**36.** $3x + y < 5$

Write the inequality that defines the shaded portion of each plane.

37. 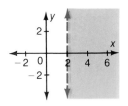　**38.** 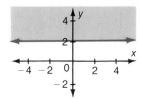　**39.**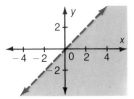

■■■■■ **MAINTAIN**

Solve and check each equation. (*Pages 302–305*)

40. $|x + 5| = 3$　**41.** $|3y| = 12$　**42.** $|4 - a| = 7$　**43.** $|-2t + 1| = 7$

Solve and graph each inequality. (*Pages 302–305*)

44. $|x| > 5$　**45.** $|n - 1| < 6$　**46.** $|y + 2| < 1$　**47.** $|3t| < 9$

Write each compound sentence as two simple sentences joined by <u>or</u> or <u>and</u>.
(*Pages 295–298*)

48. $4x \leq 24$　**49.** $-3 < t < 2$　**50.** $-2 \leq n - 1 < 4$

51. $-6a \geq 30$　**52.** $2y + 1 \leq -1$　**53.** $-11 < 3m - 2 \leq 7$

Solve each problem. (*Pages 232–234*)

54. The labor costs for a plumbing job vary directly as the number of hours a plumber works. If labor costs for 3 hours amount to $96, what would be the labor costs for 8 hours?

55. The amount of chicken used in a recipe varies directly as the number of servings. If 3 pounds of chicken are used for 12 servings, how many pounds of chicken will be needed for 20 servings?

■■■■■ **CONNECT AND EXTEND**

In Exercises 56–64, describe the graph of each inequality. Use one of the word descriptions below. In these exercises, $A \neq 0$, $B \neq 0$.

A straight line　　*An open half-plane*　　*A closed half-plane*

56. $Ax + By = C$　**57.** $Ax + By \leq C$　**58.** $Ax + By < C$

59. $Ax + By \geq C$　**60.** $Ax + By > C$　**61.** $Ax = C$

62. $By = C$　**63.** $Ax \leq C$　**64.** $By > C$

308　*Chapter 8*

8-7 Systems of Inequalities

A system of linear inequalities in two variables is usually solved by graphing.

Remember! The graph of an inequality that uses $>$ or $<$ <u>does not include</u> the graph of the related equation. To show this, the graph of the related equation is a dashed line.

EXAMPLE 1 Solve by graphing: $\begin{cases} x + y > 10 \\ x - y > -4 \end{cases}$

Solution: ① Graph $x + y > 10$. Any point in half-plane E is a solution of $x + y > 10$. Note that the graph of $x + y = 10$ is dashed to show that it is not included in the half-plane.

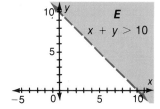

② Graph $x - y > -4$. Any point in half-plane F is a solution of $x - y > -4$. Note that the points on the graph of $x - y = -4$ are not included in the half-plane.

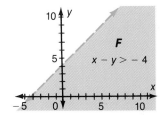

③ Any point in the intersection of the half-planes E and F (darkest region) is a solution of $x + y > 10$ <u>and</u> $x - y > -4$.

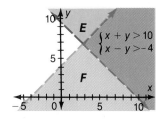

Thus, **all points in the darkest region** (but no points on the lines) are solutions of the system.

Sometimes points on a line are included in the solutions of a system of linear inequalities. You indicate these points by showing all or part of the graph of the line as a solid line (see Example 2).

EXAMPLE 2 Solve by graphing: $\begin{cases} y \geq 2x - 4 \\ x + y \leq 5 \end{cases}$

Solution: **1** Graph $y \geq 2x - 4$.

Any point in half-plane E
<u>or</u> on the line $y = 2x - 4$
(edge of half-plane E) is a
solution of $y \geq 2x - 4$.

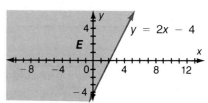

2 Graph $x + y \leq 5$.

Any point in half-plane F
<u>or</u> on the line $x + y = 5$
(edge of half-plane F) is a
solution of $x + y \leq 5$.

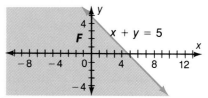

3 Any point **in the intersection of half-planes E and F**
(darkest region) and **any
point on the lines that border the intersection** is a solution of $y \geq 2x - 4$ <u>and</u>
$x + y \leq 5$.

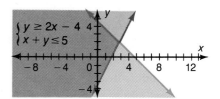

EXERCISES: Classwork/Homework

Objective: To solve systems of linear inequalities by graphing

CHECK YOUR UNDERSTANDING

Match each graph in Exercises 1–4 with one of the systems given in a–d.

1.

2.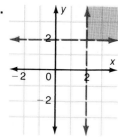

3.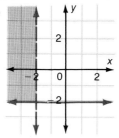

4.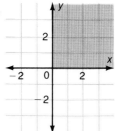

a. $\begin{cases} x \geq 0 \\ y \geq 0 \end{cases}$ **b.** $\begin{cases} x \geq 0 \\ y \leq 0 \end{cases}$ **c.** $\begin{cases} x > 2 \\ y > 2 \end{cases}$ **d.** $\begin{cases} x < -2 \\ y \geq -2 \end{cases}$

Solve each system by graphing.

5. $\begin{cases} x + y \le 2 \\ x - y \le 4 \end{cases}$ **6.** $\begin{cases} y > 3x \\ y \le -3x \end{cases}$ **7.** $\begin{cases} x - y < 8 \\ x + y > 3 \end{cases}$ **8.** $\begin{cases} x + y > 10 \\ x + y < 4 \end{cases}$

9. $\begin{cases} y > 3x \\ y > 3x + 2 \end{cases}$ **10.** $\begin{cases} 2x + 3y \ge 6 \\ y \le 4 \end{cases}$ **11.** $\begin{cases} x + 2y \ge 4 \\ 2x - y \le -2 \end{cases}$ **12.** $\begin{cases} x - 2y \le 6 \\ 3x + y \ge 9 \end{cases}$

13. $\begin{cases} 2x + y > -8 \\ y < -2 \end{cases}$ **14.** $\begin{cases} y \le 4x - 1 \\ y > 2x + 1 \end{cases}$ **15.** $\begin{cases} y < x \\ y \ge 3 - x \end{cases}$ **16.** $\begin{cases} 3x - y \le 6 \\ x - 4y \ge 8 \end{cases}$

17. $y > -x$ <u>and</u> $y > \frac{1}{2}x - 4$ **18.** $\frac{1}{3}y - x \le -9$ <u>and</u> $3x - 2y - 6 \ge 0$

19. $-2 < x < 2$ <u>and</u> $-2 < y < 2$ **20.** $0 \le x \le 6$ <u>and</u> $0 \le y \le 4$

21. $\begin{cases} y \ge x \\ y < 3 \\ x > 0 \end{cases}$ **22.** $\begin{cases} y < x + 1 \\ y - 2x > 1 \\ y \le 1 \end{cases}$ **23.** $\begin{cases} x + y < 3 \\ x - y > 1 \\ 2x + y > -4 \end{cases}$ **24.** $\begin{cases} 2y > x + 2 \\ 2y + x < 6 \\ y > 0 \end{cases}$

25. The distance between two cities on a map varies directly with the actual distance between the cities. If 2.5 centimeters on the map represent 50 kilometers, what does 6 centimeters represent? (*Pages 232–234*)

26. The regular admission price at the movies is \$4.50. Admission for senior citizens is \$3.50. One evening, 284 tickets were sold for a total of \$1226. How many tickets were sold to senior citizens? (*Pages 270–274*)

Solve and graph each inequality on a number line. (*Pages 302–305*)

27. $|x| > 6$ **28.** $|n - 3| > 5$ **29.** $|a + 2| < 9$ **30.** $|4t| \le 8$

Find the slope of each line from its graph. (*Pages 207–211*)

31. 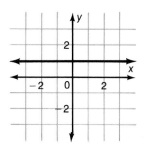   **32.** 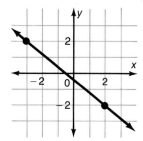   **33.**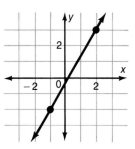

Solve by graphing.

34. $\begin{cases} x \ge 0 \\ x \le 2 \\ y \ge 0 \\ y \le 2 \end{cases}$ **35.** $\begin{cases} x \le -2 \\ x \ge -5 \\ y \le 6 \\ y \ge 4 \end{cases}$ **36.** $\begin{cases} y = x \\ x \le 4 \\ y \ge 0 \end{cases}$ **37.** $\begin{cases} y - x > 0 \\ x > -1 \\ y < 5 \end{cases}$

8-8   Making a Model: Linear Programming

Linear programming is a method of solving problems that contain restrictions, called **constraints,** which are often expressed as linear inequalities.

You can use a graph as a **model** to determine the solution or solutions to the system of linear inequalities.

EXAMPLE   A small company has five 3-ton trucks and four 5-ton trucks for hauling gravel. Only 7 crews are available at any one time to operate the trucks. How many of each kind of truck should be used to haul the maximum amount of gravel per trip?

Solution: **1** Use two variables to represent the unknowns.

Let x = the number of 3-ton trucks used.
Let y = the number of 5-ton trucks used.
Then the number of tons of gravel hauled per trip is $3x + 5y$.

2 Write a system of inequalities to represent the constraints.

$$\begin{cases} x \leq 5 \\ y \leq 4 \\ x + y \leq 7 \\ x \geq 0 \\ y \geq 0 \end{cases}$$

←——— Only five 3-ton trucks are available.
←——— Only four 5-ton trucks are available.
←——— Only 7 crews are available.
←——— A negative number of trucks is not possible.

3 Graph these inequalities on the same coordinate axes. The intersection of the solution sets forms the shaded region (called a **polygonal region**) shown in the graph. *Any point in the region satisfies the system of inequalities.*

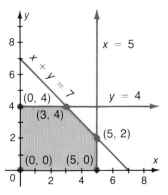

4 To find how many of each kind of truck are needed to haul the maximum amount of gravel per load means to find the ordered pair (x, y) for which the expression $3x + 5y$ is a *maximum.*

It has been proved that a maximum or minimum always occurs at one of the vertices, or corners, of the polygon. In this case, there are 5 vertices.

Check the ordered pair for each vertex in $k = 3x + 5y$.

Vertex	$k = 3x + 5y$	Value of k	
$(0, 0)$	$k = 3 \cdot 0 + 5 \cdot 0$	0	
$(5, 0)$	$k = 3 \cdot 5 + 5 \cdot 0$	15	
$(5, 2)$	$k = 3 \cdot 5 + 5 \cdot 2$	25	
$(3, 4)$	$k = 3 \cdot 3 + 5 \cdot 4$	29	← **Maximum value**
$(0, 4)$	$k = 3 \cdot 0 + 5 \cdot 4$	20	

Thus, **three 3-ton trucks** and **four 5-ton trucks** are needed.

Of course, common sense would give you the answer to the Example without the use of linear programming techniques. The techniques are shown when the answer is obvious to help you understand how to apply them when the answer is not so obvious.

EXERCISES: Classwork/Homework

Objective: To solve problems containing constraints, using linear programming methods

CHECK YOUR UNDERSTANDING

In Exercises 1–4, the vertices of a polygonal region are given. For each exercise, find the maximum and minimum values of k over the given region.

1. $(0, 0)$; $(0, 5)$; $(6, 0)$; $k = 4x + y$
2. $(0, 0)$; $(0, 6)$; $(4, 8)$; $(2, 0)$; $k = 4x + y$
3. $(1, -1)$; $(0, 2)$; $(3, 0)$; $y = 2x + 3k$
4. $(1, 1)$; $(0, 4)$; $(4, 5)$; $(3, 0)$; $y = -x + k$

PRACTICE AND APPLY

In Exercises 5–8, find the maximum and minimum values for k, given the constraints shown in the graph.

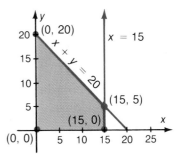

5. $k = x + 2y$
6. $k = 3x + 5y$
7. $k = 2x + 3y$
8. $k = 50x + 10y$

In Exercises 9–12:

    a. Graph the solution set of each system of inequalities and determine the coordinates of the resulting polygonal region.

    b. Find the mimimum value of $k = 2x + y$ over the region graphed.

9. $\begin{cases} x \geq 0 \\ y \geq 0 \\ x + y \leq 4 \end{cases}$
    10. $\begin{cases} y \leq 5 - \frac{1}{2}x \\ x \geq 0 \\ x \leq 7 \\ y \geq 0 \end{cases}$
    11. $\begin{cases} y \leq 5 - x \\ x \leq 4 \\ x \geq 0 \\ y \geq 0 \end{cases}$
    12. $\begin{cases} y \leq 2 - \frac{1}{2}x \\ y \geq 1 \\ x \geq 0 \end{cases}$

A manufacturer makes two models of a bicycle. The profit on Model A is $15 per bicycle and the profit on Model B is $18 per bicycle. Because of a labor shortage, the manufacturer can produce no more than 200 bicycles per week. To meet the market demand, at least 50 Model A bicycles and 80 Model B bicycles must be available each week.

Use this information in Exercises 13–17.

13. Let x represent the number of Model A bicycles and let y represent the number of Model B bicycles produced per week. Write an expression to represent the total weekly profit.

14. Write a system of inequalities that shows the constraints on x and y.

15. Graph the system of inequalities you wrote in Exercise 14.

16. State the coordinates of the vertices of the polygonal region graphed in Exercise 13.

17. What is the maximum profit possible?

The manager of a small toy shop decides to make up two types of variety packages in order to sell off 12 whistles and 32 small cars left in the shop. Each type A package contains 2 whistles and 8 small cars and sells for $6.50. Each type B package contains 3 whistles and 5 small cars and sells for $5.75.

Use this information in Exercises 18–22.

18. Let x represent the number of type A packages and let y represent the number of type B packages. Write an expression to represent the store's income from the sale of these packages.

19. Write a system of inequalities to show the constraints on x and y.

20. Graph the system of inequalities from Exercise 19.

21. State the coordinates of the vertices (corners) of the region graphed in Exercise 20.

22. What is the store's maximum possible income from the sale of the packages?

Focus on College Entrance Tests

Logical reasoning is used to solve many types of problems.

EXAMPLE Bill, Marie, and Jan each left school in their own car. The three cars were a red Hawk, a blue Cheetah, and a white Sunburst. Use the clues below to find the driver of each car.

> **CLUE A** Marie waved to the driver of the Hawk.
> **CLUE B** Bill followed the Sunburst out of the parking lot.
> **CLUE C** Marie does not drive a white car.

Solution: Make a table to show all the possibilities.
Use an X to show that a possibility cannot be true.
Use a $\sqrt{}$ when you are certain that a possibility is true.

1 Read Clue A.
Is Marie the driver of the Hawk?
Place an X next to Marie's name in the Hawk column.

	Hawk	Cheetah	Sunburst
Bill			
Marie	X		
Jan			

2 Read Clue B.
Is Bill the driver of the Sunburst?
Place an X next to Bill's name in the Sunburst column.

	Hawk	Cheetah	Sunburst
Bill			X
Marie	X		
Jan			

3 Read Clue C.
Is Marie driving the Sunburst?
What car must Marie drive?
Place an X in the Sunburst column and a $\sqrt{}$ in the Cheetah column next to Marie's name.
Place X's next to Bill's and Jan's names in the Cheetah column.

	Hawk	Cheetah	Sunburst
Bill		X	X
Marie	X	$\sqrt{}$	X
Jan		X	

4 Who is driving the Hawk?
Who is driving the Sunburst?

Bill: Hawk   Marie: Cheetah

Jan: Sunburst

Check the answer with the clues.

	Hawk	Cheetah	Sunburst
Bill	$\sqrt{}$	X	X
Marie	X	$\sqrt{}$	X
Jan	X	X	$\sqrt{}$

For each exercise, copy the table. Use the clues to complete the table to solve each problem.

1. Ann, Beth, and Carol each took a different piece of fruit for lunch. The fruits were an apple, an orange, and a banana.

   CLUE A Carol does not like bananas.

   CLUE B Beth does not have to peel her fruit.

   Who has each fruit?

	Apple	Orange	Banana
Ann			
Beth			
Carol			

2. Darin, Kyle, and Rita each get to school in a different way. One rides the bus, one drives a car, and one walks.

   CLUE A Kyle is too young to drive.

   CLUE B Darin does not walk or drive.

   How does each get to school?

	Bus	Car	Walk
Darin			
Kyle			
Rita			

Solve. Make a table to show all the possibilities.

3. Jim, Sarah, and Jane are in the school play. One plays a teacher, one plays a detective, and one plays a town mayor.

   CLUE A Jane and the teacher ride to rehearsals together.

   CLUE B Sarah helps put on the detective's makeup.

   CLUE C Sarah walks to rehearsals.

   Who plays the detective?

4. Lisa, Diane, and David attend the same high school. One is a basketball player, one is a band member, and one is a cheerleader.

   CLUE A Lisa and the cheerleader have the same lunch period.

   CLUE B David and the basketball player's brother are friends.

   CLUE C Lisa plays no sports.

   Who is the cheerleader?

IMPORTANT TERMS

Boundary of a half-plane (p. 306)
Closed half-plane (p. 307)
Compound sentence (p. 295)
Conjunction (p. 295)
Constraints (p. 312)
Disjunction (p. 296)
Edge of a half-plane (p. 306)

Half-plane (p. 306)
Intersection of two sets (p. 296)
Linear programming (p. 312)
Open half-plane (p. 306)
Polygonal region (p. 312)
Union of two sets (p. 295)

IMPORTANT IDEAS

1. **Additional Property for Inequalities:** Adding the same number to each side of an inequality results in an equivalent inequality.

2. **Multiplication Properties for Inequalities**
   a. For all real numbers, a, b, and c, if $a > b$ and $c > 0$, then $ac > bc$.
   b. For all real numbers a, b, and c, if $a > b$ and $c < 0$, then $ac < bc$.

3. The compound sentence $x \leq a$ means $x = a$ <u>or</u> $x < a$. The solution set is the union of the solution sets of $x = a$ and $x < a$. Similarly, the compound sentence $x \geq b$ means $x = b$ <u>or</u> $x > b$. The solution set is the union of the solution sets of $x = b$ and $x > b$.

4. The compound sentence $a < x < b$ means $a < x$ <u>and</u> $x < b$. The solution set is the intersection of the solution sets of $a < x$ and $x < b$.

5. A sentence involving absolute value can be written as a compound sentence. For example, $|y| = 8$ means $y = 8$ <u>or</u> $y = -8$.

6. **a.** A sentence involving absolute value and an inequality such as $|x| < 5$ can be written as $x > -5$ <u>and</u> $x < 5$.
   b. A sentence involving absolute value and an inequality such as $|x| > 4$ can be written as $x < -4$ <u>or</u> $x > 4$.

7. The graph of a linear equation separates the coordinate plane into three sets of points—the points in the two half-planes and the points on the line.

8. The maximum or minimum value, if any, of a linear expression evaluated over a polygonal region occurs at one of the vertices of the polygon.

Chapter Review

Solve and graph each inequality. (*Pages 283–286*)

1. $y - 3 > 1$ **2.** $5 \leq 8 + r$ **3.** $-3 + 4b \leq 3b + 2$

4. $6(t + \frac{1}{2}) - 5(1 + t) \geq 0$ **5.** $3(2 - n) < 9$

Solve and graph each inequality. (*Pages 287–290*)

6. $7d < -14$ **7.** $3 - 2r > 7$ **8.** $-\frac{3}{4}y \leq -6$

Solve each inequality. (*Pages 287–290*)

9. $4x - 6 \leq 2(x + 8)$ **10.** $2(y - 4) \geq 7 - y$

11. $-6t + 2(4t - 1) \leq t + 5$ **12.** $3m - 4 < 2(5m + 6) - 3m$

Solve each problem. (*Pages 291–294*)

13. Phillip scored 18 points in one basketball game and 13 points in another. What is the least number of points he must score in the next game if his average for the 3 games is to be more than 14 points?

14. Tom plans to spend no more than $245 for a life vest and a pair of skis. Suppose the cost of the skis is $2 more than 3 times the vest. What is the greatest amount Tom can spend for the vest?

Write each compound sentence as two simple sentences joined by <u>or</u> or <u>and</u>. (*Pages 295–298*)

15. $4x \geq -12$ **16.** $c + 4 \leq 0$ **17.** $-5 < t < 1$

18. $-12 < 3p < -3$ **19.** $6s - 8 \geq 4$ **20.** $-1 < \frac{1}{4}d + 1 < 3$

Solve and graph each inequality. (*Pages 295–298*)

21. $-3 < x < 4$ **22.** $-4t \geq 0$ **23.** $-4 < m - 2 \leq 4$

Solve and check each equation. (*Pages 302–305*)

24. $|x - 2| = 7$ **25.** $|4y| - 5 = 3$ **26.** $|-\frac{1}{2}n| = 3$

27. $|6 - p| = 5$ **28.** $12 = |r| + 7$ **29.** $|2(a + 3) - a| = 5$

Solve and graph each inequality. (*Pages 302–305*)

30. $|x| < 6$ **31.** $|n - 2| < 4$ **32.** $|4t| > 16$ **33.** $|7c + 5| > -2$

Graph each inequality on the coordinate plane. (*Pages 306–308*)

34. $y > -4x$ **35.** $y \leq x - 1$ **36.** $x + y < -2$ **37.** $-x + y \geq 5$

Match each graph in Exercises 38–41 with one of the systems given in a–d.
(*Pages 309–311*)

38. 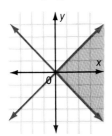 **39.** 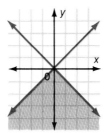 **40.** 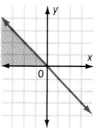 **41.**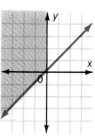

a. $\begin{cases} y \le x \\ y \le -x \end{cases}$ **b.** $\begin{cases} y \le -x \\ y \ge 0 \end{cases}$ **c.** $\begin{cases} x \le 0 \\ y \ge x \end{cases}$ **d.** $\begin{cases} y \le x \\ y \ge -x \end{cases}$

Solve each system by graphing. (*Pages 309–311*)

42. $\begin{cases} y < x + 3 \\ y < -5x \end{cases}$ **43.** $\begin{cases} y \ge 2x \\ y \ge x - 1 \end{cases}$ **44.** $\begin{cases} 3x - y > -2 \\ x + 2y < 4 \end{cases}$ **45.** $\begin{cases} x + y \ge 2 \\ x - y \le 6 \\ y \le 0 \end{cases}$

In Exercises 46–51, find the maximum
and minimum values for k, given the
constraints shown in the graph. (*Pages 312–314*)

46. $k = x + y$ **47.** $k = 3x + y$

48. $k = x + 4y$ **49.** $k = 2x - y$

50. $k = 3x - 2y$ **51.** $k = x - 3y$

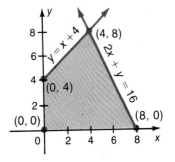

Each of three old machines can stamp out 4 parts per minute. Each of four
newer machines can stamp out 6 parts per minute. Only 5 workers are
available at any one time to operate the machines.

Use this information in Exercises 52–56.

52. Let x represent the number of old machines used and let y represent the number
of newer machines used. Write an expression to represent the total number of
parts made per minute.

53. Write a system of inequalities that shows the constraints on x and y.

54. Graph the system of inequalities you wrote in Exercise 53.

55. Write the coordinates of the vertices of the polygonal region graphed in
Exercise 54.

56. What is the maximum number of parts that can be made per minute?

Solve and graph each inequality on a number line.

1. $x + 6 < 9$

2. $-4c > 8$

3. $4r - 7 \leq -3$

Solve each problem.

4. Dale deposited $180 in his savings account, bringing his savings to over $800. What is the smallest amount that could have been in his account before this deposit?

5. The sum of two consecutive positive integers is less than 190. Find the pair with the greatest possible sum.

Write each compound sentence as two simple sentences joined by <u>or</u> or <u>and</u>.

6. $x - 3 \geq 9$

7. $3x + 2 \leq 10$

8. $-8 < 2n + 6 < -2$

Solve and graph each inequality on a number line.

9. $4x \leq 12$

10. $-3 < y + 1 < 5$

11. $|n - 2| > 3$

Solve and check each equation.

12. $|x| = 20$

13. $|t - 2| = 4$

14. Graph the inequality $2x + y \leq 4$ on the coordinate plane.

15. Solve by graphing: $\begin{cases} y < x \\ y < 3x + 6 \end{cases}$

A manufacturer makes two models of a watch. The profit on Model A is $5 per watch and the profit on Model B is $12 per watch. The manufacturer can produce no more than 300 watches per week. To meet the market demand, at least 110 Model A watches and 60 Model B watches must be available each week. Use this information for Exercises 16–20.

16. Let x represent the number of Model A watches and let y represent the number of Model B watches produced per week. Write an expression to represent the total weekly profit.

17. Write a system of inequalities that shows the constraints on x and y.

18. Graph the system of inequalities you wrote in Exercise 17.

19. State the coordinates of the vertices of the polygonal region graphed in Exercise 18.

20. What is the maximum profit possible?

Skills

Solve each inequality. (*Pages 283–286, 287–290*)

1. $5(a + 1) - 2(2a - 1) \leq 0$

2. $3(2n + 1) - 5n \geq 2n - 1$

3. $1 + n > 3(1 - n)$

4. $5(3 - n \geq 2(n + \frac{1}{2})$

Write each compound sentence as two simple sentences joined by <u>or</u> or <u>and</u>. (*Pages 295–298*)

5. $2y \geq 5 \ 2y =$

6. $\frac{1}{3}n - 2 \geq 3$

7. $-6 < 4a + 6 < -2$

Solve and graph each inequality on a number line. (*Pages 295–298*)

8. $3n \leq 12$

9. $-5 < 2p + 3 \leq 3$

10. $3(n + 1) \leq -6$

Graph each inequality on the coordinate plane. (*Pages 306–308*)

11. $y > x - 1$

12. $y \leq -2x$

13. $x + y < -4$

14. $2x - y \geq 1$

Solve each system by graphing. (*Pages 309–311*)

15. $\begin{cases} x - y < 4 \\ x + y > 0 \end{cases}$

16. $\begin{cases} y \geq 3x \\ y \geq -x + 1 \end{cases}$

17. $\begin{cases} 3x - y > 2 \\ 2x + y < -3 \end{cases}$

18. $\begin{cases} y > -x + 4 \\ y > x \end{cases}$

Problem Solving and Applications

19. A nursery had a sale on seedlings. Each customer had to buy at least 15, but no more than 100, seedlings. Represent this as an inequality, where *s* is the number of seedlings per customer. (*Pages 295–298*)

20. Jim threw the javelin four times for distances of 165, 170, 158, and 178 feet. What is the least distance he must get on his fifth throw in order to average at least 170 feet for the five throws? (*Pages 291–294*)

A group of 360 people is to be bused to the state fair. The bus company has four 60-passenger buses and six 40-passenger buses available. The cost of renting a 60-passenger bus is $200; the cost of renting a 40-passenger bus is $140. Use this information in Exercises 21–23. (*Pages 312–314*)

21. Let *x* represent the number of 60-passenger buses rented and let *y* represent the number of 40-passenger buses. Write an expression to represent the total cost.

22. Write and graph a system of inequalities showing the constraints on *x* and *y*.

23. Write the coordinates of the vertices of the polygonal region graphed in Exercise 22 and find the minimum cost possible.

Cumulative Maintenance: Chapters 1-8

Part 1

Choose the best answer. Choose *a*, *b*, *c*, or *d*.

1. Which of the following is equivalent to $4x \leq 7$?

   a. $7 > 4x$ **b.** $4x = 7$

   c. $4x < 7$ and $4x = 7$ **d.** $4x < 7$ or $4x = 7$

2. Which point is <u>not</u> on the graph of $y = |x|$?

   a. $(0, 0)$ **b.** $(-1, -1)$ **c.** $(-3, 3)$ **d.** $(12, 12)$

3. Solve the equation $\frac{1}{4}(2x - 8) = 4x + 5$.

   a. $x = -2$ **b.** $x = 1\frac{5}{9}$ **c.** $x = 2$ **d.** $x = -1\frac{5}{9}$

4. For all rational numbers, a, b, and c, if $a > b$ and $c > 0$, which of the following statements is true?

   a. $ac < bc$ **b.** $ac > bc$ **c.** $ac < b$ **d.** $ac = bc$

5. Simplify: $3ab + 2a^2b - 4(ab - 3a^2b) + a^2b$

   a. ab **b.** $-ab + a^2b$ **c.** $15a^2b - ab$ **d.** $7ab - a^2b$

6. 30% of a number is 21. What is the number?

   a. 90   **b.** 70   **c.** 80   **d.** 60

7. If y varies directly as x and $y = 3.2$ when $x = 1.2$, find y when $x = 8.4$.

   a. 22.4   **b.** 2.0   **c.** 19.2   **d.** -22.4

8. Which ordered pair is a solution of the system $\begin{cases} 2x + y = 3? \\ x - 2y = 4 \end{cases}$

   a. $(2, 2)$ **b.** $(2, 1)$ **c.** $(2, -1)$ **d.** $(2, 0)$

9. Which system has no solutions?

   a. $\begin{cases} 4x + y = 6 \\ y = 4x + 9 \end{cases}$ **b.** $\begin{cases} 3x - 2y = 8 \\ 2y = 5x + 7 \end{cases}$ **c.** $\begin{cases} 7y - 4x = 3 \\ y = \frac{4}{7}x - 2 \end{cases}$ **d.** $\begin{cases} x - y = 15 \\ 3x + 5y = 17 \end{cases}$

10. Solve: $-\frac{2}{3}x > 4$

    a. $x < 6$ **b.** $x > 6$ **c.** $x > -6$ **d.** $x < -6$

11. Solve $|4y| = 16$.

    a. $\{-4\}$ **b.** $\{4\}$ **c.** $\{16\}$ **d.** $\{-4, 4\}$

12. Which property is illustrated by this statement?

    $$a(b + c) = ab + ac$$

    a. associative   **b.** distributive   **c.** commutative   **d.** reflexive

13. Solve $4 - 3x \leq -11$

    a. $x \geq 5$ **b.** $x \leq 5$ **c.** $x \leq -5$ **d.** $x \geq -5$

14. Solve $2t + 4 > 6t - 8$.

    a. $t > 3$ **b.** $t < 3$ **c.** $t < 1$ **d.** $t > 1$

15. What is the solution set of $|2(x - 1) - 8| = 4$?

    a. $\{-7, 3\}$ **b.** $\{7, 3\}$ **c.** $\{7\}$ **d.** $\{3\}$

16. What is the meaning of the inequality $-4 < x < 7$?

    a. $-4 < x$ <u>or</u> $x < 7$ **b.** $-4 < x$ <u>and</u> $x < 7$

    c. $x > 7$ <u>or</u> $x > -4$ **d.** $x > 7$ <u>and</u> $x < -4$

17. What is the equation of the line that passes through the points $(0, 0)$ and $(4, 4)$?

    a. $y = x$ **b.** $y = x + 4$ **c.** $y = x - 4$ **d.** $y = 4x$

18. Which point is on the line parallel to the x axis and 4 units below it?

    a. $(4, 0)$ **b.** $(1, 4)$ **c.** $(2, -4)$ **d.** $(-4, 0)$

Part 2

Solve each problem.

19. Cliff Stevens earns $1750 per month plus a 4% commission on the sales he makes. Last month he earned a total of $2325. What were his sales that month?

20. The sum of the digits of a two-digit number is 10. When 54 is added to the number, the result is the original number with its digits reversed. Find the number.

21. Two trains 1240 kilometers apart start at the same time and travel toward each other. One travels at a rate of 70 kilometers per hour and the other at a rate of 85 kilometers per hour. In how many hours will they meet?

22. Jay's had sales of $7500 which were deposited into a checking account. Then an additional $2000 was deposited. If over $12,000 are now in the account, what is the smallest amount that could have been in the account originally?

23. Ted Simms borrowed $25,000 for one year, part at 8% and the rest at 10%. If the rates of interest were interchanged, Ted would have paid $50 more in interest. Find the amount he borrowed at each rate.

24. James can ride his mountain bike at a rate of 0.2 miles per minute. How many hours will it take him to travel a distance of 54 miles?

25. The shortest side of a triangular sail is one-fifth the length of the longest side. The third side is four feet shorter than the longest side. Find the lengths of the sides of the sail if the perimeter is 40 feet.

26. The amount of money Helen earns varies directly with the number of orders she fills. Last week, for 217 orders, she earned $737.80. How much will Helen earn by filling 176 orders?

Exponents and Polynomials

Each circuit on a silicon chip can be as small as 5×10^{-4} millimeter or 2×10^{-6} inch. The measures, 5×10^{-4} and 2×10^{-6}, are expressed in **scientific notation,** a method often used to write very large or very small numbers.

9-1 Exponents

Suppose that you have a choice between two jobs. The first job pays $20 per hour. Your monthly salary for a 35-hour week would be about $2800.

The second job pays 1¢ on the first day of work. Then for each day after the first, you would receive double the preceding day's wage. Which job would you choose?

The partial table below shows how to compute each day's wages for the second job.

Day	Wages in Cents	Powers of Two	
		Factor Form	Exponent Form
1	1		2^0
2	2	2	2^1
3	4	2×2	2^2
4	8	$2 \times 2 \times 2$	2^3
5	16	$2 \times 2 \times 2 \times 2$	2^4
6	32	$2 \times 2 \times 2 \times 2 \times 2$	2^5
.	.	.	.
.	.	.	.
.	.	.	.
29	268,435,456	$\underbrace{2 \times 2 \times 2 \cdots \times 2 \times 2}_{\textbf{28 factors}}$	2^{28}
30	536,870,912	$\underbrace{2 \times 2 \times \cdots \times 2 \times 2}_{\textbf{29 factors}}$	2^{29}

POWERS

Each day's wages for the second job can be expressed as a power of 2. For example, the 6th day's wages can be written as

$$2^5 = \underbrace{2 \times 2 \times 2 \times 2 \times 2}_{\textbf{5 factors}} = 32¢$$

The wages on day 30 are 2^{29}¢, or over 5 million dollars!
Note how powers are read.

For 2^2, read "two squared" or "the second power of 2."

For 2^3, read "two cubed" or "the third power of 2."

For 2^4, read "two to the fourth" or "the fourth power of 2."

For 2^n, read "two to the *n*th" or "the *n*th power of 2."

Exponents and Polynomials   **325**

Examples of exponents used with other bases are given below.

Expression	Base	Exponent	Meaning
3^2	3	2	$3 \cdot 3$
5^4	5	4	$5 \cdot 5 \cdot 5 \cdot 5$
15^1	15	1	15
$(-3)^2$	-3	2	$(-3)(-3)$
x^7	x	7	$x \cdot x \cdot x \cdot x \cdot x \cdot x \cdot x$
x^a	x	a	$\underbrace{x \cdot x \cdot x \cdot \;\cdots\; \cdot x}_{a \text{ factors}}$

DEFINITIONS

If x is a real number and a is an integer greater than 1, then
$$x^a = \underbrace{x \cdot x \cdot x \cdot \;\cdots\; \cdot x,}_{a \text{ factors}}$$
When $a = 1$, $x^a = x$. That is, $x^1 = x$.

EXPONENTIAL FORM

Example 1 shows how the definition is used to write a number in exponential form.

EXAMPLE 1   Write 10,000 in exponential form.

Solution: $10,000 = 10 \cdot 10 \cdot 10 \cdot 10$ ⟵ **Write as factors of 10.**

$= 10^4$ ⟵ **By definition**

The definition can also be used to write certain products as a base with a single exponent.

EXAMPLE 2   Write $2^5 \cdot 2^3$ as a base with a single exponent.

Solution: $2^5 \cdot 2^3 = \underbrace{2 \cdot 2 \cdot 2 \cdot 2 \cdot 2}_{\textbf{Five factors}} \cdot \underbrace{2 \cdot 2 \cdot 2}_{\textbf{Three factors}}$

$\underbrace{}_{\textbf{Eight factors}}$

$= 2^8$

Example 3 shows how the definition is applied when evaluating expressions.

EXAMPLE 3 Find the value of x^3y^2 when $x = -2$ and $y = 3$.

 Solution: Replace x with -2 and y with 3.

$$x^3y^2 = (-2)^3(3)^2$$
$$= (-2)(-2)(-2)\,(3)(3) \quad \longleftarrow \quad \textbf{By definition}$$
$$= \quad\quad (-8) \quad \cdot \quad 9 \quad = -72$$

EXERCISES: Classwork/Homework

 Objective: To evaluate expressions with exponents

CHECK YOUR UNDERSTANDING

1. How many factors of 2 are there in 2^{17}?

2. How many factors of 5 are there in 5^{10}?

3. How many factors of 4 are there in $4^3 \cdot 4^4$?

4. How many factors of 7 are there in $7^5 \cdot 7^6$?

PRACTICE AND APPLY

 Complete.

	Expression	Base	Exponent	Meaning
5.	5^6	?	?	?
6.	10^3	?	?	?
7.	2^6	?	?	?
8.	a^5	?	?	?
9.	?	10	5	?
10.	?	2	3	?
11.	?	?	?	$10 \cdot 10 \cdot 10 \cdot 10$
12.	?	?	?	$x \cdot x \cdot x \cdot x \cdot x \cdot x \cdot x$
13.	?	?	?	x

 Evaluate.

14. 10^2 **15.** 10^4 **16.** 10^1 **17.** 10^5 **18.** 10^7 **19.** 10^{10}

20. How many zeros follow the "1" in the decimal numeral for 10^{13}?

21. How many zeros follow the "1" in the decimal numeral for 10^a?

Exponents and Polynomials **327**

Evaluate.

22. $(-1)^3$ 23. $(-1)^7$ 24. $(-1)^9$ 25. $(-1)^5$ 26. $(-1)^{11}$ 27. $(-1)^{99}$

28. $(-1)^2$ 29. $(-1)^6$ 30. $(-1)^4$ 31. $(-1)^{10}$ 32. $(-1)^{30}$ 33. $(-1)^{100}$

Write in exponential form.

34. 100   35. 100,000   36. 1,000,000   37. 1 million   38. 1 billion

39. 1 thousand   40. 10 billion   41. 1,000,000,000   42. 10   43. 1 trillion

Write each product as a base with a single exponent.

44. $10^3 \cdot 10^2$ 45. $2^3 \cdot 2^4$ 46. $5^2 \cdot 5^3$ 47. $10 \cdot 10^4$

48. $5^3 \cdot 5^2$ 49. $2^3 \cdot 2^3$ 50. $15^2 \cdot 15^4$ 51. $2^{15} \cdot 2^2$

52. $x^2 \cdot x^3$ 53. $a^4 \cdot a^2$ 54. $y^5 \cdot y^4$ 55. $m^6 \cdot m^2$

Find the value when $a = 1$, $b = 2$, and $c = -3$.

56. a^5 57. $(-b)^2$ 58. c^3 59. $a^2 b$

60. ab^2 61. $a^2 c^2$ 62. $b^2 c^2$ 63. abc

64. $a^2 b^2 c^2$ 65. abc^2 66. $a^{25} b^2$ 67. $a^{100} b^3 c$

━━━ **MAINTAIN**

Solve each system by graphing. (*Pages 309–311*)

68. $\begin{cases} x + 3y \geq 6 \\ 2x - y \leq -3 \end{cases}$

69. $\begin{cases} y < x + 2 \\ y \leq -2x \end{cases}$

70. $\begin{cases} y > x - 5 \\ x \leq -4 \end{cases}$

71. $\begin{cases} x + y > 3 \\ y > x \end{cases}$

Solve.

72. The sum of the digits of a two-digit number is 10. When 54 is added to the number, the result is the original number with its digits reversed. Find the number. (*Pages 266–269*)

73. In the last three weeks, Carla earned $38, $45, and $52. How much must she earn this week in order to have average earnings of at least $48 per week for four weeks? (*Pages 291–294*)

──── **REVIEW CAPSULE FOR SECTION 9-2** ────

Multiply. (*Pages 70–73*)

1. $(-40)(-5)$ 2. $18(-21)$ 3. $2(-3)(-3)(-3)$ 4. $(-1)(-1)(-1)(-1)$

5. $(-18)(-20)0$ 6. $(-6)(15)(20)(-2)$ 7. $4(-1)(-7)(-10)$ 8. $(-1)(-1)(-1)$

9-2 Multiplying Monomials

When exponential expressions have the *same base*, their product can be expressed using the same base and a single exponent by applying the definition of exponent.

a. $4^3 \cdot 4^2 = 4 \cdot 4 \cdot 4 \cdot 4 \cdot 4$ **b.** $x^4 \cdot x^4 = x \cdot x \cdot x \cdot x \cdot x \cdot x \cdot x \cdot x$

$$= 4^5 \qquad\qquad\qquad\qquad = x^8$$

Note in **a** and **b** that the *sum* of the exponents equals the *single exponent* in the answer. This suggests the following property.

PRODUCT PROPERTY OF POWERS

If x is a real number and a and b are positive integers, then

$$x^a \cdot x^b = x^{a+b}$$

$x^1 \cdot x^2 = x^{1+2} = x^3$
$x^5 \cdot x^3 = x^{5+3} = x^8$

This property can be used to find products such as $(-3x^2)(2x)$.

EXAMPLE 1 Find each product.

     a. $(-3x^2)(2x)$ **b.** $(-3ab^2)(-2a^3b^5)$

Solutions:

a. $(-3x^2)(2x) = (-3 \cdot 2)(x^2 \cdot x)$ **b.** $(-3ab^2)(-2a^3b^5) = (-3 \cdot -2)(a \cdot a^3)(b^2 \cdot b^5)$
$$= -6x^{2+1} \qquad\qquad\qquad\qquad\qquad = 6a^{1+3}b^{2+5}$$
$$= -6x^3 \qquad\qquad\qquad\qquad\qquad\quad = 6a^4b^7$$

Expressions such as $-3x^2$ and $2x$ are *monomials*.

DEFINITION

A **monomial** is a number, a variable, or the product of numbers and variables with nonnegative integral exponents.

Monomial	Not a Monomial	
$\sqrt{3}x^2$	$3x^{-2}$	← **Negative exponent**
$\frac{1}{4}x^2y^2$	$3y^2 + 7y + 7$	← **Sum of monomials**
8	$4x^{\frac{1}{2}}$	← **Rational number exponent**

Exponents and Polynomials   **329**

The Product Property of Powers can also be used to write in exponential form.

EXAMPLE 2 Write in exponential form: $(4 \times 10^5)(2 \times 10^8)$

Solution: $(4 \times 10^5)(2 \times 10^8) = (4 \times 2)(10^5 \times 10^8)$

$$= 8 \times 10^{5+8} \quad \longleftarrow \quad \textbf{Product Property}$$

$$= \textbf{8} \times \textbf{10}^{\textbf{13}}$$

EXERCISES: Classwork/Homework

Objective: To multiply monomials

CHECK YOUR UNDERSTANDING

For Exercises 1–8, tell whether each product can be expressed using the same base and a single exponent. Write Yes or No.

1. $3^7 \cdot 3^4$ **2.** $2^5 \cdot 4^5$ **3.** $4 \cdot 4^6$ **4.** $5^2 \cdot 3^3$

5. $1^1 \cdot 1^2$ **6.** $6^3 \cdot 3^6$ **7.** $8 \cdot 7$ **8.** $2^{10} \cdot 2^8$

For Exercises 9–16, tell whether each expression is a monomial. Write Yes or No.

9. $2x$ **10.** $-\frac{3}{4}x^5$ **11.** $4x^2 + 6x$ **12.** $\sqrt{5}xy$

13. $-5ab^2$ **14.** $6c^{\frac{1}{4}}$ **15.** $12y^{-3}$ **16.** $4ab^2c^4$

PRACTICE AND APPLY

Find each product.

17. $(x \cdot x \cdot x \cdot x)(x \cdot x \cdot x)$ **18.** $(3 \cdot 3)(3 \cdot 3 \cdot 3 \cdot 3)$ **19.** $(-y)(y \cdot y)$

20. $x^4 \cdot x^5$ **21.** $x^2 \cdot x^4$ **22.** $m \cdot m^6$

23. $n^3 \cdot n^4$ **24.** $b \cdot b^2$ **25.** $a(a)$

26. $b^2 \cdot b^3$ **27.** $(-b)(-b)$ **28.** $b(-b)$

29. $x(-x^2)$ **30.** $(-y^2)(y^2)$ **31.** $-y(-y^2)$

32. $p^3 \cdot p^2$ **33.** $-x(-x^2)$ **34.** $3^6 \cdot 3^4$

35. $2(2^3)(2^4)$ **36.** $3(3^2)(3^4)$ **37.** $5^2(-5^2)(5^3)$

38. $(-4x^2y)(-5xy)$ **39.** $(-3a^2b)(ab)(-2ab)$ **40.** $(8mn^2)(-3m^2y^4)$

41. $(2x)(3x^4)(-6x^3)$ **42.** $(4c^2d)(5cd)(cd^2)$ **43.** $-1(x^3)(-x)$

44. $10^3 \cdot 10^2 \cdot 10^4$ **45.** $10^5 \cdot 10^8 \cdot 10$ **46.** $10 \cdot 10^5 \cdot 10^9$

Write each product in exponential form.

47. $(2 \times 10^2)(3 \times 10^4)$ **48.** $(7 \times 10)(9 \times 10^5)$ **49.** $(1.5 \times 10^3)(2 \times 10^6)$

50. $(2.4 \times 10^7)(3.9 \times 10)$ **51.** $(2.8 \times 10^9)(a \times 10^2)$ **52.** $(a \times 10^x)(b \times 10^y)$

Identify the number named by each product as positive, $\underline{P}$, or negative, $\underline{N}$.

53. $(-1)^4(-1)^3$ **54.** $(-1)^{10}(-1)^8$ **55.** -10^4 **56.** -3^{15} **57.** $(-3)^{15}$ **58.** $(-4)^{25}$

■■■■■ **MAINTAIN**

Evaluate. (*Pages 325–328*)

59. 10^4 **60.** 10^2 **61.** 10^6 **62.** $(-1)^4$ **63.** $(-1)^7$ **64.** $(-1)^{23}$

In Exercises 65–68:

a. Graph the solution set of each system of inequalities and determine the coordinates of the resulting polygonal region.

b. Find the minimum values of $k = x + 3y$ over the region graphed. (*Pages 309–311*)

65. $\begin{cases} x \geq 0 \\ y \geq 0 \\ x + y \leq 6 \end{cases}$ **66.** $\begin{cases} y \leq 9 - x \\ x \geq 0 \\ x \leq 7 \\ y \geq 0 \end{cases}$ **67.** $\begin{cases} y \leq 1 + \frac{1}{2}x \\ x \leq 6 \\ x \geq 0 \\ y \geq 0 \end{cases}$ **68.** $\begin{cases} y \leq 6 - \frac{3}{2}x \\ y \geq 1 \\ x \geq 0 \end{cases}$

Use the substitution method to solve each system. (*Pages 249–251*)

69. $\begin{cases} x = y + 3 \\ 2x - 6y = 26 \end{cases}$ **70.** $\begin{cases} 5c = d \\ c = 2d - 18 \end{cases}$ **71.** $\begin{cases} m = n + 2 \\ 2m + 2n = 8 \end{cases}$

■■■■■ **CONNECT AND EXTEND**

Write each product in exponential form. All exponents are positive integers.

72. $x^a \cdot x^2$ **73.** $y^2 \cdot y^b$ **74.** $x^a \cdot x^b$

75. $a^{x-2} \cdot a^5$ **76.** $x^{3a} \cdot x^{2a}$ **77.** $(x^{2a+7})(x^{2a-8})^0$

78. $3^x \cdot 3^2$ **79.** $2^{4a} \cdot 2^{3a}$ **80.** $(2^{2a+7})(2^{7a-6})$

81. $(x + 2)^2 \cdot (x + 2)^4$ **82.** $(x + 2)^a \cdot (x + 2)^6$ **83.** $(x + 2)^{2a} \cdot (x + 2)^{b-a}$

■■■■■ **NON-ROUTINE PROBLEM**

84. This cube was painted on all sides and then cut into 27 equal smaller cubes.

a. How many smaller cubes have paint on only 2 sides?

b. How many smaller cubes have paint on only 1 side?

9-3 Powers of Monomials

The Product Property of Powers can be used to write expressions such as $(5^4)^2$ with a single exponent.

a. $(5^4)^2 = 5^4 \cdot 5^4$
$\quad\quad\quad = 5^{4+4}$
$\quad\quad\quad = 5^8$

b. $(t^3)^4 = t^3 \cdot t^3 \cdot t^3 \cdot t^3$
$\quad\quad\quad = t^{3+3+3+3}$
$\quad\quad\quad = t^{12}$

The examples suggest this property.

POWER OF A POWER

If x is a real number and a and b are positive numbers, then

$$(x^a)^b = x^{ab}.$$

$(x^4)^2 = x^8$
$(x^2)^3 = x^6$

Example 1 shows you how to apply this property.

EXAMPLE 1 Simplify: **a.** $(6^3)^9$ **b.** $(z^5)^{10}$

Solutions: **a.** $(6^3)^9 = 6^{3 \cdot 9}$ **b.** $(z^5)^{10} = z^{5 \cdot 10}$
$\quad\quad\quad\quad\quad\quad\quad = 6^{27}$ $= z^{50}$

The following examples suggest a method for multiplying an exponential expression having a monomial base.

c. $(3r)^3 = (3r)(3r)(3r)$
$\quad\quad\quad = (3 \cdot 3 \cdot 3)(r \cdot r \cdot r)$
$\quad\quad\quad = 3^3 r^3$, or $27r^3$

d. $(xy)^5 = (xy)(xy)(xy)(xy)(xy)$
$\quad\quad\quad = (x \cdot x \cdot x \cdot x \cdot x)(y \cdot y \cdot y \cdot y \cdot y)$
$\quad\quad\quad = x^5 y^5$

Thus, a power of a product of two or more factors equals the product of the powers of each factor.

POWER OF A PRODUCT

If x and y are real numbers and a is a positive integer, then

$$(xy)^a = x^a y^a.$$

$(xy)^4 = x^4 y^4$
$(4a)^2 = 4^2 a^2$, or
$16a^2$

Recall that $-x = -1 \cdot x$. Thus, two factors of $-x$ are -1 and x.

EXAMPLE 2 Simplify: **a.** $(-x)^6$ **b.** $\left(-\frac{2}{3}x^5y^2\right)^3$

    Solutions: **a.** $(-x)^6 = (-1 \cdot x)^6$ **b.** $\left(-\frac{2}{3}x^5y^2\right)^3 = \left(-\frac{2}{3}\right)^3(x^5)^3(y^2)^3$

$\qquad\qquad\qquad\quad = (-1)^6(x)^6$

$\qquad\qquad\qquad\quad = x^6 \qquad\qquad\qquad\qquad\qquad\qquad\qquad = -\frac{8}{27}x^{15}y^6$

NOTE: Raising a negative number to an *even-numbered* exponent gives a *positive* number. Raising a negative number to an *odd-numbered* exponent gives a *negative* number.

EXERCISES: Classwork/Homework

    Objective: To raise an expression to a power

CHECK YOUR UNDERSTANDING

Classify each sentence as true, <u>T</u>, or false, <u>F</u>. When a sentence is false, tell why it is false.

1. $(y^2)^3 = y^2 \cdot y^3$ **2.** $(x^5)^2 = x^{10}$ **3.** $(-4a)^3 = 64a^3$ **4.** $(xy^2)^4 = xy^8$

5. $(3b^2)^2 = 9b^4$ **6.** $(-5c^3)^3 = -125c^9$ **7.** $(-x^4y^2)^2 = -x^8y^4$ **8.** $(2a^2b^2)^5 = 2a^7b^7$

PRACTICE AND APPLY

Simplify. No denominator equals zero.

9. $(x^3)^2$ **10.** $(x^2)^6$ **11.** $(x^4)^2$ **12** $(a^3)^4$

13. $(x^3)^5$ **14.** $(x^7)^3$ **15.** $(x^5)^2$ **16.** $(x^2)^5$

17. $(y^3)^3$ **18.** $(a^5)^6$ **19.** $(b^4)^6$ **20.** $(y^4)^8$

21. $(ab)^3$ **22.** $(xy)^2$ **23.** $(2x)^2$ **24.** $(2xy)^2$

25. $(xyz)^4$ **26.** $(-5)^2$ **27.** $(-6)^2$ **28.** $(-x)^4$

29. $(-x)^5$ **30.** $(-y)^2$ **31.** $(-4x)^2$ **32.** $(-ab)^3$

33. $(3a^2b)^2$ **34.** $(6a^2)^3$ **35.** $(-3b)^3$ **36.** $(2x^3y^2)^3$

37. $(3^2a^2b^4)^2$ **38.** $(4x^3y^2)^3$ **39.** $(2m^3n^2)^4$ **40.** $(2a^2b)^3$

41. $(4a^4c^2d^3)^3$ **42.** $(16x^3y^2)^2$ **43.** $(2x^3y^2)^6$ **44.** $(a^2b)^3$

45. $(-x^4y^3)^2$ **46.** $(-x^4y^2)^3$ **47.** $(2 \times 10^3)^2$ **48.** $(3 \times 10^5)^4$

49. $\left(\frac{2}{3}\right)^3$ **50.** $\left(\frac{1}{3}\right)^4$ **51.** $\left(\frac{c}{d}\right)^7$ **52.** $\left(\frac{ab}{c}\right)^5$ **53.** $\left(\frac{x^2}{y^3}\right)^2$

54. $\left(\frac{b^2}{a}\right)^2$ **55.** $\left(\frac{c^2}{d}\right)^3$ **56.** $\left(\frac{a^2}{b^3}\right)^3$ **57.** $\left(\frac{a^3}{b}\right)^6$ **58.** $\left(\frac{x^3}{y^2}\right)^2$

Exponents and Polynomials   **333**

Match each expression in Column I with an equivalent expression in Column II.

Column I

59. $(x^2)^n$

60. $(-3x^a)^3$

61. $(x^n)^n$

62. $(3x^a)^3$

63. $(xy^a)^b$

64. $\frac{3}{2}\left(\frac{m}{n}\right)^c$

65. $\left(\frac{x}{y^a}\right)^b$

66. $\left(\frac{3m}{2n}\right)^c$

Column II

a. x^{n^2}

b. $-27x^{3a}$

c. $\frac{3m^c}{2n^c}$

d. $\frac{x^b}{y^{ab}}$

e. $27x^{3a}$

f. $x^b y^{ab}$

g. $\frac{3^c m^c}{2^c n^c}$

h. $\frac{x^b}{y^a}$

i. x^{2n}

j. xy^{ab}

███████ **MAINTAIN**

Find each product. (*Pages 329–331*)

67. $x^4 \cdot x^6$

68. $(-y)(y^2)$

69. $(-4ab)(ab)(2b^2)$

70. $-1(xy^2)(4x^2y^3)$

Write in exponential form. (*Pages 325–328*)

71. 100

72. 100,000

73. 10 million

74. 10 billion

Solve each system. (*Pages 249–255*)

75. $\begin{cases} 2x - y = 15 \\ x + y = 6 \end{cases}$

76. $\begin{cases} r - 3s = 15 \\ -r = 6 \end{cases}$

77. $\begin{cases} a = 4b + 3 \\ a = -4b - 11 \end{cases}$

78. $\begin{cases} 5y = -3x + 15 \\ -6y = 3x - 10 \end{cases}$

79. $\begin{cases} 3x + 6y = 9 \\ -6y = -6 \end{cases}$

80. $\begin{cases} -4x + y = 0 \\ 4x - 3y = 0 \end{cases}$

███████ **CONNECT AND EXTEND**

Simplify. All variables represent positive integers.

81. $\left(\frac{a^2}{bc^3}\right)^4$

82. $\left(\frac{r^3}{s^2t}\right)^5$

83. $\left(\frac{a^3b^2}{c^4}\right)^3$

84. $\left(\frac{xy^6}{z^2}\right)^2$

85. $(-2a^3b^2)(3a^4b^6)$

86. $x \cdot x^2(x^3)^2$

87. $\left(\frac{-3x^2}{4y^2}\right)^3$

88. $(a^n)^m$

89. $(x^n)^n$

90. $(a^6)^m$

91. $\left(\frac{m}{n}\right)^k$

92. $\left(\frac{x^2}{y}\right)^c$

93. $\left(\frac{3x^n}{5y^m}\right)^c$

94. $\left(\frac{3x^3}{4y^2}\right)^m$

95. $\left(\frac{3a^mb^n}{2xy}\right)^k$

96. $\left(\frac{2ab}{4xy}\right)^d$

──────── **REVIEW CAPSULE FOR SECTION 9-4** ────────

Find each quotient. (*Pages 78–82*)

1. $\frac{1}{4} \div (-1)$

2. $z \div (-1)$

3. $-8 \div \frac{1}{x}, x \neq 0$

4. $-r \div (-r), r \neq 0$

9-4 Dividing Monomials

The quotient of two exponential expressions can be written with a single exponent *if the expressions have the same base.*

a. $\dfrac{2^5}{2^3} = \dfrac{2 \cdot 2 \cdot 2 \cdot 2 \cdot 2}{2 \cdot 2 \cdot 2}$ ⟵ **By definition** ⟶ **b.** $\dfrac{x^6}{x^4} = \dfrac{x \cdot x \cdot x \cdot x \cdot x \cdot x}{x \cdot x \cdot x \cdot x}$

$\qquad = \left(\dfrac{2 \cdot 2 \cdot 2}{2 \cdot 2 \cdot 2}\right)(2 \cdot 2)$ ⟵ **By the Associative Property** ⟶ $= \left(\dfrac{x \cdot x \cdot x \cdot x}{x \cdot x \cdot x \cdot x}\right)(x \cdot x)$

$\qquad = \quad 1 \quad \cdot \quad 2^2 \qquad\qquad\qquad\qquad\qquad\qquad = \quad 1 \quad \cdot \quad x^2$

$\qquad = 2^2 \quad ⟵ \quad 2^2 = 2^{5-3} \qquad\qquad\qquad\quad = x^2 \quad ⟵ \quad x^2 = x^{6-4}$

NOTE: In **a** and **b**, subtracting the exponent of the denominator from the exponent of the numerator gives the single exponent in the answer. This suggests the following property.

QUOTIENT PROPERTY OF POWERS

> If x is a real number, $x \neq 0$, and a and b are positive integers such that $a \geq b$ then
>
> $$\dfrac{x^a}{x^b} = x^{a-b}$$
>
> $\dfrac{x^7}{x^3} = x^4$
>
> $\dfrac{x^5}{x^2} = x^3$

This property can be used to simplify quotients such as $\dfrac{x^4 y^3}{x^2 y}$.

EXAMPLE Simplify: **a.** $\dfrac{x^4 y^3}{x^2 y}$ **b.** $\dfrac{-6a^5 b^3 c^2}{2a^3 b^2 c}$

Solutions: **a.** $\dfrac{x^4 y^3}{x^2 y} = \left(\dfrac{x^4}{x^2}\right)\left(\dfrac{y^3}{y}\right)$

$\qquad\qquad\qquad = x^{(4-2)} y^{(3-1)}$

$\qquad\qquad\qquad = x^2 y^2$

b. $\dfrac{-6a^5 b^3 c^2}{2a^3 b^2 c} = \left(\dfrac{-6}{2}\right)\left(\dfrac{a^5}{a^3}\right)\left(\dfrac{b^3}{b^2}\right)\left(\dfrac{c^2}{c}\right)$

$\qquad\qquad\qquad = -3a^{(5-3)} b^{(3-2)} c^{(2-1)}$

$\qquad\qquad\qquad = -3a^2 bc$

NOTE: When $a = b$, it follows from the Quotient Property of Powers that

$$\dfrac{x^a}{x^b} = x^{a-b} = x^0 = 1.$$

This means that the zero power of any number equals 1.

ARGUMENT For example, $\dfrac{2}{2} = 1$ and $\dfrac{2^1}{2^1} = 1$. Since $\dfrac{2^1}{2^1} = 2^{1-1}$, $2^0 = 1$.

Objective: To divide monomials

▮▮▮▮▮ **CHECK YOUR UNDERSTANDING**

Simplify. No denominator equals zero.

1. $\dfrac{x^{12}}{x^6}$ 2. $\dfrac{a^{10}}{a^{10}}$ 3. $\dfrac{-x^3y^5}{x^2y^3}$ 4. $\dfrac{-56c^6}{-7c^2}$ 5. $\dfrac{8^{21}}{8^{19}}$ 6. $\dfrac{x^3y^5}{x^3y^5}$

▮▮▮▮▮ **PRACTICE AND APPLY**

Simplify. No denominator equals zero.

7. $\dfrac{2^3}{2}$ 8. $\dfrac{3^5}{3^2}$ 9. $\dfrac{5^6}{5^3}$ 10. $\dfrac{x^5}{x^5}$ 11. $\dfrac{a^6}{a}$ a^5 12. $\dfrac{a^9}{a^7}$

13. $\dfrac{x^8}{x^7}$ 14. $\dfrac{x^3y^2}{xy}$ 15. $\dfrac{a^3y^3}{a^2y}$ 16. $\dfrac{y^3}{y^2}$ 17. $\dfrac{a^3b^5}{ab^2}$ 18. $\dfrac{2x^7}{3x^7}$

19. $\dfrac{k^5m^3}{k^3m^2}$ 20. $\dfrac{18x^3y^4}{2xy^2}$ 21. $\dfrac{-15x^7y^5}{-3x^2y^4}$ 22. $\dfrac{-36a^2b^2c^4}{4abc^3}$

23. $\dfrac{-27r^5s^8}{-3r^3s^6}$ 24. $\dfrac{-2k^4m^3}{4k^2}$ 25. $\dfrac{8 \times 10^2}{2 \times 10^2}$ 26. $\dfrac{8 \times 10^{11}}{4 \times 10}$

Classify each quotient as positive, _P_, or negative, _N_.

27. $\dfrac{(-1)^8}{(-1)^2}$ 28. $\dfrac{(-5)^{15}}{(-5)^5}$ 29. $\left(\dfrac{-8}{-4}\right)^2$ 30. $\dfrac{(-3)^{19}}{(-3)^9}$

Classify each quotient as positive, _P_, or negative, _N_, when $x = -1$ and $y = -3$.

31. $\dfrac{x^5}{x^2}$ 32. $\dfrac{y^{10}}{y^3}$ 33. $\dfrac{x^2y}{x^2y}$ 34. $\dfrac{x^{95}}{x^3}$

Simplify. No denominator equals zero.

Example: $\dfrac{9xy(-4x^2y^3)}{-18x^2y^2} = \dfrac{-36x^3y^4}{-18x^2y^2} = \mathbf{2xy^2}$

35. $\dfrac{4ab(7a^2b^3)}{-14a^3b^3}$ 36. $\dfrac{4ab^2(-5ab^3)}{10a^2b^2}$ 37. $\dfrac{(-3ab^2)^2}{6ab}$ 38. $\dfrac{(3ab^2)^2(-6a^3b)}{(3a^2b^2)^2}$

39. $\dfrac{(5ab)^2(-20a^3b)}{4a^2b^3}$ 40. $\dfrac{(5a^2b)^2(-100b^3)}{(5^2b)^2}$ 41. $\dfrac{(5 \times 10^2)^3}{5 \times 10^2}$ 43. $\dfrac{(11 \times 10)^5}{(11 \times 10^2)^2}$

▮▮▮▮▮ **MAINTAIN**

Simplify. (*Pages 332–334*)

43. $(x^2)^4$ 44. $(a^7)^2$ 45. $(-4)^3$ 46. $(3a^2b^2c^3)^2$ 47. $(2 \times 10^4)^4$

Write each product in exponential form. (*Pages 329–331*)

48. $(2 \times 10^1)(4 \times 10^2)$ **49.** $(6 \times 10^2)(7 \times 10^3)$ **50.** $(1.7 \times 10^4)(a \times 10^3)$

51. $(1.5 \times 10^5)(2.9 \times 10)$ **52.** $(4.1 \times 10^7)(a \times 10^3)$ **53.** $(a \times 10^x)(c \times 10^y)$

Solve each system. (*Pages 256–259*)

54. $\begin{cases} 2x + y = 6 \\ 3x + y = 4 \end{cases}$ **55.** $\begin{cases} 7a - s = -3 \\ 7a + 4s = -18 \end{cases}$ **56.** $\begin{cases} 2m + 3n = 8 \\ 6m + 3n = 4 \end{cases}$

57. $\begin{cases} 2x + 3y = 2 \\ 3x + y = -4 \end{cases}$ **58.** $\begin{cases} 4a + 6b = 4 \\ 3a - 4b = 20 \end{cases}$ **59.** $\begin{cases} 3t + 2s = 9 \\ 3t + 3s = 15 \end{cases}$

▮▮▮▮ CONNECT AND EXTEND

Simplify. All exponents are positive integers. No denominator equals zero.

60. $\dfrac{a^x b^2 y}{a^x b y}$ **61.** $\dfrac{a^x b^4}{a^y}$ **62.** $\dfrac{a^t b^w}{a^v b^{25}}$ **63.** $\dfrac{x^{u-v} y^{w-z}}{x^{2r-u} y^w}$

64. $\dfrac{x^{3u-2v} y^3}{x^{2u+2v} y^2}$ **65.** $\dfrac{a^{3x}}{a^{2x}}$ **66.** $\dfrac{a^{2x} b^{3y} c^k}{abc}$ **67.** $\dfrac{ab^2 c^4 d^{2-k}}{ac^3 d^k}$

68. $\dfrac{(x^{2a+1})^2}{(x^{a-1})}$ **69.** $\dfrac{(y^{3a-9})^6}{y^{2a-4}}$ **70.** $\left(\dfrac{(x^{2a-4})^2}{x^{a+5}} \right)^3$ **71.** $\dfrac{(1.69 \times 10^3)^a}{(1.3 \times 10^a)^2}$

▮▮▮▮ NON-ROUTINE PROBLEM

72. There are six glasses in a row. Three of the glasses are empty and three are full. The arrangement of the glasses is empty, empty, empty, full, full, full. By moving one glass, change the arrangement to empty, full, empty, full, empty, full.

——— REVIEW CAPSULE FOR SECTION 9-5 ———

Find each product. (*Pages 329–331*)

1. $a^7 \cdot a^3$ **2.** $-c(c^3)$ **3.** $4^2 \cdot 4^5$ **4.** $x^2 \cdot x$

5. $(x^2 y)(xy)$ **6.** $(c^3 d)(3c^4)$ **7.** $10^5 \cdot 10^2 \cdot 10^3$ **8.** $10^5 \cdot 10 \cdot 10^2$

Write each product in exponential form. (*Pages 329–331*)

9. $(2 \times 10^2)(3 \times 10^4)$ **10.** $(7 \times 10^3)(1.5 \times 10^2)$ **11.** $(6.12 \times 10^5)(1.1 \times 10^3)$

Find the value when $a = -1$, $b = 3$, and $c = -4$. (*Pages 325–328*)

1. ab^2 **2.** a^2b **3.** abc^2 **4.** a^3c^3 **5.** a^3b^2c

Find each product. (*Pages 329–331*)

6. $n \cdot n^3$ **7.** $x^2(-x^3)$ **8.** $-(3a^3)(4a^4)$ **9.** $(2d)(3c^2d)(cd^2)$

Simplify. No denominator equals zero. (*Pages 332–334*)

10. $(y^2)^4$ **11.** $(-a^2b)^4$ **12.** $(2 \times 10^4)^2$ **13.** $\left(\dfrac{r^2}{st}\right)^3$

Simplify. No denominator equals zero. (*Pages 335–337*)

14. $\dfrac{a^8}{a^6}$ **15.** $\dfrac{xy^4}{xy^3}$ **16.** $\dfrac{-12b^2c^2}{4b}$ **17.** $\dfrac{4a(-2ab^2)}{2a^2}$

Historical Digest: **Population Growth**

In the early 1800's Thomas Malthus, an English economist, was concerned that the world's food supply would not be able to keep up with the growth of the population. The formula $A = p(1 + r)^t$, where A = the ending population, p = the beginning population, r = rate of growth, and t = time in years, can be used to find how fast a population can grow. For example, if a country has a population of one million people and a growth rate of 3% per year, the population will increase as follows.

Year	Population	Change per Year
1	1,000,000	—
2	1,030,000	30,000
3	1,060,900	30,900
4	1,092,727	31,727

You can see from the table that the population change increases each year. After 100 years, a population of one million people will increase to over 19 million people!

Suppose a certain country has a population of 5 million people. Use the formula given above and your calculator to find what the population will be in 100 years if the growth rate is 3% per year.

Compound Interest Formulas

Compound interest paid by a bank on deposits is computed on the total of the **principal** (amount deposited) plus the **interest** previously earned. The interest is usually paid more than once a year. This formula is used to compute compound interest.

$$A = p(1 + r)^n$$

A = amount of the new balance
r = rate of interest per period
p = principal
n = number of interest periods per year

EXAMPLE: The First City Bank pays 5% interest compounded quarterly (four times a year) on regular savings accounts. Anthony deposited $400 in a regular savings account. What will be the amount of his new balance after one year?

Solution: $A = p(1 + r)^n$

$p = \$400, n = 4, r = 0.0125$ ◄——— **$r = 0.05 \div 4$, or 0.0125**

$A = (400)(1 + 0.0125)^4$, or $400(1.0125)^4$

400 ☒× ☒(1.0125

☒y^x 4 ☒) ☒= ▐ 420.37813 ◄——— **Round to the nearest cent.**

Anthony will have **$420.38** in his account after one year.

EXERCISES For Exercises 1–3, find the new balance after one year.

1. $200; 6% interest
   Compounded
   quarterly

2. $500; 7% interest
   Compounded
   twice a year

3. $600; 6% interest
   Compounded
   monthly

4. Juan has $900 in a savings account. The bank pays 6% interest compounded twice a year. What will be the new balance after one year?

5. Cynthia has $300 in a savings account. The bank pays 5% interest compounded quarterly. What will be the new balance after one year?

9-5 Negative Exponents

Suppose that the Quotient Property of Powers holds for positive integers a and b, when $a < b$. That is, for any real number x, $x \neq 0$,

$$\frac{x^a}{x^b} = x^{a-b}, \text{ for } a < b.$$

Suppose the Quotient Property Holds	You Already Know	Reasonable Definition
$\dfrac{10^8}{10^{10}} = 10^{8-10} = 10^{-2}$	$\dfrac{10^8}{10^{10}} = \dfrac{10^8}{10^8} \cdot \dfrac{1}{10^2} = \dfrac{1}{10^2}$	$10^{-2} = \dfrac{1}{10^2}$
$\dfrac{10^7}{10^8} = 10^{7-8} = 10^{-1}$	$\dfrac{10^7}{10^8} = \dfrac{10^7}{10^7} \cdot \dfrac{1}{10^1} = \dfrac{1}{10}$	$10^{-1} = \dfrac{1}{10}$
$\dfrac{x^5}{x^8} = x^{5-8} = x^{-3}$	$\dfrac{x^5}{x^8} = \dfrac{x^5}{x^5} \cdot \dfrac{1}{x^3} = \dfrac{1}{x^3}$	$x^{-3} = \dfrac{1}{x^3}$
$\dfrac{y}{y^5} = y^{1-5} = y^{-4}$	$\dfrac{y}{y^5} = \dfrac{y}{y} \cdot \dfrac{1}{y^4} = \dfrac{1}{y^4}$	$y^{-4} = \dfrac{1}{y^4}$

The examples in the table suggest this definition.

DEFINITION

> If x is any real number except zero and a is a positive integer, then
> $$x^{-a} = \frac{1}{x^a}.$$
>
> $3^{-4} = \dfrac{1}{3^4}$
>
> $x^{-2} = \dfrac{1}{x^2}$

You can use this definition to simplify expressions having negative exponents. To **simplify such an expression** means to rewrite it without exponents or with positive exponents only.

EXAMPLE 1 Simplify: **a.** $(-5)^{-3}$ **b.** $3y^{-2}$ **c.** $\dfrac{x^2}{y^{-2}}$

Solutions: Write each expression with positive exponents. Simplify the result when possible.

a. $(-5)^{-3} = \dfrac{1}{(-5)^3}$ **b.** $3y^{-2} = 3 \cdot y^{-2}$ **c.** $\dfrac{x^2}{y^{-2}} = x^2 \div y^{-2}$

$= \dfrac{1}{-125}$ $= 3 \cdot \dfrac{1}{y^2}$ $= x^2 \div \dfrac{1}{y^2}$

$= -\dfrac{1}{125}$ $= \dfrac{3}{y^2}$ $= x^2 \cdot y^2 = x^2 y^2$

The Product and Quotient Properties of Powers apply to negative exponents as well as to positive exponents.

EXAMPLE 2 Simplify: **a.** $y^{-5} \cdot y^3$ **b.** $\dfrac{c^{-7}}{c^{-2}}$ **c.** $\dfrac{r^4 \cdot r^{-2}}{r^6}$

Solutions: **a.** $y^{-5} \cdot y^3 = y^{-5+3}$ ⟵ **Product Property of Powers**

$$= y^{-2}$$

$$= \frac{1}{y^2}$$

b. $\dfrac{c^{-7}}{c^{-2}} = c^{-7-(-2)}$ ⟵ **Quotient Property of Powers**

$$= c^{-5}$$

$$= \frac{1}{c^5}$$

c. $\dfrac{r^4 \cdot r^{-2}}{r^6} = \dfrac{r^2}{r^6}$ ⟵ **Product Property of Powers**

$$= r^{-4}$$ ⟵ **Quotient Property of Powers**

$$= \frac{1}{r^4}$$

EXERCISES: Classwork/Homework

Objective: To simplify powers and products and quotients of powers involving positive and negative exponents

CHECK YOUR UNDERSTANDING

1. *Complete:* The expression $x^2 y^{-3}$ can be rewritten as $\dfrac{x^2}{y^3}$ so that the expression has _?_ exponents only.

2. When simplifying the expression $\dfrac{a^{-3}}{a^4}$, would you add or subtract the exponents?

Write each expression as a power with a positive exponent.

3. 3^{-2} 4. 2^{-3} 5. 5^{-4} 6. $(-6)^{-2}$

7. $(-7)^{-5}$ 8. 12^{-4} 9. 30^{-2} 10. 15^{-6}

For Exercises 11–42, simplify. No variable equals zero.

11. 4^{-2}

12. 3^{-3}

13. r^{-4}

14. t^{-8}

15. $(-2)^{-3}$

16. $(-4)^{-3}$

17. $(\frac{1}{2})^{-4}$

18. $(\frac{3}{4})^{-3}$

19. $3x^{-5}$

20. $2y^{-4}$

21. $a^{-3}b^2$

22. ac^{-4}

23. $(2x)^{-2}$

24. $(3y)^{-3}$

25. ab^{-3}

26. rs^{-2}

27. $4^{-2} \cdot 4^3$

28. $8^{-3} \cdot 8^5$

29. $a^5 \cdot a^{-3}$

30. $b^{-2} \cdot b^7$

31. $x^{-3} \cdot x^{-2}$

32. $y^{-1} \cdot y^{-2}$

33. $\dfrac{n^2}{n^3}$

34. $\dfrac{m^5}{m^7}$

35. $\dfrac{r^{-2}}{r^{-5}}$

36. $\dfrac{s^{-6}}{s^{-3}}$

37. $\dfrac{p^{-8}}{p^7}$

38. $\dfrac{n^2}{n^{-5}}$

39. $\dfrac{c^7 \cdot c^{-9}}{c^{-6}}$

40. $\dfrac{s^{-2} \cdot s^{-3}}{s^{-7}}$

41. $\dfrac{m^{-10} \cdot m^8}{m^{-2}}$

42. $\dfrac{r^3 \cdot r^{-5}}{r^3}$

Simplify. No denominator equals zero. (*Pages 332–337*)

43. $\dfrac{2^4}{2}$

44. $\dfrac{x^7}{x^3}$

45. $\dfrac{x^2y}{xy}$

46. $\dfrac{-24a^4b^2c^3}{4a^2bc^2}$

47. $\dfrac{9 \times 10^{12}}{3 \times 10^2}$

48. $(x^3)^4$

49. $(a^4)^5$

50. $(-5)^3$

51. $(4c^2d)^2$

52. $(3 \times 10^4)^3$

Choose two variables to represent the unknowns. Then write each equation and solve. (*Pages 263–265*)

53. One number is 8 more than a second number. The sum of the numbers is 22. Find the numbers.

54. The sum of two numbers is 24. One number is 6 less than the other. Find the numbers.

55. The difference between two numbers is 9. Two times the larger is two more than four times the smaller. Find the numbers.

56. The length of a rectangle is 3 feet more than the width. The perimeter is 38 feet. Find the length and width.

Simplify. No variable equals zero.

57. $(a^4)^{-2}$

58. $(x^3)^{-1}$

59. $(a^{-7}b^3)^{-3}$

60. $(r^2s^{-3})^{-4}$

61. $\left(\dfrac{a}{b}\right)^{-1}$

62. $\left(\dfrac{d}{c}\right)^{-2}$

63. $\left(\dfrac{w^{-2}}{w^{-5}}\right)^{-3}$

64. $\left(\dfrac{d^{-5}}{d^{-9}}\right)^{-2}$

65. $\dfrac{7x^2y^{-2}}{z^{-2}}$

66. $\dfrac{a^{-2}b^3}{c^4d^{-5}}$

67. $\dfrac{2r^{-3}s^2t^{-7}}{8fs^{-3}t^4}$

68. $\dfrac{c^{-3}d^{-5}f^{-2}}{c^{-9}d^{-2}f^{-3}}$

9-6 Scientific Notation

The planet Jupiter is approximately 768,000,000 kilometers from the sun.

Very large and very small numbers are used in many scientific areas. For convenience, these numbers are expressed as the product of some power of 10 and a number from 1 to 10. This representation is called **scientific notation.**

$$768,000,000 = 7.68 \times 10^8 \quad \longleftarrow \text{Scientific Notation}$$

Number between 1 and 10   Power of 10

Decimal Notation	Scientific Notation
Number	$(1 \leq x < 10) \times 10^a$
95,672	9.5672×10^4
9567.2	9.5672×10^3
956.72	9.5672×10^2
95.672	9.5672×10^1
9.5672	9.5672×10^0
0.95672	9.5672×10^{-1}
0.095672	9.5672×10^{-2}
0.0095672	9.5672×10^{-3}
0.00095672	9.5672×10^{-4}

Numbers greater than 1 (rows 1–5); Numbers less than 1 (rows 6–9).

NOTE: When the given number is *greater than 10,* the power of 10 at the right in the table has a *positive exponent.*

When the number is *less than 1,* the power of 10 at the right in the table has a *negative exponent.*

When the given number is *between 1 and 10,* the power of 10 has a *zero exponent.*

EXAMPLE 1 Write each number in scientific notation.

    a. 867,000,000,000   **b.** 0.00000305

Solutions: **a.** 867,000,000,000. ◄————— The number is greater than 10.

             11 places ◄————— Count the number of places the decimal point must be moved to get a number between 1 and 10.

             8.67×10^{11} ◄————— Write as a product.

    b. 0.00000305 ◄————— The number is less than 1.

             6 places ◄————— Count the number of places the decimal point must be moved to get a number between 1 and 10.

             3.05×10^{-6} ◄————— Write as a product.

EXAMPLE 2 Express the product or quotient in scientific notation.

    a. $(2 \times 10^3)(8 \times 10^2)$ **b.** $\dfrac{1.5 \times 10^6}{0.3 \times 10^9}$

Solutions: **a.** $(2 \times 10^3)(8 \times 10^2) =$ **b.** $\dfrac{1.5 \times 10^6}{0.3 \times 10^9} =$

           $(2)(8) \times (10^3)(10^2) =$ $\left(\dfrac{1.5}{0.3}\right) \times \left(\dfrac{10^6}{10^9}\right) =$

           $16 \times 10^5 =$

           1.6×10^6 5×10^{-3}

CALCULATOR

You can use a scientific calculator with an exponential shift key, EE or EXP , to perform multiplication and division of numbers written in scientific notation. For example,

a. $(3.2 \times 10^3)(4.5 \times 10^5)$

3.2 EE 3 × 4.5 EE 5 = | 1.44 09 | ◄——— 1.44×10^9

b. $(6.3 \times 10^2) \div (1.5 \times 10^6)$

6.3 EE 2 ÷ 1.5 EE 6 = | 4.2 -04 | ◄——— 4.2×10^{-4}

EXERCISES: Classwork/Homework

Objective: To write numbers in scientific notation

■■■■■■ CHECK YOUR UNDERSTANDING

Complete.

1. Writing a number as the product of a power of 10 and a number from 1 to 10 is writing that number in __?__ .

2. When writing a number greater than 10 in scientific notation, the power of 10 has a __?__ exponent.

3. When writing a number less than 1 in scientific notation, the power of 10 has a __?__ exponent.

4. When writing a number between 1 and 10 in scientific notation, the power of 10 has a __?__ exponent.

■■■■■■ PRACTICE AND APPLY

Write each number in scientific notation.

5. 4600

6. 20,500,000

7. 67,000,000

8. 100,000

9. 24,000,000,000,000

10. 0.0043

11. 0.00057

12. 0.0000008

13. 0.00002

14. 0.07

15. 0.0008

16. 0.005

17. $\frac{2}{10,000}$

18. $\frac{7}{10,000,000}$

19. 6 million

20. 4 billion

21. 3 thousand

22. 2.6 billion

23. 40 million

24. 400 billion

25. 5 thousandths

Write each number in scientific notation.

26. The star Alpha Centauri is 40,000,000,000,000 kilometers from the earth.

27. In one year, light travels about 10 trillion kilometers.

28. The center of our galaxy is 30,000 light years away.

29. Astronomers have detected objects so far away that the light from these objects has taken 10 billion years to reach us.

30. The diameter of our galaxy is 100,000 light years.

32. Our galaxy has about a hundred billion stars.

31. The sun is about 150,000,000 kilometers from the earth.

33. Special balances can weigh something as small as 0.00000001 gram.

Express the product or quotient in scientific notation.

34. $(4 \times 10^3)(7 \times 10^2)$ **35.** $(8.2 \times 10^{-2})(1.5 \times 10^8)$ **36.** $(6 \times 10^{-3})(8.6 \times 10^{-7})$

37. $\dfrac{8 \times 10^{-9}}{2 \times 10^3}$ **38.** $\dfrac{2.25 \times 10^2}{1.5 \times 10^{-9}}$ **39.** $\dfrac{4.5 \times 10^{-7}}{9 \times 10^{-2}}$

40. The sun is approximately 1.49×10^8 kilometers from the earth. The speed of light is about 2.98×10^5 kilometers per second. Find the time it takes light from the sun to reach the earth.

41. The earth's mass is approximately 6×10^{24} kilograms. If the mass of the sun is 3.3×10^5 times the mass of the earth, what is the mass of the sun?

42. Marine animals convert the sugar acquired from food into energy. For each molecule of sugar converted, 1×10^{-20} calories are released. How many calories would be released if 1.2×10^3 molecules of sugar were converted?

43. The volume of a droplet of water in a fog is about 8×10^{-8} cubic centimeters. If the volume of the earth is 1.08×10^{27} cubic centimeters, how many times as great is the volume of earth than the volume of a droplet of water in a fog?

Write each number in decimal notation.

44. The sun has a mass of 2.2×10^{27} tons.

45. The temperature of the sun is about 6×10^3 degrees Celsius.

46. If one foot of copper wire is heated 1° Celsius, it expands 1.6×10^{-5} feet.

47. A helium atom has a diameter of 2.2×10^{-8} centimeters.

■■■■■■ **MAINTAIN**

Simplify. No variable equals zero. (*Pages 340–342*)

48. 10^{-3} **49.** $(-2)^{-4}$ **50.** a^{-6} **51.** $3x^{-7}$

52. $x^3 \cdot x^{-4}$ **53.** $7^{-3} \cdot 7^1$ **54.** $\dfrac{x^{-3}}{x^{-1}}$ **55.** $\dfrac{n^{-8}}{n^2}$

Simplify. No denominator equals zero. (*Pages 335–337*)

56. $\dfrac{3^4}{3}$ **57.** $\dfrac{x^9}{x^4}$ **58.** $\dfrac{a^3b^5}{ab}$ **59.** $\dfrac{-12r^4s^7t^2}{4r^2s^3t}$ **60.** $\dfrac{8 \times 10^{15}}{2 \times 10^3}$

■■■■■■ **NON-ROUTINE PROBLEM**

61. In a shop class of ten students, exactly two students are given the responsibility of cleaning the shop each day after class. A schedule is made pairing each student with every other student in the class exactly once. How many pairs of students are listed on the schedule?

9-7 Addition and Subtraction of Polynomials

To find the *perimeter of a polygon,* you add the lengths of its sides.

Polygon	Perimeter
$5x^2 - 6$ (top) $2x^2$ (left) $2x^2$ (right) $5x^2 - 6$ (bottom)	$5x^2 - 6$ $5x^2 - 6$ $2x^2$ $2x^2$ ——— $14x^2 - 12$
$3y^2$ $4y^2$ $6y^2 - 2$	$3y^2$ $4y^2$ $6y^2 - 2$ ——— $13y^2 - 2$

The length of each side of each polygon is expressed as a *monomial* or as the sum of monomials. Recall from the definition on page 329 that expressions such as $13y^2$ and -2 are *monomials.*

A **polynomial** is a monomial or the sum of monomials. A polynomial with two terms is called a **binomial;** a polynomial with three terms is called a **trinomial.**

Monomial	Binomial	Trinomial
$7x^2y^2$	$4a + 3$	$3x^2 - 6x + 9$
-9	$9x^2 - 25z^2$	$6a - 7b - 3c$

To add polynomials, you add monomials that are *like terms.*

EXAMPLE 1 Add: $(4a + 6b) + (2a - 3b)$

Solution: First group the like terms. Then apply the Distributive Property.

$(4a + 6b) + (2a - 3b) = (4a + 2a) + (6b - 3b)$

$= (4 + 2)a + (6 - 3)b$ ⟵ By the Distributive Property

$= \mathbf{6a + 3b}$

It is often convenient to arrange like terms in the same column before adding or subtracting, as shown in Examples 2 and 3.

EXAMPLE 2 Add: $(-3x^2 + 7xy - 6y^2) + (5xy + 3y^2 - 4x^2)$

Solution:

$$\begin{array}{r} -3x^2 + 7xy - 6y^2 \\ -4x^2 + 5xy + 3y^2 \\ \hline -7x^2 + 12xy - 3y^2 \end{array}$$

←——— Arrange like terms in the same column.
←——— Add like terms.

To subtract a polynomial, you add its additive inverse.

EXAMPLE 3 Subtract $(x^3 + 2x^2 - 8x) - (-2x^2 + 7x - 5)$

Solution:

$$\begin{array}{r} x^3 + 2x^2 - 8x + 0 \\ 2x^2 - 7x + 5 \\ \hline x^3 + 4x^2 - 15x + 5 \end{array}$$

←——— Arrange like terms in the same column.
←——— Additive inverse of $-2x^2 + 7x - 5$.
←——— Add like terms.

EXERCISES: Classwork/Homework

Objective: To add and subtract polynomials

CHECK YOUR UNDERSTANDING

Classify each of the following polynomials as a monomial, a binomial, or a trinomial.

1. $2x + 1$

2. $6x^2yz^2$

3. $5a^2 - 2a + 4$

4. -6

5. $7c + 4d - 3e$

6. $18s^3 - 5t^2$

Add or subtract as indicated.

7. $(4a - 3b) + (8a + 5b)$

8. $(6r + 9s) - (4r + 3s)$

9. $(4a^2 - 5ab - 6b^2) + (10ab - 6a^2 - 6b^2)$ **10.** $(h^2 + 6h + 9) - (25 - 10h + h^2)$

PRACTICE AND APPLY

For Exercises 11–22, add.

11. $\begin{array}{r} 4a - 3b + 5c \\ 8a + 5b - 9c \end{array}$

12. $\begin{array}{r} 4r + 3s + t \\ 6r + 9s + 5t \end{array}$

13. $\begin{array}{r} 6p - 4t + x \\ -7p + 8t + 6x \end{array}$

14. $5b + 4c + 8d, 8b - 7c - 6d, 3b - 4c$

15. $7x - 2y + 5z, 8y - 9z, 7x - 5y$

16. $5x + 7y - 10, 8y - 2x + 3, 2x - 10y + 4$

17. $4a^2 - 5ab - 6b^2$, $10ab - 6a^2 - 8b^2$, $10b^2 - 3a^2 - 7ab$

18. $a - b + c$, $b - c - a$, $c - a + b$, $a - 2b - c$

19. $4ab - 5bc + 6ac$, $6bc - 7ab - 8ac$, $10ab - bc - ac$

20. $x^2 + y^2 - z^2$, $3z^2 - 2x^2 - 4y^2$, $4y^2 + x^2 + z^2$

21. $x^2 - 6x + 7$, $8x - 15 - x^2$, $4x^2 + 6x - 9$, $7x + 10$

22. $a^2 - 2ab + b^2$, $2ab + a^2 + b^2$, $4a^2 - 4ab - b^2$, $a^2 - b^2$

Find the perimeter of each polygon.

23.

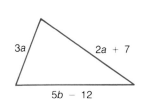

$3a$ $2a + 7$ $5b - 12$

24.

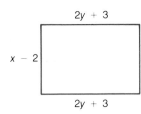

$2y + 3$ $x - 2$ $x - 2$ $2y + 3$

25.

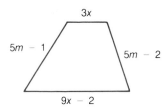

$3x$ $5m - 1$ $5m - 2$ $9x - 2$

26.

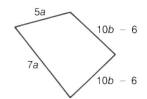

$5a$ $10b - 6$ $7a$ $10b - 6$

27.

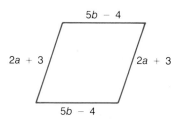

$5b - 4$ $2a + 3$ $2a + 3$ $5b - 4$

28.

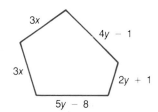

$3x$ $4y - 1$ $3x$ $2y + 1$ $5y - 8$

Subtract.

29. $\begin{array}{r} 3a + 4 \\ 2a + 9 \\ \hline \end{array}$

30. $\begin{array}{r} 7b - 5 \\ 10b - 8 \\ \hline \end{array}$

31. $\begin{array}{r} r + 8s \\ r - 5s \\ \hline \end{array}$

32. $\begin{array}{r} 8a - 9xy \\ -a + 9xy \\ \hline \end{array}$

33. $\begin{array}{r} a - b + c \\ a + b - c \\ \hline \end{array}$

34. $\begin{array}{r} x^2 + 2x + 1 \\ x^2 - 2x + 1 \\ \hline \end{array}$

35. $\begin{array}{r} 2a + 0 \\ a - b \\ \hline \end{array}$

36. $\begin{array}{r} 2x^2 \quad - 4 \\ x + 2 \\ \hline \end{array}$

37. $\begin{array}{r} x^3 + 0 + 0 + 8 \\ x^3 + x^2 - 2x + 0 \\ \hline \end{array}$

38. $\begin{array}{r} x^2 + 6 \\ x^3 \quad - 3 \\ \hline \end{array}$

39. $\begin{array}{r} 3x^2 - 6x \\ 2x^2 \quad + 7 \\ \hline \end{array}$

40. $\begin{array}{r} -4x^2 - x + 9 \\ 3x^3 \quad + x \\ \hline \end{array}$

41. $(5x + y) - (2x - y)$

42. $(a + 5b) - (4a - 3b)$

43. $(3x^2 - 4y^2) - (2x^2 + 5y^2)$

44. $(4x^2 - 2x - 3) - (-5x - 4)$

45. $(5x^2 - 10y^2) - (3x^2 + 2xy - 6y^2)$

46. $(-4x^3 - 6x^2 + 3x - 1) - (8x^3 + 4x^2 - 2x + 3)$

47. $(-5a + 2b - 3c + 8d) - (4a - b + 3c + 5d)$

48. From $3a - 2b + 5c$, take $-2a + 5b - c$.

49. Subtract $6x^2 - 3xy + y^2$ from $8x^2 + 5xy - y^2$.

50. From $6ab - 2ac + 5bc$, take $10ab - 2bc + 3ac$.

████████ **MAINTAIN**

Write each number in scientific notation. (*Pages 343–346*)

51. 48,000,000 **52.** 0.000031 **53.** 0.000001 **54.** 6,000,000,000

55. 230 **56.** 180,000 **57.** 0.0396 **58.** 0.000104

Solve each problem. (*Pages 266–269*)

59. A two-digit number is 4 times the sum of its digits. When 18 is added to the number, the result is the original number with its digits reversed. Find the number.

60. The units digit of a two-digit number is 6 less than the tens digit. The number is 7 more than 8 times the sum of the digits. Find the number.

████████ **CONNECT AND EXTEND**

61. From the sum of $x + 3y$ and $-3x - y$, subtract $x - y$.

62. Subtract $x^2 - y^2 - z^2$ from the sum of $2x^2 + 3y^2 - z^2$ and $4x^2 - 3y^2 + 5z^2$.

63. Take $a - b + 1$ from the sum of $a + c + 1$ and $a + b + 1$.

64. Subtract the sum of $(4x^3 + 2x^2 - 5)$ and $(15x - x^3 - x^2)$ from the difference of $(9 + 6x - 2x^2)$ and $(4x - 1 - 5x^3 + x^2)$.

65. If x is 3 meters, which is greater: the perimeter of a square whose sides are each $(3x - 1)$ units or the perimeter of a rectangle whose length is $x + 9$ and whose width is $2x - 3$? How much greater?

——— **REVIEW CAPSULE FOR SECTION 9-8** ———

Multiply. (*Pages 34–37, 329–331*)

1. $3(2a + 5b - 4)$ **2.** $-7(2x - y + 5)$ **3.** $(-1)(2a - 6b + 1)$

4. $-5(-4k + 3s - 2)$ **5.** $(-1)(21 - 5t - 3r)$ **6.** $(-1)(-6u + 10w - 11z)$

7. $a^4 \cdot a^5$ **8.** $q \cdot q^2$ **9.** $(-t^4)(t^3)$ **10.** $-a^5(-a^5)$ **11.** $3x^2y(-9xy^5)$

Simplify. (*Pages 64–68*)

12. $7a - (6a - 3 + b)$ **13.** $9b + (3c + 2) - b$ **14.** $5n - (-n + 2 - 3n)$

9-8 Products of Polynomials

AREA   To find the **area of a rectangle,** you multiply its length and width.

Rectangle	Area
$3x$ $7x - 9$	$\begin{aligned} 3x(7x - 9) &= 3x[7x + (-9)] \\ &= 3x(7x) + 3x(-9) \\ &= 21x^2 + (-27x) \\ &= \mathbf{21x^2 - 27x} \end{aligned}$
$4y + 2$ $4y + 2$	$\begin{aligned} (4y + 2)(4y + 2) &= (4y + 2)4y + (4y + 2)2 \\ &= 4y(4y) + 2(4y) + 4y(2) + 2(2) \\ &= 16y^2 + 8y + 8y + 4 \\ &= \mathbf{16y^2 + 16y + 4} \end{aligned}$

You can see from the table that you use the Distributive Property and the properties of exponents to multiply polynomials.

EXAMPLE 1 Multiply: $7y(-6y - 9)$

Solution: $\begin{aligned} 7y(-6y - 9) &= 7y[-6y + (-9)] \\ &= 7y(-6y) + 7y(-9) \quad \longleftarrow \textbf{By the Distributive} \\ &\qquad\qquad\qquad\qquad\qquad\quad\; \textbf{Property} \\ &= (7)(-6)(y \cdot y) + (7)(-9)y \\ &= \mathbf{-42y^2 - 63y} \end{aligned}$

Example 1 shows how to multiply a monomial and a binomial. To multiply two binomials, you use the Distributive Property twice.

EXAMPLE 2 Multiply: $(x + 2)(x - 5)$

Solution: $\begin{aligned} (x + 2)(x - 5) &= (x + 2)[x + (-5)] \\ &= (x + 2)x + (x + 2)(-5) \quad \longleftarrow \textbf{By the Distributive Prop.} \\ &= (x)(x) + (2)(x) + (x)(-5) + (2)(-5) \quad \longleftarrow \\ &= x^2 + 2x - 5x - 10 \\ &= \mathbf{x^2 - 3x - 10} \end{aligned}$

It is often easier to use a vertical format to multiply.

EXAMPLE 3 Multiply: $(5n + 2t)(7n + 3t)$

Solution: Arrange the polynomials vertically. Write like terms in the same column.

$$
\begin{array}{r}
5n + 2t \\
7n + 3t \\
\hline
15nt + 6t^2 \\
35n^2 + 14nt \\
\hline
35n^2 + 29nt + 6t^2
\end{array}
$$

$\longleftarrow$ $3t(5n + 2t)$

$\longleftarrow$ $7n(5n + 2t)$

$\longleftarrow$ $35n^2 + (15nt + 14nt) + 6t^2$

EXERCISES: Classwork/Homework

Objective: To multiply polynomials

CHECK YOUR UNDERSTANDING

Complete. Use the Distributive Property.

1. $3x(x + 9) = 3x(\underline{\ ?\ }) + 3x(\underline{\ ?\ })$
2. $4x(-2x - 6) = (\underline{\ ?\ })(-2x) - (\underline{\ ?\ })(6)$
3. $(-2n^3 - 5n)6n = (\underline{\ ?\ })(6n) - (\underline{\ ?\ })(6n)$
4. $(a^3 + 1)2a = (a^3)(\underline{\ ?\ }) + 1(\underline{\ ?\ })$
5. $(a + 2)(a + 9) = (a + 2)(\underline{\ ?\ }) + (a + 2)(\underline{\ ?\ })$
6. $(x + y)(x - y) = (\underline{\ ?\ })(x) - (\underline{\ ?\ })(y)$

PRACTICE AND APPLY

For Exercises 7–69, multiply.

7. $2x(x + 5)$ 8. $3x(-x - 4)$ 9. $(t^3 + 2t)(3t)$
10. $a(2a + 3)$ 11. $x^2(3x + 4)$ 12. $3y(y - 8)$
13. $2y(3y - 4)$ 14. $-2y(y + 6)$ 15. $-3x(x + 9)$
16. $m(5m - 2)$ 17. $r(r^2 - 9)$ 18. $s(7s - 8)$
19. $3x^2(2x - 6)$ 20. $-4a(3a - 5b)$ 21. $5mn(7m - 2n)$
22. $2a(a^2 - 4a + 3)$ 23. $-3x(x^2 + 5x + 2)$ 24. $y^2(y^2 - 6y + 3)$
25. $-2ab(6a^2 - 4ab + 5b^2)$ **26.** $3xy(-x^4 - 4x^2y + 5xy^2)$ **27.** $(3a^2 - 2a - 9)(-a)$

28. $(a + 7)(a + 3)$ **29.** $(x + 9)(x + 5)$ **30.** $(2a + 4)(a + 5)$

31. $(7x + 3)(x + 1)$ **32.** $(a + 3)(a - 4)$ **33.** $(2a + 3b)(a - b)$

34. $(2a - 5)(3a + 2)$ **35.** $(a + 3)(a + 2)$ **36.** $(2a + 3)(3a - 2)$

37. $(a - 3b)(2a + 3b)$ **38.** $(a + b)(c + d)$ **39.** $(a - b)(c + d)$

40. $(a - b)(c - d)$ **41.** $(a + b)(c - d)$ **42.** $(3b - 4c)(3b + 4c)$

43. $(3b - 4c)(2c + 3d)$ **44.** $(4x - 5)(4x + 5)$ **45.** $(7n - 3)(7n + 3)$

46. $(3x - 4)(3x - 4)$ **47.** $(2a - 3b)(a - 4b)$ **48.** $(5x - 3y)(3x + 4y)$

49. $(a + b)(a - b)$ **50.** $(\frac{1}{2}x - y)(2x + y)$ **51.** $(\frac{1}{3}t - 5)(\frac{1}{3}t + 6)$

52. $(1.6n - 9)(0.2n - 5)$ **53.** $(a^2 + b)(a^2 - 2b)$ **54.** $(x^2 - y^2)(x^2 + y^2)$

55. $(m^2 - 2n^2)(m^2 - 2n^2)$ **56.** $(4s - 3)(2s^2 + 3)$ **57.** $(a^3 + b^3)(3a^3 + b^3)$

58. $(2x^2 + 3y^2)(3x^2 + 2y^2)$ **59.** $(x - 3)^2$ **60.** $(2x + 3y)^2$

61. $(x + 5)(x + 7)$ **62.** $x + 5(x + 7)$ **63.** $y - 6(2y + 8)$

64. $(y - 6)(2y + 8)$ **65.** $2x + y(8x - 4y)$ **66.** $(2x + y)(8x - 4y)$

67. $(7x - 9)(3x - 4)$ **68.** $4 - (5x + 2)$ **69.** $5 - 2(8x + 3)$

Find the area of each region outlined in red.

70.

71.

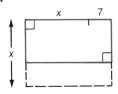

72.

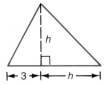

73.

74.

75.

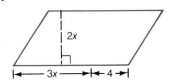

76. Which has the greater area, a square with sides x units long or a rectangle with length $(x + 1)$ units and width $(x - 1)$ units. How much greater is it?

77. Which has the greater area, a square with sides x units long, or a rectangle with length $(x + 2)$ units and width $(x - 2)$ units? How much greater is it?

78. Which has the greater area, a square with sides $(x + 1)$ units long or a rectangle with length $(x + 2)$ units and width x units? How much greater is it?

79. Which has the greater area, a square with sides $(x + 1)$ units long or a rectangle with length x units and width $(x - 2)$ units? How much greater is it?

Solve each problem. (*Pages 270–274*)

80. Maria makes a bank deposit of $590 with 70 five- and ten-dollar bills. How many of each kind of bill did she deposit?

81. Marianne has 60 coins in dimes and quarters. The total value of the coins is $12.90. How many coins of each kind does she have?

■■■■■ **CONNECT AND EXTEND**

Multiply.

82. $(x^2 + 2x + 1)(x + 1)$

83. $(x^2 + 2x + 1)(x - 1)$

84. $(n^3 - 5n^2 + 2)(n^2 - 2n)$

85. $(x^2 - xy + y^2)(x + y)$

86. $(x^2 - 6xy + 9y)(x - 3y)$

87. $(2 - 3a^2 - a)(a - 1)$

88. $(c - 2c^2 + 3)(2 + c)$

89. $(x^3 + 3x^2 + 2x - 1)(x - 1)$

■■■■■ **REVIEW** ■■■■■

Simplify. No denominator equals zero. (*Pages 340–342*)

1. 8^{-2}

2. t^{-8}

3. $(-5)^{-3}$

4. $5x^{-2}$

5. $x^{-6} \cdot x^{-4}$

6. $\left(\frac{2}{3}\right)^{-2}$

7. $\dfrac{s^{-9}}{s^{-2}}$

8. $\dfrac{m^{-5} \cdot m^3}{m^8}$

Write each number in scientific notation. (*Pages 343–346*)

9. 0.0000043

10. 189.3

11. 2,000,000

12. 0.00806

Express the product or quotient in scientific notation. (*Pages 343–346*)

13. $(5 \times 10^{-4})(7 \times 10^7)$

14. $(6 \times 10^7)(3.5 \times 10^{20})$

15. $\dfrac{(4.2 \times 10^3)}{(1.4 \times 10^6)}$

Add or subtract as indicated. (*Pages 347–350*)

16. $(3a + 4b) + (2a - 6b)$

17. $(5x^2y + 4xy^2) - (x^2y - 3xy^2)$

18. $(4d^2 + 2d - 4) - (5d + d^2)$

19. $(2x^3 + x^2 - 4x) - (x^3 + x^2)$

Multiply. (*Pages 351–353*)

20. $3(4x - 1)$

21. $2y^2(2y + 4)$

22. $(c - 4)(2c + 1)$

23. $(2c + 3)(2c + 3)$

24. $(4a^2 - 2c)(a^2 - c)$

25. $4b - 3(b - 1)$

9-9   Products of Binomials

FOIL METHOD   You can use the Distributive Property to develop a pattern for multiplying two binomials. This pattern is sometimes called the *FOIL method*.

EXAMPLE 1   Multiply: $(2x + 5)(3x + 4)$

Solution:

Product of first terms	$+$	Product of outer terms	$+$	Product of inner terms	$+$	Product of last terms
F		O		I		L

$(2x + 5)(3x + 4)$ $(2x + 5)(3x + 4)$ $(2x + 5)(3x + 4)$ $(2x + 5)(3x + 4)$

$(2x)(3x)$ $+$ $(2x)(4)$ $+$ $5(3x)$ $+$ $5(4)$

$6x^2$ $+$ $8x$ $+$ $15x$ $+$ 20

$(2x + 5)(3x + 4) = 6x^2 + 8x + 15x + 20$ ◄——— **Combine like terms.**

$= 6x^2 + 23x + 20$

You can use the FOIL method to multiply any two binomials by inspection.

EXAMPLE 2   Multiply by inspection: **a.** $(4x + 1)(2x - 3)$ **b.** $(5x - 4)(2x + 7)$

Solutions:

 F   O   I   L

a. $(4x + 1)(2x - 3) = 8x^2 - 12x + 2x - 3 = 8x^2 - 10x - 3$

 F   O   I   L

b. $(5x - 4)(2x + 7) = 10x^2 + 35x - 8x - 28 = 10x^2 + 27x - 28$

EXERCISES: Classwork/Homework

Objective: To find the product of two binomials by inspection

▬▬▬ CHECK YOUR UNDERSTANDING

Complete.

 F   O   I   L

1. $(x + 5)(x - 3) = \underline{?} - \underline{?} + \underline{?} - \underline{?}$

$= \underline{?}$

 F   O   I   L

2. $(5a - 3)(2a - 2) = \underline{?} - \underline{?} - \underline{?} + \underline{?}$

$= \underline{?}$

$$\begin{array}{cccc} & \text{F} & \text{O} & \text{I} \quad \text{L} \end{array}$$

3. $(8x - 3)(4x + 5) = \underline{?} + \underline{?} - \underline{?} - \underline{?}$ **4.** $(2x - 1)(x + 4) = \underline{?} + \underline{?} - \underline{?} - \underline{?}$
$$= \underline{?}$$
$$= \underline{?}$$

5. $(3x - 2y)(2x + 5y) = \underline{?} + \underline{?} - \underline{?} - \underline{?}$ **6.** $(x - 1)(6x + 7) = \underline{?} + \underline{?} - \underline{?} - \underline{?}$
$$= \underline{?}$$
$$= \underline{?}$$

▬▬▬ PRACTICE AND APPLY

Find each product.

7. $(x + 5)(x + 3)$ **8.** $(x - 5)(x + 7)$ **9.** $(x + 2)(x - 2)$

10. $(x + 3)(x + 2)$ **11.** $(a - 2)(a + 3)$ **12.** $(y - 5)(y + 1)$

13. $(b - 7)(b + 3)$ **14.** $(d + 4)(d - 5)$ **15.** $(p + 9)(p + 11)$

16. $(2x + 5)(5x + 6)$ **17.** $(d - 4)(d + 5)$ **18.** $(m + n)(m - n)$

19. $(3y + 2)(4y + 3)$ **20.** $(2x + 5)(3x + 1)$ **21.** $(x + 3)(2x + 7)$

22. $(p - 9)(p - 11)$ **23.** $(3x - 4)(3x + 4)$ **24.** $(m - n)(p - q)$

25. $(b + 4)(b + 4)$ **26.** $(n - 2)(n + 2)$ **27.** $(m + 7)(m - 11)$

28. $(a + b)(2a - b)$ **29.** $(a - 2c)(a + 2c)$ **30.** $(3x - 2y)(3x + 2y)$

31. $(3x + 2)(x - 1)$ **32.** $(x^2 + 2y)(x^2 - 2y)$ **33.** $(y^2 + 3)(y^2 + 3)$

34. $(2b + 3)(4b - 7)$ **35.** $(4y - 3)(4y - 3)$ **36.** $(4y - 3)(4y + 3)$

37. $(2a + 5)(2a + 3)$ **38.** $(4c - 7)(5c + 9)$ **39.** $(5x + 3)(x + 1)$

40. $(2f + 9)(3f + 7)$ **41.** $(7b + 2)(5b - 1)$ **42.** $(10p + 3)(6p - 1)$

43. $(8x + 3)(3x - 4)$ **44.** $(8r - 5)(7r + 5)$ **45.** $(2c - 9)(3c - 8)$

46. $(4x + 7)(5x - 3)$ **47.** $(x^2 - 4)(x^2 + 4)$ **48.** $(y^2 - 2)(y^2 + 2)$

49. $(7a - 2)(a + 8)$ **50.** $(a^2 - 3b)(a^2 + 2b)$ **51.** $(3x - 5y)(2x + 3y)$

52. $(\frac{1}{2}x + 5)(6x - 10)$ **53.** $(\frac{1}{2}x - 3)(7x + 8)$ **54.** $(5a + 1)(\frac{1}{2}a + 4)$

55. $(\frac{1}{3}t + 8)(\frac{1}{4}t + 6)$ **56.** $(5x + \frac{2}{3})(6x + \frac{3}{2})$ **57.** $(\frac{1}{5}x - 7)(\frac{1}{7}x - 5)$

58. $(0.3u - 0.4)(0.5u - 0.1)$ **59.** $(1.8w - 2.4)(0.2w + 0.5)$ **60.** $(1.4t + 3n)(t + 1.2n)$

Write a polynomial to represent each area.

61. A rectangular tennis court has a length of $(x + 7)$ units and a width of $(x - 3)$ units.

62. The length of a rectangular garden is $(2x + 3)$ units. The width of the garden is $(x + 2)$ units.

63. Each side of a square table cloth has a length of $(x + 5)$ units.

64. Which has the greater area, a rectangle with length $(a + 2)$ units and width $(a + 1)$ units, or a rectangle with length $(a + 4)$ units and width $(a - 1)$ units? How much greater is it?

65. Which has the greater area, a rectangle with length $(2a + 1)$ units and width $(a - 5)$ units, or a rectangle with length $(2a + 3)$ units and width $(a - 6)$ units? How much greater is it?

▬▬▬▬ **MAINTAIN**

Multiply. (*Pages 351–353*)

66. $x(3x + 2)$

67. $-2y(y^2 - 4y + 7)$

68. $(2c - 1)(3c + 5)$

Subtract. (*Pages 347–350*)

69. $6a + 8$
  $4a + 5$

70. $2x^2 \quad - 9$
  $\underline{5x + 2}$

71. $x^2 + 4x + 6$
  $\underline{x^2 - 4x + 6}$

72. $(6x + y) - (3x - y)$

73. $(b + 3c) - (7b - c)$

74. $(4x^2 - 5y^2) - (3x^2 + 2y^2)$

75. $(8e^2 - 4e - 1) - (-6e - 5)$

Solve the problems. (*Pages 270–274*)

76. An alloy that is 5% copper is mixed with a second alloy that is 8% copper. How many kilograms of each alloy must be melted to obtain 45 kilograms of an alloy that is 7% copper?

77. How many kilograms of pecans selling at \$4.10 per kilogram must be mixed with 15 kilograms of peanuts selling at \$2.50 per kilogram to produce a mixture that is worth \$3.10 per kilogram?

▬▬▬▬ **CONNECT AND EXTEND**

Find each product.

Example: $(x + 2)^3 = (x + 2)(x + 2)^2$
$$= (x + 2)(x^2 + 4x + 4)$$
$$= x^3 + 6x^2 + 12x + 8$$

78. $(x + 5)^3$

79. $(2x + 3)^3$

80. $(x - 3)^3$

81. $(3x - 1)^3$

82. $(x + y)^3$

83. $(x - y)^3$

84. $(3x + y)^3$

85. $(2x - 7y)^3$

▬▬▬▬ **NON-ROUTINE PROBLEM**

86. A building has six stories that are each the same height. It takes an elevator 6 seconds to rise to the third floor. How many additional seconds will it take the elevator to rise from the third floor to the sixth floor?

9-10 Squaring Binomials

Study the table to find the pattern for squaring binomials.

Square of a Sum	Square of a Difference
$(x + 4)^2 = (x + 4)(x + 4)$	$(x - 4)^2 = (x - 4)(x - 4)$
$= x^2 + 4x + 4x + 16$	$= x^2 - 4x - 4x + 16$
$2(4x)$	$2(-4x)$
$= x^2 + 8x + 16$	$= x^2 - 8x + 16$
$(m + 3n)^2 = (m + 3n)(m + 3n)$	$(m - 3n)^2 = (m - 3n)(m - 3n)$
$= m^2 + 3mn + 3mn + 9n^2$	$= m^2 - 3mn - 3mn + 9n^2$
$2(3mn)$	$2(-3mn)$
$= m^2 + 6mn + 9n^2$	$= m^2 - 6mn + 9n^2$

The pattern in the table suggests the following procedure.

PROCEDURE

> **To square a binomial:**
> 1. Square the first term.
> 2. Add to this twice the product of the first and last terms when the binomial is of the form $(a + b)$.
>
>   Subtract twice the product of the first and last terms when the binomial is of the form $(a - b)$.
> 3. Add to this the square of the last term.

EXAMPLE 1 Write the square of each binomial as a trinomial.

    a $(5x + 2y)^2$ **b.** $(2y - 3)^2$

Solutions: **a.** $(5x + 2y)^2 = (5x)^2 + 2(5x)(2y) + (2y)^2$

                     $= 25x^2 + 20x + 4y^2$

    b. $(2y - 3)^2 = (2y)^2 - 2(2y)(3) + 3^2$

                     $= 4y^2 - 12y + 9$

You can square a number by writing it as the sum or as the difference of two numbers.

EXAMPLE 2 Square each number: **a.** $(32)^2$ **b.** $(49)^2$

Solutions: **a.** $(32)^2 = (30 + 2)^2$ **b.** $(49)^2 = (50 - 1)^2$

$$= (30)^2 + 2(30)(2) + 2^2 \qquad = (50)^2 - 2(50)(1) + 1^2$$
$$= 900 + 120 + 4 \qquad\qquad = 2500 - 100 + 1$$
$$= 1024 \qquad\qquad\qquad\quad = 2401$$

You will find it useful to memorize these special binomial products.

SUMMARY

> **Square of a Binomial Sum: $(a + b)^2 = a^2 + 2ab + b^2$**
>
> **Square of a Binomial Difference: $(a - b)^2 = a^2 - 2ab + b^2$**

EXERCISES: Classwork/Homework

Objective: To square binomials

CHECK YOUR UNDERSTANDING

1. *Complete*: When a binomial is squared, the middle term of the resulting trinomial is twice the __?__ of the first and last terms.

2. When writing the trinomial for the expression $(x + 2)^2$, would you add or subtract the middle term?

Find the missing term.

3. $(x - 10)^2 = \underline{\ ?\ } - 20x + 100$

4. $(x + 3)^2 = x^2 + \underline{\ ?\ } + 9$

5. $(3y - 5)^2 = 9y^2 - 30y + \underline{\ ?\ }$

6. $(2p + 3)^2 = 4p^2 + \underline{\ ?\ } + 9$

7. $(m^2 - 6)^2 = \underline{\ ?\ } - 12m^2 + 36$

8. $(x + 2y)^2 = x^2 + \underline{\ ?\ } + 4y^2$

PRACTICE AND APPLY

Write the square of each binomial as a trinomial.

9. $(a + 3)^2$

10. $(a - 2)^2$

11. $(a + 5)^2$

12. $(x - 3)^2$

13. $(a - 5)^2$

14. $(n - 6)^2$

15. $(x - y)^2$

16. $(2a + 3)^2$

17. $(2a + 1)^2$

18. $(4a - 1)^2$

19. $(5m - 1)^2$

20. $(7m - 4)^2$

21. $(n + 3)^2$

22. $(5m + 3)^2$

23. $(3x - y)^2$

24. $(x + 2)^2$

25. $(2x - 3)^2$ **26.** $(2x - 5)^2$ **27.** $(2x + y)^2$ **28.** $(y + 10)^2$

29. $(2x - 3y)^2$ **30.** $(3a - 2b)^2$ **31.** $(10a + 2)^2$ **32.** $(5c + 3d)^2$

33. $(2x^2 + 3y^2)^2$ **34.** $(5c + 4y^3)^2$ **35.** $(a^2 - 3b^2)^2$ **36.** $(x^2y - 5)^2$

37. $(a^2 - 3)^2$ **38.** $(2a^2 + 3)^2$ **39.** $(11a^2 + c^2)^2$ **40.** $(8x^2 - 5d^2)^2$

Square each number.

41. $(20 - 1)^2$ **42.** $(100 - 1)^2$ **43.** $(50 + 2)^2$ **44.** $(100 + 5)^2$

45. $(21)^2$ **46.** $(29)^2$ **47.** $(999)^2$ **48.** $(98)^2$ **49.** $(101)^2$ **50.** $(19)^2$

 You can use the program on page 617 to compute the square of a given binomial.

Write each binomial in the form $Ax + B$. Then use the program to square each binomial

51. $9 + x$ **52.** $8 + 4x$ **53.** $x - 4$ **54.** $5 - 7x$

Write the square of each binomial as a trinomial.

55. $\left(x + \frac{1}{2}\right)^2$ **56.** $\left(x + \frac{1}{3}\right)^2$ **57.** $\left(x - \frac{1}{6}\right)^2$ **58.** $\left(2y + \frac{1}{2}\right)^2$ **59.** $\left(6b + \frac{1}{2}\right)^2$

60. $\left(9a + \frac{1}{6}\right)^2$ **61.** $\left(x - \frac{a}{2}\right)^2$ **62.** $\left(y - \frac{1}{2}p\right)^2$ **63.** $\left(x + \frac{y}{2}\right)^2$ **64.** $\left(\frac{x}{2} + 4\right)^2$

MAINTAIN

Find each product. (*Pages 351–357*)

65. $(x + 3)(x + 6)$ **66.** $(x - 4)(x + 5)$ **67.** $(x - 2)(x - 3)$

68. $(2x + 3)(5x + 1)$ **69.** $(2x - y)(4x - 7y)$ **70.** $(a^2 + 2b)(a^2 + 6b)$

71. $a(a + 4)$ **72.** $x^2(2x - 1)$ **73.** $y(2y - 5)$

74. $-4a(7a - 3b)$ **75.** $-s(s^2 - 3s + 5)$ **76.** $(11a^2 - 7a + 2)(-a)$

Solve each system by graphing. Check your solutions. (*Pages 243–248*)

77. $\begin{cases} y = -x + 7 \\ y = \frac{1}{3}x - 1 \end{cases}$ **78.** $\begin{cases} x + y = 2 \\ y = x + 2 \end{cases}$ **79.** $\begin{cases} 4x - 2y = 4 \\ y + 3x = 8 \end{cases}$

NON-ROUTINE PROBLEM

80. Eight square sheets of paper, all the same size, are placed on top of each other. They overlap as shown in the drawing at the right. The top sheet, labeled 1, is shown completely. Number the other sheets in order from top to bottom.

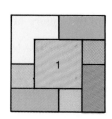

9-11 Product of (*a* + *b*) and (*a* − *b*)

Study the table to find the pattern for finding the product of the sum
and difference of the same two numbers.

(*a* + *b*)(*a* − *b*)	Multiply by inspection.	Simplify.
$(x + 7)(x - 7)$	$x^2 + 7x - 7x - 49$	$x^2 - 49$
$(y + 10)(y - 10)$	$y^2 + 10y - 10y - 100$	$y^2 - 100$
$(2x + 5)(2x - 5)$	$4x^2 + 10x - 10x - 25$	$4x^2 - 25$

The pattern in the table suggests the following procedure for finding
the product of (*a* + *b*) and (*a* − *b*).

> To find the product of the sum and difference of the same two
> numbers:
>
> **1** Square the first term of either binomial.
>
> **2** Subtract the square of the second term of either binomial.

EXAMPLE 1 Write each product as a binomial.

a. $\left(\frac{1}{3} + y\right)\left(\frac{1}{3} - y\right)$ b. $(3r + 7t)(3r - 7t)$

Solutions: a. $\left(\frac{1}{3} + y\right)\left(\frac{1}{3} - y\right) = \left(\frac{1}{3}\right)^2 - y^2$ ⟵ **(First term)² − (Second term)²**

$$= \frac{1}{9} - y^2$$

b. $(3r + 7t)(3r - 7t) = (3r)^2 - (7t)^2$ ⟵ **(First term)² −
(Second term)²**

$$= 9r^2 - 49t^2$$

This procedure is useful in finding certain products.

EXAMPLE 2 Find the product: 42×38

Solution: $42 \times 38 = (40 + 2)(40 - 2)$ ⟵ **Write 42 and 38 as the sum and
difference of the same two numbers.**

$$= (40^2) - (2)^2$$
$$= 1600 - 4 = 1596$$

You will find it useful to memorize this special binomial product.

Product of a Sum and Difference
$$(a + b)(a - b) = a^2 - b^2 \qquad (x + 2)(x - 2) = x^2 - 4$$

EXERCISES: Classwork/Homework

Objective: To find the product of the sum and difference of the same two numbers

CHECK YOUR UNDERSTANDING

Write each product as a binomial.

1. $(x + 1)(x - 1)$ **2.** $(a + 3)(a - 3)$ **3.** $(2r - 5)(2r + 5)$
4. $(1 - 6q)(1 + 6q)$ **5.** $(3h + 4s)(3h - 4s)$ **6.** $(0.2s - 0.1t)(0.2s + 0.1t)$

Write the factors as the sum and difference of the same two numbers.

7. 32×28 **8.** 18×22 **9.** 27×33 **10.** 59×61
11. 101×79 **12.** 83×77 **13.** 41×39 **14.** 159×81

PRACTICE AND APPLY

Write each product as a binomial.

15. $(p + 7)(p - 7)$ **16.** $(p - 5)(p + 5)$ **17.** $(p + 8)(p - 8)$
18. $(2p + 5)(2p - 5)$ **19.** $(b + c)(b - c)$ **20.** $(c - 2)(c + 2)$
21. $(2p + 3)(2p - 3)$ **22.** $(3p + 5)(3p - 5)$ **23.** $(R - r)(R + r)$
24. $(2x + y)(2x - y)$ **25.** $(5x + 4y)(5x - 4y)$ **26.** $(7x - 6y)(7x + 6y)$
27. $(6x^2 - 7y)(6x^2 + 7y)$ **28.** $(a^2 + b^2)(a^2 - b^2)$ **29.** $(ab - c)(ab + c)$
30. $(y - x^2)(x^2 + y)$ **31.** $(\frac{1}{2} - 2x)(\frac{1}{2} + 2x)$ **32.** $(y + 0.5)(y - 0.5)$
33. $(2c + d)(2c - d)$ **34.** $(3c + 2d)(3c - 2d)$ **35.** $(5y - 4)(4 + 5y)$
36. $(x^2 + y^2)(x^2 - y^2)$ **37.** $(x^3 - y^3)(x^3 + y^3)$ **38.** $(x^4 - y^4)(x^4 + y^4)$

Find each product.

39. $(20 + 1)(20 - 1)$ **40.** $(30 + 1)(30 - 1)$ **41.** $(100 + 2)(100 - 2)$
42. $(50 + 4)(50 - 4)$ **43.** $(10 + 5)(10 - 5)$ **44.** $(1000 + 1)(1000 - 1)$
45. $18 \cdot 22$ **46.** $101 \cdot 99$ **47.** $51 \cdot 49$

Find the area of the region bounded by the red closed curve.

48.

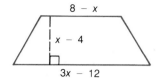

49.

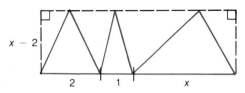

50. Which has the greater area, a square each of whose sides is x units long or a rectangle having the same perimeter but with width 5 units shorter than the width of the square?

51. Which has the greater area, a square each of whose sides is y units long or a rectangle having the same perimeter but with length 4 units longer than the side of the square? How much greater is it?

▨▨▨▨ **MAINTAIN**

Write the square of each binomial as a trinomial. (*Pages 358–360*)

52. $(x + 5)^2$ **53.** $(a - 3)^2$ **54.** $(2a + 3)^2$ **55.** $(3x - 5)^2$

56. $(x + 2y)^2$ **57.** $(a^2 + 2b^2)^2$ **58.** $(10r + 8s^2)^2$ **59.** $(7c^2 - 3d)^2$

Find each product. (*Pages 355–357*)

60. $(d + 5)(d + 6)$ **61.** $(2x - 7)(3x - 8)$ **62.** $(8p + 5)(7p - 2)$

63. $(y^2 + 1)(y^2 + 1)$ **64.** $(x^2 - 3)(x^2 + 4)$ **65.** $(\frac{1}{2}t + 7)(3t - 4)$

Solve each problem. (*Pages 263–269*)

66. The distance from New London to Bluepoint is 216 miles more than the distance from Lake Patricia to Cheyenne City. The sum of the two distances is 406 miles. Find the distance from New London to Bluepoint.

67. The tens digit of a two-digit number is 17 less than four times the units digit. The number is 11 more than three times the sum of the digits of the numbers. Find the number.

▨▨▨▨ **CONNECT AND EXTEND**

Write each product as a binomial.

68. $(x^n + 1)(x^n - 1)$ **69.** $(1 - y^{2a})(1 + y^{2a})$ **70.** $(x^a - y^b)(x^a + y^b)$

71. $(a^2b^8 - 5)(a^2b^8 + 5)$ **72.** $(0.2 + x^3y^5)(0.2 - x^3y^5)$ **73.** $(b^n + c^{2n})(b^n - c^{2n})$

74. $(c^n + d^n)(c^n - d^n)$ **75.** $(x^{2n} - 2y^n)(x^{2n} + 2y^n)$ **76.** $(3y^n - 4^{2n})(3y^n + 4^{2n})$

▨▨▨▨ **NON-ROUTINE PROBLEM**

77. Would it be cheaper for you to take one friend to the movies twice, or two friends at the same time?

9-12 Division of Polynomials

Division of one polynomial by another is similar to long division in arithmetic.

Arithmetic

$$\boxed{1}\ \ 28\overline{)537}$$

$$\quad \underline{1}$$

$$\quad \underline{28}$$

$$\quad \ 25$$

Think: $(28)(\underline{\ ?\ }) \le 53$

$\longleftarrow$ $1 \cdot 28$

$\longleftarrow$ $53 - 28$

$$\boxed{2}\ \ 28\overline{)537}$$

$$\quad \ \ \underline{19}$$

$$\quad \ \underline{28}$$

$$\quad 257$$

$$\quad \underline{252}$$

$$\quad \ \ \ 5$$

$\longleftarrow$ Think: $(28)(\underline{\ ?\ }) \le 257$

$\longleftarrow$ Remainder

Answer: $19 + \dfrac{5}{28}$, or $19\dfrac{5}{28}$

Algebra

$$\boxed{1}\ \ x + 3\overline{)x^2 + x - 1}$$

$$\quad \ \ \ \underline{x}$$

$$\quad \ \underline{x^2 + 3x}$$

$$\quad \ \ \ \ \ -2x$$

Think: $(x)(\underline{\ ?\ }) = x^2$

$\longleftarrow$ $x(x + 3)$

$\longleftarrow$ $x - 3x$

$$\boxed{2}\ \ x + 3\overline{)x^2 + x - 1}$$

$$\quad \ \ \ \underline{x - 2}$$

$$\quad \ \underline{x^2 + 3x}$$

$$\quad \ \ \ \ -2x - 1$$

$$\quad \ \ \ \ \underline{-2x - 6}$$

$$\quad \ \ \ \ \ \ \ \ \ 5$$

$\longleftarrow$ Think: $(x)(\underline{\ ?\ }) = -2x$

$\longleftarrow$ Remainder

Answer: $x - 2 + \dfrac{5}{x + 3}$

As these examples show, a division problem can be expressed in general form.

$$\frac{\textbf{Dividend}}{\textbf{Divisor}} = \textbf{Quotient} + \frac{\textbf{Remainder}}{\textbf{Divisor}}, \text{ or}$$

$$\textbf{Dividend} = \textbf{(Divisor)(Quotient)} + \textbf{Remainder}$$

Example 1 shows how to use this general form to check a division problem.

EXAMPLE 1 Divide $x^3 - x^2 - 2x + 10$ by $x + 2$.

Solution:

$$\boxed{1}\ \ x + 2\overline{)x^3 - x^2 - 2x + 10}$$

$$\quad \ \ \ \ \underline{x^2}$$

$$\quad \ \ \underline{x^3 + 2x^2}$$

$$\quad \ \ \ \ \ -3x^2 - 2x + 10$$

$\longleftarrow$ Think: $(x)(\underline{\ ?\ }) = x^3$

$\longleftarrow$ $x^2(x + 2)$

$\longleftarrow$ $x^3 - x^2 - 2x + 10 - (x^3 + 2x^2)$

$$\boxed{2}\ \ x + 2\overline{)x^3 - x^2 - 2x + 10}$$

$$\quad \ \ \ \ \underline{x^2 - 3x}$$

$$\quad \ \ \underline{x^3 + 2x^2}$$

$$\quad \ \ \ \ -3x^2 - 2x + 10$$

$$\quad \ \ \ \ \underline{-3x^2 - 6x}$$

$$\quad \ \ \ \ \ \ \ \ 4x + 10$$

$\longleftarrow$ Think: $x(\underline{\ ?\ }) = -3x^2$

$\longleftarrow$ $(-3x)(x + 2)$

$\longleftarrow$ $(-3x^2 - 2x + 10) - (-3x^2 - 6x)$

$$\boxed{3} \quad x + 2 \overline{)\begin{array}{l} x^2 - 3x + 4 \\ x^3 - x^2 - 2x + 10 \end{array}} \quad \longleftarrow \quad \text{Think: } (x)(\underline{\ ?\ }) = 4x$$

$$\begin{array}{r} x^3 + 2x^2 \\ \hline -3x^2 - 2x + 10 \\ -3x^2 - 6x \\ \hline 4x + 10 \\ 4x + 8 \\ \hline 2 \end{array}$$

$4(x + 2)$ $\longleftarrow$

Remainder $\longleftarrow$

Thus, $x^3 - x^2 - 2x + 10 \div x + 2 = x^2 - 3x + 4 + \dfrac{2}{x + 2}$.

Check: Dividend = (Divisor)(Quotient) + Remainder

$x^3 - x^2 - 2x + 10 \overset{?}{=} (x + 2)(x^2 - 3x + 4) + 2$

$x^3 - x^2 - 2x + 10 \overset{?}{=} (x^3 - x^2 - 2x + 8) + 2$

$x^3 - x^2 - 2x + 10 \overset{?}{=} x^3 - x^2 - 2x + 10$ Yes ✔

When you divide polynomials, always be sure that the terms of each polynomial are arranged in descending order of the exponents of the variable. Also, when one of the terms in the dividend is "missing," insert 0 as the coefficient of the variable.

EXAMPLE 2 Divide $2a^2 + a^3 - 75$ by $a - 5$.

Solution: Write $2a^2 + a^3 - 75$ as $a^3 + 2a^2 + 0a - 75$. $\longleftarrow$ **Descending order of exponents**

$$a - 5 \overline{)\begin{array}{l} a^2 + 7a + 35 \\ a^3 + 2a^2 + 0a - 75 \end{array}}$$

$$\begin{array}{r} a^3 - 5a^2 \\ \hline 7a^2 + 0a \\ 7a^2 - 35a \\ \hline 35a - 75 \\ 35a - 175 \\ \hline 100 \end{array}$$

Answer: $a^2 + 7a + 35 + \dfrac{100}{a - 5}$

The check is left for you.

EXERCISES: Classroom/Homework ▰▰▰▰▰▰

Objective: To divide one polynomial by another

▰▰▰▰ **CHECK YOUR UNDERSTANDING**

Write the missing terms to be inserted in the dividend before dividing.

1. $t + 5 \overline{)t^2 - 25}$ **2.** $x - 3 \overline{)x^2 - 12}$ **3.** $2a - 1 \overline{)4a^3 - 8a^2 + 10}$

4. $x + 2\overline{)x^3 + 8}$ **5.** $2x^2 + 2x + 1\overline{)4x^4 + 1}$ **6.** $3x - 1\overline{)12x^3 - 9x^2 + 7}$

Write the terms of the dividend in descending order of the exponents of the variable.

7. $2r - 1\overline{)10r - 9r^2 + 5 + 2r^3}$ **8.** $4k - 1\overline{)7 + 8k^2 - 30k}$ **9.** $z - 3\overline{)2 - 13z + 6z^2}$

▓▓▓▓▓▓▓ **PRACTICE AND APPLY**

Divide the first polynomial by the second.

10. $x^2 + 10x + 21; x + 3$ **11.** $y^2 + 13y + 22; y + 2$

12. $c^2 - 3c - 28; c - 7$ **13.** $p^2 - p + 32; p + 5$

14. $3n^2 + 14n + 8; n + 4$ **15.** $2a^2 - 11a + 14; a - 2$

16. $4y^2 + 19y + 21; y + 1$ **17.** $3c^2 - 24c + 9; c - 3$

18. $2x^2 - 11x - 40; 2x + 5$ **19.** $6a^2 - 13a + 7; 2a - 3$

20. $8x^2 - 14x - 30; 2x - 6$ **21.** $15n^2 + 16n + 10; 3n + 2$

22. $x^2 + xy - 3y^2; x - y$ **23.** $a^3 - 5a^2 + 2a + 8; a - 2$

24. $c^3 + 2c^2 - 2c + 24; c + 4$ **25.** $6x^3 + x^2 - 19x + 6; 2x - 3$

26. $8p^3 - 2p^2 - 5p - 4; 4p + 1$ **27.** $3a^3 + 8a^2b + 7ab^2; 3a + 2b$

28. $6y^3 - 10y^2 + 2y - 10; 3y + 1$ **29.** $x^2 + 25; x + 5$

30. $6a^2 - ab + b^2; 2a + b$ **31.** $a^3 - 8b^3; a - 2b$

32. $x^3 - 6x^2 + 1; x + 2$ **33.** $x^3 - 2x - 21; x - 3$

34. $x^3 - 125; x - 5$ **35.** $x^3 + 27; x + 3$

▓▓▓▓▓▓▓ **MAINTAIN**

Write each product as a binomial. (*Pages 361–363*)

36. $(x + 6)(x - 6)$ **37.** $(p + 8)(p - 8)$ **38.** $(y + 1)(y - 1)$

39. $(x + 3y)(x - 3y)$ **40.** $(2a - b)(2a + b)$ **41.** $(2c + 5d)(2c - 5d)$

Solve each system. (*Pages 256–259*)

42. $\begin{cases} 5p + c = -2 \\ p + 2c = -22 \end{cases}$ **43.** $\begin{cases} 6r - 5t = -4 \\ 9r + 11t = 31 \end{cases}$ **44.** $\begin{cases} 3c + 4z = 130 \\ 2c - 3z = 132 \end{cases}$

▓▓▓▓▓▓▓ **CONNECT AND EXTEND**

45. Find the value of k for which $(3t + 2)$ is a factor of $15t^2 - 2t + k$.

46. Find the value of k for which $(x - 3)$ is a factor of $2x^3 - x^2 - 17x + k$.

47. A rectangle of width $(4x - 9y)$ units has an area of $(12x^2 - 11xy - 36y^2)$ square units. Find the perimeter of the rectangle.

48. When $6p^3 - 22p + c$ is divided by $2p - 4$, the remainder is 5. Find c.

Focus on College Entrance Tests

When comparing two quantities or expressions, it is sometimes helpful to choose real numbers that satisfy the conditions of the problem and substitute them in the given expressions.

EXAMPLE   If n is a real number and $n < 0$, which of the following statements must be true?

a. $n > \dfrac{1}{n}$ **b.** $(n^2 - 1) > (1 - n^2)$ **c.** $(n - 1) > (1 - n)$ **d.** $n^2 > n$

Think: Two choices involve n^2, and n^2 is always positive. Thus, check the choices involving n^2 first.

Solution: **b.** $(n^2 - 1) > (1 - n^2)$ ⟵ Not true when $n = -\dfrac{1}{2}$

d. $n^2 > n$ ⟵ Always true, since $n < 0$ and $n^2 > 0$

a. $n > \dfrac{1}{n}$ ⟵ Not true when $n = -2$

c. $(n - 1) > (1 - n)$ ⟵ Never true, since $(n - 1) < 0$ and $(1 - n) > 0$

Answer: **d**

TRY THESE

Choose the best answer. Choose a, b, c, or d. (Assume that all variables represent real numbers.)

1. If $y > 0$, which of the following must be true?

a. $y^2 > y$ **b.** $y > \dfrac{1}{y}$ **c.** $(y + 1) > (y - 1)$ **d.** $\dfrac{1}{y} > \dfrac{1}{y^2}$

2. If $y < 0$, which of the following must be true?

a. $y^4 > y^2$ **b.** $y^3 > y$ **c.** $y^3 > y^2$ **d.** $y^4 > y$

3. If $p > 2$, which of the following must be true?

a. $\dfrac{p - 2}{2} > \dfrac{p}{2}$ **b.** $\dfrac{p + 2}{2} > \dfrac{p}{2}$ **c.** $\dfrac{2}{p + 2} > \dfrac{2}{p}$ **d.** $\dfrac{2}{p} > \dfrac{2}{p - 2}$

4. If $q \neq 0$, which of the following must be true?

a. $\dfrac{q - (q + q)}{q} > 1$ **b.** $\dfrac{q - (q - q)}{q} > 1$ **c.** $\dfrac{q + (q + q)}{q} > 1$ **d.** $\dfrac{q + (q - q)}{q} > 1$

5. If $w > 1$, which of the following must be true?

a. $\dfrac{1}{w - 1} > \dfrac{1}{1 - w}$ **b.** $\dfrac{1}{w - 1} > \dfrac{-1}{1 - w}$ **c.** $\dfrac{1}{1 - w} > \dfrac{-1}{w - 1}$ **d.** $\dfrac{1}{1 - w} > \dfrac{-1}{1 - w}$

Chapter Summary

IMPORTANT IDEAS

1. If x is a real number and a is an integer greater than 1, then

$$x^a = \underbrace{x \cdot x \cdot x \cdot \cdots \cdot x.}_{a \text{ factors}}$$

When $a = 1$, $x^a = x$, that is, $x^1 = x$.

2. **Product Property of Powers:** If x is a real number and a and b are positive integers, then

$$x^a \cdot x^b = x^{a+b}.$$

3. **Property of the Power of a Power:** If x is a real number and a and b are positive integers, then

$$(x^a)^b = x^{ab}.$$

4. **Property of the Power of a Product:** If x and y are real numbers and a is a positive integer, then

$$(xy)^a = x^a y^a.$$

5. **Quotient Property of Powers:** If x is a real number, $x \neq 0$, and a and b are positive integers such that $a \geq b$, then

$$\frac{x^a}{x^b} = x^{a-b}.$$

6. If x is any real number except zero and a is a positive integer, then

$$x^{-a} = \frac{1}{x^a}.$$

7. To add polynomials, add monomials that are like terms. To subtract a polynomial, add its additive inverse.

8. **The FOIL Method for Finding the Product of Two Binomials**
   Add the product of the **first** terms, the product of the **outer** terms, the product of the **inner** terms, and the product of the **last** terms.

9. **Steps in Squaring a Binomial**
   1 Square the first term.
   2 Add to this twice the product of the first and last terms when the binomial is of the form $(a + b)$.

   Subtract twice the product of the first and last terms when the binomial is of the form $(a - b)$.

3 Add to this the square of the last term.

$$(a + b)^2 = a^2 + 2ab + b^2$$
$$(a - b)^2 = a^2 - 2ab + b^2$$

10. **Steps in Finding the Product of the Sum and Difference of the Same Two Numbers**

   1 Square the first term of either binomial.

   2 Subtract the square of the second term of either binomial.

$$(a + b)(a - b) = a^2 - b^2$$

Chapter Review

Evaluate. (*Pages 325–328*)

1. $(-2)^3$
2. $(-3)^2$
3. 5^0
4. 10^8
5. $(-1)^{13}$

Find the value when $a = 2$, $b = -4$, and $c = 5$. (*Pages 325–328*)

6. a^2c
7. a^3b^2
8. abc^2
9. ab^3
10. a^3b^2c

Find each product. (*Pages 329–331*)

11. $a^2(a^6)$
12. $x^2 \cdot x^7$
13. $p^4 \times p$
14. $(-h)(-y)$
15. $10^3 \cdot 10^3$
16. $(3x^2)(-4x^3)$
17. $(-3mn)(-m^2)$
18. $(-st)(s^2t^3)$

Raise to the indicated power. No denominator equals zero. (*Pages 332–334*)

19. $(x^3)^5$
20. $(x^5)^3$
21. $(3y)^3$
22. $(-ab^2)^3$
23. $(3cd^4)^3$
24. $(-3 \times 10^3)^2$
25. $\left(\dfrac{m^2}{pn^3}\right)^3$
26. $\left(\dfrac{q^2r}{s^3}\right)^2$

Simplify. All exponents are positive integers and no denominator equals zero. (*Pages 335–337*)

27. $\dfrac{3c^3}{c^3}$
28. $\dfrac{m^3n^2}{m^2n}$
29. $\dfrac{-18a^2b^4}{-6ab}$
30. $\dfrac{6p(3p^3)}{9p^2}$
31. $\dfrac{(-6x^3y)(-xy)^2}{-2x^2y^2}$
32. $\dfrac{q^{c+1}}{q^c}$
33. $\dfrac{s^{2x}t^{3y}}{st^2}$
34. $\dfrac{(y^{3k+4})^3}{y^{2k+12}}$

Simplify. No variable equals zero. (*Pages 340–342*)

35. 3^{-4} **36.** $(-4)^3$ **37.** y^{-6} **38.** $\left(-\frac{2}{3}\right)^{-3}$ **39.** $3n^{-2}$

Write each number in scientific notation. (*Pages 343–346*)

40. 800,000,000   **41.** 29,000,000,000   **42.** 0.0000038

Express the product or quotient in scientific notation. (*Pages 343–346*)

43. $(6.2 \times 10^2)(1.4 \times 10^{-7})$ **44.** $\dfrac{1.2 \times 10^{-7}}{4.8 \times 10^5}$ **45.** $\dfrac{9 \times 10^{-2}}{1.5 \times 10^{-6}}$

Add or subtract as indicated. (*Pages 347–350*)

46. $(6x + 3y) - (2x + 5y)$ **47.** $(2a^2b - ab^2) + (ab^2 - 4a^2b)$

48. $(m^2 + 6m) + (2m^2 - m)$ **49.** $(2cd + c + 5) - (d - cd - 6)$

Multiply. (*Pages 351–354*)

50. $5(6y + 3)$ **51.** $-6a(3a^2 - 2)$ **52.** $(2x - y)(x + 4y)$

53. $(\frac{1}{2}x - 1)(2x + 4)$ **54.** $(x - y)(y - x)$ **55.** $(c^2 + 2d)(2c^2 + d)$

Find each product by inspection. (*Pages 355–357*)

56. $(p - 4)(p + 1)$ **57.** $(3y - 4)(y - 2)$ **58.** $(2a + 3b)(3a - 4b)$

59. $(2x^2 + 1)(x^2 + 4)$ **60.** $(2d - h)(d + 3h)$ **61.** $(0.5r + s)(1.4r - s)$

Write the square of each binomial as a trinomial. (*Pages 358–360*)

62. $(c + 6)^2$ **63.** $(6p - 1)^2$ **64.** $(x^2 + 3)^2$ **65.** $(4a - 3b)^2$

Write each product as a binomial. (*Pages 361–363*))

66. $(d - 5)(d + 5)$ **67.** $(8 + a)(8 - a)$ **68.** $(f - g)(f + g)$

69. $(4w - 5)(4w + 5)$ **70.** $(5m + 2n)(5m - 2n)$ **71.** $(2b^2 - 7)(2b^2 + 7)$

Divide the first polynomial by the second. (*Pages 364–366*)

72. $x^2 + x - 6$; $x + 3$ **73.** $a^2 - 6a + 9$; $a - 3$

74. $4y^2 - 25$; $2y - 5$ **75.** $4x^2 - 5x - 6$; $4x + 3$

76. $b^3 + 4b + 5$; $b + 1$ **77.** $2n^3 + 3n^2 + 3n + 1$; $2n + 1$

78. $y^3 + 3y^2 + 16$; $y + 4$ **79.** $4a^3 - 4a^2 - 15a + 1$; $2a - 3$

Find the value when $a = -1$, $b = 2$, and $c = -4$.

1. a^2b **2.** bc^3 **3.** abc^2

Simplify. No denominator equals zero.

4. $\dfrac{n^4}{n}$ **5.** $\dfrac{-15a^2bc^2}{3ab}$ **6.** $\dfrac{x^2(4xy)^2}{4x^2y}$

Simplify. No variable equals zero.

7. 2^{-3} **8.** $(-3)^{-2}$ **9.** y^{-5} **10.** $(-\tfrac{1}{3})^{-3}$ **11.** $3x^{-4}$

Write each number in scientific notation.

12. 650,000,000   **13.** 0.00003   **14.** 7 million

Express the product or quotient in scientific notation.

15. $(8 \times 10^{-3})(1.9 \times 10^4)$ **16.** $\dfrac{5.5 \times 10^3}{2.75 \times 10^4}$ **17.** $\dfrac{1.6 \times 10^{-3}}{8 \times 10^{12}}$

Add or subtract as indicated.

18. $(3m - 4n) - (2n + m)$ **19.** $(x^2 + x - 4) + (3x - 1 - x^2)$

Raise to the indicated power.

20. $(-cd^2)^3$ **21.** $(x - 4)^2$ **22.** $(3a + 4b^2)^2$

Multiply.

23. $w^3(-w^4)$ **24.** $(-4x^2)(-2x^5)$

25. $3b(2b - 1)$ **26.** $3t(t^2 - 5t + 2)$

27. $(3y + 2x)(y - 3x)$ **28.** $(3c - 3d)(c - d)$

29. $(y + 4)(y - 4)$ **30.** $(2a - b)(2a + b)$

31. Divide $x^2 + 5x + 6$ by $x + 3$.   **32.** Divide $y^3 - 7y + 6$ by $y - 2$.

33. Divide $2y^2 - 3y - 27$ by $2y - 9$.   **34.** Divide $5x^3 + 3x^2 - 25x - 15$ by $x^2 - 5$.

Additional Practice

Skills

Find the value when $a = 1$, $b = -2$, and $c = 5$. (*Pages 325–328*)

1. a^2b **2.** b^2c **3.** abc **4.** a^2b^3c **5.** $a^3b^4c^2$

Find each product. (*Pages 329–331*)

6. $c^2(c^3)$ **7.** $(-3x)(4x)$ **8.** $-(-4b^2)(-3)$ **9.** $3n(2mn)(3n^2)$

Raise to the indicated power. No denominator equals zero. (*Pages 332–334*)

10. $(x^3)^2$ **11.** $(ab^4)^3$ **12.** $\left(\dfrac{n^2p}{2m^3}\right)^4$ **13.** $\left(\dfrac{ab^3}{c^4}\right)^5$

Simplify. All exponents are positive integers and no denominator equals zero. (*Pages 335–337*)

14. $\dfrac{x^7}{x^4}$ **15.** $\dfrac{a^2b^4}{ab^2}$ **16.** $\dfrac{(2mn^2)(5m^3n^2)}{(2mn^2)^2}$ **17.** $\dfrac{p^{5k-1}}{p^{3k-4}}$

Simplify. No variable equals zero. (*Pages 340–342*)

18. $(-2)^{-3}$ **19.** r^{-2} **20.** $4a^{-6}$ **21.** $(ax)^{-4}$

Write in scientific notation. (*Pages 343–346*)

22. 0.0000024 **23.** $320,000,000$ **24.** 2500 **25.** 0.0000652

Multiply. (*Pages 351–353*)

26. $3x(2x - 1)$ **27.** $(a + 1)(a - 5)$ **28.** $(3n - 4)(5n - 1)$

Write each product as a binomial. (*Pages 361–363*)

29. $(2y - 9)(2y + 9)$ **30.** $(xy + 1)(xy - 1)$ **31.** $(6s - \tfrac{1}{2})(6s + \tfrac{1}{2})$

Divide the first polynomial by the second. (*Pages 364–366*)

32. $x^2 - 8x + 15$; $x - 3$ **33.** $y^3 - 3y^2 - 4y$; $y + 1$

Problem Solving and Applications

34. Find the perimeter of a square if the length of each of its four equal sides is $(2b + 3)$ units. (*Pages 347–350*)

35. Which has the greater area, a rectangle with length $(n + 1)$ units and width $(n - 1)$ units or a square with the same perimeter as the rectangle? How much greater is it? (*Pages 361–363*)

Part 1

Choose the best answer. Choose *a*, *b*, *c*, or *d*.

1. If y varies directly as x and $y = 9$ when $x = 4$, then what is y when $x = 5$?
   a. 10 **b.** 2.25 **c.** 11.25 **d.** 4

2. Which ordered pair is a solution of the system $\begin{cases} 2x - 3y = 4 \\ 4x + y = 8? \end{cases}$
   a. $(-1, -2)$ **b.** $(3, -4)$ **c.** $(1, 4)$ **d.** $(2, 0)$

3. What is the mean of the numbers $3, -3, 2, 1, -1, 0, 4, -2$?
   a. $\frac{4}{7}$ **b.** $\frac{1}{2}$ **c.** 2 **d.** 0

4. What is the theoretical probability that when a die is rolled, the number showing is greater than 4?
   a. $\frac{1}{6}$ **b.** $\frac{1}{2}$ **c.** $\frac{1}{3}$ **d.** $\frac{1}{4}$

5. Which of the following is equivalent to $2^3 \cdot 4^4$?
   a. 8^{12} **b.** 2^{11} **c.** 8^7 **d.** 4^{10}

6. Solve $3 - 4x \geq -9$.
   a. $x \leq -3$ **b.** $x \geq 3$ **c.** $x \leq 3$ **d.** $x \geq -3$

7. What is the slope of every line that is parallel to the x axis?
   a. 1 **b.** -1 **c.** 0 **d.** undefined

8. The number of solutions to the equation $|x - 3| = 5$ is
   a. 0 **b.** 1 **c.** 2 **d.** infinitely many

9. What is the y intercept of the line with equation $2x + 3y - 5 = 0$?
   a. 3 **b.** 2 **c.** $\frac{5}{3}$ **d.** $-\left(\frac{2}{3}\right)$

10. Solve the equation $2x - \frac{1}{3} = 3\left(x - \frac{2}{9}\right)$.
    a. $x = \frac{1}{9}$ **b.** $x = \frac{1}{3}$ **c.** $x = \frac{2}{9}$ **d.** $x = 1$

11. Find the value of $(-3x^2)(-2x^3)$ when $x = -1$.
    a. $-\frac{1}{6}$ **b.** $\frac{1}{6}$ **c.** 6 **d.** -6

12. What is the meaning of the inequality $|x| > 3$?
    a. $x < 3$ and $x > -3$ **b.** $x > 3$ and $x < -3$
    c. $x < 3$ or $x > -3$ **d.** $x > 3$ or $x < -3$

13. Solve the system $\begin{cases} x - 3y = 11 \\ 2x + y = 8. \end{cases}$
    a. $(5, -2)$ **b.** $(5, 2)$ **c.** $(-2, 5)$ **d.** $(2, 5)$

14. What is the equation of the line that is parallel to the line with equation $3x + 4y = 2$ and has y intercept 2?

a. $y = \frac{3}{4}x + 8$

b. $y = -\frac{3}{4}x + 8$

c. $y = \frac{3}{4}x - 2$

d. $y = -\frac{3}{4}x + 2$

15. If x and y are real numbers and a is a positive integer, then $(xy)^a$ is equivalent to

a. $x(y^a)$

b. $(x^a)y$

c. $x^a y^a$

d. x^{ay}

16. Solve $-3(x - 2) \geq 2(4 - x)$.

a. $x \leq 2$

b. $x \geq -2$

c. $x \leq -2$

d. $x \geq 2$

17. Which point does not lie on the graph of $y = |x - 2|$?

a. $(-1, 3)$

b. $(0, 2)$

c. $(1, -1)$

d. $(2, 0)$

18. Which line passes through the points $(1, 4)$ and $(-1, 3)$?

a. $x + 2y + 7 = 0$

b. $x - 2y + 7 = 0$

c. $x - 2y - 7 = 0$

d. $y = \frac{1}{2}x + 7$

19. If $a = -4.5$, what is the value of $a + |a|$?

a. -9

b. 9

c. 0

d. 4.5

20. Which of the following is equivalent to $\dfrac{-(3x^2y)^2(4xy^2)}{6xy^3}$?

a. $-2x^2$

b. $6x^4y$

c. $6x^2y$

d. $-6x^4y$

21. What is the solution set of $|2(x + 1) - 5| = 9$?

a. $\{6\}$

b. $\{-3\}$

c. $\{6, -3\}$

d. $\{6, 3\}$

22. 18 is 24% of what number?

a. 70

b. 80

c. 75

d. 85

23. Which property is illustrated by this statement:

$$a + (b + c) = (a + b) + c?$$

a. Associative

b. Distributive

c. Commutative

d. Reflexive

24. Perform the indicated multiplication: $(2x^2 + 3y)(3x - 2y^2)$.

a. $6x^3 - 6y^3$

b. $6x^3 - 4x^2y^2 + 9xy - 6y^3$

c. $6x^2 - 4x^2y^2 + 9xy - 6y^2$

d. $2x^2 + 9xy - 2y^2$

25. Simplify: $3x^2y + 4x(x + y) - 3y(x^2 + x) - (2x)^2$.

a. $8x^2 + xy$

b. xy

c. $-xy$

d. $6x^2y - xy$

26. Which of the following is the remainder after dividing $x^3 - 3x^2 - 5$ by $x + 2$?

a. -5

b. 25

c. -20

d. -25

27. Which of the following is equivalent to $(2x^2 - 3y^2)^2$?

    a. $4x^4 - 9y^4$ **b.** $36x^4y^4$

    c. $4x^4 - 6x^2y^2 + 9y^4$ **d.** $4x^4 - 12x^2y^2 + 9y^4$

Part 2

Solve each problem.

28. Jim bought a pair of shoes and received a 15% discount from the list price. If his bill was $55.25, what was the list price for the shoes?

29. The length of a rectangle is 3 ft less than twice its width. If the perimeter is 24 ft, find the length and width.

30. Sue has taken three tests in mathematics this term; her grades were 86, 87 and 92. If her goal is to have a test average of at least 90, what is the lowest score she can get on the fourth and last test?

31. The weight of a cable varies directly as its length. If a 2-ft section weighs 1.5 pounds, how heavy is a 500-ft reel of cable?

32. A clerk mistakenly reverses the two digits in the price of a paperback book, overcharging the customer $0.18. If the sum of the digits is 16, determine the correct price of the book.

33. If it takes 8 hours to complete a journey when a car travels at 45 mph, how long will it take to complete the same journey if the car travels at 60 mph?

34. Which has the greater area, a square each of whose sides is x units long, or a rectangle having the same perimeter, but with length 3 units longer than the sides of the square?

35. Paul invested twice as much money at 5% per year as he did at 4% per year. How much did he invest at each rate if his annual return totaled $280?

36. A rectangle of width $2x - 5y$ has an area of $(6x^2 - 11xy - 10y^2)$ sq. units. Find the perimeter of the rectangle.

37. A shipment of 18 cars, some weighing 3000 pounds apiece and the others 5000 pounds apiece, has a total weight of 30 tons. Find the number of each kind of car.

10 **Factoring Polynomials**

The application of the formula for the area of a rectangle, $A = l\,w$, to solving problems in algebra often leads to a **trinomial expression** of degree 2. For example, the expression $x^2 + 4x = 192$ can be used to find the area of a flower garden whose length is 4 meters greater than its width and whose area is 192 square meters.

10-1 Factoring Integers

To *factor* a number or a polynominal means to write it as a product.

$$174 = 2 \cdot 3 \cdot 29$$ **Factors of 174**

Each number below has only two whole-number factors, the number itself and 1. These numbers are called *prime numbers*.

2, 3, 5, 7, 11, 13, 17, 19, 23, 29, 31

DEFINITION

> A **prime number** is an integer greater than 1 that has exactly two positive integral factors, itself and 1.

Numbers such as 4, 9, 10, 16, 25, and so on, are *composite numbers*.

DEFINITION

> A **composite number** is any integer greater than 1 that is not prime.

Every composite number can be expressed as a product of prime-number factors.

When a composite number is written as a product of prime-number factors or of powers of prime-number factors, the number is in **prime-factorization form.**

EXAMPLE

Write each number in prime-factorization form.

a. 500 **b.** 756

Solutions: Divide by the prime numbers in order.

Divide by each prime number as many times as possible, before dividing by the next prime number.

a. $500 = 2 \cdot 250$ ◄────── **Divide by 2 again.**

$= 2 \cdot 2 \cdot 125$ ◄────── **125 is not divisible by 3. Try 5.**

$= 2 \cdot 2 \cdot 5 \cdot 25$ ◄────── **Divide by 5 again.**

$= 2 \cdot 2 \cdot 5 \cdot 5 \cdot 5$ ◄────── **Stop! All factors are prime factors.**

$= 2^2 \cdot 5^3$ ◄────── **Prime factorization.**

b. $756 = 2 \cdot 378$ ◄————— Divide by 2 again.

$= 2 \cdot 2 \cdot 189$ ◄————— Divide by 3.

$= 2 \cdot 2 \cdot 3 \cdot 63$ ◄————— Divide by 3 again.

$= 2 \cdot 2 \cdot 3 \cdot 3 \cdot 21$ ◄————— Divide by 3 again.

$= 2 \cdot 2 \cdot 3 \cdot 3 \cdot 3 \cdot 7$ ◄————— Stop! All factors are prime factors.

$= 2^2 \cdot 3^3 \cdot 7$ ◄————— Prime factorization

The *Unique Factorization Property,* also called the *Fundamental Property of Arithmetic,* states that there is *one and only one way* to factor positive integers such as 500 and 756 into primes.

> **Unique Factorization Property**
>
> The factorization of any positive integer into primes is unique, disregarding the order of the factors.

When you are asked to find the factors of a number, you must know whether you are to find the whole-number, integral, rational, or real-number factors. For example,

$$\tfrac{1}{2} \text{ and } 36 \text{ are } rational\text{-}number\ factors \text{ of } 18.$$

Unless told otherwise in this text, assume that you are factoring over the set of integers.

EXERCISES: Classwork/Homework

Objective: To write a number in prime factorization form and to write all of its whole number factors

CHECK YOUR UNDERSTANDING

Complete.

1. An integer greater than 1 that has exactly two positive integral factors, iself and 1, is a __?__ number.

2. Any integer greater than 1 that is not prime is a __?__ number.

Determine whether the second number is a factor of the number in parentheses. Answer <u>Yes</u> or <u>No</u>.

3. $(3^3 \cdot 5)$; $3 \cdot 5$ **4.** $(2 \cdot 5 \cdot 7)$;   3   **5.** $(8 + 2)$;   8

6. $(5 \cdot 6^2 \cdot 8)$;   6   **7.** $(3 \cdot 4 \cdot 7)$;   4   **8.** $(8^2 \cdot 7 \cdot 4)$; $8 \cdot 7 \cdot 4$

9. $(5^2 \cdot 6^2 \cdot 8)$; $5^2 \cdot 8$ **10.** $(3^2 + 1)$;   3   **11.** $(9^2 + 1)$;   9

Identify each number as prime **P**, or composite, **C**.

12. 15	**13.** 9	**14.** 7	**15.** 29	**16.** 31	**17.** 51
18. 37	**19.** 33	**20.** 18	**21.** 43	**22.** 49	**23.** 11
24. 13	**25.** 100	**26.** 23	**27.** 17	**28.** 48	**29.** 101

Write each number in prime-factorization form.

30. 18	**31.** 36	**32.** 21	**33.** 15	**34.** 42	**35.** 32
36. 45	**37.** 49	**38.** 25	**39.** 28	**40.** 33	**41.** 44
42. 500	**43.** 625	**44.** 300	**45.** 1000	**46.** 960	**47.** 72

Write each number as the product of two rational-number factors.

48. 4	**49.** 6	**50.** 3	**51.** 10	**52.** 7	**53.** 9
54. 8	**55.** 11	**56.** $\frac{1}{8}$	**57.** $\frac{1}{16}$	**58.** $\frac{1}{10}$	**59.** $\frac{1}{2}$

60. A marching band has 72 members. What rectangular formations are possible if each row and each column must have at least 6 players?

61. The Cobb City marching band has 100 members. What rectangular formations are possible if each row and each column must have at least 5 players?

62. Ann sets out 100 tomato plants in her garden. In what ways can she arrange them so that she has the same number in each row and there are at least 5 rows and 5 columns?

63. Use a calculator to determine whether $2^3 \cdot 3^3 \cdot 5^2 \cdot 7$ is the prime factorization of 18,900. If it is not, then find the correct prime factorization.

Divide the first polynomial by the second. (*Pages 364–366*)

64. $2x^2 + x - 15; x + 3$ **65.** $3x^2 - 5x - 12; x - 3$ **66.** $x^2 - 3x - 7; x + 2$

Write each product as a binomial. (*Pages 361–363*)

67. $(x + 3)(x - 3)$ **68.** $(y - 12)(y + 12)$ **69.** $(2t - 4)(2t + 4)$

Solve and graph each inequality. (*Pages 295–298*)

70. $x + 2 > 4$ **71.** $a - 5 < -6$ **72.** $b - 3 \leq 1$

Use the Distributive Property to find each product. (*Pages 34–37, 149–151*)

1. $3(x + 4)$ **2.** $-2(a + b)$ **3.** $-5(2s + t)$ **4.** $6(4 + y)$

5. $a(b + c)$ **6.** $y(w - z)$ **7.** $ab(3 - c)$ **8.** $cd(p + r)$

10-2 Common Factors

The Distributive Property is used to find products. It is also used to find factors of polynomials.

Multiplying	Factoring
$6(x + y) = 6x + 6y$	$6x + 6y = 6(x + y)$
$a(b + c) = ab + ac$	$ab + ac = a(b + c)$
$5x(3x^2 - 4x - 1) = 15x^3 - 20x^2 - 5x$	$15x^3 - 20x^2 - 5x = 5x(3x^2 - 4x - 1)$
$(x + 2)(x + 3) = x(x + 3) + 2(x + 3)$	$x(x + 3) + 2(x + 3) = (x + 2)(x + 3)$

Thus, since $6(x + y) = 6x + 6y$, then $6x + 6y = 6(x + y)$.

When you factor **over the integers,** you rewrite the polynomial as the product of factors that have integral coefficients only.

To identify the factors of the polynomial, first look for the greatest common factor of the terms of the polynomial. The **greatest common factor (GCF)** of two or more terms is the product of all the factors shared by the terms.

EXAMPLE 1 Factor.

a. $3x + 3y$ **b.** $x^2 - x$ **c.** $7x^3 - 21x$ **d.** $2y^3 + 4y^2 + 6y$

Solutions: Look for the greatest common factor in each term of the polynomial.

a. $3x + 3y = 3(x + y)$ ◄——— The GCF is 3.

b. $x^2 - x = x(x - 1)$ ◄——— The GCF is x.

c. $7x^3 - 21x = 7x(x^2 - 3)$ ◄——— The GCF is 7x.

d. $2y^3 + 4y^2 + 6y = 2y(y^2 + 2y + 3)$ ◄——— The GCF is 2y.

When a polynomial has no polynomial factors with integral coefficients except itself and 1, it is a **prime polynomial with respect to the integers.** For example, the polynomial

$$6x + 5y$$

is a prime polynomial over the integers because $6x$ and $5y$ have *no common factors with integral coefficients other than 1.*

Some polynomials have a common binomial factor.

EXAMPLE 2 Factor: $a(r + t) + b(r + t)$

Solution: Think of $(r + t)$ as a monomial.

$$a(r + t) + b(r + t) = ax + bx \qquad \longleftarrow \quad \text{Let } x = (r + t).$$
$$= x(a + b) \qquad \longleftarrow \quad \text{The common factor is } x.$$
$$= (r + t)(a + b) \qquad \longleftarrow \quad \text{Replace } x \text{ with } (r + t).$$

Sometimes you have to group terms in order to find the common binomial factor.

EXAMPLE 3 Factor: $ax + cy + xy + ac$

Solution: The terms of the polynomial can be grouped in two ways.

Method I: $ax + cy + xy + ac = (ax + xy) + (cy + ac) \quad \longleftarrow \quad$ Group terms with a common factor.

$$= x(a + y) + c(y + a) \quad \longleftarrow \quad \text{Common monomial factors: } x \text{ and } c$$
$$= x(a + y) + c(a + y) \quad \longleftarrow \quad y + a = a + y$$
$$= (a + y)(x + c) \quad \longleftarrow \quad (a + y) \text{ is the common factor.}$$

Method II: $ax + cy + xy + ac = (ax + ac) + (cy + xy) \quad \longleftarrow \quad$ Group terms with a common factor.

$$= a(x + c) + y(c + x) \quad \longleftarrow \quad \text{Common monomial factors: } a \text{ and } y$$
$$= a(x + c) + y(x + c) \quad \longleftarrow \quad c + x = x + c$$
$$= (x + c)(a + y) \quad \longleftarrow \quad (x + c) \text{ is the common factor.}$$

Objective: To factor polynomials by finding common monomial or binomial factors

▬▬▬▬ **CHECK YOUR UNDERSTANDING**

One factor is given for each polynomial. Write the other factor.

1. $8a + 8b = \underline{?}\ (a + b)$

2. $xy + y^2 = \underline{?}\ (x + y)$

3. $3x^3 + 3x = \underline{?}\ (x^2 + 1)$

4. $8x^3 - 4xy^2 = \underline{?}\ (2x^2 - y^2)$

5. $15a^2 + 15ab^2 = 15a(\underline{?}\ )$

6. $x^3y - y = y(\underline{?}\ )$

7. $-2ab + 8bc - 4ac = -2(\underline{?}\ )$

8. $pq + qr + q^2 = q(\underline{?}\ )$

9. $3(x - y) + a(x - y) = (\underline{?}\ )(3 + a)$

10. $t(x - 4) + w(x - 4) = (\underline{?}\ )(x - 4)$

▬▬▬▬ **PRACTICE AND APPLY**

One factor is given for each polynomial. Write the other factor.

11. $3x + 6y = 3(\underline{?}\ + 2y)$

12. $4n - 2 = 2(2n - \underline{?}\ )$

13. $3b^2 - 24b = 3b(\underline{?}\ - 8)$

14. $15ab^2 - 3b^2 = 3b^2(\underline{?}\ - \underline{?}\ )$

15. $-3ax + 6ay = -3a(\underline{?}\ - \underline{?}\ )$

16. $p^2 - p = p(\underline{?}\ - \underline{?}\ )$

17. $8y - 24 = 8(y - \underline{?}\ )$

18. $8x^2y^2 - xy^2 = xy^2(\underline{?}\ - \underline{?}\ )$

19. $x^2 - 3x^2y = x^2(\underline{?}\ - \underline{?}\ )$

20. $6a^2b - 3ab^2 = 3ab(\underline{?}\ - \underline{?}\ )$

21. $5x + 20 = \underline{?}\ (x + 4)$

22. $3x^2 - 6xy + 9y = 3(\underline{?}\ - \underline{?}\ + \underline{?}\ )$

23. $400x - x^2 = \underline{?}\ (400 - x)$

24. $1000x^3 - x = x(\underline{?}\ - \underline{?}\ )$

25. $4ab - b = b(\underline{?}\ - \underline{?}\ )$

26. $8x^2 - 28x - 4 = \underline{?}\ (2x^2 - 7x - 1)$

27. $25x^2 - 20y^2 = \underline{?}\ (5x^2 - 4y^2)$

28. $5m - 10mn - 15 = \underline{?}\ (m - 2mn - 3)$

29. $7x + 49xy = 7x(\underline{?}\ + \underline{?}\ )$

30. $4x^3 + 6x^2 - 2x = 2x)\underline{?}\ + \underline{?}\ - \underline{?}\ )$

31. $a(x + y) + b(x + y) = (x + y)(\underline{?}\ + \underline{?}\ )$

32. $t(a + 3) - y(a + 3) = (a + 3)(\underline{?}\ - \underline{?}\ )$

33. $10 + 2t + 5s + st = (\underline{?}\ + \underline{?}\ )(5 + t)$

34. $tx - wx + ty - wy = (\underline{?}\ - \underline{?}\ )(x + y)$

For Exercises 35–57, factor.

35. $7x + 7y$

36. $3a + 9b$

37. $8x - 4y$

38. $ax + bx$

39. $3x - awx$

40. $9x^2 - 6y^2$

41. $4c + ac + bc$

42. $ay + by + 3y$

43. $d^2 + 2d + ad$

44. $ax - ay + a^2$

45. $5x - 10y + 15z^2$

46. $5t + 10t^2 + t^3$

47. $2\pi r^2 + 2\pi rh$

48. $a^2b + ab^2 + a^3b^3$

49. $cdh^3 + c^2dh + c^3d^2h^2$

50. $d(e + f) + g(e + f)$

51. $a(b - c) + d(b - c)$

52. $3(x + y) - g(x + y)$

53. $a(q - r) - s(q - r)$

54. $(vx + xz) + sv + sz$

55. $kp - kn + (pr - rn)$

56. $6w - 15 - 14hw + 35h$

57. $2ax^2 + bx^2 - 2ay^2 - by^2$

Factor. If a polynomial cannot be factored over the integers, write <u>Prime</u>.

58. $3a + b$

59. $7a^2b - 7ab$

60. $18r^2 - 6 + 24r$

61. $8x^2 - 3y^2$

62. $64ab - 16b^2$

63. $10a^2 + 33ab + 17b^2$

64. $12n^2 - 4 + 16n$

65. $9p^2 - 5q^2$

66. $36x^2 - 18xy$

67. $14x^2 + 7xy + 21y^2$

68. $7n^2 - 8mn + 3n^2$

69. $9ab + a^2 + 2b^2$

70. $39a^3 - 52ab^2 + 65ac^2$

71. $27x^4 + 3x^3 + 9ax$

72. $9s - 13s^2 + 5t$

73. $25xy - 50xz + 100x$

74. $4x^2 - 8x + 6$

75. $3x^2 + 6xy - 2x^3$

76. $a^3 + 3a^2b + 3ab^2$

77. $14 - 42p + 7$

78. $3ab^2 - ab + 2a^2$

79. $8x^2 - 12xy - 16xz$

80. $ay^2 + ab + 3a$

81. $3x^3 - 15x^2 - 6x$

82. $8a^3 - 4ax^2 - 12a^2x^2$

83. $3a^2 + 4a^3 - 5a^4b$

84. $6x^3 - 2x^2y + z^3$

████████ **MAINTAIN**

Write each number in prime-factorization form. (*Pages 377–379*)

85. 16   **86.** 36   **87.** 40   **88.** 120   **89.** 200   **90.** 350

Divide. (*Pages 364–366*)

91. $(2x^2 + 3x - 17) \div (x + 4)$

92. $(4x^2 - 11x - 1) \div (x - 3)$

93. $(3x^3 - 2x^2 - 5x + 5) \div (x - 1)$

94. $(8x^3 + 2x^2 - 11x + 36) \div (2x + 3)$

Solve and graph each inequality. (*Pages 295–298*)

95. $-8n \leq -24$

96. $2y - 3 > -1$

97. $3t + 4 \geq -2$

████████ **CONNECT AND EXTEND**

Find the missing factor.

98. $x^{n+3} + x^n = x^n(\underline{\ ?\ })$

98. $2y^{n+1} + 4y^n = 2y^n(\underline{\ ?\ })$

100. $4w^{n-1} + 6w^{n+1} = (\underline{\ ?\ })(2w^{n-2} + 3w^n)$

101. $9z^{2n} + 21z^{2n+1} = (\underline{\ ?\ })(3z^n + 7z^{n+1})$

———— **REVIEW CAPSULE FOR SECTION 10–3** ————

Multiply. (*Pages 361–363*)

1. $(b + 5)(b - 5)$

2. $(2a + 1)(2a - 1)$

3. $(3x - 2)(3x + 2)$

Factoring Polynomials   **383**

10-3 Factoring the Difference of Two Squares

MAKING A MODEL

The area of the large square at the right is a^2. The area of the small square is b^2. The area of the shaded portion of the figure is the difference of the areas of the two squares, or $a^2 - b^2$.

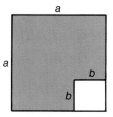

Figure 1

Suppose the shaded portion of the figure is cut along a dashed line (Figure 2). Regions I and II can then be repositioned to form a rectangle (Figure 3).

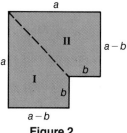

Figure 2

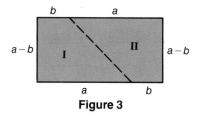

Figure 3

In Figure 3, the length of the rectangle is $a + b$ and the width is $a - b$. Therefore, the area of the rectangle can be expressed as $(a + b)(a - b)$. Since this is the same as the area of the shaded portion in Figure 1, the area of the shaded portion can also be expressed as $(a + b)(a - b)$.

This suggests the following pattern for factoring $a^2 - b^2$.

Factoring the Difference of Two Squares

$$a^2 - b^2 = (a + b)(a - b) \qquad\qquad x^2 - 49 = (x - 7)(x + 7)$$

EXAMPLE   Factor: $25x^2 - 36y^2$

Solution: **Think:** $25x^2 = (5x)^2$ and $36y^2 = (6y)^2$.

$25x^2 - 36y^2 = (5x)^2 - (6y)^2$ ⟵ **Write as the difference of squares.**

$= (5x + 6y)(5x - 6y)$ ⟵ **Write as the product of a sum and difference.**

NOTE: You can check your answers by multiplying the factors.

EXERCISES: Classwork/Homework

Objective: To factor the difference of two squares

CHECK YOUR UNDERSTANDING

Determine whether each of the following is the difference of two squares. Answer <u>Yes</u> or <u>No</u>.

1. $m^2 - 1$ **2.** $x^2 - 8$ **3.** $r^2 - 4$ **4.** $9 - y^2$

5. $a^2 - 120$ **6.** $2t^2 - 100$ **7.** $4 - y^2$ **8.** $x^2 - 81$

PRACTICE AND APPLY

Factor each polynomial. When a polynomial cannot be factored over the integers, write <u>Prime.</u>

9. $y^2 - 9$ **10.** $x^2 - 4$ **11.** $x^2 - 25$ **12.** $y^2 - 36$

13. $4x^2 - 9$ **14.** $9x^2 - 4$ **15.** $16y^2 - 36$ **16.** $-64 + 4x^2$

17. $x^2y^2 - a^2$ **18.** $y^6 - 100$ **19.** $9x^4y^2 - b^2$ **20.** $1 - 81y^2$

21. $x^2y^2 - z^2$ **22.** $-25 + 4x^2y^2$ **23.** $x^2 + y^2$ **24.** $x^2 - y^4$

25. $4x^2 + 16y^2$ **26.** $81x^2 - 64y^2$ **27.** $25x^2 - 49$ **28.** $49 - 25x^2$

Solve.

29. Within a large square whose side is a units is a small square whose side is 3 units. What is the area of the large square? What is the area of the small square? What is the area of the shaded surface between the two squares? Factor the expression for the shaded area.

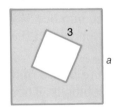

30. A small circle whose radius is r units is drawn within a large circle whose radius is R units. What is the area of the large circle? What is the area of the shaded part? Factor the expression for the shaded area.
(HINT: First, factor out the common monomial factor, π. Then factor the binomial.)

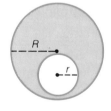

31. If four circular holes (radius r) are cut in a large circular plate of radius R, what is the area of the remaining surface in terms of R and r? Factor the expression for the shaded area. (See the hint for Exercise 30.)

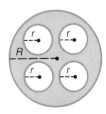

Factor. (*Pages 380–383*)

32. $5x + 5y$ **33.** $6a - 12b$ **34.** $8r - 4t$

35. $ac + bc$ **36.** $d^2 + 3d + cd$ **37.** $10 + 5t + 5t^2$

Identify each number as prime, **P**, or composite, **C**. (*Pages 377–379*)

38. 6   **39.** 12   **40.** 17   **41.** 35   **42.** 41   **43.** 64

Solve each problem. (*Pages 291–294*)

44. The sum of two consecutive positive integers is less than 40. Find the pair with the greatest sum.

45. The sum of two consecutive even integers is greater than 80. Find the pair with the smallest sum.

CONNECT AND EXTEND

Factor.

46. $(a + b)^2 - c^2$ **47.** $c^2 - (a + b)^2$ **48.** $(r + s)^2 - t^2$

49. $(r + s)^2 - (t + u)^2$ **50.** $(x - a)^2 - (y - b)^2$ **51.** $4(x - a)^2 - 9(y + b)^2$

NON-ROUTINE PROBLEMS

52. Cory mistakenly multiplies a number on his calculator by 35 instead of dividing by 35. If the calculator displays the number 51,450, what is the correct answer to the problem?

53. Mr. Thomas plans to drive his car 45,000 miles. Each of the tires he buys will last a maximum of 30,000 miles. Find the fewest number of tires he will have to buy to travel 45,000 miles.

54. The figure at the right shows a stack of 8 identical building blocks. There is no block in the center of the figure. For each of the eight building blocks, answer the following.

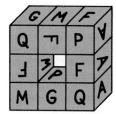

  a. What letter is opposite the letter *F*?
  b. What letter is opposite the letter *P*?
  c. What letter is opposite the letter *A*?

————— **REVIEW CAPSULE FOR SECTION 10–4** —————

Square each binomial. (*Pages 358–360*)

1. $(a - 3)^2$ **2.** $(x + 4)^2$ **3.** $(2x - 5)^2$ **4.** $(9 + b)^2$

5. $(2a + 5t)^2$ **6.** $(3p^2 - 2)^2$ **7.** $(0.1 + z)^2$ **8.** $(\frac{1}{2} - bc)^2$

10-4 Factoring a Perfect Square Trinomial

A **perfect square trinomial** is the square of a binomial. That is, since

$$(x + 7)(x + 7) = (x + 7)^2 = x^2 + 14x + 49$$

and

$$(x - 7)(x - 7) = (x - 7)^2 = x^2 - 14x + 49,$$

both $x^2 + 14x + 49$ and $x^2 - 14x + 49$ are perfect square trinomials. To determine whether a trinomial is a perfect square, follow this procedure.

PROCEDURE

> To determine whether a trinomial is a perfect square, check these two conditions:
>
> **1** The first and last terms must be squares of monomials.
>
> **2** The middle term must be twice the product of the monomials.

EXAMPLE 1 Determine which of the following is a perfect square trinomial.

    a. $x^2 - 14x + 49$ **b.** $4p^2 + 10pq + 9q^2$

Solutions:

a. $x^2 - 14x + 49$ **b.** $4p^2 + 10pq + 9q^2$

  $x^2 = (x)^2$; $49 = (7)^2$ ←— **Check Condition 1.** —→ $4p^2 = (2p)^2$; $9q^2 = (3q)^2$

  $14x = 2(x)(7)$ ←— **Check Condition 2.** —→ $10pq \neq 2(2p)(3q)$

The trinomial in **a** is a perfect square; the trinomial in **b** is not.

To factor a perfect square trinomial, you reverse the procedure for squaring a binomial. First, you find the first and last monomial terms. The sign between these terms is the *same as the sign of the middle term* of the trinomial.

EXAMPLE 2 Factor: **a.** $4x^2 + 12x + 9$ **b.** $25y^2 - 20y + 4$

  a. $4x^2 = (2x)^2$; $9 = (3)^2$; $12x = 2(2x)(3)$ ←— **Check for a perfect square trinomial.**

    $4x^2 + 12x + 9 = (2x \quad 3)(2x \quad 3)$ ←— **Write the monomial terms.**

               $= (2x + 3)(2x + 3)$ ←— **Write the same sign as the middle terms of the trinomial.**

               $= (2x + 3)^2$

b. $25y^2 = (5y)^2; 4 = (2)^2; 20y = 2(5y)(2)$ ← **Check for a perfect square trinomial**

$25y^2 - 20y + 4 = (5y \quad 2)(5y \quad 2)$ ← **Write the monomial terms.**

$= (5y - 2)(5y - 2)$ ← **Write the same sign as the middle term of the trinomial.**

$= (5y - 2)^2$

Memorizing these formulas will help you to factor perfect square trinomials.

> **Factoring Perfect Square Trinomials**
>
> $a^2 + 2ab + b^2 = (a + b)(a + b) = (a + b)^2$
>
> $a^2 - 2ab + b^2 = (a - b)(a - b) = (a - b)^2$

EXERCISES: Classwork/Homework

Objective: To factor a perfect square trinomial

CHECK YOUR UNDERSTANDING

1. In a perfect square trinomial, the first and last terms must be squares of __?__.

2. In a perfect square trinomial, the middle term must be twice the __?__ of the monomials.

Determine whether each of the following is a perfect square trinomial. Answer **Yes** or **No**.

3. $x^2 - 2xy + y^2$

4. $x^2 - 5x + 16$

5. $1 - 6x + 9x^2$

6. $b^2 - 20b + 20$

7. $4a^2 - 4ab + b^2$

8. $x^2 - 8x + 8$

PRACTICE AND APPLY

Write each perfect square trinomial as the square of a binomial. One term of the binomial is written for you.

9. $a^2 + 4ab + 4b^2 = (a + \underline{\;?\;})^2$

10. $x^2 + 2xy + y^2 = (\underline{\;?\;} + y)^2$

11. $4x^2 - 4x + 1 = (2x - \underline{\;?\;})^2$

12. $b^2 - 8bc + 16c^2 = (b - \underline{\;?\;})^2$

13. $s^2 + 6st + 9t^2 = (s + \underline{\;?\;})^2$

14. $n^2 - 12n + 36 = (\underline{\;?\;} - 6)^2$

15. $4x^2 + 20x + 25 = (2x + \underline{\;?\;})^2$

16. $64x^2 - 16xy + y^2 = (\underline{\;?\;} - y)^2$

17. $25 - 10y + y^2 = (\underline{\;?\;} - y)^2$

18. $9a^2 - 24a + 16 = (\underline{\;?\;} - 4)^2$

Replace __?__ with + or − to make the square of the binomial equal the trinomial.

19. $x^2 - 16x + 64 = (x \underline{} 8)^2$

20. $p^2 - 10pq + 25q^2 = (p \underline{} 5q)^2$

21. $n^2 - 12n + 36 = (n \underline{} 6)^2$

22. $4x^2 - 12x + 9 = (2x \underline{} 3)^2$

Factor.

23. $x^2 + 6x + 9$ **24.** $x^2 - 6x + 9$ **25.** $n^2 + 14n + 49$

26. $4x^2 - 12xy + 9y^2$ **27.** $4x^2 + 12xy + 9y^2$ **28.** $x^2 - 10x + 25$

29. $1 + 8x + 16x^2$ **30.** $1 - 8x + 16x^2$ **31.** $a^2 + 8a + 16$

32. $4x^2 - 4x + 1$ **33.** $4x^2 + 4x + 1$ **34.** $a^2 - 16a + 64$

35. $9y^2 + 12y + 4$ **36.** $9y^2 - 12y + 4$ **37.** $b^2 - 6b + 9$

38. $4a^2 - 4a + 1$ **39.** $9a^2 - 12a + 4$ **40.** $9 + 12x + 4x^2$

41. $49a^2 - 84a + 36$ **42.** $4m^2 - 12m + 9$ **43.** $x^2 - 18x + 81$

Factor.

Example: $x^2 + 2xy + y^2 - z^2 = (x + y)^2 - z^2 = (x + y + z)(x + y - z)$

44. $(a^2 + 2ab + b^2) - c^2$ **45.** $c^2 - (a^2 + 2ab + b^2)$

46. $(x^2 - 2xy + y^2) - 9$ **47.** $16 - (x^2 - 2xy + y^2)$

48. $a^2 - 9 + 2ab + b^2$ **49.** $x^2 - 16 - 2xy + y^2$

▬▬▬ MAINTAIN

Solve each problem. (*Pages 291–294*)

50. Elliot plans to spend no more than $100 for a skateboard and a helmet. Suppose that the cost of the skateboard is $20 less than 3 times the cost of the helmet. What is the greatest amount Elliot can spend for the skateboard?

51. Margaret's grades on four tests were 85, 92, 84, and 95. She wants her mean score on five tests to be greater than 90. Find the lowest score she can get on the fifth test.

▬▬▬ CONNECT AND EXTEND

52. The area of a square can be represented by $x^2 - 28x + 196$. Find the length of a side of the square.

53. The area of a square can be represented by $x^2 + 6x + 9$. Find the perimeter of the square.

Probability / Making a Model

Life scientists are specialists in living things. Since biology is the science of life, many life scientists call themselves **biologists.** However, most are named by the type of living thing that they study or by the nature of the work that they perform. Some life scientist careers are agronomist, biochemist, botanist, horticulturist, microbiologist, nutritionist, and zoologist.

In the study of **genetics,** life scientists learn that the traits of parents are transmitted to their offspring by tiny particles called **genes.** Each living thing has two genes for each trait—one gene from each parent.

The genes for tall and short pea plants are represented below.

TT	Pure tall	
tt	Pure short	T = gene for tallness
Tt	Hybrid tall	t = gene for shortness

When a pure tall pea plant and a pure short pea plant are crossed, all offspring are hybrid tall.

Suppose that two hybrid tall pea plants are crossed. This problem is related to the algebra problem of squaring a binomial.

Let $(\frac{1}{2}T + \frac{1}{2}t)$ represent the two genes for tallness and shortness in each hybrid tall pea plant. Then

$$(\tfrac{1}{2}T + \tfrac{1}{2}t)(\tfrac{1}{2}T + \tfrac{1}{2}t) = \tfrac{1}{4}TT + \tfrac{1}{2}Tt + \tfrac{1}{4}tt.$$

This result indicates the following probabilities.

The probability (chances) that an offspring will be pure tall (TT) is 1 out of 4.

This means that, over a long enough period of time, you can expect about one fourth of all such offspring to be pure tall.

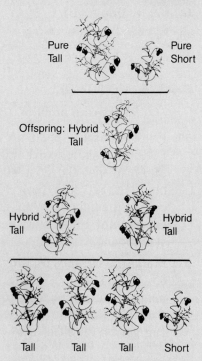

Pure Tall — Pure Short

Offspring: Hybrid Tall

Hybrid Tall — Hybrid Tall

Tall   Tall   Tall   Short

The probability (chances) that an offspring will be hybrid tall (Tt) is 1 out of 2.

That is, over a long period of time about one half of all such offspring can be expected to be hybrid tall.

The probability (chances) that an offspring will be pure short (tt) is 1 out of 4.

EXAMPLE 1: There are 24 offspring of two hybrid tall parent pea plants. Find the probable number of each type.

Solution: Refer to the trinomial on page 390.

$$\frac{1}{4}TT + \frac{1}{2}Tt + \frac{1}{4}tt \begin{cases} \frac{1}{4} \times 24 = 6 \text{ pure tall} \\ \frac{1}{2} \times 24 = 12 \text{ hybrid tall} \\ \frac{1}{4} \times 24 = 6 \text{ pure short} \end{cases}$$

In guinea pigs, a rough coat gene R is **dominant** to a smooth coat gene r. This means that guinea pigs will have coats as shown below.

RR: Pure rough coat Rr: Hybrid rough coat rr: Pure smooth coat

EXAMPLE 2: A guinea pig with a pure rough coat (RR) is mated with a guinea pig which has a hybrid rough coat (Rr). There are 36 offspring. Find the probable number of each type.

Solution: $(\frac{1}{2}R + \frac{1}{2}R)(\frac{1}{2}R + \frac{1}{2}r) = \frac{1}{4}RR + \frac{1}{4}Rr + \frac{1}{4}RR + \frac{1}{4}Rr$

$$= \frac{1}{2}RR + \frac{1}{2}Rr$$

$\frac{1}{2} \times 36 = 18$ pure rough coat (RR) $\frac{1}{2} \times 36 = 18$ hybrid rough coat (Rr)

All of the offspring will have rough coats.

EXERCISES

There are 128 offspring of two pea plants. Find the probable number of pure tall (TT), pure short (tt), and hybrid tall (Tt) for each combination of parent plants.

1. Hybrid tall and pure short
2. Pure short and pure short
3. Pure tall and hybrid tall
4. Pure tall and pure short

There are 56 offspring of two guinea pigs. Find the probable number of offspring with pure rough coats (RR), hybrid rough coats (Rr), and pure smooth coats (rr) for each combination of parents.

5. Hybrid rough coat; hybrid rough coat
6. Pure rough coat; pure smooth coat
7. Pure rough coat; hybrid rough coat

Multiply. (*Pages 355–357*)

1. $(a + 1)(a + 2)$
2. $(x - 3)(x - 2)$
3. $(y + 4)(y - 3)$
4. $(2 - t)(5 + t)$
5. $(y - 5z)(y + 2z)$
6. $(d - 8g)(d + 11g)$

10-5 Factoring $x^2 + bx + c$

GUESS AND CHECK

Since $(x + 2)(x + 3) = x^2 + 5x + 6$, it should be possible to factor $x^2 + 5x + 6$ as $(x + 2)(x + 3)$. The procedure lies in using the guess and check strategy to identify two integers such that their product is 6 and their sum is 5.

EXAMPLE 1 Factor: $x^2 + 5x + 6$

Solution: ① $x^2 + 5x + 6 = (x \quad)(x \quad)$ ◄——— **The factors of x^2 are x and x.**

② Write the integral factors of 6.
$(1, 6); \quad (-1, -6); \quad (2, 3); \quad (-2, -3)$

③ **Guess and check:** Test the sum of the factors. Stop when you find two whose sum is 5.

$$\begin{array}{ccc} 1 & -1 & 2 \\ \underline{6} & \underline{-6} & \underline{3} \\ 7 & -7 & 5 \end{array}$$

7 No −7 No 5 Yes ✔ Thus, $x^2 + 5x + 6 = (x + 2)(x + 3)$.

Example 1 illustrates that when the product of the two integral factors is positive *and* their sum is positive, the two factors will both be positive.

EXAMPLE 2 Factor: $t^2 - 7t + 12$

Solution: ① $t^2 - 7t + 12 = (t \quad)(t \quad)$ ◄——— **The factors of t^2 are t and t.**

② Integral factors of 12:
$(1, 12); \quad (-1, -12); \quad (2, 6); \quad (-2, -6); \quad (3, 4); \quad (-3, -4)$

③ Test the sum of the factors to find two whose sum is -7.
$$-3 + (-4) = -7$$

Thus, $t^2 - 7t + 12 = (t - 3)(t - 4)$. ◄——— **Check by multiplying.**

Example 2 illustrates that when the product of the two integral factors is positive *and* their sum is negative, the two factors will both be negative.

EXAMPLE 3 Factor: $x^2 - 5x - 14$

Solution:
1. $x^2 - 5x - 14 = (x\ \ \ )(x\ \ \ )$
2. Integral factors of -14: $(1, -14)$; $(-1, 14)$; $(2, -7)$; $(-2, 7)$
3. Determine which two factors have a sum of -5.

$$2 + (-7) = -5$$

Thus, $x^2 - 5x - 14 = (x + 2)(x - 7)$.

Example 3 illustrates that when the product of two integral factors is negative *and* their sum is negative, one factor will be positive and one will be negative.

EXAMPLE 4 Factor.

a. $x^2 - 6x + 8$ b. $t^2 - 10t - 24$ c. $t^2 + 6rt - 27r^2$

Solutions: a. $x^2 - 6x + 8 = (x - 4)(x - 2)$ ⟵   Since $-4(-2) = 8$ and $-4 + (-2) = -6$

b. $t^2 - 10t - 24 = (t - 12)(t + 2)$ ⟵   Since $-12(2) = -24$ and $-12 + 2 = -10$

c. $t^2 + 6rt - 27r^2 = (t - 3r)(t + 9r)$ ⟵   Since $-3(9) = -27$ and $-3 + 9 = 6$

EXERCISES: Classwork/Homework

Objective: To factor a polynomial of the form $x^2 + bx + c$

CHECK YOUR UNDERSTANDING

For each of the following, identify two integers such that their sum equals the first number and their product equals the second number.

1. 7; 12   **2.** -5; 6   **3.** 5; -24 **4.** -6; 5   **5.** -6; 9   **6.** -2; -15
7. -9; 18   **8.** 4; -32 **9.** -4; -32 **10.** -1; -72 **11.** 1; -72 **12.** -13; 36

Factor each trinomial.

13. $x^2 + 7x + 12$

14. $x^2 + 6x + 8$

15. $y^2 + 8y + 15$

16. $m^2 + 10m + 21$

17. $a^2 + 3a - 4$

18. $x^2 + 3x - 10$

19. $y^2 + 7y - 8$

20. $b^2 + 2b - 8$

21. $x^2 - 5x + 6$

22. $x^2 - 6x + 5$

23. $x^2 - 13x + 36$

24. $x^2 - 9x + 18$

25. $x^2 - 2x - 15$

26. $x^2 - 4x - 32$

27. $x^2 - x - 72$

28. $x^2 - 5x - 14$

29. $x^2 + 5x - 24$

30. $x^2 + 6x + 5$

31. $x^2 + 4x - 32$

32. $x^2 + x - 72$

33. $x^2 - 10x + 21$

34. $x^2 - 6x + 8$

35. $x^2 + 14x + 48$

36. $x^2 - 8x + 15$

37. $x^2 + 9x + 8$

38. $x^2 + 10x + 16$

39. $x^2 + 2x - 8$

40. $y^2 + 9y + 18$

41. $y^2 - 17y + 66$

42. $x^2 + 2x - 15$

43. $y^2 - y + 156$

44. $x^2 + x - 56$

45. $y^2 + 6y - 72$

46. $3 - 4t + t^2$

47. $20 + 12v + v^2$

48. $-30 + 13w + w^2$

49. $51 - 20k + k^2$

50. $x^2 + 5xy + 4y^2$

51. $r^2 - 6rt + 8t^2$

52. $16p^2 - 8pq + q^2$

53. $a^2 - 14ab + 24b^2$

54. $y^2 - 6yz - 16z^2$

55. Find the length of the rectangle.

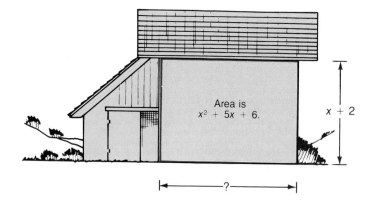

Area is $x^2 + 5x + 6$.

$x + 2$

?

56. Find the missing factor.

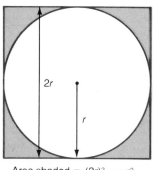

$2r$

r

Area shaded $= (2r)^2 - \pi r^2$
$= 4r^2 - \pi r^2$
$= (4 - \pi)(?)$

For Exercises 57–59, find the dimensions of each rectangle if the lengths of the sides are expressed as binomials with integral coefficients.

57.

Area = $x^2 - 169$

58.

Area = $x^2 + 13x + 12$

59.

Area = $x^2 - 4x + 4$

▄▄▄▄▄ **MAINTAIN**

Factor. (*Pages 384–395*)

60. $x^2 + 4x + 4$

61. $b^2 - 24b + 144$

62. $4m^2 - 4m + 1$

63. $9b^2 - 49$

64. $x^2y^2 - 100$

65. $36 - 4y^2$

Write each compound sentence as two simple sentences joined by <u>or</u> or <u>and</u>. (*Pages 295–298*)

66. $x - 1 \geq 6$

67. $-2 < y < 4$

68. $t + 4 \leq 8$

69. $2a - 1 \leq 9$

70. $-6 < 3x < 9$

71. $0 < 2x - 1 < 5$

▄▄▄▄▄ **CONNECT AND EXTEND**

Find the value of k that will make the second polynomial a factor of the first.

72. $x^2 + kx + 6; x + 3$

73. $x^2 - kx + 10; x + 5$

74. $x^2 - kx + 24; x - 6$

Factor.

75. $(x + y)^2 + 5(x + y) + 6$ **76.** $(c + d)^2 - 3(c + d) + 18$ **77.** $x^4 + 7x^2y^2 + 10y^4$

▄▄▄▄▄ **NON-ROUTINE PROBLEM**

78. Complete the **magic square** below. The sum of each row, column, and diagonal is $3a^2 + 12a$. Each entry must be given in factored form.

$(a + 3)(a + 4)$	___?___	$(a + 4)(a + 1)$
___?___	___?___	___?___
___?___	$(a + 4)(a + 4)$	$(a - 3)(a + 4)$

——— **REVIEW CAPSULE FOR SECTION 10–6** ———

Multiply. (*Pages 355–357*)

1. $(2x + 3)(3x + 4)$

2. $(b - 5)(3b + 7)$

3. $(y - 2)(5y + 8)$

4. $(5a + 7b)(5a + 3b)$

5. $(3a + b)(2a - 3b)$

6. $(7c - 2d)(c + 5d)$

Identify each number as prime, P, or composite, C. (*Pages 377–379*)

1. 25   **2.** 17   **3.** 32   **4.** 75   **5.** 83   **6.** 105

Write each number in prime-factorization form. (*Pages 377–379*)

7. 45   **8.** 48   **9.** 56   **10.** 78   **11.** 250   **12.** 720

Factor. If a polynomial cannot be factored over the integers, write Prime.
(*Pages 380–383*)

13. $5a + 10b$ **14.** $3x + ax + dx$ **15.** $pr^2 - p^2r$

16. $y^2 + 3y$ **17.** $3m^2 + 13n^2$ **18.** $s^3t^2 + s^2t^3 - s^2t$

19. $a(b + c) - 2(b + c)$ **20.** $kx + wy + wx + ky$ **21.** $2y + xy + 2x + 4$

Factor. If a polynomial cannot be factored over the integers, write Prime.
(*Pages 384–386*)

22. $1 - m^2$ **23.** $-9 + a^2$ **24.** $9b^2 - 16$

25. $5m^2 - p^2$ **26.** $4a^2 - b^4$ **27.** $x^2y^2 - 9$

Factor. (*Pages 387–389, 392–395*)

28. $x^2 + 8x + 16$ **29.** $64 - 16a + a^2$ **30.** $9x^2 + 6x + 1$

31. $x^2 + 4x + 3$ **32.** $b^2 - 6b + 8$ **33.** $r^2 - 4r - 12$

Historical Digest: **Secret Codes**

Prime numbers are of interest today to people who make up secret codes (cryptographers). A message is often translated into a code by assigning a single digit to each letter. The message then becomes a long number which can be factored into prime numbers. This makes the message easier to decipher since it is in smaller pieces.

A major development in code breaking occurred in 1988 when 400 computers took one month to factor a number 100 digits long. This resulted in a 41-digit prime number and a 61-digit prime number.

What type of businesses or government agencies do you think might use codes?

10-6 Factoring $ax^2 + bx + c$

In the previous lesson, you factored trinomials where the x^2-term had a coefficient of 1. You can also factor some trinomials in which the x^2-term has a coefficient that is not 1.

EXAMPLE 1 Factor: $2x^2 - 5x - 3$

Solution: **1** $2x^2 - 5x - 3 = (2x\quad)(x\quad)$ ←— **Write the factors of $2x^2$. The only possibilities are 2x and x.**

2 Integral factors of -3: $(-1, 3)$; $(1, -3)$

3 Write all possible binomials. Test the sum of the outer and inner products to find those with a sum of $-5x$.

Binomials	Outer Product + Inner Product
$(2x - 1)(x + 3)$	$6x - x = 5x$ **No**
$(2x + 3)(x - 1)$	$-2x + 3x = x$ **No**
$(2x - 3)(x + 1)$	$2x - 3x = -x$ **No**
$(2x + 1)(x - 3)$	$-6x + x = -5x$ **Yes** ✔

Thus, $2x^2 - 5x - 3 = \mathbf{(2x + 1)(x - 3)}$.

In Example 2, all three terms of the trinomial have positive coefficients. Thus, its binomial factors will also have positive coefficients. This reduces the number of possible binomial factors to be tested.

EXAMPLE 2 Factor: $6x^2 + 7x + 2$

Solution: **1** $6x^2 + 7x + 2 = (6x\quad)(x\quad)$ ←——— **Write the factors of $6x^2$.**
$\qquad\qquad\qquad\qquad\quad (3x\quad)(2x\quad)$

2 Integral factors of 2: $(2, 1)$

Binomials	Outer Product + Inner Product
$(6x + 1)(x + 2)$	$12x + x = 13x$ **No**
$(6x + 2)(x + 1)$	$6x + 2x = 8x$ **No**

Binomials	Outer Product + Inner Product
$(3x + 1)(2x + 2)$	$6x + 2x = 8x$ **No**
$(3x + 2)(2x + 1)$	$3x + 4x = 7x$ **Yes** ✔

Thus, $6x^2 + 7x + 2 = (3x + 2)(2x + 1)$.

As the Examples show, you may have to write several pairs of factors before you find the pair that works. With experience, you will be able to find the pair that works after only a few trials.

EXAMPLE 3 Factor: $8x^2 - 35x + 12$

Solution: **1** $8x^2 - 35x + 12 = (8x\ \ \ )(x\ \ \ )$ ◄——— **Write the factors of $8x^2$.**
$= (4x\ \ \ )(2x\ \ \ )$

Since the middle term of the trinomial is preceded by $-$ and the third term is preceded by $+$, both factors of 12 will be negative.

2 Integral factors of 12: $(-1, -12)$; $(-2, -6)$; $(-3, -4)$

3 Test the possible binomials.

Binomials	Outer Product + Inner Product
$(8x - 1)(x - 12)$	$-96x - x = -97x$ **No**
$(8x - 12)(x - 1)$	$-8x - 12x = -20x$ **No**
$(8x - 2)(x - 6)$	$-48x - 2x = -50x$ **No**
$(8x - 6)(x - 2)$	$-16x - 6x = -22x$ **No**
$(8x - 3)(x - 4)$	$-32x - 3x = -35x$ **Yes** ✔

Thus, $8x^2 - 35x + 12 = (8x - 3)(x - 4)$. ◄——— **Check by multiplying.**

In Example 3, the correct binomial factors were found on the fifth trial. Thus, the six possibilities involving $4x$ and $2x$ did not have to be checked.

EXERCISES: Classwork/Homework

Objective: To factor a polynomial of the form $ax^2 + bx + c$

CHECK YOUR UNDERSTANDING

Write the factors of each monomial.

1. $3x^2$ **2.** $2a^2$ **3.** $6y^2$ **4.** $7b^2$ **5.** $9t^2$ **6.** $8y^2$

Write the integral factors for each integer.

7. 2   **8.** 15   **9.** -35 **10.** 6   **11.** 10   **12.** -12

Match each trinomial in Column I with its corresponding factorization in Column II.

Column I

13. $2a^2 + 7ab - 15b^2$

14. $3a^2 + 10a - 8$

15. $12a^2 + 17a + 6$

16. $6a^2 - 43a + 72$

17. $4a^2 - 4ab - 15b^2$

Column II

a. $(3a - 2)(a + 4)$

b. $(2a - 9)(3a - 8)$

c. $(2a - 5b)(2a + 3b)$

d. $(2a - 3b)(a + 5b)$

e. $(3a + 2)(4a + 3)$

▮▮▮▮▮▮ PRACTICE AND APPLY

Factor. One factor is written for you.

18. $3a^2 + 5a + 2 = (3a + 2)(a + \underline{?})$

19. $4y^2 + 13y - 35 = (y + 5)(4y - \underline{?})$

20. $8a^2 + 18a - 5 = (2a + 5)(\underline{?} - 1)$

21. $5x^2 + 9x - 18 = (5x - 6)(x + \underline{?})$

22. $18n^2 + 21n - 4 = (6n - \underline{?})(3n + 4)$

23. $40n^2 + n - 6 = (\underline{?} - 3)(\underline{?} + 2)$

24. $2a^2 + 7ab - 15b^2 = (2a - \underline{?})(a + \underline{?})$

25. $5a^2 + 2a - 7 = (5a + \underline{?})(a - \underline{?})$

26. $x^2 + x - 72 = (x + \underline{?})(x - \underline{?})$

27. $5x^2 + 9x - 2 = (5x - \underline{?})(x + \underline{?})$

28. $6x^2 + x - 12 = (3x - \underline{?})(2x + \underline{?})$

Factor.

29. $2x^2 + 5x + 2$

30. $3x^2 + 11x + 10$

31. $9y^2 + 3y - 2$

32. $15y^2 - y - 2$

33. $6y^2 - 17y + 12$

34. $21x^2 + 5x - 6$

35. $6x^2 + 5x - 4$

36. $9x^2 + 6x - 8$

37. $5x^2 - 16x + 3$

38. $8y^2 - 2y - 1$

39. $3y^2 + 4y - 7$

40. $x^2 - 4x - 32$

41. $2y^2 + 7y + 5$

42. $12y^2 + 7y + 1$

43. $3x^2 - 11x + 6$

44. $2b^2 + 13b + 15$

45. $3a^2 - 10a - 25$

46. $2n^2 + 9n - 5$

47. $8x^2 - 10xy + 3y^2$

48. $14x^2 - 57xy - 27y^2$

49. $18 - 9y - 35y^2$

50. $-21x^2 - 3x - 8$

51. $2x^2 + 7x + 6$

52. $40c^2 + 39cd - 40d^2$

53. $12x^2 - 29xy + 14y^2$

54. $56x^2 + 15x - 56$

55. $16a^2 + 56ab + 49b^2$

56. $3x^2 - 8xy - 3y^2$

57. $64a^2 + 112ab + 49b^2$

58. $18x^2 - 57x + 35$

Graph the solution set of each compound sentence. (*Pages 295–298*)

59. $x > 3$ <u>or</u> $x < -3$ **60.** $1 < y$ <u>and</u> $y < 4$ **61.** $c > -2$ <u>and</u> $c < 3$

62. $a > -1$ <u>and</u> $a \leq 5$ **63.** $t > -2$ <u>or</u> $t = -2$ **64.** $b < 1$ <u>or</u> $b < 0$

■■■■ CONNECT AND EXTEND

Factor.

Example: $2(x - 1)^2 + 5(x - 1) - 3 = [2(x - 1) - 1][(x - 1) + 3]$
$$= (2x - 2 - 1)(x - 1 + 3)$$
$$= (2x - 3)(x + 2)$$

65. $3(a - 1)^2 + 5(a - 1) + 2$ **66.** $2(x - 2)^2 - 3(x - 2) - 2$

67. $6(x + 1)^2 - 13(x + 1) - 5$ **68.** $2(n + 2)^2 - 3(n + 2) - 14$

69. $6(y - 3)^2 - 8(y - 3) - 8$ **70.** $10(t + 3)^2 + 7(t + 3) + 1$

■■■■ NON-ROUTINE PROBLEMS

For Exercises 71–74, look for a pattern in the products in the box at the right. Then use the pattern to evaluate each expression without using pencil and paper.

$999 \times 2 = 1998$
$999 \times 3 = 2997$
$999 \times 4 = 3996$
$999 \times 5 = 4995$

71. 999×6 **72.** 999×8 **73.** $6993 \div 999$ **74.** $8991 \div 999$

75. In the figure below, a belt runs over six wheels in the direction of the arrows. How many wheels are turning clockwise?

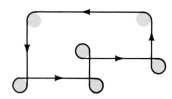

76. Jim and Todd each ran two laps around a track. When Jim completed the first lap, he noted that he was 50 meters behind Todd. Jim then began to run a distance of eight meters for every seven meters that Todd ran. The two boys were tied after completing the second lap. How long was the track?

——— REVIEW CAPSULE FOR SECTION 10–7 ———

State the greatest common monomial factor for each expression. (*Pages 380–383*)

1. $sr - st$ **2.** $3x^2 - 6x - 30$ **3.** $rs^2 - 2r$ **4.** $10x - 15x^3$

5. $18a - 27b$ **6.** $21a^3b^2 - 14a^2b$ **7.** $2x^2 + 8x + 4$ **8.** $t^3 - t^2 + t$

10-7　Factoring Completely

A polynomial is **factored completely** when it is expressed as the product of prime polynomials. The following procedure will help you to factor polynomials completely.

PROCEDURE

> To factor polynomials completely:
>
> **1** Look for common monomial factors.
>
> **2** Look for a difference of squares.
>
> **3** Look for a perfect square trinomial.
>
> **4** Look for a factorable trinomial of the form $x^2 + bx + c$ or $ax^2 + bx + c$.
>
> **5** When a polynomial has four or more terms, look for a way to group the terms in pairs to find a common binomial factor. Also, look for a group of three terms to find a perfect square trinomial.
>
> **6** Check each factor to be sure that it is prime. Check your work by multiplying the factors.

EXAMPLE 1　Factor completely.

　　　　　　a. $2x^2 - 10x + 12$　　　　　　**b.** $5k^2 + 55kn + 90n^2$

Solutions:　**a.** $2x^2 - 10x + 12 = 2(x^2 - 5x + 6)$　　←　Common monomial factor: 2

　　　　　　　　　　　　　$= 2(x - 3)(x - 2)$

　　　　　　b. $5k^2 + 55kn + 90n^2 = 5(k^2 + 11kn + 18n^2)$　←　Common monomial factor: 5

　　　　　　　　　　　　　$= 5(k + 9n)(k + 2n)$

Remember to check whether the factors in your final answer are prime over the integers.

EXAMPLE 2

　　　　　　a. $4x^2 - 4x^4$　　　　**b.** $4x^3 + x^2 - x$　　　　**c.** $8a^2 + 16a + 8$

Solutions:　**a.** $4x^2 - 4x^4 = 4x^2(1 - x^2)$　　←　The common factor is $4x^2$.

　　　　　　　　　　　　$= 4x^2(1 + x)(1 - x)$　←　$(1 - x^2) = (1 + x)(1 - x)$

Factoring Polynomials　　**401**

b. $4x^3 + x^2 - x = x(4x^2 + x - 1)$ ⟵ The common factor is **x.**

Since $4x^2 + x - 1$ is a prime polynomial over the integers,

$4x^3 + x^2 - x = \mathbf{x(4x^2 + x - 1)}.$

c. $8a^2 + 16a + 8 = 8(a^2 + 2a + 1)$ ⟵ The common factor is **8.**

$= 8(a + 1)(a + 1)$ ⟵ **a² + 2a + 1 = (a + 1)(a + 1)**

$= \mathbf{8(a + 1)^2}$

EXERCISES: Classwork/Homework

Objective: To factor a polynomial completely over the integers

CHECK YOUR UNDERSTANDING

Find the missing factor.

1. $3x^2 + 6x = \underline{\ ?\ }(x + 2)$

2. $2x^2 + 2x + 2 = 2(\underline{\ ?\ })$

3. $8a^2 - 12ab - 16ac = 4a(\underline{\ ?\ })$

4. $5n^3 + 5n^2 - 15n = \underline{\ ?\ }(n^2 + n - 3)$

Classify each of the following as a difference of squares, $\underline{D}$, a perfect square trinomial, $\underline{P}$, or neither of these, $\underline{N}$.

5. $a^2 + b^2$　　　**6.** $y^2 - 9$　　　**7.** $a^2 - 2a + 1$　　　**8.** $t^2 + t - 20$

9. $25 - r^2t^2$　　**10.** $x^2 + xy + y^2$　　**11.** $b^2 + 16b + 64$　　**12.** $n^2 - 30n + 225$

PRACTICE AND APPLY

Factor completely.

13. $5b^2 + 20b - 60$ 　　**14.** $2x^2 + 10x - 28$ 　　**15.** $6x^2 - 21x - 12$

16. $4b^2 + 26b - 14$ 　　**17.** $12x^2 - 10x - 12$ 　　**18.** $18a^2 + 21a - 9$

19. $3x^2 - 3y^2$ 　　**20.** $24a^2 - 54b^2$ 　　**21.** $3b^2 - 3b$

22. $2y^3 - 4y^2 - 48y$ 　　**23.** $2m^3 - 20m^2 + 18m$ 　　**24.** $6z^3 - 3z^2 - 30z$

25. $2a^3 - 2a$ 　　**26.** $4b^2 - 24b + 20$ 　　**27.** $12m^2 + 33m - 9$

28. $3t^3 - 27t$ 　　**29.** $3x^2 + 6x - 24$ 　　**30.** $4x^2 - 32x + 60$

31. $2x^2 + 12x - 80$ 　　**32.** $5y^2 - 45y - 110$ 　　**33.** $2t^2 - 28t + 98$

34. $3x^3 - 33x^2 + 84x$ 　　**35.** $x^4 - 9x^2$ 　　**36.** $5x^2 + 60x - 140$

37. $2a^2 + 14a + 24$ 　　**38.** $5y^2 - 45$ 　　**39.** $st^2 - st - 20s$

40. $7a^2 - 14a - 105$ 　　**41.** $3x^2 + 12x + 45$ 　　**42.** $x^2 - 6x + 9$

43. $6t^2 - 15t^3$ 　　**44.** $2 - 128t^2$ 　　**45.** $ab^2 - ab - 72a$

46. $n^2 + 5n + 7$ 　　**47.** $3a^2 + a - 2$ 　　**48.** $2a^2 - 5a + 3$

49. $a^2 + 25$ **50.** $q^2 - 12q - 28$ **51.** $2x^2 - 14x + 24$

52. $y^4 - 6y^2 - 16$ **53.** $49c^2 + 70c + 25$ **54.** $5a^2 - 80$

55. $x^3 - x$ **56.** $a^4 - 16$ **57.** $1 - 4y^2$

58. $x^2 + 4y^2$ **59.** $2xy + 2yz + z^2 - x^2$ **60.** $2 - 2y^2$

61. $x^2a + x^2b - 16a - 16b$ **62.** $y^2x + 2y^2 - 100x - 200$

63. $5r(r + 1)(r - 6) + 8(r - 6)$ **64.** $p(p - 5)(p + 1) + 9(p + 1)$

65. $x^2 - 2xy + y^2 - 3x + 3y$ **66.** $a^3 - 4a^2b + 2a^2 - 8b^2$

▬▬▬ MAINTAIN

Solve and check each equation. (*Pages 302–305*)

67. $|a - 1| = 3$ **68.** $|3x| = 12$ **69.** $|-4y| = 20$

70. $|2k - 7| = 5$ **71.** $|w + 4| = 6$ **72.** $|3p + 2| = 7$

▬▬▬ CONNECT AND EXTEND

Factor completely.

73. $z^4 - 81z^2q^2 - 4z^2 + 324q^2$ **74.** $y^3 - y^2 - 4y + 4$

75. $(x^2 - 25)^2 - (5 - x)^2$ **76.** $16x^2y^2 - (x^2 + y^2 - g^2)^2$

77. $(x + y)^2 - (x - y)^2$ **78.** $(4x^2 - 12x + 9) - x^4$

79. $k^3 + k^2 - k - 1$ **80.** $p^3 - p^2 - 8p + 8$

81. $t^4 + t^2 - 2$ **82.** $b^4 - 10b^2 + 9$

83. $h^2 - (a^2 - 6a + 9)$ **84.** $p^2 - 10p + 25 - q^2$

85. $(2a + 3)^2 - (a - 1)^2$ **86.** $16d^8 - 8d^4 + 1$

87. $(x + y)^4 - 16(x + y)^2 + 63$ **88.** $(a + b)^2 - (x^2 - 2xy + y^2)$

▬▬▬ NON-ROUTINE PROBLEMS

89. Susan dug up 100 flower bulbs and separated them into five paper bags. The number of bulbs put in the first and second bags totaled 48. In the second and third bags, the bulbs totaled 32; in the third and fourth bags, the bulbs totaled 27; and in the fourth and fifth bags, the bulbs totaled 41. How many bulbs were put in each bag?

90. Trace the figure below. Connect all the points in the figure by drawing exactly four line segments without lifting your pencil off the paper. Do not draw through any one point more than once.

Solve and check each equation. (*Pages 95–98, 118–121*)

1. $x - 4 = 0$ **2.** $y + 6 = 0$ **3.** $2x - 3 = 0$ **4.** $3x + 5 = 0$

Write the common monomial factor for each polynomial. (*Pages 380–383*)

5. $3x^5 + 27x^3$ **6.** $5y^5 - 10y^6$ **7.** $2a^6 + 4a^5 + 6a^4$ **8.** $9t^4 - 12t^3 - 15t^2$

10-8   Using Factoring to Solve Equations

Some equations can be solved by factoring. The factoring method applies the Factors of Zero Property.

FACTORS OF ZERO PROPERTY

> **If the product of two real numbers *a* and *b* is zero, then**
> **$a = 0$ or $b = 0$ or both *a* and *b* equal 0.**

Thus, by the Factors of Zero Property, if

$(x + 9)(x - 4) = 0$, then $x + 9 = 0$ or $x - 4 = 0$. That is,

$$x = -9 \text{ or } \quad x = 4.$$

Example 1 shows how this property is applied in solving equations.

EXAMPLE 1 Solve by factoring: $x^2 - 7x + 12 = 0$

Solution: $x^2 - 7x + 12 = 0$ ⟵ Factor $x^2 - 7x + 12$.

$(x - 3)(x - 4) = 0$

$x - 3 = 0$ or $x - 4 = 0$ ⟵ By the Factors of Zero Property

$x = 3$ or $x = 4$

Check: $x^2 - 7x + 12 = 0$ ⟵ Replace x with 3. $x^2 - 7x + 12 = 0$ ⟵ Replace x with 4.

$(3)^2 - 7(3) + 12 \overset{?}{=} 0$ $(4)^2 - 7(4) + 12 \overset{?}{=} 0$

$9 - 21 + 12 \overset{?}{=} 0$ $16 - 28 + 12 \overset{?}{=} 0$

$0 \overset{?}{=} 0$ Yes ✔ $0 \overset{?}{=} 0$ Yes ✔

Solution set: {**3, 4**}

When an equation is not in the form $ax^2 + bx + c = 0$, rewrite it in that form before using the factoring method.

EXAMPLE 2   Solve by factoring: $2x^2 = -4x$

Solution: $2x^2 = -4x$ ⟵——— Add 4x to each side.

$2x^2 + 4x = 0$ ⟵——— Factor 2x² + 4x.

$2x(x + 4) = 0$

$2x = 0$ or $x + 4 = 0$ ⟵——— By the Factors of Zero Property

$x = 0$ or $x = -4$ The check is left for you.

Solution set: $\{-4, 0\}$

EXERCISES: Classwork/Homework

Objective: To solve equations by factoring

CHECK YOUR UNDERSTANDING

Write each equation in the form $ax^2 + bx + c = 0$.

1. $x^2 + 3x = 4$ **2.** $x^2 + 2x = 8$ **3.** $x^2 - 4x = 32$

4. $15x^2 - x = 2$ **5.** $9x^2 + 6x = 8$ **6.** $3x^2 - 11x = -6$

Solve for the variable.

7. $b(b - 1) = 0$ **8.** $z(z + 6) = 0$ **9.** $(q - 3)(q - 7) = 0$

PRACTICE AND APPLY

In Exercises 10–51, solve by factoring.

10. $x^2 - 5x - 6 = 0$ **11.** $x^2 - 5x + 6 = 0$ **12.** $x^2 - 3x - 10 = 0$

13. $x^2 = 100$ **14.** $n^2 + n = 0$ **15.** $y^2 + 7y = 0$

16. $y^2 - 8y - 9 = 0$ **17.** $a^2 - 36 = 0$ **18.** $c^2 - 49 = 0$

19. $3x^2 = 75$ **20.** $y^2 = 4y + 12$ **21.** $y^2 = -7y - 10$

22. $5a^2 + 3a - 2 = 0$ **23.** $3a^2 - 10a - 8 = 0$ **24.** $6a^2 + a - 2 = 0$

25. $9x^2 - 36x = 0$ **26.** $n^2 = 7n$ **27.** $y^2 = 8y$

28. $3n^2 + 7n = 0$ **29.** $15a^2 = 13a + 20$ **30.** $4a^2 - 9a = 0$

31. $3x^2 - 2 = x^2 + 6$ **32.** $24a^2 + 26a - 63 = 0$ **33.** $5x^2 - 2x = 3$

34. $0 = 9w^2 + 6w - 27w^3$ **35.** $23p - 6 = -4p^2$ **36.** $4y^2 + 4y = -1$

37. $p^3 - 13p^2 + 36p = 0$ **38.** $y^3 - 16y^2 = 0$ **39.** $3z^3 + 2z^2 = z$

40. $3r^3 - 3r^2 - 3r + 3 = 0$ **41.** $a^3 + a^2 = 4a + 4$ **42.** $w^3 - 2w^2 = 15w$

43. $(b - 2)(b + 3) = 6$ **44.** $(b + 2)(b - 3) = 6$ **45.** $(x - 2)(x - 1) = 6$

46. $(z + 1)(z + 8) = -12$ **47.** $(t - 5)(t - 2) = 4$ **48.** $3x^5 = 27x^3$

49. $(x - 5)^2 = 16$ **50.** $(a + 9)^2 = 25$ **51.** $(2a - 4)^2 = 81$

▰▰▰▰▰▰ **MAINTAIN**

Solve each system by graphing. (*Pages 306–308*)

52. $\begin{cases} x - y < 4 \\ x + y > 0 \end{cases}$ **53.** $\begin{cases} y \geq 3x \\ y \geq -x + 1 \end{cases}$ **54.** $\begin{cases} 3x - y > 2 \\ 2x + y < -3 \end{cases}$

▰▰▰▰▰▰ **CONNECT AND EXTEND**

Solve by factoring.

55. $(a - 1)^2 - 5(a - 1) + 6 = 0$

56. $(t + 3)^2 - (t + 3) - 12 = 0$

57. $16(z - 1)^2 - 16(z - 1) = 0$

58. $6(r + 2)^2 - 5(r + 2) = 6$

59. $(2a - 1)(3a + 4) - 3(a - 1)(a + 2) = 18$

60. $(3r - 1)(3r + 1) - (2r - 1)(2r + 1) = 45$

▰▰▰▰▰▰ **NON-ROUTINE PROBLEM**

61. What follows next in the sequence of **a–f** below? (HINT: Factor each numerator.)

a. $\dfrac{x^2 - 16x + 60}{x - 6}$ **b.** $\dfrac{2x^2 + 17x + 30}{x + 6}$ **c** $\dfrac{3x^2 - 22x + 40}{x - 4}$

d. $\dfrac{4x^2 + 21x + 20}{x + 4}$ **e.** $\dfrac{25x^2 - 100}{5x + 10}$ **f.** $\underline{\;?\;}$

──────── **REVIEW CAPSULE FOR SECTION 10–9** ────────

Represent each word expression by an algebraic expression (*Pages 1–4*)

1. The difference of 12 and n **2.** 15 more than x

3. 3 increased by p **4.** Four times m

5. The quotient of y and 5   **6.** q decreased by 12.5

7. The product of a and 14   **8.** b divided by 50

10-9 Using Factoring

DRAWING A DIAGRAM

Some problems can be represented by equations that can be solved by factoring. However, some solutions may not satisfy the conditions of the problem. For example, the length of a rectangle cannot be a negative number. In such cases, you disregard these solutions.

EXAMPLE 1 The Calhoun Marching Band uses a rectangular formation with 8 rows and 10 columns. When 40 new members joined the band, an equal number of rows and columns were added to the formation. How many rows and how many columns were added?

Solution: **1** **Find:** The number of rows and columns added

Given: There were 8 rows and 10 columns (80 members). Forty new members were added in an equal number of rows and columns.

Columns

x x x x x x x x x x
x x x x x x x x x x
x x x x x x x x x x
Rows x x x x x x x x x x
x x x x x x x x x x
x x x x x x x x x x
x x x x x x x x x x
x x x x x x x x x x

2 Draw a diagram to show the 8 rows and 10 columns.

Represent the unknowns:

Let n = the number of rows added.
Then n = the number of columns added.

Write an equation for the problem.

Think: $\left(\dfrac{\text{Number of}}{\text{Rows}}\right)\left(\dfrac{\text{Number of}}{\text{Columns}}\right) = \dfrac{\text{Total}}{}$

Translate: $(8 + n) \cdot (10 + n) = 120$

3 Solve the equation.

$(8 + n)(10 + n) = 120$
$80 + 18n + n^2 = 120$
$n^2 + 18n - 40 = 0$ ⟵ **Factor.**
$(n - 2)(n + 20) = 0$
$n - 2 = 0$ or $n + 20 = 0$
$n = 2$ or $n = -20$ ⟵ **The number of rows cannot be negative.**

Factoring Polynomials **407**

4 **Check:** Does $10(12) = 120$ Yes ✓

Two rows and **two columns** were added.

Remember that equations with an x^2-term must be written in the form $x^2 + bx + c = 0$ or $ax^2 + bx + c = 0$ before factoring.

EXAMPLE 2 A photograph is 14 centimeters long and 11 centimeters wide. A white border of uniform width is placed around the photo. The area of the border is 116 square centimeters. What is the width of the border?

Solution: **1** **Find:** The width of the border

Given: The photograph is 14 centimeters long and 11 centimeters wide. The area of the border is 116 square centimeters.

2 Draw and label a figure.

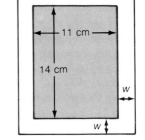

Let w = the width of the border.
Then the new length is $14 + 2w$.
The new width is $11 + 2w$.

Write an equation for the problem.

Think: $\left(\begin{array}{c}\text{New}\\\text{Length}\end{array}\right) \cdot \left(\begin{array}{c}\text{New}\\\text{Width}\end{array}\right) = \begin{array}{c}\text{Area of}\\\text{Photo}\end{array} + \begin{array}{c}\text{Area of}\\\text{Border}\end{array}$

Translate: $(14 + 2w) \cdot (11 + 2w) = 11(14) + 116$

3 $(14 + 2w)(11 + 2w) = 270$

$154 + 50w + 4w^2 = 270$

$4w^2 + 50w - 116 = 0$

$2(2w^2 + 25w - 58) = 0$ ◄——— **Factor.**

$2(2w + 29)(w - 2) = 0$ ◄——— $2 \neq 0$

$2w + 29 = 0$ or $w - 2 = 0$

$w = -14.5$ or $w = 2$ ◄——— **The width cannot equal -14.5.**

4 **Check:** Total area: $(14 + 4)(11 + 4) = 11(14) + 116$?   Yes ✓

The width of the border is **2 centimeters.**

EXERCISES: Classwork/Homework

Objective: To solve word problems using equations that can be solved by factoring

■■■■■■ CHECK YOUR UNDERSTANDING

In Exercises 1–4:
a. Represent the unknowns.
b. Write the equation you would use to solve the problem.

1. The length of a hallway is four times its width. The area is 144 square meters. Find the length and the width.

2. A living room is 3 feet longer than it is wide. Its area is 180 square feet. Find its length and width.

3. Find two consecutive integers whose product is 182.

4. The sum of an integer and its square is 156. Find the integer.

■■■■■■ PRACTICE AND APPLY

Solve each problem.

5. The sum of two numbers is 12. The sum of their squares is 74. What are the numbers?

6. The difference of two numbers is 3. The sum of their squares is 117. What are the numbers?

7. Find two consecutive integers whose product is 210.

8. Find two consecutive even integers whose product is 80.

9. Find two consecutive negative integers such that the sum of their squares is 113.

10. The square of a certain positive integer is 30 more than the integer. Find the integer.

11. Twice the square of a certain number equals 144 more than twice the number. What is the number?

12. The square of a certain number is 4 more than three times the number. What is the number?

13. The area of a rectangular flower garden is 192 square meters. The length of the garden is 4 meters more than its width. Find the length and width.

14. A rectangular parking lot is 20 meters longer than it is wide. The area of the lot is 1056 square meters. Find the dimensions (length and width).

15. Find two consecutive odd integers such that the square of the second decreased by the first is 14.

16. A farmer planted 360 apple trees so that there were 9 more trees in a row than the number of rows. How many rows were there?

17. 55 band members are arranged in a formation so that there are 6 more rows than the number of persons per row. How many rows are there?

18. A fife-and-drum band has 120 members. When they are arranged in a rectangular formation, the number of players in each row is 7 less than the number of rows. How many players are there in each row?

19. A brass band uses a marching formation of 10 rows and 10 columns. When 54 new members joined the band, the new marching formation had 3 more rows than columns. How many rows were added to the old formation?

20. The length of a rectangle is 3 times its width. Increasing the width by 2 centimeters and the length by 4 centimeters doubles the area of the original rectangle. What are the dimensions of the original rectangle?

21. The length of a square lot is increased by 10 meters and the width is increased by 5 meters. The area of the resulting rectangular lot is 3 times the area of the square. What was the area of the square?

22. A real estate agency wishes to double the size (area) of its ad in a telephone directory by adding the same amount to the length and width of its present ad. The present ad is 4 centimeters wide and 6 centimeters long. What will be the new dimensions of the ad?

23. A billboard is 7 meters long and 5 meters high. An advertiser wishes to increase its size by adding the same amount to its length and width. The new area will be 63 square meters. How much must be added to the length and width of the billboard to do this?

24. The perimeter of a picture frame is 80 centimeters. The area is 396 square centimeters. Find the dimensions of the frame.

25. The area of a rectangular heating panel is 192 square centimeters. Its perimeter is 56 centimeters. Find the length and width of the panel.

26. A city lot is 12 meters wide and 42 meters long. How wide a strip must be cut off one end and one side to make the area of the lot 400 square meters?

27. A creek runs along one side of a rectangular lot with an area of 4800 square feet. A fence on three sides requires 200 feet of fencing. What are the length and width of the lot?

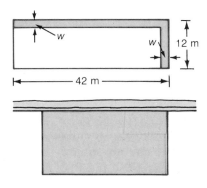

In Exercises 28–29, find the mean, median, and mode(s). (*Pages 74–77*)

28. 6, 7, 8, 6, 6, 7, 6, 8

29. 4, 18, 8, 2, 3, 4, 10

Solve each proportion. (*Pages 103–106*)

30. $\dfrac{x+5}{3} = \dfrac{7}{21}$

31. $\dfrac{m+2}{4} = \dfrac{m-1}{3}$

32. $\dfrac{4}{t} = \dfrac{8}{t+3}$

33. $\dfrac{1}{x} = \dfrac{-2}{6-x}$

A group of 250 people is to be bused to the state fair. The bus company has four 50-passenger buses and six 25-passenger buses available. The cost of renting a 50-passenger bus is $150; the cost of renting a 25-passenger bus is $100. Use this information in Exercises 34–36. (*Pages 312–314*)

34. Let x represent the number of 50-passenger buses rented and let y represent the number of 25-passenger buses. Write an expression to represent the total cost.

35. Write and graph a system of inequalities showing the constraints on x and y.

36. Write the coordinates of the vertices of the polygonal region graphed in Exercise 35 and find the minimum cost possible.

CONNECT AND EXTEND

37. A courtyard is designed so that the central rectangle with an area of 1000 square feet is surrounded by a walk which is 4 feet wide. The area of the walk is 624 square feet. Find the dimensions of the central rectangle.

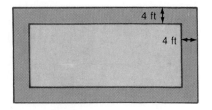

38. Squares 4 inches wide are cut out of a square sheet of metal at each corner. The sides are then turned up to form an open box. If the volume of the box is 1024 cubic inches, what was the original length of each side?

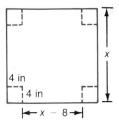

NON-ROUTINE PROBLEM

39. A five-digit number contains the digits shown at the right. Use the clues below to find the number.

Clue 1: The number is less than 30,000.
Clue 2: The number is even.
Clue 3: The 0 is next to the 1.
Clue 4: The 3 is not next to the 2 or 0.

Focus on College Entrance Tests

Given a system of equations (or a compound sentence with "and"), you can sometimes answer questions on College Entrance tests without solving the system. The key is in recognizing a binomial product or the factors of such a product.

EXAMPLE   If $a + b = 5$ and $a - b = 3$, find $a^2 - b^2$.

    a. 2   **b.** 3   **c.** 15   **d.** 16

Think: $a^2 - b^2 = (a + b)(a - b)$

Solution: $a^2 - b^2 = (a + b)(a - b)$ ⟵   **From the given equations:** $a + b = 5; a - b = 3.$

                  $= (5)(3) = 15$ **Answer: c**

TRY THESE

Choose the best answer. Choose *a*, *b*, *c*, or *d*.

1. If $x - y = 6$ and $x + y = -1$, find $x^2 - y^2$.

  a. -6 **b.** 5   **c.** 6   **d.** 35

2. If $m + 2p = 4$ and $m - 2p = 6$, find $m^2 - 4p^2$.

  a. -8 **b.** 10   **c.** 24   **d.** 26

3. If $3c - d = 1$ and $3c + d = \frac{1}{2}$, find $9c^2 - d^2$.

  a. $\frac{1}{2}$ **b.** $\frac{3}{4}$ **c.** $1\frac{1}{2}$ **d.** 2

4. If $s^2 - t^2 = 6$ and $s + t = 3$, find $s - t$.

  a. 2   **b.** 3   **c.** 6   **d.** 18

5. If $a - b = 2$ and $a^2 - b^2 = 12$, find $a + b$.

  a. $\frac{1}{6}$ **b.** 6   **c.** 14   **d.** 24

6. If $4p^2 - 9r^2 = 3$ and $2p + 3r = 3$, find $2p - 3r$.

  a. -1 **b.** 1   **c.** 3   **d.** 9

7. If $(a + b)^2 = 6$ and $ab = 8$, find $a^2 + b^2$. (HINT: $(a + b)^2 = a^2 + 2ab + b^2$.)

  a. 22   **b.** 20   **c.** -2 **d.** -10

8. If $x + y = 8$ and $xy = 4$, find $x^2 + y^2$.

  a. 0   **b.** 56   **c.** 60   **d.** 72

9. If $(a - b)^2 = 49$ and $ab = 30$, find $a^2 + b^2$.

  a. 109   **b.** 79   **c.** 67   **d.** -11

Composite number (p. 377)   Prime-factorization form (p. 377)
Factor (p. 377)   Prime number (p. 377)
Factor completely (p. 401)   Prime polynomial with respect
Perfect square trinomial (p. 387)   to the integers (p. 381)

IMPORTANT
IDEAS

1. **Unique Factorization Property (Fundamental Property of Arithmetic)**
   The factorization of any positive integer into primes is unique, disregarding the order of the factors.

2. **Formula for Factoring the Difference of Two Squares**
   $$a^2 - b^2 = (a + b)(a - b)$$

3. **Conditions Under Which a Trinomial Is a Perfect Square**
   a. The first and last terms must be squares of monomials.
   b. The middle term must be twice the product of the monomials.

4. **Formulas for Factoring Perfect Square Trinomials**
   $$a^2 + 2ab + b^2 = (a + b)(a + b) = (a + b)^2$$
   $$a^2 - 2ab + b^2 = (a - b)(a - b) = (a - b)^2$$

5. **Steps for Factoring Polynomials Completely**
   1 Look for common monomial factors.

   2 Look for a difference of squares.

   3 Look for a perfect square trinomial.

   4 Look for a factorable trinomial of the form $x^2 + bx + c$ or $ax^2 + bx + c$.

   5 When a polynomial has four or more terms, look for a way to group the terms in pairs to find a common binomial factor. Also, look for a group of three terms to find a perfect square trinomial.

   6 Check each factor to be sure that it is prime. Check your work by multiplying the factors.

6. **Factors of Zero Property** If the product of two real numbers a and b is zero, then $a = 0$, or $b = 0$, or both a and b equal 0.

Chapter Review

Write each number in prime-factorization form. (*Pages 377–379*)

1. 27   **2.** 75   **3.** 94   **4.** 180   **5.** 360   **6.** 630

Write all the whole-number factors of each expression. Do not include 1.
(Pages 377–379)

7. $3^2 \cdot 5$ **8.** $2 \cdot 3 \cdot 11$ **9.** $2 \cdot 7^2$ **10.** $2 \cdot 3^2 \cdot 5$

Factor. If a polynomial cannot be factored over the integers, write <u>Prime</u>.
(Pages 380–383)

11. $3a - 6b$ **12.** $2c^3 - 4c$ **13.** $5q - 8p^3$

14. $x^2y^3 + x^3y$ **15.** $4n + mn - n^2$ **16.** $xy^3 - x^2y^4 + x^3y^3$

(Pages 384–386)

17. $9 - x^2$ **18.** $4a^2 - 36$ **19.** $-1 + n^2$ **20.** $4c^2 + d^2$

21. $100 - 16x^2$ **22.** $9x^4 - y^2$ **23.** $m^2n^2 - c^2$ **24.** $d^6 - 1$

Factor. *(Pages 387–389)*

25. $y^2 - 10y + 25$ **26.** $100 + 20b + b^2$ **27.** $16x^2 - 24x + 9$

28. $9c^2 + 24cd + 16d^2$ **29.** $4m^2 - 4mn + n^2$ **30.** $144 - 48a + 4a^2$

(Pages 392–395)

31. $a^2 + 6a + 8$ **32.** $c^2 - 9c + 8$ **33.** $s^2 - 3s - 10$

34. $t^2 + 4t - 45$ **35.** $-16 + 6y + y^2$ **36.** $w^2 - w - 2$

37. $-36 + 5n + n^2$ **38.** $6a^2 - 5ab + b^2$ **39.** $t^2 + 2st - 15s^2$

(Pages 397–400)

40. $3x^2 - x - 2$ **41.** $5y^2 - 13y + 6$ **42.** $12y^2 + 16y + 5$

43. $8x^2 - 25x + 3$ **44.** $8c^2 - 43c - 30$ **45.** $16n^2 - 2n - 3$

46. $4d^2 + d - 5$ **47.** $-10 + t + 24t^2$ **48.** $-12h^2 + 11h - 2$

Factor completely. *(Pages 401–403)*

49. $2h^2 + 4h + 2$ **50.** $3b^2 - 27$ **51.** $4p^2 - 16p + 16$

52. $6r^2 + 18r + 12$ **53.** $5c^2 - 125$ **54.** $8r^2 - 56r - 64$

55. $y^3 + 2y^2 - 8y$ **56.** $6a^3 - 30a^2 + 24a$ **57.** $8n^4 + 6n^3 - 9n^2$

Solve by factoring. *(Pages 404–406)*

58. $x^2 = x$ **59.** $3y^2 + 12y = 0$ **60.** $m^2 + 2m - 8 = 0$

61. $b^2 = 9$ **62.** $9q^2 + 4 = 12q$ **63.** $t^2 + 10t = 24$

64. $3d^2 + 5d - 2 = 0$ **65.** $y^3 = 36y$ **66.** $2a^3 - 2a^2 - 12a = 0$

Solve each problem. *(Pages 407–411)*

67. Find three consecutive positive integers such that the square of the greatest of the three is equal to the sum of the squares of the other two.

68. Find three consecutive even integers such that the square of the greatest of the three is 148 more than the product of the other two.

69. There are 396 seats in a theater. The number of seats in each row is 4 more than the number of rows. How many seats are there in each row?

70. A patio is twice as long as it is wide. Its area can be doubled by adding 3 meters to its length and 1 meter to its width. Find the dimensions of the patio.

71. A marching band has 154 members. When they are arranged in a rectangular formation, the number of players in each row is 3 more than the number of rows. How many players are there in each row?

72. A rectangular lot is 6 meters wide and 10 meters long. When the length and width are increased by the same amount, the area of the lot is increased by 80 square meters. How much must be added to the length and width to do this?

Chapter Test

Write each number in prime-factorization form.

1. 96   **2.** 300   **3.** 13   **4.** 55   **5.** 220

Factor completely.

6. $2x^2 + 6xy$

7. $9b^2 - 1$

8. $a^2 + 12a + 36$

9. $y^2 + 11y + 24$

10. $2x^2 - 4x + 2$

11. $a^2b^3 - a^3b$

12. $4 - 4n + n^2$

13. $n^2 + n - 56$

14. $x^4 - 4$

15. $6b^2 + 4b - 2$

16. $4x^2 - 20xy + 25y^2$

17. $a^2b^2 - 16c^2$

18. $2m^2 + 20m + 50$

19. $a^3 - a^2 - 6a$

20. $m^3 - m$

Solve by factoring.

21. $x^2 + 2x - 15 = 0$

22. $2a^2 = 72$

23. $4p^2 + 8p - 12 = 0$

24. Four times the square of an integer is 6 more than twice the integer. What is the integer?

25. A rectangle is three times as long as it is wide. Its area is 48 square centimeters. Find its length and width.

Additional Practice

Skills   Write each number in prime-factorization form. (*Pages 377–379*)

1. 63 **2.** 44 **3.** 60 **4.** 273 **5.** 375 **6.** 612

Factor. (*Pages 380–383*)

7. $15a - 12a^2$ **8.** $x^2y - x^2y^3 + 2x^3y$ **9.** $9a^2 - 18a^3$

(*Pages 384–386*)

10. $a^2 - 1$ **11.** $16m^2 - 49n^2$ **12.** $a^2b^2 - 100$ **13.** $x^{10} - y^2$

(*Pages 387–389*)

14. $x^2 - 18x + 81$ **15.** $4x^2 + 12x + 9$ **16.** $9a^2 - 24ab + 16b^2$

(*Pages 392–395*)

17. $x^2 - 5x - 14$ **18.** $x^2 - 10x + 9$ **19.** $a^2 + ab - 12b^2$

(*Pages 397–400*)

20. $3n^2 - 11n - 4$ **21.** $4x^2 + 6x - 10$ **22.** $8x^2 - 19x + 6$

Factor completely. (*Pages 401–403*)

23. $5x^2 - 45$ **24.** $3x^2 - 3x - 18$ **25.** $18n^3 - 6n^2 - 4n$

Solve by factoring. (*Pages 404–406*)

26. $y^2 - 9y = 0$ **27.** $n^2 - 2n - 24 = 0$ **28.** $2y^2 - y - 36 = 0$

Problem Solving and Applications

29. Two hundred forty folding chairs are arranged in a rectangular array for an outdoor concert. What formations are possible, if there must be at least 10 rows and at least 10 chairs in each row? (*Pages 377–379*)

30. Each side of a square picture is $2m$ units long. The picture is centered over a square mat with each side $3n$ units long. Express the uncovered area of the mat in terms of m and n. Factor the expression. (*Pages 384–386*)

31. The area of a rectangle is $(x^2 - 5x - 36)$ square units. Express the length and width of the rectangle as binomials. (*Pages 392–395*)

32. It takes 170 one-foot square tiles to cover a floor. The length of the floor is 3 feet less than twice the width. What are its dimensions? (*Pages 407–411*)

Part 1

Choose the best answer. Choose *a*, *b*, *c*, or *d*.

1. If $6x^2 + 5x - 6$ is divided by $(2x + 3)$, then the quotient is

   a. $3x - 6$ **b.** $3x + 5$ **c.** $3x - 2$ **d.** $3x + 2$

2. Solve $14 - 3x > -7$.

   a. $x > -7$ **b.** $x < 7$ **c.** $x > 7$ **d.** $x < -7$

3. Factor: $3a^2bc^3 + 27ab^3c^2 + 9a^2b^2c^2$

   a. $3abc(ac^2 + 27b^2c + 9abc)$ **b.** $3abc^2(ac + 9a^2 + 3ab)$
   c. $3abc^2(ac + 9b^2 + 3ab)$ **d.** $3abc(3ac + 9b^2 + 3ab)$

4. Which of the following real numbers is not a solution of $|x - 2| > 5$?

   a. 8   **b.** -2 **c.** -4 **d.** -6

5. Write the following compound sentence as two simple sentences joined by <u>or</u> or <u>and</u>: $0 < x - 2 < 3$

   a. $x - 2 < 3$ or $x - 2 > 0$ **b.** $x < 5$ and $x > 2$
   c. $x - 2 < 3$ and $x > 0$ **d.** $x < 5$ or $x > 2$

6. Which of the following is not a perfect square trinomial?

   a. $9x^2 - 12xy + 4y^2$ **b.** $16a^2 - 20ab + 25b^2$
   c. $4s^2 + 28st + 49t^2$ **d.** $x^2 - 4xy + 4y^2$

7. Solve $|x - 3| = 8$.

   a. $\{-5, 11\}$ **b.** $\{11\}$ **c.** $\{5\}$ **d.** $\{5, 11\}$

8. Which of the following pairs does not satisfy the system
   $\begin{cases} 2x - 3y > 7 \\ x + y < 1 \end{cases}$?

   a. $(3, -3)$ **b.** $(0, -4)$ **c.** $(1, -5)$ **d.** $(4, 0)$

9. What is the equation of the line that is parallel to $4x - 3y + 8 = 0$ and passes through the point $(1, 1)$?

   a. $4x - 3y + 1 = 0$ **b.** $y = \frac{4}{3}x - \frac{1}{3}$
   c. $4x - 3y - 8 = 0$ **d.** $y = \frac{4}{3}x - \frac{8}{3}$

10. What is the theoretical probability that when one card is selected at random from an ordinary deck of 52 playing cards, it is a 2?

   a. $\frac{1}{10}$ **b.** $\frac{1}{4}$ **c.** $\frac{1}{52}$ **d.** $\frac{1}{13}$

11. Which of the following is equivalent to $4^2 2^4$?

   a. 2^8 **b.** 8^8 **c.** 2^6 **d.** 6^8

12. If the area of a square can be represented by $4x^2 + 36x + 81$, find the perimeter of the square.

   a. $2x + 9$ **b.** $4x + 18$ **c.** $6x + 27$ **d.** $8x + 36$

13. Find the value of $(-x^2)(y^3)$ when $x = -2$ and $y = -3$.

   a. -72 **b.** 72 **c.** 108 **d.** -108

14. One of the factors of $x^2 + 8x + 7$ is $x + 1$. The other factor is

   a. $x + 8$ **b.** $x + 7$ **c.** $x - 7$ **d.** $x - 8$

15. Simplify: $(2x - 3y)^2 - (3x + 2y)^2$

   a. $x^2 + 10xy + 25y^2$ **b.** $-(x^2 + 10xy + 25y^2)$
   c. $5x^2 + 24xy - 5y^2$ **d.** $-(5x^2 + 24xy - 5y^2)$

16. What is the slope of the line which passes through $(-1, -3)$ and $(-1, 5)$?

   a. 0 **b.** no slope **c.** -4 **d.** 1

17. Find the value of $|x^3| - x^3 - |x^3 - 1|$ when $x = -1$.

   a. 2 **b.** -2 **c.** 0 **d.** -1

18. Find the value of k that will make $(2x + 3)$ a factor of $8x^2 + kx + 6$.

   a. 16 **b.** 6 **c.** 2 **d.** 8

19. What is the equation of the line with slope $\frac{2}{3}$ and passing through the point $(-1, 3)$?

   a. $y = \frac{1}{3}(2x + 11)$ **b.** $y = \frac{2}{3}x + 11$
   c. $3y = 6x + 33$ **d.** $2x - 3y - 11 = 0$

20. Solve for x: $7 - \frac{2}{3}x = 11$.

   a. 6 **b.** -6 **c.** $\frac{10}{3}$ **d.** 27

21. Solve the system: $\begin{cases} x - 2y = 10 \\ 2x + y = 5 \end{cases}$

   a. $x = 10, y = 0$ **b.** $x = 1, y = 3$
   c. $x = 4, y = -3$ **d.** $x = -4, y = 3$

22. If s varies directly as t and $s = 5$ when $t = 9$, find s when $t = 12$.

   a. 8 **b.** $\frac{5}{9}$ **c.** $\frac{20}{3}$ **d.** $\frac{9}{5}$

23. If the product of two real numbers a and b is zero, then which of the following statements is always true?

   a. $a = 0$ **b.** $b = 0$
   c. $a = 0$ or $b = 0$ **d.** $a = 0$ and $b = 0$

24. If $k < 0$, which of the following is positive?

    a. k^3 **b.** $0 - k$ **c.** $-|-k^3|$ **d.** $k - 1$

25. What is the slope of the line with equation $2x - 3y - 7 = 0$?

    a. $\frac{3}{2}$ **b.** $-\frac{3}{2}$ **c.** $\frac{2}{3}$ **d.** $-\frac{7}{3}$

Part 2

Solve each problem.

26. Maureen plans to spend no more than $55 for a skirt and blouse. If the cost of the skirt is $5 less than twice the cost of the blouse, what is the largest amount Maureen can spend for the skirt?

27. The sum of two consecutive even integers is greater than 70. Find the pair with the smallest sum.

28. A rectangle has an area of $6x^3 + 2x^2 - 9x - 3$; its length is $2x^2 - 3$. Find its perimeter.

29. The sum of an integer and its square is 56. Find the integer. (HINT: there are two solutions.)

30. A rectangular field has a length which is twice its width. If both the width and length are increased by 3 feet, the area of the largest field is three times bigger than that of the original field. What were the dimensions of the original field?

31. The members of a civic club decided to make a gift of $2000 to a shelter for the homeless, with each member contributing the same amount. If the club had 20 more members, each would have contributed $5 less. How many members does the club currently have?

32. An 8% salt solution is mixed with a 12% salt solution. How many grams of each solution are needed to obtain 200 grams of a 10% solution?

33. Tom's clothing store is selling pants at $28.75 a pair and jackets for $54.50 each. If 22 items were sold for a total of $735.50, how many pants and how many jackets were sold?

34. Sylvia has some money invested at 8% per year. If she adds $500 to her account, the new total will return the same amount each year at 6% as her original investment does at 8%. How much does she have invested at 8%?

35. In an electrical system, the electromotive force (emf) varies directly as the current. When an electric current is 36 amperes, the emf is 315 volts. Find the emf when the current is 42 amperes.

11 Rational Expressions

To determine the most efficient use of shovels to excavate the foundation for a building, the rates of work for each shovel can be modeled by equations involving **rational expressions**.

11-1   Simplifying Rational Expressions

A *rational expression* is a ratio having polynomials as its terms. The following are rational expressions.

$$\frac{5}{9} \qquad \frac{3}{x} \qquad \frac{x^2 + y^2}{a^2} \qquad \frac{a^2 - b^2}{a + 5b}$$

DEFINITION

> A **rational expression** is an expression of the form $\frac{P}{Q}$, where P and Q are polynomials and $Q \neq 0$.

SIMPLEST FORM

A rational expression is in **simplest form** when the numerator and denominator of the expression have no common factors other than 1 and -1. Thus, to simplify a rational expression, first factor the numerator and denominator. Then identify any common factors.

EXAMPLE 1 Simplify: $\dfrac{x^2 + xy}{x^2 - xy}$

Solution: Factor the numerator and denominator.

$$\frac{x^2 + xy}{x^2 - xy} = \frac{x(x + y)}{x(x - y)} \qquad \longleftarrow \quad \text{The common factor is x.}$$

$$= \frac{x}{x} \cdot \frac{x + y}{x - y} \qquad \longleftarrow \quad \frac{x}{x} = 1$$

$$= \frac{x + y}{x - y} \qquad \longleftarrow \quad \text{Simplest form}$$

Recall that *division by zero is not defined.* Thus, the values of the variables must be restricted so that the denominator cannot equal zero. In Example 1, x cannot equal zero or y.

EXAMPLE 2 Simplify: $\dfrac{a^2 - 9}{a^2 + 5a + 6}$

Solution: $\dfrac{a^2 - 9}{a^2 + 5a + 6} = \dfrac{(a + 3)(a - 3)}{(a + 3)(a + 2)} \qquad \longleftarrow \quad \text{The common factor is } (a + 3).$

$$= \frac{a + 3}{a + 3} \cdot \frac{a - 3}{a + 2} \qquad \longleftarrow \quad \frac{\overset{1}{\cancel{a + 3}}}{\underset{1}{\cancel{a + 3}}} = 1$$

$$= \frac{a - 3}{a + 2} \qquad \longleftarrow \quad \text{Simplest form}$$

NOTE: In Example 2, a cannot equal -2 or -3.

When simplifying rational expressions watch for factors that are opposites of each other. Recall that

$$-(5y - x) = (-1)(5y - x) = x - 5y.$$

EXAMPLE 3 Simplify: $\dfrac{3x^2 - 15xy + 18y^2}{9y^2 - x^2}$

Solution: $\dfrac{3x^2 - 15xy + 18y^2}{9y^2 - x^2} = \dfrac{3(x^2 - 5xy + 6y^2)}{9y^2 - x^2}$

$= \dfrac{3(x - 3y)(x - 2y)}{(3y - x)(3y + x)}$ $\longleftarrow$ **(x − 3y) and (3y − x) are opposites.**

$= \dfrac{3(x - 3y)(x - 2y)}{-(x - 3y)(x + 3y)}$ $\longleftarrow$ **(3y − x) = −(x − 3y)**

$= \dfrac{\overset{1}{\cancel{x - 3y}}}{\underset{1}{\cancel{x - 3y}}} \cdot \dfrac{3(x - 2y)}{-(x + 3y)}$ $\longleftarrow$ **The common factor is (x − 3y)**

$= \dfrac{3(x - 2y)}{-(x + 3y)}$, or $-\dfrac{3(x - 2y)}{(x + 3y)}$ $\longleftarrow$ **Simplest form**

NOTE: In Example 3, x cannot equal $3y$ or $-3y$.

EXERCISES: Classwork/Homework

Objective: To simplify rational expressions

CHECK YOUR UNDERSTANDING

Find the common factor in the numerator and denominator of each rational expression. If none exists, write "none."

1. $\dfrac{10}{15}$

2. $\dfrac{10 + 1}{15 + 1}$

3. $\dfrac{4 \cdot 9}{4 \cdot 10}$

4. $\dfrac{4 \cdot 9 - 5}{4 \cdot 10 - 5}$

5. $\dfrac{a^2b^3}{ab}$

6. $\dfrac{a^2b^3 + 1}{ab}$

7. $\dfrac{(x - y)(x + y)}{(x + y)^2}$

8. $\dfrac{(a - b)^2}{(a + b)^2}$

PRACTICE AND APPLY

Simplify. No denominator equals zero.

9. $\dfrac{3 \cdot 5}{3 \cdot 4}$

10. $\dfrac{3 \cdot 4 \cdot 5}{3 \cdot 4}$

11. $\dfrac{6xy}{6}$

12. $\dfrac{6xy}{6x}$

13. $\dfrac{12}{18}$

14. $\dfrac{9}{12}$

15. $\dfrac{a^2}{ab}$

16. $\dfrac{24a}{36b}$

17. $\dfrac{12x}{15xy}$

18. $\dfrac{25x^2}{30x}$

19. $\dfrac{18x^2y}{24xy}$

20. $\dfrac{3xy}{24y}$

21. $\dfrac{4(x + y)}{7(x + y)}$

22. $\dfrac{5(x - y)}{2(x - y)}$

23. $\dfrac{4(a + b)}{8(a + b)}$

24. $\dfrac{a(x + y)}{x(x + y)}$

25. $\dfrac{24}{15(x + y)}$

26. $\dfrac{m(x - y)^2}{e(x - y)}$

27. $\dfrac{3(x - y)^2}{x - y}$

28. $\dfrac{4(a + 2b)^2}{4(a + 2b)}$

29. $\dfrac{7(x - 6y)^2}{7x}$

30. $\dfrac{36x}{15(x + 2)}$

31. $\dfrac{15(a + b)}{6(2a + b)}$

32. $\dfrac{8(x - 2y)}{18(2x - y)}$

33. $\dfrac{3x - 6y}{9x + 12y}$

34. $\dfrac{a^2b - ab^2}{a^2b^2 + ab^2}$

35. $\dfrac{2ab + b^2}{a^2 - b^2}$

36. $\dfrac{4x - 4y}{x + y}$

37. $\dfrac{3a + 3b}{3(a + b)}$

38. $\dfrac{x^2 - y^2}{x^2 - 2xy + y^2}$

39. $\dfrac{a + b}{a^2 + 2ab + b^2}$

40. $\dfrac{x - 1}{x^2 - 2x + 1}$

41. $\dfrac{x + 1}{x^2 + 2x + 1}$

42. $\dfrac{5a + 5}{a^2 + 7a + 6}$

43. $\dfrac{a^2 + a}{a}$

44. $\dfrac{3a^2 - 3}{a - 1}$

45. $\dfrac{5 - v}{v - 5}$

46. $\dfrac{2(a - 1)(a + 7)}{(1 - a)(a + 7)}$

47. $\dfrac{b + 9}{81 - b^2}$

48. $\dfrac{c - d}{(d - c)^2}$

49. $\dfrac{(t - 1)^2}{1 - t^2}$

50. $\dfrac{(x - y)^2}{(y - x)}$

51. $\dfrac{k - n}{(n - k)^3}$

52. $\dfrac{(5a - c)^5}{(c - 5a)^5}$

53. $\dfrac{2x^3 - 12x^2 + 2x}{x^2 - 6x + 1}$

54. $\dfrac{3a + 3b}{a^2 + 2ab + b^2}$

55. $\dfrac{2x^2 + 6x + 4}{4x^2 - 12x - 16}$

56. $\dfrac{2x^3 - 2x^2 - 4x}{3x^3 + 3x^2 + 18x}$

57. $\dfrac{6x + 12}{x^2 - x - 6}$

58. $\dfrac{x^2y - y}{x + 1}$

59. $\dfrac{3a^2 - 3}{1 - a}$

60. $\dfrac{a^2 + 1}{a + 1}$

61. $\dfrac{R^2 - r^2}{3r + 3R}$

62. $\dfrac{6a^2 + a - 15}{6a^2 - 13a + 6}$

63. $\dfrac{2a^2 - ab - b^2}{2a^2 + ab - b^2}$

64. $\dfrac{6a^2 + 42a + 72}{18 - 2a^2}$

65. $\dfrac{3x^2 - 27}{24 - 11x + x^2}$

66. $\dfrac{(a + b)^2(a - b)}{a^2 - b^2}$

■■■■■■■ **MAINTAIN**

Solve each problem. (*Pages 407–411*)

67. Find two consecutive odd integers such that the square of the first decreased by the second is 4.

68. Twice the square of a positive number equals 112 more than twice the number. What is the number?

69. The area of a rectangular flower bed is 384 square meters. The length of the garden is 8 more than twice its width. Find the length and width.

70. A rectangular parking lot is 15 meters longer than it is wide. The area of the lot is 250 square meters. Find the dimensions (length and width).

Solve by factoring. (*Pages 404–406*)

71. $a^2 - 16 = 0$

72. $2a^2 = -17a - 35$

73. $x^2 = 7x$

74. $r^2 + 8r = 0$

75. $3a^2 - 13a = -14$

76. $9m^2 - 81 = 0$

Write each product as a base with a single exponent. (*Pages 325–328*)

77. $5^3 \cdot 5^8$

78. $x^2 \cdot x^4$

79. $2^{12} \cdot 2$

80. $7^2 \cdot 7$

81. $a^6 \cdot a^3$

82. $10 \cdot 10^3$

83. $2^3 \cdot 2^2$

84. $m \cdot m$

CONNECT AND EXTEND

Simplify. No denominator equals zero.

85. $\dfrac{(x + y)^2 + (x + y) - 2}{x + y + 2}$

86. $\dfrac{(x + y)^2 - (r + t)^2}{x + y - r - t}$

87. $\dfrac{(a + b)^2 + 2(a + b) - 35}{a + b + 7}$

88. $\dfrac{(m + n)^2 - 2(m + n)}{m + n - 2}$

89. $\dfrac{(c + d)^2 - (r + s)^2}{c + d + r + s}$

90. $\dfrac{(2x + y)^2 - 6(2x + y) - 27}{2x + y + 3}$

NON-ROUTINE PROBLEMS

91. The number of single-cell organisms in a jar doubles every minute. The jar is full in one hour. When was the jar half-full?

92. How many rectangles are there in the figure below?

REVIEW CAPSULE FOR SECTION 11-2

Simplify. (*Pages 329–331, 335–337*)

1. $(4n)(3n)$

2. $(2a^2b)(a^2b^3)$

3. $(\frac{1}{2}c^3)(-4c^7)$

4. $(4x^2yz^3)(-3xy^2z^5)$

5. $\dfrac{x^{12}}{x^2}$

6. $\dfrac{-8ab}{-32ab^3}$

7. $\dfrac{14r^2st^3}{35rs^2t}$

8. $\dfrac{(3x^5)(2x^4)}{(6x^2)^3}$

9. $\dfrac{36a^2b^3}{8a^5b}$

10. $\dfrac{36a^2b^3}{7ab^9}$

11. $\dfrac{36x^2y^3}{6x^2y^2}$

12. $\dfrac{63x^2y^2}{28a^6b^6}$

Factor. (*Pages 380–383, 387–389*)

13. $3x^3y^2 - 2x^2y^3$

14. $100z^2 - 1$

15. $16x^3 - 4x$

16. $9t^2 + 18t + 9$

17. $z^2 - 7z - 18$

18. $4q^2 + 11q - 3$

11-2 Multiplying Rational Expressions

Multiplying two rational expressions is similar to multiplying two rational numbers. The method is generalized below.

PRODUCT OF RATIONAL EXPRESSIONS

If $\dfrac{P}{Q}$ and $\dfrac{R}{S}$ are rational expressions, then

$$\frac{P}{Q} \cdot \frac{R}{S} = \frac{P \cdot R}{Q \cdot S}$$

$$\frac{a}{x} \cdot \frac{x^2}{4} = \frac{a \cdot \overset{x}{\cancel{x^2}}}{\underset{1}{\cancel{4 \cdot x}}}$$

$$= \frac{ax}{4}$$

EXAMPLE 1 Multiply $\dfrac{3a^2b}{2ab^2} \cdot \dfrac{4abx}{9a^2by}$. Express the product in simplest form.

Solution:
$$\frac{3a^2b}{2ab^2} \cdot \frac{4abx}{9a^2by} = \frac{(3a^2b)(4abx)}{(2ab^2)(9a^2by)}$$

$$= \frac{12a^3b^2x}{18a^3b^3y} \qquad \longleftarrow \quad \textbf{Simplify the product.}$$

$$= \frac{\overset{2\ 1\ 1}{\cancel{12a^3b^2}x}}{\underset{3\ 1\ b}{\cancel{18a^3b^3}y}} \qquad \longleftarrow \quad \dfrac{2 \cdot 1 \cdot 1 \cdot x}{3 \cdot 1 \cdot b \cdot y} = \dfrac{2x}{3by}$$

$$= \frac{2x}{3by} \qquad \longleftarrow \quad \textbf{Simplest form}$$

When multiplying rational expressions whose numerators and denominators are not monomials, it is usually easier to simplify first. Example 2 shows how to do this.

EXAMPLE 2 Multiply: $\dfrac{3a + 3b}{a - b} \cdot \dfrac{a + 2b}{a^2 + 2ab + b^2}$. Simplify the product.

Solution: Factor any polynomials that are not prime over the integers.

$$\frac{3a + 3b}{a - b} \cdot \frac{a + 2b}{a^2 + 2ab + b^2} = \frac{3(a + b)}{a - b} \cdot \frac{(a + 2b)}{(a + b)(a + b)}$$

$$= \frac{3(\overset{1}{\cancel{a + b}})}{a - b} \cdot \frac{a + 2b}{(\underset{1}{\cancel{a + b}})(a + b)} \qquad \longleftarrow \quad \textbf{Simplify.}$$

$$= \frac{3(a + 2b)}{(a - b)(a + b)} = \frac{3a + 6b}{a^2 - b^2}$$

Unless otherwise indicated, assume throughout the remainder of this text that no denominator equals zero.

EXERCISES: Classwork/Homework

Objective: To multiply rational expressions

CHECK YOUR UNDERSTANDING

Multiply. Express each product in simplest form.

1. $\dfrac{5}{7} \cdot \dfrac{3}{4}$

2. $8 \cdot \dfrac{3}{4}$

3. $\dfrac{6}{25} \cdot \dfrac{5}{3}$

4. $\dfrac{a}{b} \cdot \dfrac{b}{d}$

5. $\dfrac{5}{x} \cdot \dfrac{x}{9}$

6. $\dfrac{a}{b} \cdot \dfrac{b}{a}$

7. $\dfrac{a}{2} \cdot 12$

8. $\dfrac{x^2}{y} \cdot \dfrac{y}{x^3}$

PRACTICE AND APPLY

Multiply. Express each product in simplest form.

9. $\dfrac{x}{y} \cdot \dfrac{my}{nx}$

10. $\dfrac{3}{x} \cdot \dfrac{x^2}{3}$

11. $\dfrac{3x}{d} \cdot \dfrac{c}{3x}$

12. $\dfrac{ab^2}{2} \cdot \dfrac{c}{abd}$

13. $\dfrac{ab}{xy} \cdot \dfrac{x}{a^3b^2}$

14. $\dfrac{xy^2}{m^3n} \cdot \dfrac{m^2}{y^3}$

15. $\dfrac{7xy^2}{8x^2y} \cdot \dfrac{16xz^2}{49y^2z}$

16. $\dfrac{a}{b} \cdot \dfrac{c}{d} \cdot \dfrac{ax}{by} \cdot \dfrac{y^2}{x^2}$

17. $\dfrac{4 \cdot 6}{2 \cdot 3^2} \cdot \dfrac{27}{2^2 \cdot 3}$

18. $(x + 2) \cdot \dfrac{x + 3}{x + 1}$

19. $(2x + 5) \cdot \dfrac{2x + 3}{2x - 5}$

20. $\dfrac{(x - 5)^2}{3(x - 5)}$

21. $\dfrac{a + 1}{a + 2} \cdot \dfrac{a + 2}{a + 1}$

22. $\dfrac{a + 3}{a - 3} \cdot \dfrac{1}{a + 3}$

23. $(n + 3) \cdot \dfrac{n + 3}{n + 5}$

24. $(2x - 5) \cdot \dfrac{x + 7}{2x - 5}$

25. $x^2y \cdot \dfrac{8}{2x + 2xy}$

26. $\dfrac{3a - 3b}{10ab} \cdot \dfrac{50a^2b^2}{a^2 - b^2}$

27. $n(a + b) \cdot \dfrac{1}{m(a + b)}$

28. $\dfrac{a^2 - 4b^2}{a^2 - b^2} \cdot \dfrac{3a^2b^2}{a + b}$

29. $\dfrac{a^2 + 5a}{a^2 - 16} \cdot \dfrac{a^2 - 4a}{a^2 - 25}$

30. $\dfrac{3x - 48y^2}{2x^2 - 8y^2} \cdot \dfrac{3x + 6y}{3x + 12y}$

31. $\dfrac{x^2 + 8x + 16}{x^2 - 9} \cdot \dfrac{x - 3}{x + 4}$

32. $\dfrac{a^2 - 3a - 10}{(a - 2)^2} \cdot \dfrac{a - 2}{a - 5}$

33. $\dfrac{9 - x^2}{x + 3} \cdot \dfrac{x}{3 - x}$

34. $\dfrac{24x^2}{3(x^2 - 4x + 4)} \cdot \dfrac{3x - 6}{2x}$

35. $\dfrac{x^2 - 6x + 5}{x - 1} \cdot \dfrac{x - 1}{x - 5}$

36. $\dfrac{c^2 - 6c}{c - 6} \cdot \dfrac{c + 3}{c}$

37. $\dfrac{x^2 - 24 - 2x}{x^2 - 30 - x} \cdot \dfrac{x + 5}{x^2 - 16}$

38. $\dfrac{a^2 + 7ab + 10b^2}{a^2 + 6ab + 5b^2} \cdot \dfrac{a + b}{a^2 + 4ab + 4b^2} \cdot \dfrac{a + 2b}{1}$

39. $\dfrac{x^2 - y^2}{x^2 - 3xy + 2y^2} \cdot \dfrac{xy - 2y}{y^2 + xy} \cdot \dfrac{x(x - y)}{(x - y)^2}$

40. $\dfrac{2a - 3b}{a^2 + 4ab + 4b^2} \cdot \dfrac{4a^2 - 4b^2}{4a^2 - 9b^2} \cdot \dfrac{5a^2 + 10ab}{3ab - 3b^2}$

41. $\dfrac{6x - 3y}{4x^2 + 4xy + y^2} \cdot \dfrac{2x + y}{4x^2 - 4xy + y^2}$

42. $\dfrac{5m + 5n}{m^2 - n^2} \cdot \dfrac{m^2 - mn}{(m + n)^2}$

43. $\dfrac{x^2 - 3x - 18}{x^2 - x - 2} \cdot \dfrac{3x + 3}{x^2 - 2x - 15}$

44. $\dfrac{a^2 + 6a + 5}{a - 3} \cdot \dfrac{5a - 15}{a^2 + 4a - 5}$

45. $\dfrac{3a + 9}{3a^2 - 5a + 2} \cdot \dfrac{6a^2 - 7a + 2}{2a^2 + 3a - 18}$

46. $\dfrac{4x^2 - 9y^2}{6x^2 - 9xy} \cdot \dfrac{6xy}{4xy + 6y^2}$

47. $\dfrac{x^2 + 6x + 8}{x^2 + 4x + 14} \cdot \dfrac{x^2 + 5x + 6}{x^2 + 7x + 12}$

48. $\dfrac{a^2 + a - 2}{a^2 - 3a - 10} \cdot \dfrac{a^2 - 2a - 8}{a^2 - 7a + 12}$

49. $\dfrac{x^2 - 2xb + b^2}{b - 1} \cdot \dfrac{b^2 - 5b + 4}{x^2 - b^2}$

50. $\dfrac{x^2 - x - 1}{x - 1} \cdot \dfrac{x^2 - 1}{x} \cdot \dfrac{x^2 - x - 1}{x - 1}$

MAINTAIN

Solve each problem. (*Pages 407–411*)

51. A rectangular picture is 7 centimeters longer than its width. The area of the picture frame is 260 square centimeters. Find the length and width.

52. A band has 112 members. When they are arranged in a rectangular formation, the number of players in each row is 6 less than the number of rows. How many players are there in each row?

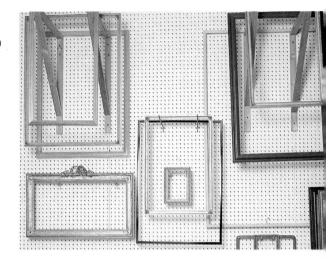

Find each product. (*Page 329–331*)

53. $c \cdot c^3$
54. $-a^2(a^3)$
55. $3^3 \cdot 3^4$
56. $b(-b)$

57. $(2x)(4x^2)$
58. $(-x^5)(3x^2)(7x)$
59. $10^5 \cdot 10 \cdot 10^7$
60. $(-6x^2y)(5x)$

▰▰▰▰ **CONNECT AND EXTEND**

Multiply. Express each product in simplest form.

61. $\dfrac{a^2 - 5a + 6}{6a^2 - 17s + 5} \cdot \dfrac{6a^2 + 7a - 3}{2a^2 - 7a + 3} \cdot \dfrac{a^2 - 7a + 5}{a^2 - 3a + 2}$

62. $\dfrac{4x^2 + x - 14}{6xy - 14y} \cdot \dfrac{4x^2}{x^2 - 4} \cdot \dfrac{x - 2}{4x - 7} \cdot \dfrac{3x^2 - x - 14}{2x^2 - 14}$

63. $\dfrac{(a + b)^2 - c^2}{a^2 + ab - ac} \cdot \dfrac{a}{(a + c)^2 - b^2} \cdot \dfrac{(a - b)^2 - c^2}{ab - b^2 - bc}$

64. $\dfrac{4b^2 - 16b + 15}{2b^2 + 3b + 1} \cdot \dfrac{b^2 - 6b - 7}{2b^2 - 17b + 21} \cdot \dfrac{4b^2 - 1}{4b^2 - 20b + 25}$

65. $\dfrac{6x^2 - 8x - 8}{8 - 16x - 10x^2} \cdot \dfrac{5x^2 - 2x}{8x^2 - 22x + 12} \cdot \dfrac{8x^2 + 10x - 12}{6x^2 + 25x + 14}$

66. $\dfrac{6 - 4b - 2b^2}{15b^2 - b - 6} \cdot \dfrac{5b^2 + 13b + 6}{b^2 + 7b + 12} \cdot \dfrac{3b^2 - 11b + 6}{2b^2 - 12b + 10}$

▰▰▰▰ **NON-ROUTINE PROBLEMS**

67. In a marching formation, there is always one majorette marching in front of two majorettes and one majorette marching behind two majorettes. Another majorette marches between two majorettes. What is the least possible number of majorettes marching?

68. Grace has two minutes to get to the bus station before her bus departs. The bus station is two miles from her home. She drives at a speed of 30 miles per hour for the first mile traveled. Will she get to the bus station before her bus departs? Explain.

───── **REVIEW CAPSULE FOR SECTION 11-3** ─────

Divide. Express the answers in simplest form. (*Pages 78–82*)

1. $\dfrac{1}{2} \div \dfrac{1}{4}$
2. $-10 \div \dfrac{2}{5}$
3. $-\dfrac{5}{6} \div 25$
4. $\dfrac{3}{5} \div \dfrac{3}{15}$

5. $\dfrac{3}{4} \div \dfrac{3}{4}$
6. $8 \div -\dfrac{1}{4}$
7. $-9 \div \dfrac{1}{3}$
8. $-\dfrac{7}{8} \div -\dfrac{5}{2}$

11-3 Division of Rational Expressions

To divide by a real number, you multiply by the reciprocal of the divisor.

$$\frac{2}{3} \div \frac{1}{4} = \frac{2}{3} \cdot \frac{4}{1}$$

$$= \frac{8}{3}, \text{ or } 2\frac{2}{3}.$$

The procedure for dividing by a rational expression is similar.

DIVISION OF RATIONAL EXPRESSIONS

To divide a rational expression $\frac{P}{Q}$ by a rational expression $\frac{R}{S}$, multiply $\frac{P}{Q}$ by the multiplicative inverse, or reciprocal, of $\frac{R}{S}$. That is, for $R \neq 0$,

$$\frac{P}{Q} \div \frac{R}{S} = \frac{P}{Q} \cdot \frac{S}{R}.$$

$$\frac{4x}{mp} \div \frac{5}{b} = \frac{4x}{mp} \cdot \frac{b}{5}$$

$$= \frac{4xb}{5mp}$$

EXAMPLE 1 Divide: $\frac{5y}{9xz^3} \div \frac{15y^3}{18x^2z^3}$. Express the answer in simplest form.

Solution: Multiply by the reciprocal of the divisor.

$$\frac{5y}{9xz^3} \div \frac{15y^3}{18x^2z^3} = \frac{5y}{9xz^3} \cdot \frac{18x^2z^3}{15y^3}$$

$$= \frac{\overset{1}{\cancel{5y}}}{\underset{1}{\cancel{9xz^3}}} \cdot \frac{\overset{2x}{\cancel{18x^2z^3}}}{\underset{3 \cdot y^2}{\cancel{15y^3}}} \longleftarrow \text{Simplify.}$$

$$= \frac{2x}{3y^2} \longleftarrow \text{Simplest form}$$

When dividing rational expressions having numerators and denominators that are not monomials, look for polynomials that can be factored.

EXAMPLE 2 Divide: $\dfrac{x^2 - 4x + 4}{3x - 6} \div (x - 2)$

Solution: $\dfrac{x^2 - 4x + 4}{3x - 6} \div (x - 2) = \dfrac{x^2 - 4x + 4}{3x - 6} \cdot \dfrac{1}{x - 2}$

$$= \dfrac{\overset{1}{(x - 2)}\overset{1}{(x - 2)}}{3\underset{1}{(x - 2)}} \cdot \dfrac{1}{\underset{1}{(x - 2)}} \longleftarrow \quad \dfrac{1 \cdot 1 \cdot 1}{3 \cdot 1 \cdot 1} = \dfrac{1}{3}$$

$$= \dfrac{1}{3}$$

**COMPLEX
FRACTIONS**

To simplify an expression such as

$$\dfrac{\dfrac{x^2}{y^2}}{\dfrac{x}{y}} \qquad \text{write it in the form} \qquad \dfrac{x^2}{y^2} \div \dfrac{x}{y}.$$

Then divide as shown in Examples 1 and 2.

A second method of simplifying such an expression uses the multi-plicative inverse postulate. For example, to simplify the expression above, multiply both numerator and denominator by $\dfrac{y}{x}$, the multipli-cative inverse of $\dfrac{x}{y}$. This will result in a denominator of 1.

$$\dfrac{\dfrac{x^2}{y^2}}{\dfrac{x}{y}} = \dfrac{\dfrac{x^2}{y^2} \cdot \dfrac{y}{x}}{\dfrac{x}{y} \cdot \dfrac{y}{x}} = \dfrac{\dfrac{x^2 \cdot y}{y^2 \cdot x}}{1} = \dfrac{\overset{x}{\cancel{x^2 y}}}{\underset{1y}{\cancel{xy^2}}} = \dfrac{x}{y}$$

EXERCISES: Classwork/Homework

Objective: To divide rational expressions

CHECK YOUR UNDERSTANDING

Complete.

1. To divide a rational expression, $\dfrac{a}{b}$, by a rational expression, $\dfrac{c}{d}$, multiply by the __?__ of $\dfrac{c}{d}$.

2. When dividing rational expressions having numerators and denominators that are not monomials, look for polynomials that can be __?__.

Write the reciprocal of each expression.

3. $\dfrac{c}{d}$

4. $5x^2$

5. $\dfrac{21a^2}{15b^2}$

6. $\dfrac{a - b}{x + y}$

7. $6x - 3$

8. $\dfrac{3a - 12}{2a + 14}$

In Exercises 9–14, write each division problem as a multiplication problem.

9. $\dfrac{5}{x} \div y$

10. $\dfrac{2xy}{5} \div \dfrac{x}{10}$

11. $\dfrac{abc^2}{xy} \div \dfrac{a}{x}$

12. $\dfrac{3a - 5}{4} \div \dfrac{a - 5}{7}$

13. $\dfrac{6a - 7}{4} \div 3a - 9$

14. $\dfrac{2x + y}{x^2 + 4} \div \dfrac{x}{x - 2}$

▇▇▇▇▇▇ PRACTICE AND APPLY

Divide. Express the answers in simplest form.

15. $\dfrac{x}{2} \div \dfrac{x}{4}$

16. $\dfrac{x}{4} \div \dfrac{x}{a}$

17. $\dfrac{2}{x} \div \dfrac{4}{x}$

18. $\dfrac{4}{x} \div \dfrac{2}{x}$

19. $\dfrac{x}{y} \div \dfrac{3}{y}$

20. $\dfrac{ad}{bc} \div \dfrac{a}{b}$

21. $\dfrac{a}{b} \div \dfrac{c}{d}$

22. $\dfrac{xy}{ab} \div \dfrac{xy}{bc}$

23. $\dfrac{1}{a} \div \dfrac{a}{b}$

24. $\dfrac{a}{x} \div \dfrac{c}{x}$

25. $\dfrac{1}{f} \div \dfrac{1}{g}$

26. $\dfrac{a}{x} \div \dfrac{x}{c}$

27. $\dfrac{8}{3a} \div 16$

28. $\dfrac{9ab^2}{8xy^2} \div \dfrac{3b^2}{2xy}$

29. $\dfrac{14a^2}{10b^2} \div \dfrac{21a^2}{15b^2}$

30. $\dfrac{5x}{12yz^2} \div \dfrac{15x^3}{18y^2z^2}$

31. $\dfrac{4a - 16}{3a} \div (3a - 12)$

32. $\dfrac{6z - 27}{4z} \div (4z - 18)$

33. $\dfrac{x^2 + x}{a} \div x^2$

34. $\dfrac{(a - b)(a + b)}{(x - y)(x + y)} \div \dfrac{a + b}{x + y}$

35. $\dfrac{a^2 - b^2}{x^2 - y^2} \div \dfrac{a + b}{x - y}$

36. $\dfrac{(2x)^3}{(4yz)^3} \div \dfrac{16x^2}{8y^2z^3}$

37. $\dfrac{3(x + y)^2}{x - y} \div 6(x + y)$

38. $\dfrac{x - y}{x + y} \div \dfrac{5x^2 - 5y^2}{3x - 3y}$

39. $\dfrac{x^2 + 2x + 1}{3x} \div (x + 1)$

40. $\dfrac{a^3 - 6a^2 + 8a}{5a} \div \dfrac{2a - 4}{10a - 40}$

41. $\dfrac{5a^2 - 5ab}{ab + b^2} \div \dfrac{5a^2 - 5b^2}{b}$

42. $\dfrac{k}{k^2 - 6k + 9} \div \dfrac{1}{k - 3}$

43. $\dfrac{a^2 - 49}{(a + 7)^2} \div \dfrac{3a - 21}{2a + 14}$

44. $(b^2 - 9) \div \dfrac{b^2 + 8b + 15}{2b + 10}$

Write each expression as a problem in division using the division symbol. (The heavier line shows the main division.) Then divide and simplify.

45. $\dfrac{\dfrac{b}{a}}{b}$

46. $\dfrac{\dfrac{x}{4}}{\dfrac{3}{2}}$

47. $\dfrac{\dfrac{ab^2}{x}}{\dfrac{x^2}{ab}}$

48. $\dfrac{\dfrac{3x}{y}}{\dfrac{5y^2}{2x^3}}$

Rational Expressions **431**

49. $\dfrac{\dfrac{x^2}{y}}{\dfrac{x}{y}}$

50. $\dfrac{\dfrac{a^2b}{c}}{\dfrac{c}{a}}$

51. $\dfrac{\dfrac{r^2}{t}}{\dfrac{t^2}{r}}$

52. $\dfrac{\dfrac{rt}{s}}{\dfrac{s^3}{t^2}}$

▮▮▮▮▮▮ MAINTAIN

Simplify. No denominator equals zero. (*Pages 332–334*)

53. $(x^4)^5$

54. $\left(\dfrac{2}{5}\right)^3$

55. $(-4b^5)^2$

56. $(-3a^2b^4)^4$

57. $\left(\dfrac{x^3}{y^4}\right)^9$

▮▮▮▮▮▮ CONNECT AND EXTEND

Perform the indicated operations. Express the answers in simplest form.

58. $\dfrac{x^2 - y^2}{x^2} \cdot \dfrac{x + y}{x - y} \div \dfrac{x^2 - y^2}{yx}$

59. $\dfrac{a^2 - 2ab + b^2}{ab} \cdot \dfrac{a + b}{a - b} \div \dfrac{a^2 - b^2}{a^2}$

60. $\dfrac{a^3b^3}{a^3 - ab^2} \div \dfrac{abc}{a - b} \cdot \dfrac{ab + bc}{ab}$

61. $\dfrac{xy - xz - x^2}{xyz} \cdot \dfrac{x^2y^2z^3}{xy - xz} \div x^3$

62. $\dfrac{2x^3}{2a + b} \div \dfrac{10a^2}{4a^2 + 4ab + b^2} \cdot \dfrac{12a + 3b}{2a^2 + ab}$

63. $\dfrac{k + n}{k^2 + n^2} \cdot \dfrac{k}{k - n} \div \dfrac{(k + n)^2}{k^4 - n^4}$

You can use a calculator to evaluate rational expressions.

EXAMPLE: Evaluate $\dfrac{2x^3 + 3x^2 - 4x + 5}{4x^2 + 5x - 10}$ when $x = 5$.

Solution: Rewrite the numerator and denominator so that each exponent is 1.

Factor using x:

$$\dfrac{(2x^2 + 3x - 4)x + 5}{(4x + 5)x - 10} = \dfrac{[(2x + 3)x - 4]x + 5}{(4x + 5)x - 10}$$

Evaluate the denominator first. Store its value.

$\boxed{4}\ \boxed{\times}\ \boxed{5}\ \boxed{+}\ \boxed{5}\ \boxed{=}\ \boxed{\times}\ \boxed{5}\ \boxed{-}\ \boxed{10}\ \boxed{=}\ \boxed{\text{STO}}\ \boxed{2}\ \boxed{\times}\ \boxed{5}\ \boxed{+}\ \boxed{3}\ \boxed{=}\ \boxed{\times}\ \boxed{5}$

$\boxed{-}\ \boxed{4}\ \boxed{=}\ \boxed{\times}\ \boxed{5}\ \boxed{+}\ \boxed{5}\ \boxed{=}\ \boxed{\div}\ \boxed{\text{RCL}}\ \boxed{=}\ \ \boxed{\mathbf{2.6956521}}$

Evaluate each expression below when the variable equals 6.

64. $\dfrac{3y^2 + 16y - 35}{5y^2 + 33y - 14}$

65. $\dfrac{6d^3 - 4d^2 - 8d + 2}{3d^2 + d - 2}$

66. $\dfrac{2a^3 + 4a^2 + 3a + 7}{a^3 + 2a^2 - 9a - 18}$

67. $\dfrac{z^3 - 5z^2 - 2z + 8}{z^3 - z^2 - 4z + 4}$

11-4　Least Common Denominator

To find the sum or difference of rational expressions such as

$$\frac{2}{a} + \frac{3}{a^2b} \quad \text{and} \quad \frac{3}{5x-10} - \frac{2}{x^2-4},$$

you replace the rational expressions with equivalent expressions having a *common denominator*. For example, a^3b^2 is a common denominator of a and a^2b because a^3b^2 is divisible by *both* a and a^2b. For convenience, however, the *least common denominator*, or LCD, is most often used. The **LCD** of two or more rational expressions is the smallest positive common multiple, called the **least common multiple (LCM),** of the denominators of the rational expressions.

EXAMPLE 1　Find the LCD of two rational expressions having 8 and 36 as the denominators.

Solution:　
[1] Write the prime factorization of each number.
$$8 = 2 \cdot 2 \cdot 2, \text{ or } 2^3 \qquad\qquad 36 = 2 \cdot 2 \cdot 3 \cdot 3, \text{ or } 2^2 \cdot 3^2$$
[2] Write a product using each prime factor only once:　$2 \cdot 3$
[3] For each factor, write the greatest exponent used in the prime factorizations:　$2^3 \cdot 3^2$
[4] Simplify.　　$2^3 \cdot 3^2 = 8 \cdot 9 = 72$　　**LCD: 72**

The method of Example 1 can be used when the denominators of the rational expressions contain variables.

EXAMPLE 2　Find the LCD of two rational expressions having $6x^5y$ and $9x^2y^2$ as denominators.

Solution:　
[1] $6x^5y = 2 \cdot 3 \cdot x^5 \cdot y$
$9x^2y^2 = 3^2 \cdot x^2 \cdot y^2$
[2] $2 \cdot 3 \cdot x \cdot y$　◄——— **Write each prime factor only once.**
[3] $2 \cdot 3^2 \cdot x^5 \cdot y^2$　◄—— **Write the greatest exponent of each prime factor.**
[4] $\mathbf{18x^5y^2}$　◄——— **LCD**

When one or more of the factors is a binomial, you can write the LCD in factored form.

EXAMPLE 3 Find the LCD of rational expressions having the given denominators.

$$a^2 - 9; \qquad 3a^2 + 3a - 18; \qquad a^2 - 4a + 4$$

Solution: ☐1 $a^2 - 9 = (a + 3)(a - 3)$
$3a^2 + 3a - 18 = 3(a^2 + a - 6) = 3(a + 3)(a - 2)$
$a^2 - 4a + 4 = (a - 2)(a - 2)$, or $(a - 2)^2$

☐2 Product using each prime factor once: $3(a + 3)(a - 3)(a - 2)$

☐3 Product having the greatest exponent for each factor:
$$3(a + 3)(a - 3)(a - 2)^2 \longleftarrow \textbf{Factored form}$$
Thus, the **LCD is $3(a + 3)(a - 3)(a - 2)^2$.**

The following is a summary of the procedure used to find the LCD of rational expressions.

SUMMARY

To find the LCD of rational expressions:
☐1 Express each denominator as a product of prime factors.
☐2 Write a product using each prime factor only once.
☐3 For each factor, write the greatest exponent used in any prime factorization.
☐4 Simplify where necessary. The result is the LCD.

EXERCISES: Classwork/Homework

Objective: To find the least common denominator of rational expressions

CHECK YOUR UNDERSTANDING

Complete.

1. To find the sum or difference of rational expressions such as $\frac{8}{y}$ and $\frac{9}{2x^2}$, you replace the rational expressions with equivalent expressions having a common __?__.

2. The smallest positive common multiple of the denominators of two or more rational expressions is the __?__.

3. The expression $6ab^2$ is a common denominator of both $3ab$ and $6b^2$ because $6ab^2$ is __?__ by both $3ab$ and $6b^2$.

4. The least common denominator of the rational expressions $\frac{8}{1}$ and $\frac{5}{x^2}$ is __?__ .

In Exercises 5–10, complete the prime factorization of each number.

5. 6, 9
$6 = 2 \cdot \underline{\ ?\ }$
$9 = 3^2$

6. $2x, 2y$
$2x = \underline{\ ?\ } \cdot x$
$2y = 2 \cdot \underline{\ ?\ }$

7. ab^2, a^2b
$ab^2 = \underline{\ ?\ } \cdot b^2$
$a^2b = \underline{\ ?\ } \cdot b$

8. $2a^2, 12b^2$
$2a^2 = 2 \cdot \underline{\ ?\ }$
$12b^2 = \underline{\ ?\ } \cdot 3 \cdot b^2$

9. $5x^2y, 4xy, 10x^3y^3$
$5x^2y = 5 \cdot \underline{\ ?\ } \cdot \underline{\ ?\ }$
$4xy = \underline{\ ?\ } \cdot x \cdot \underline{\ ?\ }$
$10x^3y^3 = \underline{\ ?\ } \cdot \underline{\ ?\ } \cdot x^3 \cdot \underline{\ ?\ }$

10. $2x^2, xy, 3y^3$
$2x^2 = 2 \cdot \underline{\ ?\ }$
$xy = \underline{\ ?\ } \cdot y$
$3y^3 = 3 \cdot \underline{\ ?\ }$

■■■■■■ **PRACTICE AND APPLY**

Find the LCD of rational expressions having the given denominators.

11. 6; 12
12. 3; 4
13. 2; 15

14. 5; 6
15. 8; 12
16. a; b

17. ab; b^2
18. $2a^2$; $12b^2$
19. $2a$; $3a$

20. $6p$; $4p$
21. $2x$; $3y$
22. ab^2; a^2b

23. 8; 4; 3
24. 5; 2; 4
25. 5; 4; 10

26. 16; 12; 3
27. x^2; y; y^2
28. x; y; z

29. $(x - y)$; $(x + y)$
30. $(x^2 - y^2)$; $(x - y)$

31. $(4a - 8b)$; $(3a - 6b)$
32. $(9a^2 - 6)$; $(15a^2 - 10)$

33. $(2x + 2y)$; $(x + y)$
34. $(x^2 - 4)$; $(x + 2)^2$

35. $(x^2 - 5x + 6)$; $(x^2 - 4x + 3)$
36. $(6a^2 - 5a - 6)$; $(12a^2 + 11a + 2)$

37. $(x^2 - 2x - 8)$; $(x^2 - 6x + 8)$
38. $(a^2 + 12a + 36)$; $(a^2 + 3a - 18)$

39. $(4x^2 - 9y^2)$; $(4x + 6y)$
40. $(r^2 - 25t^2)$; $(3r - 15t)$

41. $(2b^2 - b - 3)$; $(3b^2 + 5b + 2)$
42. $(3z^2 - 13z + 4)$; $(2z^2 - 5z - 12)$

■■■■■■ **MAINTAIN**

Divide. Express the answers in simplest form. *(Pages 429–432)*

43. $\dfrac{x^2y}{x} \div \dfrac{x}{y^2}$

44. $\dfrac{5a^2}{7b} \div \dfrac{15a^2}{14b^2}$

45. $\dfrac{x - y}{x + y} \div \dfrac{x^2 - y^2}{2}$

46. $8kn \div \dfrac{24k}{n}$

47. $\dfrac{6r^2t^2}{8s} \div 3rt$

48. $\dfrac{3c + 12}{18} \div \dfrac{c - 2}{2}$

49. $\dfrac{1}{x} \div \dfrac{1}{x^2}$

50. $\dfrac{(n - 1)^2}{4} \div (n - 1)$

51. $\dfrac{a - x}{y} \div \dfrac{a^2 - x^2}{xy}$

Rational Expressions **435**

Multiply. Express each product in simplest form. (*Pages 425–428*)

52. $\dfrac{9x^2y}{16xy^2} \cdot \dfrac{8xz^2}{27x^2z}$

53. $(3x - 2) \cdot \dfrac{5x + 4}{3x - 2}$

54. $\dfrac{a}{b} \cdot \dfrac{c}{d} \cdot \dfrac{x^2}{y} \cdot \dfrac{y}{a^3}$

55. $\dfrac{4a + 4b}{12ab} \cdot \dfrac{36a^3b^3}{a^2 - b^2}$

56. $\dfrac{5 + a}{a - 9} \cdot \dfrac{1}{5 + a}$

57. $\dfrac{25 - x^2}{x + 5} \cdot \dfrac{x}{5 - x}$

Simplify. No denominator equals zero. (*Pages 335–337*)

58. $\dfrac{2^9}{2}$

59. $\dfrac{x^6}{x^2}$

60. $\dfrac{x^3y^5}{xy^2}$

61. $\dfrac{5c^2d}{15cd}$

62. $\dfrac{-45b^3d^5}{9b^2}$

63. $\dfrac{24r^6s^3t^5}{-8r^6t^3}$

■■■■■■■ **CONNECT AND EXTEND**

Find the LCD of rational expressions having the given denominators.

64. $(a^2 - 1)$; $(3a + 3)$; $(5a - 5)$

65. $(a + 3)$; $(a - 2)$; $(a^2 - 2a - 15)$

66. $(3c + 3d)$; $(c - d)$; $(c^2 - d^2)$

67. $(m^2 - n^2)$; $(3m + 3n)$; $(4m - 4n)$

68. $(5s + 5t)$; $(5s)$; $(s^2 + 2st + t^2)$

69. $(a - 2)$; $(4a^2 - 9)$; $(2a^2 - a - 6)$

70. The LCD of two rational expressions is $24cd$. The denominator of one rational expression is $8d$. Must the denominator of the other rational expression be $3c$? Explain.

71. If the least common multiple of the polynomials $2x^2 - 32$ and $ax - 4a$ is $6(x - 4)(x + 4)$, find two possible values for a.

■■■■■■■ **NON-ROUTINE PROBLEM**

72. An ant climbs up a pole five feet during the day and slides back four feet during the night. The pole is 30 feet high. How many days will it take the ant to climb from ground level to the top of the pole?

——— **REVIEW CAPSULE FOR SECTION 11-5** ———

Combine like terms. (*Pages 64–68*)

1. $8r + 4 - 2r$

2. $7xy + 18 + 9xy - 3$

3. $6t + 7 - 3t - 9$

4. $9 - 9x^2y + 4x^2y - 4$

5. $5r - 3m + 9r - 2m$

6. $4a - 9b - 7a - 7b$

11-5 Rational Expressions: Addition/Subtraction

Adding or subtracting rational expressions with like denominators is similar to adding or subtracting fractions with like denominators.

If $\frac{P}{Q}$ and $\frac{R}{Q}$ are rational expressions then

$$\frac{P}{Q} + \frac{R}{Q} = \frac{P+R}{Q}$$

and

$$\frac{P}{Q} - \frac{R}{Q} = \frac{P-R}{Q}$$

Arithmetic

$$\frac{1}{5} + \frac{3}{5} = \frac{1+3}{5} = \frac{4}{5}$$

Algebra

$$\frac{4}{a} - \frac{2}{a} = \frac{4-2}{a} = \frac{2}{a}$$

EXAMPLE 1 Add or subtract as indicated. Express answers in simplest form.

Problem: **a.** $\dfrac{a+5}{x} + \dfrac{a-2}{x}$

Solution:

$$\frac{a+5}{x} + \frac{a-2}{x} = \frac{a+5+a-2}{x}$$

$$= \frac{2a+3}{x} \quad \longleftarrow \quad \text{Simplest form}$$

Problem: **b.** $\dfrac{3a}{2} - \dfrac{a+7}{2}$

Solution:

$$\frac{3a}{2} - \frac{a+7}{2} = \frac{3a-(a+7)}{2}$$

$$= \frac{3a-a-7}{2} \quad \longleftarrow \quad -(a+7) = (-1)(a+7) = -a-7$$

$$= \frac{2a-7}{2} \quad \longleftarrow \quad \text{Simplest form}$$

Adding or subtracting rational expressions with unlike denominators is similar to adding or subtracting fractions with unlike denominators. To add or subtract with unlike denominators, the first step is to find the LCD. The same is true for rational expressions.

Arithmetic	**Algebra**

$$\frac{2}{3} + \frac{4}{5} \longleftarrow \text{LCD: 15} \qquad\qquad \frac{a}{3x} + \frac{c}{2y} \longleftarrow \text{LCD: 6xy}$$

$$\frac{2}{3} + \frac{4}{5} = \left(\frac{2}{3}\cdot\frac{5}{5}\right) + \left(\frac{4}{5}\cdot\frac{3}{3}\right) \qquad \frac{a}{3x} + \frac{c}{2y} = \left(\frac{a}{3x}\cdot\frac{2y}{2y}\right) + \left(\frac{c}{2y}\cdot\frac{3x}{3x}\right)$$

$$= \frac{10}{15} + \frac{12}{15} \qquad\qquad\qquad\qquad = \frac{2ay}{6xy} + \frac{3cx}{6xy}$$

$$= \frac{22}{15}, \text{ or } 1\frac{7}{15} \qquad\qquad\qquad = \frac{2ay + 3cx}{6xy}$$

EXAMPLE 2 Add or subtract as indicated: $\dfrac{3}{x^2} + \dfrac{5}{2xy} - \dfrac{4}{3y^2}$

Solution: ☐1 Find the LCD.   LCD: $6x^2y^2$

☐2 Write equivalent expressions having $6x^2y^2$ as the denominator. That is,

multiply $\dfrac{3}{x^2}$ by $\dfrac{6y^2}{6y^2}$ because $(x^2)(6y^2) = 6x^2y^2$;

multiply $\dfrac{5}{2xy}$ by $\dfrac{3xy}{3xy}$ because $(2xy)(3xy) = 6x^2y^2$; and

multiply $\dfrac{4}{3y^2}$ by $\dfrac{2x^2}{2x^2}$ because $(3y^2)(2x^2) = 6x^2y^2$.

$$\frac{3}{x^2} + \frac{5}{2xy} - \frac{4}{3y^2} = \left(\frac{3}{x^2}\cdot\frac{6y^2}{6y^2}\right) + \left(\frac{5}{2xy}\cdot\frac{3xy}{3xy}\right) - \left(\frac{4}{3y^2}\cdot\frac{2x^2}{2x^2}\right)$$

$$= \frac{18y^2}{6x^2y^2} + \frac{15xy}{6x^2y^2} - \frac{8x^2}{6x^2y^2}$$

☐3 $$= \frac{18y^2 + 15xy - 8x^2}{6x^2y^2}$$

NOTE: Recall that multiplying a rational expression by an expression such as $\dfrac{6y^2}{6y^2}$ ($y \neq 0$) is equivalent to multiplying by 1.

EXAMPLE 3 Add or subtract as indicated: $\dfrac{x+1}{x^2-9} + \dfrac{4}{x+3} - \dfrac{x-1}{x-3}$

Solution: Factor the denominator, $x^2 - 9$. Then find the LCD.

$$\frac{x+1}{x^2-9} + \frac{4}{x+3} - \frac{x-1}{x-3} = \frac{x+1}{(x+3)(x-3)} + \frac{4}{x+3} - \frac{x-1}{x-3} \longleftarrow \text{LCD: } (x+3)(x-3)$$

$$= \frac{x + 1}{(x + 3)(x - 3)} + \left(\frac{4}{x + 3} \cdot \frac{x - 3}{x - 3}\right) - \left(\frac{x - 1}{x - 3} \cdot \frac{x + 3}{x + 3}\right)$$

$$= \frac{x + 1}{(x + 3)(x - 3)} + \frac{4(x - 3)}{(x + 3)(x - 3)} - \frac{(x - 1)(x + 3)}{(x + 3)(x - 3)}$$

$$= \frac{x + 1 + 4(x - 3) - (x - 1)(x + 3)}{(x + 3)(x - 3)}$$

$$= \frac{x + 1 + 4x - 12 - (x^2 + 2x - 3)}{(x + 3)(x - 3)} \longleftarrow \quad \textbf{Simplify.}$$

$$= \frac{5x - 11 - x^2 - 2x + 3}{(x + 3)(x - 3)}$$

$$= \frac{-x^2 + 3x - 8}{(x + 3)(x - 3)} \longleftarrow \quad \textbf{Simplest form}$$

The following is a summary of the procedure used to add or subtract rational expressions.

**UNLIKE
DENOMINATORS**

To add or subtract rational expressions:

1 Find the LCD of the denominators.

2 Write equivalent rational expressions having the LCD as denominators.

3 Add or subtract as indicated.

4 Write the answer in simplest form.

EXERCISES: Classwork/Homework

Objective: To add and subtract rational expressions

CHECK YOUR UNDERSTANDING

Complete.

1. $\frac{2}{x}\left(\frac{?}{?}\right) = \frac{2x}{x^2}$ 2. $\frac{3a}{2b}\left(\frac{?}{?}\right) = \frac{18a^2b}{12ab^2}$ 3. $\frac{5}{12xy}\left(\frac{?}{?}\right) = \frac{15xy}{36x^2y^2}$ 4. $\frac{5}{x + 1}\left(\frac{?}{?}\right) = \frac{5(x - 1)}{x^2 - 1}$

Find the missing numerator.

5. $\frac{3x}{4} = \frac{?}{12}$ 6. $\frac{3}{2t} = \frac{?}{12t}$ 7. $\frac{7x}{8} = \frac{?}{8xy^2}$ 8. $\frac{2x - 3}{x^2} = \frac{?}{x^2y}$

Add or subtract as indicated. Write the answers in simplest form.

9. $\dfrac{7}{b} + \dfrac{9}{b}$

10. $\dfrac{10}{c} - \dfrac{3}{c}$

11. $\dfrac{27}{q} + \dfrac{23}{q} - \dfrac{1}{q}$

12. $\dfrac{3a}{2} + \dfrac{(a+9)}{2}$

13. $\dfrac{17b}{3} + \dfrac{(2a-6)}{3}$

14. $\dfrac{(2a+6)}{4} + \dfrac{(3a-9)}{4}$

15. $\dfrac{17m}{6} + \dfrac{(3m+4)}{6}$

16. $\dfrac{(2a-3)}{2} - \dfrac{(6a+5)}{2}$

17. $\dfrac{(2a+9)}{4} - \dfrac{(2a-6)}{4}$

18. $\dfrac{(3x-2y)}{6} - \dfrac{(4x-5y)}{6}$

19. $\dfrac{(2a-7b)}{12} - \dfrac{(6a+6b)}{12}$

20. $\dfrac{2a}{x+5} + \dfrac{3a}{x+5}$

21. $\dfrac{m}{x-y} + \dfrac{n}{x-y}$

22. $\dfrac{2a}{x-4} - \dfrac{5a}{x-4}$

23. $\dfrac{7m}{2y+5} - \dfrac{6m}{2y+5}$

24. $\dfrac{x^2}{7} + \dfrac{x^2}{6}$

25. $\dfrac{2x}{3} + \dfrac{5y}{2}$

26. $\dfrac{x^2y}{6} + \dfrac{xy^2}{5}$

27. $\dfrac{7ab}{10} - \dfrac{3a}{4}$

28. $\dfrac{2a+3}{6} - \dfrac{5a-7}{9}$

29. $\dfrac{3x-5}{4} + \dfrac{5x-3}{3}$

30. $\dfrac{1}{a} + \dfrac{1}{b}$

31. $\dfrac{2}{a} + \dfrac{3}{b}$

32. $\dfrac{1}{a} - \dfrac{1}{b}$

33. $\dfrac{4}{x} - \dfrac{5}{y}$

34. $\dfrac{a}{b} - \dfrac{c}{d}$

35. $\dfrac{3}{2c} + \dfrac{4}{6c}$

36. $\dfrac{5}{4a} - \dfrac{3}{8a}$

37. $\dfrac{7a}{10p} - \dfrac{2b}{5p}$

38. $\dfrac{5r}{4c} + \dfrac{4s}{5d}$

39. $\dfrac{3}{x} + \dfrac{5}{x^2}$

40. $\dfrac{4a}{b^2} - \dfrac{3a}{b}$

41. $\dfrac{3}{x} + \dfrac{5}{x^3} + \dfrac{2}{x^2}$

42. $\dfrac{9}{mn} + \dfrac{3}{mn^2}$

43. $\dfrac{8}{x} + \dfrac{3}{xy}$

44. $\dfrac{1}{6p} - \dfrac{1}{4p} + \dfrac{1}{3p}$

45. $\dfrac{3}{b} + \dfrac{5}{2b} - \dfrac{11}{3b}$

46. $\dfrac{a+b}{b} - \dfrac{a-b}{a}$

47. $\dfrac{x+1}{2x} + \dfrac{2}{x}$

48. $\dfrac{5}{x+2} + \dfrac{3}{x-2}$

49. $\dfrac{5}{x+5} - \dfrac{3}{x-5}$

50. $\dfrac{2}{a+3} + \dfrac{5}{a+5}$

51. $\dfrac{2x}{x-y} - \dfrac{3y}{x+y}$

52. $\dfrac{a}{2a+2b} - \dfrac{b}{3a+3b}$

53. $\dfrac{4a}{6a-2b} + \dfrac{3b}{9a-3b}$

54. $\dfrac{2}{3t+3s} + \dfrac{3}{5t-5s}$

55. $\dfrac{3x}{2y-3} - \dfrac{2x}{3y-2}$

56. $\dfrac{x+3}{x-5} + \dfrac{x-5}{x+3}$

You can use the program on page 619 to add two fractions. Use the program to find $\frac{A}{B} + \frac{C}{D}$ for the given values of A, B, C, and D.

57. $A = 3; B = 4;$ $C = 2; D = 3$

58. $A = 7; B = 8;$ $C = 3; D = 5$

59. $A = 6; B = 7;$ $C = 4; D = 5$

■■■■ MAINTAIN

Divide. Express the answers in simplest form. (*Pages 429–432*)

60. $\frac{a}{y} \div \frac{y}{t}$ **61.** $\frac{xt}{ab} \div \frac{xt}{bc}$ **62.** $\frac{1}{r} \div \frac{1}{g}$ **63.** $\frac{5x^2}{21xz^3} \div \frac{25x}{27yz}$

Simplify. No variable equals zero. (*Pages 340–342*)

64. 4^3 **65.** 10^5 **66.** 8^0 **67.** $4a^{-3}$ **68.** 10^{-2}

Write in scientific notation. (*Pages 343–346*)

69. 46,500 **70.** 0.00023 **71.** 200,500

72. 0.0000008 **73.** 169 million **74.** 6 thousandths

■■■■ CONNECT AND EXTEND

Add or subtract as indicated. Write the answers in simplest form.

75. $\frac{4a}{2a + 6} - \frac{a - 1}{a + 3}$

76. $\frac{x - 6y}{2x^2 - 5xy + 2y^2} - \frac{7}{x + 2y}$

77. $\frac{2x}{x^2 - 25} - \frac{4(x - 5)}{x - 5}$

78. $\frac{7}{a^2 + a - 2} - \frac{5}{a^2 - 4a + 3}$

79. Write a rational expression that, when subtracted from $\frac{3x - 7}{2x + 3}$, gives a difference of $\frac{x - 5}{2x + 3}$.

80. Write a rational expression that, when added to $\frac{3}{x + 4}$, gives a sum of $\frac{7x + 5}{x^2 + 4x}$.

■■■■ NON-ROUTINE PROBLEMS

81. A train is one mile long and is traveling at a rate of one mile per minute. How long will it take the train to pass through a tunnel one mile long?

82. Alberto has a 3-liter jar and a 5-liter jar. Using these two jars only, how can he measure exactly 4 liters of water?

Simplify. No denominator equals zero. (*Pages 421–424*)

1. $\dfrac{16c}{28cd}$

2. $\dfrac{2a + b}{4a^2 - b^2}$

3. $\dfrac{3x + 3y}{x^2 + 2xy + y^2}$

4. $\dfrac{6x^2 - 13xy + 6y^2}{6y^2 - 7xy + 2x^2}$

Multiply. Write each product in simplest form. (*Pages 425–428*)

5. $\dfrac{ah}{4x} \cdot \dfrac{x}{h}$

6. $(x + 1) \cdot \dfrac{x - 3}{x - 1}$

7. $\dfrac{x^2 - 3x - 10}{x^2 - 2x} \cdot \dfrac{x^2 - 3x + 2}{x^2 - 25}$

Divide. Write each answer in simplest form. (*Pages 429–432*)

8. $\dfrac{x}{3} \div \dfrac{x}{a}$

9. $\dfrac{4ab}{x} \div \dfrac{8a^2}{x^2}$

10. $\dfrac{a^2 - 2a - 3}{a^2 + a - 2} \div \dfrac{a - 3}{2a^2 + 2a - 4}$

Find the LCD of the rational expressions having the given denominators. (*Pages 433–436*)

11. $3; 11$

12. $2ab^2; 4a^2$

13. $(x^2 - 2x - 8); (x^2 - 3x - 4)$

Add or subtract as indicated. Write each answer in simplest form. (*Pages 437–441*)

14. $\dfrac{2a + 4}{a + b} + \dfrac{3a - 5}{a + b}$

15. $\dfrac{3}{xy^2} + \dfrac{2}{x^2y}$

16. $\dfrac{x}{x^2 - 4} + \dfrac{1}{x^2 + 2x}$

17. $\dfrac{s}{r^2 - s^2} - \dfrac{r + s}{r - s}$

18. $\dfrac{a}{2(a - 3)} - \dfrac{5}{a^2 - 9}$

19. $\dfrac{5}{x + 4} - \dfrac{3}{x - 3}$

Historical Digest: Galileo

The formula, d = $16t^2$, where distance is measured in feet and time is measured in seconds, can be used to find the distance traveled by a falling object. **Galileo Galilei,** an Italian astronomer, worked on this formula about four hundred years ago in his home-town of Pisa, Italy. He dropped two balls of the same size but different weights from the Leaning Tower of Pisa. Just as he thought, they hit the ground at the same time. Notice that this should make sense from the formula since there is no variable needed for the weight of the object.

Suppose you had seen Galileo drop a ball from a tower and it took 3 seconds for the ball to hit the ground. How tall was the tower?

Perform the indicated operations. (*Pages 64–65, 351–352*)

1. $5 - (t - 1)(t - 1)$ **2.** $(b + 1)(b + 1) + 1$ **3.** $a(a - 1) - 1$

4. $2(c + d) + 2c + 2d$ **5.** $12(a - 2) + a + 2$ **6.** $(x - 5)(x + 3) - x$

7. $7(y + z) + 2y$ **8.** $5r - 2(r^2 - 4)$ **9.** $5t + 1 + (t - 4)(t + 4)$

11-6   Mixed Expressions: Addition/Subtraction

Recall that numbers such as $4\frac{1}{2}$ and $5\frac{2}{3}$ are called **mixed numbers.** They indicate the sum of a whole number and a fraction.

$$4\tfrac{1}{2} = 4 + \tfrac{1}{2} \qquad\qquad 5\tfrac{2}{3} = 5 + \tfrac{2}{3}$$

The sum or difference of rational expressions where one rational expression has a denominator of 1 is called a **mixed expression.**

EXAMPLE 1   Add: $t + \dfrac{5}{2t}$

Solution: Write t as $\frac{t}{1}$. Then identify the LCD.

$$t + \frac{5}{2t} = \frac{t}{1} + \frac{5}{2t} \quad\longleftarrow\quad \textbf{LCD: 2t}$$

$$= \left(\frac{t}{1} \cdot \frac{2t}{2t}\right) + \frac{5}{2t}$$

$$= \frac{2t^2}{2t} + \frac{5}{2t}$$

$$= \frac{2t^2 + 5}{2t} \quad\longleftarrow\quad \textbf{Simplest form}$$

The method of Example 1 can also be used when the operation is subtraction.

Rational Expressions   **443**

EXAMPLE 2 Subtract: $a + 1 - \dfrac{1}{a - 1}$

Solution: $\quad a + 1 - \dfrac{1}{a - 1} = \dfrac{a + 1}{1} - \dfrac{1}{a - 1}$ ⟵ **LCD: (a − 1)**

$$= \left(\dfrac{a + 1}{1} \cdot \dfrac{a - 1}{a - 1} \right) - \dfrac{1}{a - 1}$$

$$= \dfrac{(a + 1)(a - 1)}{1(a - 1)} - \dfrac{1}{a - 1}$$

$$= \dfrac{a^2 - 1}{a - 1} - \dfrac{1}{a - 1}$$

$$= \dfrac{a^2 - 1 - 1}{a - 1}$$

$$= \dfrac{a^2 - 2}{a - 1}$$

EXERCISES: Classwork/Homework

Objective: To add or subtract a polynomial and a rational expression

CHECK YOUR UNDERSTANDING

Complete.

1. Numbers that indicate the sum of a whole number and a fraction, such as $2\frac{1}{2}$ and $5\frac{6}{7}$, are called __?__.

2. A mixed expression is the sum or difference of rational expressions where one rational expression has a denominator of __?__.

Replace each __?__ with the correct polynomial.

3. $4 + \dfrac{1}{d} = \left(\dfrac{4}{1} \cdot \dfrac{?}{d} \right) + \dfrac{1}{d}$

$\qquad = \dfrac{?}{d} + \dfrac{1}{d}$

$\qquad = \dfrac{?}{d}$

4. $2 - \dfrac{3}{2p} = \left(\dfrac{2}{1} \cdot \dfrac{?}{2p} \right) - \dfrac{3}{2p}$

$\qquad = \dfrac{?}{2p} - \dfrac{3}{2p}$

$\qquad = \dfrac{?}{2p}$

PRACTICE AND APPLY

Add or subtract as indicated. Write the answers in simplest form.

5. $3 + \dfrac{1}{a}$

6. $s - \dfrac{5}{3s}$

7. $3 + \dfrac{a}{b}$

8. $1 + \dfrac{3}{x + 1}$

9. $7 - \dfrac{4}{a - b}$

10. $7 + \dfrac{2x}{y + z}$

11. $a + \dfrac{1}{a + 1}$

12. $a - \dfrac{1}{a - 1}$

13. $9 - \dfrac{2r}{r + s}$

14. $\dfrac{4}{z - 2} + 4$

15. $10 + \dfrac{c + 2}{c - 3}$

16. $18 - \dfrac{a + b}{a - b}$

17. $ax + \dfrac{b}{x}$

18. $2x - \dfrac{x + y}{y}$

19. $a - \dfrac{b}{c}$

20. $\dfrac{a}{x} - (a - 1)$

21. $a^2 + \dfrac{1}{a}$

22. $\dfrac{4a}{(a - 2)^2} + 1$

23. $\dfrac{3r}{r^2 - 9} - 2$

24. $2 + \dfrac{2x + 3y}{x + y}$

25. $(a + 1) + \dfrac{1}{a + 1}$

26. $6 + \dfrac{5}{4x - 2}$

27. $\dfrac{8}{3x - 1} - 6$

28. $\dfrac{5}{t - 1} - (t - 1)$

29. $(x - 5) - \dfrac{x}{x + 3}$

30. $\dfrac{2a - 1}{a + 2} + (2a - 3)$

31. $(2t - 1) - \dfrac{4t}{t + 6}$

32. $\dfrac{x - 7}{2x + 5} + (x - 4)$

33. $\dfrac{5t + 1}{t - 4} + (t + 4)$

34. $(a + 6) + \dfrac{3a - 4}{a + 6}$

35. $(a + 2) + \dfrac{5}{a - 2}$

36. $4 - \dfrac{3}{t - 1} - \dfrac{1}{t + 1}$

37. $\dfrac{x}{x + 2} + \dfrac{x}{x - 2} - 1$

▬▬▬▬ **MAINTAIN**

Add or subtract as indicated. Write the answers in simplest form.
(*Pages 437–441*)

38. $\dfrac{16c}{5} + \dfrac{(9c - 2)}{5}$

39. $\dfrac{(3a - 2c)}{9} - \dfrac{(7a + 5c)}{9}$

40. $\dfrac{4r}{7} + \dfrac{r + s}{3}$

41. $\dfrac{9m}{5y + 3} - \dfrac{2m}{5y + 3}$

42. $\dfrac{6x}{3} + \dfrac{2y}{5}$

43. $\dfrac{1}{c} - \dfrac{1}{d}$

44. $\dfrac{x + 1}{x} - \dfrac{x - 1}{6x}$

45. $\dfrac{x^2 y}{7d} + \dfrac{x^2 y}{4d}$

46. $\dfrac{1}{6a} + \dfrac{1}{3a} - \dfrac{1}{2a}$

Find the LCD of rational expressions having the given denominators.
(*Pages 433–436*)

47. $4;\ 15$

48. $5c;\ 8cd$

49. $6;\ 3;\ 8$

50. $r^2 s;\ st;\ s^2$

51. $(m + n);\ (m - n)$

52. $(x^2 - 1);\ (x + 1)$

53. $(a^2 - 4);\ (a + 2)^2$

Subtract. (*Pages 347–350*)

54. $9x - 3$
$\underline{7x + 9}$

55. $m - n + b$
$\underline{m + n - b}$

56. $2x^2 y - 4x$
$\underline{17x^2 y \qquad + 8}$

Rational Expressions **445**

Find the perimeter of each polygon. (*Pages 347–350*)

57.

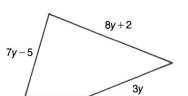

58.

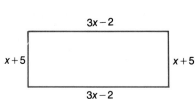

59.

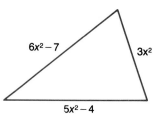

CONNECT AND EXTEND

Add or subtract as indicated. Write the answers in simplest form.

60. $\dfrac{x^2}{x + y} - \dfrac{y^2}{x - y} - (x - y)$

61. $\dfrac{7}{x - 5} + (x^2 + 2x - 3)$

62. $(a^2 + 3a + 1) + \dfrac{4}{a - 5}$

63. $\dfrac{7}{x - 2} + x^2 + \dfrac{4}{x + 2} + 4$

64. $\dfrac{\frac{1}{2} - \frac{1}{3}}{\frac{1}{2} + \frac{1}{3}}$

65. $\dfrac{\frac{3}{4} + \frac{2}{5}}{\frac{3}{4} - \frac{2}{5}}$

66. $\dfrac{\frac{1}{a} - \frac{1}{2a}}{\frac{2}{a}}$

67. $\dfrac{1 - \frac{9}{x^2}}{x + 3}$

68. $\dfrac{\frac{a}{b} + 1}{\frac{a}{b} - 1}$

69. $\dfrac{\frac{3a}{2} + 1}{\frac{3a}{4} - \frac{1}{3a}}$

70. $\dfrac{\frac{r^2 + t^2}{rt} + 2}{\frac{r^2 - t^2}{2rt}}$

71. $\dfrac{1 + \frac{2r}{r^2 + 1}}{1 - \frac{2r + 2}{r^2 + 1}}$

NON-ROUTINE PROBLEM

72. The 5 short pieces of chain shown below must be linked together to form one long chain. Explain how the pieces can be linked together by cutting only three of the rings.

——— **REVIEW CAPSULE FOR SECTION 11-7** ———

Solve and check each equation. (*Pages 103–107, 404–406*)

1. $9a - 2a = 42$

2. $6c + 8 = 4c$

3. $12 - 4x = 8x$

4. $7n + 4 - 3n - 6 = 10$

5. $15x = 56 + x^2$

6. $6b - 15 = -9b + 45$

7. $y^2 = -6y + 27$

8. $4x^2 - 9 = 0$

9. $2y^2 + 7 = y^2 - 2y + 10$

11-7   Equations with Rational Expressions

The following example shows how to solve equations containing rational expressions.

EXAMPLE 1   Solve: $\frac{n}{3} + \frac{n}{2} = 1$

Solution:

$$\frac{n}{3} + \frac{n}{2} = 1 \qquad \longleftarrow \qquad \textbf{The LCD is 6.}$$
$$\textbf{Multiply each side by 6.}$$

$$6\left(\frac{n}{3} + \frac{n}{2}\right) = 6(1)$$

$$6 \cdot \frac{n}{3} + 6 \cdot \frac{n}{2} = 6 \cdot 1 \qquad \longleftarrow \qquad \textbf{By the distributive postulate}$$

$$2n + 3n = 6 \qquad \longleftarrow \qquad \textbf{Solve for } \textbf{\textit{n}}.$$

$$5n = 6$$

$$n = \frac{6}{5}$$

Check: $\frac{n}{3} + \frac{n}{2} = 1$

$$\frac{\frac{6}{5}}{3} + \frac{\frac{6}{5}}{2} \stackrel{?}{=} 1 \qquad \longleftarrow \qquad \textbf{Simplify each addend.}$$

$$\frac{\frac{6}{5}}{3} = \frac{6}{5} \div 3 = \frac{\overset{2}{\cancel{6}}}{5} \cdot \frac{1}{\underset{1}{\cancel{3}}} = \frac{2}{5} \quad \text{and}$$

$$\frac{\frac{6}{5}}{2} = \frac{6}{5} \div 2 = \frac{\overset{3}{\cancel{6}}}{5} \cdot \frac{1}{\underset{1}{\cancel{2}}} = \frac{3}{5}.$$

$$\frac{2}{5} + \frac{3}{5} \stackrel{?}{=} 1$$

$$1 = 1 \quad \text{Yes} \checkmark \qquad \textbf{Solution set: } \left\{\frac{6}{5}\right\}$$

REMEMBER: Multiply each side of an equation containing rational expressions by the LCD.

The equation in Example 2 contains rational expressions that have a variable in the denominator. Recall that values of the variable that could make a denominator equal zero must be excluded. Thus, in Example 2, x cannot equal 2 or 4.

EXAMPLE 2 Solve: $\dfrac{7}{x-4} - \dfrac{5}{x-2} = 0$

Solution: $\dfrac{7}{x-4} - \dfrac{5}{x-2} = 0$ ⟵ The LCD is $(x-4)(x-2)$ $x \neq 4$, $x \neq 2$. Multiply each side by $(x-4)(x-2)$.

$$(x-4)(x-2)\left(\frac{7}{x-4} - \frac{5}{x-2}\right) = (x-4)(x-2)(0)$$

$7(x-2) - 5(x-4) = 0$ ⟵ Simplify.

$7x - 14 - 5x + 20 = 0$

$2x + 6 = 0$

$2x = -6$

$x = -3$ ⟵ Remember: $x \neq 2$ and $x \neq 4$

Check: $\dfrac{7}{x-4} - \dfrac{5}{x-2} = 0$ ⟵ Replace x with -3.

$\dfrac{7}{-3-4} - \dfrac{5}{-3-2} \overset{?}{=} 0$

$\dfrac{7}{-7} - \dfrac{5}{-5} \overset{?}{=} 0$ ⟵ $-\left(\dfrac{5}{-5}\right) = -(-1) = 1$

$-1 + 1 \overset{?}{=} 0$ Yes ✔ **Solution set: $\{-3\}$.**

APPARENT SOLUTION Sometimes the number obtained as a solution to an equation does not check in the original equation. The number is only an **apparent solution** (not a solution at all). This is why it is important to check.

EXAMPLE 3 Solve: $\dfrac{x}{10} + \dfrac{1}{x-1} = \dfrac{x+1}{2x-2}$

Solution: $\dfrac{x}{10} + \dfrac{1}{x-1} = \dfrac{x+1}{2x-2}$ ⟵ Factor $2x - 2$.

$\dfrac{x}{10} + \dfrac{1}{x-1} = \dfrac{x+1}{2(x-1)}$ ⟵ LCD: $10(x-1)$, $x \neq 1$

$$10(x-1)\left(\frac{x}{10} + \frac{1}{x-1}\right) = [10(x-1)]\left[\frac{x+1}{2(x-1)}\right]$$

$$10(x - 1)\left(\frac{x}{10}\right) + 10(x - 1)\left(\frac{1}{x - 1}\right) = 5(x + 1)$$

$$(x - 1)x + 10 = 5(x + 1)$$

$$x^2 - x + 10 = 5x + 5 \quad \longleftarrow \quad \text{Write in the form } x^2 + bx + c = 0.$$

$$x^2 - 6x + 5 = 0 \quad \longleftarrow \quad \text{Factor } x^2 - 6x + 5.$$

$$(x - 5)(x - 1) = 0$$

$$x - 5 = 0 \quad \text{or} \quad x - 1 = 0$$

$$x = 5 \quad \text{or} \quad x = 1 \quad \longleftarrow \quad \text{Remember: } x \neq 1$$

Note what happens when you check both solutions.

Check: $\dfrac{x}{10} + \dfrac{1}{x - 1} = \dfrac{x + 1}{2x - 2}$ $\longleftarrow$ **Replace x with 5.** $\dfrac{x}{10} + \dfrac{1}{x - 1} = \dfrac{x + 1}{2x - 2}$ $\longleftarrow$ **Replace x with 1.**

$$\frac{5}{10} + \frac{1}{4} \overset{?}{=} \frac{6}{8} \qquad\qquad\qquad \frac{1}{10} + \frac{1}{0} \overset{?}{=} \frac{2}{0}$$

$$\frac{1}{2} + \frac{1}{4} \overset{?}{=} \frac{3}{4} \qquad\qquad \text{Since division by 0 is not defined, 1 is not a solution.}$$

$$\frac{3}{4} \overset{?}{=} \frac{3}{4} \quad \text{Yes} \checkmark \qquad \textbf{Solution set: } \{5\}$$

To solve equations containing rational expressions, follow these steps.

Steps for Solving Equations with Rational Expressions

1 Multiply **each side** of the equation by the LCD.

2 Follow the usual procedures to solve the resulting equation.

3 Check the answers.

EXERCISES: Classwork/Homework

Objective: To solve equations containing rational expressions

CHECK YOUR UNDERSTANDING

1. *Complete:* To solve equations containing rational expressions, first multiply each side of the equation by the __?__ .

2. In the equation $\dfrac{8}{x - 3} + \dfrac{9}{x - 5} = 0$, why can x not equal 3 or 5?

In Exercises 3–8, by what polynomial would you multiply each side of the equation in order to obtain an equation without rational expressions?

3. $\dfrac{7}{n} - \dfrac{1}{2} = 3$

4. $\dfrac{5}{6x} + 3 = \dfrac{1}{2x}$

5. $\dfrac{x+2}{x-1} = 2$

6. $\dfrac{6}{x+3} = \dfrac{3}{8}\,8$

7. $\dfrac{8}{x} - \dfrac{4}{2x} = 1$

8. $\dfrac{10}{x-3} = \dfrac{9}{x-5}$

■■■■■■ **PRACTICE AND APPLY**

Solve each equation.

9. $\dfrac{a}{3} - \dfrac{a}{4} = 2$

10. $\dfrac{b}{4} - \dfrac{b}{5} = 2$

11. $\dfrac{3a}{5} + \dfrac{3}{2} = \dfrac{7a}{10}$

12. $\dfrac{4d}{7} + \dfrac{5}{4} = \dfrac{17d}{28}$

13. $\dfrac{3t}{4} + \dfrac{5}{3} = \dfrac{7t}{6}$

14. $\dfrac{3m}{2} + \dfrac{5}{3} = \dfrac{7m}{6}$

15. $\dfrac{2}{x} = 3$

16. $\dfrac{3}{a} = -4$

17. $\dfrac{2}{3x} = \dfrac{1}{9}$

18. $\dfrac{3}{2x} - \dfrac{1}{3} = \dfrac{5}{6x}$

19. $\dfrac{5}{6x} + 3 = \dfrac{1}{2x}$

20. $\dfrac{3}{10x} - \dfrac{3}{5} = \dfrac{2}{5x}$

21. $\dfrac{5}{n} - \dfrac{1}{2} = 2$

22. $\dfrac{4}{x} + \dfrac{3}{2x} = \dfrac{11}{6}$

23. $\dfrac{2n+1}{2n} - \dfrac{3n-2}{3n} = \dfrac{7}{12}$

24. $\dfrac{4}{2x} - 3 = \dfrac{-2}{5x} - \dfrac{3}{5}$

25. $\dfrac{4}{3x} - \dfrac{5}{2x} = 5 - \dfrac{1}{6x}$

26. $\dfrac{7}{4x} - 2 = \dfrac{3}{2x} - 4$

27. $\dfrac{3}{2} = \dfrac{x}{x+2}$

28. $\dfrac{b-2}{b+3} = \dfrac{3}{8}$

29. $\dfrac{x-7}{x+2} = \dfrac{1}{4}$

30. $\dfrac{5}{a+3} = \dfrac{2}{2}$

31. $\dfrac{a-1}{a-2} = 1.5$

32. $\dfrac{y}{y-3} = \dfrac{6}{3}$

33. $\dfrac{2}{x+3} = \dfrac{5}{x}$

34. $\dfrac{t+1}{t-1} = \dfrac{2}{t-1} + \dfrac{t}{8}$

35. $\dfrac{b}{6} + \dfrac{1}{b-1} = \dfrac{b+1}{2b-2}$

36. $\dfrac{x}{3} + \dfrac{2x^2}{3x-4} = \dfrac{9x-2}{9}$

37. $\dfrac{2x-1}{2} - \dfrac{x+2}{2x+5} = \dfrac{6x-5}{6}$

38. $\dfrac{7}{x-4} = \dfrac{5}{x-2}$

39. $\dfrac{10}{x-3} = \dfrac{9}{x-5}$

40. $\dfrac{x+5}{x-3} + \dfrac{4}{x-3} = 5$

41. $\dfrac{x+2}{x+4} = \dfrac{x+6}{x-8}$

42. $\dfrac{x-1}{x+1} = \dfrac{x+3}{x+10}$

43. $\dfrac{x-3}{x+5} = \dfrac{x-2}{x+2}$

44. $\dfrac{x}{x-3} + \dfrac{2}{x+4} = 1$

45. $\dfrac{3x}{x-2} - 3 = \dfrac{4}{x+2}$

46. $\dfrac{2x}{x-4} - \dfrac{4}{x+5} = 2$

47. $\dfrac{5x}{x+1} - \dfrac{x}{x+6} = 4$

48. $\dfrac{x-1}{x+1} - \dfrac{2x}{x-1} = -1$ **49.** $\dfrac{6}{4x} = \dfrac{x+2}{x^2-3x}$

50. $6 + \dfrac{20}{x^2-1} = \dfrac{10}{x-1}$

Add or subtract as indicated. Write the answers in simplest form.
(*Pages 443–446*)

51. $3x - \dfrac{x - y}{x}$

52. $ay + \dfrac{b}{x}$

53. $12 + \dfrac{a - 3}{a + 7}$

54. $\dfrac{9}{x - 1} - 4$

55. $(m + 1) + \dfrac{1}{m + 1}$

56. $5c - \dfrac{c + d}{d}$

Add or subtract as indicated. Write the answers in simplest form.
(*Pages 437–441*)

57. $\dfrac{(4m - 8b)}{15} - \dfrac{(9m + 6b)}{15}$

58. $\dfrac{r + 2}{4r} + \dfrac{3}{r}$

59. $\dfrac{6x + 3y}{9} - \dfrac{2x + 4y}{6}$

60. $\dfrac{6d}{c + 9} + \dfrac{8d}{c + 9}$

Multiply. (*Pages 351–354*)

61. $-4xy(6x - 2y)$

62. $-2mn(5m^2 - 4mn + 6n^2)$

63. $(y - 9)(y + 7)$

64. $(3b + 4c)(2b - c)$

CONNECT AND EXTEND

Solve each equation.

65. $\dfrac{3}{3x^2 - 3x - 28} = \dfrac{5}{5x^2 - x - 20}$

66. $\dfrac{2x + 1}{x - 1} - \dfrac{3x}{x + 2} = \dfrac{-x^2 - 2}{x^2 + x - 2}$

67. $\dfrac{a}{a - 2} = \dfrac{a + 3}{a + 2} - \dfrac{a}{a^2 - 4}$

68. $\dfrac{3(x - 4)}{4x^2 - 9} = \dfrac{3x}{4x^2 - 16x + 15}$

69. For what value of k will the solution set of $\dfrac{a - 2}{5a} = \dfrac{1}{k} - \dfrac{4}{15a}$ be {4}?

70. For what value of k will the solution set of $\dfrac{k}{3t} = \dfrac{t - 5}{t^2 - 4t}$ be $\left\{\dfrac{5}{2}\right\}$?

NON-ROUTINE PROBLEMS

71. A three-digit number is between 300 and 500. The sum of the digits is 12. The sum of the hundred's digit and the one's digit equals the ten's digit. Find the number.

72. Two shirts and one jacket cost the same amount as two sweaters. One sweater and two shirts cost the same amount as one jacket. Which costs the least—a shirt, a jacket, or a sweater?

Rational Expressions **451**

Dimensional Analysis

At automobile proving grounds, **test engineers** study the performance of new cars under all kinds of road conditions. Instruments installed in the cars measure the efficiency of springs, shock absorbers, seat cushions, and other equipment. Test engineers also use human-size dummies to learn how to make cars both comfortable and safe.

While testing the effect of braking on a new type of tire, an engineer used these facts to change miles per hour to feet per second.

$$1 \text{ h} = 60 \text{ min} \qquad 1 \text{ min} = 60 \text{ s}$$
$$1 \text{ mi} = 5{,}280 \text{ ft}$$

EXAMPLE 1: A car is traveling at 84 miles per hour. How many feet per second is this?

Solution:

1️⃣ Change mi/h to mi/min.

$$84 \, \frac{\text{mi}}{\cancel{\text{h}}} \cdot \frac{1 \, \cancel{\text{h}}}{60 \, \text{min}} \quad \longleftarrow \quad \textbf{The "hours" cancel to give mi/min.}$$

$$\frac{84}{60} \, \frac{\text{mi}}{\text{min}}, \text{ or } \frac{7}{5} \, \text{mi/min}$$

2️⃣ Change mi/min to mi/s.

$$\frac{7}{5} \, \frac{\text{mi}}{\cancel{\text{min}}} \cdot \frac{1 \, \cancel{\text{min}}}{60 \, \text{s}} = \frac{7}{300} \, \text{mi/s}$$

3️⃣ Change mi/s to ft/s.

$$\frac{7}{300} \, \frac{\cancel{\text{mi}}}{\text{s}} \cdot \frac{5{,}280 \, \text{ft}}{1 \, \cancel{\text{mi}}} = \frac{7(5{,}280)}{300} \, \frac{\text{ft}}{\text{s}}$$

$$= \textbf{123.2 ft/s}$$

So 84 mi/h = **123.2 ft/s.**

In Example 1, you could also have solved the problem by first changing miles per hour to feet per hour. Then you would change feet per hour to feet per second. The procedure is shown below in one step.

$$84 \, \frac{\text{mi}}{\text{h}} \cdot \frac{5{,}280 \, \text{ft}}{1 \, \text{mi}} \cdot \frac{1 \, \text{h}}{60 \, \text{min}} \cdot \frac{1 \, \text{min}}{60 \, \text{s}} = \frac{84 \cdot 5{,}280}{60 \cdot 60} \, \frac{\text{ft}}{\text{s}}$$

$$= \textbf{123.2 ft/s}$$

The procedure of converting measurements from one unit to another is called **dimensional analysis.** When working with area and volume, dimensional analysis may also be used in converting measurements with square units and cubic units respectively. The procedure has the advantage of reducing the number of measurement facts that must be memorized.

EXAMPLE 2: Find the number of square feet (ft^2) in 8 square yards (yd^2).

Think: 3 ft = 1 yd, or 3 ft/yd, or $\dfrac{3 \text{ ft}}{1 \text{ yd}}$.

Solution: $\dfrac{8 \text{ yd}^2}{1} \cdot \left(\dfrac{3 \text{ ft}}{1 \text{ yd}}\right)^2 = \dfrac{8 \cancel{\text{ yd}^2}}{1} \cdot \dfrac{9 \text{ ft}^2}{1 \cancel{\text{ yd}^2}}$

$\qquad\qquad = \textbf{72 ft}^2$

EXERCISES

Use dimensional analysis to solve each problem.

1. Convert 26.2 miles, the average length of a marathon, to inches.

2. Convert 144 inches to yards.

3. How many square inches are there in 24 ft^2?

4. How many cubic yards are there in 135 ft^3?

5. Convert 60 miles per hour to miles per second.

6. Convert 10 ounces per pint to pounds per quart.

7. A skydiver "free falls" at a rate of 120 miles per hour. How many feet per second is this?

8. A secretary can type a page of manuscript in 4 minutes. How many hours will it take to type 45 manuscript pages?

9. Jeff drove for 8 hours at an average speed of 50 miles per hour. The car averaged 25 miles per gallon of gas. What was the cost of fuel if it is selling at $1.05 per gallon?

10. A construction crew uses 135 ft^3 of sand per day. If sand weighs 1.2 tons per cubic yard, how many pounds of sand is used per day? (HINT: 1 ton = 2000 pounds)

11-8   Number Problems

Some number problems can be represented by equations involving rational expressions.

EXAMPLE 1   When the same number is subtracted from the numerator and added to the denominator of $\frac{17}{22}$ (Condition 1), the result is $\frac{5}{8}$ (Condition 2). What is the number?

Solution: **1 Find:**   The number to be subtracted from 17 and added to 22

Given: The same number is subtracted from the numerator and added to the denominator. ◄——— **Condition 1**

The new fraction equals $\frac{5}{8}$. ◄——— **Condition 2**

Represent the unknowns.
Let x = the number to be added and subtracted.

Original fraction: $\frac{17}{22}$ New fraction: $\frac{17 - x}{22 + x}$

2 Write an equation to "connect" Condition 1 and Condition 2.

$$\frac{17 - x}{22 + x} = \frac{5}{8}$$

3 Solve the equation.

$$8(22 + x)\left(\frac{17 - x}{22 + x}\right) = 8(22 + x)\left(\frac{5}{8}\right)$$ ◄——— **LCD: 8(22 + x), x ≠ −22**

$$8(17 - x) = (22 + x)5$$ ◄——— **Multiply**

$$136 - 8x = 110 + 5x$$ ◄——— **Solve for x**

$$2 = x$$

4 Check: $\frac{17 - 2}{22 + 2} \overset{?}{=} \frac{5}{8}$

$\frac{15}{24} \overset{?}{=} \frac{5}{8}$ Yes ✔   The number is **2.**

Recall that any two numbers whose product is 1 are *reciprocals* or *multiplicative inverses* of each other.

Thus, $\frac{2}{3}$ and $\frac{3}{2}$ are **reciprocals** because $\frac{2}{3} \cdot \frac{3}{2} = 1.$

Also, -5 **and** $-\frac{1}{5}$ are **reciprocals** because $-5\left(-\frac{1}{5}\right) = 1.$

EXAMPLE 2 One positive number is three times another positive number (Condition 1). The difference of their reciprocals is $\frac{1}{6}$ (Condition 2). Find the numbers.

Solution: **1** **Find:** Two positive numbers

Given: One positive number is three times another.

The difference of their reciprocals is $\frac{1}{6}$.

Let $a =$ the smaller positive number.
Then $3a =$ the larger number.

Reciprocals: $\frac{1}{a}$ and $\frac{1}{3a}$, $a \neq 0$

2 **Think:** You know that $3a > a$. Therefore, $\frac{1}{a} > \frac{1}{3a}$.
Subtract $\frac{1}{3a}$ from $\frac{1}{a}$.

$$\underbrace{\text{Larger number}}_{\dfrac{1}{a}} \; \underbrace{\text{minus}}_{-} \; \underbrace{\text{smaller number}}_{\dfrac{1}{3a}} \; \text{is} \; \frac{1}{6}$$

Translate: $\quad \dfrac{1}{a} \quad - \quad \dfrac{1}{3a} \quad = \dfrac{1}{6}$

3 $6a\left(\dfrac{1}{a} - \dfrac{1}{3a}\right) = 6a\left(\dfrac{1}{6}\right)$

$\qquad 6 - 2 = a$

$\qquad\quad 4 = a \quad \longleftarrow \quad$ **Don't forget to find 3a.**

$\qquad 12 = 3a$

4 **Check:** **Condition 1** Does $12 = 3 \cdot 4$? Yes ✔

Condition 2 Does $\frac{1}{4} - \frac{1}{12} = \frac{1}{6}$? Yes ✔

The numbers are **4** and **12**.

Objective: To solve number problems involving rational expressions

▬▬▬▬ CHECK YOUR UNDERSTANDING

Complete. Use >, = , or < to compare the numbers.

1. If $5 > 3$, then $\frac{1}{5}$ __?__ $\frac{1}{3}$.

2. If $2 < 6$, then $\frac{1}{2}$ __?__ $\frac{1}{6}$.

3. If $12a > a$, then $\frac{1}{12a}$ __?__ $\frac{1}{a}$

4. If $p < 3p$, then $\frac{1}{a}$ __?__ $\frac{1}{3p}$.

5. If $x < x + 2$, then $\frac{1}{x}$ __?__ $\frac{1}{x + 2}$.

6. If $b > b - 1$, then $\frac{1}{b - 1}$ __?__ $\frac{1}{b}$.

In Exercises 7–10:
a. Use Condition 1 to represent the unknown(s).
b. Use Condition 2 to write an equation for the problem.

7. What number added to both numerator and denominator of the fraction $\frac{3}{7}$ (Condition 1) results in a fraction equal to $\frac{3}{5}$ (Condition 2)?

8. What number added to both the numerator and denominator of the fraction $\frac{4}{9}$ (Condition 1) results in a fraction equal to $\frac{2}{3}$ (Condition 2)?

9. One positive number is 4 times another (Condition 1). The difference of their reciprocals is $\frac{3}{8}$ (Condition 2). Find the numbers.

10. A positive number is twice another (Condition 1). The sum of their reciprocals is $\frac{1}{2}$ (Condition 2). Find the numbers.

▬▬▬▬ PRACTICE AND APPLY

Solve each problem.

11. What number must be added to both the numerator and denominator of the fraction $\frac{5}{8}$ to make a fraction equal to $\frac{3}{4}$?

12. What number must be subtracted from both the numerator and denominator of the fraction $\frac{7}{12}$ to make a fraction equal to $\frac{1}{2}$?

13. One positive number is 5 times another positive number. The difference of their reciprocals is $\frac{2}{5}$. Find the numbers.

14. One positive number is 3 times another positive number. The sum of their reciprocals is $\frac{2}{3}$. Find the numbers.

15. What number must be added to the numerator and subtracted from the denominator of $\frac{17}{32}$ to make a fraction equal to $\frac{3}{4}$?

16. What number must be subtracted from the numerator and added to the denominator of $\frac{13}{23}$ to make a fraction equal to $\frac{1}{3}$?

17. The numerator of a fraction is 3 less than its denominator. If 2 is added to the numerator, the value of the fraction becomes $\frac{3}{4}$. What is the fraction?

18. The denominator of a fraction is 4 more than its numerator. If 6 is added to the denominator, the value of the fraction becomes $\frac{1}{3}$. What is the fraction?

19. One number is 4 more than another. The quotient of the greater divided by the smaller is $\frac{5}{2}$. Find the numbers.

20. One number is 7 less than another. The quotient of the greater divided by the smaller is $\frac{4}{3}$. Find the numbers.

21. The sum of two fractions is $\frac{11}{16}$ and one of them is $\frac{5}{6}$ of the other. Find the fractions.

22. The difference between two fractions is $\frac{1}{8}$. One fraction is $\frac{2}{3}$ of the other. Find the fractions.

23. Two integers are consecutive. If 6 is added to the first and 2 is subtracted from the second, the quotient of the resulting integers is $4\frac{1}{2}$. Find them.

24. Two integers are consecutive. If 5 is added to the first and 3 is subtracted from the second, the quotient of the resulting integers is $2\frac{2}{5}$. Find them.

25. The sum of two numbers is 11. The sum of their reciprocals is $\frac{11}{30}$. Find the numbers.

26. The difference of two numbers is 5. The difference of their reciprocals is $\frac{5}{126}$. Find the numbers.

27. The sum of a positive number and its reciprocal is $\frac{41}{20}$. Find the number.

28. The difference of a positive number and its reciprocal is $\frac{24}{35}$. Find the number.

━━━━━━ **MAINTAIN**

Write the square of each binomial as a trinomial. (*Pages 358–360*)

29. $(a - 7)^2$ **30.** $(3x - 4)^2$ **31.** $(2c - d)^2$ **32.** $(5x - 2y)^2$

33. $(x^2 - y^2)^2$ **34.** $(2a^2 - 3b^2)^2$ **35.** $(xy^2 - 9)^2$ **36.** $(100 + 2)^2$

Write each product as a binomial. (*Pages 361–363*)

37. $(r + 4)(r - 4)$ **38.** $(2x - 3)(2x + 3)$ **39.** $(3x - 2b)(3x + 2b)$

40. $(a^2 + b^2)(a^2 - b^2)$ **41.** $(\frac{1}{3} - 3x)(\frac{1}{3} + 3x)$ **42.** $(y^2 + 0.9)(y^2 - 0.9)$

━━━━━━ **CONNECT AND EXTEND**

Solve each problem.

43. The numerator of a fraction is 1 less than the denominator. The reciprocal of the fraction is $\frac{7}{12}$ more than the fraction. Find the fraction.

44. The denominator of a fraction is 3 more than the numerator. The fraction is $\frac{21}{10}$ less than its reciprocal. Find the fraction.

Solve and check each equation. *(Pages 118–121)*

1. $7d + 9 = 16d$ **2.** $8(5d + 4) = 48$ **3.** $18t = 12(5 - t)$

4. $4x + 8 = 9(x - 3)$ **5.** $5x + 3(2 + x) = 5$ **6.** $55(x + 5) = 45(x + 55)$

7. $30(25 - x) = 20(25 + x)$ **8.** $15(3 - c) = 3(3 + c)$ **9.** $3x = 2(x + 10)$

■■■■ **PROBLEM SOLVING AND APPLICATIONS** ■■■■

11-9   Organizing Data: Motion Problems

Motion problems are based on the distance/rate/time formula.

Distance = rate × time,   or $d = rt$

Organizing information in a table is a useful strategy in solving motion problems.

EXAMPLE 1 David Blaisdell spends 5 hours traveling to and from work each day. If his average rate driving his moped to work is 18 miles per hour and his average rate returning is 12 miles per hour (Condition 1), how far is it from his home to his place of work (Condition 2)?

Solution:

1 **Find:** The distance from David's home to his work

     Given: David travels 5 hours to and from work each day. His rate of speed to work is 18 miles per hour and his rate of speed returning is 12 miles per hour.

Represent the unknowns.

Let t = time going.
Let $5 - t$ = time returning.

2   Organize the given information in a table.

	Rate (r)	Time (t)	Distance $d = rt$
Going	18 mph	t	$18t$
Returning	12 mph	$5 - t$	$12(5 - t)$

Use the table to write an equation.

Think: **Distance going** = **Distance returning**

Translate: $18t$ = $12(5 - t)$

3 Solve the equation.

$$18t = 12(5 - t)$$
$$18t = 60 - 12t$$
$$30t = 60$$
$$t = 2 \longleftarrow \text{ It takes 2 hours to drive to work.}$$

4 **Check:** Does the total time going to and from work equal 5 hours?

Does $2 + 3 = 5$? Yes ✔

Does the distance to work equal the distance returning from work?

Does $18 \cdot 2 = 12 \cdot 3$? Yes ✔

The distance from home to work is $2 \cdot 18$, or **36 miles.**

Suppose that a boat travels at a rate of 30 kilometers per hour in still water and that the rate of the current is 4 kilometers per hour.

Then,

rate traveling upstream is 30 − 4, or 26 km/h,

and

rate traveling downstream is 30 + 4, or 34 km/h.

EXAMPLE 2 A motorboat can travel at a rate of 25 kilometers per hour in still water. Find the rate of the current of a river if the boat takes $\frac{2}{3}$ as much time to travel 100 kilometers downstream as it takes to travel the same distance upstream.

Solution:

1 **Find:** The rate of current of the river

Given: A motorboat travels 25 kilometers per hour in still water. The time it takes to travel 100 kilometers downstream is $\frac{2}{3}$ the time it takes to travel 100 kilometers upstream.

Let x = the rate of the current.
Then $25 + x$ = the rate downstream and
$25 - x$ = the rate upstream.

Rational Expressions **459**

Organize the given information is a table.

	Rate (r)	Distance (d)	Time $t = d \div r$
Downstream	$25 + x$	100	$\dfrac{100}{25 + x}$
Upstream	$25 - x$	100	$\dfrac{100}{25 - x}$

Think: Time downstream $= \dfrac{2}{3}$ (Time upstream)

Translate: $\dfrac{100}{25 + x} = \dfrac{2}{3}\left(\dfrac{100}{25 - x}\right)$ ⬅——— LCD: $3(25 + x)(25 - x)$

3

$$3(25 + x)(25 - x)\left(\dfrac{100}{25 + x}\right) = 3(25 + x)(25 - x)\left(\dfrac{2}{3}\right)\left(\dfrac{100}{25 - x}\right)$$

$$3(25 - x)(100) = (25 + x)(2)(100)$$

$$300(25 - x) = 200(25 + x)$$

$$7500 - 300x = 5000 + 200x$$

$$2500 = 500x$$

$$5 = x$$

4 **Check:**   The check is left for you.   Rate of the current: **5 km/h**

EXERCISES: Classwork/Homework

Objective: To solve motion problems

█████ CHECK YOUR UNDERSTANDING

A jet had been flying for 2 hours when it encountered headwinds which reduced its speed by 64 kilometers per hour. The plane took 5 hours to travel 2304 kilometers.

Use this information in Exercises 1–3.

1. Complete the table.

	Rate (r)	Time (t)	Distance $d = rt$
Before headwinds	x	2	?
After headwinds	?	?	?

2. Write the equation you would use to find the plane's rate before encountering the headwinds.

■■■■■■ **PRACTICE AND APPLY**

Solve each problem.

4. A tanker takes $\frac{1}{2}$ hour to go from a refinery to a delivery point and back. If its rate going is 30 mph and its rate returning is 40 mph, how far is it from the refinery to the delivery point?

6. Jim drove his car 500 kilometers in the same time that Ed drove his car 450 kilometers. Jim drove 5 kilometers an hour faster than Ed. Find the speed of each.

8. Millan drives 30 miles to work and Sharon drives 20 miles. Both take the same time to get to work since Millan drives 15 mph faster than Sharon. Find the speed of each person.

10. Tim can average 12 mph with his motor boat in still water. Find the rate of the current of a river if the boat takes twice as long to go 48 miles upstream as it does to travel the same distance downstream.

12. A boat goes 36 kilometers upstream in the same time that it takes to travel 45 kilometers downstream. The current is flowing at 3 kilometers per hour. Find the rate of the boat in still water.

14. Allan can drive his car over a route in 5 hours, and Carla can drive her car over the same route in 4 hours. How long would it take to meet if they started at opposite ends at the same time?

3. What was the rate of the plane after encountering the headwinds?

5. Laurie takes 3 hours to travel from Ahmes to Billings on her moped. Brian covers the same distance in 2 hours, traveling 10 kilometers per hour faster. How far is it from Ahmes to Billings?

7. A sight-seeing bus travels 90 kilometers to its destination. If the rate returning is twice the rate going and the time for a round trip is 3 hours, find the rate of travel each way.

9. Karen can row 10 kilometers per hour in still water. In a river where the current is 5 kilometers per hour, it takes her 4 hours longer to row x kilometers upstream than the same distance downstream. Find x.

11. A boat that sails at the rate of 30 kilometers per hour in still water can go 104 kilometers down a river in the same time it takes to travel 91 kilometers up the river. Find the rate of the current of the river.

13. A plane can fly 600 kilometers with the wind in the same time that it can fly 520 kilometers against the wind. The wind is blowing at 30 kilometers per hour. Find the rate of the plane in still air.

15. On a trip, June drove at a rate of 55 mph. She decided to return by a route that was 5 miles longer. Her rate returning was 45 mph. If it took her 1 hour longer returning, how long was the second route?

16. An airplane flew 200 kilometers with a tailwind of 60 kilometers per hour. Then it returned against the wind. Find the rate of the plane in still air if the trip took 45 minutes.

17. A plane flies 852 kilometers with a tailwind in half the time it takes to fly 1560 kilometers against the same wind. If the rate in still air is 408 kilometers per hour, find the speed of the wind.

▋▋▋▋▋▋ **MAINTAIN**

Solve each problem. (*Pages 433–436*)

18. What number must be subtracted from both the numerator and denominator of the fraction $\frac{7}{9}$ to make a fraction equal to $\frac{2}{3}$?

19. One positive number is 5 times another number. The sum of their reciprocals is $\frac{2}{5}$. Find the numbers.

20. One number is 6 more than another. The quotient of the larger divided by the smaller is $\frac{26}{14}$.

21. The difference between two fractions is $\frac{4}{7}$. One fraction is $\frac{2}{3}$ of the other. Find the fractions.

(*Pages 107–110*)

22. An art dealer bought an oil painting for $1200 and then sold it at an auction for a 40% profit. What was the selling price of the painting?

23. The list price (regular price) of a typewriter is $355. A discount (reduction in price) of $106.50 is given. What percent of the list price is the discount?

Divide the first polynomial by the second. (*Pages 364–366*)

24. $c^2 - 2c - 63;\ c - 9$ **25.** $x^2 + 4x - 32;\ x + 8$ **26.** $2n^2 - 14n - 36;\ 2n + 4$

▋▋▋▋▋▋ **CONNECT AND EXTEND**

27. Rhonda can swim in still water at twice the rate of the current in the river near her home. She swam one kilometer upstream and then back in 40 minutes. Find the rate of the current.

28. Two cars race on a 6.4-kilometer track. The faster car gains a lap in 40 minutes. The sum of the rates of the cars is 320 kilometers per hour. Find the rate of each car.

11-10   Organizing Data: Work Problems

Work problems usually deal with persons or machines working at different rates of speed. The first step in solving these problems involves determining how much of the work an individual or a machine can do in a given unit of time.

For example, suppose Freida takes 3 hours to type a term paper.

Part of job done in 1 hour: $\frac{1}{3}$

Part of job done in 2 hours: $\frac{1}{3} \cdot 2$, or $\frac{2}{3}$

Part of job done in n hours: $\frac{1}{3} \cdot n$, or $\frac{n}{3}$

Many work problems involve this formula.

rate of work $\times$ time = work done,   or

$$r \quad \cdot \quad t \quad = \quad w$$

EXAMPLE 1 Gloria can clear the snow from a sidewalk in 60 minutes. Marsha can clear the same area in 30 minutes. How long will it take them to do the job if they work together?

Solution: **1** **Find:** The time it will take both Gloria and Marsha to do the job if they work together

Given: Gloria can clear the snow in 60 minutes. Marsha can clear the same area in 30 minutes.

Let t = the number of minutes for both to do the job working together.

2 Organize the given information in a table.

Worker	Rate of Work per Minute (r)	Time Spent Working Together (t)	Part of Work Done ($r \cdot t = w$)
Gloria	$\frac{1}{60}$	t	$\frac{1}{60}t$, or $\frac{t}{60}$
Marsha	$\frac{1}{30}$	t	$\frac{1}{30}t$, or $\frac{t}{30}$

Rational Expressions   **463**

Use the table to write an equation for the problem.

Think: $\dfrac{\text{Work done by Gloria}}{} + \dfrac{\text{Work done by Marsha}}{} = \dfrac{\text{Total job}}{}$

Translate: $\dfrac{t}{60} + \dfrac{t}{30} = 1$

3 Solve the equation. The LCD is 60.

$$60\left(\frac{t}{60} + \frac{t}{30}\right) = 60(1)$$

$$60\left(\frac{t}{60}\right) + 60\left(\frac{t}{30}\right) = 60$$

$$t + 2t = 60 \quad \longleftarrow \quad \textbf{Solve for } t.$$

$$3t = 60$$

$$t = 20 \quad \longleftarrow \quad \textbf{Number of minutes they work together}$$

4 Check: Gloria does $\frac{20}{60}$, or $\frac{1}{3}$ of the work in 20 minutes.

Marsha does $\frac{20}{30}$, or $\frac{2}{3}$ of the work in 20 minutes.

Total work done: $\frac{1}{3} + \frac{2}{3} = \frac{3}{3}$, or 1

Working together, Gloria and Marsha can complete the job in **20 minutes.**

REMEMBER: When a job is completed, the sum of the fractional parts of the job done by each worker equals 1.

CALCULATOR   Here is a way to solve Example 1 using a calculator.

Rewrite the equation $\frac{t}{60} + \frac{t}{30} = 1$ as $\frac{1}{60} + \frac{1}{30} = \frac{1}{t}$.

1 $\boxed{\div}$ 60 $\boxed{=}$ $\boxed{+}$ 1 $\boxed{\div}$ 30 $\boxed{=}$ $\boxed{0.05}$ $\longleftarrow$ $\frac{1}{t} = 0.05$

To find t, you must use the inverse key, $\boxed{^1\!/_x}$.

$\boxed{^1\!/_x}$ $\boxed{20}$ $\longleftarrow$ **20 minutes**

464   *Chapter 11*

EXAMPLE 2 Bill can do a certain job in 8 days. After working alone for 4 days, he is joined by Tony. Together they finish the job in 2 more days. How long would it take Tony to do the job alone?

Solution:

$\boxed{1}$ **Find:** The time it would take Tony to do the job alone

Given: Bill can do a job in 8 days. Bill worked alone for 4 days and then worked with Tony for two days to finish the job.

Let d = the number of days for Tony to do the job alone.

Then $\frac{1}{d}$ = Tony's rate of work.

$\boxed{2}$ Organize the given information in a table. Use the table to write an equation for the problem.

Worker	Rate of Work Per Day	Time Working Alone	Time Working Together	Work Done ($r \cdot t = w$)
Bill	$\frac{1}{8}$	4 days	2 days	$\frac{1}{8}(4) + \frac{1}{8}(2) = \frac{3}{4}$
Tony	$\frac{1}{d}$	0 days	2 days	$\frac{1}{d} \cdot 2$, or $\frac{2}{d}$

Think: $\dfrac{\text{Work done by Bill}}{} + \dfrac{\text{Work done by Tony}}{} = \dfrac{\text{Total job}}{}$

Translate: $\frac{3}{4} \quad + \quad \frac{2}{d} \quad = \quad 1 \longleftarrow$ LCD: **4d**

$\boxed{3}$
$$4d\left(\frac{3}{4} + \frac{2}{d}\right) = 4d(1)$$
$$4d\left(\frac{3}{4}\right) + 4d\left(\frac{2}{d}\right) = 4d$$
$$3d + 8 = 4d$$
$$8 = d \longleftarrow \text{Number of days if Tony worked alone}$$

$\boxed{4}$ **Check:** Work done by Bill: $\frac{3}{4}$

Work done by Tony: $\frac{2}{d} = \frac{2}{8} = \frac{1}{4}$

Total work done: $\frac{3}{4} + \frac{1}{4} = 1$

It will take Tony **8 days** to do the job alone.

Objective: To solve work problems

████ CHECK YOUR UNDERSTANDING

Pipe A can empty a pool in 5 hours. Pipe B can empty the pool in 3 hours. Use this information in Exercises 1–7.

1. What part of the pool can Pipe A empty in 1 hour?

2. What part of the pool can Pipe A empty in 4 hours?

3. What part of the pool can Pipe B empty in 1 hour?

4. What part of the pool can Pipe B empty in 3 hours?

5. What part of the pool is drained in 1 hour by both pipes?

6. What part of the pool can be emptied in x hours by both pipes?

7. Write an equation whose solution would give the number of hours that it would take both pipes to empty the pool.

████ PRACTICE AND APPLY

Solve each problem.

8. Ken can build a fence in 4 days. His niece Sara can do it in 4.5 days. How long would it take them working together?

9. Jill can paint a house in 2 days. Her brother can paint it in 4 days. How long would it take them to paint the house if they work together?

10. A large pipe can empty a tank in 5 minutes, and a smaller pipe can empty it in 8 minutes. How long would it take both pipes to empty the tank?

11. Marge can do a piece of work in 3 days, Mae in 5 days, and Gina in 8 days. If all three work together, how long will it take them to do the work?

12. To remove the dirt from a building foundation, a contractor is using a large diesel shovel and a small one. If the large shovel can do the entire job in 6 days and the small shovel can do it in 9 days, how long will it take them together?

13. Gwen Hall estimates that she can paint the Smiths' house in 6 days. Her brother Doug can paint it in 8 days and her sister Laura can paint it in 10 days. How long will it take all three working together?

14. Jim can shovel the driveway in 2 hours. Lucy can shovel it in 4 hours. Jim shovels for 1 hour and then Lucy helps him finish the job. How long does it take the two of them to finish?

15. If one pipe can fill a tank in 3 hours, a second pipe in 5 hours and a third pipe in 6 hours, how long will it take to fill the tank if all three pipes are being used?

16. One machine can complete an order for bolts in 7 hours and another machine can do it in 5 hours. How long will it take both machines to finish the job after the slower machine has been working alone for $3\frac{1}{2}$ hours?

17. Juan can paint a room in 3 hours. Anita can paint the same room in 5 hours. Anita paints alone for 2 hours and then Juan helps her finish. How long does it take them to finish painting the room?

18. Kate can type a manuscript in 6 hours. If Mark helps her they can type the complete manuscript in 4 hours. How long would it take Mark if he did all the typing?

19. Jacques can spade a garden in 5 hours. After working alone for 2 hours, he is joined by Dave. Together they finish the job in 1 hour. How long would it take Dave to spade the garden alone?

20. It takes 10 minutes to fill a certain tank and 15 minutes to empty it when it is full. With the drain open and the tank empty, how long would it take to fill it?

21. Janette can make an afghan in 10 days, Bill in 6 days, and Sue in 15 days. Bill and Janette work for 3 days. How long will it take Janette and Sue to finish the afghan?

■■■■■ **MAINTAIN**

22. Laurie rode her bicycle 32 kilometers in the same time that Alyssa rode her bicycle 40 kilometers. Alyssa rode 2 kilometers an hour faster than Laurie. Find the speed of each person. (*Pages 458–462*)

23. A boat that sails at a rate of 26 miles per hour in still water can go 150 miles down a river in the same time it takes to travel 110 miles up the river. Find the rate of the current of the river. (*Pages 458–462*)

24. One positive number is 7 times another number. The sum of their reciprocals is $\frac{1}{7}$. Find the numbers. (*Pages 454–457*)

25. The sum of two fractions is $\frac{25}{27}$ and one of them is $\frac{2}{3}$ of the other. Find the fractions. (*Pages 454–457*)

Subtract. (*Pages 347–350*)

26. $7r + s$
$\underline{3r - 2s}$

27. $x^2 + 4y^2$
$\underline{5x^2 - y^2}$

28. $m + p + 6s$
$\underline{\quad -p - 9s}$

■■■■■ **CONNECT AND EXTEND**

29. A swimming pool can be filled by a large pipe in 4 hours and by a small pipe in 6 hours. A third pipe can empty the pool in 3 hours. How long would it take to fill the pool if all three were open at the same time?

Focus on College Entrance Tests

On College Entrance tests, it is important to recognize problems that can be solved by using proportions.

If c cans of stew make x servings, how many cans are need to make y servings?

      a. $\dfrac{xy}{c}$ **b.** $\dfrac{cx}{y}$ **c.** $\dfrac{c}{xy}$ **d.** $\dfrac{cy}{x}$

Solution: Let $n =$ the number of cans needed for y servings.

$$\dfrac{c}{x} = \dfrac{n}{y} \quad \longleftarrow \text{ Cans}$$
$$\qquad\qquad \longleftarrow \text{ Servings}$$

$$xn = cy$$

$$n = \dfrac{cy}{x} \quad \textbf{Answer: d}$$

TRY THESE

Choose the best answer. Choose a, b, c, or d.

1. If a machine fills c cans in h hours, how many hours will it take to fill d cans?

    a. $\dfrac{hd}{c}$ **b.** $\dfrac{h}{cd}$ **c.** $\dfrac{d}{hc}$ **d.** $\dfrac{cd}{h}$

2. If Beth earns d dollars in h hours, how many dollars will she earn in 10 hours?

    a. $\dfrac{10h}{d}$ **b.** $\dfrac{10d}{h}$ **c.** $10 + \dfrac{d}{h}$ **d.** $\dfrac{10 + d}{h}$

3. A car travels a kilometers in b hours. At that rate, how many hours will it take the car to go 200 kilometers?

    a. $200\dfrac{a}{b}$ **b.** $\dfrac{b}{200a}$ **c.** $\dfrac{200}{a} + b$ **d.** $\dfrac{200b}{a}$

4. If c cups of flour are used to make p pie crusts, how many cups of flour are needed to make $2p$ pie crusts?

    a. $2p$ **b.** $\dfrac{c}{2}$ **c.** $2c$ **d.** $\dfrac{2}{p}$

5. If p pounds of potatoes cost d dollars, how many pounds of potatoes can be bought with $3d$ dollars?

    a. $3p$ **b.** $3d$ **c.** $\dfrac{3d^2}{p}$ **d.** $\dfrac{3p}{d} + 1$

IMPORTANT TERMS

Apparent solution (p. 448)
Least common denominator, or LCD (p. 433)
Mixed expression (p. 443)

Mixed number (p. 443)
Rational expression (p. 421)
Simplest form (p. 421)

IMPORTANT IDEAS

1. **Product of Rational Expressions Theorem** If $\frac{P}{Q}$ and $\frac{R}{S}$ are rational expressions, then

$$\frac{P}{Q} \cdot \frac{R}{S} = \frac{P \cdot R}{Q \cdot S}.$$

2. **Division of Rational Expressions Theorem** To divide a rational expression $\frac{P}{Q}$ by a rational expression $\frac{R}{S}$, multiply $\frac{P}{Q}$ by the multiplicative inverse, or reciprocal, of $\frac{R}{S}$. That is, for $R \neq 0$,

$$\frac{P}{Q} \div \frac{R}{S} = \frac{P}{Q} \cdot \frac{S}{R}.$$

3. **Steps for finding the LCD of rational expressions**
   1. Express each denominator as a product of prime factors.
   2. Write a product using each prime factor only once.
   3. For each factor, write the greatest exponent used in any prime factorization.
   4. Simplify where necessary. The result is the LCD.

4. **Addition and Subtraction of Rational Expressions Theorem**
   If $\frac{P}{Q}$ and $\frac{R}{Q}$ are rational expressions, then

$$\frac{P}{Q} + \frac{R}{Q} = \frac{P + R}{Q} \quad \text{and} \quad \frac{P}{Q} - \frac{R}{Q} = \frac{P - R}{Q}.$$

5. **Steps for Adding or Subtracting Rational Expressions**
   1. Find the LCD of the denominators.
   2. Write equivalent rational expressions having the LCD as denominators.
   3. Add or subtract as indicated.
   4. Write the answer in simplest form.

6. **Steps for Solving Equations with Rational Expressions**
   1. Multiply each side of the equation by the LCD.
   2. Follow the usual procedures to solve the resulting equation.

7. **Work formula:** rate of work $\times$ time = work done, or $r \cdot t = w$.

Simplify. (*Pages 421–424*)

1. $\dfrac{39}{65}$

2. $\dfrac{12ab}{30b^2}$

3. $\dfrac{3(x + y)}{9(x - y)}$

4. $\dfrac{6(c + 2d)^2}{8(c + 2d)}$

5. $\dfrac{5x}{5x + 10}$

6. $\dfrac{2a - 4b}{6a + 4b}$

7. $\dfrac{4x^2 - 16y^2}{8y^2 - 2x^2}$

8. $\dfrac{6a^2 - 15ab + 9b^2}{3b^2 - 4ab + a^2}$

Multiply. Write each product in simplest form. (*Pages 425–428*)

9. $\dfrac{x^2}{2a} \cdot \dfrac{a}{x}$

10. $(2x + 1) \cdot \dfrac{x + 5}{6x + 3}$

11. $\dfrac{3a + 3}{4a - 4} \cdot \dfrac{a - 1}{a + 1}$

12. $\dfrac{4x}{x^2 - y^2} \cdot \dfrac{x - y}{2x^2 + 2xy}$

13. $\dfrac{2x}{x + 2} \cdot \dfrac{x^2 + 5x + 6}{2x + 2}$

14. $\dfrac{3a + b}{a^2 - b^2} \cdot \dfrac{a - b}{3a^2 + 4ab + b^2}$

Divide. Write each answer in simplest form. (*Pages 429–432*)

15. $\dfrac{3}{a} \div \dfrac{6}{b}$

16. $\dfrac{ax}{by} \div \dfrac{x}{y}$

17. $\dfrac{6a^2b}{5c} \div \dfrac{3ac}{5b}$

18. $\dfrac{(5xy)^2}{12z} \div \dfrac{10x}{9z^3}$

19. $\dfrac{x^2 + xy}{a^2 - b^2} \div \dfrac{x + y}{(a - b)^2}$

20. $(x^2 - a^2) \div \dfrac{ax - a^2}{x + a}$

Find the LCD of rational expressions having the given denominators. (*Pages 433–436*)

21. $7; 9$

22. $4; 10$

23. $3x^2y^2; 9xy^2$

24. $(x + 3); (x - 3)$

25. $(a^2 - b^2); (a + b)$

26. $(y^2 + 2y + 1); (y^2 - y - 2)$

Add or subtract as indicated. Write each answer in simplest form. (*Pages 437–441*)

27. $\dfrac{3x + 5}{x + 2} - \dfrac{2x + 3}{x + 2}$

28. $\dfrac{a + 1}{6} + \dfrac{a + 1}{9}$

29. $\dfrac{a + b}{ab} - \dfrac{3}{2a}$

30. $\dfrac{1 - 3y}{3xy} - \dfrac{2x - 1}{6x^2y}$

31. $\dfrac{2}{a + 3} - \dfrac{1}{a - 1}$

32. $\dfrac{x}{x + 2} - \dfrac{8}{x^2 - 4}$

33. $\dfrac{x - y}{3x + 3y} - \dfrac{x - y}{2x + 2y}$

34. $\dfrac{x + 1}{2xy} - \dfrac{2y - 1}{4y^2}$

Add or subtract as indicated. Write each answer in simplest form. (*Pages 443–446*)

35. $3 + \dfrac{x}{y}$

36. $b + \dfrac{3}{2b}$

37. $x - \dfrac{2y}{3x}$

38. $\dfrac{3}{x} + 2x$

39. $a - \dfrac{ab}{a + b}$

40. $x - \dfrac{3}{x + 2}$

41. $1 + \dfrac{2x + 1}{x - 1}$

42. $(a + 1) + \dfrac{1}{a - 1}$

Solve each equation. (*Pages 447–451*)

43. $\dfrac{n}{2} - \dfrac{2n}{9} = 5$

44. $\dfrac{24}{3x} = \dfrac{4}{9}$

45. $\dfrac{12}{5x} - \dfrac{7}{5x} = \dfrac{1}{2}$

46. $\dfrac{y}{6} = \dfrac{y}{2(2 - y)}$

47. $\dfrac{a}{3} = \dfrac{4}{a + 4}$

48. $\dfrac{1}{y} + \dfrac{1}{2y} = \dfrac{1}{y + 2}$

49. $\dfrac{4}{x} = \dfrac{x}{x + 1} - \dfrac{1}{x^2 + x}$

50. $\dfrac{3}{x - 3} + \dfrac{4}{x} = \dfrac{x}{x - 3}$

51. $\dfrac{a}{1 + 3a} = \dfrac{2}{a + 5}$

52. $\dfrac{x - 1}{x + 2} - \dfrac{6}{x^2 + 2x} = \dfrac{2}{x}$

53. $\dfrac{y}{y + 14} = \dfrac{2}{y + 5}$

54. $\dfrac{n + 1}{n} = \dfrac{2}{2n - 3} + \dfrac{2}{n}$

Solve each problem. (*Pages 454–457*)

55. The sum of two fractions is $\frac{11}{12}$. One fraction is $\frac{3}{8}$ of the other. Find the fractions.

56. The sum of two positive integers is 14. The difference of their reciprocals is $\frac{1}{24}$. Find the integers.

(*Pages 458–462*)

57. Miriam drove 400 kilometers in the same amount of time that it took Ruth to drive 320 kilometers. Miriam drove 15 kilometers per hour faster than Ruth. Find the speed of each.

58. Bob paddles his canoe at a rate of 6 kilometers per hour in still water. Find the rate of the current if it takes Bob twice as long to paddle 20 kilometers upstream as to paddle 20 kilometers downstream.

(*Pages 463–467*)

59. An old machine can produce an order for bottle caps in 7.5 hours. A newer machine can produce the same number of caps in 5 hours. How long would it take to fill the order using both machines together?

60. One outboard motor uses up a tank of fuel in 6 hours. A larger motor uses the same amount of fuel in 4 hours. How long can both motors be run if they are connected to the same tank that is filled to capacity?

Perform the indicated operations. Express answers in simplest form.

1. $\dfrac{4x^2}{3y} \div \dfrac{x}{y}$

2. $3 - \dfrac{2}{a}$

3. $\dfrac{9x^2}{4} \cdot \dfrac{2}{15x}$

4. $\dfrac{3b^3}{4} \div \dfrac{26}{8}$

5. $\dfrac{a^2 + ab}{a^2 - b^2} \cdot \dfrac{a - b}{a + ab}$

6. $\dfrac{2x + 3y}{x - y} + \dfrac{x - 6y}{x - y}$

7. $\dfrac{x^2 - y^2}{3xy} \div \dfrac{x^2 - 2xy + y^2}{6x}$

8. $\dfrac{c - d}{cd} + \dfrac{c + d}{c^2}$

9. $\dfrac{3}{2x + 2y} - \dfrac{x}{x^2 - y^2}$

10. $\dfrac{x^2 - 9}{x^2 + 2x} \cdot \dfrac{x + 2}{x^2 + 6x + 9}$

11. $\dfrac{3}{a + 1} + 1$

12. $\dfrac{y^2 - 3y + 2}{2y + 2} \cdot \dfrac{y + 1}{y - 1}$

13. $\dfrac{a + 1}{4a^2} - \dfrac{1 - a}{2a}$

Solve each equation.

14. $\dfrac{x}{6} + \dfrac{2x}{9} = 7$

15. $\dfrac{3y}{y + 9} + \dfrac{3}{4y} = 1$

16. $\dfrac{a}{a - 2} = \dfrac{2}{a - 3}$

Solve each problem.

17. What number must be added to the numerator and subtracted from the denominator of $\frac{13}{38}$ to make a fraction equal to $\frac{7}{10}$?

18. One positive number is four times another number. The difference of their reciprocals is $\frac{1}{4}$. Find the numbers.

19. Jan drove 160 kilometers in the same time that Karen drove 150 kilometers. Jan drove 5 kilometers per hour faster than Karen. Find the speed of each.

20. It takes David 30 minutes to load a truck. Matthew can do the job in 20 minutes. How long will it take them to load the truck if they work together?

Skills

Simplify. No denominator equals zero. (*Pages 421–424*)

1. $\dfrac{24a^2 b}{56a}$
2. $\dfrac{36xy}{60wx}$
3. $\dfrac{3a + 3b}{3a^2 - 3b^2}$
4. $\dfrac{x^2 - x - 6}{x^2 + x - 12}$

Multiply. Write each product in simplest form. (*Pages 425–428*)

5. $\dfrac{x + y}{12} \cdot \dfrac{3}{x}$
6. $(2x - 3) \cdot \dfrac{x}{4x - 6}$
7. $\dfrac{a^2 - b^2}{4a + 2b} \cdot \dfrac{2}{a - b}$

Divide. Write each answer in simplest form. (*Pages 429–432*)

8. $\dfrac{18}{c} \div \dfrac{36}{c^2}$
9. $\dfrac{9x^2 - 4y^2}{2x^2} \div \dfrac{3x - 2y}{8x}$
10. $\dfrac{n^2 + 2n + 1}{3n - 3} \div \dfrac{n + 1}{3}$

Add or subtract as indicated. Write each answer in simplest form. (*Pages 437–441*)

11. $\dfrac{3a + b}{a + b} - \dfrac{a - b}{a + b}$
12. $\dfrac{x + 1}{6x} + \dfrac{4x}{8x^2}$
13. $\dfrac{x}{x^2 - x - 6} - \dfrac{1}{x^2 - 3x}$

(*Pages 443–446*)

14. $3 + \dfrac{1}{2a}$
15. $x - \dfrac{1}{x + 1}$
16. $\dfrac{2}{y + 3} - (y - 3)$

Solve. (*Pages 447–451*)

17. $\dfrac{y}{6} + \dfrac{y}{9} = 5$
18. $\dfrac{2}{x} + \dfrac{3}{4} = \dfrac{4x + 5}{4x}$
19. $\dfrac{n}{n + 1} = \dfrac{3}{n - 1} - \dfrac{6}{n^2 - 1}$

Problem Solving and Applications

20. Two integers are consecutive. If 5 is subtracted from the lesser integer and added to the greater integer, their quotient is equal to $\frac{1}{2}$. Find the integers. (*Pages 454–457*)

21. Kim drove her car 100 kilometers in the same time that Sue drove her car 110 kilometers. Sue's average rate was 6 kilometers per hour faster than Kim's. Find the average rate for each person. (*Pages 458–462*)

22. A plane can fly 1050 kilometers with a tailwind in the same time that it can fly 900 kilometers against the wind. If the wind speed is 25 kilometers per hour, what is the speed of the plane in still air? (*Pages 458–462*)

23. Janet can type a manuscript in 6 days. After working alone one day, Ted helps her to complete the job. Together, they finish the typing in 3 more days. How long would it take Ted to do the job alone? (*Pages 463–467*)

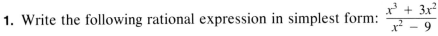

Part 1 Choose the best answer. Choose *a, b, c,* or *d.*

1. Write the following rational expression in simplest form: $\dfrac{x^3 + 3x^2}{x^2 - 9}$

   a. $\dfrac{x + 3}{x - 3}$ **b.** $x - \frac{1}{3}x^2$

   c. $\dfrac{x^2}{x - 3}$ **d.** $\dfrac{x + 3}{9}$

2. Use factoring to find the solutions of the equation $x^2 = 24 - 5x$.

   a. $\{-3, 8\}$ **b.** $\{-8, 3\}$ **c.** $\{-2, 12\}$ **d.** $\{-12, 2\}$

3. Express the product $9 \cdot 3^5$ as one base with a single exponent.

   a. 27^6 **b.** 27^5 **c.** 3^{10} **d.** 3^7

4. Which of the following is not in simplest form?

   a. $\dfrac{x + y}{x - y}$ **b.** $\dfrac{x + y}{x^2 - y^2}$ **c.** $\dfrac{x^2 + x + 1}{x^2 + x}$ **d.** $\dfrac{x^2 + 4}{x + 2}$

5. Find the value of $(-x^3y)(2x^2y^3)$ when $x = -1$ and $y = -2$.

   a. 64   **b.** -64 **c.** 32   **d.** -32

6. What is the theoretical probability that if a six-sided die is tossed, the number which shows has 3 as a prime factor?

   a. $\frac{1}{6}$ **b.** $\frac{1}{4}$ **c.** $\frac{1}{3}$ **d.** $\frac{1}{2}$

7. Perform the indicated division and express the result in simplest form:

   $\dfrac{x^3 - 4x}{x^3(x + 2)} \div \dfrac{x + 2}{x}$

   a. $\dfrac{x^2 - 4}{x}$ **b.** $\dfrac{x^3}{x^2 - 4}$ **c.** $\dfrac{x(x + 2)}{x - 2}$ **d.** $\dfrac{x - 2}{x(x + 2)}$

8. What is the slope of the line with equation $5x = 3y - 8$?

   a. $\frac{3}{5}$ **b.** $\frac{8}{3}$ **c.** $\frac{5}{3}$ **d.** 8

9. Solve the inequality $-3(1 - 2x) > 2(x - 1)$.

   a. $x > \frac{1}{4}$ **b.** $x > -\frac{1}{4}$ **c.** $x < -\frac{1}{4}$ **d.** $x < \frac{1}{4}$

10. What is the solution set of $|3(x - 1) + 5| = 1$?

    a. $\{-1\}$ **b.** $\{\frac{1}{3}\}$ **c.** $\{-1, -\frac{1}{3}\}$ **d.** $\{-1, \frac{1}{3}\}$

11. Find the least common denominator of the three rational expressions whose denominators are $3x^2 + 10x - 8$, $9x^2 - 4$, and $x^2 + 8x + 16$.

    a. $(x + 4)(3x + 2)(3x - 2)$ **b.** $(x + 4)(3x - 2)^2$
    c. $(x + 4)^2(3x + 2)$ **d.** $(x + 4)^2(3x + 2)(3x - 2)$

12. If y varies directly as x and $y = 12.5$ when $x = 3.75$, find x when y is 18.75.

    a. 5.625   **b.** 62.5   **c.** 56.25   **d.** 10

13. Find the numerator of the sum of the rational expressions $\dfrac{x}{x^2 - 1}$ and $\dfrac{x}{x - 1}$.

   a. $x^2 + 2x$ **b.** $x^2 + x$ **c.** $2x$ **d.** $x^3 + x^2 - 2x$

14. Which point is not on the graph of $y = |x - 1|$?

   a. $(1, 0)$ **b.** $(0, 1)$ **c.** $(3, -2)$ **d.** $(-1, 2)$

15. Solve the equation: $\dfrac{3}{x + 2} - \dfrac{4}{x - 3} = 0$.

   a. $x = 3$ **b.** $x = -2$ **c.** $x = 17$ **d.** $x = -17$

16. How many solutions are there for the system $\begin{cases} 2x - 3y - 1 = 0 \\ 6y - 4x - 2 = 0 \end{cases}$

   a. none   **b.** many   **c.** infinite   **d.** one

17. Find the mean of $-3, \frac{1}{2}, 0, -\frac{1}{2}, -2, \frac{3}{2}, 0, -1, \frac{1}{2}, 2$.

   a. $-\frac{1}{4}$ **b.** $-\frac{1}{5}$ **c.** $\frac{1}{4}$ **d.** $\frac{1}{5}$

18. Solve the system: $\begin{cases} 8x - 3y = 2 \\ 4x + y = 6 \end{cases}$

   a. $\{1, 2\}$ **b.** $\{1, -2\}$ **c.** $\{-1, 2\}$ **d.** $\{-1, -2\}$

Part 2

Solve each problem.

19. What number must be subtracted from both the numerator and the denominator of the fraction $\frac{9}{13}$ to make a fraction equal to $\frac{1}{3}$?

20. The length of a rectangular poster is 8 in longer than its width. The area of the poster is 308 in². Find the length and width.

21. A speedboat traveled 80 miles downstream in 2.5 hours. The return trip took 4 hours against the current. What is the speed of the boat in still water, and what is the speed of the current?

22. Jim leaves home at 8 A.M. and rides due east on his bike at 6.5 mph; his brother leaves at the same time but rides due west at 5.5 mph. At what time will they be exactly 30 miles apart?

23. Bill can paint his barn in 15 hours, while his brother Tom would take 18 hours to complete the job. If Bill paints for 7 hours alone and then is joined by Tom, how much longer will it take the two of them to complete the job?

24. The high temperatures in Boston on four consecutive days in January were 28, 30, 29 and 30, measured in degrees Fahrenheit. In order for the average high temperature for five consecutive days to be at least 32°F, what is the minimum high temperature that must be reached on the fifth day?

CHAPTER 152

Roots of Numbers

If you were in a plane at an altitude of 1000 meters, you could see a distance of about 113 kilometers to the horizon. However, this does not mean that you could see about 226 kilometers if you were in a plane at an altitude of 2 kilometers. To find this distance, you could solve this equation.

$$D = 3.56 \sqrt{A}$$

A is the altitude in meters.

12-1 Roots of Numbers

To square a number, you multiply it by itself. The inverse operation is taking the *square root*.

$$\text{Since } 5^2 = 25, \sqrt{25} = 5.$$ ⟵ **Read: "The square root of 25 is 5."**

RADICAL

In the expression $\sqrt{25}$, $\sqrt{}$ is the **radical symbol**, 25 is the **radicand**, and $\sqrt{25}$ is the **radical.**

Since $9^2 = 81$ and $(-9)^2 = 81$, the number 81 has two square roots, 9 and -9. Every positive real number has two square roots, one positive and one negative.

DEFINITION

> The **principal square root** of a positive real number is the positive square root of the number. The principal square root is indicated by the radical symbol $\sqrt{}$.

From the definition,

$$\sqrt{\frac{49}{9}} = \frac{7}{3} \quad \text{and} \quad \sqrt{0.36} = \mathbf{0.6}$$

A negative square root is associated with the symbol $-\sqrt{}$. The symbol $\pm\sqrt{}$, indicates both square roots.

EXAMPLE 1 Simplify: **a.** $\sqrt{400}$ **b.** $\pm\sqrt{\dfrac{49}{625}}$

Solutions: **a.** $\sqrt{400} = 20$ ⟵ **Since $(20)^2 = 400$**

b. $\pm\sqrt{\dfrac{49}{625}} = \pm\dfrac{7}{25}$ ⟵ **Since $\left(\dfrac{7}{25}\right)^2 = \dfrac{49}{625}$ and $\left(-\dfrac{7}{25}\right)^2 = \dfrac{49}{625}$**

A negative number has no real-number square root.

$$\sqrt{-225} \neq -15 \text{ because } (-15)^2 = 225.$$

Thus, for $\sqrt{a}$ to represent a nonnegative real number, a must be a positive real number or zero. Since $|a| \geq 0$ for all real numbers, absolute value notation can be used to ensure that $\sqrt{a^2}$ is a nonnegative real number.

DEFINITION

> For any real number a, $\sqrt{a^2} = |a|$.

EXAMPLE 2 Simplify: **a.** $\sqrt{r^2 t^2}$ **b.** $\sqrt{81a^4}$

    Solutions: **a.** $\sqrt{r^2 t^2} = |rt|$ ⟵   **By definition**

                   b. $\sqrt{81a^4} = 9|a^2| = 9a^2$ ⟵   **Since a² cannot be negative**

EXERCISES: Classwork/Homework

        Objective: To find the square root of numbers of expressions

■■■■■■■ **CHECK YOUR UNDERSTANDING**

      For Exercises 1–3, complete the sentence.

1. The inverse operation of squaring a number is taking its __?__ .

2. Every positive real number has two square roots, one __?__ and one __?__ .

3. The positive square root of a number is called the __?__ .

4. Assume that $\sqrt{a}$ represents a nonnegative real number. Explain why a cannot be a negative real number.

      Write the two square roots of each number.

5. 64   **6.** 121   **7.** $\frac{25}{36}$ **8.** $\frac{1}{4}$ **9.** 10,000   **10.** $\frac{9}{100}$

■■■■■■ **PRACTICE AND APPLY**

      In Exercises 11–70, simplify.

11. $\sqrt{16}$ **12.** $-\sqrt{25}$ **13.** $\sqrt{49}$ **14.** $\pm\sqrt{144}$

15. $\pm\sqrt{100}$ **16.** $\pm\sqrt{81}$ **17.** $\sqrt{10,000}$ **18.** $\sqrt{40,000}$

19. $-\sqrt{4^2}$ **20.** $\pm\sqrt{8^2}$ **21.** $\pm\sqrt{100^2}$ **22.** $\sqrt{125^2}$

23. $\sqrt{\frac{9}{49}}$ **24.** $\sqrt{\frac{4}{81}}$ **25.** $\pm\sqrt{\frac{25}{36}}$ **26.** $\pm\sqrt{\frac{121}{100}}$

27. $-\sqrt{\frac{64}{25}}$ **28.** $\pm\sqrt{\frac{144}{169}}$ **29.** $\sqrt{\left(\frac{81}{100}\right)^2}$ **30.** $\sqrt{\left(\frac{196}{49}\right)^2}$

31. $(\sqrt{17})^2$ **32.** $(\sqrt{13})^2$ **33.** $(\sqrt{25})^2$ **34.** $(\sqrt{46})^2$

35. $\sqrt{b^2}$ **36.** $\sqrt{c^4}$ **37.** $\pm\sqrt{t^{10}}$ **38.** $\pm\sqrt{d^6}$

39. $\sqrt{c^4 d^6}$ **40.** $-\sqrt{f^{10} t^4}$ **41.** $-\sqrt{h^8 s^{12}}$ **42.** $\sqrt{r^{12} t^6}$

43. $\sqrt{9c^2}$ **44.** $\sqrt{81t^8}$ **45.** $-\sqrt{64c^6}$ **46.** $-\sqrt{49b^4}$

47. $\pm\sqrt{25d^4}$ **48.** $\pm\sqrt{100r^{12}}$ **49.** $\sqrt{4x^2 y^2}$ **50.** $\sqrt{9a^2 b^2}$

51. $\sqrt{0.49}$ **52.** $\sqrt{0.25}$ **53.** $-\sqrt{2.25}$ **54.** $-\sqrt{1.44}$

55. $\sqrt{0.64b^2}$ **56.** $\sqrt{1.69a^2}$ **57.** $\pm\sqrt{6.25t^4}$ **58.** $\pm\sqrt{4.41a^6}$

59. $\sqrt{25r^8s^{16}t^{12}}$ **60.** $\pm\sqrt{49c^{10}d^6f^{12}}$ **61.** $-\sqrt{81a^{12}b^8d^{16}}$ **62.** $\sqrt{16f^4g^{10}h^{18}}$

63. $\pm\sqrt{\dfrac{49t^4}{25b^6}}$ **64.** $\pm\sqrt{\dfrac{16d^8}{121f^2}}$ **65.** $\sqrt{\dfrac{49a^4b^2}{9}}$ **66.** $\sqrt{\dfrac{25x^2y^2}{36}}$

67. $\sqrt{(13c^3)^2}$ **68.** $\sqrt{(468d^7)^2}$ **69.** $\sqrt{(2a^2)^4}$ **70.** $\sqrt{(3b^3)^6}$

■■■■■■ MAINTAIN

Solve each problem. (*Pages 458–467*)

71. Steven can paint a room in 3 hours. Kevin requires 5 hours to complete the job. How long would it take them to paint the room if they worked together?

72. Mr. Braun took 45.5 minutes to drive from his house to the post office and back. His rate going was 35 mph and his rate returning was 30 mph. How long did it take Mr. Braun to drive from the post office back to his house?

Determine whether the second number is a factor of the number in parentheses. Answer <u>Yes</u> or <u>No</u>. (*Pages 377–379*)

73. $(4 \cdot 6^2 \cdot 8)$; 4   **74.** $(2^2 + 1)$; 5   **75.** $(6^2 + 1)$; 6

Identify each number as prime, <u>P</u>, or composite, <u>C</u>. (*Pages 377–379*)

76. 121   **77.** 7   **78.** 10   **79.** 42   **80.** 63   **81.** 23

■■■■■■ CONNECT AND EXTEND

Simplify.

Examples: $\sqrt[3]{8} = 2$ **Since** $2^3 = 8$ $\sqrt[4]{81} = 3$ **Since** $3^4 = 81$

82. $\sqrt[3]{27}$ **83.** $\sqrt[3]{125}$ **84.** $\sqrt[4]{256}$ **85.** $\sqrt[4]{625}$

86. $\sqrt[3]{a^6b^3}$ **87.** $\sqrt[3]{d^6t^9}$ **88.** $\sqrt[3]{c^{12}f^{18}g^6}$ **89.** $\sqrt[3]{r^9s^3t^6}$

90. $\sqrt[4]{(14b^2)^4}$ **91.** $\sqrt[3]{(23d^4)^3}$ **92.** $\sqrt[3]{(16f^6)^3}$ **93.** $\sqrt[4]{(21t^3)^4}$

■■■■■■ NON-ROUTINE PROBLEM

94. Copy the addition problem at the right and find the sum. Then replace six of the digits in the problem with a zero so that the sum is 1,111.

$$\begin{array}{r} 111 \\ 333 \\ 555 \\ 777 \\ +999 \end{array}$$

Write an infinite repeating decimal for each of the following. (*Pages 26–29*)

1. $\frac{5}{9}$ 2. $\frac{9}{11}$ 3. $\frac{13}{33}$ 4. $1\frac{2}{3}$ 5. $4\frac{1}{6}$ 6. $\frac{1}{3}$

Square each of the following (*Pages 9–13*)

7. 15   8. 1.5   9. 4   10. 0.4   11. $\frac{2}{3}$ 12. $\frac{3}{4}$

12-2   Real Numbers

PERFECT SQUARES

Rational numbers such as the following are <u>perfect squares</u>.

$$25 \qquad \frac{4}{9} \qquad 0.16 \qquad 144 \qquad 1\frac{7}{9}$$

DEFINITION

A rational number is a **perfect square** if it is the square of a rational number

$$\frac{4}{9} = \frac{2}{3} \cdot \frac{2}{3}$$
$$\mathbf{0.16} = (0.4)(0.4)$$
$$\mathbf{144} = 12 \cdot 12$$

Rational numbers such as 5, $\frac{3}{8}$, and 0.7 are <u>not</u> perfect squares. This means there is no rational number whose square is 5, no rational number whose square is $\frac{3}{8}$, and no rational number whose square is 0.7. Thus, $\sqrt{5}$, $\sqrt{\frac{3}{8}}$, and $\sqrt{0.7}$ are *irrational* numbers.

IRRATIONAL SQUARE ROOT

A rational number that is not a perfect square has an **irrational** square root.

EXAMPLE 1   Identify each square root as rational or irrational. Give a reason.

   a. $\sqrt{15}$ **b.** $-\sqrt{49}$ **c.** $\sqrt{3}$

Solutions: Check whether the radicand is a perfect square.

   a. Since 15 is <u>not</u> a perfect square, $\sqrt{15}$ is **irrational.**
   b. Since 49 is a perfect square, $-\sqrt{49}$ is **rational.**
   c. Since 3 is <u>not</u> a perfect square, $\sqrt{3}$ is **irrational.**

EXAMPLE 2 Identify each square root as rational or irrational. Give a reason.

a. $-\sqrt{0.81}$ **b.** $\sqrt{\dfrac{9}{16}}$ **c.** $\sqrt{1\dfrac{2}{3}}$

Solutions: **a.** Since 0.81 is a perfect square, $-\sqrt{0.81}$ is **rational.**

b. Since $\dfrac{9}{16}$ is a perfect square, $\sqrt{\dfrac{9}{16}}$ is **rational.**

c. $\sqrt{1\dfrac{2}{3}} = \sqrt{\dfrac{5}{3}}$. Since $\dfrac{5}{3}$ is <u>not</u> a perfect square, $\sqrt{1\dfrac{2}{3}}$ is **irrational.**

Recall that every rational number can be written as an infinite repeating decimal.

$$2\dfrac{1}{2} = 2.5000\cdots \qquad \dfrac{2}{3} = 0.666\cdots \qquad \dfrac{3}{11} = 0.\overline{27}$$

The decimal equivalents of irrational numbers are non-repeating.

Some Irrational Numbers

$\sqrt{3} = 1.7320508\cdots$ $\sqrt{2} = 1.4142135\cdots$ $\sqrt{5} = 2.2360679\cdots$ $\longleftarrow$ **There is no repeating pattern.**
$\sqrt{7} = 2.6457513\cdots$ $\sqrt{6} = 2.4494897\cdots$ $-\sqrt{8} = -2.8284271\cdots$

Numbers such as 2, $-\sqrt{2}$, 14, -3.4, 0, and $0.\overline{6}$ are *real numbers*.

DEFINITION

> The set of *real numbers* contains all the rational numbers and all the irrational numbers.

Recall that there is a one-to-one correspondence between the points on the number line and the real numbers.

EXAMPLE 3 How many real numbers are there between $\dfrac{1}{3}$ and $\dfrac{3}{5}$?

Solution: Find a number halfway between $\dfrac{1}{3}$ and $\dfrac{3}{5}$. $\dfrac{1}{2}(\dfrac{1}{3} + \dfrac{3}{5}) = \dfrac{7}{15}$

Find a number halfway between $\dfrac{1}{3}$ and $\dfrac{7}{15}$. $\dfrac{1}{2}(\dfrac{1}{3} + \dfrac{7}{15}) = \dfrac{6}{15}$, or $\dfrac{2}{5}$

Find a number halfway between $\dfrac{1}{3}$ and $\dfrac{2}{5}$. $\dfrac{1}{2}(\dfrac{1}{3} + \dfrac{2}{5}) = \dfrac{11}{30}$

Conclusion: There are an **infinite number** of real numbers between $\dfrac{1}{2}$ and $\dfrac{3}{5}$.

Example 3 suggests the following property.

DENSITY PROPERTY

> Between any two real numbers, there is another real number.

EXERCISES: Classwork/Homework

Objective: To identify a square root of a number as rational or irrational

CHECK YOUR UNDERSTANDING

For Exercises 1–3, complete the sentence.

1. A rational number is a perfect square if it is the square of a __?__ number.

2. Since 30 is not a perfect square, $\sqrt{30}$ is an __?__ number.

3. The set that contains all the rational numbers and all the irrational numbers is the set of __?__ .

4. Name the property which states that between any two real numbers there is another real number.

5. Explain why $1.4142135\cdots$ is not a rational number.

6. How many real numbers are there between $\frac{1}{2}$ and $\frac{7}{8}$?

PRACTICE AND APPLY

For Exercises 7–36, identify each square root as <u>rational</u> or <u>irrational</u>.   Give a reason.

7. $\sqrt{25}$

8. $-\sqrt{3}$

9. $\sqrt{100}$

10. $\sqrt{22}$

11. $-\sqrt{18}$

12. $-\sqrt{96}$

13. $\sqrt{121}$

14. $\sqrt{7}$

15. $-\sqrt{400}$

16. $\sqrt{529}$

17. $-\sqrt{\frac{1}{10}}$

18. $\sqrt{\frac{1}{100}}$

19. $-\sqrt{2.56}$

20. $\sqrt{1.44}$

21. $\sqrt{4\frac{1}{6}}$

22. $-\sqrt{\frac{7}{12}}$

23. $-\sqrt{\frac{8}{9}}$

24. $\sqrt{\frac{9}{36}}$

25. $\sqrt{0.81}$

26. $\sqrt{1.69}$

27. $-\sqrt{5}$

28. $\sqrt{5\frac{1}{8}}$

29. $\sqrt{\frac{81}{25}}$

30. $-\sqrt{130}$

31. $\sqrt{3.61}$

32. $\sqrt{112}$

33. $\sqrt{0.05}$

34. $-\sqrt{\frac{1}{36}}$

35. $\sqrt{\frac{9}{47}}$

36. $\sqrt{3\frac{1}{5}}$

For Exercises 37–42, find three real numbers between the two given numbers.

37. $\frac{1}{4}$ and $\frac{1}{2}$

38. $\frac{2}{5}$ and $\frac{3}{5}$

39. $\frac{7}{6}$ and $\frac{3}{2}$

40. 0.3 and 0.4

41. 0.51 and 0.532

42. 3.26 and 3.265

Simplify. (*Pages 477–479*)

43. $\pm\sqrt{9r^8s^6}$ **44.** $-\sqrt{\dfrac{25}{49}}$ **45.** $\sqrt{25^2}$ **46.** $\sqrt{81c^{10}}$

Solve each problem. (*Pages 463–467*)

47. Mary Ellen can set up a lab experiment in 4 hours. Maureen can set it up in 3 hours. Mary Ellen works alone for $\frac{1}{2}$ hour and then Maureen helps her finish. How long does it take them to finish?

48. Ron can assemble a bookshelf unit in 10 hours. Bob can assemble it in 8 hours. How long would it take them to assemble the unit if they worked together?

Factor. (*Pages 380–383*)

49. $7x - rsx$ **50.** $9r^2s + 9r^2sb$ **51.** $m^2 + 3m + cm$
52. $ab^2c + abc^3 - a^3bc$ **53.** $8mx - mx + 3x$ **54.** $a(w - x) - c(w - x)$

CONNECT AND EXTEND

Find the expression for a real number that is halfway between each given pair of expressions.

55. $-4a$ and $\frac{7a}{3}$ **56.** $\frac{5c}{9}$ and $2c$ **57.** $\frac{-3r}{5}$ and $\frac{r}{4}$

58. $(7a + 2)$ and $(5a - 6)$ **59.** $(-16 - 7m)$ and $(-8 + 3m)$ **60.** $(4r - 3)$ and $(2r + 5)$

NON-ROUTINE PROBLEMS

61. Suppose a person was born on the 25th day of the year 35 B.C. and died on the 25th day of the year 15 A.D. How many years did the person live?

62. Use four 4's and one or more of the operation symbols, $+$, $-$, $\div$, or $\times$, to express the whole numbers from 1 to 4.
Example: $(4 \div 4) + 4 - 4 = 1$

REVIEW CAPSULE FOR SECTION 12–3

Write each rational number in the form $\dfrac{a}{b}$ when a and b are integers and b is not equal to 0. (*Pages 26–29*)

1. 0.3 **2.** 0.25 **3.** -8 **4.** -3.5 **5.** $3\frac{1}{3}$ **6.** $-1\frac{1}{5}$

12-3 Rational Approximations of Square Roots

You learned in Chapter 1 that every rational number can be represented by an infinite repeating decimal or by a terminating decimal.

$$\frac{1}{3} = 0.333 \cdots, \text{ or } \mathbf{0.\overline{3}} \qquad\qquad 1\frac{3}{5} = \frac{8}{5} = \mathbf{1.6}$$

The bar indicates the digits that repeat.

You also learned that any rational number can be represented in the form $\frac{a}{b}$, where a is an integer and b is a natural number.

$$0 = \frac{0}{1} \qquad 5.61 = \frac{561}{100} \qquad 0.001 = \frac{1}{1000}$$

Example 1 shows how to represent an infinite repeating decimal in the form $\frac{a}{b}$.

EXAMPLE 1 Write $0.\overline{3}$ in the form $\frac{a}{b}$.

Solution: Let $n = 0.\overline{3}$ ◄——— **Multiply each side by 10^1, or 10.**

$10n = 3.\overline{3}$ ◄——— **Subtract $n = 0.\overline{3}$ from this equation.**

$\underline{\quad n = 0.\overline{3}\quad}$

$9n = 3.0$ ◄——— **Solve for n.**

$n = \frac{3}{9}, \text{ or } \frac{1}{3}$ \qquad Thus, $0.\overline{3} = \mathbf{\frac{1}{3}}$.

EXAMPLE 2 Write $9.\overline{18}$ in the form $\frac{a}{b}$.

Solution: Let $n = 9.\overline{18}$ ◄——— **Multiply each side by 10^2, or 100.**

$100n = 918.\overline{18}$ ◄——— **Subtract $n = 9.\overline{18}$ from this equation.**

$\underline{\quad n = \quad 9.\overline{18}\quad}$

$99n = 909.00$

$n = \frac{909}{99} = \frac{101}{11}$ \qquad Thus, $9.\overline{18} = \mathbf{\frac{101}{11}}$.

Recall that a rational number that is not a perfect square has an **irrational square root**. Thus, the following numbers are irrational.

$$\sqrt{2} \qquad \sqrt{5} \qquad -\sqrt{17} \qquad \sqrt{31}$$

An irrational square root is often left in radical form. However, you can always approximate an irrational square root between consecutive integers.

$$2 < \sqrt{7} < 3 \quad \longleftarrow \quad \textbf{Since } \sqrt{4} < \sqrt{7} < \sqrt{9}$$

$$9 < \sqrt{84} < 10 \quad \longleftarrow \quad \textbf{Since } \sqrt{81} < \sqrt{84} < \sqrt{100}$$

You can use a calculator or the Table of Squares and Square Roots on page 636 to find a closer approximation to the square root of an irrational number.

EXAMPLE 3 The area of a square is 55 square meters. What is the length of each side to the nearest tenth of a meter?

Solution: Let s = the length of each side.

$$s^2 = 55 \quad \longleftarrow \quad \textbf{Area = s · s}$$

$$s = \pm\sqrt{55} \quad \longleftarrow \quad \begin{array}{l}\textbf{Since } s^2 = \underline{55}, s = \sqrt{55}, \\ \textbf{or } s = -\sqrt{55}.\end{array}$$

$$s = \sqrt{55} \quad \longleftarrow \quad \textbf{s must be positive.}$$

Using the table on page 636 yields:

$$s \approx 7.416$$

$$s \approx 7.4 \quad \longleftarrow \quad \begin{array}{l}\textbf{Rounded to the} \\ \textbf{nearest tenth}\end{array}$$

Using the calculator yields:

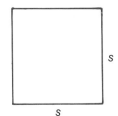

55 $\boxed{\sqrt{x}}$ $\boxed{7.4161985}$

$$\longrightarrow \quad s \approx 7.4$$

The length of each side is about **7.4 meters.**

EXERCISES: Classwork/Homework

Objectives: To write repeating decimals in the form $\frac{a}{b}$
To find rational approximations of square roots

CHECK YOUR UNDERSTANDING

For Exercises 1–3, complete the sentence.

1. Every rational number can be represented by an infinite repeating decimal or by a __?__ decimal.

2. To write $0.\overline{13}$ in the form $\frac{a}{b}$, first multiply both sides of the equation $n = 0.\overline{13}$ by __?__.

3. To write $0.\overline{125}$ in the form $\frac{a}{b}$, first multiply both sides of the equation $n = 0.\overline{125}$ by __?__.

4. Explain why $\sqrt{8}$ is between the consecutive integers 2 and 3.

Determine the consecutive integers x and y between which each square root lies.

5. $x < \sqrt{67} < y$

6. $x < \sqrt{47} < y$

7. $x < \sqrt{27} < y$

8. $x < \sqrt{101} < y$

9. $x < \sqrt{123} < y$

10. $x < \sqrt{150} < y$

11. $x < \sqrt{136} < y$

12. $x < \sqrt{46} < y$

13. $x < \sqrt{56} < y$

14. $x < \sqrt{14} < y$

15. $x < \sqrt{260} < y$

16. $x < \sqrt{901} < y$

17. $x < \sqrt{10,001} < y$

18. $x < \sqrt{1,000,001} < y$

19. $x < \sqrt{8101} < y$

■■■■■■■ **PRACTICE AND APPLY**

Write each rational number in the form $\frac{a}{b}$.

20. $0.\overline{4}$

21. $0.\overline{8}$

22. $0.\overline{15}$

23. $0.\overline{81}$

24. $0.\overline{72}$

25. $0.\overline{23}$

26. $0.\overline{186}$

27. $0.\overline{296}$

28. $0.\overline{543}$

29. $0.\overline{262}$

30. $1.\overline{2}$

31. $3.\overline{4}$

32. $2.\overline{51}$

33. $6.\overline{23}$

34. $3.\overline{14}$

35. $6.\overline{34}$

36. $1.3\overline{78}$

37. $4.2\overline{54}$

38. $3.70\overline{4}$

39. $2.82\overline{9}$

Use the Table of Square Roots on page 636 or a calculator to determine an approximation to each square root. Round each answer to the nearest tenth.

40. $\sqrt{8}$ **41.** $\sqrt{21}$ **42.** $\sqrt{13}$ **43.** $\sqrt{26}$ **44.** $\sqrt{92}$ **45.** $\sqrt{59}$

46. $\sqrt{50}$ **47.** $\sqrt{85}$ **48.** $\sqrt{101}$ **49.** $\sqrt{125}$ **50.** $\sqrt{76}$ **51.** $\sqrt{132}$

For Exercises 52–58, solve each problem.
Use the Table of Squares and Square Roots on page 636 or a calculator. Round answers to the nearest tenth.

52. The area of a square garden is 74 square meters. What is the length of one side of the garden?

53. The area of a square poster is 630 square centimeters. What is the length of a side of the poster?

54. The area of a circle is 67 square centimeters. What is the radius? (HINT: Area $= \pi r^2$; use $\pi = 3.14$.)

55. The area of a circular rug is 7 square meters. What is the diameter of the rug? (Use $\pi = 3.14$.)

56. The formula $d = 4.9t^2$ gives the approximate distance in meters traveled in t seconds by an object falling from rest. How long will an object take to fall 490 meters from rest?

57. The length of a rectangle is 5 times its width. The area of the rectangle is 204 square inches. Find the length and width of the rectangle.

58. The formula $D = 3.56\sqrt{a}$ gives the approximate distance to the horizon (in kilometers) from the viewpoint of an aircraft a meters above the ground. Find the distance to the horizon from the cockpit of an airplane 2025 meters off the ground. (HINT: Use the "Squares" column in the Table of Squares and Square Roots.)

 You can use the program on page 620 to calculate the square root of any positive integer.

Use the program for the following values of x.

59. $x = 5$ **60.** $x = 13$ **61.** $x = 26$ **62.** $x = 36$

63. $x = 42$ **64.** $x = 100$ **65.** $x = 9$ **66.** $x = 115$

MAINTAIN

Identify each square root as <u>rational</u> or <u>irrational</u>. Give a reason. (*Pages 480–483*)

67. $\sqrt{16}$ **68.** $\sqrt{7}$ **69.** $-\sqrt{900}$ **70.** $-\sqrt{25}$ **71.** $\sqrt{3\frac{1}{2}}$ **72.** $\sqrt{\frac{1}{5}}$

Simplify. (*Pages 477–479*)

73. $-\sqrt{64t^2}$ **74.** $\sqrt{r^{20}t^6}$ **75.** $-\sqrt{49c^{10}}$ **76.** $\sqrt{25c^{12}d^8}$

Factor each polynomial. When a polynomial cannot be factored, write <u>Prime</u>. (*Pages 384–386*)

77. $r^2 - s^4$ **78.** $-36 + c^2$ **79.** $2a^2 + 9$ **80.** $a^2b^2 - c^2$

CONNECT AND EXTEND

Simplify. Approximate the answer to the nearest tenth.

81. $5\sqrt{17} + 9$ **82.** $\sqrt{15} - \sqrt{6}$ **83.** $4\sqrt{87}$ **84.** $\frac{2}{5}\sqrt{14}$

85. $29 - 4\sqrt{10}$ **86.** $9\sqrt{30} - 2\sqrt{6}$ **87.** $\frac{3\sqrt{18} - 4}{5}$ **88.** $\frac{20 - 3\sqrt{42}}{8}$

NON-ROUTINE PROBLEM

89. Look at the figure at the right. Name two different things that you see.

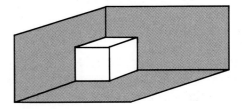

Simplify. (*Pages 477–479*)

1. $\sqrt{9c^4}$ **2.** $-\sqrt{121y^{10}}$ **3.** $-\sqrt{81r^8}$ **4.** $-\sqrt{25x^6}$ **5.** $\sqrt{49r^4}$

12-4 Simplifying Radicals

The following illustrates an important property of radicals.

$$\sqrt{9 \cdot 4} = \sqrt{36} = 6 \qquad\qquad \sqrt{9} \cdot \sqrt{4} = 3 \cdot 2 = 6$$

PRODUCT PROPERTY OF RADICALS

> The square root of the product of two nonnegative numbers is the product of their square roots. That is, if a and b are real numbers and $a \geq 0$, $b \geq 0$, then
>
> $$\sqrt{ab} = \sqrt{a} \cdot \sqrt{b}.$$

This property is used to simplify radicals. A radical is in **simplest form** when the radicand does not contain a perfect square factor other than 1.

EXAMPLE   Simplify.

    a. $\sqrt{50}$ **b.** $3\sqrt{8}$ **c.** $\sqrt{4d^5}$

Solutions: Identify the perfect square factors in the radicand.

    a. $\sqrt{50} = \sqrt{25 \cdot 2}$ ←——— **25 is the greatest perfect square factor of 50.**

           $= \sqrt{25} \cdot \sqrt{2}$ ←——— $\sqrt{25 \cdot 2} = \sqrt{25} \cdot \sqrt{2}$

           $= 5\sqrt{2}$ ←——— **Simplest form**

    b. $3\sqrt{8} = 3\sqrt{4 \cdot 2}$

           $= 3 \cdot \sqrt{4} \cdot \sqrt{2}$ ←——— $\sqrt{4 \cdot 2} = \sqrt{4} < \sqrt{2}$

           $= 3 \cdot 2 \cdot \sqrt{2}$

           $= 6\sqrt{2}$ ←——— **Simplest form**

    c. $\sqrt{4d^5} = \sqrt{4d^4 \cdot d}$ ←——— $4d^4$ **is the greatest perfect square factor of** $4d^5$.

           $= \sqrt{4d^4} \cdot \sqrt{d}$

           $= 2d^2\sqrt{d}$ ←——— **Simplest form**

Objective: To simplify radicals

CHECK YOUR UNDERSTANDING

Complete.

1. To simplify a radical, first factor the radicand to find the greatest __?__ factor.

2. A radical is in simplest-form when the radicand does not contain a perfect square factor other than __?__ .

Write each number as the product of the greatest possible perfect square integer and another factor.

3. $18 = $ __?__ $\times 2$

4. $27 = $ __?__ $\times 3$

5. $200 = $ __?__ $\times 2$

6. $125 = $ __?__ $\times$ __?__

7. $288 = $ __?__ $\times$ __?__

8. $300 = $ __?__ $\times$ __?__

9. $98 = $ __?__ $\times$ __?__

10. $243 = $ __?__ $\times$ __?__

11. $320 = $ __?__ $\times$ __?__

PRACTICE AND APPLY

Simplify. Assume that all variables represent positive real numbers.

12. $\sqrt{8}$

13. $\sqrt{40}$

14. $\sqrt{20}$

15. $\sqrt{24}$

16. $\sqrt{100}$

17. $\sqrt{98}$

18. $\sqrt{32}$

19. $2\sqrt{4}$

20. $\sqrt{242}$

21. $\sqrt{64}$

22. $\sqrt{196}$

23. $\sqrt{28}$

24. $4\sqrt{72}$

25. $2\sqrt{20}$

26. $3\sqrt{28}$

27. $4\sqrt{49}$

28. $\sqrt{56}$

29. $3\sqrt{18}$

30. $9\sqrt{50}$

31. $6\sqrt{72}$

32. $8\sqrt{12}$

33. $-6\sqrt{9}$

34. $-3\sqrt{16}$

35. $-2\sqrt{32}$

36. $-5\sqrt{32}$

37. $4\sqrt{200}$

38. $3\sqrt{1000}$

39. $\sqrt{1 \text{ million}}$

40. $3\sqrt{1 \text{ million}}$

41. $\sqrt{1,000,000,000,000}$

42. $3\sqrt{1,000,000,000}$

43. $4\sqrt{10,000,000,000}$

44. $\sqrt{10^2}$

45. $\sqrt{10^4}$

46. $\sqrt{10^7}$

47. $\sqrt{9t^7}$

48. $\sqrt{36b^3}$

49. $\sqrt{25m^9}$

50. $\sqrt{18p^5}$

51. $\sqrt{24c^7}$

52. $\sqrt{75q^{11}}$

53. $\sqrt{12r^5s^7}$

54. $\sqrt{32a^9b^3}$

55. $\sqrt{72c^9d^{13}}$

Approximations for $\sqrt{2}$, $\sqrt{3}$, and $\sqrt{5}$ are given below.

$$\sqrt{2} \approx 1.414 \qquad \sqrt{3} \approx 1.732 \qquad \sqrt{5} \approx 2.236$$

Using these approximations, you can find the square root of many numbers without using a calculator or the Table of Square Roots. Find the nonnegative square root of each number.

Example: 300 $\qquad \sqrt{300} = \sqrt{100} \cdot \sqrt{3} = 10\sqrt{3} \approx 10(1.732) = $ **17.32**

56. 8

57. 12

58. 20

59. 45

60. 98

61. 147   **62.** 320   **63.** 192   **64.** 216   **65.** 360

![MAINTAIN]

Write each rational number in the form $\frac{a}{b}$. (*Pages 484–498*)

66. $0.\overline{7}$ **67.** $0.\overline{1}$ **68.** $3.\overline{2}$

69. $0.2\overline{4}$ **70.** $0.\overline{16}$ **71.** $0.\overline{407}$

Find three real numbers between the two given numbers. (*Pages 480–483*)

72. $\frac{1}{2}$ and $\frac{6}{8}$ **73.** $\frac{7}{6}$ and $\frac{5}{3}$ **74.** 0.24 and 0.242

Factor. (*Pages 387–389*)

75. $x^2 - 4x + 4$ **76.** $b^2 - 18b + 81$ **77.** $16a^2 + 40a + 25$

78. $36t^2 - 12t + 1$ **79.** $9 - 30x + 25x^2$ **80.** $49 - 42y + 9y^2$

![CONNECT AND EXTEND]

Simplify. Assume that all variables represent positive real numbers.

81. $\sqrt{3(x + y)^2}$ **82.** $\sqrt{5(t - r)^2}$ **83.** $\sqrt{28(c^2 + d^2)^3}$

84. $\sqrt{48(a^2 - b^2)^5}$ **85.** $\sqrt{x^2 + 2xy + y^2}$ **86.** $\sqrt{d^2 + 6d + 9}$

![NON-ROUTINE PROBLEM]

87. A man is shipwrecked on an island and a crate of apples washed ashore with him. He calculates that if he eats one apple per day, the apples will last 14 days longer than if he eats two apples per day for two days and no apples on the third day. How many apples are in the crate?

——— **REVIEW CAPSULE FOR SECTION 12–5** ———

Simplify. (*Pages 9–13, 358–360, 477–479*)

1. 10^2 **2.** 15^2 **3.** 7^2 **4.** $(a - 1)^2$

5. $(a + 1)^2$ **6.** $(2t + 5)^2$ **7.** $(\sqrt{2})^2$ **8.** $(\sqrt{5})^2$

9. $(\sqrt{9})^2$ **10.** $(\sqrt{16})^2$ **11.** $(\sqrt{7})^2$ **12.** $(\sqrt{25})^2$

Solve for a^2. (*Pages 95–98*)

13. $a^2 + 25 = 144$ **14.** $18 + a^2 = 225$ **15.** $72 - a^2 = 15$ **16.** $21 = 169 - a^2$

Solve for a. (*Pages 404–406*)

17. $a^2 = 81$ **18.** $a^2 = 36$ **19.** $a^2 - 144 = 0$ **20.** $121 - a^2 = 0$

Simplify. (*Pages 477–479*)

1. $\sqrt{64}$ **2.** $-\sqrt{400}$ **3.** $\sqrt{100x^2}$ **4.** $\pm\sqrt{a^8b^4}$

Identify each square root as rational or irrational. (*Pages 480–483*)

5. $\sqrt{3\frac{1}{5}}$ **6.** $-\sqrt{2\frac{1}{8}}$ **7.** $\sqrt{0.01}$ **8.** $-\sqrt{1.72}$ **9.** $-\sqrt{\frac{9}{21}}$ **10.** $\sqrt{\frac{36}{225}}$

Find the real number halfway between the two given numbers.
(*Pages 480–483*)

11. 23.12 and 24.68 **12.** $2\frac{6}{7}$ and $\frac{1}{5}$ **13.** $\frac{8}{9}$ and $2\frac{1}{4}$

Solve each problem. (*Pages 484–487*)

14. The area of a square is 7 square meters. What is the length of one side of the square to the nearest tenth of a meter?

15. The length of a rectangle is twice its width. The area of the rectangle is 218 square units. Find the dimensions to the nearest tenth.

Simplify. Variables represent positive numbers. (*Pages 488–490*)

16. $\sqrt{28}$ **17.** $\sqrt{80}$ **18.** $-\sqrt{24x^5}$ **19.** $2\sqrt{36d^3}$

Historical Digest: ***Radicals***

The word ''radical'' comes from a Latin word meaning root. The radical symbol, $\sqrt{}$, probably comes from an old European lower case letter ''r.''

About 500 B.C., the Greek philosopher and mathematician Pythagoras formed a society devoted to the mysteries of mathematics, music, and astronomy. This society believed that everything in the universe was based on counting numbers and that every number could be written as the ratio of two of these numbers. Then they discovered the existence of $\sqrt{2}$. Since this did not fit in with their concept of number and they could not explain it, they tried to hide their discovery.

Meteorology is the study of the atmosphere. The best known activity of meteorologists is **weather forecasting.**

The table at the right shows the **Temperature-Humidity Index,** or **THI.** THI is a measure of how comfortable (or uncomfortable) people feel under given conditions of temperature and humidity during the warm season.

EXAMPLE 1:

Find the temperature-humidity index above which most people feel uncomfortable.

Solution:

Locate the curved band in the table for "nearly everyone feels uncomfortable." The band passes through the number 79.

Temperature-Humidity Index: **79**

THE TEMPERATURE-HUMIDITY INDEX

Temperature	Relative Humidity 10% 20% 30% 40% 50% 60% 70% 80% 90% 100%
68°	63 64 64 65 65 66 67 67 68 68
69°	64 64 65 65 66 67 67 68 68 69
70°	64 65 65 66 67 67 68 69 69 70
71°	65 65 66 67 67 68 69 70 70 71
72°	65 66 67 67 68 69 70 71 71 72
73°	66 66 67 68 69 70 70 71 72 73
74°	66 67 68 69 70 71 71 72 73 74
75°	67 67 68 69 70 71 72 73 74 75
76°	67 68 69 70 71 72 73 74 75 76
77°	68 69 70 71 72 73 74 75 76 77
78°	68 69 70 71 73 74 75 76 77 78
79°	69 70 71 72 73 74 76 77 78 79
80°	69 70 72 73 74 75 76 78 79 80
81°	70 71 72 73 75 76 77 78 80 81
82°	70 72 73 74 75 77 78 79 81 82
83°	71 72 73 75 76 78 79 80 82 83
84°	71 73 74 75 77 78 79 81 83 84
85°	72 73 75 76 78 79 80 82 84 85
86°	72 74 75 77 78 80 81 83 84 86
87°	73 74 76 77 79 81 82 84 85 87
88°	73 75 76 78 80 81 83 85 86 88
89°	74 75 77 79 81 82 84 86 87 89
90°	74 76 77 79 81 83 85 87 88 90
91°	75 76 78 80 82 84 85 87 89 91
92°	75 77 79 81 83 85 86 88 90 92
93°	76 78 80 81 83 85 87 89 91 93
94°	76 78 80 82 84 86 88 90 92 94
95°	77 79 81 83 85 87 89 91 93 95

few people feel uncomfortable ↓

about one-half of all people feel uncomfortable ↓

nearly everyone feels uncomfortable ↓

rapidly decreasing work efficiency ↓

extreme danger ⇩

In cold climates, the combined effect of high winds and cold temperatures can make a person feel colder than the actual thermometer reading. This is called **wind chill.**

EXAMPLE 2:

Find the wind chill temperature when the thermometer reading is −5°F and the wind speed is 10 miles per hour.

Solution:

Locate the wind speed, 10 miles per hour, along the left side of the table. Look horizontally to the right to the column headed "−5."

Wind Chill Temperature: **−27°F**

WIND CHILL TEMPERATURE TABLE

Wind Speed (mph)	Thermometer Reading (°F) −25	−20	−15	−10	−5	0	5	10	15	20
5	−31	−26	−21	−15	−10	−5	0	6	11	16
10	−52	−46	−40	−34	−27	−22	−15	−9	−3	3
15	−65	−58	−51	−45	−38	−31	−25	−18	−11	−5
20	−74	−67	−60	−53	−46	−39	−31	−24	−17	−10
25	−81	−74	−66	−59	−51	−44	−36	−29	−22	−15
30	−86	−79	−71	−64	−56	−49	−41	−33	−25	−18
35	−89	−82	−74	−67	−58	−52	−43	−35	−27	−20
40	−92	−84	−76	−69	−68	−53	−45	−37	−29	−21

The following formula can be used to approximate the wind chill temperature in degrees Celsius.

$$C = 33 - \frac{(10\sqrt{r} + 10.45 - r)(33 - t)}{22.1}$$

C: wind chill temperature in degrees Celsius
t: air temperature in degrees Celsius
r: wind speed in meters per second

EXAMPLE 3: On a fall day the air temperature is 5°C. The wind speed is 8 meters per second. Find the wind chill temperature.

Solution: $C = 33 - \dfrac{(10\sqrt{r} + 10.45 - r)(33 - t)}{22.1}$

$C = 33 - \dfrac{(10\sqrt{8} + 10.45 - 8)(33 - 5)}{22.1}$ ← $r = 8$ $t = 5$

$= 33 - \dfrac{(10\sqrt{8} + 10.45 - 8)(28)}{22.1}$

8 $\boxed{\sqrt{}}$ $\boxed{\times}$ 10 $\boxed{+}$ 10.45 $\boxed{-}$ 8 $\boxed{\times}$

28 $\boxed{\div}$ 22.1 $\boxed{=}$ $\boxed{+/-}$ $\boxed{+}$ 33 $\boxed{=}$ $\boxed{-5.939347}$

The wind chill temperature is **about −6°C.**

EXERCISES

In Exercises 1–4, refer to the tables on page 492.

1. Find the temperature-humidity index above which about 50% of most people feel uncomfortable.

2. Find the temperature-humidity index when the temperature is 90°F and the relative humidity is 80%.

3. What wind speed produces a wind chill temperature of −53°F when the thermometer reading is −10°F?

4. Does the wind chill temperature increase or decrease when the wind speed increases and the thermometer reading stays the same?

Use the formula above to find the wind chill temperature to the nearest degree Celsius (°C).

5. Air temperature: −3°C
   Wind speed: 7 meters per second

6. Air temperature: 12°C
   Wind speed: 6 meters per second

12-5 The Pythagorean Theorem

Test each triangle below to determine whether the sum of the squares of the shorter sides equals the square of the longest side. (The symbol ⌐ means that an angle is a right angle.)

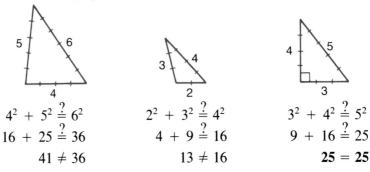

$$4^2 + 5^2 \stackrel{?}{=} 6^2$$
$$16 + 25 \stackrel{?}{=} 36$$
$$41 \neq 36$$

$$2^2 + 3^2 \stackrel{?}{=} 4^2$$
$$4 + 9 \stackrel{?}{=} 16$$
$$13 \neq 16$$

$$3^2 + 4^2 \stackrel{?}{=} 5^2$$
$$9 + 16 \stackrel{?}{=} 25$$
$$\mathbf{25 = 25}$$

RIGHT TRIANGLE

The sentence is true for the third triangle only because it is a *right triangle*. A **right triangle** is a triangle with one angle of 90°. The relationship between the two shorter sides (legs) and the longest side (hypotenuse) of every right triangle is known as the *Pythagorean Theorem*.

Many number properties have been stated earlier in this book. Some of these properties are often called **postulates,** that is, statements assumed to be true. A **theorem** is a statement that can be proved from postulates and definitions.

PYTHAGOREAN THEOREM

> If a, b, and c are the lengths of the sides of a right triangle and c is the length of the **hypotenuse** (longest side), then
> $$a^2 + b^2 = c^2$$

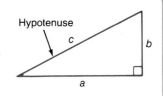

The proof is outlined in Exercises 57–60 on page 498.

EXAMPLE 1 The shorter sides of a right triangle are 12 and 5. Find the length of the hypotenuse.

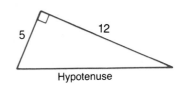

Solution: Since the triangle is a right triangle, use the Pythagorean Theorem.

$$a^2 + b^2 = c^2 \longleftarrow \quad \text{Replace } a \text{ with 5 and } b \text{ with 12.}$$
$$5^2 + 12^2 = c^2$$
$$25 + 144 = c^2$$
$$169 = c^2 \longleftarrow \quad \text{Since } c^2 = 169,\, c = 13 \text{ or } c = -13.$$
$$13 = c \longleftarrow \quad \text{The length of a side of the triangle must be positive.}$$

The length of the hypotenuse is **13.**

The Pythagorean Theorem is useful in solving problems related to right triangles.

EXAMPLE 2 The top of a 6-meter ladder reaches a window ledge. The ledge is 5 meters above the ground. To the nearest tenth of a meter, how far from the house is the foot of the ladder?

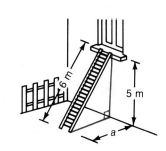

Solution: Since the ladder, the ground and the side of the house form a right triangle, use the Pythagorean Theorem.

$$c^2 = a^2 + b^2 \longleftarrow \quad \text{Replace } c \text{ with 6 and } b \text{ with 5.}$$
$$6^2 = a^2 + 5^2$$
$$36 = a^2 + 25 \longleftarrow \quad \text{Solve for } a^2.$$
$$11 = a^2$$
$$\pm\sqrt{11} = a \longleftarrow \quad \text{The distance, } a, \text{ cannot be negative.}$$
$$a \approx 3.317 \longleftarrow \quad \text{Use the Table of Square Roots} \quad \text{or} \quad 11 \;\boxed{\sqrt{x}} \;\; \boxed{3.3166248}$$

The foot of the ladder is about **3.3 meters** from the house.

When you know the lengths of three sides of a triangle, you can use this theorem to determine whether it is a right triangle.

THEOREM

> If the sum of the squares of the lengths of the two shorter sides (legs) of a triangle is equal to the square of the length of the longest side (hypotenuse), then the triangle is a right triangle.

EXAMPLE 3

Determine whether a triangle whose sides are 10, 15, and 20 units long is a right triangle.

Solution: $c^2 = a^2 + b^2$ ←———— **Replace c with 20, a with 10, and b with 15.**

$20^2 \overset{?}{=} 10^2 + 15^2$

$400 \overset{?}{=} 100 + 225$

$400 \neq 325$ The triangle is **not** a right triangle.

EXERCISES: Classwork/Homework

Objective: To use the Pythagorean Theorem to find the length of a side of a right triangle

CHECK YOUR UNDERSTANDING

1. *Complete:* A triangle with one angle of 90° is a __?__ triangle.

2. *Complete:* The longest side of a right triangle is the __?__.

3. The lengths of the sides of a right triangle are 3 inches, 4 inches, and 5 inches. What is the length of the hypotenuse?

4. The lengths of the sides of a triangle are 5, 6, and 8 units. Explain how you would determine if this triangle is a right triangle.

PRACTICE AND APPLY

In Exercises 5–14, refer to the diagram at the right. Use the Pythagorean Theorem to find the unknown side. Use the Square Root Table on page 636 or a calculator. Round answers to the nearest tenth.

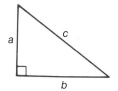

5. $a = 6, b = 8, c = $ __?__

6. $a = 24, b = 10, c = $ __?__

7. $a = 14, b = 7, c = $ __?__

8. $a = 9, b = 5, c = $ __?__

9. $a = 10, b = 12, c = $ __?__

10. $a = 8, b = 10, c = $ __?__

11. $a = 12, b = $ __?__$, c = 17$

12. $a = 10, b = $ __?__$, c = 13$

13. $a = $ __?__$, b = 16, c = 25$

14. $a = $ __?__$, b = 10, c = 19$

Use the Pythagorean Theorem and a calculator to find the unknown side. Round answers to the nearest tenth.

15. $a = 5.6, b = 2.3, c = $ __?__

16. $a = 8.3, b = 3.7, c = $ __?__

17. $a = 6.2, b = $ __?__$, c = 10.5$

18. $a = $ __?__$, b = 3.6, c = 14.2$

In Exercises 19–30, the lengths of three sides of a triangle are given. State whether or not they form a right triangle. Answer *Yes* or *No.*

19. 12, 5, 13

20. 9, 12, 15

21. 4, 5, 7

22. 3, 10, 12

23. 9, 40, 41

24. 16, 20, 24

25. 2, 9, 10

26. 3, 4, 5

27. 7, 10, 12

28. 1, 1, $\sqrt{2}$

29. $\sqrt{3}$, 1, 2

30. $\sqrt{2}$, $\sqrt{2}$, 2

In Exercises 31–38, draw a diagram for each problem. Use the Table of Square Roots on page 636 or a calculator. Round answers to the nearest tenth.

31. A pipeline is built diagonally across a square field. Each side of the field is 7 kilometers long. What is the length of the pipeline?

32. A wire stretches from the top of a pole 22 feet high to a stake in the ground which is 10 feet from the foot of the pole. Find the length of the wire.

33. A ladder 40 feet long leans against a building and reaches a ledge. The foot of the ladder is 16 feet from the building. How high is the ledge?

34. Sean took a homing pigeon 10 kilometers due east of his home and then 5 kilometers north. When he let the pigeon go, if flew straight home. How far did it fly?

35. A diagonal of a square is 10 centimeters long. Find the length of each side of the square.

36. The diagonal of a rectangle is 20 inches long. The rectangle's length is 3 times its width. Find the dimensions of the rectangle.

37. Two telephone poles, 30 feet and 39 feet high, respectively, are 60 feet apart. How long is the wire from the top of one pole to the top of the other pole?

38. In a swimming pool 70 feet long and 25 feet wide, how many feet will be saved by swimming diagonally across the pool instead of along its sides?

■■■■■■■ MAINTAIN

Simplify. (*Pages 488–490*)

39. $\sqrt{44}$

40. $\sqrt{27}$

41. $\sqrt{48}$

42. $\sqrt{80}$

43. $2\sqrt{28}$

Determine an approximation to each square root. Round each answer to the nearest tenth. (*Pages 484–487*)

44. $\sqrt{26}$

45. $\sqrt{83}$

46. $\sqrt{5}$

47. $\sqrt{123}$

48. $\sqrt{90}$

Factor each trinomial. (*Pages 392–395*)

49. $x^2 + 16x + 63$

50. $r^2 - 2r - 3$

51. $a^2 - 9a + 18$

52. $b^2 - 6b - 16$

53. $c^2 + 5c - 36$

54. $36 + 13x + x^2$

Solve each problem.

55. A rectangle of height 12 centimeters is inscribed in a circle with a radius of 10 centimeters. Find the area of the rectangle.

56. A man on a wharf 12 meters above the water pulls in a boat on the end of a rope. He had 20 meters of rope out and the pulled in 7 meters of rope. How far did he move the boat?

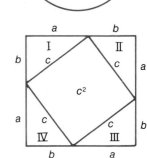

10 cm   12 cm

The figure at the right suggests a proof of the Pythagorean Theorem. Note that each side of the larger square is $(a + b)$ units long. The area of this square is made up of four triangles and a smaller square each of whose sides is c units long.

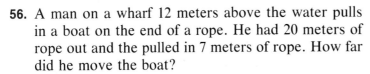

In Exercises 57–60, give a reason for each statement.

57. $(a + b)^2 = c^2 + 4(\frac{1}{2}ab)$ (Why?)

58. $a^2 + 2ab + b^2 = c^2 + 4(\frac{1}{2}ab)$ (Why?)

59. $a^2 + 4(\frac{1}{2}ab) + b^2 = c^2 + 4(\frac{1}{2}ab)$ (Why?)

60. $a^2 + b^2 = c^2$ (Why?)

61. Derive a formula for the length of the altitude, h, of the equilateral triangle shown at the right.

62. Derive a formula for the area of an equilateral triangle in terms of a side, s.

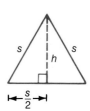

63. Prove: A triangle with sides $2pq$, $(p^2 - q^2)$, and $(p^2 + q^2)$ is a right triangle.

─────── **REVIEW CAPSULE FOR SECTION 12–6** ───────

Evaluate. (*Pages 9–13, 53–61*)

1. $|-8|$ **2.** $|15 - 12|$ **3.** $|-8 + 6|$ **4.** $|-8 - (-7)|$ **5.** $|9 - (-1)|$
6. $[9 - (-7)]^2$ **7.** $(21 - 8)^2$ **8.** $(1 - 3)^2$ **9.** $[7 - (-5)]^2$ **10.** $[-3 - (-5)]^2$

Evaluate $(x_2 - x_1)^2 + (y_2 - y_1)^2$ for the given values of (x_1, y_1) and (x_2, y_2).
(*Pages 9–13, 58–61*)

11. $x_1 = 7, y_1 = 0$; $x_2 = 3, y_2 = -1$ **12.** $x_1 = 0, y_1 = -1$; $x_2 = 3, y_2 = -1$
13. $x_1 = -4, y_1 = -5$; $x_2 = -2, y_2 = -2$ **14.** $x_1 = 2, y_1 = -5$; $x_2 = 4, y_2 = 2$

12-6 The Distance Formula

Two points that lie on a line parallel to the *x* axis (horizontal line) have the same *y* coordinate. To find the distance between two such points, determine the absolute value of the difference of their *x* coordinates. Thus, in Figure 1,

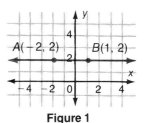

Figure 1

$$AB = |-2 - 1| = |-3| = \textbf{3}.$$

Similarly, two points that lie on a line parallel to the *y* axis (vertical line) have the same *x* coordinate. To find the distance between two such points, determine the absolute value of the difference of their *y* coordinates. Thus, in Figure 2,

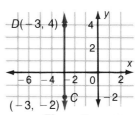

Figure 2

$$CD = |4 - (-2)| = |4 + 2| = |6|$$
$$= \textbf{6}.$$

Suppose that you wish to find the distance between the points $A(-2, 3)$ and $B(4, -5)$ shown in Figure 3. First you draw the horizontal and vertical line segments intersecting at *C* to form right triangle *ABC*. After finding the lengths of *AC* and *BC*, you can use the Pythagorean Theorem to find the length of *AB*. Thus,

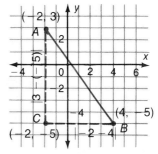

Figure 3

$$BC = |-2 - 4| = |-6| = \textbf{6} \quad \text{and} \quad AC = |3 - (-5)| = |8| = \textbf{8}$$

$$(AB)^2 = \underbrace{(BC)^2}_{} + \underbrace{(AC)^2}_{} \quad \longleftarrow \quad \textbf{By the Pythagorean Theorem}$$

$$(AB)^2 = \quad 6^2 \quad + \quad 8^2$$

$$(AB)^2 = \quad 36 \quad + \quad 64$$

$$(AB)^2 = 100 \quad \text{and} \quad AB = 10 \qquad \text{Thus, } AB \text{ is } \textbf{10 units} \text{ long.}$$

This procedure can be generalized as a formula to find the distance between any two points $P_1(x_1, y_1)$ and $P_2(x_2, y_2)$ in the coordinate plane. You are asked to prove this formula in the Exercises.

DISTANCE FORMULA	If $P_1(x_1, y_1)$ and $P_2(x_2, y_2)$ are any two points in the coordinate plane, the distance, d, between the points is given by the formula $$d = \sqrt{(x_2 - x_1)^2 + (y_2 - y_1)^2}.$$

EXAMPLE   Find the distance between $P(7, 3)$ and $Q(2, -5)$.

Solution: Use the Distance Formula.

$d = \sqrt{(x_2 - x_1)^2 + 1\,(y_2 - y_1)^2}$ ← **Replace x_2 with 2 and x_1 with 7.**
Replace y_2 with -5 and y_1 with 3.

$d = \sqrt{(2 - 7)^2 + (-5 - 3)^2}$

$d = \sqrt{(-5)^2 + (-8)^2}$

$d = \sqrt{25 + 64}$, or $\sqrt{89}$ ← **Simplest form**

It does not matter which point is considered (x_1, y_1) and which one is considered (x_2, y_2). The distance will be the same.

CALCULATOR   You can also use a calculator and the Distance Formula to find the distance in the Example above.

$d = \sqrt{(2 - 7)^2 + (-5 - 3)^2}$

$\boxed{(}$ $\mathbf{2}$ $\boxed{-}$ $\mathbf{7}$ $\boxed{)}$ $\boxed{x^2}$ $\boxed{+}$

$\boxed{(}$ $\mathbf{5}$ $\boxed{+/-}$ $\boxed{-}$ $\mathbf{3}$ $\boxed{)}$ $\boxed{x^2}$ $\boxed{=}$ $\boxed{89}$

To find the distance to the nearest tenth, use the $\boxed{\sqrt{x}}$ key.

$\boxed{89}$ $\boxed{\sqrt{x}}$ $\boxed{9.433911}$ The distance is about **9.4 units.**

EXERCISES: Classwork/Homework

Objective: To find the distance between two points on the coordinate plane

CHECK YOUR UNDERSTANDING

1. Robert used the Distance Formula to find the distance between $A(-2, 4)$ and $B(3, 5)$. The first step of his work is shown below.

$$d = \sqrt{(-2 - 4)^2 + (3 - 5)^2}$$

Will Robert's answer be correct? Explain.

Find the distance between each pair of points.

2. $A(0, 0)$ and $B(-5, 0)$ **3.** $P(0, 0)$ and $Q(0, -5)$ **4.** $C(-3, 5)$ and $D(-3, -3)$

5. $D(6, 8)$ and $E(0, 0)$ **6.** $M(0, 0)$ and $N(2, 3)$ **7.** $S(1, 3)$ and $T(4, 7)$

8. $U(5, 10)$ and $V(2, 6)$ **9.** $X(2, 1)$ and $Y(-3, -4)$ **10.** $L(-2, 4)$ and $M(-1, 2)$

11. $C(3, 1)$ and $D(-1, 6)$ **12.** $A(2, 2)$ and $B(2, -7)$ **13.** $P(9, 6)$ and $R(-5, 6)$

14. $N(-2, -3)$ and $T(1, 2)$ **15.** $E(3, 2)$ and $F(8, -10)$ **16.** $J(-2, 4)$ and $K(7, -8)$

Use the given figure to answer each question.

17.

18.

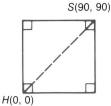

19.

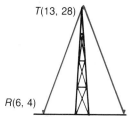

What is the distance between the objects on the teeter-totter?

How far is it from home plate to second base?

How long is the guy wire of the radio antenna?

Find the perimeter of each triangle.

20.

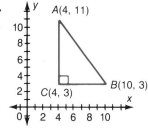

21.

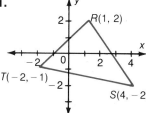

22.

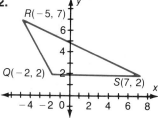

Simplify. Assume that all variables represent positive real numbers. (*Pages 488–490*)

23. $\sqrt{72}$ **24.** $\sqrt{90}$ **25.** $4\sqrt{28}$ **26.** $-3\sqrt{4}$ **27.** $\sqrt{32d^5}$

Factor. (*Pages 397–400*)

28. $2x^2 - 5x - 12$ **29.** $5y^2 + 33y - 14$ **30.** $6a^2 + 7a - 5$

31. Use the Pythagorean Theorem to prove the Distance Formula.

Simplify. (*Pages 488–490*)

1. $\sqrt{18}$ **2.** $\sqrt{300}$ **3.** $\sqrt{50}$ **4.** $\sqrt{8}$

5. $\sqrt{32}$ **6.** $\sqrt{12}$ **7.** $\sqrt{24}$ **8.** $\sqrt{1000}$

9. $(\sqrt{7})^2$ **10.** $(\sqrt{3})^2$ **11.** $(\sqrt{6})^2$ **12.** $(\sqrt{2})^2$

12-7   Multiplication of Radicals

To multiply two radicals such as $4\sqrt{2}$ and $3\sqrt{5}$, you use the Commutative and Associative Properties of Multiplication.

EXAMPLE 1   Multiply: $-3\sqrt{6} \cdot 4\sqrt{3}$. Express the answer in simplest form.

Solution: $-3\sqrt{6} \cdot 4\sqrt{3} = (-3 \cdot 4) \cdot (\sqrt{6} \cdot \sqrt{3})$ ◄——— **By the Commutative and Associative Properties**

$= -12 \cdot \sqrt{6 \cdot 3}$

$= -12 \cdot \sqrt{18}$ ◄——— $\sqrt{18}$ **can be simplified.**

$= -12 \cdot \sqrt{9} \cdot \sqrt{2}$ ◄——— $\sqrt{18} = \sqrt{9} \cdot \sqrt{2}$

$= -12 \cdot 3 \cdot \sqrt{2}$

$= -36\sqrt{2}$ ◄——— **Simplest form**

When a radical can be simplified, it is usually easier to do this before multiplying by other factors.

EXAMPLE 2   Multiply: $\sqrt{8} \cdot \sqrt{6}$. Express the answer in simplest form.

Solution: $\sqrt{8} \cdot \sqrt{6} = \sqrt{4 \cdot 2} \cdot \sqrt{6}$ ◄——— $\sqrt{8}$ **can be simplified.**

$= 2 \cdot \sqrt{2} \cdot \sqrt{6}$ ◄——— $\sqrt{2} \cdot \sqrt{6} = \sqrt{12}$

$= 2 \cdot \sqrt{12}$ ◄——— $\sqrt{12}$ **can be simplified.**

$= 2 \cdot \sqrt{4 \cdot 3}$

$= 2 \cdot \sqrt{4} \cdot \sqrt{3}$

$= 2 \cdot 2 \cdot \sqrt{3}$

$= 4\sqrt{3}$ ◄——— **Simplest form**

CALCULATOR

You can use a scientific calculator to find a decimal approximation for the product of two radicals.

Multiply: $4\sqrt{6} \cdot -2\sqrt{5}$

4 ⬜×⬜ 6 ⬜√x⬜ ⬜=⬜ ⬜×⬜ 2 ⬜+/-⬜ ⬜×⬜ 5 ⬜√x⬜ ⬜=⬜ ⬜-43.817805⬜

The product is about **−43.8.**

EXERCISES: Classwork/Homework

Objective: To multiply radicals

CHECK YOUR UNDERSTANDING

Replace each __?__ with the correct number.

1. $\sqrt{8} \cdot \sqrt{3} = \sqrt{\underline{?} \cdot 2} \cdot \sqrt{3}$
   $= \sqrt{\underline{?}} \cdot \sqrt{2} \cdot \sqrt{3}$

2. $\sqrt{50} \cdot \sqrt{2} = \sqrt{\underline{?} \cdot 2} \cdot \sqrt{2}$
   $= \sqrt{\underline{?}} \cdot \sqrt{2} \cdot \sqrt{2}$

3. $6\sqrt{8} \cdot 5\sqrt{6} = (6 \cdot 5) \cdot (\sqrt{8} \cdot \sqrt{\underline{?}})$
   $= 30 \cdot \sqrt{\underline{?}}$

4. $5\sqrt{10} \cdot 4\sqrt{5} = (5 \cdot \underline{?}) \cdot (\sqrt{10} \cdot \sqrt{5})$
   $= \underline{?} \cdot \sqrt{50}$

PRACTICE AND APPLY

Multiply and simplify.

5. $\sqrt{5} \cdot \sqrt{2}$
6. $\sqrt{3} \cdot \sqrt{5}$
7. $\sqrt{7} \cdot \sqrt{2}$
8. $\sqrt{6} \cdot \sqrt{2}$
9. $\sqrt{3} \cdot \sqrt{6}$
10. $3\sqrt{3} \cdot \sqrt{2}$
11. $\sqrt{5} \cdot \sqrt{10}$
12. $\sqrt{8} \cdot \sqrt{2}$
13. $\sqrt{9} \cdot \sqrt{4}$
14. $\sqrt{4} \cdot \sqrt{2}$
15. $\sqrt{3} \cdot \sqrt{12}$
16. $\sqrt{10} \cdot \sqrt{20}$
17. $\sqrt{25} \cdot \sqrt{3}$
18. $\sqrt{50} \cdot \sqrt{2}$
19. $\sqrt{7} \cdot \sqrt{7}$
20. $\sqrt{30} \cdot \sqrt{3}$
21. $2\sqrt{3} \cdot \sqrt{2}$
22. $\sqrt{3} \cdot 5\sqrt{7}$
23. $4\sqrt{2} \cdot \sqrt{5}$
24. $3\sqrt{2} \cdot 4\sqrt{3}$
25. $5\sqrt{2} \cdot 3\sqrt{5}$
26. $4\sqrt{5} \cdot 3\sqrt{2}$
27. $7\sqrt{6} \cdot 2\sqrt{2}$
28. $8\sqrt{5} \cdot 3\sqrt{6}$
29. $-7\sqrt{12} \cdot 4\sqrt{3}$
30. $8\sqrt{6} \cdot -3\sqrt{3}$
31. $3\sqrt{6} \cdot 4\sqrt{10}$
32. $-2\sqrt{12} \cdot -3\sqrt{2}$
33. $-8\sqrt{6} \cdot -3\sqrt{7}$
34. $-6\sqrt{8} \cdot 3\sqrt{6}$
35. $-9\sqrt{10} \cdot 7\sqrt{3}$
36. $-4\sqrt{14} \cdot 2\sqrt{7}$

Use a calculator to find each product. Round each answer to the nearest tenth.

37. $2\sqrt{5} \cdot 6\sqrt{3}$
38. $-4\sqrt{8} \cdot 6\sqrt{2}$
39. $-6\sqrt{5} \cdot -3\sqrt{3}$
40. $5\sqrt{10} \cdot \sqrt{8}$
41. $3\sqrt{6} \cdot -2\sqrt{5}$
42. $-8\sqrt{3} \cdot 4\sqrt{7}$
43. $\sqrt{8} \cdot 4\sqrt{3}$
44. $-2\sqrt{5} \cdot 9\sqrt{2}$

Multiply. Variables represent positive numbers.

45. $\sqrt{a} \cdot \sqrt{ab}$
46. $\sqrt{cd} \cdot \sqrt{c}$
47. $\sqrt{8bc} \cdot \sqrt{4bc}$
48. $\sqrt{6ax} \cdot \sqrt{9ax}$
49. $\sqrt{6m^4} \cdot \sqrt{3mn^2}$
50. $\sqrt{2a^2c} \cdot \sqrt{2c^2x}$
51. $\sqrt{a^3b} \cdot \sqrt{bc^3}$
52. $\sqrt{c^3} \cdot -\sqrt{5cd}$
53. $\sqrt[3]{4} \cdot \sqrt[3]{2}$
54. $\sqrt[3]{9} \cdot \sqrt[3]{3}$
55. $\sqrt[3]{4^2} \cdot \sqrt[3]{4}$
56. $\sqrt[3]{7} \cdot \sqrt[3]{7^2}$
57. $\sqrt[3]{10} \cdot \sqrt[3]{10^2}$
58. $\sqrt[3]{8} \cdot \sqrt[3]{2}$
59. $\sqrt[3]{12} \cdot \sqrt[3]{2}$
60. $\sqrt[3]{24} \cdot \sqrt[3]{2}$

Find the distance between each pair of points. (*Pages 499–501*)

61. $P(4, 3)$ and $Q(0, 0)$ **62.** $A(0, 0)$ and $C(-5, 9)$ **63.** $Q(-1, 2)$ and $R(8, -2)$

64. $P(1, 4)$ and $S(6, 9)$ **65.** $T(-3, 2)$ and $R(2, -7)$ **66.** $S(4, 0)$ and $V(4, 9)$

In Exercises 67–68, draw a diagram for each problem. Use the Table of Square Roots on page 636 or a calculator. Round answers to the nearest tenth. (*Pages 494–498*)

67. A ladder 50 feet long leans against a building and reaches a window ledge that is 30 feet above the ground. How far is it from the building to the foot of the ladder?

68. Karl jogged 8 miles due east of his house and then 5 miles due north. He returned on a path that led straight to his house. How far did he jog home?

Factor. (*Pages 401–403*)

69. $5x^2 + 15x - 20$ **70.** $3x^2 + 6x - 72$ **71.** $d^3 - d$

72. $6m^2 - 24$ **73.** $12y^2 - 42y + 18$ **74.** $8 - 8z^2$

CONNECT AND EXTEND

Multiply. Variables represent positive numbers.

75. $-3a\sqrt{ab} \cdot 2a\sqrt{ab}$ **76.** $-2\sqrt{7y} \cdot 5\sqrt{2y}$ **77.** $y^2\sqrt{xy} \cdot 2x\sqrt{y}$

78. $3b\sqrt{b^2e} \cdot 2e\sqrt{be^2}$ **79.** $5t^2\sqrt{k^3} \cdot 2t\sqrt{k}$ **80.** $2\sqrt{r} \cdot 3\sqrt{r^3} \cdot 3\sqrt{r^5}$

NON-ROUTINE PROBLEM

81. Which triangle below has the greater area? (HINT: Use the Pythagorean Theorem.)

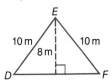
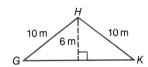

REVIEW CAPSULE FOR SECTION 12–8

Simplify. (*Pages 477–479*)

1. $\sqrt{\dfrac{4}{25}}$ **2.** $\sqrt{\dfrac{9}{16}}$ **3.** $\sqrt{\dfrac{25}{49}}$ **4.** $\sqrt{\dfrac{16}{81}}$ **5.** $\sqrt{\dfrac{49}{100}}$ **6.** $\sqrt{\dfrac{121}{25}}$

12-8   Quotients of Radicals

Since $\sqrt{\dfrac{16}{81}} = \dfrac{4}{9}$ and $\dfrac{\sqrt{16}}{\sqrt{81}} = \dfrac{4}{9}$, $\sqrt{\dfrac{16}{81}} = \dfrac{\sqrt{16}}{\sqrt{81}}$.

Since $\sqrt{\dfrac{4}{25}} = \dfrac{2}{5}$ and $\dfrac{\sqrt{4}}{\sqrt{25}} = \dfrac{2}{5}$, $\sqrt{\dfrac{4}{25}} = \dfrac{\sqrt{4}}{\sqrt{25}}$.

These statements suggest the following property.

Division Property for Square Roots

If a and b are real numbers where $a \geq 0$ and $b > 0$, then

$$\sqrt{\dfrac{a}{b}} = \dfrac{\sqrt{a}}{\sqrt{b}}.$$

EXAMPLE 1 Simplify: **a.** $\sqrt{\dfrac{8}{49}}$ **b.** $4\sqrt{\dfrac{5}{16}}$

Solutions: a. $\sqrt{\dfrac{8}{49}} = \dfrac{\sqrt{8}}{\sqrt{49}}$ ⟵ Division Property for Square Roots

$= \dfrac{\sqrt{4 \cdot 2}}{7}$ ⟵ $\sqrt{8} = \sqrt{4 \cdot 2} = \sqrt{4} \cdot \sqrt{2}$

$= \dfrac{2\sqrt{2}}{7}$ ⟵ Simplest form

b. $4\sqrt{\dfrac{5}{16}} = 4 \cdot \dfrac{\sqrt{5}}{\sqrt{16}}$ ⟵ Division Property for Square Roots

$= \overset{1}{4} \cdot \dfrac{\sqrt{5}}{\underset{1}{4}}$ ⟵ $\dfrac{1 \cdot \sqrt{5}}{1}$

$= \sqrt{5}$

The following definition will help you to determine whether a radical is in simplest form.

DEFINITION

A radical is in simplest form when:

1 The radicand contains no factor that is a perfect square.

2 The radicand does not contain a fraction.

3 No radical appears in a denominator.

To simplify a fraction such as $\dfrac{\sqrt{7}}{\sqrt{3}}$, write an equivalent fraction having a rational denominator. This is called **rationalizing the denominator.**

EXAMPLE 2 Simplify: **a.** $\sqrt{\dfrac{7}{3}}$ **b.** $\dfrac{5\sqrt{2}}{2\sqrt{18}}$

Solutions: **a.** $\sqrt{\dfrac{7}{3}} = \dfrac{\sqrt{7}}{\sqrt{3}}$

$= \dfrac{\sqrt{7}}{\sqrt{3}} \cdot \dfrac{\sqrt{3}}{\sqrt{3}}$ ⟵ Multiplying by $\dfrac{\sqrt{3}}{\sqrt{3}}$ will give an equivalent fraction with no radical in the denominator.

$= \dfrac{\sqrt{21}}{3}$ ⟵ $\sqrt{3} \cdot \sqrt{3} = (\sqrt{3})^2 = 3$

b. $\dfrac{5\sqrt{2}}{2\sqrt{18}} = \dfrac{5\sqrt{2}}{2\sqrt{18}} \cdot \dfrac{\sqrt{2}}{\sqrt{2}}$ ⟵ Multiplying by $\dfrac{\sqrt{2}}{\sqrt{2}}$ will give an equivalent fraction with no radical in the denominator.

$= \dfrac{5\sqrt{4}}{2\sqrt{36}}$

$= \dfrac{5 \cdot 2}{2 \cdot 6}$

$= \dfrac{10}{12}$, or $\dfrac{5}{6}$

Follow the method of Example 2 to rationalize a denominator containing variables.

EXAMPLE 3 Simplify: **a.** $\sqrt{\dfrac{1}{b^5}}$ **b.** $\sqrt{\dfrac{2}{10x}}$

Solutions: **a.** $\sqrt{\dfrac{1}{b^5}} = \dfrac{\sqrt{1}}{\sqrt{b^5}}$

$= \dfrac{1}{\sqrt{b^5}} \cdot \dfrac{\sqrt{b}}{\sqrt{b}}$ ⟵ Multiplying by $\dfrac{\sqrt{b}}{\sqrt{b}}$ will give an equivalent rational expression with no radical in the denominator.

$= \dfrac{\sqrt{b}}{\sqrt{b^6}}$

$= \dfrac{\sqrt{b}}{b^3}$, or $\dfrac{1}{b^3}\sqrt{b}$

b. $\sqrt{\dfrac{2}{10x}} = \sqrt{\dfrac{1}{5x}}$ ← $\dfrac{2}{10} = \dfrac{1}{5}$

$$= \dfrac{1}{\sqrt{5x}}$$

$$= \dfrac{1}{\sqrt{5x}} \cdot \dfrac{\sqrt{5x}}{\sqrt{5x}}$$

$$= \dfrac{\sqrt{5x}}{5x}$$ ← $(\sqrt{5x} \cdot \sqrt{5x}) = (\sqrt{5x})^2 = 5x$

EXERCISES: Classwork/Homework

Objective: To divide radicals

CHECK YOUR UNDERSTANDING

Complete.

1. The quotient $\dfrac{\sqrt{3}}{\sqrt{25}}$ is not in simplest form because there is a __?__ in the denominator.

2. To rationalize the denominator of $\dfrac{\sqrt{2}}{\sqrt{3}}$, you would multiply both the numerator and the denominator by __?__.

Determine which quotients are in simplest form. Answer <u>Yes</u> or <u>No</u>.

3. $\dfrac{\sqrt{6}}{3}$ **4.** $\dfrac{5}{\sqrt{5}}$ **5.** $\dfrac{\sqrt{9}}{2\sqrt{2}}$ **6.** $\dfrac{2\sqrt{7}}{3}$ **7.** $\dfrac{14}{3\sqrt{5}}$

PRACTICE AND APPLY

Simplify.

8. $\sqrt{\dfrac{4}{25}}$ **9.** $\sqrt{\dfrac{3}{49}}$ **10.** $\sqrt{\dfrac{7}{36}}$ **11.** $\sqrt{\dfrac{10}{81}}$ **12.** $\sqrt{\dfrac{6}{16}}$

13. $2\sqrt{\dfrac{7}{25}}$ **14.** $5\sqrt{\dfrac{9}{196}}$ **15.** $3\sqrt{\dfrac{6}{100}}$ **16.** $7\sqrt{\dfrac{11}{144}}$ **17.** $6\sqrt{\dfrac{3}{64}}$

18. $2\sqrt{\dfrac{12}{225}}$ **19.** $7\sqrt{\dfrac{18}{49}}$ **20.** $5\sqrt{\dfrac{24}{121}}$ **21.** $9\sqrt{\dfrac{27}{169}}$ **22.** $7\sqrt{\dfrac{75}{625}}$

Rationalize the denominators and simplify. All variables represent positive numbers.

23. $\dfrac{3}{\sqrt{5}}$ **24.** $\dfrac{2}{\sqrt{3}}$ **25.** $\dfrac{5}{\sqrt{2}}$ **26.** $\dfrac{2}{\sqrt{6}}$ **27.** $\dfrac{\sqrt{3}}{\sqrt{2}}$

28. $\dfrac{\sqrt{7}}{\sqrt{2}}$ **29.** $\dfrac{\sqrt{8}}{\sqrt{3}}$ **30.** $\dfrac{\sqrt{7}}{\sqrt{5}}$ **31.** $\dfrac{2\sqrt{3}}{\sqrt{2}}$

32. $\dfrac{3\sqrt{2}}{\sqrt{3}}$ **33.** $\dfrac{4\sqrt{2}}{\sqrt{5}}$ **34.** $\dfrac{3\sqrt{3}}{\sqrt{2}}$ **35.** $\dfrac{5\sqrt{8}}{\sqrt{7}}$

36. $\dfrac{3\sqrt{9}}{\sqrt{2}}$ **37.** $\dfrac{2\sqrt{4}}{\sqrt{3}}$ **38.** $\dfrac{8\sqrt{5}}{\sqrt{15}}$ **39.** $\dfrac{3\sqrt{6}}{2\sqrt{2}}$

40. $\dfrac{2\sqrt{7}}{5\sqrt{3}}$ **41.** $\dfrac{5\sqrt{3}}{\sqrt{18}}$ **42.** $\dfrac{4\sqrt{2}}{3\sqrt{32}}$ **43.** $\dfrac{4}{\sqrt{a}}$

44. $\dfrac{7}{\sqrt{y}}$ **45.** $\dfrac{21}{\sqrt{2b}}$ **46.** $\dfrac{14}{\sqrt{4c}}$ **47.** $\dfrac{8}{\sqrt{2d}}$

48. $\sqrt{\dfrac{3}{b^3}}$ **49.** $\sqrt{\dfrac{4}{c^5}}$ **50.** $\sqrt{\dfrac{3}{12x^3}}$ **51.** $\sqrt{\dfrac{14}{8x^5}}$

52. $\sqrt{\dfrac{21}{27d^3}}$ **53.** $\dfrac{\sqrt{ax}}{\sqrt{a}}$ **54.** $\dfrac{\sqrt{b^3 d^4}}{\sqrt{bd}}$ **55.** $\dfrac{\sqrt{24b^3}}{\sqrt{6b}}$

Simplify.

56. $\sqrt{\dfrac{2}{3}} \cdot \sqrt{\dfrac{3}{4}}$ **57.** $\sqrt{\dfrac{3}{5}} \cdot \sqrt{\dfrac{2}{5}}$ **58.** $\sqrt{\dfrac{7}{2}} \cdot \sqrt{\dfrac{7}{5}}$ **59.** $\sqrt{\dfrac{7}{8}} \cdot \sqrt{\dfrac{3}{8}}$

60. $\sqrt{\dfrac{3}{5}} \cdot \sqrt{\dfrac{6}{7}}$ **61.** $\sqrt{\dfrac{10}{13}} \cdot \sqrt{\dfrac{1}{2}}$ **62.** $\sqrt{\dfrac{6}{7}} \cdot \sqrt{\dfrac{7}{6}}$ **63.** $\sqrt{\dfrac{3}{5}} \cdot \sqrt{\dfrac{3}{5}}$

64. $\sqrt{3 - \dfrac{1}{2}}$ **65.** $\sqrt{7 + \dfrac{3}{4}}$ **66.** $\sqrt{25 - \dfrac{25}{4}}$ **67.** $\sqrt{4^2 - \left(\dfrac{1}{4}\right)^2}$

■■■■■■ **MAINTAIN**

Multiply and simplify. (*Pages 502–504*)

68. $\sqrt{7} \cdot \sqrt{3}$ **69.** $\sqrt{12} \cdot \sqrt{3}$ **70.** $\sqrt{5} \cdot \sqrt{15}$ **71.** $\sqrt{8} \cdot \sqrt{6}$

72. $5\sqrt{3} \cdot \sqrt{8}$ **73.** $6\sqrt{4} \cdot 3\sqrt{9}$ **74.** $-3\sqrt{7} \cdot -2\sqrt{6}$ **75.** $\sqrt{12} \cdot -4\sqrt{5}$

Find the distance between each pair of points. (*Pages 499–501*)

76. L(0, −3) and M(4, 0)   **77.** A(−3, 1) and B(−3, 8)

78. T(5, −3) and S(9, −4)   **79.** C(1, 1) and D(3, 2)

Factor completely. (*Pages 401–403*)

80. $2x^2 + 4x - 96$ **81.** $5a^2 - 5a$ **82.** $m^2 p + 12mp + 27p$

83. $2t^2 - 72$ **84.** $6s^2 + 9s - 105$ **85.** $2b^2 + 6b + 2$

Rationalize the denominators and simplify. All variables represent positive numbers.

86. $\sqrt{\dfrac{1}{a+b}}$ **87.** $\dfrac{x+1}{\sqrt{x+1}}$ **88.** $\sqrt{\dfrac{n+3}{n^2+6n+9}}$ **89.** $\sqrt{\dfrac{y-2}{y^2-4y+4}}$

NON-ROUTINE PROBLEMS

90. Dan has only a 9-quart pail, a 3-quart pail, and a 2-quart pail to carry water. How can Dan measure exactly eight quarts of water if he completely fills each of the pails just once?

91. A customer wanted a 25-foot piece of wire. The clerk incorrectly measured the wire with a yardstick that was 2 inches too short. How many inches were missing from the customer's length of wire?

92. The time now is between 10:00 A.M. and 11:00 A.M. Fourteen minutes from now, it will be as many minutes before 12:00 noon as it is past 10:00 A.M. now. What time is it right now?

93. Sally's grandfather has lived a sixth of his life in Ohio, a fourth of his life in Iowa, a third of his life in Illinois, and the other 21 years of his life in Wisconsin. How old is Sally's grandfather?

REVIEW

The lengths of the legs of a right triangle are *a* and *b*, and *c* is the length of the hypotenuse. Use the Pythagorean Theorem to find the length of the unknown side to the nearest tenth. (*Pages 494–498*)

1. $a = 9$, $b = 12$, $c = \underline{\quad ? \quad}$ **2.** $b = 5$, $c = 9$, $a = \underline{\quad ? \quad}$

Find the distance between each pair of points. (*Pages 499–501*)

3. $A(4, -6)$ and $B(1, -6)$ **4.** $K(7, 3)$ and $L(-4, -5)$

Multiply and simplify. Variables represent positive numbers. (*Pages 502–504*)

5. $\sqrt{3} \cdot \sqrt{12}$ **6.** $-3\sqrt{14} \cdot 2\sqrt{6}$ **7.** $\sqrt{x} \cdot \sqrt{xy}$ **8.** $\sqrt{6a} \cdot \sqrt{3a}$

Simplify. Variables represent positive numbers. (*Pages 505–508*)

9. $\sqrt{\dfrac{4}{9}}$ **10.** $\dfrac{1}{\sqrt{6}}$ **11.** $\sqrt{\dfrac{2}{5}}$ **12.** $\sqrt{\dfrac{5}{x^3}}$

12-9 Addition and Subtraction of Radicals

Terms such as $-5x^3y^2$ and $3x^3y^2$ are like terms because their variable factors, x and y, are the same and they have the same exponents. Similarly, $2\sqrt{3}$ and $7\sqrt{3}$ are **like terms** because their radicals are the same.

Like Radicals	**Unlike Radicals**
$\sqrt{5}$ and $6\sqrt{5}$	$\sqrt{3}$ and $\sqrt{5}$
$3\sqrt{a}$ and $-2\sqrt{a}$	$3\sqrt{a}$ and $2\sqrt{b}$

To add or subtract like radicals, you apply the Distributive Property.

$$5\sqrt{y} + 7\sqrt{y} = (5 + 7)\sqrt{y} = \mathbf{12\sqrt{y}}$$

EXAMPLE 1 Add or subtract as indicated: $3\sqrt{5} + 6\sqrt{2} - \sqrt{5}$

Solution: Group the like terms.

$$\begin{aligned}
3\sqrt{5} + 6\sqrt{2} - \sqrt{5} &= (3\sqrt{5} - \sqrt{5}) + 6\sqrt{2} \\
&= (3 - 1)\sqrt{5} + 6\sqrt{2} \quad \longleftarrow \quad \substack{\textbf{By the Distributive} \\ \textbf{Property}} \\
&= \mathbf{2\sqrt{5} + 6\sqrt{2}}
\end{aligned}$$

Always express each radical in simplest form before adding or subtracting. This will help you to identify like radicals.

EXAMPLE 2 Add or subtract as indicated: $\sqrt{48} + 6\sqrt{27} - 5\sqrt{12}$

Solution: Simplify the radicals before adding or subtracting.

$$\begin{aligned}
\sqrt{48} + 6\sqrt{27} - 5\sqrt{12} &= \sqrt{16 \cdot 3} + 6\sqrt{9 \cdot 3} - 5\sqrt{4 \cdot 3} \quad \longleftarrow \quad \substack{\sqrt{16 \cdot 3} = 4\sqrt{3}; \\ \sqrt{9 \cdot 3} = 3\sqrt{3}; \\ \sqrt{4 \cdot 3} = 2\sqrt{3}} \\
&= 4\sqrt{3} + 6 \cdot 3\sqrt{3} - 5 \cdot 2\sqrt{3} \\
&= 4\sqrt{3} + 18\sqrt{3} - 10\sqrt{3} \\
&= (4 + 18 - 10)\sqrt{3} \\
&= \mathbf{12\sqrt{3}} \quad \longleftarrow \quad \textbf{Simplest form}
\end{aligned}$$

You can also use the Distributive Property to simplify products of radical expressions.

EXAMPLE 3 Simplify each expression. **a.** $\sqrt{5}(3 + \sqrt{10})$ **b.** $(3 - \sqrt{5})(3 + \sqrt{5})$

Solutions: **a.** $\sqrt{5}(3 + \sqrt{10}) = \sqrt{5} \cdot 3 + \sqrt{5} \cdot \sqrt{10}$ ← **By the Distributive Property**

$= 3\sqrt{5} + \sqrt{50}$ ← **Simplify.**

$= 3\sqrt{5} + \sqrt{25 \cdot 2}$

$= \mathbf{3\sqrt{5} + 5\sqrt{2}}$ ← **Simplest form**

b. $(3 - \sqrt{5})(3 + \sqrt{5}) = (3)^2 - (\sqrt{5})^2$ ← **(a + b)(a − b) = a² − b²**

$= 9 - 5 = \mathbf{4}$ ← **(√5)² = 5**

CONJUGATES In Example 3b, note that the product of $(3 - \sqrt{5})$ and $(3 + \sqrt{5})$ is a rational number. Expressions of the form $(a + \sqrt{b})$ and $(a - \sqrt{b})$ are called **conjugates**. Since

$$(a + \sqrt{b})(a - \sqrt{b}) = a^2 - b,$$

you can use conjugates to rationalize some binomial denominators. (See the Example for Exercises 45–48.)

EXERCISES: Classwork/Homework

Objective: To add and subtract radicals

CHECK YOUR UNDERSTANDING

For each of Exercises 1–4, identify the like terms.

1. $\sqrt{2} + 2\sqrt{2} + 3\sqrt{5}$ **2.** $5\sqrt{3} + \sqrt{3} - 2\sqrt{7}$

3. $7\sqrt{5} - 3\sqrt{3} + 5\sqrt{5}$ **4.** $8\sqrt{7} + 2\sqrt{3} + 4\sqrt{3}$

PRACTICE AND APPLY

Add or subtract as indicated.

5. $3\sqrt{2} + 2\sqrt{2} - 4\sqrt{2}$ **6.** $5\sqrt{3} - 2\sqrt{3} - 6\sqrt{3}$

7. $-3\sqrt{3} + 4\sqrt{3} - 10\sqrt{3}$ **8.** $5\sqrt{7} + 6\sqrt{7} - 11\sqrt{7}$

9. $8\sqrt{5} + 6\sqrt{5} + 2\sqrt{3} + 7\sqrt{3}$ **10.** $10\sqrt{2} + 7\sqrt{3} - 4\sqrt{2} - 5\sqrt{3}$

11. $\sqrt{12} + 3\sqrt{3}$ **12.** $\sqrt{8} + 5\sqrt{2} - 6\sqrt{2}$

13. $-6\sqrt{5} + 7\sqrt{5} - \sqrt{20}$ **14.** $\sqrt{12} - \sqrt{27} + \sqrt{48}$

15. $10\sqrt{8} - \sqrt{72} + 3\sqrt{98}$ **16.** $10\sqrt{8} - 3\sqrt{98} + 6\sqrt{72}$

17. $6\sqrt{54} - 3\sqrt{24} - 2\sqrt{6}$ **18.** $\sqrt{125} + 2\sqrt{80} - 3\sqrt{20}$

19. $\sqrt{2}(\sqrt{3} + 3)$

20. $\sqrt{7}(\sqrt{2} + 5)$

21. $\sqrt{3}(\sqrt{3} + 2)$

22. $\sqrt{4}(\sqrt{8} + 2)$

23. $\sqrt{8}(2\sqrt{3} - 5)$

24. $\sqrt{5}(\sqrt{2} - \sqrt{3})$

25. $(8 + \sqrt{7})(8 - \sqrt{7})$

26. $(\sqrt{5} - 2)(\sqrt{5} + 2)$

27. $(\sqrt{6} + 9)(\sqrt{6} - 9)$

28. $\sqrt{\dfrac{2}{3}} + \sqrt{\dfrac{8}{3}}$

29. $5\sqrt{\dfrac{1}{6}} - 3\sqrt{\dfrac{3}{2}}$

30. $\sqrt{\dfrac{2}{3}} - 3\sqrt{\dfrac{1}{6}}$

31. $\sqrt{\dfrac{2}{36}} - 3\sqrt{\dfrac{2}{49}} - 6\sqrt{\dfrac{2}{25}}$

32. $\sqrt{\dfrac{8}{9}} + 2\sqrt{\dfrac{1}{2}} - 3\sqrt{\dfrac{9}{8}}$

33. $\sqrt{\dfrac{3}{4}} - 2\sqrt{\dfrac{19}{16}} + \sqrt{\dfrac{3}{8}}$

34. $\sqrt{100x} - \sqrt{9x}$

35. $2a\sqrt{ab} + 4\sqrt{a^3b}$

36. $3\sqrt{2b^3} - \sqrt{8b^3}$

37. $4\sqrt{12r^2} + 2\sqrt{75r^2} - 3\sqrt{27r^2}$

38. $\sqrt{12a^3} - 2\sqrt{3a^3} + \sqrt{27a^3}$

39. $x\sqrt{xy^3} + xy\sqrt{xy} + y\sqrt{x^3y}$

40. $2b\sqrt{25b} + b\sqrt{4b} - 3b\sqrt{9b}$

Write the conjugate of each radical expression.

41. $1 + \sqrt{2}$

42. $3 - \sqrt{5}$

43. $2\sqrt{3} + 5\sqrt{7}$

44. $1 - \sqrt{x}$

Rationalize the denominator and simplify.

Example: $\dfrac{5}{1 - 2\sqrt{5}} = \dfrac{5}{1 - 2\sqrt{5}} \cdot \dfrac{1 + 2\sqrt{5}}{1 + 2\sqrt{5}} = \dfrac{5 + 10\sqrt{5}}{1 - 4(5)} = \dfrac{\mathbf{5 + 10\sqrt{5}}}{\mathbf{-19}}$

45. $\dfrac{2}{1 + \sqrt{2}}$

46. $\dfrac{4}{\sqrt{7} - 2}$

47. $\dfrac{7}{5 - \sqrt{3}}$

48. $\dfrac{2}{\sqrt{6} - 3}$

■■■■■■ **MAINTAIN**

Simplify. (*Pages 505–509*)

49. $\sqrt{\dfrac{3}{25}}$

50. $2\sqrt{\dfrac{5}{49}}$

51. $\dfrac{2}{\sqrt{5}}$

52. $\dfrac{\sqrt{8}}{\sqrt{3}}$

53. $\dfrac{3\sqrt{7}}{5\sqrt{5}}$

Multiply and simplify. (*Pages 502–504*)

54. $\sqrt{2} \cdot \sqrt{7}$

55. $\sqrt{6} \cdot \sqrt{3}$

56. $2\sqrt{3} \cdot 5\sqrt{5}$

57. $-4\sqrt{10} \cdot 2\sqrt{5}$

Solve each problem. (*Pages 407–411*)

58. The square of a certain positive number is 24 more than five times the number. What is the number?

59. The area of a rectangular garden is 24 square meters. The length of the garden is 2 meters more than its width. Find the length and width.

Rationalize the denominator and simplify.

60. $\dfrac{3\sqrt{5} + 2\sqrt{3}}{2\sqrt{5} - 5\sqrt{3}}$

61. $\dfrac{2\sqrt{5} + 3\sqrt{2}}{4\sqrt{5} - \sqrt{2}}$

62. $\dfrac{\sqrt{a} + \sqrt{b}}{\sqrt{a} - \sqrt{b}}$

63. $\dfrac{3\sqrt{x} - 1}{\sqrt{x} + 1}$

Factor over the real numbers.

Example: $x^2 - 5 = x^2 - (\sqrt{5})^2 = (x + \sqrt{5})(x - \sqrt{5})$

64. $y^2 - 7$ **65.** $d^2 - 10$ **66.** $2b^2 - 12$ **67.** $5x^2 - 25$

68. $27 - r^2$ **69.** $1 - 2x^2$ **70.** $t^2 - 5v^2$ **71.** $a^2 - 2a\sqrt{5} + 5$

■■■■■■ **NON-ROUTINE PROBLEMS**

72. Copy the figure shown at the right. Then arrange the digits 2 through 9 in the empty boxes so that the sum of the number formed by the first row and the number formed by the second row equals the number formed by the third row.

73. A jet leaves St. Louis for New York at the same time a twin-engine plane leaves New York for St. Louis. The jet travels at a speed of 600 miles per hour. The twin-engine plane travels at a speed of 300 miles per hour. Which is closer to St. Louis when they meet?

74. Alicia Robbins drove 70 kilometers per hour on a trip. She arrived at her destination one hour earlier than she would have if she had driven 60 kilometers per hour. How far did she drive?

———— **REVIEW CAPSULE FOR SECTION 12–10** ————

Simplify. (*Pages 477–479*)

1. $(\sqrt{5})^2$ **2.** $(\sqrt{15})^2$ **3.** $(\sqrt{11})^2$ **4.** $(\sqrt{565})^2$ **5.** $(\sqrt{x})^2$

6. $(\sqrt{a - 1})^2$ **7.** $(\sqrt{2b - 1})^2$ **8.** $(3\sqrt{x})^2$ **9.** $(4\sqrt{2b})^2$ **10.** $(5\sqrt{a - 1})^2$

Determine whether the given number is a solution of the given equation. Answer <u>Yes</u> or <u>No</u>. (*Pages 22–25*)

11. $2 + \sqrt{x} = 4;\quad 4$ **12.** $2 - 4\sqrt{y} = 3;\quad \frac{1}{16}$ **13.** $1 + \sqrt{x} = 0;\quad -1$

14. $\sqrt{y} - 48 = 2;\quad 2500$ **15.** $2\sqrt{a} - 14 = 0;\quad 7$ **16.** $3\sqrt{b + 1} = 8;\quad \frac{55}{9}$

12-10 Solving Radical Equations

An equation such as $3 + \sqrt{x} = 6$ is a radical equation. A **radical equation** contains a radical that includes a variable.

EXAMPLE 1 Solve: $3 + \sqrt{x} = 6$

Solution: Add -3 to each side in order to get the radical alone on the left side.

$$3 + \sqrt{x} = 6$$
$$-3 + 3 + \sqrt{x} = -3 + 6$$
$$\sqrt{x} = 3 \quad \longleftarrow \quad \textbf{Now square both sides.}$$
$$(\sqrt{x})^2 = (3)^2 \quad \longleftarrow \quad \textbf{(}\sqrt{\textbf{x}}\textbf{)}^2 = \textbf{x}$$
$$x = 9$$

Check: $3 + \sqrt{x} = 6 \quad \longleftarrow \quad \textbf{Replace x with 9.}$
$$3 + \sqrt{9} \overset{?}{=} 6$$
$$3 + 3 \overset{?}{=} 6$$
$$6 \overset{?}{=} 6 \quad \text{Yes} \; \checkmark$$

Solution set: $\{9\}$

In Example 2, the radicand of $3\sqrt{2a - 1}$ is a binomial.

EXAMPLE 2 Solve: $3\sqrt{2a - 1} + 4 = 7$

Solution: $3\sqrt{2a - 1} + 4 = 7 \quad \longleftarrow \quad \textbf{Add (}-\textbf{4) to each side.}$
$$3\sqrt{2a - 1} + 4 + (-4) = 7 + (-4)$$
$$3\sqrt{2a - 1} = 3 \quad \longleftarrow \quad \textbf{Multiply each side by } \tfrac{1}{3}.$$
$$\sqrt{2a - 1} = 1 \quad \longleftarrow \quad \textbf{Square both sides.}$$
$$(\sqrt{2a - 1})^2 = 1^2$$
$$2a - 1 = 1 \quad \longleftarrow \quad \textbf{Solve for a.}$$
$$2a = 2$$
$$a = 1$$

The check is left for you.

Solution set: $\{1\}$

Squaring both sides of an equation sometimes results in an "apparent solution" that does not check in the original equation. An "apparent solution" is not a member of the solution set. This is why it is important to check all your answers in the original equation.

EXAMPLE 3 Solve: $6 + \sqrt{x - 5} = 3$

Solution:

$$6 + \sqrt{x - 5} = 3 \qquad \longleftarrow \text{Add } (-6) \text{ to each side.}$$
$$\sqrt{x - 5} = -3 \qquad \longleftarrow \text{Square both sides.}$$
$$(\sqrt{x - 5})^2 = (-3)^2 \qquad \longleftarrow (\sqrt{x - 5})^2 = x - 5$$
$$x - 5 = 9$$
$$x = 14$$

Check:

$$6 + \sqrt{x - 5} = 3 \qquad \longleftarrow \text{Replace } x \text{ with 14.}$$
$$6 + \sqrt{14 - 5} \overset{?}{=} 3$$
$$6 + \sqrt{9} \overset{?}{=} 3 \quad \text{No} \longleftarrow \text{14 is not a solution.}$$

Solution set: ϕ

EXERCISES: Classwork/Homework

Objective: To solve radical equations

CHECK YOUR UNDERSTANDING

1. *Complete*: A radical equation contains a radical that includes a ___?___ .

2. When $3 + \sqrt{x} = 0$ is solved, the result is $x = 9$. Is 9 a solution? Why?

State the first step you would use to solve each equation. Do *not* solve the equation.

3. $3\sqrt{y} = 1$

4. $12 + 3\sqrt{x} = 0$

5. $\sqrt{3x} + 4 = 7$

6. $\sqrt{x} + 9 = 20$

PRACTICE AND APPLY

For Exercises 7–33, solve and check each equation. If an apparent solution does not check in the original equation, give the solution set as ϕ.

7. $\sqrt{x} = 6$

8. $\sqrt{x} = \frac{3}{4}$

9. $\sqrt{\frac{n}{5}} = 2$

10. $8 = \sqrt{x - 9}$

11. $8 = \sqrt{5r + 1}$

12. $\sqrt{x + 5} = 4$

13. $3 + \sqrt{x - 1} = 5$

14. $6 + \sqrt{x} = 13$

15. $6 - \sqrt{x - 5} = 3$

16. $5 + \sqrt{x} = 3$

17. $8 + 2\sqrt{x} = 0$

18. $2\sqrt{x} = 5$

19. $5\sqrt{x} = 2$

20. $-\sqrt{x} = 6$

21. $-7 = \sqrt{y}$

22. $-\sqrt{m} = -5$

23. $-9 = -\sqrt{y}$

24. $-\sqrt{x} = \frac{3}{4}$

25. $\sqrt{x} = -3$

26. $\sqrt{x} = \sqrt{5}$

27. $-1 = \sqrt{x} - 5$

28. $\sqrt{a - 1} = \sqrt{3}$

29. $\sqrt{7 + 3x} = -4$

30. $-9 = \sqrt{6 - x}$

31. $\sqrt{3y + 2} = 2\sqrt{y}$

32. $5 = \dfrac{15}{\sqrt{2a - 3}}$

33. $\sqrt{\dfrac{9}{16}} = x$

34. Five times the square root of a number is 2. Find the number.

35. Eight less than the square root of a number is 0. What is the number?

36. Three more than the square root of a number is 7. What is the number?

37. A number is increased by 3. The square root of this sum is 5. Find the number.

38. Twice a number is decreased by 3. The square root of this difference equals 6. Find the number.

39. The quotient of the square root of a number and 5 equals $\frac{3}{4}$. What is the number?

40. The formula
$$s = \sqrt{30fd}$$
can be used to estimate the speed, s, in miles per hour that a car was traveling when it skidded d feet after the brakes were applied. In the formula, f is the coefficient of friction. Find the distance a car will travel on a wet concrete road ($f = 0.4$) if the car is traveling 50 miles per hour when the brakes are applied.

41. The formula
$$T = 2\pi\sqrt{\dfrac{L}{9.8}}$$
relates the time, T, in seconds that it takes for a pendulum to swing back and forth once with the length, L, of the pendulum in meters. What is the length of a pendulum that takes 3 seconds to swing back and forth once? Use $\pi = 3.14$. Round the answer to the nearest tenth.

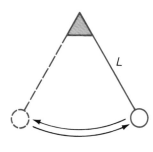

42. The formula
$$t = \sqrt{\dfrac{d^2}{216}}$$
relates the time, t, in hours that a storm with diameter, d, in miles will last. What is the diameter of a storm that lasts one hour?

43. The time, t, in seconds that it takes a body to fall a distance of s feet from rest is given by the formula
$$t = \sqrt{\dfrac{2s}{g}}$$
where g is the acceleration due to gravity. Find s when $t = 6.25$ and $g = 32$.

Solve and check each equation.

44. $\sqrt{x^2 + 5} = x + 1$ **45.** $\sqrt{x^2 - 5} = x - 5$ **46.** $\sqrt{x^2 + 24} = x + 12$

47. $\sqrt{3b^2 - 5} = 11$ **48.** $\sqrt{y^2 + 4y} = \sqrt{5}$ **49.** $\sqrt{a^2 - 7a} = \sqrt{18}$

▬▬▬ MAINTAIN

Add or subtract as indicated. (*Pages 510–513*)

50. $8\sqrt{5} - \sqrt{5} + 3\sqrt{5}$ **51.** $3\sqrt{2} + 7\sqrt{3} - 5\sqrt{2}$

52. $-2\sqrt{7} + 12\sqrt{7} - 3\sqrt{5} - \sqrt{7}$ **53.** $9\sqrt{3} - \sqrt{27} - 6\sqrt{3}$

Factor. (*Pages 392–395*)

54. $y^2 + 9y + 20$ **55.** $r^2 + 3r - 54$ **56.** $x^2 - 4x + 4$

57. $x^2 + 20x + 100$ **58.** $-6 + 5t + t^2$ **59.** $21 - 10a + a^2$

▬▬▬ CONNECT AND EXTEND

Solve and check each equation. If an apparent solution does not check in the original equation, give the solution set as φ.

60. $4\sqrt{2a + 2} - 9 = 2\sqrt{2a + 2}$ **61.** $\sqrt{4b - 3} - \sqrt{3b + 4} = 0$

62. $5\sqrt{3t - 1} - 4 = 3\sqrt{3t - 1}$ **63.** $\sqrt{2q + 6} - \sqrt{5q} = 0$

Determine whether each pair of equations is equivalent (has the same solution set). Give a reason for each answer.

64. $x^2 + y^2 = 1$; $y = \sqrt{1 - x^2}$ **65.** $x^2 + y^2 = 1$; $\sqrt{x^2 + y^2} = 1$

▬▬▬ NON-ROUTINE PROBLEM

66. Copy the figure at the right. Then place 8 dots on the figure so that two dots are on each of the three lines and two dots are on each of the four circles.

───── **REVIEW CAPSULE FOR SECTION 12–11** ─────

Write each product as a base with a single exponent. (*Pages 329–331*)

1. $x^3 \cdot x^4$ **2.** $a \cdot a^6$ **3.** $c^2 \cdot c$ **4.** $5^3 \cdot 5^2$ **5.** $10^2 \cdot 10^5$

Simplify. (*Pages 332–334*)

6. $(x^2)^2$ **7.** $(x^2)^3$ **8.** $(x^3)^2$ **9.** $(x^3)^3$ **10.** $(4b^3)^2$

11. $(z^4)^3$ **12.** $(\frac{1}{2}z)^2$ **13.** $(4t)^3$ **14.** $(-4c^2)^3$ **15.** $(0.5d)^2$

12-11 Rational Exponents

The properties of positive and negative integral exponents can be extended to rational exponents. Consider the following.

You already know that
$$\sqrt{5} \cdot \sqrt{5} = (\sqrt{5})^2 = 5.$$

If the exponent properties hold for rational exponents, then
$$5^{\frac{1}{2}} \cdot 5^{\frac{1}{2}} = 5^{\frac{1}{2}+\frac{1}{2}} = 5^1, \text{ or } 5.$$

Thus, it seems reasonable to define
$$\sqrt{5} = 5^{\frac{1}{2}}.$$

The following expresses the definition in general form.

DEFINITION

> ### Rational Exponents
>
> For any positive odd integer n where a is any real number, or for any positive even integer n where $a \geq 0$,
> $$a^{\frac{1}{n}} = \sqrt[n]{a}.$$

EXAMPLE 1 Simplify: **a.** $81^{\frac{1}{2}}$ **b.** $-(81)^{\frac{1}{2}}$ **c.** $81^{\frac{1}{4}}$ **d.** $(-8)^{\frac{1}{3}}$

Solutions: **a.** $81^{\frac{1}{2}} = \sqrt{81}$ **b.** $-(81)^{\frac{1}{2}} = -\sqrt{81}$
           $= 9$ $= -9$

    c. $81^{\frac{1}{4}} = \sqrt[4]{81}$ **d.** $(-8)^{\frac{1}{3}} = \sqrt[3]{-8}$
           $= 3 \longleftarrow$ **Since $3^4 = 81$** $= -2$

By the definition of rational exponents, $\sqrt[5]{7} = 7^{\frac{1}{5}}$. Then, by the laws of exponents,
$$\sqrt[5]{7^3} = (7^3)^{\frac{1}{5}} = 7^{3 \cdot \frac{1}{5}} = 7^{\frac{3}{5}} \quad \text{Thus,} \quad \sqrt[5]{7^3} = 7^{\frac{3}{5}}.$$

When the conditions of the definition are satisfied, rational exponents may be viewed in two ways. Thus,
$$7^{\frac{3}{5}} = (\sqrt[5]{7})^3 \quad \text{or} \quad \sqrt[5]{7^3}.$$

Example 2 illustrates the value of taking the root first.

EXAMPLE 2 Simplify: **a.** $4^{\frac{3}{2}}$ **b.** $-(27)^{\frac{2}{3}}$ **c.** $(16)^{\frac{5}{4}}$

Solutions: **a.** $4^{\frac{3}{2}} = (4^{\frac{1}{2}})^3 = (\sqrt{4})^3 = 2^3 = \mathbf{8}$

b. $-(27)^{\frac{2}{3}} = -(27^{\frac{1}{3}})^2 = -(\sqrt[3]{27})^2 = -3^2 = \mathbf{-9}$

c. $16^{\frac{5}{4}} = [(16)^{\frac{1}{4}}]^5 = (\sqrt[4]{16})^5 = (2)^5 = \mathbf{32}$

CALCULATOR

You can use a scientific calculator to simplify expressions with rational exponents. For example, to evaluate $4^{\frac{3}{2}}$, press

4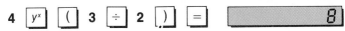

NOTE: Many calculators will not raise a negative number to a exponent. Entering $(-\frac{1}{27})^{\frac{1}{3}}$, for example, will result in an error message.

EXERCISES: Classwork/Homework

Objective: To simplify expressions containing rational exponents

CHECK YOUR UNDERSTANDING

Write using rational exponents.

1. $\sqrt{7}$ **2.** $\sqrt[3]{2}$ **3.** $\sqrt{5^3}$ **4.** $\sqrt[5]{6^2}$ **5.** $\sqrt[4]{9^3}$

Use a radical to name each of the following.

6. $3^{\frac{1}{2}}$ **7.** $10^{\frac{1}{3}}$ **8.** $2^{\frac{3}{2}}$ **9.** $8^{\frac{5}{3}}$ **10.** $24^{\frac{3}{4}}$

PRACTICE AND APPLY

Simplify.

11. $9^{\frac{1}{2}}$ **12.** $125^{\frac{1}{3}}$ **13.** $16^{\frac{1}{4}}$ **14.** $(-27)^{\frac{1}{3}}$ **15.** $81^{\frac{1}{4}}$

16. $625^{\frac{1}{4}}$ **17.** $121^{\frac{1}{2}}$ **18.** $144^{\frac{1}{2}}$ **19.** $-(36)^{\frac{1}{2}}$ **20.** $-(81)^{\frac{1}{4}}$

21. $-(\frac{1}{4})^{\frac{1}{2}}$ **22.** $(\frac{1}{27})^{\frac{1}{3}}$ **23.** $-(\frac{1}{27})^{\frac{1}{3}}$ **24.** $(-\frac{1}{27})^{\frac{1}{3}}$ **25.** $27^{\frac{1}{3}}$

26. $-(27)^{\frac{1}{3}}$ **27.** $(\frac{4}{9})^{\frac{1}{2}}$ **28.** $(-\frac{8}{125})^{\frac{1}{3}}$ **29.** $-(\frac{8}{125})^{\frac{1}{3}}$ **30.** $-(25)^{\frac{1}{2}}$

31. $-(64)^{\frac{1}{2}}$ **32.** 15^0 **33.** $-(9)^{\frac{1}{2}}$ **34.** $-(16)^{\frac{1}{4}}$ **35.** $25^{\frac{1}{2}}$

36. $81^{\frac{1}{2}}$ **37.** $8^{\frac{1}{3}}$ **38.** $64^{\frac{1}{3}}$ **39.** $32^{\frac{1}{5}}$ **40.** $-(16)^{\frac{1}{2}}$

41. $64^{\frac{1}{2}}$ **42.** $27^{\frac{1}{3}}$ **43.** $-(49^{\frac{1}{2}})$ **44.** $(-8)^{\frac{1}{3}}$ **45.** $-(125)^{\frac{1}{3}}$

46. $(\frac{1}{16})^{\frac{1}{2}}$ **47.** $(\frac{4}{25})^{\frac{1}{2}}$ **48.** $-(\frac{1}{36})^{\frac{1}{2}}$ **49.** $(-\frac{1}{8})^{\frac{1}{3}}$ **50.** $(\frac{1}{64})^{\frac{1}{3}}$

51. $27^{\frac{4}{3}}$ **52.** $(\frac{1}{64})^{\frac{2}{3}}$ **53.** $16^{\frac{3}{4}}$ **54.** $4^{\frac{3}{2}}$ **55.** $49^{\frac{3}{2}}$

Use a radical to name each of the following. Variables represent positive integers.

56. $7^{\frac{1}{2}}$ **57.** $(-8)^{\frac{1}{3}}$ **58.** $16^{\frac{1}{4}}$ **59.** $93^{\frac{1}{n}}$ **60.** $x^{\frac{1}{2}}$

61. $y^{\frac{1}{3}}$ **62.** $a^{\frac{1}{4}}$ **63.** $(x^2)^{\frac{1}{3}}$ **64.** $(xy)^{\frac{1}{2}}$ **65.** $(ab)^{\frac{1}{3}}$

66. To simplify $8^{\frac{5}{3}}$ on her calculator, Alicia pressed the following keys:

$$8 \quad \boxed{y^x} \quad 5 \quad \boxed{\div} \quad 3 \quad \boxed{=}$$

  a. What keys did she forget to press? ( )
  b. What answer did she get?
  c. Since $8^1 = 8$ and $8^2 = 64$, is her answer reasonable?

Evaluate each expression for $a = 8$, $b = 9$, and $c = 1$.

67. $a^{\frac{1}{3}} - b^{\frac{1}{2}}$ **68.** $(a + c)^{\frac{1}{2}}$ **69.** $-a^{\frac{1}{3}}$ **70.** $-(b)^{\frac{1}{2}}$ **71.** $a^{\frac{5}{3}}$

72. $b^{\frac{3}{2}}$ **73.** $-(bc)^{\frac{3}{2}}$ **74.** $c^{\frac{1}{8}}$ **75.** $(a - b)^{\frac{1}{3}}$ **76.** $(ab + c)^{\frac{1}{2}}$

■■■■■■ **MAINTAIN**

Solve and check each equation. If an apparent solution does not check in the original equation, give the solution set as ɸ. (*Pages 514–517*)

77. $\sqrt{x} = 5$ **78.** $7 + \sqrt{x} = 9$ **79.** $\sqrt{x - 3} = 5$

80. $\sqrt{2x + 1} = 7$ **81.** $\sqrt{x} = -4$ **82.** $6 - 2\sqrt{x} = 0$

Simplify. (*Pages 502–504*)

83. $\sqrt{5}(\sqrt{4} + 3)$ **84.** $\sqrt{2}(\sqrt{8} - \sqrt{2})$ **85.** $(6 - \sqrt{5})(6 + \sqrt{5})$

Factor. (*Pages 384–386*)

86. $x^2 - 1$ **87.** $16 - y^2$ **88.** $4a^2 - 9$ **89.** $81 - 25x^2$

■■■■■■ **NON-ROUTINE PROBLEMS**

90. A square handkerchief is folded in half horizontally as shown below. The folded rectangle has a perimeter of 42 inches. What is the area of the square handkerchief?

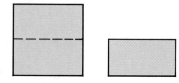

91. A cardboard strip is one inch wide and 48 inches long. It is cut with scissors at one-inch intervals, making 48 square inches. If each cut takes one second, how long will it take to make all the cuts?

Focus on College Entrance Tests

Some items on College Entrance tests are designed so that one or more of several given statements are correct, or no statement is correct. In such cases, you must examine each of the possibilities before deciding on the answer.

If n is a rational number, which of the following must be rational numbers?

$$\text{I. } \sqrt{n} \qquad \text{II. } n^2 \qquad \text{III. } \sqrt{n^2}$$

a. II only   **b.** I and II only

c. II and III only   **d.** I, II, and III

Solution: I is not always true. (For example, $\sqrt{2}$ is not rational.)
II is true, since n^2 means $n \cdot n$, and the product of two rational numbers is rational.
III is true, since $\sqrt{n^2} = |n|$, which is rational when n is rational.
Answer: c

Choose the best answer. Choose a, b, c, or d.

1. If x is an integer greater than 1, which of the following statements are true?

$$\text{I. } \sqrt{x} < x \qquad\qquad \text{II. } \sqrt{x} < x^2 \qquad\qquad \text{III. } \frac{1}{x} < \sqrt{x}$$

a. I and II only   **b.** I and III only   **c.** II and III only   **d.** I, II, and III

2. If y is an integer less than 0, which of the following statements are true?
$$\text{I. } \sqrt[3]{y} < 0 \qquad\qquad \text{II. } \sqrt{1 - y} < 0 \qquad\qquad \text{III. } \sqrt{1 + y^2} < 0$$
a. I only   **b.** II only   **c.** I and III only   **d.** None of these

3. If $\sqrt{p}$ is a rational number, which of the following must be rational numbers?
$$\text{I. } \sqrt{p + 1} \qquad\qquad \text{II. } \sqrt{p + 4} \qquad\qquad \text{III. } \sqrt{p + 9}$$
a. II only   **b.** III only   **c.** I and II only   **d.** None of these

4. If k is an integer, which of the following must be integers?

$$\text{I. } \frac{k}{2} \qquad\qquad \text{II. } k - 2 \qquad\qquad \text{III. } \sqrt{k}$$

a. I only   **b.** II only   **c.** I and II only   **d.** II and III only

5. If x is a nonzero real number, which of the following statements must be true?

$$\text{I. } \left(\frac{x}{x}\right)^x = 1 \qquad\qquad \text{II. } x^{\frac{x}{x}} = 1 \qquad\qquad \text{III. } x^{x - x} = 1$$

a. I only   **b.** II only   **c.** I and II only   **d.** I and III only

Chapter Summary

IMPORTANT TERMS

Conjugates (p. 511)
Density (p. 482)
Hypotenuse (p. 494)
Irrational square root(p. 480)
Perfect square (p. 480)
Principal square root (p. 477)
Radical (p. 477)

Radical equation (p. 514)
Radical symbol, $\sqrt{}$ (p. 477)
Radicand (p. 477)
Rational exponent (p. 518)
Rationalizing the
   denominator (p. 506)
Right triangle (p. 494)

IMPORTANT TERMS

1. For any real number a, $\sqrt{a^2} = |a|$.

2. **Density property:** Between any two real numbers, there is another real number.

3. If a and b are real numbers and $a \geq 0$, ≥ 0, then
$$\sqrt{ab} = \sqrt{a} \cdot \sqrt{b}.$$

4. **Pythagorean Theorem:** If a, b, and c are the lengths of the sides of a right triangle and c is the hypotenuse (longest side), then
$$a^2 + b^2 = c^2.$$

5. If the sum of the squares of the lengths of the two shorter sides (legs) of a triangle is equal to the square of the length of the longest side (hypotenuse), then the triangle is a right triangle.

6. **Distance Formula:** See page 500.

7. If a and b are real numbers where $a \geq 0$ and $b > 0$, then $\sqrt{\dfrac{a}{b}} = \dfrac{\sqrt{a}}{\sqrt{b}}$.

8. A radical is in simplest form when
   1 The radicand contains no factor that is a perfect square.
   2 The radicand does not contain a fraction.
   3 No radical appears in a denominator.

9. For any positive odd integer n where a is any real number, or for any positive even integer n where $a \geq 0$, $a^{\frac{1}{n}} = \sqrt[n]{a}$.

Chapter Review

Simplify. (*Pages 477–479*)

1. $\sqrt{121}$ **2.** $-\sqrt{y^{12}}$ **3.** $\sqrt{9x^2y^6}$ **4.** $\sqrt{(37d^3)^2}$

Identify each square root as rational or irrational. (*Pages 480–483*)

5. $\sqrt{\dfrac{1}{9}}$ **6.** $\sqrt{\dfrac{4}{10}}$ **7.** $\sqrt{1.44}$ **8.** $\sqrt{0.09}$ **9.** $-\sqrt{101}$ **10.** $-\sqrt{0.49}$

Find the real number halfway between the two given numbers. (*Pages 480–483*)

11. 0.45 and 0.455   **12.** 4.23 and $5\frac{1}{4}$ **13.** $8\frac{2}{5}$ and $7\frac{1}{2}$

Write each rational number in the form $\dfrac{a}{b}$. (*Pages 484–487*)

14. $0.\overline{5}$ **15.** $0.\overline{18}$ **16.** $0.1\overline{6}$ **17.** $0.\overline{407}$

18. The area of a square is 20 square meters. Find the length of a side to the nearest tenth of a meter.

19. The area of the face of an old coin is 6.28 square centimeters. Find the radius of the coin to the nearest tenth. (Use $A = \pi r^2$, $\pi = 3.14$.)

Simplify. All variables represent positive numbers. (*Pages 488–490*)

20. $\sqrt{18}$ **21.** $6\sqrt{32}$ **22.** $\sqrt{54x^3}$ **23.** $-2\sqrt{4a^3b^5}$

The lengths of the legs of a right triangle are a and b, and c is the length of the hypotenuse. Use the Pythagorean Theorem to find the length of the unknown side to the nearest tenth. (*Pages 494–498*)

24. $a = 12$, $b = 16$, $c = \underline{\ \ ?\ \ }$ **25.** $a = \underline{\ \ ?\ \ }$, $b = 7$, $c = 10$

26. A lane is built diagonally across a rectangular park 200 meters long and 300 meters wide. Find the length of the lane to the nearest meter.

27. The diagonal of a square rug is 3 meters in length. Find the length of each side of the square to the nearest tenth of a meter.

Find the distance between each pair of points. (*Pages 499–501*)

28. $C(3, -4)$ and $D(6, 0)$ **29.** $R(6, 2)$ and $S(-1, 2)$ **30.** $W(3, -6)$ and $X(-6, 3)$

Multiply and simplify. All variables represent positive numbers. (*Pages 502–504*)

31. $\sqrt{2} \cdot \sqrt{6}$ **32.** $3\sqrt{8} \cdot (-5\sqrt{12})$ **33.** $\sqrt{2a^2} \cdot \sqrt{2b^2}$ **34.** $-\sqrt{3n^3} \cdot \sqrt{6n^2}$

Simplify. All variables represent positive real numbers. (*Pages 505–509*)

35. $\pm\sqrt{\dfrac{36}{25}}$ **36.** $\dfrac{1}{\sqrt{10}}$ **37.** $\sqrt{\dfrac{12}{8y^5}}$ **38.** $\dfrac{\sqrt{30a^3b}}{\sqrt{5a}}$

Add or subtract as indicated. (*Pages 510–513*)

39. $6\sqrt{7} - 4\sqrt{7} - \sqrt{7}$ **40.** $4\sqrt{18} + 5\sqrt{2}$ **41.** $4\sqrt{24x^2} - 2\sqrt{54x^2}$

Rationalize the denominator. (*Pages 510–513*)

42. $\dfrac{1}{3 + \sqrt{2}}$ **43.** $\dfrac{3}{4 - \sqrt{3}}$ **44.** $\dfrac{4}{\sqrt{5} + 1}$ **45.** $\dfrac{2}{\sqrt{8} - 4}$

Solve and check each equation. (*Pages 514–517*)

46. $\sqrt{x - 3} = 1$ **47.** $6 + \sqrt{3x - 5} = 2$ **48.** $\sqrt{2x - 1} = \sqrt{x + 4}$

49. Nine more than the square root of a number is 14. Find the number.

50. Twelve, divided by the square root of a number, equals $1\frac{1}{2}$. Find the number.

Simplify. (*Pages 518–520*)

51. $100^{\frac{1}{2}}$ **52.** $(-27)^{\frac{1}{3}}$ **53.** $144^{\frac{1}{2}}$ **54.** $625^{\frac{3}{4}}$ **55.** $-(1000)^{\frac{2}{3}}$

Chapter Test

Simplify.

1. $\pm\sqrt{100}$ **2.** $3\sqrt{63}$ **3.** $-\sqrt{108}$ **4.** $(-8)^{\frac{1}{3}}$ **5.** $27^{\frac{2}{3}}$

Identify each square root as rational or irrational.

6. $\sqrt{\dfrac{2}{5}}$ **7.** $\sqrt{\dfrac{100}{121}}$ **8.** $-\sqrt{4}$ **9.** $\sqrt{0.25}$ **10.** $\sqrt{2\dfrac{1}{3}}$

The lengths of the sides of a right triangle are a and b, and c is the length of the hypotenuse. Find the length of the unknown side.

11. $a = 15, b = 20, c = \underline{\ ?\ }$ **12.** $a = 24, b = \underline{\ ?\ }, c = 25$

Find the distance between each pair of points.

13. $A(3, 6)$ and $B(0, 2)$ **14.** $K(6, -2)$ and $L(-3, -2)$

Perform the indicated operations. Simplify the answers.

15. $\sqrt{5} \cdot \sqrt{8}$ **16.** $-3\sqrt{2} \cdot \sqrt{10}$ **17.** $6\sqrt{2} + 3\sqrt{8}$

18. $\dfrac{3\sqrt{12}}{2\sqrt{18}}$ **19.** $\sqrt{2n} \cdot \sqrt{6n}$ **20.** $6\sqrt{5x^2} - \sqrt{45x^2}$

Solve and check each equation.

21. $\sqrt{x - 2} = 3$ **22.** $4\sqrt{x + 6} = 8$

23. The length of a parking lot is 24 meters and the width is 10 meters. Find the length of a diagonal of the lot.

24. Four less than the square root of a number is 6. What is the number?

Skills

Simplify. (*Pages 477–479*)

1. $-\sqrt{144}$ **2.** $\sqrt{0.36}$ **3.** $\pm\sqrt{19^2}$ **4.** $\sqrt{9a^2b^4}$ **5.** $\sqrt{\dfrac{64}{81}}$

Write each rational number in the form $\dfrac{a}{b}$. (*Pages 484–487*)

6. $0.\overline{7}$ **7.** $0.\overline{81}$ **8.** $1.\overline{3}$ **9.** $0.\overline{297}$ **10.** $0.41\overline{6}$

Simplify. All variables represent positive numbers. (*Pages 488–490*)

11. $\sqrt{54}$ **12.** $2\sqrt{75}$ **13.** $-3\sqrt{80x^3}$ **14.** $4\sqrt{63}$ **15.** $5\sqrt{180a^4b^5}$

Find the distance between each pair of points. (*Pages 499–501*)

16. $A(2, 3)$ and $B(2, -5)$ **17.** $P(0, 3)$ and $Q(-8, -3)$ **18.** $S(2, 12)$ and $T(-3, 0)$

Multiply and simplify. Variables represent positive numbers. (*Pages 502–504*)

19. $\sqrt{6} \cdot \sqrt{18}$ **20.** $\sqrt{75} \cdot \sqrt{2}$ **21.** $\sqrt{14a} \cdot \sqrt{2a}$ **22.** $\sqrt{15xy} \cdot \sqrt{3xy}$

Simplify. Variables represent positive numbers. (*Pages 505–509*)

23. $\sqrt{\dfrac{3}{16}}$ **24.** $\dfrac{3\sqrt{6}}{2\sqrt{3}}$ **25.** $\dfrac{\sqrt{6}}{\sqrt{8}}$ **26.** $\sqrt{\dfrac{35a^2}{7}}$ **27.** $\dfrac{\sqrt{12x^3}}{\sqrt{3x}}$

Add or subtract as indicated. (*Pages 510–513*)

28. $2\sqrt{3} + \sqrt{3} + 4\sqrt{3}$ **29.** $3\sqrt{5} - 2\sqrt{20}$ **30.** $6\sqrt{8} + 3\sqrt{18} - \sqrt{32}$

Problem Solving and Applications

31. The length of a rectangle is twice its width. The area of the rectangle is 60 square meters. Find the length and width to the nearest tenth of a meter. (*Pages 484–487*)

32. The foot of a ladder lies 1.5 meters from the base of a wall. The top lies against the wall, 3.5 meters above the ground. Find the length of the ladder (nearest tenth). (*Pages 494–498*)

33. The diagonal of a square measures 12 centimeters. Find the length of each side of the square to the nearest tenth of a centimeter. (*Pages 494–498*)

34. Twice a number is increased by 6. The square root of this sum is 8. Find the number. (*Pages 514–517*)

Part 1

Choose the best answer. Choose *a, b, c,* or *d.*

1. Solve for x: $\dfrac{4}{x-3} = x$. (Assume that $x \neq 3$.)

   a. no solution   **b.** $\{4\}$ **c.** $\{-1\}$ **d.** $\{-1, 4\}$

2. What is the theoretical probability that if one card is drawn from an ordinary deck of playing cards, it is an ace?

   a. $\dfrac{4}{13}$ **b.** $\dfrac{1}{4}$ **c.** $\dfrac{1}{52}$ **d.** $\dfrac{1}{13}$

3. What is the common factor of $3x^4y^2 + 6x^3yz + 12x^2y^2z$?

   a. $3xy^2$ **b.** $3xyz$ **c.** $3x^2y$ **d.** $3xy$

4. Simplify: $(x^2)^3 \cdot \sqrt{x^8}$.

   a. x^{13} **b.** $\sqrt{x^{13}}$ **c.** x^{10} **d.** x^5

5. Find the value of k that will make $3x - 1$ a factor of $6x^2 + kx - 3$.

   a. 3   **b.** 7   **c.** 2   **d.** -3

6. Which pair is not a solution of the system $\begin{cases} 3x - 4y \geq 6 \\ 2x + y \geq 4 \end{cases}$?

   a. $(4, 1)$ **b.** $(2, 0)$ **c.** $(8, 3)$ **d.** $(3, 1)$

7. Solve for x: $-3(\frac{1}{2} - 3x) < \frac{1}{3}(x + 2)$.

   a. $x < \dfrac{3}{26}$ **b.** $x < \dfrac{1}{4}$ **c.** $x > \dfrac{3}{26}$ **d.** $x > \dfrac{1}{4}$

8. Simplify: $(a^2 - b^2) - (a - b)^2$.

   a. $a - b$ **b.** $a + b$ **c.** $2b(a + b)$ **d.** $2b(a - b)$

9. Which of the following triples does not represent the sides of a right triangle?

   a. 5, 12, 13   **b.** $\sqrt{3}, \sqrt{5}, \sqrt{8}$ **c.** 7, 12, $\sqrt{193}$ **d.** 10, 15, 18

10. What is the equation of the line that is parallel to $y = \frac{3}{4}x - 5$ and has a y intercept equal to 3?

    a. $4y = 3x + 3$ **b.** $3x + 4y = 3$ **c.** $4y = 3x + 12$ **d.** $y = 3x - 5$

11. Calculate the distance between the points $(-2, 3)$ and $(4, -1)$.

    a. $\sqrt{8}$ **b.** $\sqrt{50}$ **c.** $\sqrt{52}$ **d.** 52

12. Which of the following is equivalent to $9 \div 3^5$?

    a. $\dfrac{1}{3^3}$ **b.** $\dfrac{1}{3^4}$ **c.** $\dfrac{1}{3^2}$ **d.** $\dfrac{3}{9^5}$

13. Solve the equation $3\sqrt{x} - 1 = \frac{2}{3}$.

    a. $\dfrac{85}{81}$ **b.** $\dfrac{2}{9}$ **c.** $\dfrac{4}{81}$ **d.** $\dfrac{101}{85}$

14. What is the mean of the numbers 3, 4, 4, 6, 7, 9, 9, 12?

    a. 9   **b.** 6.75   **c.** 6.5   **d.** 5.125

15. Express $\dfrac{2 + \sqrt{3}}{4 - \sqrt{3}}$ in simplest form.

    a. $\dfrac{5 + 2\sqrt{3}}{19}$ **b.** $\dfrac{5 - 2\sqrt{3}}{19}$ **c.** $\dfrac{11 + 6\sqrt{3}}{13}$ **d.** $\dfrac{11 - 6\sqrt{3}}{13}$

16. Which of the following is equivalent to $|x - 1| > 2$?

    a. $x > 2$ or $x < -2$ **b.** $-2 < x < 2$

    c. $x > 3$ or $x < -1$ **d.** $-1 < x < 3$

17. Evaluate $3xy^2z[3 - 2x^3y^2z] + 2x^2yz$ for $x = -1$, $y = 2$ and $z = 1$.

    a. 12   **b.** 8   **c.** 24   **d.** 0

18. Solve $|x + 3| = 3$.

    a. $\{0\}$ **b.** $\{-6\}$ **c.** $\{3\}$ **d.** $\{-6, 0\}$

Part 2

Solve each problem.

19. One pump can empty a pool in 6 hours; a smaller pump will take 9 hours to empty the same pool. If the larger pump has been in operation for $1\frac{1}{2}$ hours before the smaller pump is turned on, how much longer will it take for the two pumps to empty the pool?

20. Sean drove 90 miles to visit his sister. His average speed on the return trip was 15 mph more than his average speed going to his sister's house. If the total travel time was $3\frac{1}{2}$ hours, what was his average speed going and coming?

21. How many grams of a solution containing 10% sugar must be combined with how many grams of a solution containing 60% sugar to make 250 grams of a solution containing 50% sugar?

22. Brian had $2000 invested at an interest rate of 7% per year. How much must he invest at 8% per year to make his yearly income from both investments $300?

23. Eastville is 32 miles east of Centerville and Northtown is directly north of Centerville. If the distance between Northtown and Eastville is 56 miles, what is the distance between Centerville and Northtown, to the nearest mile?

24. The length of a poster is 3 times greater than its width. If the area of the poster is 258 square inches, find the width to the nearest tenth of an inch.

Quadratic Functions and Equations

The path of the bouncing ball above forms a parabola. A **parabola** is a model of a quadratic function of this form.

$$y = ax^2 + bx + c, a \neq 0$$

13-1 Quadratic Equations

Equations such as the following are *quadratic equations*.

$$a^2 = 5 \qquad g^2 - 9 = 0 \qquad y^2 + 5y = 0 \qquad x^2 - 4x + 4 = 0$$

DEFINITION

> A **quadratic equation** is an equation that can be written in the form **(standard form)**
>
> $$ax^2 + bx + c = 0$$
>
> where a, b, and c are real numbers and $a \neq 0$.

In Chapter 10, you solved certain quadratic equations by factoring. Quadratic equations of the form $x^2 = k$ where $k \geq 0$ can be solved by factoring or by taking the square root of each side of the equation. This last procedure results in two linear equations which *together* are equivalent to the original quadratic equation.

> If $x^2 = k$, then $x = \sqrt{k}$ <u>or</u> $x = -\sqrt{k}$
> for any real number k, $k \geq 0$.

EXAMPLE 1   Solve: $x^2 - 7 = 0$

Solution: **Method 1**   By factoring

$$x^2 - 7 = 0$$
$$(x - \sqrt{7})(x + \sqrt{7}) = 0 \longleftarrow \textbf{By the Factors of Zero Property}$$
$$x = \sqrt{7} \quad \underline{\text{or}} \quad x = -\sqrt{7}$$

Method 2   By taking the square root

$$x^2 - 7 = 0$$
$$x^2 = 7$$
$$x = \pm\sqrt{7}$$

Check: Replace x in $x^2 - 7 = 0$ with $\sqrt{7}$ and then with $-\sqrt{7}$.

Thus, the **solution set** is $\{-\sqrt{7}, \sqrt{7}\}$.

Quadratic equations such as $(x - 5)^2 = 36$ can also be solved by taking the square root of each side of the equation.

EXAMPLE 2 Solve: $(x - 5)^2 = 36$

Solution: $(x - 5)^2 = 36$ ◄——— **Take the square root of both sides.**

$$x - 5 = \pm 6$$

$x - 5 = 6$ or $x - 5 = -6$

$x = 11$ or $x = -1$

The check is left for you.   **Solution set: $\{-1, 11\}$**

EXERCISES: Classwork/Homework

Objective: To solve quadratic equations by factoring or by taking the square root of each side of the equation

■■■■■■ CHECK YOUR UNDERSTANDING

Complete.

1. The linear equation $x - 3 = \pm 5$ means $x - 3 = 5$ or $x - 3 = \underline{?}$.

2. An equation written in the form $ax^2 + bx + c = 0$ is called a $\underline{?}$ equation.

3. The quadratic equation, $x^2 - 5 = 0$, can be solved by factoring. The two factors are $(x - \sqrt{5})$ and $\underline{?}$.

4. The quadratic equation, $(x - 3)^2 = 4$, can be solved by taking the $\underline{?}$ of both sides of the equation.

5. When $x^2 - 5 = 0$ is solved by taking the square root, $x = \pm\sqrt{5}$. The solution set is $\underline{?}$.

6. Each side of the quadratic equation, $3(x - 9)^2 = 75$, can be divided by 3. The resulting equation is $\underline{?}$.

■■■■■■ PRACTICE AND APPLY

Solve each equation.

7. $x^2 = 16$

8. $y^2 - 4 = 0$

9. $x^2 - 11 = 0$

10. $n^2 - 7 = 12$

11. $m^2 + 2 = 3$

12. $7 - 2x^2 = -15$

13. $4x^2 = 36$

14. $3x^2 + 5 = 26$

15. $2r^2 = 200$

16. $2s^2 - 18 = 0$

17. $z^2 = 32$

18. $y^2 - 19 = 0$

19. $x^2 - \frac{1}{4} = 0$

20. $2x^2 = \frac{1}{2}$

21. $99 = b^2 - 22$

22. $3n^2 - n = 15 - n$

23. $4m^2 - 3 = 9$

24. $3y^2 - 9 = 0$

25. $3z^2 = \frac{12}{9}$

26. $r - r^2 = 5r^2 + r$

27. $(x - 2)^2 = 0$

28. $(x + 5)^2 = 16$

29. $(x - 3)^2 = 25$

30. $3(a + 6)^2 = 27$

31. $5(b - 2)^2 = 125$

32. $3(z - 6)^2 = 48$

33. $(b + \frac{3}{4})^2 = 16$

34. $(c + \frac{3}{2})^2 = \frac{1}{4}$

35. $(x - \frac{1}{4})^2 = \frac{1}{16}$

36. $(x + \frac{3}{7})^2 = \frac{1}{49}$

37. $(2m + 4)^2 = 1$

38. $(2k - 6)^2 = 16$

39. $5(2y - 1)^2 = 80$

40. $4(3x - 2)^2 = 36$

41. $3(2v + 7)^2 = 27$

▬▬▬ MAINTAIN

Simplify. (*Pages 518–520*)

42. $4^{\frac{1}{2}}$

43. $(-8)^{\frac{1}{3}}$

44. $-(121)^{\frac{1}{2}}$

45. $(\frac{1}{49})^{\frac{1}{2}}$

46. $(\frac{27}{64})^{\frac{1}{3}}$

Solve and check each equation. If an apparent solution does not check in the original equation, give the solution set as φ. (*Pages 514–517*)

47. $\sqrt{x} = 9$

48. $\sqrt{r} = \frac{1}{2}$

49. $\sqrt{n + 2} = 6$

50. $5 + \sqrt{a} = -2$

Simplify. No denominator equals zero. (*Pages 421–424*)

51. $\dfrac{24abc}{36bc}$

52. $\dfrac{10(a + b)}{10a - 10b}$

53. $\dfrac{a(r - s)^2}{b(r - s)}$

54. $\dfrac{2x^2 + 12x - 54}{3x^2 - 24x + 45}$

▬▬▬ CONNECT AND EXTEND

55. If $r = 3$ and the solution set of $(x + r)^2 = s$ is $\{-1, -5\}$, what is the value of s?

56. If $r = -2$ and the solution set of $(x + r)^2 = s$ is $\{\frac{1}{2}, \frac{7}{2}\}$, what is the value of s?

Solve for x where a, b, and c are nonnegative constants.

57. $x^2 = a + b$

58. $\dfrac{x^2}{a} = 1$

59. $\dfrac{x^2}{a} = b$

60. $x^2 - 2a = 0$

61. $(x + a)^2 = b$

62. $(x - a)^2 = b$

63. $(2x + a)^2 = b$

64. $(3x - c)^2 = d$

▬▬▬ NON-ROUTINE PROBLEMS

65. It takes Eric 6 minutes to cut a log into 3 pieces. At that rate, how long would it take him to cut a log into 4 pieces?

66. A special ball is dropped from the top of a building 64 meters high. Each time the ball bounces, it bounces $\frac{1}{2}$ the distance that it fell. The ball is caught when it bounces 1 meter high. Find the total distance the ball travels before being caught.

Quadratic Functions and Equations   **531**

Express each trinomial as the square of a binomial. When a trinomial is not a perfect square, write *NP*. (*Pages 387–389*)

1. $m^2 - 4m + 4$

2. $v^2 + 4v + 8$

3. $h^2 + h + 1$

4. $t^2 + 0.2t + 0.01$

5. $q^2 - 0.6q + 0.09$

6. $p^6 - 12p^3 + 36$

7. $r^2 + \frac{2}{3}r + \frac{1}{9}$

8. $y^2 - \frac{7}{6}y + \frac{49}{36}$

9. $b^2 - \frac{7}{2}b + \frac{49}{16}$

10. $t^2 - \frac{1}{3}t + \frac{1}{36}$

11. $a^2 + \frac{6}{5}a + \frac{9}{25}$

12. $c^2 + \frac{3}{4}c + \frac{9}{64}$

13-2 Completing the Square

When a quadratic equation cannot be easily solved by factoring or by taking the square root of each side, a method called **completing the square** can be used. Recall that

$$(x + 7)^2 = x^2 + 2 \cdot 7 \cdot x + 49 = x^2 + 14x + 49.$$

Note that the last term, 49, is the square of one-half the coefficient of the middle term, $14x$. That is,

$$49 = \left(\frac{1}{2} \cdot 14\right)^2.$$

EXAMPLE 1 Complete the square.

    a. $a^2 + 8a$
                    b. $x^2 - 10x$

Solutions: **a.** **Think:** What is $\left(\frac{1}{2} \cdot 8\right)^2$?
                b. **Think:** What is $\left[\frac{1}{2}(-10)\right]^2$?

           $\left(\frac{1}{2} \cdot 8\right)^2 = 4^2 = 16$
              $\left[\frac{1}{2}(-10)\right]^2 = (-5)^2 = 25$

           $a^2 + 8a + 16 = (a + 4)^2$
            $x^2 - 10x + 25 = (x - 5)^2$

The following procedure summarizes the steps for completing the square of $x^2 + bx$.

PROCEDURE

> **To complete the square of $x^2 + bx$:**
>
> **1** Find one-half the coefficient of x. $\longrightarrow \dfrac{b}{2}$
>
> **2** Square the result of step 1. $\longrightarrow \left(\dfrac{b}{2}\right)^2 = \dfrac{b^2}{4}$
>
> **3** Add the result of step 2 to $x^2 + bx$. $\longrightarrow x^2 + bx + \dfrac{b^2}{4}$

You can solve a quadratic equation by completing the square.

EXAMPLE 2 Solve $x^2 + 6x + 8 = 0$ by completing the square.

Solution:

$\boxed{1}$ Write the equation in the form $x^2 + bx = c$.

$$x^2 + 6x + 8 = 0$$
$$x^2 + 6x = -8$$

$\boxed{2}$ Complete the square for $x^2 + 6x$.

Think: $\left(\frac{1}{2} \cdot 6\right)^2 = 9$

Add this number to each side of the equation.

$$x^2 + 6x + 9 = -8 + 9$$
$$x^2 + 6x + 9 = 1$$

$\boxed{3}$ Write the left member as a perfect square. Solve the equation.

$$(x + 3)^2 = 1$$
$$x + 3 = 1 \quad \text{or} \quad x + 3 = -1$$
$$x = -2 \quad \text{or} \quad x = -4$$

$\boxed{4}$ The check is left for you. **Solution set:** $\{-4, -2\}$

Before attempting to solve a quadratic equation by completing the square, be sure that the equation is in the form $x^2 + bx + c = 0$, where the coefficient of the x^2 term is 1.

EXAMPLE 3 Solve $4x^2 - 4x - 7 = 0$ by completing the square.

Solution: Since the coefficient of $4x^2$ is not 1, divide *each side* of the equation by 4, the coefficient by $4x^2$.

$$4x^2 - 4x - 7 = 0 \quad \longleftarrow \quad \textbf{Divide each side by 4.}$$

$$x^2 - x - \frac{7}{4} = 0 \quad \longleftarrow \quad \textbf{Add } (\tfrac{7}{4}) \textbf{ to each side.}$$

$$x^2 - x = \frac{7}{4} \quad \longleftarrow \quad [\tfrac{1}{2}(-1)]^2 = \tfrac{1}{4}. \textbf{ Add } \tfrac{1}{4} \textbf{ to each side.}$$

$$x^2 - x + \frac{1}{4} = \frac{7}{4} + \frac{1}{4} \quad \longleftarrow \quad \tfrac{7}{4} + \tfrac{1}{4} = \tfrac{8}{4} = 2$$

$$\left(x - \frac{1}{2}\right)^2 = 2$$

$$x - \frac{1}{2} = \sqrt{2} \quad \text{or} \quad x - \frac{1}{2} = -\sqrt{2}$$

$$x = \frac{1}{2} + \sqrt{2} \quad \text{or} \quad x = \frac{1}{2} - \sqrt{2}$$

Check:

$$4x^2 - 4x - 7 = 0$$
$$4(\tfrac{1}{2} + \sqrt{2})^2 - 4(\tfrac{1}{2} + \sqrt{2}) - 7 \overset{?}{=} 0$$
$$4(\tfrac{1}{4} + \sqrt{2} + 2) - 2 - 4\sqrt{2} - 7 \overset{?}{=} 0$$
$$1 + 4\sqrt{2} + 8 - 2 - 4\sqrt{2} - 7 \overset{?}{=} 0$$
$$0 \overset{?}{=} 0 \quad \text{Yes}$$

$$4x^2 - 4x - 7 = 0$$
$$4(\tfrac{1}{2} - \sqrt{2})^2 - 4(\tfrac{1}{2} - \sqrt{2}) - 7 \overset{?}{=} 0$$
$$4(\tfrac{1}{4} - \sqrt{2} + 2) - 2 + 4\sqrt{2} - 7 \overset{?}{=} 0$$
$$1 - 4\sqrt{2} + 8 - 2 + 4\sqrt{2} - 7 \overset{?}{=} 0$$
$$0 \overset{?}{=} 0$$
Yes

$$\text{Solution set: } \left\{ \tfrac{1}{2} + \sqrt{2}, \tfrac{1}{2} - \sqrt{2} \right\}$$

EXERCISES: Classwork/Homework

Objective: To solve quadratic equations by completing the square

CHECK YOUR UNDERSTANDING

Write the term needed to complete the square.

1. $x^2 + 4x + \underline{\ ?\ }$
2. $x^2 - 2x + \underline{\ ?\ }$
3. $x^2 + 8x + \underline{\ ?\ }$
4. $c^2 - 14c + \underline{\ ?\ }$
5. $x^2 - x + \underline{\ ?\ }$
6. $d^2 - \frac{4}{5}d + \underline{\ ?\ }$
7. $t^2 + \frac{1}{2}t + \underline{\ ?\ }$
8. $x^2 + bx + \underline{\ ?\ }$
9. $x^2 + \frac{b}{a}x + \underline{\ ?\ }$

PRACTICE AND APPLY

Complete the square. Then write the trinomial as the square of a binomial.

10. $x^2 + 10x$
11. $y^2 - 8y$
12. $m^2 + 4m$
13. $r^2 - r$
14. $x^2 + 12x$
15. $r^2 - 20r$
16. $x^2 + 5x$
17. $x^2 - 11x$
18. $x^2 - \frac{2}{5}x$

Solve by completing the square.

19. $x^2 + 4x = 12$
20. $x^2 + 6x = 27$
21. $n^2 - 2n - 8 = 0$
22. $a^2 - 6a + 8 = 0$
23. $a^2 + 4a = 5$
24. $b^2 + 10b = -16$
25. $x^2 - 12x = -35$
26. $x^2 - 10x = -24$
27. $x^2 - 16x = -60$
28. $x^2 - 16x = 17$
29. $x^2 - 7x + 10 = 0$
30. $x^2 - 9x = -18$
31. $n^2 + 6 = -5n$
32. $n^2 - 12 = n$
33. $x^2 + x = 6$
34. $x^2 - x = 30$
35. $y^2 - y = 2$
36. $p^2 + 5p = 0$

Solve by completing the square. Irrational solutions may be left in simplified radical form.

37. $3n^2 - 2n = 1$

38. $2n^2 = n + 3$

39. $3x^2 - 2x = 8$

40. $2y^2 - 3y = 35$

41. $6p^2 - 9p = 27$

42. $2x^2 - 7x + 3 = 0$

43. $2a^2 - 5a - 12 = 0$

44. $3x^2 - x - 2 = 0$

45. $2a^2 + 3a = 17$

46. $3 = 6x^2 - x$

MAINTAIN

Solve each equation. (*Pages 529–531*)

47. $x^2 = 25$

48. $c^2 - 15 = 0$

49. $7 - 3a^2 = -14$

50. $4d^2 - 16 = 0$

51. $r^2 - \frac{1}{9} = 0$

52. $8z^2 = \frac{32}{9}$

53. $(y - 3)^2 = 49$

54. $4(s + 6)^2 = 36$

Simplify. (*Pages 518–520*)

55. $1000^{\frac{1}{3}}$

56. $-(25)^{\frac{1}{2}}$

57. $(-32)^{\frac{1}{5}}$

58. $4^{\frac{5}{2}}$

Use a radical to name each of the following. Variables represent positive integers. (*Pages 518–520*)

59. $x^{\frac{1}{4}}$

60. $(ab)^{\frac{2}{3}}$

61. $(c^2)^{\frac{1}{3}}$

62. $(t)^{\frac{1}{2}}$

Multiply. Express each product in simplest form. (*Pages 425–428*)

63. $\dfrac{35x^2y}{8x} \cdot \dfrac{24y^2}{45xy}$

64. $\dfrac{r}{s} \cdot \dfrac{t}{v} \cdot \dfrac{as}{r} \cdot \dfrac{p^2}{s^2}$

65. $\dfrac{a^2 - 2a - 35}{(a + 5)^2} \cdot \dfrac{a + 5}{a - 7}$

66. $\dfrac{6r^2 - 96s^2}{2r^2 - 8s^2} \cdot \dfrac{4r + 8s}{12r + 48s}$

CONNECT AND EXTEND

Solve. Irrational solutions may be left in simplified radical form.

67. $\frac{1}{4}x^2 - \frac{3}{2}x - 1 = 0$

68. $1 + \dfrac{7}{x} + \dfrac{2}{x^2} = 0$

69. $x^2 + bx + 1 = 0$

70. $x^2 + bx = -c$

71. $\dfrac{5x + 7}{x - 1} = 3x + 2$

72. $\dfrac{5x - 1}{x + 1} = \dfrac{3x}{2}$

73. $\dfrac{a + 3}{2a - 7} - \dfrac{2a - 1}{a - 3} = 0$

74. $\dfrac{1}{3 - b} - \dfrac{4}{5} = \dfrac{1}{9 - 2b}$

75. $(x - 3)^2 + (x + 1)^2 = 26$

76. $c^2 + c\sqrt{5} - 5 = 0$

Factoring / Using a Geometric Model

An algebraic method for solving a quadratic equation by **completing the square** was shown on pages 532–534. The following method of completing the square used a **geometric model.** This method works for finding positive solutions only to quadratic equations of the form $ax^2 + bx + c = 0$ where $a > 0$, $b > 0$, and $c < 0$.

EXAMPLE: Solve $x^2 + 4x - 12 = 0$ by completing the square.

Solution:

1 Write the equation in the form $x^2 + bx = -c$. ⟶ $x^2 + 4x = 12$

2 Represent x^2 as a square with sides of length x.

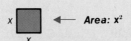

◄— **Area: x²**

3 Represent $4x$ as two rectangles, each with an area of $\frac{1}{2}(4x)$, or $2x$.

Position the rectangles as shown.

Area of the L-shaped figure: $2x + x^2 + 2x$, or $x^2 + 4x$

From step 1, $x^2 + 4x = 12$.
Thus, the area of the L-shaped figure is 12.

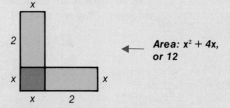

◄— **Area: x² + 4x, or 12**

4 Complete the square by adding the red region shown.

Why must the lengths of the sides of the red region equal 2?

What is the area of the red square?

$$\frac{\text{Area of}}{\text{L-shaped Region}} + \frac{\text{Area of}}{\text{Red Square}} = \underline{\quad?\quad}$$

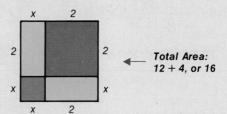

◄— **Total Area: 12 + 4, or 16**

5 Since the large square has a total area of 16, the length of each side must equal 4. Why?

Thus, $x + 2 = 4$, or $x = $ **2.**

6 **Check:** Does $(2)^2 + 4(2) - 12 = 0$?

Does $4 + 8 - 12 = 0$?   Yes ✔

EXERCISES

For Exercise 1, replace each __?__ to solve $2x^2 + 5x - 3 = 0$ by completing the square.

1. **1** Write the equation in the form $x^2 + \frac{b}{a}x = -\frac{c}{a}$. ⟶ $x^2 + \frac{5}{2}x = $ __?__

2 Represent x^2.

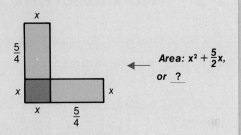

← **Area: x²**

3 Represent $\frac{5}{2}x$ as two rectangles, each with an area of $\frac{1}{2}(\frac{5}{2}x)$, or __?__ .

Area of L-shaped figure:
$\frac{5}{4}x + x^2 + \frac{5}{4}x = $ __?__

From step 1, $x^2 + \frac{5}{2}x = \frac{3}{2}$.

Thus, the area of the L-shaped figure = __?__ .

← **Area: x² + $\frac{5}{2}$x, or ?**

4 Complete the square.

The area of the red square equals __?__ .

$$\text{Area of L-shaped Region} + \text{Area of Red Square} = \text{?}$$

← **Total Area: $\frac{3}{2} + \frac{25}{16}$, or ?**

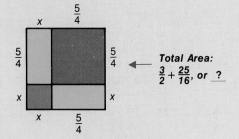

5 Since the large square has a total area of $\frac{49}{16}$, the length of each side must equal __?__ .

Thus, $x + \frac{5}{4} = \frac{7}{4}$, or $x = $ __?__ .

2. Why does the method of Exercise 1 work only for finding a positive solution of a quadratic equation?

Use the geometric method of completing the square to find a positive solution for each quadratic equation.

3. $x^2 + 2x - 3 = 0$

4. $x^2 + 4x - 21 = 0$

5. $x^2 + 6x - 16 = 0$

6. $x^2 + 8x - 20 = 0$

7. $2x^2 + 5x - 12 = 0$

8. $2x^2 + 3x - 9 = 0$

Simplify. (*Pages 488–490*)

1. $\sqrt{54}$ 2. $-\sqrt{24}$ 3. $9\sqrt{48}$ 4. $5\sqrt{18}$ 5. $-2\sqrt{32}$

6. $7\sqrt{50}$ 7. $-\sqrt{8}$ 8. $-3\sqrt{40}$ 9. $-4\sqrt{50}$ 10. $5\sqrt{44}$

13-3   The Quadratic Formula

By completing the square of the standard form of the quadratic equation,

$$ax^2 + bx + c = 0,$$

you can determine the **solutions** or **roots** of the equation.

Compare the method for the specific case shown on the left with that for the general case shown on the right.

Specific Case		**General Case**

Specific Case

$3x^2 - 2x - 2 = 0$

$x^2 - \frac{2}{3}x - \frac{2}{3} = 0$

$x^2 - \frac{2}{3}x = \frac{2}{3}$

$\frac{1}{2}\left(-\frac{2}{3}\right) = -\frac{1}{3}; \left(-\frac{1}{3}\right)^2 = \frac{1}{9}$

$x^2 - \frac{2}{3}x + \frac{1}{9} = \frac{2}{3} + \frac{1}{9}$

$\left(x - \frac{1}{3}\right)^2 = \frac{7}{9}$

$x - \frac{1}{3} = \pm\sqrt{\frac{7}{9}}$

$x = \frac{1}{3} \pm \frac{\sqrt{7}}{3}$

$x = \frac{1 \pm \sqrt{7}}{3}$

Solution set: $\left\{\dfrac{1 + \sqrt{7}}{3}, \dfrac{1 - \sqrt{7}}{3}\right\}$

← **Divide each side by the coefficient of the x²-term.** →

← $\left[\frac{1}{2}\text{(coefficient of x)}\right]^2$ →

← **Complete the square.** →

← **Solve for x.** →

General Case

Solve $ax^2 + bx + c = 0.$

$x^2 + \frac{b}{a}x + \frac{c}{a} = 0$

$x^2 + \frac{b}{a}x = -\frac{c}{a}$

$\frac{1}{2}\left(\frac{b}{a}\right) = \frac{b}{2a}; \left(\frac{b}{2a}\right)^2 = \frac{b^2}{4a^2}$

$x^2 + \frac{b}{a}x + \frac{b^2}{4a^2} = \frac{b^2}{4a^2} - \frac{c}{a}$

$\left(x + \frac{b}{2a}\right)^2 = \frac{b^2 - 4ac}{4a^2}$

$x + \frac{b}{2a} = \pm\sqrt{\frac{b^2 - 4ac}{4a^2}}$

$x = -\frac{b}{2a} \pm \frac{\sqrt{b^2 - 4ac}}{2a}$

$x = \frac{-b \pm \sqrt{b^2 - 4ac}}{2a}$

Solution set: $\left\{\dfrac{-b + \sqrt{b^2 - 4ac}}{2a}, \dfrac{-b - \sqrt{b^2 - 4ac}}{2a}\right\}$

The solutions for the general equation are usually referred to as the *quadratic formula*.

> **Quadratic Formula**
>
> For the quadratic equation $ax^2 + bx + c = 0$, where a, b, and c are real numbers and $a \neq 0$,
>
> $$x = \frac{-b \pm \sqrt{b^2 - 4ac}}{2a}.$$

EXAMPLE Use the quadratic formula to solve $3x^2 + 2x - 3 = 0$.

Solution: Identify a, b, and c. Then use the quadratic formula.

$3x^2 + 2x - 3 = 0$ ⟵ $a = 3; b = 2; c = -3$

$x = \dfrac{-b \pm \sqrt{b^2 - 4ac}}{2a}$ ⟵ **Quadratic formula**

$x = \dfrac{-2 \pm \sqrt{(2)^2 - 4(3)(-3)}}{2(3)}$

$x = \dfrac{-2 \pm \sqrt{4 + 36}}{6}$

$x = \dfrac{-2 \pm \sqrt{40}}{6}$ ⟵ **Simplify $\sqrt{40}$.**

$x = \dfrac{-2 \pm 2\sqrt{10}}{6}$ ⟵ **Factor the numerator.**

$x = \dfrac{2(-1 \pm \sqrt{10})}{6}$ ⟵ **Simplify.**

$x = \dfrac{-1 \pm \sqrt{10}}{3}$ ⟵ **The check is left for you.**

Solution set: $\left\{ \dfrac{-1 + \sqrt{10}}{3}, \dfrac{-1 - \sqrt{10}}{3} \right\}$

CALCULATOR

You can use a calculator to find decimal approximations for the solutions of quadratic equations. For example,

$\dfrac{-1 + \sqrt{10}}{3}$: 1 $\boxed{+/-}$ $\boxed{+}$ 10 $\boxed{\sqrt{x}}$ $\boxed{=}$ $\boxed{\div}$ 3 $\boxed{=}$ $\boxed{0.7207592}$

$\dfrac{-1 - \sqrt{10}}{3}$: 1 $\boxed{+/-}$ $\boxed{-}$ 10 $\boxed{\sqrt{x}}$ $\boxed{=}$ $\boxed{\div}$ 3 $\boxed{=}$ $\boxed{-1.3874259}$

You then round each answer as needed.

Be sure to write a quadratic equation in the form $ax^2 + bx + c = 0$ before using the quadratic formula. To solve $2x^2 - x = 3$, for example, first write the equation in the form

$$2x^2 - x - 3 = 0.$$

EXERCISES: Classwork/Homework

Objective: To solve quadratic equations using the quadratic formula

CHECK YOUR UNDERSTANDING

For each quadratic equation, identify a, b, and c.

1. $x^2 - 4x - 5 = 0$
2. $3x^2 - 5x - 4 = 0$
3. $4x^2 + 12x = 7$
4. $3x^2 = 7 + 3y$
5. $7 - a^2 = 3a$
6. $4t^2 = 9 + 2t$
7. $3x^2 = 45$
8. $5b^2 = 3b + 2$
9. $5y^2 - 1 = 2y$

PRACTICE AND APPLY

Solve each equation. Write irrational roots in simplest radical form.

10. $x^2 - 4x = 21$
11. $x^2 + 6x = 16$
12. $2x^2 - x - 3 = 0$
13. $x^2 = 3x$
14. $p^2 - 4p = 0$
15. $n^2 - 2n - 8 = 0$
16. $a^2 + 4a = 5$
17. $6a^2 + 13a + 6 = 0$
18. $n^2 + 6 = -5n$
19. $2y^2 = 5y - 3$
20. $2x^2 + x = 3$
21. $y^2 + 3y = 4$
22. $y^2 - y = 2$
23. $10b^2 + 7b - 12 = 0$
24. $x^2 + 6x = -9$
25. $x^2 - 2x = 4$
26. $x^2 + 2x = 1$
27. $x^2 + 4x = -2$
28. $x^2 + 6x + 3 = 0$
29. $x^2 - x - 1 = 0$
30. $x^2 + 3x + 1 = 0$
31. $2x^2 - 4x - 3 = 0$
32. $2x^2 + x - 5 = 0$
33. $3x^2 - 2x = 1$
34. $2x^2 + 7x + 2 = 0$
35. $6x^2 - 3x - 4 = 0$
36. $3x^2 + 10x + 5 = 0$
37. $2x^2 - 7x + 2 = 0$
38. $2x^2 - x - 1 = 0$
39. $3x^2 - 2x = 7$
40. $2y^2 - 3y = 4$
41. $4n^2 - 4 = n$
42. $7x^2 - 3x - 1 = 0$
43. $9n^2 + 2 + 9n = 0$
44. $8n^2 + 7n - 2 = 0$
45. $4a^2 - 5 = 3a$
46. $4 + \dfrac{9}{b^2} - \dfrac{12}{b} = 0$
47. $\dfrac{6d + 10}{d} = -\dfrac{3}{d^2}$
48. $\dfrac{3}{t - 1} - 4 = \dfrac{1}{t + 1}$

Solve each equation. Use the Table of Square Roots on page 636 or use a calculator to approximate irrational roots to the nearest tenth.

49. $3n^2 - 2n = 2$
50. $3x^2 - x - 3 = 0$
51. $2a^2 - 5a - 1 = 0$
52. $2n^2 = n + 2$
53. $5n^2 + 3 = 11n$
54. $3b^2 + 5b + 1 = 0$

You can use the program on page **621** to solve quadratic equations of the form $ax^2 + bx + c = 0$.

Write each equation in the form $ax^2 + bx + c = 0$. Then use the program to find the roots.

55. $x^2 + 5x = 7$

56. $3x^2 = 8 + 2x$

57. $12x = 4x^2 + 9$

MAINTAIN

Solve by completing the square. Irrational square roots may be left in simplified radical form. (*Pages 532–535*)

58. $x^2 + 10x = 24$

59. $a^2 + 12a = 45$

60. $r^2 = 5r$

61. $3n^2 - 4n = 2$

62. $2a^2 + 3 = -8a$

63. $5x^2 - x - 9 = 0$

Solve each equation. (*Pages 529–531*)

64. $m - m^2 = 8m^2 + m$

65. $6(z - 12)^2 = 48$

66. $8(t + 5)^2 = 120$

Divide. Express the answers in simplest form. (*Pages 429–432*)

67. $\dfrac{7a}{14bc} \div 14a$

68. $\dfrac{8a - 32}{5a} \div (3a - 12)$

69. $\dfrac{s^2 - t^2}{x^2 - y^2} \div \dfrac{s + t}{x - y}$

CONNECT AND EXTEND

In Exercises 70–74, refer to the quadratic equation $ax^2 + bx + c = 0$, where $a \neq 0$ and $b^2 - 4ac > 0$.

70. Show that the sum of the roots of the equation is $-\dfrac{b}{a}$.

71. Show that the product of the roots of the equation is $\dfrac{c}{a}$.

72. Write a quadratic equation whose roots are $1 \pm \sqrt{3}$. (HINT: Use the results of Exercises 70 and 71 to find the sum and product of the roots and thus to find the relationship between a, b, and c.)

73. Write a quadratic equation whose roots are $2 \pm \sqrt{5}$.

74. Write two quadratic equations whose solutions are $2 \pm \sqrt{3}$.

NON-ROUTINE PROBLEM

75. Jerome and his sister Latasha walk to school every day. They start at the same time and walk at the same speed. Who gets to school first? Explain. Refer to the figure at the right.

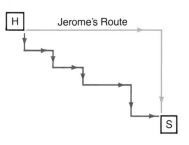

13-4   Using Quadratic Equations

When the conditions of a problem can be represented by a quadratic equation, the equation can then be solved by one of the methods you have learned.

EXAMPLE 1   In a school auditorium, the number of seats in each row is 8 fewer than the number of rows (Condition 1). The auditorium seats 609 persons (Condition 2). How many seats are there in each row?

Solution:

1 **Find:**   **The number of seats in each row.**

    Given: The number of seats in each row is 8 fewer than the number of rows. ◄——— **Condition 1**

             The auditorium seats 609 persons ◄——— **Cor.dition 2**

Represent the unknowns.

         Let s = the number of seats in each row.
         Then $s + 8$ = the number of rows.

2 Write an equation to "connect" Condition 1 and Condition 2.

Think:	**Number of Seats per Row**	·	**Number of Rows**	=	**Total Seats**
	↓		↓		↓
Translate:	s	·	$(s + 8)$	=	609

3 Solve the equation.

$$s(s + 8) = 609$$
$$s^2 + 8s = 609$$
$$s^2 + 8s - 609 = 0 \quad \longleftarrow \quad a = 1, b = 8, c = -609.$$
$$s = \frac{-b \pm \sqrt{b^2 - 4ac}}{2a}$$
$$s = \frac{-8 \pm \sqrt{64 + 2436}}{2}$$
$$s = \frac{-8 \pm \sqrt{2500}}{2}$$

$$s = \frac{-8 + 50}{2}$$ ◄──────── **The number of seats cannot be negative.**

$$s = \frac{-8 + 50}{2} = \frac{42}{2}, \text{ or } \mathbf{21}$$ ◄──────── **Number of seats per row**

4 The check is left for you.   There are **21 seats** per row.

When the solutions to a quadratic equation are irrational numbers, use the Table of Square Roots on page 636 or use a calculator to approximate the solutions to the nearest tenth, to the nearest hundredth, and so on, as directed.

EXAMPLE 2   The **Golden Rectangle,** discovered by the Greeks in the fifth century B.C., was considered to have the most "pleasing" shape. In a golden rectangle, the length is about 1.6 times the width (Condition 1). Find, to the nearest tenth, the dimensions of the golden rectangle with an area of 48 square centimeters.

Solution: **1** **Find:**   The dimensions of the rectangle

Given: The length of a golden rectangle is about 1.6 times the width. The area is 48 square centimeters.

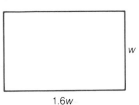
w

1.6w

Let w = the width.
Then $1.6w$ = the length.

2 **Think:**   **Length** · **Width** = **Area**

Translate: w · $1.6w$ =   48

3 $w(1.6w) = 48$

$1.6w^2 = 48$

$w^2 = 30$

$w = \pm\sqrt{30}$ ◄──────── **The width cannot be negative.**

$w \approx 5.5$ ◄──────── **Don't forget to find the length.**

$1.6w \approx 8.8$

4 **Check:**   Is $(5.5)(8.8) \approx 48$?   Yes ✔

The width is about **5.5 centimeters;** the length is about **8.8 centimeters.**

Objective: To solve problems using quadratic equations

CHECK YOUR UNDERSTANDING

In Exercises 1–6:
a. Use Condition 1 to represent the variables.
b. Use Condition 2 to write an equation for the problem.

1. The length of a rectangle is 3 meters longer than the width. The area is 40 square meters.

2. The base of a triangle is 3 feet longer than the altitude. The area is 44 square feet.

3. The product of two consecutive odd integers is 35.

4. A certain number exceeds its square by 15.

5. The square of a number is 10 more than three times the number.

6. The sum of a number and six times its reciprocal is 5.

PRACTICE AND APPLY

Use a quadratic equation to represent the conditions of each problem. Then solve the equation. Approximate irrational roots to the nearest hundredth.

7. In a theater, the number of seats in each row is 16 fewer than the number of rows. How many seats are in each row of a 1161-seat theater?

8. The length of a rectangular piece of sheet metal is 3 times its width. What is its length if its area is 192 square centimeters?

9. Find the dimensions of a golden rectangle with an area of 40 square centimeters.

10. One number is 3 more than another. The product of the numbers is 54. Find the numbers.

11. The square of a number is 56 more than the number itself. What is the number?

12. The length of a rectangle is 3 meters longer than its width. Its area is 40 square meters. Find its dimensions.

13. The perimeter of a rectangle is 30 meters and its area is 54 square meters. What are its dimensions?

14. What is the length of the diagonal of a square if it is 3 centimeters longer than a side of the square?

15. A number exceeds its square by $\frac{2}{9}$. Find the number.

16. The square of a number exceeds the number by 42. Find the number.

17. The hypotenuse of a right triangle is 2 centimeters longer than one side and 4 centimeters longer than the other side. How long is the hypotenuse?

18. A rectangular strip of asphalt paving is 5 meters longer than it is wide. Its area is 300 square meters. Find the length and width of the strip.

19. The numerator of a fraction is 1 less than its denominator. If the fraction is increased by 2 times its reciprocal, the sum will be $3\frac{5}{12}$. Find the numerator and the denominator.

20. The denominator of a fraction is 2 more than its numerator. If the fraction is increased by 3 times its reciprocal, the sum will be $5\frac{3}{5}$. Find the numerator and the denominator.

21. The figure below shows a rectangular park with a border of chestnut trees. The border has an area of 225 square meters. How wide is this border if the outside length is 25 meters and the outside width is 15 meters?

22. A box is to be made by cutting squares measuring 4 centimeters on a side from the square piece of cardboard shown below. If the volume of the box is to be 100 cubic centimeters, find the length of a side of the original square.

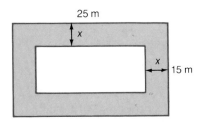

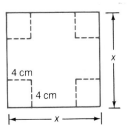

(Pages 538–541)

MAINTAIN

Use the quadratic formula to solve each equation. Write irrational roots in simplest radical forms. *(Pages 538–541)*

23. $x^2 + 7x - 5 = 0$ **24.** $x^2 - x = 7$ **25.** $c^2 = 4c$

Solve by completing the square. *(Pages 532–535)*

26. $p^2 - 16p = -4$ **27.** $y^2 + 22y = 1$ **28.** $x^2 - 24x + 30 = 0$

Find the LCD of rational expressions having the given denominators. *(Pages 433–436)*

29. $2a; 3ay$ **30.** $xy; xy^2$ **31.** $2a; 3b; 5c$ **32.** $4xy; 6xy^2; 15x^2$

CONNECT AND EXTEND

Solve each problem.

33. Sam and his mother drove 294 miles to the State Fair. Sam drove the farm truck at an average speed of 7 miles per hour slower than his mother drove the family car. It took Sam an hour longer than it took his mother. What was Sam's rate?

34. Mrs. and Mr. Murphy can do a piece of work together in 5 hours. Alone Mrs. Murphy can do the job in 3 hours less than Mr. Murphy can do it alone. How many hours, to the nearest tenth, will it take each to do the job?

Solve each equation. Irrational solutions may be left in simplified radical form. (*Pages 529–531*)

1. $x^2 = 64$

2. $y^2 + 6 = 7$

3. $3x^2 = 36$

4. $4n^2 + 5 = 21$

5. $(x - 4)^2 = 0$

6. $4(a - 5)^2 = 16$

Solve each equation. Irrational solutions may be left in simplified form. (*Pages 532–541*)

7. $x^2 - 2x - 15 = 0$

8. $x^2 + 5x + 6 = 0$

9. $n^2 - 2n = 8$

10. $a^2 - a = 2$

11. $2t^2 + t - 6 = 0$

12. $3s^2 - 6s = 1$

13. $a^2 - 4a - 21 = 0$

14. $c^2 = 4c$

15. $y^2 - 2y = 8$

16. $3b^2 + 2b = 3$

17. $2x^2 + 4x = 1$

18. $2y^2 = y + 2$

Solve each problem. Approximate irrational roots to the nearest tenth. (*Pages 542–545*)

19. On a pegboard, the number of pegs in each row is 4 more than the number of rows. There are 96 pegs in all. How many pegs are in each row?

20. The hypotenuse of a right triangle is one meter longer than one leg and 3 meters longer than the other leg. How long is the hypotenuse?

Historical Digest: Quadratic Equations

In about 2000 B.C., the Babylonians were solving second degree (quadratic) equations by completing the square and by using a formula. For hundreds of years, mathematicians worked to develop formulas for solving equations of the third, fourth, fifth, and higher degrees. In the 1500's, formulas for equations of the third and fourth degrees were published by the Italian mathematician Girolamo Cardano. Then in the 1800's, Évariste Galois, a French mathematician, and Niels Henrik Abel, a Norwegian mathematician, both discovered that the roots of equations to the fifth, sixth, and higher degrees cannot be solved in the same way as equations of the second, third, and fourth degrees.

Try to find the roots of these equations.

$$y = x^3 - 3x^2 + 2x \qquad y = 4x^4 + 7x^3 + 3x^2$$

Complete the table of ordered pairs for each function. (*Pages 188–190*)

1. $y = x^2 - x + 6$

x	−2	−1	0	1	2	3
y	?	?	?	?	?	?

2. $y = 2x^2 - 9x + 11$

x	−4	−2	0	2	4	6
y	?	?	?	?	?	?

13-5 Graphing Quadratic Functions

Each of these equations defines a *quadratic function.*

$$y = 2x^2 \qquad y = -3x^2 + 5 \qquad y = 2x^2 + 5x - 9$$

DEFINITION

> A function defined by the equation $y = ax^2 + bx + c$, where a, b, and c are real numbers and $a \neq 0$ is a **quadratic function.**

PARABOLA

The graph of a quadratic function is a **parabola.** To sketch the graph of a parabola, make a table of ordered pairs. Then graph the points and draw a smooth curve connecting them.

EXAMPLE 1 Graph the function $y = x^2 - 2x - 3$.

Solution: ☐1 Make a table of values.   ☐2 Graph the ordered pairs. Draw a smooth curve.

x	$x^2 - 2x - 3$	y
−2	$(-2)^2 - 2(-2) - 3$	5
−1	$(-1)^2 - 2(-1) - 3$	0
0	$0^2 - 2(0) - 3$	−3
1	$1^2 - 2(1) - 3$	−4
2	$2^2 - 2(2) - 3$	−3
3	$3^2 - 2(3) - 3$	0
4	$4^2 - 2(4) - 3$	5

x	y
−2	5
−1	0
0	−3
1	−4
2	−3
3	0
4	5

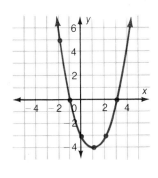

X INTERCEPT

The x coordinate of a point where the curve intersects the x axis is called an **x intercept.** In Example 1, the x intercepts are -1 and 3.

Quadratic Functions and Equations **547**

To find the *zeros* of a function, you find the values of x that make y equal to 0. This can be done by graphing to find the x intercepts.

DEFINITION

> The **zeros** of a function are the values of x for which the function equals zero.

EXAMPLE 2 Graph the function $y = 2x - x^2$.

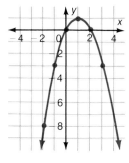

Determine the zeros of the function.

Solution:

x	−2	−1	0	1	2	3
y	−8	−3	0	1	0	−3

The zeros of the function are **0** and **2**.

CALCULATOR

If you want to evaluate a quadratic function for a decimal, it would be more efficient to use a calculator. For example, evaluate $y = x^2 - 2x - 3$ when $x = 1.5$.

1.5 $\boxed{x^2}$ $\boxed{-}$ 2 $\boxed{\times}$ 1.5 $\boxed{-}$ 3 $\boxed{=}$ ▭ $\boxed{-3.75}$

When $x = 1.5$, $y = -3.75$.

EXERCISES: Classwork/Homework

Objective: To graph quadratic functions and read the zeros of each function from its graph

CHECK YOUR UNDERSTANDING

Write *Yes* or *No* to indicate whether each function is quadratic.

1. $y = -5x$ **2.** $y = 3x^2$ **3.** $y = -5x^2 + 9$ **4.** $x + 2y - 3 = 0$
5. $3x^2 + 5x - 7 = y$ **6.** $x^2 + x = 2 + y$ **7.** $y = 4$ **8.** $x^2 + x = y$

Complete.

9. The graph of a quadratic function is a ___?___ .

10. To find the zeros of a function, you find the values of x that make y equal to ___?___ .

Graph each quadratic function.

11. $y = x^2 + 8x + 12$ **12.** $y = x^2 + 6x + 8$ **13.** $y = x^2 - 6x + 8$

14. $y = x^2 - 8x + 12$ **15.** $y = x^2 - 2x - 8$ **16.** $y = x^2 - 2x - 24$

17. $y = x^2 - 16$ **18.** $y = x^2 - 25$ **19.** $y = x^2 - x - 6$

20. $y = x^2 + 2x - 3$ **21.** $y = x^2 - 6x + 8$ **22.** $y = x^2 - 49$

In Exercises 23–28:
a. Determine the x intercepts from the graph of the function.
b. Write the zeros of the function.

23.

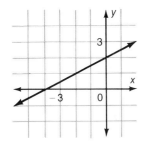

24.

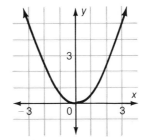

25.

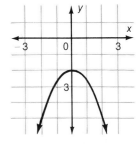

26.

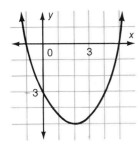

27.

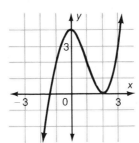

28.

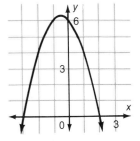

Graph each function. Determine the zeros of each function.

29. $y = x^2 + x - 6$ **30.** $y = x^2 - 15x + 54$ **31.** $y = x^2 - 9$

32. $y = x^2 + 3x - 10$ **33.** $y = x^2 + 2x + 1$ **34.** $y = x^2 - 5x - 36$

35. $y = 13 + 12x - x^2$ **36.** $y = 10 + 3x - x^2$ **37.** $y = 5 - 4x - x^2$

Use a quadratic equation to represent the conditions of each problem. Then solve the equation. Approximate irrational roots to the nearest hundredth. (*Pages 542–545*)

38. The hypotenuse of a right triangle is 3 inches longer than one side and 4 inches longer than the other side. How long is the hypotenuse?

39. In a theater, the number of seats in each row is 12 fewer than the number of rows. How many seats are in each row of a 1900-seat auditorium?

Use the quadratic formula to solve each equation. Write irrational roots in simplest radical form. (*Pages 538–541*)

40. $x^2 - 11x = -4$

41. $10n^2 + 2n - 5 = 0$

42. $y^2 + 4y = -3$

43. $7a^2 - 10a = 2$

44. $x^2 + 4x = 9$

45. $3x^2 - 8x = 7$

Add or subtract as indicated. Write the answers in simplest form. (*Pages 437–441*)

46. $\dfrac{c^2 + d^2}{2b} - \dfrac{c^2 - d^2}{2b}$

47. $\dfrac{4x - 7}{5} - \dfrac{6x + 3}{4}$

48. $\dfrac{1}{2c} + \dfrac{1}{6c} - \dfrac{1}{4c}$

49. $\dfrac{4s - 1}{t} - \dfrac{s + 2}{3t}$

50. $\dfrac{4}{3a^2} + \dfrac{5}{6ab} - \dfrac{8}{2b^2}$

51. $\dfrac{6y - 5m}{-x^2} + \dfrac{2y + 7m}{-2x^2}$

▬▬▬ CONNECT AND EXTEND

Graph each function. Determine the zeros of each function.

52. $y = 2x^2 - x - 15$

53. $y = 3x^2 - x - 2$

54. $y = 2x^2 - 9x - 11$

55. $y = x^2 + \frac{1}{4}x - \frac{3}{8}$

56. $y = x^2 - 0.5x - 8.4$

57. $y = 15 - 4x - 4x^2$

▬▬▬ NON-ROUTINE PROBLEM

58. How many triangles are shown in the figure at the right?

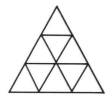

─── REVIEW CAPSULE FOR SECTION 13-6 ───

Classify each number as *rational* or *irrational*. (*Pages 484–487*)

1. $-\frac{1}{2}$
 2. $\sqrt{5}$
 3. $\sqrt{81}$
 4. $-\sqrt{100}$
 5. $2\sqrt{3}$
 6. $5 - 6\sqrt{2}$

Solve each quadratic equation by factoring. (*Pages 529–531*)

7. $a^2 - 121 = 0$

8. $16x^2 = 9$

9. $12y^2 + 11y + 2 = 0$

10. $3b^2 - 10b + 3 = 0$

11. $29d + 7 = -4d^2$

12. $4t^2 + 25 = 20t$

Use the quadratic formula to solve each equation. (*Pages 538–541*)

13. $x^2 - 10x + 25 = 0$

14. $9 = b^2 - 6b$

15. $r^2 = 5$

16. $3z - 5z^2 + 1 = 0$

17. $2q^2 - 3q - 1 = 0$

18. $5d^2 + 7d = 10$

13-6 The Discriminant

Note where the zeros occur in each of these functions.

Two x Intercepts	One x Intercept	No x Intercepts
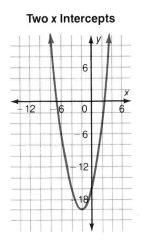	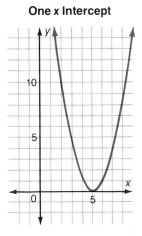	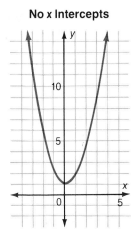
$y = x^2 + 5x - 14$	$y = x^2 - 10x + 25$	$y = x^2 + 1$

Function	x Intercepts	Nature of the Solutions
$y = x^2 + 5x - 14$	Two distinct points	Two real zeros
$y = x^2 - 10x + 25$	One point	One real zero
$y = x^2 + 1$	None	No real zeros

The number and kind of solutions of quadratic equations can be determined from a part of the quadratic formula, that is, from

$$b^2 - 4ac.$$

DISCRIMINANT   This portion of the formula that determines the nature of the solutions of a quadratic equation is called the **discriminant.**

Equation	$\sqrt{b^2 - 4ac}$	Nature of $b^2 - 4ac$	Solutions
$x^2 + 5x - 14 = 0$	$\sqrt{25 + 56}$	Positive: two real-number solutions	$\{2, -7\}$
$x^2 - 10x + 25 = 0$	$\sqrt{100 - 100}$	Zero: one real-number solution	$\{5\}$
$x^2 + 1 = 0$	$\sqrt{0 - 4}$	Negative: no real-number solutions	ϕ

For convenience, the solutions of $x^2 - 10x + 25 = 0$ are said to be equal since factoring $x^2 - 10x + 25 = 0$ as $(x - 5)(x - 5) = 0$ gives $+5$ and $+5$ as solutions. However, there is only one distinct solution, 5.

Quadratic Functions and Equations   **551**

For $x^2 + 1 = 0$, there is no solution in the set of real numbers. The number $\sqrt{0 - 4}$, or simply $\sqrt{-4}$, is not a real number.

> ### Nature of the solutions of $ax^2 + bx + c = 0$
> **1** If $b^2 - 4ac > 0$, there are two distinct, real solutions.
> **2** If $b^2 - 4ac = 0$, there is one distinct, real solution.
> **3** If $b^2 - 4ac < 0$, there are no real solutions.

EXAMPLE Use the discriminant to determine the nature of the solutions of each equation.

   a. $3x^2 - 11 = 0$ **b.** $-x^2 + x - 5 = 0$ **c.** $-x^2 + 6x - 9 = 0$

Solutions: **a.** $3x^2 - 11 = 0$ ⟵ $a = 3, b = 0, c = -11$
$$b^2 - 4ac = 0 - 4(3)(-11)$$
$$= 132$$
Since $b^2 - 4ac > 0$ there are **two real-number solutions.**

   b. $-x^2 + x - 5 = 0$ ⟵ $a = -1, b = 1, c = -5$
$$b^2 - 4ac = 1 - 4(-1)(-5)$$
$$= -19$$
Since $b^2 - 4ac < 0$, there are **no real-number solutions.**

   c. $-x^2 + 6x - 9 = 0$ ⟵ $a = -1, b = 6, c = -9$
$$b^2 - 4ac = 6^2 - 4(-1)(-9)$$
$$= 0$$
Since $b^2 - 4ac = 0$, there is **one distinct real-number solution.**

EXERCISES: Classwork/Homework

Objective: To state the nature of the solutions of a quadratic equation by evaluating the discriminant

CHECK YOUR UNDERSTANDING

Complete.

1. In the quadratic formula, the expression $b^2 - 4ac$ is called the __?__.

2. A quadratic function that intersects the x axis in two distinct points has __?__ real-number solutions.

3. When $b^2 - 4ac$ is 0, the quadratic equation has __?__ solution(s).

4. When $b^2 - 4ac < 0$, the quadratic equation has __?__ solutions.

Evaluate $b^2 - 4ac$ for each equation.

5. $x^2 + 9x + 5 = 0$

6. $x^2 + 8x - 4 = 0$

7. $x^2 + 6x + 9 = 0$

8. $x^2 - 4x + 4 = 0$

9. $2x^2 + x + 6 = 0$

10. $2x^2 + 7x + 9 = 0$

11. $x^2 - 9 = 0$

12. $x^2 - 16 = 0$

13. $-5x^2 - 2x - 3 = 0$

Without solving, give the nature of the solutions of each equation.

14. $x^2 + 2x + 8 = 0$

15. $3x^2 - 3x - 4 = 0$

16. $3y^2 - \frac{1}{3}y = \frac{2}{5}$

17. $x^2 = 5x + 5$

18. $3x^2 + 4x - \frac{3}{4} = 0$

19. $2y^2 - 4y = -2$

20. $x^2 - x + \frac{6}{25} = 0$

21. $20x = x^2 + 100$

22. $-x^2 + 7x - 15 = 0$

23. For what values of k will the equation $x^2 + kx + 25 = 0$ have only one solution?

24. For what values of k are the solutions of $x^2 + 4x + k = 0$ real numbers?

25. For what values of k will the equation $x^2 + kx + 3 = 0$ have two real solutions?

26. For what values of k are the solutions of $x^2 + 6x + k = 0$ not real numbers?

Use a quadratic equation to represent the conditions of each problem. Then solve the equation. Approximate irrational roots to the nearest hundredth. (*Pages 542–545*)

27. There are two numbers such that one is 4 more than half the other. The difference of the squares of the two numbers is 320. What are the numbers?

28. An auditorium has 550 seats. There are 3 more rows of seats than seats in each row. How many rows are there?

Add or subtract as indicated. Write the answers in simplest form. (*Pages 443–446*)

29. $a - \frac{10}{7b}$

30. $7 + \frac{4}{x + 2}$

31. $\frac{b}{c} - (b - 1)$

32. $\frac{2}{t - 3} - (t - 3)$

In Exercises 33–36, describe the solutions of the quadratic equation $ax^2 + bx + c = 0$ according to the given conditions.

33. $b^2 = 4ac$

34. $a \neq 0, b \neq 0, c = 0$

35. $b = 0$, a and c have opposite signs

36. $b = 0$, a and c have the same sign

13-7 Maximum and Minimum

AXIS OF SYMMETRY

In the graph at the right, the dashed line through $P(1, -4)$, is called the **axis of symmetry** of the parabola. The equation of the axis of symmetry is $x = 1$. If the parabola is folded along this line, the left side of the parabola will fit exactly over the right side. The axis of symmetry is halfway between *any* two points on the parabola that have the same y coordinate. Thus, the line $x = 1$ is halfway between the points $(-1, 0)$ and $(3, 0)$, and the points are said to be **mirror images** of each other.

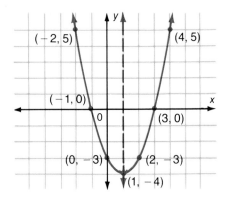

MINIMUM

The minimum (least) value of the quadratic function shown above is the value of y on the axis of symmetry. Thus, the minimum value is -4.

The axis of symmetry for the function $y = ax^2 + bx + c$ is midway between the two roots. To find this point, find the *mean*, or *average*, of the roots.

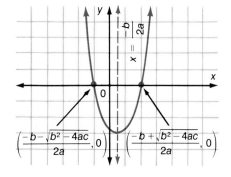

$$\frac{\dfrac{-b + \sqrt{b^2 - 4ac}}{2a} + \dfrac{-b - \sqrt{b^2 - 4ac}}{2a}}{2} = -\frac{b}{2a}$$

Thus, the axis of symmetry is a line parallel to the y axis; its equation is $x = -\dfrac{b}{2a}$.

For the quadratic function, $y = ax^2 + bx + c$, the equation of the axis of symmetry is $x = -\dfrac{b}{2a}$.

NOTE: The maximum or minimum point of a quadratic function is the *only* point of the function that lies on the axis of symmetry; it occurs at the **vertex,** or **turning point,** of the parabola, where $x = -\dfrac{b}{2a}$.

EXAMPLE 1 For the parabola $y = x^2 + x - 6$, find each of the following.

a. The equation of the axis of symmetry.

b. The coordinates of the vertex

c. The minimum value of the function

Solutions: **a.** Equation of axis of symmetry:

$$x = -\frac{b}{2a}$$

$x = -\frac{1}{2}$ ⟵ $a = 1; b = 1$

b. Since the vertex of the parabola lies on the axis of symmetry, find y when $x = -\frac{1}{2}$.

$y = x^2 + x - 6$

$y = (-\frac{1}{2})^2 - \frac{1}{2} - 6$

$y = \frac{1}{4} - \frac{1}{2} - 6 = -6\frac{1}{4}$

Coordinates of vertex: $(-\frac{1}{2}, -6\frac{1}{4})$

c. Minimum value: $-6\frac{1}{4}$

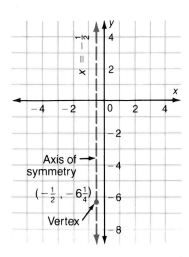

You can use the results of Example **1a** and **1b** to sketch the graph.

EXAMPLE 2 Sketch the graph of $y = x^2 + x - 6$.

Solution: Use the information from Example 1 and the zeros of the function.

Axis of symmetry: $x = -\frac{1}{2}$

Vertex: $\left(-\frac{1}{2}, -6\frac{1}{4}\right)$

Zeros of the function: -3 and 2

Sketch the parabola.

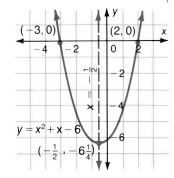

When the coefficient of the square term of a quadratic function is positive, the graph of the function opens upward; when the coefficient is negative, the graph opens downward.

$y = x^2 - 4x + 3$

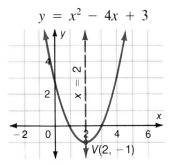

$y = 4x - x^2$

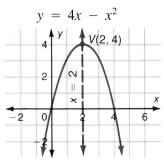

For the quadratic function $y = ax^2 + bx + c$,

a. the graph opens **upward when a > 0**, and

b. the graph opens **downward when a < 0**.

EXERCISES: Classwork/Homework

Objective: To find the maximum or minimum value of a quadratic function

CHECK YOUR UNDERSTANDING

1. *Complete:* The axis of symmetry of a parabola is halfway between any two points on the parabola that have the same __?__ coordinate.

2. When a parabola opens upward, does it have a maximum point or a minimum point?

3. When a parabola opens downward, does it have a maximum point or a minimum point?

4. Since the coefficient of the square term of the function $y = -x^2 + 3x$ is negative, the graph of the function opens __?__.

State whether each function will have a maximum value or a minimum value.

5. $y = 3x^2$

6. $y = 2x + x^2$

7. $y = 6 + x - x^2$

8. $y = 9 + x^2$

9. $y = -(1 - x)^2$

10. $y = (x + 1)^2$

For each parabola in Exercises 11–25:

a. Write the equation of the axis of symmetry.

b. Write the coordinates of the vertex and tell whether it is a maximum or minimum point.

c. Sketch the parabola.

11. $y = 2x^2$ **12.** $y = 4x^2$ **13.** $y = x^2 + 4$

14. $y = x^2 - 6x + 5$ **15.** $y = x^2 + 8x + 7$ **16.** $y = x^2 - 2x - 8$

17. $y = x^2 - 3x$ **18.** $y = x^2 + 2x - 8$ **19.** $y = x^2 - 2x$

20. $y = -2x^2$ **21.** $y = -x^2 + 1$ **22.** $y = -x^2 + 3x$

23. $y = -x^2 - 2x + 8$ **24.** $y = -x^2 - 2x + 3$ **25.** $y = -x^2 + 3x - 2$

Find the indicated value of y.

26. Find the minimum value of y if $y = x^2 - 6x + 8$.

27. Find the maximum value of y if $y = 5 - x^2$.

28. Find the maximum value of y if $y = -x^2 + 3x - 2$.

29. Find the minimum value of y if $y = x^2 - 2x - 24$.

Myra wishes to use 100 feet of fencing to build a rectangular pen for her dog. The sum of the length and width of the yard will be 50 feet. The area, y, of the yard will equal $x(50 - x)$.

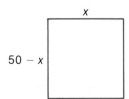

30. Find x so that the area, y, is a maximum.

31. Find the maximum area.

32. A farmer uses 250 feet of fence to enclose a rectangular garden. What should be the length and width of the garden if the farmer is to have the maximum area to plant?

A homeowner wishes to make a rectangular garden surrounded on three sides by a decorative fence. (The house forms the fourth side.) The owner buys 60 feet of fence.

33. If x represents the width of the garden, represent the second width and the length in terms of x.

34. Find the width that will make the area a maximum.

35. What is the maximum area that can be enclosed with the fence?

36. Suppose the homeowner in Exercises 33–35 had 40 feet of fence. What would be the dimensions of the garden that would make the area a maximum?

Without solving, give the nature of the solutions of each equation. (*Pages 551–553*)

37. $x^2 + x = 5$ **38.** $x^2 + x = -7$ **39.** $4x^2 = 12x - 9$

40. $9x^2 = 24x + 16$ **41.** $x^2 + 6x + 3 = 0$ **42.** $7x^2 = -2x - 10$

In Exercises 43–48:
a. Graph each quadratic function.
b. Write the zeros of the function. (*Pages 547–550*)

43. $y = x^2 - x - 6$ **44.** $y = x^2 + 4x - 12$ **45.** $y = x^2 - 9x + 20$

46. $y = x^2 + 8x + 15$ **47.** $y = 9x^2 - 36$ **48.** $y = x^2 - 1$

Solve each equation. (*Pages 447–451*)

49. $\dfrac{5}{x} = \dfrac{4}{x - 3}$ **50.** $\dfrac{2}{3} + \dfrac{3}{6x} = \dfrac{5}{2x}$ **51.** $\dfrac{3}{4} + \dfrac{1}{x} = \dfrac{5}{8}$

52. $\dfrac{8}{3x} - \dfrac{1}{15} = \dfrac{2}{x} - \dfrac{2}{5}$ **53.** $\dfrac{x + 4}{x + 6} = \dfrac{1}{2}$ **54.** $\dfrac{1}{3} + \dfrac{1}{a + 2} = \dfrac{a - 2}{6a + 12}$

55. Determine a formula that will give the maximum or minimum value of the quadratic function $y = ax^2 + bx + c$.

56. Graph the given quadratic functions on the same set of coordinate axes. Determine what happens to the graph of $y = ax^2 + bx + c$ as a increases.

$$y = \tfrac{1}{2}x^2 \qquad y = x^2 \qquad y = 2x^2$$

57. Graph the given quadratic functions on the same set of coordinate axes. Determine what happens to the graph of $y = ax^2 + bx + c$ as the value of c changes.

$$y = x^2 + 5 \qquad y = x^2 + 1 \qquad y = x^2 - 3$$

58. Tommy forgot his locker number at school. The school secretary reminds him that the digits in his locker number are all odd numbers and that, when added, they total 11. There are 120 lockers. What is Tommy's locker number?

59. In the addition problem below, the letters P, K, and N represent three different digits. Identify the digits.

$$\begin{array}{r} P\ K \\ +\ \ K\ N \\ \hline K\ N\ K \end{array}$$

Graph each inequality in the coordinate plane. (*Pages 306–308*)

1. $y > x + 2$ **2.** $y \geq -x + 5$ **3.** $y \leq 2x - 5$

4. $y < -x - 3$ **5.** $y - 3x > -4$ **6.** $y + 4x > +3$

13-8 Quadratic Inequalities

The graph of an equation such as $y = -x^2 + 1$ divides the coordinate plane into three sets of points:

> **a.** the set of points on the curve,
> **b.** the set of points inside the curve, and
> **c.** the set of points outside the curve.

The solution of an inequality such as $y > -x^2 + 1$ is made up of one or two of these sets of points.

To determine the solution set of $y > -x^2 + 1$, first graph the related equation $y = -x^2 + 1$. Then test points inside and outside the curve to find those that satisfy the inquality.

EXAMPLE   Graph: $y > -x^2 + 1$

Solutions: **1** Graph $y = -x^2 + 1$.

Use a dashed line to show that the solutions of $y > -x^2 + 1$ are *not* on the graph of $y = -x^2 + 1$.

2 Test points inside and outside the parabola.

Inside: Test $(0, 0)$ Outside: Test $(0,3)$

$\quad y > -x^2 + 1 \qquad\qquad y > -x^2 + 1$

$\quad 0 > 0 + 1? \qquad\qquad\ \ 3 > 0 + 1?$

$\quad 0 > 1? \quad$ No $\qquad\quad\ 3 > 1? \quad$ Yes ✔

3 Shade the region outside the parabola.

The graph of $y > -x^2 + 1$ is the **set of points outside the parabola.**

NOTE: The inequality is *never* satisfied by the set of points inside the curve <u>and</u> the set of points outside the curve.

You can test points inside and outside the graph of $y = -x^2 + 1$ to show that the shaded region on each graph below represents the given set of points.

$y < -x^2 + 1$ $y \geq -x^2 + 1$ $y \leq -x^2 + 1$

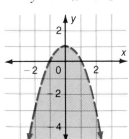 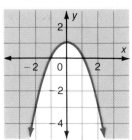 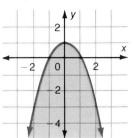

EXERCISES: Classwork/Homework

Objective: To solve quadratic inequalities

CHECK YOUR UNDERSTANDING

For each parabola in Exercises 1–8:
a. State whether the graph will include a solid, <u>S</u>, or a dashed, <u>D</u>, curve.
b. State whether the graph includes the region inside the curve or outside the curve.

1. $y > x^2$ **2.** $y \geq x^2$ **3.** $y \leq x^2 - 1$ **4.** $y < x^2 - 1$

5. $y \geq 2x - x^2$ **6.** $y \leq 1 - x^2$ **7.** $y < x^2 - 3x$ **8.** $y > x^2 + 5x + 6$

PRACTICE AND APPLY

Graph each inequality.

9. $y \leq x^2$ **10.** $y > x^2 - 1$ **11.** $y \geq x^2 + 4$ **12.** $y < -x^2$

13. $y > -2x^2$ **14.** $y > x^2 - 2x$ **15.** $y \leq x^2 - 3x$ **16.** $y \geq 1 - x^2$

17. $y \leq x^2 - 4x + 4$ **18.** $y \geq x^2 - 2x + 1$ **19.** $y < 2 - x^2$ **20.** $y \leq 5 - x^2 + 3$

21. $y > x^2 + 2x - 8$ **22.** $y \leq x^2 - 5x - 6$ **23.** $y \geq 6 - x^2$ **24.** $y \geq 5 - x^2$

Graph the solution set of each system.

25. $\begin{cases} y \geq x^2 \\ y < 4 \end{cases}$ **26.** $\begin{cases} y \geq x^2 \\ x \leq 0 \end{cases}$ **27.** $\begin{cases} y < -x^2 + 1 \\ y \geq 0 \end{cases}$ **28.** $\begin{cases} y \geq -x^2 \\ x \geq 0 \end{cases}$

29. $\begin{cases} y > x^2 - 3 \\ y < x \end{cases}$ **30.** $\begin{cases} y > -x^2 + 4 \\ y \geq x \end{cases}$ **31.** $\begin{cases} y \leq x^2 + 2 \\ y \geq x \end{cases}$ **32.** $\begin{cases} y \leq 2x^2 \\ y \geq 2x - 3 \end{cases}$

33. $\begin{cases} y > x^2 - 4 \\ y \leq 4 \end{cases}$ **34.** $\begin{cases} y < x^2 + 5 \\ y < 5 \end{cases}$ **35.** $\begin{cases} y < -x^2 + 5 \\ y \geq 0 \end{cases}$ **36.** $\begin{cases} y > -x^2 + 2 \\ y \leq -5 \end{cases}$

For each parabola in Exercises 37–42:
a. Write the equation of the axis of symmetry.
b. Write the coordinates of the vertex and tell whether it is a maximum or minimum point.
c. Sketch the parabola. (*Pages 554–558*)

37. $y = 3x^2$ **38.** $y = x^2 - 8x$ **39.** $y = x^2 - 4x - 5$

Without solving, give the nature of the solutions of each equation. (*Pages 551–553*)

40. $\frac{1}{3}x^2 = 15x + 45$ **41.** $x^2 + 4x + 4 = 0$ **42.** $25x = x^2 - 150$

Solve each problem. (*Pages 454–457*)

43. What number must be added to the numerator and denominator of $\frac{11}{17}$ to make a fraction equal to $\frac{5}{7}$?

44. One number is 6 less than another. The quotient of the larger divided by the smaller is $\frac{3}{2}$. Find the numbers.

■■■■ **CONNECT AND EXTEND**

Graph the solution set of each system.

45. $\begin{cases} y \geq x^2 \\ y \leq -x^2 \end{cases}$ **46.** $\begin{cases} y \geq x^2 - 2 \\ y \leq -x^2 + 4 \end{cases}$ **47.** $\begin{cases} y \geq x^2 - 4 \\ y \leq \frac{1}{4}x^2 \end{cases}$ **48.** $\begin{cases} y \leq 1 - x^2 \\ y \leq x^2 + 1 \end{cases}$

■■■■ **NON-ROUTINE PROBLEM**

49. Two positive integers are each less than 10. The sum of their squares, added to their product, equals a perfect square. Find the integers.

——— **REVIEW CAPSULE FOR SECTION 13-9** ———

In Exercises 1–4, write a formula to express the direct variation. Use k as the constant of variation. (*Pages 232–234*)

1. The perimeter, P, of an equilateral triangle varies directly as the length of a side, r.

2. The length, r, of a person's shadow at a given time varies directly as the height, h, of the person.

3. The total income, T, at a fixed rate of pay per hour, varies directly as the number of hours worked, h.

4. For a car traveling at a constant rate, the distance covered, d, varies directly as the time, t, that it travels.

5. If s varies directly as n, and $s = 60$ when $n = 2$, find s when $n = 7$.

6. If w varies directly as p, and $w = 5$ when $p = 10$, find p when $w = 12.5$.

13-9 Inverse Variation

The table below and the graph at the right illustrate the rate of speed required to travel 480 kilometers during various periods of time.

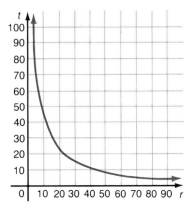

r	80	60	40	30	20	10	5
t	6	8	12	16	24	48	96

For a trip of 480 kilometers, the relationship between rate of travel (speed) and time can be defined by the equation $rt = 480$. The equation describes an *inverse variation*. It shows that r varies inversely as t or that t varies inversely as r. That is, as the values of r decrease, the values of t increase. Also, as the values cf r increase, the values of t decrease.

DEFINITION

If the product of two variables is a nonzero constant, the variables are in **inverse variation.** The equation for the inverse variation may be written as

$$xy = k \quad \text{or} \quad y = \frac{k}{x},$$

where k is the **constant of variation.**

EXAMPLE 1 Determine whether each equation is an example of inverse variation.

   a. $bh = 40$ **b.** $t = \frac{100}{r}$

Solution: Compare each equation with $xy = k$ or $y = \frac{k}{x}$.

   a. $bh = 40$ has the same form as $xy = k$. Thus, it is an example of inverse variation.

   b. $t = \frac{100}{r}$ has the same form as $y = \frac{k}{x}$. Thus, it is an example of inverse variation.

NOTE: In $bh = 40$, the constant of variation is 40. In $t = \frac{100}{r}$, the constant of variation is 100.

When you are given that a function is an inverse variation and you know one ordered pair of the function, you can determine k, the constant of variation. Then you can write the equation that shows how x and y are related.

EXAMPLE 2 If x varies inversely as y, and $x = 4$ when $y = 5$, write the equation that shows how x and y are related.

Solution: ☐1 Find k, the constant of variation.

$$xy = k \longleftarrow \text{ \textbf{x varies inversely as y.}}$$
$$\text{\textbf{Replace x with 4 and y with 5.}}$$
$$4 \cdot 5 = k$$
$$20 = k \longleftarrow \text{\textbf{Write the equation. Use k = 20.}}$$

☐2 Equation: $xy = 20$

HYPERBOLA

The graph of the inverse variation

$$xy = k, \text{ where } k > 0$$

is a **hyperbola.** Its branches are in the first and third quadrants.

$xy = 4$

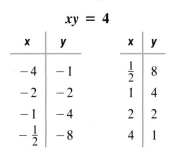

x	y		x	y
-4	-1		$\frac{1}{2}$	8
-2	-2		1	4
-1	-4		2	2
$-\frac{1}{2}$	-8		4	1

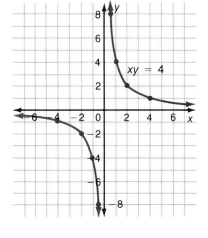

When $k < 0$, the branches of the hyperbola are in the second and fourth quadrants. In practical applications, only the branch in the first quadrant usually satisfies all the conditions of the problem.

EXAMPLE 3 The current in an electric circuit varies inversely as the resistance. When the current is 40 amps, the resistance is 12 ohms. Find the current when the resistance is 20 ohms.

Solution: ☐1 Find the constant of variation.

$$cr = k \longleftarrow \text{ \textbf{c varies inversely as r.}}$$
$$40 \cdot 12 = k \quad \text{and} \quad k = 480 \quad \textbf{Equation: } cr = 480$$

Quadratic Functions and Equations **563**

2 Find c when $r = 20$.

$$cr = 480$$
$$20c = 480$$
$$c = 24 \quad \text{The current is \textbf{24 amps}.}$$

EXERCISES: Classwork/Homework

Objective: To solve problems involving inverse variation

CHECK YOUR UNDERSTANDING

Determine whether each equation is an example of inverse variation. Answer _Yes_ or _No_.

1. $yz = 6$ **2.** $y = x$ **3.** $b + h = 40$ **4.** $ab = \frac{1}{4}$

5. $\frac{x}{y} = \frac{1}{2}$ **6.** $y = \frac{1}{x}$ **7.** $x = \frac{200}{z}$ **8.** $\frac{a}{5} = \frac{3}{b}$

In Exercises 9–12, use the equation $xy = 28$.

9. If x increases, what happens to y?

10. If x decreases, what happens to y?

11. If a certain value of x is doubled, what happens to the value of y?

12. If a certain value of y is multiplied by 4, what happens to the value of x?

PRACTICE AND APPLY

Determine whether each of the following is an example of inverse variation. Answer _Yes_ or _No_. Give a reason for each answer.

13. $xy = 6$ **14.** $x + y = 6$ **15.** $x - y = 6$ **16.** $x = 10y$

17. $\frac{x}{y} = 6$ **18.** $x = \frac{10}{y}$ **19.** $y = \frac{42}{x}$ **20.** $x + y = 10$

21. $y = 250x$ **22.** $y = 430x - 5$ **23.** $xy + y = 8$ **24.** $xy - y = 8$

In Exercises 25–30, y varies inversely as x. Write the equation that shows how x and y are related.

25. $y = 7$ when $x = 6$ **26.** $y = 4$ when $x = 12$ **27.** $y = \frac{3}{4}$ when $x = \frac{2}{3}$

28. $y = -5$ when $x = 2$ **29.** $y = -8$ when $x = -5$ **30.** $y = -5\frac{1}{4}$ when $x = -8\frac{1}{3}$

31. If x varies inversely as y, and $x = 8$ when $y = 9$, find x when $y = 18$.

32. If p varies inversely as q, and $p = 50$ when $q = 4$, find p when $q = 40$.

33. If r varies inversely as t and $r = 80$ when $t = 0.25$, find r when $t = 2$.

34. If y varies inversely as z and $y = 6$ when $z = -4$, find y when $z = -3$.

35. If a varies inversely as b and $a = 60$ when $b = \frac{1}{2}$, find b when $a = 20$.

36. If c varies invesely as d and $c = 0.40$ when $d = 100$, find d when $c = 1.6$.

In Exercises 37–38, the current varies inversely as the resistance.

37. When the resistance in a certain electrical circuit is 10 ohms, the current is 24 amps. Find the current when the resistance is 20 ohms.

38. A certain electrical circuit has a resistance of 12 ohms. The current is 15 amps. Find the current when the resistance is decreased to 4 ohms.

39. The number of days needed to finish repairing a sidewalk varies inversely as the number of people working. It takes 12 days for two people to repair the walk. How many people are needed to complete the job in 4 days?

40. The rent for an apartment varies inversely as the number of people sharing the cost. Four people sharing an apartment pay $120 each per month. How many people would be needed so that each would pay $80 per month?

41. The amount of time to make a trip varies inversely as the rate of travel. At 30 miles per hour it takes Jenny 4 hours to travel from her home to her vacation cottage. How long would it take if she drove at 50 miles per hour?

42. A jet traveling at 2200 kilometers per hour took 4 hours to fly from Boston to Paris. The time varies inversely as the rate of speed. How long would it take a plane traveling at 2500 km/hr to make the same trip?

43. The number of tomato plants in a row in George's garden varies inversely as the space between them. If the plants are spaced 15 centimeters apart, 60 plants fit in a row. How many can fit if he places them 25 centimeters apart?

44. The number of days needed to paint the outside of a house varies inversely as the number of people painting the house. It takes 2 people 8 days to paint the house. How many days will it take 4 people to paint the house?

45. The number of square tiles on a floor varies inversely as the area of the tiles. It takes 108 tiles with an area of 1 square foot to cover a certain floor. How many tiles with an area of $\frac{9}{16}$ square foot would it take to cover the same floor?

46. When the tension on a wire is kept constant, the number of vibrations per second varies inversely as the length of the wire. A wire 400 centimeters long vibrates 160 times per second. How long should a wire be to vibrate 240 times per second?

If y varies inversely as the square of x, then $y = \frac{k}{x^2}$ or $yx^2 = k$. Find the constant of variation and write the equation for each relation.

47. $y = 6$ when $x = 2$,

48. $y = 2$ when $x = 1$

49. $y = 8$ when $x = 4$

50. $y = 4$ when $x = -3$

51. $y = -5$ when $x = -4$

52. $y = 3\frac{1}{2}$ when $x = 5\frac{3}{4}$

Graph each inequality. (*Pages 559–561*)

53. $y > -x^2 + 2x$ **54.** $y \geq x^2 + 4x + 1$ **55.** $y \leq -2x^2 - 3$ **56.** $y < x^2 - 2x + 4$

For each parabola in Exercises 57–59:
a. Write the equation of the axis of the symmetry.
b. Write the coordinates of the vertex and tell whether it is a maximum or minimum point.
c. Sketch the parabola. (*Pages 554–558*)

57. $y = -3x^2$ **58.** $y = x^2 + 6x + 5$ **59.** $y = x^2 + 4x$

60. Carol can type a manuscript in 7 hours. Terri can type the same manuscript in 5 hours. How long would it take them to type the manuscript if they work together? (*Pages 463–467*)

61. One printing press can complete an order in 5 hours, and another in 3 hours. How long will it take both printing presses to finish the job after the slower press has been working alone for 1 hour? (*Pages 463–467*)

62. The frequency, f, of vibration of a wire (of uniform length and tension) varies inversely as the square root of its weight, w. Express this relation in a formula, using k to represent the constant of variation. Given that k is 508, what is f when w is 4?

63. The intensity, I, of a light varies inversely as the square of the distance, d, from the light. How far should a book be placed from a light to receive four times as much intensity of illumination as it received when it was 2 meters from the light?

In Exercises 64–65, use the formula $fp = v$, where f is the frequency, p is the wavelength and v is the speed of sound (about 335 meters per second in air).

64. An open pipe produces a sound wave whose length is twice that of the pipe. What is the frequency of the sound from a pipe whose length is 1 meter?

65. A stopped pipe produces a sound wave whose length is four times that of the pipe. Find the length of a pipe that produces a sound with a frequency of 220.

13-10 Joint and Combined Variation

JOINT VARIATION

When one variable varies directly as the product of two or more variables, the variation is called a **joint variation.**

EXAMPLE 1 The volume, V, of a pyramid varies jointly as the area of its base, B, and its altitude h. When $B = 18$ and $h = 4$, $V = 24$. Find V when $B = 7$ and $h = 12$.

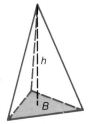

Solution: $V = kBh$ ◄——— *V varies jointly as B and h.*

To find k, replace V with 24, B with 18, and h with 4.

$24 = k(18)(4)$

$24 = 72k$

$\frac{1}{3} = k$ ◄——— **Write the equation for the joint variation. Use $k = \frac{1}{3}$.**

Thus, $V = \frac{1}{3}Bh$. ◄——— **Replace B with 7 and h with 12.**

$V = \frac{1}{3}(7)(12)$

$V = \textbf{28 cubic units}$ ◄——— **Volume is measured in cubic units.**

COMBINED VARIATION

When a variable varies directly as one variable and inversely as another, the variation is sometimes called **combined variation.** Thus, if x varies directly as y and inversely as z, then

$$x = ky\left(\frac{1}{z}\right) \quad \text{or} \quad x = \frac{ky}{z}.$$

EXAMPLE 2 Suppose that y varies directly as x and inversely as w. If $y = 2$ when $x = 7$ and $w = 14$, find y when $x = 10$ and $w = 8$.

Solution: $y = \frac{kx}{w}$ ◄——— **y varies directly as x and inversely as w.**

To find k, replace y with 2, x with 7, and w with 14.

$$2 = \frac{7k}{14}$$

$$2 = \frac{1}{2}k$$

$$4 = k \quad \longleftarrow \quad \text{Write the equation for the variation.}$$

$$y = \frac{4x}{w} \quad \longleftarrow \quad \text{Replace } x \text{ with 10 and } w \text{ with 8.}$$

$$y = \frac{4 \cdot 10}{8}$$

$$y = 5$$

EXERCISES: Classwork/Homework

Objective: To solve problems involving joint or combined variation

CHECK YOUR UNDERSTANDING

Write a formula for each statement. Use k as the constant of variation.

1. a varies jointly as b and c.

2. t varies jointly as s and v.

3. m varies directly as n and inversely as p.

4. h varies directly as g and inversely as l.

5. s varies directly as n and inversely as the square of r.

6. x varies directly as the square of y and inversely as the cube of w.

PRACTICE AND APPLY

7. If t varies jointly as s and r, and $t = 120$ when $s = 15$ and $r = 4$, find t when $s = 12$ and $r = 9$.

8. If q varies jointly as n and p, and $q = 12$ when $n = 14$ and $p = 6$, find q when $n = 21$ and $p = 8$.

9. If x varies jointly as w, y, and z, and $x = 15$ when $w = 2$, $y = 10$, and $z = 3$, find x when $w = 8$, $y = 5$, and $z = 7$.

10. If a varies jointly as b, c, and d, and $a = 75$ when $b = 1$, $c = 5$, and $d = 5$, find a when $b = 3$, $c = 7$, and $d = 9$.

11. If q varies directly as h and inversely as j, and $q = 14$ when $h = 28$ and $j = 7$, find q when $h = 14$ and $j = 6$.

12. If f varies directly as d^2 and inversely as b, and $f = 3$ when $d = 6$ and $b = 4$, find f when $d = 9$ and $b = 5$.

13. If A varies directly as B and inversely as C^2, and $A = 9$ when $B = 9$ and $C = 4$, find A when $B = 5$ and $C = 2$.

14. If G varies directly as H^3 and inversely as F^2, and $G = 4$ when $H = 2$ and $F = 4$, find G when $H = 6$ and $F = 12$.

15. If m varies jointly as p and r^2, and $m = 28$ when $p = 7$ and $r = 8$, find m when $p = 10$ and $r = 4$.

16. If x varies jointly as y and z and inversely as m, and $x = 60$ when $y = 2$, $z = 5$, and $m = 4$, find x when $y = 3$, $z = 9$, and $m = 6$.

17. The area of a triangle varies jointly as the base and the height. A triangle with a base of 5 inches and a height of 6 inches has an area of 15 square inches. Find the area when the base is 7 inches and the height is 4 inches.

18. The mass, m, of a rectangular sheet of wood varies jointly as the length, l, and the width, w. When l is 40 centimeters and w is 20 centimeters, m is 400 grams. Find m when l is 30 centimeters and w is 20 centimeters.

19. The volume of a pyramid, V, varies jointly as the area of the base, B, and the height, h. When B is 12 square centimeters and h is 9 centimeters, V is 36 cubic centimeters. Find V when B is 14 square centimeters and h is 6 centimeters.

20. The volume of a cone varies jointly as the area of the base, B_1 and the height, h. The volume is 50 cubic centimeters when the area of the base is 30 square centimeters and the height is 5 centimeters. Find V when $h = 9$ centimeters and $B = 40$ square centimeters.

21. The glide ability of a hang glider depends on a ratio called the **aspect ratio**, R. R varies directly as the square of the wingspread, S^2, and inversely as the wing area, A. When A is 30 square feet and, S is 9 feet, R is 2.7. Find R when A is 40 square feet and S is 10 feet.

22. The force of attraction, F, of a body varies directly as its mass, m, and inversely as the square of the distance, d, from the body. When $m = 8$ kilograms and $d = 5$ meters, $F = 100$ Newtons. Find F when $m = 2$ kilograms and $d = 15$ meters.

23. The electrical resistance in a wire varies directly as its length, L, and inversely as the square of its diameter, d. A wire 5 kilometers long with a diameter of 6 millimeters has a resistance of 20 ohms. Find the resistance of a wire of the same material with a length of 6 kilometers and a diameter of 4 millimeters.

24. The crushing load, L, of a square wooden post varies directly as the fourth power of its thickness, t^4, and inversely as its length squared, l^2. A post 10 centimeters thick and 4 meters high is crushed by a load of 22.5 tons. What is the crushing load of a post 5 centimeters thick and 3 meters high?

▬▬▬▬ **MAINTAIN**

Graph each inequality. (*Pages 559–561*)

25. $y > x^2 + 2x + 2$ 　　　**26.** $y \geq -4x^2$ 　　　　　　**27.** $y \leq x^2 + 6x$

Add or subtract as indicated. Write the answers in simplest form. (*Pages 443–446*)

28. $\dfrac{q}{r-7} - \dfrac{s}{r-7}$ 　　　**29.** $\dfrac{2}{xy} + \dfrac{3}{yx}$ 　　　　**30.** $\dfrac{x}{a-b} - \dfrac{y}{a-b}$

Focus on College Entrance Tests

Instead of solving a given equation, it is sometimes easier to try each of the given "solutions" to see which one makes the equation true.

EXAMPLE Which of the following numbers is in the solution set for $3x^2 - 14x + 16 = 0$?

    a. 4   **b.** 2   **c.** -4 **d.** -8

Think: If $3x^2 - 14x + 16 = 0$, then $3x^2 = 14x - 16$.
But $3x^2$ is positive. Therefore, $14x - 16$ must be positive.
Thus, $14x - 16 > 0$, or $14x > 16$ and $x > 1$.
This eliminates choices **c** and **d**. Test choices **a** and **b**.

Solution: Test **a.**: $3(4)^2 - 14(4) + 16 = 8 \neq 0$ ⟵ **4 is not a solution.**

             Test **b.**: $3(2)^2 - 14(2) + 16 = 0$ ⟵ **2 is a solution.**   **Answer: b**

TRY THESE

Choose the best answer. Choose _a_, _b_, _c_, or _d_.

1. Which of the following numbers is in the solution set for $x^2 + 13x + 12 = 0$?

    a. -4 **b.** -1 **c.** 1   **d.** 6

2. Which of the following numbers is in the solution set for $x^2 - 14x + 24 = 0$?

    a. -12 **b.** -2 **c.** 2   **d.** 8

3. Which of the following numbers is in the solution set for $2x^2 + 11x + 12 = 0$?

    a. -4 **b.** -1 **c.** 2   **d.** 4

4. Which of the following numbers is in the solution set for $3x^2 + 4x - 4 = 0$?

    a. -4 **b.** -2 **c.** $\frac{1}{3}$ **d.** 4

5. Which of the following numbers is in the solution set for $x^2 + 16x - 36 = 0$?

    a. -18 **b.** -1 **c.** 4   **d.** 6

6. Which of the following numbers is in the solution set for $6x^2 - 23x - 4 = 0$?

    a. -4 **b.** -1 **c.** $\frac{1}{2}$ **d.** 4

7. If $\dfrac{1}{2 + \dfrac{1 + x}{2}} = \dfrac{1}{2}$, what is the value of x? (HINT: $\dfrac{1 + x}{2}$ must equal 0.)

    a. -2 **b.** -1 **c.** 0   **d.** 1

Chapter Summary

IMPORTANT TERMS

Combined variation (p. 567)
Completing the square (p. 532)
Discriminant (p. 551)
Hyperbola (p. 563)
Inverse variation (p. 562)
Joint variation (p. 567)

Parabola (p. 547)
Quadratic equation (p. 529)
Quadratic function (p. 547)
Roots of an equation (p. 538)
Zeros of a function (p. 548)

IMPORTANT IDEAS

1. If $x^2 = k$, then $x = \sqrt{k}$ <u>or</u> $x = -\sqrt{k}$ for any real number k, $k \geq 0$.
2. **Steps for Completing the Square of $x^2 + bx$**
   - **1** Find one-half the coefficient of x.
   - **2** Square the result of Step 1.
   - **3** Add the result of Step 2 to $x^2 + bx$.
3. **Quadratic Formula:** For the quadratic equation $ax^2 + bx + c = 0$, where a, b, and c are real numbers and $a \neq 0$,
$$x = \frac{-b \pm \sqrt{b^2 - 4ac}}{2a}.$$
4. **The Nature of the Solutions of $ax^2 + bx + c = 0$**
   - **1** If $b^2 - 4ac > 0$, there are two distinct, real solutions.
   - **2** If $b^2 - 4ac = 0$, there is one distinct, real solution.
   - **3** If $b^2 - 4ac < 0$, there are no real solutions.

Chapter Review

Solve each equation. Irrational solutions may be left in simplified radical form. (*Pages 529–531*)

1. $x^2 = 121$

2. $4n^2 = 32$

3. $2y^2 - 8 = 10$

4. $(y - 5)^2 = 0$

5. $6(t + 3)^2 = 24$

6. $(3b - 1)^2 = 81$

7. $(6y + 3)^2 = 1$

8. $(x - \frac{3}{4})^2 = \frac{9}{16}$

9. $2(x - 3)^2 = \frac{8}{25}$

Solve by completing the square. Irrational solutions may be left in simplified radical form. (*Pages 532–535*)

10. $x^2 + 6x = 7$

11. $a^2 - 6a - 7 = 0$

12. $y^2 + 3y = 4$

13. $x^2 - x = 30$

14. $r^2 + 4r = -2$

15. $b^2 = 3b + 10$

Use the quadratic formula to solve each equation. Irrational solutions may be left in simplified radical form. (*Pages 538–541*)

16. $y^2 + 6y - 16 = 0$ **17.** $x^2 - 3x = 0$ **18.** $b^2 = 5 - 4b$

19. $9c^2 + 2 + 9c = 0$ **20.** $2x^2 + 11x + 5 = 0$ **21.** $2y^2 - 7y + 4 = 0$

Solve each problem. Approximate irrational roots to the nearest tenth. (*Pages 542–545*)

22. The sum of a positive number and its square is 72. Find the number.

23. The sum of the squares of two consecutive positive integers is 85. Find the integers.

24. The perimeter of a rectangle is 32 meters, and its area is 48 square meters. What are its dimensions?

25. The length of a rectangular sign is one meter longer than its width. Its area is 11 square meters. Find its dimensions.

Graph each quadratic function. Write the zeros of the function. (*Pages 547–550*)

26. $y = x^2 + 2x - 8$ **27.** $y = x^2 - 3x$ **28.** $y = x^2 + 4x + 4$

29. $y = x^2 - 5x + 4$ **30.** $y = x^2 - 4$ **31.** $y = -x^2 + 6x - 9$

Without solving, give the nature of the solutions of each equation. (*Pages 551–553*)

32. $x^2 - 5x - 5 = 0$ **33.** $2x^2 - 3x = 0$ **34.** $y^2 - 20y + 100 = 0$

35. $3y^2 = 1 + 2y$ **36.** $x^2 - 14x + 48 = 0$ **37.** $a^2 + 2 = 2a$

38. $x^2 = 8x - 16$ **39.** $3n = 4n^2 + 1$ **40.** $x^2 + x + \frac{1}{4} = 0$

y varies inversely as *x*. Write the equation that shows how *x* and *y* are related. (*Pages 562–566*)

41. $y = 36$ when $x = -3$ **42.** $y = 7$ when $x = 1$ **43.** $y = 6$ when $x = 16$

44. $y = 9$ when $x = \frac{1}{2}$ **45.** $y = -2\frac{1}{2}$ when $x = 3$ **46.** $y = -\frac{9}{2}$ when $x = \frac{2}{3}$

47. A rectangular garden is to have a given area. When the length is 8 meters, the width is 3.5 meters. What is the width when the length is 5.6 meters?

48. A rectangular box is to have a given volume. When the area of the base of the box is 144 square units, the height is 8 units. What is the height when the area of the base is 256 square units?

For Exercises 49–52, solve each problem. (*Pages 567–569*)

49. If *c* varies jointly as *p* and *q*, and *c* = 84 when $p = 3$ and $q = 7$, find *c* when $p = \frac{1}{2}$ and $q = 9$.

50. If *r* varies directly as *w* and inversely as y^2, and $r = 2$ when $w = 6$ and $y = 3$, find *r* when $w = 10$ and $y = 2$.

51. If b varies jointly as c and d and inversely as f^2, and $b = 80$ when $c = 10$, $d = 2$, and $f = 4$, find b when $c = 5$, $d = 6$, and $f = 2$.

52. If h varies jointly as j^2 and k and inversely as g, and $h = 50$ when $j = 2$, $k = 5$, and $g = \frac{1}{2}$, find h when $j = 4$, $k = 10$, and $g = \frac{1}{4}$.

Chapter Test

Solve each equation. Irrational solutions may be left in simplified radical form.

1. $2x^2 + 3 = 11$

2. $(y - 1)^2 = 9$

3. $3(x + 4)^2 = 48$

4. $x^2 + 3x + 2 = 0$

5. $x^2 - 9x = -18$

6. $4y^2 - 2y - 1 = 0$

7. $y^2 + 3y - 4 = 0$

8. $n^2 + 32 = 12n$

9. $c^2 - 4c + 2 = 0$

Write the zeros of the functions graphed below.

10.

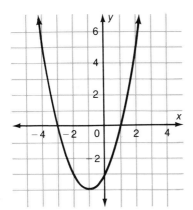

11.

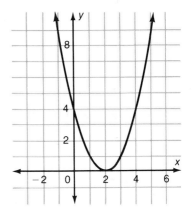

Without solving, give the nature of the solutions of each equation.

12. $x^2 - 8x + 16 = 0$

13. $x^2 + 5x + 8 = 0$

14. $6x^2 + 13x - 5 = 0$

15. $9x^2 + 1 = 6x$

16. The width of a picture window is 2 feet more than its height. If the area of the window is 24 square feet, what are its width and height?

17. In a right triangle, one leg is 2 meters shorter than the hypotenuse. The other leg is 4 meters shorter than the hypotenuse. Find the length of the hypotenuse.

18. If c varies inversely as d, and $c = 4$ when $d = -6$, find c when $d = 2$.

19. If p varies inversely as t, and $p = 3$ when $t = 6$, find p when $t = 9$.

20. Given that c varies jointly as n and p and inversely as t, and $n = 4$, $p = 6$, and $t = 12$ when $c = 1$, find c when $n = 5$, $p = 18$, and $t = 15$.

Additional Practice

Skills

Solve each equation. Irrational solutions may be left in simplified radical form. (*Pages 529–531*)

1. $y^2 = 81$

2. $7(y - 4)^2 = 343$

3. $2x^2 + 5 = 155$

Solve by completing the square. Irrational solutions may be left in simplified radical form. (*Pages 532–535*)

4. $x^2 - 4x = 0$

5. $x^2 - 6x = 0$

6. $x^2 + 2x - 4 = 0$

Use the quadratic formula to solve each equation. Irrational solutions may be left in simplified radical form. (*Pages 538–541*)

7. $x^2 - 3x = 40$

8. $y^2 + 64 = 16y$

9. $2a^2 - a = 3$

Graph each quadratic function. Determine the zeros of each function. (*Pages 547–550*)

10. $y = x^2 - 3x - 4$

11. $y = x^2 + 2x + 1$

12. $y = x^2 - 36$

Without solving, give the nature of the solutions of each equation. (*Pages 551–553*)

13. $x^2 = 8x + 20$

14. $x^2 + 5 = x$

15. $x^2 + 15x + 36 = 0$

Problem Solving and Applications

Solve each problem. (*Pages 542–545*)

16. In a theater, the number of seats in each row is 2 more than the number of rows. The theater seats 624 people. How many seats are there in each row?

17. A driveway is 10 meters longer than it is wide. Its area is 35 square meters. Find its length and width to the nearest tenth of a meter.

18. The combined areas of two square flower gardens is 65 square meters. Each side of the larger garden is 3 feet longer than a side of the smaller garden. Find the length of a side of each garden.

19. A small city lot is in the shape of a right triangle. The hypotenuse is 40 meters longer than one leg and 5 meters longer than the other leg. Find the length of each side of the lot.

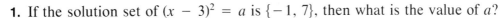

Part 1 Choose the best answer. Choose a, b, c, or d.

1. If the solution set of $(x - 3)^2 = a$ is $\{-1, 7\}$, then what is the value of a?

   a. 4 **b.** 16 **c.** -4 **d.** -16

2. What negative value for b will make $x^2 + bx + \frac{1}{4}$ the square of a binomial?

   a. -1 **b.** $-\frac{1}{2}$ **c.** $-\frac{1}{4}$ **d.** -2

3. Evaluate $|-x^3 + 1| - |x^5 - 1|$ when $x = -1$.

   a. 4 **b.** 0 **c.** -4 **d.** 2

4. Express $\dfrac{a^2 - b^2}{x^2 - y^2} \div \dfrac{a + b}{x - y}$ in simplest form. (Assume $x \neq y$.)

   a. $\dfrac{a - b}{x - y}$ **b.** $\dfrac{x + y}{a - b}$ **c.** $\dfrac{x - y}{a - b}$ **d.** $\dfrac{a - b}{x + y}$

5. What is the equation of the line that is parallel to $5x - 2y = 3$ and has y-intercept -4?

   a. $y = -\frac{5}{2}x + 4$ **b.** $y = -\frac{5}{2}x - 4$
   c. $y = \frac{5}{2}x + 4$ **d.** $y = \frac{5}{2}x - 4$

6. Complete the square and write the resulting trinomial as the square of a binomial: $x^2 + 3x$.

   a. $(x + \frac{9}{4})^2$ **b.** $(x - \frac{9}{4})^2$ **c.** $(x + \frac{3}{2})^2$ **d.** $(x - \frac{3}{2})^2$

7. What are the solutions of the inequality $|x - 2| < 3$?

   a. $x < 3$ <u>and</u> $x > -3$ **b.** $x < 2$ <u>and</u> $x > -2$
   c. $x < 5$ <u>and</u> $x > -1$ **d.** $x > 5$ <u>or</u> $x < -1$

8. Find the least common denominator of the two rational expressions whose denominators are $x^2 - 9$ and $2x^2 - 3x - 9$.

   a. $(x - 3)(x + 3)^2$ **b.** $(x^2 - 9)(2x^2 - 3x - 9)$
   c. $(x^2 - 9)(2x + 3)$ **d.** $(x - 3)(2x + 3)$

9. Which of the following is equivalent to $\dfrac{4^{\frac{3}{2}}}{8^{\frac{2}{3}}}$?

   a. $\frac{1}{2}^{\frac{5}{6}}$ **b.** $32^{\frac{3}{2}}$ **c.** 2 **d.** $\frac{1}{2}$

10. Find the solutions of the equation $2x^2 - x = 2$.

   a. $\dfrac{1 \pm \sqrt{17}}{4}$ **b.** $\dfrac{-1 \pm \sqrt{17}}{4}$ **c.** $\dfrac{1 \pm \sqrt{17}}{2}$ **d.** $\dfrac{-1 \pm \sqrt{17}}{2}$

11. Which of the following numbers is irrational?

   a. $\sqrt{36}$ **b.** $-\sqrt{169}$ **c.** $\dfrac{189}{\sqrt{4}}$ **d.** $\sqrt{124}$

Quadratic Functions and Equations **575**

12. Without solving the equation $6x^2 - 8x + 3 = 0$, determine how many solutions it has.

   a. 0   **b.** 1   **c.** 2   **d.** 3

13. If a varies directly as b and $a = 10.2$ when $b = 8.1$, find a when $b = \frac{9}{17}$.

   a. $\frac{2}{3}$ **b.** $\frac{34}{27}$ **c.** 1.3   **d.** 0.8

14. Find the value of k that will make $(3x - 5)$ a factor of $6x^2 + kx - 35$.

   a. 7   **b.** 11   **c.** -6 **d.** 3

15. What is the theoretical probability that if a ten-sided die is tossed, the number showing is divisible by 3?

   a. $\frac{1}{3}$ **b.** $\frac{1}{10}$ **c.** $\frac{1}{5}$ **d.** $\frac{3}{10}$

16. Solve for x: $x + \frac{2}{x} = 4$.

   a. $2 \pm \sqrt{2}$ **b.** $-2 \pm \sqrt{2}$ **c.** $2 \pm 2\sqrt{2}$ **d.** $-2 \pm 2\sqrt{2}$

17. Which of the following is the equation of the axis of symmetry of the graph of $y = -3x^2 + 5x - 4$?

   a. $x = -\frac{5}{6}$ **b.** $x = \frac{5}{6}$ **c.** $x = -\frac{4}{3}$ **d.** $x = \frac{4}{3}$

18. Solve for x: $8(3 - 2x) > 2(x - 1)$.

   a. $x > \frac{13}{9}$ **b.** $x > -\frac{13}{9}$ **c.** $x < \frac{13}{9}$ **b.** $x < -\frac{13}{9}$

19. Simplify $(a + 2b)^2 - (2a - b)^2$.

   a. $-3(a^2 - b^2)$ **b.** $-(3a^2 - 8ab - 3b^2)$
   c. $a^2 - 2ab + b^2$ **d.** $3a^2 + 8ab + 3b^2$

20. If the graph of $y = ax^2 + bx + c$ opens downward, then which of the following is always true?

   a. $a > 0$ **b.** $a = 0$ **c.** $a = -1$ **d.** $a < 0$

21. Calculate the distance between the points $(-3, -1)$ and $(2, 6)$.

   a. $\sqrt{26}$ **b.** $2\sqrt{5}$ **c.** 20   **d.** $\sqrt{74}$

22. Find the maximum value of the quadratic function $y = 5 + 8x - 2x^2$.

   a. -19 **b.** 21   **c.** 13   **d.** 0

23. Find the solution set of $|2(1 - 3x) - 5| = 4$.

   a. $\{-\frac{7}{6}\}$ **b.** $\{\frac{1}{6}\}$ **c.** $\{-\frac{7}{6}, \frac{1}{6}\}$ **d.** $\emptyset$

24. Which point does not satisfy the system $\begin{cases} y \le 3x - x^2 \\ y + x \ge 0 \end{cases}$?

   a. $(3, -1)$ **b.** $(0, 0)$ **c.** $(2, 1)$ **d.** $(1, -2)$

25. What is the equation of the line which passes through $(-3, -1)$ and $(2, 6)$?

   a. $5x - 7y + 8 = 0$ **b.** $7x - 5y + 16 = 0$

   c. $5x - 7y - 8 = 0$ **d.** $7x - 5y - 16 = 0$

26. If s varies directly as t and inversely as v, then which of the following equations describes the relation among the three variables s, t, and v?

   a. $s = \dfrac{k}{tv}$ **b.** $s = \dfrac{kv}{t}$

   c. $\dfrac{1}{s} = \dfrac{kt}{v}$ **d.** $s = \dfrac{kt}{v}$

Part 2

Solve each problem.

27. The town of Acton is due west of Baxter, and Carter is due north of Baxter. If the (straight line) distance between Acton and Carter is 3 miles greater than the distance between Baxter and Carter, and is 6 miles greater than the distance between Acton and Baxter, how far apart are Acton and Carter?

28. A large pool can be emptied in 15 hours by opening both of two outlet pipes. With the pool full, one pipe is opened; then, after 5 hours the second pipe is opened, and the pool is then emptied by both pipes in 13 additional hours. How long would it take for each pipe alone to empty the pool?

29. Jason's new river boat can travel at a rate of 18 miles per hour in still water. He finds that on the Columbia River he can go 63 miles down the river in the same time it takes to go 45 miles up the river. What is the speed of the current in the river?

30. A farmer will use 120 feet of fence to surround three sides of a rectangular field; a river will be the fourth boundary. If he wishes to enclose as large an area as possible, how much of the fence should be used for one width? What is the maximum area that can be enclosed?

31. If current is flowing through a wire, the resistance varies inversely as the square of the diameter. If a $\frac{5}{8}$-inch diameter wire has 56 ohms resistance, how much resistance does the same length of $\frac{1}{2}$-inch wire have?

32. A new auto-focus camera has a list price of $249.50; Shutter's Camera Mart is selling it for $219.95. What percent discount is Shutter's offering?

33. A theater has 720 seats. The number of seats in each row is 6 more than the number of rows. How many seats are there in each row?

34. How many ounces of a 5% salt solution must be added to 30 ounces of a 10% salt solution to produce an 8% salt solution?

14 Other Applications of Algebra

The fundamental concepts of trigonometry are extensions of the concepts of ratio, proportion, and similarity. The trigonometric ratios connect these ideas to the properties of right triangles. One application of these ratios is to **indirect measurement,** such as finding the distance across a river.

14-1 Algebra and Similar Triangles

SIMILAR TRIANGLES

CONGRUENT ANGLES

Ratio and proportion are useful in geometry for solving problems that deal with *similar triangles*. **Similar triangles** have the same shape; that is, corresponding angles have equal measures. In similar triangles, corresponding sides are opposite *congruent angles*. **Congruent angles** are angles that have the same measure.

Similar Triangles	Corresponding Angles	Corresponding Sides
	$\angle A$ and $\angle D$	$\overline{BC}$ and $\overline{EF}$
	$\angle B$ and $\angle E$	$\overline{AC}$ and $\overline{DF}$
	$\angle C$ and $\angle F$	$\overline{AB}$ and $\overline{DE}$
	$\angle K$ and $\angle X$	$\overline{LM}$ and $\overline{ZY}$
	$\angle L$ and $\angle Z$	$\overline{KM}$ and $\overline{XY}$
	$\angle M$ and $\angle Y$	$\overline{KL}$ and $\overline{XZ}$

NOTE: "$\overline{AB}$" means "segment $\overline{AB}$," and "AB" is its measure.

EXAMPLE 1 **a.** Find the ratio of each pair of corresponding sides in these similar right triangles.

b. Compare the ratios.

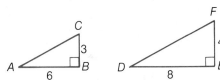

Solutions: **a.** $\dfrac{AB}{DE} = \dfrac{6}{8} = \dfrac{3}{4}; \quad \dfrac{BC}{EF} = \dfrac{3}{4}$

$AC^2 = 6^2 + 3^2$ $\qquad\qquad DF^2 = 8^2 + 4^2$

$AC^2 = 36 + 9$ $\qquad\qquad DF^2 = 64 + 16$

$AC = \sqrt{45}$ $\qquad\qquad DF = \sqrt{80}$

$AC = \sqrt{9 \cdot 5} = 3\sqrt{5}$ $\qquad DF = \sqrt{16 \cdot 5} = 4\sqrt{5}$

$$\frac{AC}{DF} = \frac{3\sqrt{5}}{4\sqrt{5}} = \frac{3}{4}$$

b. Each of the three ratios equals $\dfrac{3}{4}$.

If two triangles are similar, then their corresponding sides are proportional.

Thus, when you know that two triangles are similar, you can write a proportion to find the length of an unknown side.

EXAMPLE 2 In an isosceles triangle, the **altitude** (height) drawn from the vertex angle to the base bisects the base. Find the height, BD, of $\triangle ABC$. Write the answer in simplest radical form.

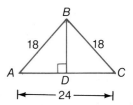

Solution: Use the Pythagorean Theorem

$$AD^2 + BD^2 = AB^2 \longleftarrow \text{ Pythagorean Theorem}$$

$$12^2 + BD^2 = 18^2 \longleftarrow AD = \tfrac{1}{2} AC = \tfrac{1}{2}(24)$$

$$BD^2 = 180$$

$$BD = \sqrt{180}$$

$$BD = \sqrt{36 \cdot 5} = \mathbf{6\sqrt{5}}$$

EXERCISES: Classwork/Homework

Objective: To find the unknown lengths in similar triangles

CHECK YOUR UNDERSTANDING

Complete.

1. If two triangles are similar then their corresponding sides are ___?___ .

2. Angles that have the same measure are ___?___ angles.

In Exercises 3–6, each pair of triangles is similar. In Exercises 3–4, find the ratio comparing corresponding known sides of each pair.

3.

4.

Write a proportion comparing corresponding sides of each pair.

5.

6.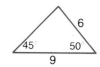

In Exercises 7–8, each pair of triangles is similar. Find the unknown length.

7.

8.

9. Norman is 1.8 meters tall. On a sunny day, Patty measured Norman's shadow and the shadow of the school. Use the similar triangles shown below to find the height of the school to the nearest tenth.

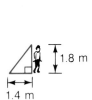

10. On the same sunny day, the shadow of a tree was 12 meters long. Use the similar triangles below to find the height of the tree to the nearest tenth.

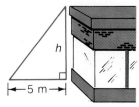

11. Jorge found the height of a street lamp by placing a mirror on the sidewalk. Then he walked backwards until he saw the top of the streetlight in the mirror. The figure below shows how he formed similar triangles. Find the height of the street lamp to the nearest tenth.

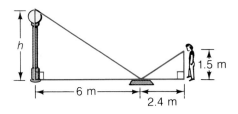

12. Find the distance across this lake to the nearest tenth of a meter.

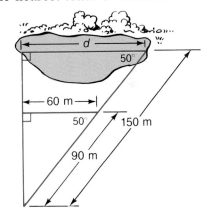

Solve.

13. Triangle ABC is similar to triangle EDC. Find the distance across the lake from point A to point B.

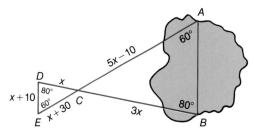

Write a decimal for each fraction. Round to four decimal places.
(*Pages 26–29*)

1. $\frac{6}{14}$ **2.** $\frac{3}{8}$ **3.** $\frac{4}{9}$ **4.** $\frac{5}{7}$ **5.** $\frac{20}{18}$

Solve each equation. (*Pages 99–102*)

6. $1.5399 = \frac{x}{10}$ **7.** $0.8391 = \frac{w}{240}$ **8.** $1.1918 = \frac{x}{18}$ **9.** $3.2205 = \frac{15}{x}$

14-2   The Tangent Ratio

These three right triangles are similar.

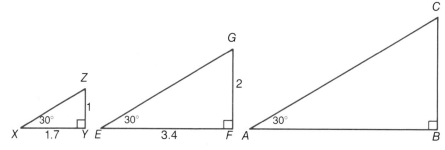

Since $\frac{YZ}{FG} = \frac{XY}{EF}$, the following proportion is true.

$$\frac{YZ}{XY} = \frac{FG}{EF}$$

Thus, for the above triangles,

$$\frac{1}{1.7} = \frac{2}{3.4} = \frac{BC}{AB}.$$

TANGENT   The ratio $\frac{BC}{AB}$ in *any* right triangle ABC, where $\angle B$ is a right angle, is the **tangent of angle C**.

DEFINITION

> In a right triangle, the **tangent of an acute angle** is the ratio
>
> $$\frac{\text{length of the leg opposite the angle}}{\text{length of the leg adjacent to the angle}}.$$

Tangent of angle A is abbreviated tan A.

EXAMPLE 1 Find each ratio. Write a decimal for the ratio.

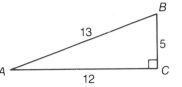

a. tan A **b.** tan B

Solutions: **a.** tan $A = \dfrac{BC}{AC}$ ◄——— $\dfrac{BC \text{ is opposite } \angle A.}{AC \text{ is adjacent to } \angle A.}$

tan $A = \dfrac{5}{12}$

tan $A = .4167$ ◄——— Rounded to 4 decimal places.

b. tan $B = \dfrac{AC}{BC}$ ◄——— $\dfrac{AC \text{ is opposite } \angle B.}{BC \text{ is adjacent to } \angle B.}$

tan $B = \dfrac{12}{5}$

tan $B = 2.4$

TRIGONOMETRIC RATIO A ratio of the lengths of two sides of a right triangle is a **trigonometric ratio.** The study of trigonometry originated in connection with real-world measurement problems that involve right triangles.

A trigonometric ratio depends only on the measure of an acute angle, *not* on the size of the right triangle. The **Table of Sines, Cosines, and Tangents** on page 637 gives these values for acute angles. You can also use a calculator to find their values.

Although most values are approximations for the ratios, the ''='' symbol is used because it is more convenient. Thus, in Example 1, write tan $A = .4167$ instead of tan $A \approx .4167$.

EXAMPLE 2 Find the tangent of 41°.

Solution: Find 41 in the **Angle-** column. Move directly right to the **Tangent**-column.

tan 41° = **.8693**

Angle	Sine	Cosine	Tangent
40°	.6428	.7660	.8391
41	.6561	.7547	.8693
42	.6691	.7431	.9004

or 41 [tan]   `0.8692867` ◄——— tan 41° = 0.8693

You can use the tangent to find the measure of an angle. The symbol ''m∠A'' means ''the measure of angle A.''

EXAMPLE 3 What is the measure of the angle whose tangent is 1.1106?

Solution: Find 1.1106 in the **Tangent**-column. Move directly left to the **Angle**-column.

Angle	Sine	Cosine	Tangent
47°	.7314	.6820	1.0724
48	.7431	.6691	1.1106
49	.7547	.6561	1.1504

The measure of the angle whose tangent is 1.1106 is **48°**.

or   **1.1106** [INV] [tan]   `47.999679`   ◄──── **48°**

You also use the tangent to find the measure of a side.

EXAMPLE 4 A flagpole is side *BC* in triangle *ABC* pictured at the right. Point *A* is 14 meters from point *C* and ∠ *A* is 47°. How high is the flagpole to the nearest meter?

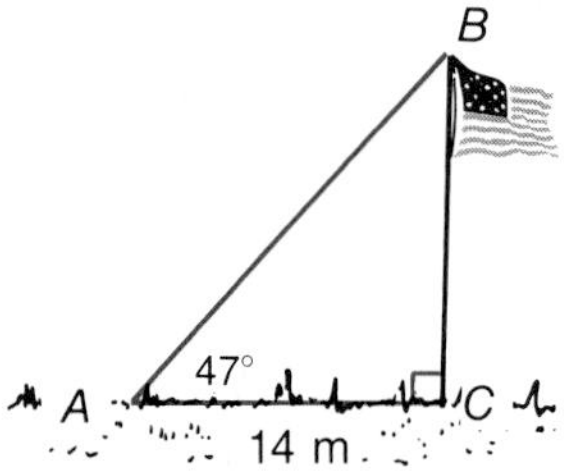

Solution: $\tan 47° = \dfrac{BC}{14}$

$1.0724 = \dfrac{BC}{14}$ ◄──── **tan 47° = 1.0724.**

$14(1.0724) = BC$ ◄──── **Solve for BC.**

$15.0136 = BC$ The height of the flagpole is about **15 meters.**

EXERCISES: Classwork/Homework

Objective: To define and use the tangent ratio

CHECK YOUR UNDERSTANDING

Complete.

1. The tangent of an acute angle is the ratio of the length of the leg opposite the angle to the length of the leg __?__ to the angle.

2. The ratio of the lengths of two sides of a right triangle is a __?__ ratio.

In Exercises 3–5, find tan _A_ and tan _B_.

3.

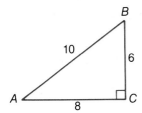

4.

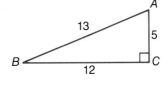

5.

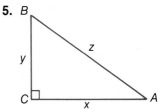

Find the tangent of each angle measure.

6. 20°	**7.** 40°	**8.** 22°	**9.** 45°	**10.** 55° 1.4281	**11.** 70°
12. 5°	**13.** 25°	**14.** 37°	**15.** 80°	**16.** 85° 11.4301	**17.** 89°

Find _x_.

18. $\tan x = .5774$

19. $\tan x = 1.7321$

20. $\tan x = .1228$

21. $\tan x = .6009$

22. $\tan x = 1.6003$

23. $\tan x = 2.2460$

24. Complete the following sentence.

> As the measure of an angle increases from 0° to 89°, the tangent of the angle measure __?__ (increases or decreases) from .0000 to __?__ .

25. The triangle at the right is a right triangle. Use the tangent ratio to find the distance between Tom's home and John's home, directly through the park.

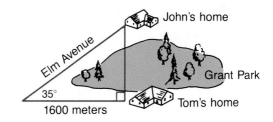

26.

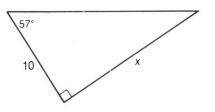

27.

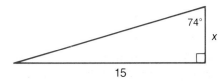

28. In right triangle XYZ, m$\angle$ X is 45°. Since the sum of $\angle$ X, $\angle$ Y, and $\angle$ Z is 180°, m$\angle$ Y is also 45°. If two angles of a triangle have the same measure, the sides opposite these angles have the same length and the triangle is isosceles.

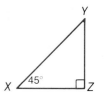

Triangle XYZ is isosceles and $XZ = YZ$.

$\tan X = \dfrac{YZ}{XZ} = \underline{\ ?\ }$ $\tan Y = \dfrac{XZ}{YZ} = \underline{\ ?\ }$ $\tan 45° = \underline{\ ?\ }$

29. To the nearest foot, how long is $\overline{DF}$ in $\triangle$ DEF below?

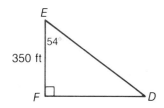 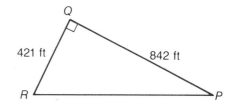

30. In $\triangle$ PQR above, what is m$\angle$ P, to the nearest degree?

31. Use Figure 1 below to find the length of $\overline{BC}$ to the nearest foot.

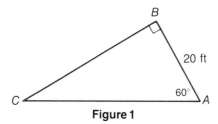 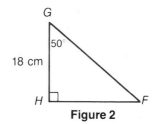

Figure 1   Figure 2

32. In Figure 2 at the right above, find the length of $\overline{HF}$ to the nearest centimeter.

33. In the figure at the right, angle C is the right angle of $\triangle$ ABC. What measurements could you make to find BC, the distance across the pond?

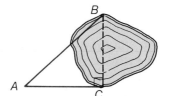

34. Using the figure for Exercise 33, find BC if m$\angle$ A is 42° and AC is 80 meters.

NON-ROUTINE PROBLEM

35. Four friends, Luise, Maria, Carol, and Glenn, are sitting in a row. Neither Maria nor Carol are sitting next to Glenn. Carol is sitting just to the right of Maria. Write the seating arrangement from left to right.

14-3   The Sine and Cosine Ratios

Suppose you wanted to determine the height of a plane or the distance across a pond as shown below.

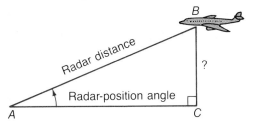
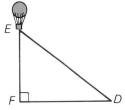

If both situations are represented by right triangles, where you know the length of the hypotenuse and the measure of one acute angle, you still would not be able to find either *BC* or *FD* using the tangent ratio. There are two other ratios that you can use.

DEFINITIONS

> In a right triangle, the **sine of an acute angle** is the ratio
>
> $$\frac{\textbf{length of opposite side}}{\textbf{length of hypotenuse}}.$$
>
> In a right triangle, the **cosine of an acute angle** is the ratio
>
> $$\frac{\textbf{length of adjacent side}}{\textbf{length of hypotenuse}}.$$

The abbreviation for sine is **sin** (pronounced "sign"). The abbreviation for cosine is **cos** (pronounced "co-sign").

EXAMPLE 1   Use the figure at the right to determine sin *A* and cos *A* for each of the triangles *ABC*, *ADE* and *AFG*, where *AB* = 5, *AD* = 10, and *AF* = 15.

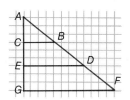

Solutions:

Triangle	sin A	cos A
ABC	$\sin A = \dfrac{BC}{AB} = \dfrac{4}{5}$	$\cos A = \dfrac{AC}{AB} = \dfrac{3}{5}$
ADE	$\sin A = \dfrac{DE}{AD} = \dfrac{8}{10} = \dfrac{4}{5}$	$\cos A = \dfrac{AE}{AD} = \dfrac{6}{10} = \dfrac{3}{5}$
AFG	$\sin A = \dfrac{FG}{AF} = \dfrac{12}{15} = \dfrac{4}{5}$	$\cos A = \dfrac{AG}{AF} = \dfrac{9}{15} = \dfrac{3}{5}$

Since the triangles in Example 1 are similar, the ratios of corresponding sides are equal. Thus, for each of the triangles,

$$\sin A = \tfrac{4}{5} \quad \text{and} \quad \cos A = \tfrac{3}{5}.$$

Now you can solve the problems mentioned at the beginning of this section.

EXAMPLE 2 The distance from the tower to the plane is 40 kilometers and the measure of angle A is 12°. Find the height of the plane to the nearest tenth.

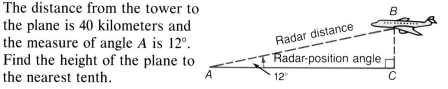

Solution: Since you know the measure of $\angle A$ and of the hypotenuse, and you want to find the side opposite $\angle A$, use $\sin A$.

$$\sin A = \frac{BC}{AB}$$

$$\sin 12° = \frac{BC}{40} \quad \longleftarrow \quad \begin{array}{l}\textbf{Find sin 12°} \\ \textbf{in the table}\end{array} \text{ or } \quad 12 \ \boxed{\text{sin}} \quad \boxed{0.2079117}$$

$$.2079 = \frac{BC}{40} \quad \longleftarrow \quad \textbf{Solve for BC.}$$

$$BC = 40(.2079)$$

$$BC = 8.3160$$

The height of the plane is about **8.3 kilometers.**

EXAMPLE 3 Find the distance across the pond shown at the right to the nearest meter.

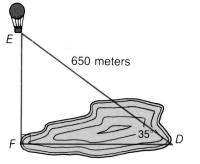

Solution: Since you know the measure of $\angle D$ and of the hypotenuse, and you want to find the side adjacent to $\angle D$, use $\cos D$.

$$\cos D = \frac{FD}{ED}$$

$$\cos 35° = \frac{FD}{650} \quad \longleftarrow \quad \begin{array}{l}\textbf{Find cos 35°} \\ \textbf{in the table.}\end{array} \text{ or } \quad 35 \ \boxed{\text{cos}} \quad \boxed{0.819152}$$

$$.8192 = \frac{FD}{650} \quad \longleftarrow \quad \textbf{Solve for FD.}$$

$$FD = 650(.8192)$$
$$FD = 532.48$$

The distance is about **532 meters**.

EXERCISES: Classwork/Homework

Objective: To define and use sine and cosine ratios

CHECK YOUR UNDERSTANDING

For Exercises 1–4, use the triangle at the right.

1. $\cos R = \dfrac{?}{TR}$

2. $\sin T = \dfrac{?}{TR}$

3. $\cos \underline{\ ?\ } = \dfrac{TS}{TR}$

4. $\sin \underline{\ ?\ } = \dfrac{RS}{TR}$

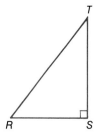

In Exercises 5–7, find the sine and cosine of angle A.

5.

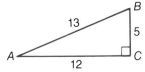

6.

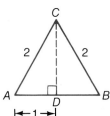

7.

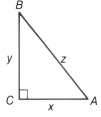

PRACTICE AND APPLY

Find approximations for the sine and cosine of the following angles.

8. $35°$ **9.** $42°$ **10.** $54°$ **11.** $83°$ **12.** $72°$ **13.** $61°$

Find x.

14. $\sin x = .1392$ **15.** $\sin x = .3907$ **16.** $\sin x = .6561$

17. $\sin x = .7547$ **18.** $\sin x = .9135$ **19.** $\sin x = .9962$

20. Look at your results for Exercises 14–19. As the size of an acute angle increases, does the sine ratio increase or decrease?

Find x.

21. $\cos x = .9336$ **22.** $\cos x = .7660$ **23.** $\cos x = .5299$

24. $\cos x = .1736$ **25.** $\cos x = .0175$ **26.** $\cos x = .9877$

27. Look at the cosine values in the table. As the size of an acute angle increases, does the value of the cosine increase or decrease?

28. Bea's kite string is 60 meters long and makes an angle of 42° with the horizontal in the figure below. How high above the ground is the kite?

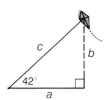

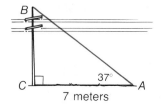

29. In the figure above, $\overline{AB}$ represents a wire supporting a pole, $\overline{BC}$. Find AB.

30. The railroad that runs to the summit of Pike's Peak makes, at the steepest place, an angle of 27° with the horizontal. How many meters would you rise in walking 30 meters up the railroad track?

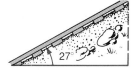

31. In △ ABC below, c is 25 meters and ∠ A is 65°. How long is b?

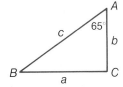

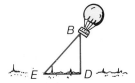

32. In the figure at the right above, the balloon at B is anchored to the ground at a point E by a wire. The wind blows the balloon so the wire makes an angle of 48° with the ground. If point D, directly under the balloon, is 85 meters from E, how long is the wire?

33. How far above the ground is the balloon in Exercise 32?

34. The scouts of the Lynx Patrol want to know the distance across a pond. They laid off $\overline{CA}$ at right angles to $\overline{BC}$. They extended $\overline{CA}$ until they came to a point A from which they could measure $\overline{AB}$. They measured $\overline{AB}$ and angle A. If AB is 195 meters and ∠ A is 57°, find BC.

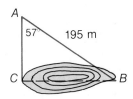

CONNECT AND EXTEND

35. The diagonals of a square are perpendicular to each other, as shown in the figure at the right. If a circle is circumscribed about the square, the diagonals are also diameters of the circle. Use the cosine ratio to find the radius of a circle circumscribed about a square whose side is 3.5 centimeters.

36. Use the Pythagorean Theorem to check your answer to Exercise 35.

Find the unknown length in each pair of similar triangles. (*Pages 579–581*)

1.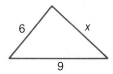

2.

Complete. (*Pages 582–586*)

3. tan 32° = __?__

4. tan 47° = __?__

5. tan 86° = __?__

6. tan x = .4040; x = __?__ **7.** tan x = 2.1445; x = __?__ **8.** tan x = 8.1443; x = __?__

9. In the figure at the right, point B is 60 meters from the base of the water tower and $\angle B$ is 41°. Find side AC, the height of the tower, to the nearest meter. (*Pages 582–586*)

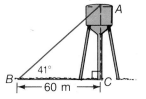

Complete. (*Pages 587–590*)

10. sin 25° = __?__

11. cos 63° = __?__

12. cos 13° = __?__

13. sin x = .3090; x = __?__ **14.** cos x = .8387; x = __?__ **15.** sin x = .9613; x = __?__

16. An airplane approaching an airport is 800 meters above the control tower. The angle of elevation from the tower to the plane is 8°. Find the distance between the plane and the tower to the nearest meter. (*Pages 587–590*)

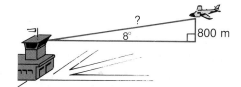

Historical Digest: *Trigonometry*

The sine, cosine, and tangent ratios are a part of a branch of mathematics called **trigonometry.** It is likely that the Egyptians used trigonometry over 4000 years ago to help build the pyramids. A Greek astronomer, Hipparcus, used trigonometry to make a table of the locations of over 800 stars. In the 1850's, the "Great Trigonometric Survey of India" estimated the height of Mount Everest, the highest mountain in the world, to be 29,028 feet. Even special space "stereophotography" methods from the space shuttle Columbia in 1983 have changed that height by only 26 feet.

14-4 Using the Sine, Cosine, and Tangent Ratios

MAKING A DIAGRAM

An important step in using trigonometric ratios to solve problems is deciding which ratio to use. When no figure is given, you should first draw one, carefully labeling what is known and what is to be found. The ratio that involves both the known parts and the part to be found is the one to use in solving the problem.

Known and Unknown Sides of the Right Triangle	Ratios to Use
opposite and adjacent	tangent
opposite and hypotenuse	sine
adjacent and hypotenuse	cosine

To describe the angles found by lines of sight to objects, two angles are used. They are the **angle of elevation** and the **angle of depression.**

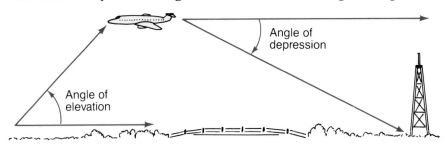

EXAMPLE 1 To find the height of a tree, a girl measures 9 meters along a straight line from its base. From the end of this line, she finds the angle of elevation to the top of tree to be 41°. How high is the tree (to the nearest meter)?

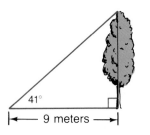

Solution: Let y = the height of the tree.

$$\tan 41° = \frac{y}{9}$$ ◄——— The opposite side is unknown; the adjacent side is known. Use the tangent ratio.

$$.8693 = \frac{y}{9}$$ ◄——— $\tan 41° = .8693$

$$y = 9(.8693)$$

$$y = 7.8237 \quad \text{The tree is about \textbf{8 meters} high.}$$

EXAMPLE 2 The diagonal of a rectangle is 8 centimeters long and makes an angle of 25° with the longer side of the rectangle. Find the length of the base to the nearest centimeter.

Solution: 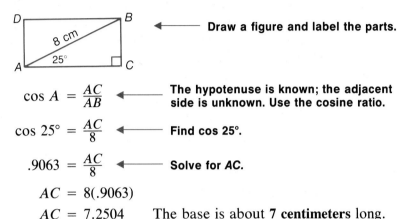 ← **Draw a figure and label the parts.**

$$\cos A = \frac{AC}{AB} \quad \leftarrow \quad \text{\textbf{The hypotenuse is known; the adjacent side is unknown. Use the cosine ratio.}}$$

$$\cos 25° = \frac{AC}{8} \quad \leftarrow \quad \text{\textbf{Find cos 25°.}}$$

$$.9063 = \frac{AC}{8} \quad \leftarrow \quad \text{\textbf{Solve for AC.}}$$

$$AC = 8(.9063)$$

$$AC = 7.2504 \quad \text{The base is about \textbf{7 centimeters} long.}$$

EXERCISES: Classwork/Homework

Objective: To use the sine, cosine, and tangent ratios to solve problems

CHECK YOUR UNDERSTANDING

Use each figure to tell which trigonometric ratio could be used to find x.

1.

2.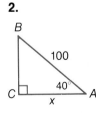

3.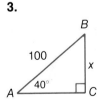

4.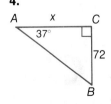

5.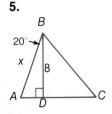

PRACTICE AND APPLY

6. To find the distance across a pond between two points, M and N, Fred measured off 250 meters on a line MR perpendicular to segment MN. He found $\angle MRN$ to be 35°. Find MN.

7. Some girl scouts measured the height of a mound. They stretched a string from a point, A, at the bottom of the mound to the top, T, finding AT to be 24 meters. The measure of the angle of elevation of the top from point A was 35°. How high was the mound?

8. If AB and BC in the figure at the right are each 30 meters, and BD is 18 meters, what is the measure of angle A?

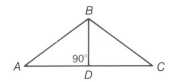

9. You are given rectangle $ABCD$ with diagonal AC drawn. The measure of the angle between $\overline{AD}$ and $\overline{AC}$ is 31° and AD is 16.3 centimeters. How long is $\overline{AC}$?

10. Find the angle of elevation of the sun to the nearest degree when a church steeple 200 feet high casts a shadow 80 feet long.

11. From the top of a cliff 1200 meters above a lake, the angle of depression of the nearest shore is 18°. Find the distance from the top of the cliff to the edge of the lake.

12. In the figure at the right, AB is 215 centimeters, $\angle A$ is 35°, $\angle C$ is 65°, and the angles at D are right angles. How long are $\overline{BD}$ and $\overline{BC}$?

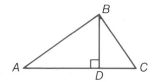

13. Use your own height in meters to find how long a shadow you will cast if the angle of elevation of the sun is 37°.

14. A tower that is 50 meters high has a support wire that makes an angle of 35° with the ground. How long is the wire? How far from the foot of the tower is the support wire attached to the ground?

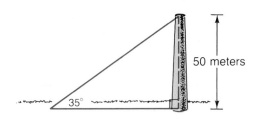

▬▬▬▬ **NON-ROUTINE PROBLEM**

15. Doris took some coins out of her bank and arranged the coins in four rows with four coins in each row. Each of the four rows, the four columns, and the two diagonals had exactly one penny, one nickel, one dime, and one quarter. Show how Doris could have arranged the coins.

14-5 The Field Postulates

POSTULATE

As you will learn in geometry, a **postulate** is a mathematical statement that is accepted without proof—just as in algebra. Postulates are important in the structure of geometry. As the following illustrates, postulates are also important in the structure of algebra.

If it is nine o'clock, then five hours from now it will be two o'clock. Although $9 + 5 = 14$, in *clock arithmetic*

$$9 + 5 = 2.$$

In clock arithmetic you only use the whole numbers 1 through 12.

$$C = \{1, 2, 3, 4, 5, 6, 7, 8, 9, 10, 11, 12\}$$

FINITE SET

Set C is a **finite set** because you can count the number of elements and the counting comes to an end.

Here is the procedure for adding numbers in clock arithmetic.

PROCEDURE

> If the sum of any two numbers named in C is greater than 12, you subtract 12 to find the clock sum.

Here is the addition table for C.

+	1	2	3	4	5	6	7	8	9	10	11	12
1	2	3	4	5	6	7	8	9	10	11	12	1
2	3	4	5	6	7	8	9	10	11	12	1	2
3	4	5	6	7	8	9	10	11	12	1	2	3
4	5	6	7	8	9	10	11	12	1	2	3	4
5	6	7	8	9	10	11	12	1	2	3	4	5
6	7	8	9	10	11	12	1	2	3	4	5	6
7	8	9	10	11	12	1	2	3	4	5	6	7
8	9	10	11	12	1	2	3	4	5	6	7	8
9	10	11	12	1	2	3	4	5	6	7	8	9
10	11	12	1	2	3	4	5	6	7	8	9	10
11	12	1	2	3	4	5	6	7	8	9	10	11
12	1	2	3	4	5	6	7	8	9	10	11	12

EXAMPLE 1 Find the clock sums: **a.** $8 + 5$ **b.** $7 + 9$

Solutions: **Method 1: Using the Procedure**

a. $8 + 5 = 13$ and $13 - 12 = 1$

b. $7 + 9 = 16$ and $16 - 12 = 4$

Method 2: Using the Table

a. Find 8 in the + column. Look directly right to the 5-column.

$$8 + 5 = 1$$

b. Find 7 in the + column. Look directly right to the 9-column.

$$7 + 9 = 4$$

The following is the procedure for multiplying numbers in clock arithmetic.

PROCEDURE

If the product of any two numbers named in C is greater than 12, you subtract 12 or a multiple of 12 to find the clock product.

Here is the multiplication table for C.

×	1	2	3	4	5	6	7	8	9	10	11	12
1	1	2	3	4	5	6	7	8	9	10	11	12
2	2	4	6	8	10	12	2	4	6	8	10	12
3	3	6	9	12	3	6	9	12	3	6	9	12
4	4	8	12	4	8	12	4	8	12	4	8	12
5	5	10	3	8	1	6	11	4	9	2	7	12
6	6	12	6	12	6	12	6	12	6	12	6	12
7	7	2	9	4	11	6	1	8	3	10	5	12
8	8	4	12	8	4	12	8	4	12	8	4	12
9	9	6	3	12	9	6	3	12	9	6	3	12
10	10	8	6	4	2	12	10	8	6	4	2	12
11	11	10	9	8	7	6	5	4	3	2	1	12
12	12	12	12	12	12	12	12	12	12	12	12	12

EXAMPLE 2 Find the clock products: **a.** 9×2 **b.** 8×4

Solutions: **Method 1: Using the Procedure**

a. $9 \times 2 = 18$ and $18 - 12 = 6$

b. $8 \times 4 = 32$ and $32 - 24 = 8$

Method 2: Using the Table

a. Find 9 in the ×-column. Look directly right to the 2-column.

$$9 \times 2 = 6$$

b. Find 8 in the ×-column. Look directly right to the 4-column.

$$8 \times 4 = 8$$

Note that in the finite set C under the operations of clock arithmetic, 12 acts the same as 0 does in the set of real numbers. That is, 12 is the additive identity element and 12 times any number is 12. Therefore, if the clock had been labeled as shown below, the pattern for addition and multiplication would be the same with 12 being replaced by 0.

FIELD

A set of numbers together with two operations for which the eleven postulates given below hold is called a **field**, *F*.

To determine if C is a field, check each postulate with the addition and multiplication tables for C.

Field Postulates	Does C satisfy the postulate?
1. $a + b$ is an element of the set. **2.** $a \times b$ is an element of the set.	**1–2.** Yes. The sum or product of any two numbers is in C.
Commutativity **3.** $a + b = b + a$ **4.** $a \times b = b \times a$	**3–4.** Yes. All cases can be checked. Draw a diagonal from upper left to lower right of the table. The pattern on either side of the diagonal is the same. This shows commutativity.
Associativity **5.** $a + (b + c) = (a + b) + c$ **6.** $a \times (b \times c) = (a \times b) \times c$	**5–6.** Yes. Check a few cases. All cases should be checked to show that these postulates hold.
Identity Element **7.** There is an identity element, 0, such that $a + 0 = a$.	**7.** Yes. The identity element is 12. 12 added to any number in C gives that number.
8. There is an identity element, 1, such that $a \times 1 = a$.	**8.** Yes. The identity element is 1. 1 times any number in C gives that number.

Field Postulates	Does C satisfy the postulate?

Inverse Element

9. For each element a in F, there is an inverse element, $-a$, such that $a + -a = 0$.

9. Yes. The additive identity element, 12, appears in each column. So each number in C has an additive inverse.

10. For each element a in F, there is an inverse element, $\frac{1}{a}$, $a \neq 0$, such that $a \times \frac{1}{a} = 1$.

10. No. There is no number in C by which to multiply 2, 3, 4, 6, 8, 9, 10, or 12 to get the identity element 1.

Distributive

11. $a \times (b + c) = a \times b + a \times c$

11. Yes. Try a few cases. All combinations should be checked.

If one postulate is not satisfied, then the set of numbers is not a field. Thus, you could have stopped after finding that Postulate 10 did not hold. The set of clock numbers is *not* a field.

EXERCISES: Classwork/Homework

Objective: To test whether a given finite set of numbers under two given operations satisfies the postulates for a field

CHECK YOUR UNDERSTANDING

1. *Complete:* A set in which the number of elements can be counted and the counting comes to an end is a __?__.

2. Explain how to determine whether a set is a field.

PRACTICE AND APPLY

Complete the following tables for a "four-hour clock."

3.

+	0	1	2	3
0	0	1	2	3
1	1	?	?	?
2	2	3	?	?
3	3	?	?	2

4.

×	0	1	2	3
0	0	0	0	0
1	0	?	?	?
2	0	2	?	?
3	0	?	?	1

5. Does the set of numbers on a "four-hour clock" meet all the requirements for a field? If not, which postulate(s) is (are) not satisfied? Give examples.

Complete the following tables for a "six-hour clock."

6.

+	0	1	2	3	4	5
0	0	1	2	3	4	5
1	1	?	?	?	?	0
2	2	?	4	?	?	?
3	3	?	?	?	?	2
4	4	?	?	?	2	?
5	5	?	1	?	?	?

7.

×	0	1	2	3	4	5
0	0	0	0	0	0	0
1	0	?	2	?	?	?
2	0	?	?	?	?	?
3	0	?	?	?	0	?
4	0	4	?	?	?	2
5	0	?	4	?	?	1

8. Does the set of numbers on a "six-hour clock" meet all the requirements for a field? Explain.

9. Is any set of numbers on an "even-number clock" a field? Explain.

Complete the following tables for a "three-hour clock."

10.

+	0	1	2
0	0	?	?
1	?	2	?
2	?	?	1

11.

×	0	1	2
0	0	0	0
1	0	?	?
2	0	?	?

12. Is the set of numbers on a "three-hour clock" a field?

13. Is the set of numbers on a "five-hour clock" a field?

14. Addition and multiplication tables for the finite set S = {E, O} are shown below. Is set S a field?

+	E	O
E	E	O
O	O	E

×	E	O
E	E	E
O	E	O

NON-ROUTINE PROBLEMS

15. Three friends ate lunch at a restaurant and split the total cost of the lunch equally. If they had paid separately, Mary would have paid $0.10 less, Sue would have paid, $0.80 more, and Audrey would have paid $2.20. What was the total cost of the lunch?

16. Write plus signs and decimal points between the digits to make each equation true.

Example: 3 4 1 2 5 6 = 12.72
3 + 4.12 + 5.6 = 12.72

a. 9 1 4 6 7 3 = 164.46

b. 4 4 3 8 6 5 = 18.03

14-6 Logic and Algebra

The study of geometry is an application of logical reasoning. An understanding of some of the elementary aspects of logic can prove to be helpful to you in geometry and in your next algebra course, particularly when dealing with theorems that are often stated in the *if–then* form.

CONDITIONAL STATEMENT

In mathematics, a statement in the *if–then* form is a **conditional statement.** You can think of a conditional statement as a *promise*.

If <u>it is cold</u>, then <u>I wear my coat</u>.

If you keep your promise, then the conditional is true; if you do not, it is false.

In the following table, T stands for *True* and F stands for *False*.

It is cold	You wore your coat.	You kept your promise.	
T	T	T	
F	T	T ←	You did not say that you wouldn't wear your coat if it wasn't cold. Thus, you kept your promise.
F	F	T ←	This case is *True* because you didn't break your promise.
T	F	F ←	This case is *False* because you broke your promise.

Notice that the only case where the conditional is false is when the if–part is true and the then–part is false. The analysis of a conditional statement suggests the truth table below. The symbol for the conditional is $p \rightarrow q$, where the $\rightarrow$ connects the then–part, q, with the if–part, p.

p	q	$p \rightarrow q$
T	T	T
F	T	T
F	F	T
T	F	F

The symbol "~" is read **"not."** Thus, in Example 1, $\sim q$ is the negation of the then–part of the statement, q.

EXAMPLE 1 Tell when the conditional is false if p is true and q is true.

If <u>it is raining</u>, then <u>I will use my umbrella</u>.

Solution: Keep p true and make q false.

p	q
It is raining.	I will *not* use my umbrella.

COMPOUND STATEMENT

A conditional statement is a **compound statement** since it is formed by combining two *simple* statements.

EXAMPLE 2 Combine these two simple statements or the negatives of these statements to form a true conditional.

<u>3 is an even number.</u>   <u>3 is a real number.</u>

Solution: There are three ways to do this.

		p	q	$p \rightarrow q$
If 3 is an even number, then 3 is a real number.		F	T	T
If 3 is an even number, then 3 is *not* a real number.		F	F	T
If 3 is *not* an even number, then 3 is a real number.		T	T	T

CONVERSE

The **converse** of a conditional statement is formed by interchanging the p and q statements.

EXAMPLE 3 Write the converse for each of the true conditionals in Example 2.

		q	p	$q \rightarrow p$
Solution: If 3 is a real number, then 3 is an even number.		T	F	F
If 3 is *not* a real number, then 3 is an even number.		F	F	T
If 3 is a real number, then 3 is *not* an even number.		T	T	T

As Example 3 shows, the converse of a true conditional is not always true. However, for a definition, *both* the conditional and its converse must be true.

EXAMPLE 4 Write this definition as a conditional and its converse.

An even number is a number divisible by 2.

If a number is an even number, then it is divisible by 2. ←——— **Conditional**

If a number is divisible by 2, then it is an even number. ←——— **Converse**

EXERCISES: Classwork/Homework

Objective: To use conditionals and their converses

■■■■■ **CHECK YOUR UNDERSTANDING**

1. *Complete:* In mathematics, a statement in the if–then form is a __?__ statement.

2. In symbols, how would you show the negation of the then–part of a statement, q?

3. *Complete:* A conditional statement formed by combining two simple statements is a __?__ statement.

4. *Complete:* If p and q are interchanged in the statement $p \rightarrow q$, the statement formed is the __?__ of $p \rightarrow q$.

■■■■■ **PRACTICE AND APPLY**

Tell when each conditional is *false*.

5. If you have no more than 2 errors, then you get an A.

6. If our team wins this game, then our team goes to the Rose Bowl.

7. If I drive over the speed limit, then I break the law.

8. If the sun is shining, then I cast a shadow.

Write *True* or *False* for each conditional.

9. If 7 is a whole number, then 7 is an even number.

10. If $\sqrt{2}$ is an irrational number, then $\sqrt{2}$ is an even number.

11. If $2 \times 3 = 8$, then $2 + 3 = 5$.

12. If $4 + 7 > 6$, then $7 > 6 - 4$.

13. If $25 + 60 = 85$, then $85 - 60 = 25$.

Combine each pair of statements to form a true conditional.

14. $\sqrt{2}$ is irrational; 7 is an even number.

15. 15 is a real number; 15 is a rational number.

16. 9 is a factor of 12; 3 is a factor of 12.

Write the converse of each conditional.

17. If I work hard, then I get tired.

18. If x is a rose, then x is a flower.

19. If Q is a triangle, then Q has exactly three sides and three angles.

Write each definition as a conditional and its converse.

20. An equilateral triangle is a triangle with three equal sides.

21. An irrational number is a number that cannot be expressed as the ratio of an integer and a natural number.

22. An acute angle is an angle whose measure is less than 90°.

23. An obtuse angle is an angle whose measure is greater than 90° and less than 180°.

24. Perpendicular lines are lines that meet at right angles.

25. Equivalent equations are equations that have the same solution set.

26. A set is a subset of a second set if all its members are also members of the second set.

27. A binomial is a polynomial of two terms.

28. A compound statement is formed by combining two simple statements.

CONNECT AND EXTEND

For Exercises 29–34, use the statements p, q, and r below to write each symbolic statement in words.

p: Paula is in Atlanta.
q: Ralph is in school.
r: Sue is at home.

29. $p \rightarrow q$
30. $p \rightarrow r$
31. $q \rightarrow r$
32. $p \rightarrow \sim q$
33. $\sim p \rightarrow \sim q$
34. $q \rightarrow \sim r$

NON-ROUTINE PROBLEMS

35. A photographer wishes to take a picture of four people standing side by side. In how many ways can these four people be arranged?

36. Rob has two jars of equal size. One is full of nickels, The other is half full of dimes. Which jar has more money in it? Explain.

Other Applications of Algebra **603**

14-7   Direct Proof and Algebra

HYPOTHESIS AND CONCLUSION

As was indicated in the previous section, theorems are often stated as conditionals. One way to prove a theorem is by a *direct proof*. A **direct proof** shows that the then-statement follows from the if-statement. In a proof, the if-statement is called the **hypothesis** and is always taken to be true. The then-statement is called the **conclusion.** It is the statement that is to be proved true.

LOGICAL REASONING

The first step in a proof states the hypothesis or what is given. Each statement thereafter is a conclusion that follows logically from the statement or statements that preceded it.

Each statement in a proof must be justified by a reason. The reason may be the hypothesis, a definition, postulate, or a theorem.

EXAMPLE 1 Prove the following theorem.

If x, y, and z are any real numbers, then $(x + y)z = xz + yz$.

Proof: **Hypothesis:** x, y, and z are any real numbers.

Conclusion: $(x + y)z = xz + yz$

Statements	Reasons
1. x, y, and z are any real numbers	1. Given (hypothesis)
2. $(x + y)z = z(x + y)$	2. Commutative postulate for multiplication
3. $z(x + y) = zx + zy$	3. Distributive postulate
4. $zx + zy = xz + yz$	4. Commutative postulate for multiplication
5. $(x + y)z = xz + yz$	5. Substitution principle

NOTE: Statements that have been proved may be used in later proofs.

To prove the next theorem, you will need these definitions.

DEFINITIONS

> An **even number** is a number of the form **$2n$, where n is an integer.**
>
> An **odd number** is a number of the form **$2n + 1$, where n is an integer.**

For example,

20 is an even number, because $20 = \mathbf{2} \cdot 10$.

$2k + 2$ is an even number, because $2k + 2 = \mathbf{2}(k + 1)$.

21 is an odd number, because $21 = (\mathbf{2} \cdot 10) + \mathbf{1}$.

$2k + 3$ is an odd number, because $2k + 3 = \mathbf{2}(k + 1) + \mathbf{1}$.

EXAMPLE 2 Prove the following theorem.

If two numbers are odd numbers, then their sum is an even number.

Proof: **Hypothesis:** a and b are any two odd numbers.

Conclusion: $a + b$ is an even number.

Statements	Reasons
1. a and b are odd numbers.	1. Given
2. Let $a = 2k + 1$; let $b = 2p + 1$; $a + b = 2k + 1 + 2p + 1$	2. Definition of odd number; addition property for equations
3. $2k + 1 + 2p + 1 = 2k + 2p + 2$	3. Addition
4. $2k + 2p + 2 = 2(k + p + 1)$	4. Distributive postulate
5. $k + p + 1$ is an integer.	5. Closure postulate for addition
6. $2(k + p + 1)$ is an even number.	6. Definition of even number
7. $a + b$ is an even number.	7. Substitution

EXERCISES: Classwork/Homework

Objective: To write a direct proof

CHECK YOUR UNDERSTANDING

1. *Complete:* In a theorem, the if-statement is called the __?__ and the then-statement is called the __?__.

2. Each statement in a proof must be justified by a reason. List four items that may be used as reasons.

PRACTICE AND APPLY

Prove each of the following.

3. $2x + 3x = 5x$

4. $n + n = 2n$

5. $3x + (5y + 7x) = 10x + 5y$

6. $3(4x) = 12x$

7. $(-2a)(-3a) = 6a^2$

8. $a(b + c + d) = ab + ac + ad$

9. $(x + 3)(x + 4) = x^2 + 7x + 12$

10. $(x + y)^2 = x^2 + 2xy + y^2$

Write a proof for each statement. Statements that have been proved may be used in later proofs.

11. The square of an even number is even.

12. The square of an odd number is odd.

13. The sum of two even numbers is an even number. (HINT: Let $2n$ be one even number and let $2k$ be the other. Then find $2n + 2k$.)

14. The sum of an even number and an odd number is an odd number.

15. The product of two odd numbers is an odd number.

16. The product of two even numbers is an even number.

17. The product of an even number and an odd number is an even number.

18. The sum of two multiples of 3 is a multiple of 3. (HINT: A multiple of 3 is a number of the form $3n$, where n is an integer.)

19. The product of two multiples of 3 is a multiple of 3.

20. The sum of two multiples of 6 is a multiple of 6.

21. If a number is divisible by 6, then it is divisible by 2. (HINT: Show that a number divisible by 6 is a multiple of 2.)

22. If a number is divisible by 6, then it is divisible by 3.

23. The product of two multiples of 5 is a multiple of 5.

24. For all real numbers a and b, $a - b$ and $b - a$ are opposites. (HINT: Prove that $(a - b) + (b - a) = 0$ is true. Then refer to the meaning of opposites.)

25. If a number is odd, then the cube of the number is odd. (HINT: $(2n + 1)^3 = (2n + 1)^2 (2n + 1))$

26. If one of two given numbers is even and the other is odd, then the square of their sum is an odd number.

27. If one of two given numbers is even and the other is odd, then the sum of the square of their sum and the odd number is an even number. (HINT: Let x be the even number and y the odd number. Prove that $(x + y)^2 + y$ is an even number.)

28. If a number is not a multiple of 4, then its square is not a multiple of 8. (HINT: Numbers that are not multiples of 4 have the form $4n + 1$, $4n + 2$, or $4n + 3$, where n is an integer.)

█████████ **NON-ROUTINE PROBLEMS**

29. Mike has 12 blue socks and 8 black socks in a drawer. Without looking, how many socks would he need to take out to be sure he gets two socks of the same color?

30. After spending $\frac{1}{4}$ of her money on food, $\frac{1}{2}$ of her money on clothing, and $\frac{1}{6}$ of her money on records, Julie had six dollars left. How much money did she have at first?

Chapter Summary

IMPORTANT TERMS

Angle of depression (p. 592)
Angle of elevation (p. 592)
Compound statement (p. 601)
Conclusion (p. 604)
Conditional (p. 600)
Congruent angles (p. 579)
Converse (p. 601)
Cosine ratio (p. 587)

Direct proof (p. 604)
Field (p. 597)
Field postulates (p. 597)
Finite set (p. 595)
Hypothesis (p. 604)
Similar triangles (p. 579)
Sine ratio (p. 587)
Tangent ratio (p. 582)

IMPORTANT IDEAS

1. If two triangles are similar, then the corresponding sides are proportional.

2. A trigonometric ratio depends only on the measure of an acute angle, *not* on the size of the right triangle.

3. In using trigonometric ratios to solve problems, use the ratio that involves both the known parts and the part to be solved.

4. For a given set to be a field, it must satisfy the field postulates.

5. Each statement in a proof must be justified by a reason. The reason may be the hypothesis, a definition, a postulate, or a previously proved theorem.

Chapter Review

1. Triangles *MRT* and *QSH* are similar:
   MR = 7, *RT* = 6, *MT* = 4, *QH* = 12.
   Find *HS* and *QS*. (*Pages 579–581*)

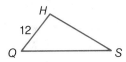

Use triangle *ABC* to determine each ratio. (*Pages 582–590*)

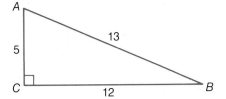

2. tan *A*   3. tan *B*

4. sin *A*   5. cos *A*

6. sin *B*   7. cos *B*

In each triangle, find *x* and *y*. Round answers to the nearest tenth.

8.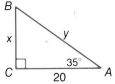

9.

In each triangle, find the measure of ∠A. Round answers to the nearest degree. (*Pages 582–590*)

10.

11.

12. If you want the top of the 10-meter ladder shown below to be 8 meters from the ground, what must be the measure of angle B? (*Pages 592–594*)

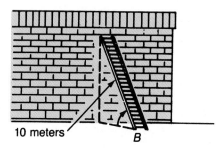

10 meters

B

13. If you want the bottom of the ladder above to be 7 meters from the building, what must be the measure of angle B? (*Pages 592–594*)

Using clock addition and multiplication, determine whether each finite set under these operations determines a field. If it does not, show by an example that at least one postulate is not satisfied. (*Pages 595–599*)

14. {0, 1, 2}   **15.** {0, 1, 2, 3}   **16.** {0, 1, 2, 3, 4}

(*Pages 600–603*)

17. Under what conditions is the following statement false?
If I use an umbrella, then it is raining.

18. Combine these two statements to make a true conditional.
6 is a factor of 12; 6 is a factor of 24.

19. State the converse of the conditional in Exercise 18. When is the converse false?

20. Write this definition as a conditional and its converse.
An odd number is a natural number that is not divisible by two.

Write a direct proof for each of the following. (*Pages 604–606*)

21. $(3x^2)(-7x^3) = -21x^5$

22. The sum of two multiples of 4 is a multiple of 4.

Find the unknown lengths in each pair of similar triangles.

1.

2.

Use triangle *ABC* to write each ratio.

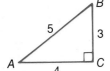

3. sin *A*

4. tan *A*

5. cos *A*

6. tan *B*

7. sin *B*

8. cos *B*

9. One angle of a right triangle measures 70° and the side adjacent to it measures 19 meters. To the nearest tenth of a meter, what is the measure of the side opposite the 70° angle?

Combine each pair of statements to form a true conditional.

10. 5 is a whole number; 5 is a rational number.

11. Today is Saturday; Saturday is the last day of the week.

12. A figure is a square; a figure is a rectangle.

13. Write the converse of each conditional in Exercises 10–12. Then write *True* or *False* for each converse.

14. Determine whether the set of integers is a field under the usual definitions of addition and multiplication. Explain your answer.

15. Prove: $5(x + 2) = 10 + 5x$

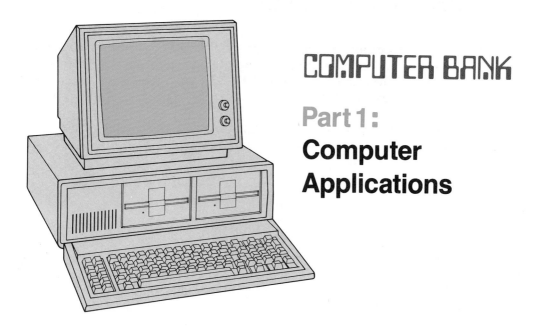

COMPUTER BANK

Part 1:
Computer Applications

The following is a listing of the computer applications activities that are included in Part I of the Computer Bank. The related textbook page for each activity is also indicated.

BASIC: FORMULAS IN PROGRAMS

The program for the following problem uses REM (short for "remark") statements. REM statements are used to add explanatory comments to a program. The computer ignores REM statements when executing a program. They are intended for the people who read the program.

Description: The program computes and prints the unit price of each item, given the total price of a purchase, p, and the number of units, n.

```
100 REM   P = TOTAL PRICE
110 REM   N = NUMBER OF UNITS
120 REM   U = UNIT PRICE OF AN ITEM
130 REM
140 PRINT "WHAT IS THE TOTAL PRICE";
150 INPUT P
160 PRINT "HOW MANY UNITS";
170 INPUT N
180 LET U = P / N
190 PRINT "THE UNIT PRICE = $"; U
200 PRINT "ANY MORE CALCULATIONS (1 = YES, 0 = NO)";
210 INPUT Z
220 IF Z = 1 THEN 140
230 END
```

TRY THESE   Run the program for the following values.

1. $p = \$1.09$; $n = 24$
2. $p = \$1.99$; $n = 46$
3. $p = \$0.99$; $n = 9$
4. $p = \$3.10$; $n = 15$
5. $p = \$0.85$; $n = 50$
6. $p = \$1.59$; $n = 36$
7. $p = \$1.88$; $n = 25$
8. $p = \$4.51$; $n = 18$
9. $p = \$2.85$; $n = 19$

Write a BASIC program for each problem.

10. Given the length of a side, s, of a square, use the formula
$$A = s^2$$
to compute and print the area.

11. Given the length, width, and height of a refrigerator car, use the formula
$$V = lwh$$
to compute and print the volume.

BASIC: SOLVING AX + B = C

Description: The program computes and prints the solution of the equation $ax + b = c$, given a, b, and c. Included in the program are the possibilities that the solution set contains all real numbers or the empty set.

```
100 PRINT "FOR THE EQUATION AX + B = C, WHAT ARE"
110 PRINT "A, B, AND C";
120 INPUT A, B, C
130 IF A = 0 THEN 170
140 LET X = (C - B)/A
150 PRINT "X = ";X
160 GOTO 210
170 IF B = C THEN 200
180 PRINT "NO SOLUTION"
190 GOTO 210
200 PRINT "ALL REAL NUMBERS ARE SOLUTIONS."
210 PRINT
220 PRINT "ANY MORE EQUATIONS TO SOLVE (1=YES, 0=NO)";
230 INPUT Z
240 IF Z = 1 THEN 120
250 END
```

TRY THESE Write each equation in the form $ax + b = c$. Then use the program to solve the equation.

1. $71 = 5x - 3$
2. $89 + 10x = 284$
3. $104 - 15x = 73$
4. $234 = 45 + 21x$
5. $804 = 66 - 34x$
6. $1245 - 125x = 1542$
7. $54 + 0x = 120$
8. $81 = 81 - 0x$
9. $99 = 12 + 0x$
10. $4x + 83 + 7x = 135$
11. $25x - 75 - 12x = 90$
12. $342 = 17x - 135 + 14x$

Write a BASIC program for each problem.

13. Given the measures of two angles of a triangle, compute and print the measure of the third angle. Use the following formula.
$$A + B + C = 180$$

14. Given the perimeter of a square, compute and print the length of the side. Use the following formula.
$$P = 4s$$

15. Given the average of three numbers and two of the numbers, compute and print the third number. Use the following formula.
$$A = \frac{x + y + z}{3}$$

BASIC: EQUATION OF A LINE

Description: The program prints the equation of a line in slope-intercept form, given the slope and the coordinates of a point on the line.

```
100 PRINT "WHAT IS THE SLOPE OF THE LINE AND THE"
110 PRINT "COORDINATES OF A POINT ON THE LINE";
120 INPUT M, X1, Y1
130 LET B = Y1 - M*X1
140 PRINT "EQUATION IS Y = ";
150 IF M = 0 THEN 240
160 IF B = 0 THEN 200
170 IF B < 0 THEN 220
180 PRINT M;"X +";B
190 GOTO 250
200 PRINT M;"X"
210 GOTO 250
220 PRINT M;"X -";ABS(B)
230 GOTO 250
240 PRINT B
250 PRINT
260 PRINT "ANY MORE LINES (1=YES, 0=NO)";
270 INPUT Z
280 IF Z = 1 THEN 120
290 END
```

TRY THESE Run the program using the following values of slope and coordinates of a point on each line.

1. Slope: 2; Point: $(0, 3)$
2. Slope: 4; Point: $(-2, -1)$
3. Slope: 3; Point: $(1, -3)$
4. Slope: 7; Point: $(3, 6)$
5. Slope: -1; Point: $(4, 0)$
6. Slope: -3; Point: $(1, 3)$
7. Slope: -10; Point: $(6, 2)$
8. Slope: 12; Point: $(0, 8)$
9. Slope: 0; Point: $(2, -5)$
10. Slope: 0; Point: $(-1, -1)$

11. The program does not handle vertical lines, since the slope of such lines is undefined. Add statements to the program so that a value of 999 for the slope is the code for a vertical line. Print the equation in the form $x = x_1$.

Write a BASIC program for each problem.

12. Given the coordinates of two points on a line, print the equation of the line in slope–intercept form.

13. Given the coordinates of a point on a line and the y intercept, print the equation of the line in slope–intercept form.

BASIC: SOLVING SYSTEMS OF EQUATIONS

Description: The program computes and prints the solution of a system of two linear equations in two variables.

```
100 REM SOLVE A1*X + B1*Y = C1
110 REM         A2*X + B2*Y = C2
120 REM
130 PRINT "ENTER THE COEFFICIENTS OF THE FIRST EQUATION";
140 INPUT A1, B1, C1
150 PRINT "ENTER THE COEFFICIENTS OF THE SECOND EQUATION";
160 INPUT A2, B2, C2
170 LET D = A1*B2 - A2*B1
180 IF D = 0 THEN 230
190 LET X = (B2*C1 - B1*C2)/D
200 LET Y = (A1*C2 - A2*C1)/D
210 PRINT "SOLUTION IS (";X;",";Y;")"
220 GOTO 240
230 PRINT "NO UNIQUE SOLUTION"
240 PRINT "ANY MORE SYSTEMS TO SOLVE (1=YES, 0=NO)";
250 INPUT Z
260 IF Z = 1 THEN 130
270 END
```

TRY THESE   In Exercises 1–12, write each system in the following form.

$$\begin{cases} A_1 x + B_1 y = C_1 \\ A_2 x + B_2 y = C_2 \end{cases}$$

Then use the program to solve each system.

1. $\begin{cases} y = 2x + 4 \\ 2x = 4 - y \end{cases}$

2. $\begin{cases} 2x + y = -2 \\ 2y = 4x - 1 \end{cases}$

3. $\begin{cases} 3y + 4x = 0 \\ 5 + 6y = 2x \end{cases}$

4. $\begin{cases} 4x - 17 = -3y \\ 3y + 2x - 13 = 0 \end{cases}$

5. $\begin{cases} y = 9 - x \\ y = 5x - 3 \end{cases}$

6. $\begin{cases} 8x + 13 = -5y \\ 3x = 2y - 1 \end{cases}$

7. $\begin{cases} 4x = 3y - 2 \\ 6 + 12x = 9y \end{cases}$

8. $\begin{cases} x = -2 \\ y = 2x + 4 \end{cases}$

9. $\begin{cases} x = 4y \\ \frac{1}{4}x = 20 - y \end{cases}$

10. $\begin{cases} x + y = 12 \\ -y = 8 \end{cases}$

11. $\begin{cases} 0.4x = 1.2 - y \\ 0.6x = y + 3.9 \end{cases}$

12. $\begin{cases} 0.5y = 0.75x - 4 \\ 0.25x + 0.5y = 2.5 \end{cases}$

13. Expand the program so that, when D = 0, it prints whether the system has no solution or infinitely many solutions. For the first set of data in the sample run of the program, the revised program should print DEPENDENT SYSTEM--INFINITELY MANY SOLUTIONS. For the second set of data in the sample run, the revised program should print INCONSISTENT SYSTEM--NO SOLUTION.

BASIC: SOLVING INEQUALITIES

Description: The program computes and prints the solution of any inequality of the following form.

$$ax + b < c$$

Included in the program are the possibilities that the solution set may be all real numbers or the empty set.

```
100 PRINT "ENTER VALUES FOR A, B, C"
110 PRINT "(IN THAT ORDER, SEPARATED BY COMMAS)";
120 INPUT A, B, C
130 IF A = 0 THEN 200
140 LET X = (C - B)/A
150 IF A < 0 THEN 180
160 PRINT "X < ";X
170 GOTO 240
180 PRINT "X > ";X
190 GOTO 240
200 IF B < C THEN 230
210 PRINT "NO SOLUTION"
220 GOTO 240
230 PRINT "ALL REAL NUMBERS ARE SOLUTIONS."
240 PRINT "ANY MORE INEQUALITIES TO SOLVE (1=YES, 0=NO)";
250 INPUT Z
260 IF Z = 1 THEN 120
270 END
```

TRY THESE   Run the program for the following values of *a*, *b*, and *c*.

1. $a = 2; b = 5; c = 9$
2. $a = 3; b = 4; c = 10$
3. $a = 2; b = -6; c = 0$
4. $a = -2; b = 5; c = 9$
5. $a = 0; b = 7; c = 8$
6. $a = 0; b = 8; c = 7$

Write each of the following inequalities in the form $ax + b < c$. Then use the program to solve the inequality.

7. $6 + 4x < 12$
8. $18 > 3x - 2$
9. $25 > 7 + 11x$
10. $112 < 16x - 123$
11. $254 < 24x + 123$
12. $82 - 9x < 233$

13. Write REM statements that can be added to the sample program above to explain what the program is doing. For example,

```
145 REM LINES 150-190 DECIDE WHETHER TO REVERSE THE < SIGN.
```

14. Change the problem in the description above to solve $ax + b \leq c$. What statements in the program must be changed and how?

BASIC: SOLVING ABSOLUTE VALUE EQUATIONS

Description: The program computes and prints the solutions of equations in the form $|Ax + B| = C$. Included in the program are the possibilities that the solution set may be all real numbers or the empty set.

```
100 PRINT "FOR THE EQUATION !AX + B! = C,"
110 PRINT "WHAT ARE A, B, AND C";
120 INPUT A, B, C
130 IF C < 0 THEN 250
140 IF C = 0 THEN 200
150 IF A = 0 THEN 230
160 LET X1 = (C - B)/A
170 LET X2 = (-C - B)/A
180 PRINT "SOLUTIONS ARE ";X1;" AND ";X2
190 GOTO 280
200 LET X = -B/A
210 PRINT "SOLUTION IS ";X
220 GOTO 280
230 IF B = C THEN 270
240 IF B = -C THEN 270
250 PRINT "NO SOLUTION"
260 GOTO 280
270 PRINT "ALL REAL NUMBERS ARE SOLUTIONS."
280 PRINT
290 PRINT "ANY MORE EQUATIONS TO SOLVE (1=YES, 0=NO)";
300 INPUT Z
310 IF Z = 1 THEN 120
320 END
```

TRY THESE   Write each equation in the form $|Ax + B| = C$. Then use the program to solve the equation.

1. $35 = |4x - 1|$ 　　　　2. $|4 - x| = 44$ 　　　　3. $|15 + 5x| = 55$

4. $0 = |6 - 2x|$ 　　　　5. $100 = |-5x|$ 　　　　6. $|4x + 2| + 8 = 0$

7. $|10 + 8x| = 0$ 　　　　8. $0 = |80 - 10x| - 8$ 　　　　9. $9 = |3x - 1| + 9$

Write a BASIC program for the problem.

10. Given the coordinates of a point, decide whether the point is in the solution set of the following system of inequalities.

$$\begin{cases} x \le 0 \\ 2x + y \ge 6 \\ 4x + y < 3 \end{cases}$$

BASIC: SQUARING BINOMIALS

Description: The program computes and prints the squares of binomials of the form *Ax* + *B*.

```
100 PRINT "FOR THE BINOMIAL TO BE SQUARED, AX + B,"
110 PRINT "WHAT ARE A AND B";
120 INPUT A, B
130 LET C = 2 * A * B
140 IF C < 0 THEN 170
150 PRINT A*A;"X↑2 +";C;"X +";B*B
160 GOTO 180
170 PRINT A*A;"X↑2 -";ABS(C);"X +";B*B
180 PRINT
190 PRINT "ANY MORE BINOMIALS TO SQUARE (1=YES, 0=NO)";
200 INPUT Z
210 IF Z = 1 THEN 120
220 END
```

TRY THESE Run the program for the following values of *A* and *B*.

1. $A = 3$; $B = 4$
2. $A = 2$; $B = 9$
3. $A = 6$; $B = -3$
4. $A = -5$; $B = 2$
5. $A = -4$; $B = -4$
6. $A = -8$; $B = 0$

Write each binomial in the form *Ax* + *B*. Then use the program to square each binomial.

7. $5 + x$
8. $10 + 3x$
9. $11 - 2x$
10. $21x$
11. $-32x$
12. $15 - 23x$

Rewrite the program to do each of the following.

13. Square binomials of the form $Ax + By$.

14. Eliminate the printing of coefficients equal to 1 or -1.

15. Test whether *A* or *B* (or both) equals 0 and change the printing of the trinomial accordingly. For example, for the binomial 5 X + 0, print the square simply as 25 X↑2 and not 25 X↑2 + 0 X + 0.

Write a BASIC program for each problem. As in the program and in Exercises 14 and 15 above, print answers as "neatly" as possible. For example, print 5 X↑2 - 9 X - 2 and not 5 X↑2 + -9 X + -2; print X↑2 + 5 X + 6 and not 1 X↑2 + 5 X + 6; print -X↑2 + 3 X - 2 and not -1 X↑2 + 3 X + -2. Also, do not print terms with 0 coefficients.

16. Multiply $(Ax + B)$ and $(Cx + D)$.

17. Add $(Ax + B)$ and $(Cx + D)$.

18. Subtract $(Cx + D)$ from $(Ax + B)$.

BASIC: FACTORING THE DIFFERENCE OF TWO SQUARES

The radical sign ($\sqrt{}$) does not usually appear on computer keyboards. Therefore, in BASIC the SQR function is used to obtain a square root. LET Y = SQR(X) means that Y will equal the square root of X (provided X ≥ 0). Another BASIC function needed in the following program is the INT ("integer") function. INT(X) gives the largest integer less than or equal to X. Thus, INT(3.5) = 3; INT(2.9) = 2; INT (-1.8) = -2; INT(81) = 81.

Description: The program computes and prints the factors of the difference of two squares, if possible.

```
100 PRINT "FOR AX↑2 - B, WHAT ARE A AND B";
110 INPUT A, B
120 IF A <= 0 THEN 140
130 IF B > 0 THEN 160
140 PRINT "A AND B MUST BE POSITIVE. TRY AGAIN."
150 GOTO 110
160 LET S = INT(SQR(A) + .5)
170 IF ABS(SQR(A)-S) >= .001 THEN 200
180 LET S = INT(SQR(B) + .5)
190 IF ABS(SQR(B)-S) < .001 THEN 220
200 PRINT "CANNOT BE FACTORED"
210 GOTO 240
220 PRINT "FACTORS ARE (";SQR(A);"X +";SQR(B);")";
230 PRINT "(";SQR(A);"X -";SQR(B);")"
240 PRINT "ANY MORE BINOMIALS TO BE FACTORED (1=YES, 0=NO)";
250 INPUT Z
260 IF Z = 1 THEN 110
270 END
```

TRY THESE   Write a BASIC program for each problem.

1. The INT function can be used to decide whether one integer is a factor of another integer. For example, if $A/B = INT(A/B)$, then B is a divisor of A. Given a positive integer A, print all the factors of A. For example, for $A = 36$, print 1 2 3 4 6 9 12 18 36.

2. Given two positive integers a and b, print all common factors of a and b.

3. For binomials of the form $Ax + B$, given integers A and B, decide whether A and B have a common factor other than 1 or -1. If they do, factor out the largest common factor of A and B. For example, for 3 X + 12, print 3 (X + 4).

4. Given nonzero integers b and c, factor trinomials of the form $x^2 + bx + c$ over the integers, if possible.

5. Given integers a, b, and c, factor $ax^2 + bx + c$ over the integers, if possible.

BASIC: ADDING FRACTIONS

A computer cannot handle fractions as you do. If you enter $2/5$ into a computer, the machine will divide 2 by 5 and return a decimal, 0.4. To program a computer to compute the sum of two fractions in fractional form, you must include the following algebra in the program.

$$\frac{a}{b} + \frac{c}{d} = \frac{ad}{bd} + \frac{bc}{bd} = \frac{ad + bc}{bd}$$

Description: This program computes and prints the sum of two fractions.

Program:
```
100 PRINT "FOR THE FRACTIONS A/B AND C/D, WHAT"
110 PRINT "ARE A, B, C, AND D (NONE 0)";
120 INPUT A, B, C, D
130 IF A*B*C*D <> 0 THEN 160
140 PRINT "NO ZERO VALUES. TRY AGAIN."
150 GOTO 120
160 LET N = A*D + B*C
170 LET D1 = B*D
180 IF N = 0 THEN 310
190 LET N1 = ABS(N)
200 LET D2 = ABS(D1)
210 IF N1 > D2 THEN 240
220 LET S = N1
230 GOTO 250
240 LET S = D2
250 FOR Y = S TO 1 STEP -1
260 IF N1/Y <> INT(N1/Y) THEN 280
270 IF D2/Y = INT(D2/Y) THEN 290
280 NEXT Y
290 LET N = N/Y
300 LET D1 = D1/Y
310 PRINT "(";A;"/";B;") + (";C;"/";D;") = ";
320 IF ABS(D1) = 1 THEN 380
330 IF N * D1 < 0 THEN 360
340 PRINT ABS(N);"/";ABS(D1)
350 GOTO 390
360 PRINT "-";ABS(N);"/";ABS(D1)
370 GOTO 390
380 PRINT N * D1
390 PRINT
400 PRINT "ANY MORE FRACTIONS (1=YES, 0=NO)";
410 INPUT Z
420 IF Z = 1 THEN 120
430 END
```

TRY THESE   Rewrite the program so that it does each of the following.

1. Subtract C/D from A/B.   2. Multiply A/B and C/D.   3. Divide A/B by C/D.

BASIC: COMPUTING SQUARE ROOTS

BASIC has the SQR function for computing square roots. But how does a function like this work? The **algorithm** (step–by–step procedure) for approximating the square root of a positive real number is shown below.

Procedure

1. Make an estimate, e, of the square root. For example, let e be the greatest integer less than or equal to $\frac{1}{2}x$.
2. Divide x by e. Call this quotient a.
3. Take the average of a and e. Let this average become e_2.
4. Repeat steps 2 and 3 until the difference between a and e becomes less than a specified tolerance (for example, 0.1). Then, that value of e is the approximate square root.

Description: The program computes and prints the square root of any positive integer without using the SQR function.

```
100 PRINT "ENTER A POSITIVE REAL NUMBER."
110 INPUT X
120 IF X <= 0 THEN 100
130 LET E = INT(X/2)              ←——— Step 1
140 LET A = X/E                   ←——— Step 2
150 LET E = (A + E)/2             ←——— Step 3
160 IF ABS(A - E) > .0001 THEN 140 ←——— Step 4 (Tolerance: 0.0001)
170 PRINT "SQUARE ROOT OF";X;" = ";E
180 PRINT
190 PRINT "ANY MORE SQUARE ROOTS (1=YES, 0=NO)";
200 INPUT Z
210 IF Z = 1 THEN 100
220 END
```

TRY THESE   Run the program for the following values of x.

1. $x = 3$ **2.** $x = 17$ **3.** $x = 89$ **4.** $x = 7$

5. Add statements to the program so that the successive values of e and a are printed in two labeled columns.

Write a BASIC program for each problem.

6. Given the area of a square, compute and print the length of a side. (See Example 3 on page 485.)

7. Given the area of a circle, compute and print the length of the radius. (Use $\pi = 3.14$) (See Exercise 54 on page 486.)

8. Given the lengths of the two legs of a right triangle, compute and print the length of the hypotenuse. (See Example 1 on page 494.)

BASIC: SOLVING QUADRATIC EQUATIONS

Description: The program computes and prints the roots of quadratic equations of the form $ax^2 + bx + c = 0$ ($a \neq 0$). If the equation has no real roots, the output will be NO REAL ROOTS.

```
100 PRINT "FOR THE EQUATION A*X↑2 + B*X + C = 0,"
110 PRINT "WHAT ARE A,B,C";
120 INPUT A, B, C
130 LET D = B↑2 - 4*A*C
140 IF D = 0 THEN 200
150 IF D < 0 THEN 230
160 LET X1 = (-B + SQR(D))/(2*A)
170 LET X2 = (-B - SQR(D))/(2*A)
180 PRINT "THE TWO ROOTS ARE ";X1;"AND ";X2
190 GOTO 240
200 LET X = -B/(2*A)
210 PRINT "DOUBLE ROOT IS ";X
220 GOTO 240
230 PRINT "NO REAL ROOTS"
240 PRINT
250 PRINT "ANY MORE EQUATIONS TO SOLVE (1=YES, 0=NO)";
260 INPUT Z
270 IF Z = 1 THEN 120
280 END
```

TRY THESE   Run the program for the following values of a, b, and c.

1. $a = 1$; $b = 1$; $c = -6$
2. $a = 1$; $b = -8$; $c = 15$
3. $a = 1$; $b = 8$; $c = -42$
4. $a = 3$; $b = 12$; $c = 10$
5. $a = -4$; $b = 2$; $c = -3$
6. $a = 4$; $b = -20$; $c = 25$

Write each equation in the form $ax^2 + bx + c = 0$. Then use the program to find the roots.

7. $4x = 3x^2 + 6$
8. $4x^2 = 5x$
9. $24x^2 = 18$
10. $2x^2 = 7x - 6$
11. $6x^2 + 3 = 7x$
12. $13x = 2x^2 + 15$

13. The program assumes that $a \neq 0$. Add statements to the program to print NOT A QUADRATIC EQUATION if 0 is entered for a.

Write a BASIC program for each problem.

14. For a function of the form $y = ax^2 + bx + c$, enter a, b, and c ($a \neq 0$). Print whether the function has 0, 1, or 2 real zeros.

15. Solve equations of the form $(ax + b)^2 = c$. If $c < 0$, print NO REAL ROOTS.

COMPUTER BANK
Part 2: Investigating Algebra

The following is a listing of the computer investigations that are included in Part II of the Computer Bank. The related textbook page for each investigation is also indicated. For each investigation, you will need the *Investigating Algebra with the Computer* software.

INVESTIGATION: Using Statistics: Predicting

Program: SCATPLOT

Objectives: To use the computer to draw scatterplots and draw the median line of fit
To have the computer predict a Y value on the median line of fit for any given X value

1. **a.** With BASIC loaded into the computer and the disk in drive 1 (or drive A), run the program SCATPLOT by typing the appropriate command.
   Apple: RUN SCATPLOT   IBM: RUN "SCATPLOT"
   Be sure to press the RETURN key after typing the command.

   b. Read the opening messages of the program.

2. Enter the pairs of values at the right into the computer. Be sure to type the comma between the pairs. Also press RETURN after entering each pair. After typing the last pair, answer PAIR #11? by typing 999, 999 (and pressing RETURN).

0.2, 70	1.1, 75
1.2, 80	1.5, 79
1.6, 83	1.9, 84
2.2, 86	2.4, 86
2.7, 89	3.0, 91

3. **a.** The computer draws the **scatterplot.** After studying the plot, press any key to see the **median line of fit.**

   b. What is the equation of the line of fit?

   c. To the question PREDICT Y VALUE FOR WHICH X VALUE? enter 3.5 (and press RETURN).

   d. What is the predicted Y value on the line of fit for X = 3.5?

   e. To ANOTHER GRAPH? enter Y (yes).

4. **a.** Enter the pairs of values below. Enter 999,999 to end the list.
   1,4   2,7   3,6   5,9   6,10   7,12   9,12   10,13   11,15   12,16

   b. Press any key to see the median line of fit.

   c. What is the equation of the line of fit?

   d. To PREDICT Y VALUE FOR WHICH X VALUE? enter 15.

   e. What is the predicted Y value for X = 15?

TRY THESE   Use the computer to draw the scatterplot of each set of data. In each case record the equation of the line of fit. Then enter the X value and record the predicted Y value for that X value.

5.

X	10	20	20	25	30	35	40	45	50	60
Y	10	12	11	14	18	23	30	29	31	35

Predict Y for X = 53.

6.

X	17.5	18.0	19.0	19.5	20.5	21.0	22.5	23.5	25.0	27.0
Y	8.7	8.5	8.4	7.9	7.8	8.0	7.4	7.1	6.8	6.1

Predict Y for X = 18.0.

INVESTIGATION: Graphing $y = |Ax + B|$

Program: ABSVAL1

Objectives: To use the computer to graph equations of the form $y = |Ax + B|$

To predict the x intercept of the graph of an equation of the form $y = |Ax + B|$

To predict the slopes of the arms of the graph of an equation of the form $y = |Ax + B|$

PART 1

1. **a.** With BASIC loaded into the computer and the disk in drive 1 (or drive A), run the program ABSVAL1 by typing the appropriate command.
   Apple: RUN ABSVAL1   IBM: RUN "ABSVAL1"
   Be sure to press the RETURN key after typing the command.

2. Have the computer graph the equation $y = |x|$. Enter 1 for A and 0 for B. With the graph on the screen, answer the following questions.
   a. The graph is shaped like what letter of the alphabet?
   b. The graph lies in which quadrants?
   c. What is the x intercept of the graph?
   d. What are the slopes of the two "arms" or "branches" of the graph?

3. **a.** Answer Y (yes) to ANOTHER GRAPH? and N (no) to CLEAR THE SCREEN?.
   b. Have the computer graph the equation $y = |2x|$. That is, enter 2 for A and 0 for B.
   c. The graph is shaped like what letter?
   d. The graph lies in which quadrants?
   e. What is the x intercept?   **f.** What are the slopes of the arms?

4. Before having the computer graph $y = |3x|$, predict the x intercept and the slopes of the arms of the graph.
   a. x intercept?   **b.** slopes?

5. Without clearing the screen, graph $y = |3x|$. (Use A $= 3$ and B $= 0$.)
   a. Was your prediction for the x intercept correct?
   b. Was your prediction for the slopes correct?

6. Answer Y to ANOTHER GRAPH? and Y to CLEAR THE SCREEN?. Then graph $y = |-2x|$. (A $= -2$, B $= 0$)
   a. What is the x intercept?   **b.** What are the slopes of the arms?
   c. The graph is the same as that of what equation graphed earlier?

7. *Complete:* For the graph of $y = |ax|$, the x intercept is __?__ and the slopes of the arms are __?__ and __?__.

Clear the screen each time and have the computer graph the following equations. In each case, predict the slopes of the arms before seeing the graph.

8. $y = |.5x|$ **9.** $y = |-4x|$ **10.** $y = |-x|$ **11.** $y = |5x|$

PART 2

1. Clear the screen and graph $y = |x + 1|$. Enter 1 for A and 1 for B.
  a. The graph is shaped like what letter?
  b. The graph is in which quadrants?
  c. What is the x intercept?   **d.** What are the slopes of the arms?

2. Graph $y = |x - 2|$. Do not clear the screen. (Enter 1 for A and -2 for B.)
  a. What is the x intercept?   **b.** What are the slopes of the arms?

3. Before graphing $y = |x + 3|$, predict the x intercept and the slopes of the arms.   **a.** x intercept?   **b.** slopes?

4. Without clearing the screen, graph $y = |x + 3|$. Were your predictions for the x intercept and the slopes correct?

TRY THESE Clear the screen and have the computer graph the following equations on the same axes. In each case, predict the x intercept before seeing the graph.

5. $y = |x - 1|$ **6.** $y = |x - 3|$
7. $y = |x + 2|$ **8.** $y = |x + 4|$

PART 3

1. Clear the screen. Then graph $y = |2x - 4|$. (Enter 2 for A and $- 4$ for B.)
  a. The graph is shaped like what letter?
  b. The graph is which quadrants?
  c. What is the x intercept?   **d.** What are the slopes of the arms?

2. Repeat step 1 for $y = |3x + 6|$.   **a.** x intercept?   **b.** slopes?

3. Before seeing the graph of $y = |2x + 8]$, predict the x intercept and the slopes of the arms.   **a.** x intercept?   **b.** slopes?

4. Clear the screen and graph $y = |2x + 8|$. Were your predictions correct?

5. Repeat steps 3–4 for $y = |-2x + 6|$. **a.** x intercept?   **b.** slopes?

6. Repeat steps 3–4 for $y = |-x + 4]$. **a.** x intercept?   **b.** slopes?

7. *Complete:* The graph of $y = |Ax + B|$ (with $a \neq 0$) is shaped like the letter
  __?__ and lies in quadrants __?__ and __?__. The x intercept is __?__ and the
  slopes of the arms are __?__ and __?__.

TRY THESE Predict the x intercept and the slopes of the arms of the graph of each equation. Then clear the screen and have the computer graph the equation. Correct your predictions if they were wrong.

8. $y = 2x + 1$ **9.** $y = 3x = 2$ **10.** $y = -5x - 4$

INVESTIGATION: Graphing y = |Ax + B| + C

Program: ABSVAL2

Objectives: To use the computer to graph equations of the form $y = |Ax + B| + C$
To predict the coordinates of the vertex and the slopes of the arms of the graph.

PART 1

1. **a.** With BASIC loaded into the computer and the disk in drive 1 (or drive A), run the program ABSVAL2 by typing the appropriate command.
   Apple: RUN ABSVAL2   IBM: RUN "ABSVAL2"
   Be sure to press the RETURN key after typing the command.

   b. Read the opening messages of the program.

2. **a.** Have the computer graph the equation $y = |x|$. Enter 1 for A, 0 for B, and 0 for C.

   b. The vertex of the graph is the endpoint where the two arms meet. What are the coordinates of the vertex of the graph? (_?_, _?_)

   c. What are the slopes of the arms of the graph?

3. **a.** Answer Y (yes) to ANOTHER GRAPH and N (no) to CLEAR THE SCREEN?.

   b. Have the computer graph $y = |x| + 3$. That is, enter 1 for A, 0 for B, and 3 for C.

   c. What are the coordinates of the vertex?

   d. What are the slopes of the arms?

4. **a.** Before having the computer graph $y = |x| - 2$, predict the coordinates of the vertex and the slopes of the arms.

   b. Without clearing the screen, graph $y = |x| - 2$. (A = 1, B = 0, C = -2)

   c. Were your predictions for the vertex and the slopes correct?

5. Answer Y to ANOTHER GRAPH? and Y to CLEAR THE SCREEN?. Then graph $y = |2x| + 4$. (A = 2, B = 0, C = 4) Give the following.
   a. coordinates of the vertex?   **b.** slopes of the arms?

6. Repeat step 5 for $y = |-3x| - 1$. (A = -3, B = 0, C = -1)

7. **a.** Before graphing $y = |4x| - 6$, predict the coordinates of the vertex and the slopes of the arms of the graph.

   b. Without clearing the screen, graph $y = |4x| - 6$. Were your predictions correct?

8. Repeat step 7 for $y = |-2x| + 5$.

Clear the screen and graph the following equations on the same screen. In each case, predict the coordinates of the vertex and the slopes of the arms before seeing the graph. Then check your predictions from the graph.

9. $y = |x| + 2$ **10.** $y = |x| + 5$ **11.** $y = |x| - 3$ **12.** $y = |x| - 7$
13. $y = |5x| + 6$ **14.** $y = |-4x| + 1$ **15.** $y = |-5x| - 7$ **16.** $y = |.5x| - 8$

PART 2

1. Clear the screen and graph $y = |x + 1| + 2$. (A = 1, B = 1, and C = 2.)

  a. What are the coordinates of the vertex?

  b. What are the slopes of the arms?

2. Repeat step 1 for $y = |x - 2| + 3$. Do not clear the screen. (A = 1, B = -2, C = 3)

3. **a.** Before having the computer graph $y = |x + 3| - 4$, predict the coordinates of the vertex and the slopes of the arms.

  b. Without clearing the screen, graph $y = |x + 3| - 4$. Were your predictions for the intercepts and the slopes correct?

4. Clear the screen and graph $y = |2x - 4| - 5$. Give the following.

  a. coordinates of the vertex? **b.** slopes of the arms?

5. Without clearing the screen, repeat step 4 for $y = |3x - 9| + 1$.

6. **a.** Before graphing $y = |4x + 12| - 2$, predict the coordinates of the vertex and the slopes of the arms.

  b. Without clearing the screen, graph $y = |4x + 12| - 2$. Were your predictions correct?

7. Repeat step 6 for $y = |-3x + 6| - 7$.

8. *Complete*: For the graph of $y = |Ax + B| + C$ (A ≠ 0), the vertex is (_?_ , _?_) and the slopes of the arms are _?_ and _?_ .

TRY THESE Clear the screen and graph the following equations on the same screen. In each case, predict the coordinates of the vertex and the slopes of the arms before seeing the graph. Then check your predictions from the graph.

9. $y = |x - 1| + 4$ **10.** $y = |x + 6| + 2$
11. $y = |2x + 8| - 1$ **12.** $y = |3x - 15| - 6$
13. $y = |-4x - 12| + 5$ **14.** $y = |-.5x + 4| - 8$

INVESTIGATION: Slope-Intercept Form of a Line

Program: SLOPEINT

Objectives: To use the computer to graph equations of the form $y = Mx + B$
To predict the slope and y intercept of a line before graphing

PART 1

1. **a.** With BASIC loaded into the computer and the disk in drive 1 (or drive A), run the program SLOPEINT by typing the appropriate command.
    Apple: RUN SLOPEINT   IBM: RUN "SLOPEINT"
    Be sure to press the RETURN key after typing the command.
   b. Read the opening messages of the program.

2. Use the program to draw the graph of $y = 2x + 3$.
   a. Type 2 for M and press RETURN.
   b. Enter 3 for B (and press RETURN).

3. With the graph on the screen, answer the following questions.
   a. Is the graph a straight line?
   b. What is the y coordinate of the point where the graph crosses the y axis? This value is called the y intercept of the graph.
   c. Use the point $(-1,1)$ and the point where the graph crosses the y axis to compute the slope. What is the slope of the graph?

4. **a.** Answer Y (yes) to the questions ANOTHER GRAPH? and CLEAR THE SCREEN?.
   b. Graph the equation $y = 4x - 1$. Enter 4 for M and -1 for B.
   c. What is the y intercept?
   d. Use the y intercept and the point $(1,3)$ to compute the slope. What is the slope?

5. Answer Y to ANOTHER GRAPH? and Y to CLEAR THE SCREEN?. Then, before having the computer graph $y = -3x + 2$, predict the y intercept and the slope of the graph.
   a. y intercept?   **b.** slope?

6. Now have the computer graph $y = -3x + 2$. (M $= -3$ and B $= 2$.)
   a. Was your prediction for the y intercept correct?
   b. Was your prediction for the slope correct?

7. Repeat steps 5 and 6 for the equation $y = .5x - 3$. Do not leave the previous graph on the screen. Were your predictions correct?

8. *Complete:* For the graph of the equation $y = Mx + B$, the slope equals __?__ and the y intercept equals __?__ .

Have the computer graph the following equations. In each case, predict the slope and *y* intercept before seeing the graph. Clear the screen before each graph is drawn.

9. $y = -.5x - 4$ **10.** $y = x + 5$

11. $y = 1.5x - 2$ **12.** $y = -x + 2.5$

PART 2   **1.** Clear the screen and graph $y = 3x$. That is, enter 3 for M and 0 for B.

      a. Does the graph go through the origin?

      b. What is the *y* intercept of the graph?

      c. Does the *y* intercept equal the value of B in the equation?

      d. What is the slope of the line?

      e. Does the slope equal the value of M in the equation?

   2. a. Before graphing $y = -2x$, predict the *y* intercept and the slope.

      b. Now clear the screen and graph $y = -2x$. Were your predictions correct?

Have the computer graph the following equations. In each case, predict the slope and *y* intercept before seeing the graph. Clear the screen before each graph is drawn.

3. $y = 2x$ **4.** $y = -3x$ **5.** $y = 2.5x$ **6.** $y = -4x$

PART 3   **1.** Clear the screen and graph $y = 4$. In this case, M = 0 and B = 4.

      a. The graph is what kind of straight line?

      b. What is the *y* intercept of the graph?

      c. Does the *y* intercept equal the value of B?

      d. What is the slope of the line?

      e. Does the slope equal the value of M for this equation?

   2. a. Before graphing $y = -2$, predict the *y* intercept and the slope.

      b. Now graph $y = -2$. (Enter 0 for M.) Were your predictions correct?

Have the computer graph these equations. In each case, predict the slope and *y* intercept before seeing the graph. Clear the screen before each graph is drawn.

3. $y = 1$ **4.** $y = -5$ **5.** $y = 2.5$ **6.** $y = -1$

INVESTIGATION: Graphing Systems of Equations

Program: SYSTEMS

Objective: To use the computer to solve systems of two linear equations by graphing

1. **a.** With BASIC loaded into the computer and the disk in drive 1 (or drive A), run the program SYSTEMS by typing the appropriate command.

   Apple: RUN SYSTEMS   IBM: RUN "SYSTEMS"

   Be sure to press the RETURN key after typing the command.

   b. Read the opening messages of the program.

2. Use the program to draw the graph of these two equations on the same axes.

$$\begin{cases} x + 2y = 5 \\ 3x - y = 1 \end{cases}$$

   a. For the first equation enter 1 for A, 2 for B, and 5 for C.

   b. Is the graph of the first equation a straight line?

   c. For the second equation enter 3 for A, -1 for B, and 1 for C.

   d. Is the graph of the second equation a straight line?

   e. At what point do the two graphs intersect? (__?__ , __?__)

   f. Substitute the x and y coordinates of the point of intersection into the first equation. Does a true sentence result?

   g. Substitute the coordinates of the intersection point into the second equation. Does a true sentence result?

3. **a.** Enter Y (yes) to the question ANOTHER SYSTEM?.

   b. Have the computer graph these equations on the same axes.

$$\begin{cases} 3x - 2y = 14 \quad\longleftarrow\quad A = 3, B = -2, C = 14 \\ 2x + 3y = -8 \quad\longleftarrow\quad A = 2, B = 3, \quad C = -8 \end{cases}$$

   c. What is the point of intersection of the two lines? (__?__ , __?__)

   d. Substitute the x and y coordinates of this point into the first equation. Do you get a true sentence?

   e. Substitute the x and y coordinates of this point into the second equation. Do you get a true sentence?

4. Repeat step 3 for this system. $\qquad \begin{cases} -3x + y = 4 \\ 10x - 7y = 5 \end{cases}$

   a. What is the point of intersection of the two lines?

   b. Substitute the x and y coordinates of the intersection point into both equations. Are both sentences true?

5. Repeat step 3 for this system.
$$\begin{cases} 6x - 2y = 12 \\ 3x - y = -4 \end{cases}$$

    a. Do the two lines intersect?

    b. Do the two equations have any common solution?

6. Repeat step 3 for this system.
$$\begin{cases} x + y = 6 \\ 2x + 2y = 12 \end{cases}$$

    a. What do you notice about the graphs of the two equations?

    b. How many common solutions do the two equations have?

TRY THESE

Have the computer graph each pair of equations on the same axes. Write the coordinates of the point of intersection of each pair or, if the lines do not intersect, write <u>no common point</u>. Check by substitution that the coordinates of the point of intersection make both equations true.

7. $\begin{cases} 3x + y = 11 \\ 2x - 3y = 11 \end{cases}$
        8. $\begin{cases} x + y = 7 \\ 2x - 3y = 14 \end{cases}$

9. $\begin{cases} 4x - 3y = 18 \\ -8x + 6y = 11 \end{cases}$
        10. $\begin{cases} -9x + 7y = -59 \\ 11x + 12y = 31 \end{cases}$

11. $\begin{cases} 2x = 14 \\ x - 2y = 3 \end{cases}$ (NOTE: B = 0)
    12. $\begin{cases} 10y = -30 \\ 4x + 2y = -2 \end{cases}$ (NOTE: A = 0)

Put each equation in the form $Ax + By = C$. Then use the program to determine the common solution, if any, of each system. Check each solution by substitution.

13. $\begin{cases} y = 3x + 2 \\ y = 6x - 1 \end{cases}$
        14. $\begin{cases} 4x = 9y - 7 \\ 3 = 3x - 4y \end{cases}$

15. $\begin{cases} 2y = 11x + 15 \\ y + 3x = 0 \end{cases}$
        16. $\begin{cases} 16 = -2x \\ 20 + x = 2y \end{cases}$

17. $\begin{cases} 3x - y = 7 \\ 4y = 12x - 15 \end{cases}$
        18. $\begin{cases} y = 5x - 2 \\ 15x - 3y = 6 \end{cases}$

INVESTIGATION: Graphing Quadratic Functions

Program: PARA1

Objectives: To use the computer to graph equations of the form $y = Ax^2 + Bx + C$ and discover that the graph is a parabola

To read the zeros of a quadratic function from its graph

1. **a.** With BASIC loaded into the computer and the disk in drive 1 (or drive A), run the program PARA1 by typing the appropriate command.
   Apple: RUN PARA1   IBM: RUN "PARA1"
   Be sure to press the RETURN key after typing the command.
   b. Read the opening messages of the program.

2. Use the program to draw the graph of $y = x^2$, as follows.
   a. Enter 1 for A and press RETURN.
   b. Enter 0 for B (and press RETURN).
   c. Enter 0 for C.
   d. Is the graph a straight line?

3. The graph of $y = x^2$ is called a **parabola.** Where does the parabola touch the x axis; that is, what is its x intercept?

4. **a.** Enter Y to ANOTHER GRAPH? and N to CLEAR THE SCREEN?.
   b. Graph $y = -3x^2$. Enter -3 for A, 0 for B, and 0 for C.

5. Answer these questions about the graph of $y = -3x^2$.
   a. Is the graph a parabola?
   b. What is the x intercept?
   c. The **zeros** of a function are the values for x which make the function equal zero. List any zeros of the function $y = -3x^2$.

6. **a.** Answer Y to ANOTHER GRAPH? and Y to CLEAR THE SCREEN?.
   b. Graph $y = x^2 + 2x$. Enter 1 for A, 2 for B, and 0 for C.

7. Answer these questions about the graph of $y = x^2 + 2x$.
   a. Is the graph a parabola?
   b. How many zeros (x intercepts) does this function have?
   c. List the zeros.

8. Clear the screen and graph $y = x^2 - 3x$. Enter $A = 1$, $B = -3$, and $C = 0$. What are the zeros of this function?

9. Clear the screen and graph $y = x^2 - x - 2$. ($A = 1$, $B = -1$, $C = -2$)
   a. How many zeros does this function have?   **b.** List the zeros.

TRY THESE Have the computer graph the following functions, each on a separate screen. List the zeros of each function. Estimate any zeros that are not integers to the nearest tenth.

10. $y = x^2 + 2x - 8$

11. $y = -x^2 + 4x$

12. $y = 2x^2 - 11x - 6$

13. $y = x^2 - 12x + 36$

INVESTIGATION: The Discriminant

Program: PARA2

Objectives: To use the computer to graph equations of the form $y = Ax^2 + Bx + C$
To use the discriminant to predict the number of zeros of the function before seeing its graph

1. **a.** With BASIC loaded into the computer and the disk in drive 1 (or drive A), run the program PARA2 by typing the appropriate command.
   Apple: RUN PARA2   IBM: RUN "PARA2"
   Be sure to press the RETURN key after typing the command.

   b. Read the opening messages of the program.

2. **a.** Use the program to graph the function $y = 3x^2 - 8x - 3$. Enter 3 for A, -8 for B, and -3 for C.

   b. After the graph is displayed, count the number of **zeros** of the function. That is, count the number of points where the graph crosses the x axis. How many zeros does it have?

   c. For a quadratic function $y = Ax^2 + Bx + C$, the value of $B^2 - 4AC$ is called the **discriminant** of the function. Compute the value of $B^2 - 4AC$ for $y = 3x^2 - 8x - 3$. Enter this value into the computer. If your value is incorrect, the computer will tell you to try again. What is the correct value?

   d. Based on the discriminant, the computer prints the number of zeros of this function. Does this number agree with your answer to part **b** above?

3. Answer Y (yes) to ANOTHER GRAPH? . Then repeat step 2 for the function $y = x^2 + x + 2$. (A = 1, B = 1, C = 2). Be sure to count the zeros from the graph before computing the discriminant.

   a. number of zeros?   **b.** discriminant?

4. Repeat step 2 for the function $y = x^2 + 4x + 4$. (A = 1, B = 4, C = 4)

   a. number of zeros?   **b.** discriminant?

5. **a.** What is the discriminant of $y = 2x^2 - x - 6$? (A = 2, B = -1, C = -6)

   b. Predict the number of zeros of the graph of $y = 2x^2 - x - 6$.

   c. Have the computer graph the function. Was your prediction correct?

   d. Enter your value for the discriminant. Was it correct?

6. Repeat step 5 for the function $y = 4x^2 - 4x + 1$.

   a. discriminant?   **b.** number of zeros?

7. Repeat step 5 for the function $y = -x^2 + 3x - 4$. Notice that A = -1.

   a. discriminant?   **b.** number of zeros?

8. *Complete*: For the quadratic function $y = Ax^2 + Bx + C$,

    a. if the discriminant is positive, the function has __?__ zero(s);

    b. if the discriminant is negative, the function has __?__ zero(s);

    c. if the discriminant is zero, the function has __?__ zero(s).

TRY THESE **Compute the discriminant of each function and predict the number of zeros. Then have the computer graph the function. Check your predictions.**

    9. $y = x^2 + 2x + 7$ **10.** $y = 2x^2 - 5x$ (NOTE: C = 0.)

    11. $y = 3x^2 + 5x - 2$ **12.** $y = 6x^2 + 5$ (NOTE: B = 0.)

    13. $y = -3x^2 + 4x + 6$ **14.** $y = -x^2 - 6x - 9$

INVESTIGATION: Maximum and Minimum

Program: PARA3

Objectives: To use the computer to graph functions of the form $y = Ax^2 + Bx + C$ and draw the axis of symmetry

To discover that the parabola opens upward when $A > 0$ and downward when $A < 0$

To discover that the x coordinate of the vertex is $\frac{-B}{2A}$ and the equation of the axis of symmetry is $x = \frac{-B}{2A}$

    1. a. With BASIC loaded into the computer and the disk in drive 1 (or drive A), run the program PARA3 by typing the appropriate command.

              Apple: RUN PARA3   IBM: RUN "PARA3"

         Be sure to press the RETURN key after typing the command.

      b. Read the opening messages of the program.

    2. a. Have the computer graph $y = x^2$. Enter 1 for A, 0 for B, and 0 for C.

      b. The computer graphs the parabola and draws the **axis of symmetry.** It also prints the equation of the axis of symmetry and the coordinates of the turning point or **vertex** of the parabola.

      c. Does the parabola open upward or downward?

      d. What are the coordinates of the vertex? (__?__ , __?__)

      e. What is the equation of the axis of symmetry? $x =$ __?__

    3. a. Enter Y (yes) for ANOTHER GRAPH?.

      b. Have the computer graph $y = -2x^2$. Enter -2 for A, 0 for B, and 0 for C.

      c. Does the parabola open upward or downward?

d. What are the coordinates of the vertex?

e. What is the equation of the axis of symmetry?

4. Repeat step 3 for $y = x^2 - 2x + 3$. (A = 1, B = −2, C = 3)

   a. open upward or downward?   **b.** coordinates of the vertex?

   c. equation of the axis of symmetry?

5. **a.** For the function $y = x^2 - 2x + 3$ above, compute $\frac{-B}{2A}$.

   b. What connection does this value have to the vertex of the parabola?

   c. What connection does this value have to the axis of symmetry equation?

6. **a.** For $y = 2x^2 - 16x + 35$, compute $\frac{-b}{2a}$.

   b. Before graphing the function, predict whether it will open up or down.

   c. Predict the equation of the axis of symmetry.

7. Have the computer graph $y = 2x^2 - 16x + 35$.

   a. Does the parabola open the way you predicted?

   b. Was your prediction of the equation of the axis of symmetry correct?

   c. What are the coordinates of the vertex?

8. Before graphing $y = -3x^2 + 6x - 2$, make predictions about the graph.

   a. open upward or downward?   **b.** equation of the axis of symmetry?

   c. x coordinate of the vertex?

9. Have the computer graph $y = -3x^2 + 6x - 2$. Were your predictions correct?

10. Complete for the parabola $y = Ax^2 + Bx + C$. (A ≠ 0)

    a. The parabola opens upward if $A > \underline{\ ?\ }$.

    b. The parabola opens downward if $\underline{\ ?\ }$.

    c. The x coordinate of the vertex of the parabola equals $\underline{\ ?\ }$.

    d. The equation of the axis of symmetry is $\underline{\ ?\ }$.

TRY THESE   Before having the computer graph each parabola, predict whether it will open upward or downward. Also predict the x coordinate of the vertex and the equation of the axis of symmetry. Check your predictions from the computer's graph. Also list the y coordinate of the vertex.

11. $y = x^2 + 6x + 7$ 12. $y = -2x^2 - 4x - 3$

13. $y = -5x^2 - 30x - 45$ 14. $y = x^2 + 2$

15. $y = 4x^2 - 8x$ 16. $y = -3x^2 + 4$

Table of Squares and Square Roots

No.	Square	Square Root	No.	Square	Square Root	No.	Square	Square Root
1	1	1.000	51	2601	7.141	101	10,201	10.050
2	4	1.414	52	2704	7.211	102	10,404	10.100
3	9	1.732	53	2809	7.280	103	10,609	10.149
4	16	2.000	54	2916	7.348	104	10,816	10.198
5	25	2.236	55	3025	7.416	105	11,025	10.247
6	36	2.449	56	3136	7.483	106	11,236	10.296
7	49	2.646	57	3249	7.550	107	11,449	10.344
8	64	2.828	58	3364	7.616	108	11,664	10.392
9	81	3.000	59	3481	7.681	109	11,881	10.440
10	100	3.162	60	3600	7.746	110	12,100	10.488
11	121	3.317	61	3721	7.810	111	12,321	10.536
12	144	3.464	62	3844	7.874	112	12,544	10.583
13	169	3.606	63	3969	7.937	113	12,769	10.630
14	196	3.742	64	4096	8.000	114	12,996	10.677
15	225	3.873	65	4225	8.062	115	13,225	10.724
16	256	4.000	66	4356	8.124	116	13,456	10.770
17	289	4.123	67	4489	8.185	117	13,689	10.817
18	324	4.243	68	4624	8.246	118	13,924	10.863
19	361	4.359	69	4761	8.307	119	14,161	10.909
20	400	4.472	70	4900	8.367	120	14,400	10.954
21	441	4.583	71	5041	8.426	121	14,641	11.000
22	484	4.690	72	5184	8.485	122	14,884	11.045
23	529	4.796	73	5329	8.544	123	15,129	11.091
24	576	4.899	74	5476	8.602	124	15,376	11.136
25	625	5.000	75	5625	8.660	125	15,625	11.180
26	676	5.099	76	5776	8.718	126	15,876	11.225
27	729	5.196	77	5929	8.775	127	16,129	11.269
28	784	5.292	78	6084	8.832	128	16,384	11.314
29	841	5.385	79	6241	8.888	129	16,641	11.358
30	900	5.477	80	6400	8.944	130	16,900	11.402
31	961	5.568	81	6561	9.000	131	17,161	11.446
32	1024	5.657	82	6724	9.055	132	17,424	11.489
33	1089	5.745	83	6889	9.110	133	17,689	11.533
34	1156	5.831	84	7056	9.165	134	17,956	11.576
35	1225	5.916	85	7225	9.220	135	18,225	11.619
36	1296	6.000	86	7396	9.274	136	18,496	11.662
37	1369	6.083	87	7569	9.327	137	18,769	11.705
38	1444	6.164	88	7744	9.381	138	19,044	11.747
39	1521	6.245	89	7921	9.434	139	19,321	11.790
40	1600	6.325	90	8100	9.487	140	19,600	11.832
41	1681	6.403	91	8281	9.539	141	19,881	11.874
42	1764	6.481	92	8464	9.592	142	20,164	11.916
43	1849	6.557	93	8649	9.644	143	20,449	11.958
44	1936	6.633	94	8836	9.695	144	20,736	12.000
45	2025	6.708	95	9025	9.747	145	21,025	12.042
46	2116	6.782	96	9216	9.798	146	21,316	12.083
47	2209	6.856	97	9409	9.849	147	21,609	12.124
48	2304	6.928	98	9604	9.899	148	21,904	12.166
49	2401	7.000	99	9801	9.950	149	22,201	12.207
50	2500	7.071	100	10,000	10.000	150	22,500	12.247

Table of Sines, Cosines, and Tangents

Angle	Sin	Cos	Tan	Angle	Sin	Cos	Tan
0°	.0000	1.0000	.0000	45°	.7071	.7071	1.0000
1	.0175	.9998	.0175	46	.7193	.6947	1.0355
2	.0349	.9994	.0349	47	.7314	.6820	1.0724
3	.0523	.9986	.0524	48	.7431	.6691	1.1106
4	.0698	.9976	.0699	49	.7547	.6561	1.1504
5	.0872	.9962	.0875	50	.7660	.6428	1.1918
6	.1045	.9945	.1051	51	.7771	.6293	1.2349
7	.1219	.9925	.1228	52	.7880	.6157	1.2799
8	.1392	.9903	.1405	53	.7986	.6018	1.3270
9	.1564	.9877	.1584	54	.8090	.5878	1.3764
10	.1736	.9848	.1763	55	.8192	.5736	1.4281
11	.1908	.9816	.1944	56	.8290	.5592	1.4826
12	.2079	.9781	.2126	57	.8387	.5446	1.5399
13	.2250	.9744	.2309	58	.8480	.5299	1.6003
14	.2419	.9703	.2493	59	.8572	.5150	1.6643
15	.2588	.9659	.2679	60	.8660	.5000	1.7321
16	.2756	.9613	.2867	61	.8746	.4848	1.8040
17	.2924	.9563	.3057	62	.8829	.4695	1.8807
18	.3090	.9511	.3249	63	.8910	.4540	1.9626
19	.3256	.9455	.3443	64	.8988	.4384	2.0503
20	.3420	.9397	.3640	65	.9063	.4226	2.1445
21	.3584	.9336	.3839	66	.9135	.4067	2.2460
22	.3746	.9272	.4040	67	.9205	.3907	2.3559
23	.3907	.9205	.4245	68	.9272	.3746	2.4751
24	.4067	.9135	.4452	69	.9336	.3584	2.6051
25	.4226	.9063	.4663	70	.9397	.3420	2.7475
26	.4384	.8988	.4877	71	.9455	.3256	2.9042
27	.4540	.8910	.5095	72	.9511	.3090	3.0777
28	.4695	.8829	.5317	73	.9563	.2924	3.2709
29	.4848	.8746	.5543	74	.9613	.2756	3.4874
30	.5000	.8660	.5774	75	.9659	.2588	3.7321
31	.5150	.8572	.6009	76	.9703	.2419	4.0108
32	.5299	.8480	.6249	77	.9744	.2250	4.3315
33	.5446	.8387	.6494	78	.9781	.2079	4.7046
34	.5592	.8290	.6745	79	.9816	.1908	5.1446
35	.5736	.8192	.7002	80	.9848	.1736	5.6713
36	.5878	.8090	.7265	81	.9877	.1564	6.3138
37	.6018	.7986	.7536	82	.9903	.1392	7.1154
38	.6157	.7880	.7813	83	.9925	.1219	8.1443
39	.6293	.7771	.8098	84	.9945	.1045	9.5144
40	.6428	.7660	.8391	85	.9962	.0872	11.4301
41	.6561	.7547	.8693	86	.9976	.0698	14.3007
42	.6691	.7431	.9004	87	.9986	.0523	19.0811
43	.6820	.7314	.9325	88	.9994	.0349	28.6363
44	.6947	.7193	.9657	89	.9998	.0175	57.2900
45	.7071	.7071	1.0000	90	1.0000	.0000	

GLOSSARY

Abscissa   In an ordered pair, the first number, or x coordinate, is the *abscissa*. (Page 175)

Absolute value   The *absolute value* of a real number x is the distance of x from 0. It is written $|x|$. (Page 53)

Additive inverses   *Additive inverses* are the same distance from zero on the number line. Their sum is zero. (Page 58)

Algebraic expression   An *algebraic expression* contains at least one variable. (Page 1)

Arithmetic mean   The *arithmetic mean* of a set of numbers, scores, and so on, is the sum of the elements in the set divided by the number of values. (Page 79)

Axis of symmetry   A parabola can be folded so that its right side fits exactly over its left side. The line on which this fold can be made is called the *axis of symmetry*. (Page 554)

Binomial   A *binomial* is the sum or difference of two monomials. (Page 347)

Combining like terms   To *combine like terms* means to add or subtract like terms. (Page 64)

Composite number   A *composite number* is any integer greater than 1 that is not prime. (Page 377)

Compound sentence   A *compound sentence* can be written as two simple sentences joined by a connective, such as <u>and</u> or <u>or</u>. (Page 295)

Conditional statement   In mathematics, a statement in the if-then form is a *conditional statement*. (Page 600)

Congruent angles   *Congruent angles* are angles that have the same measure. (Page 579)

Conjunction   A compound sentence with <u>and</u> is a *conjunction*. (Page 296)

Consistent system   A system of equations that has a solution set is *consistent*. (Page 244)

Constant of variation   In the direct variation $y = kx$, k is called the *constant of variation*. (Page 227)

Converse   The *converse* of a conditional statement is formed by interchanging the p and q statements. (Page 601)

Coordinate plane   A plane that associates number pairs or coordinates with points is called a *coordinate plane*. The x and y axes separate the coordinate plane into four regions or quadrants. (Page 175)

Cosine ratio   In a right triangle, the *cosine* of an acute angle is the ratio $\dfrac{\text{length of adjacent side}}{\text{length of hypotenuse}}$. (Page 587)

Counting numbers   The set of *counting numbers* or natural numbers is the set of numbers whose members are 1 and every number found by adding 1 to a member of the set. (Page 26)

Density Property   Between any two real numbers there is another real number. (Page 482)

Direct proof   A *direct proof* of a theorem shows that the then-statement follows from the if-statement. (Page 604)

Direct variation   The equation $y = kx$, where k is a constant, expresses *direct variation* between x and y. (Page 227)

Discriminant   The *discriminant* of the quadratic equation $ax^2 + bx + c = 0$ is the number $b^2 - 4ac$. (Page 551)

Disjunction   A compound sentence with <u>or</u> is a *disjunction*. (Page 295)

Distance Formula   If $P_1(x_1, y_1)$ and $P_2(x_2, y_2)$ are any two points in the coordinate plane, then the *distance*, d, between the points is given by the formula $d = \sqrt{(x_2 - x_1)^2 + (y_2 - y_1)^2}$. (Page 499)

Domain   For ordered pairs of a relation, the set of all first coordinates is the *domain* of the relation. (Page 181)

Equation A mathematical sentence that contains the symbol "=" is an *equation*. (Page 22)

Equivalent equations *Equivalent equations* have the same solutions for the same replacement set. (Page 95)

Equivalent inequalities Inequalities that have the same solution set are called *equivalent inequalities*. (Page 283)

Equivalent systems Systems of equations that have the same solution set are *equivalent systems*. (Page 249)

Evaluate To *evaluate* means to find the value. (Page 2)

Even number An *even number* is a number of the form 2*n*, where *n* is an integer. (Page 604)

Exponent The second power of 3 is written as 3^2. The raised two is called an *exponent*. The *exponent* indicates how many times a number is used as a factor. (Page 9)

Factor Since $35 = 7 \cdot 5$, 7 and 5 are *factors* of 35. (Page 377)

Field A set of numbers for which the field postulates hold for addition and multiplication is called a *field*. (Page 597)

Formula In a *formula*, variables and symbols are used to show how quantities are related. (Page 10)

Function A *function* is a relation for which no two ordered pairs have the same first element. (Page 181)

Half-plane If a line is drawn on the coordinate plane, a *half-plane* is the set of points that is on one side of the line. (Page 306)

Hypotenuse In a right triangle, the longest side is the *hypotenuse*. (Page 494)

Hypothesis In a proof, the if-statement is called the *hypothesis*. It is always taken to be true. (Page 604)

Inconsistent system A system of equations having no solution is *inconsistent*. (Page 244)

Inequality A mathematical sentence that uses $>$, $<$, or $\neq$ is an *inequality*. (Page 22)

Integers The set of *integers* consists of the set of whole numbers and their opposites. (Page 26)

Intersection of two lines The *intersection of two lines* is the set of points common to both lines. (Page 244)

Inverse variation If the product of two variables is a nonzero constant, the variables are in *inverse variation*. This can be expressed by the equation $xy = k$ or $y = \dfrac{k}{x}$, where k is the constant of variation. (Page 562)

Irrational number *Irrational numbers* cannot be represented in the form $\dfrac{a}{b}$, where a is an integer and b is a natural number. (Page 30)

Joint variation When one variable varies directly as the product of two or more variables, the variation is called *joint variation*. This can be expressed by the equation $x = kyz$. (Page 567)

Least common denominator The *least common denominator* (LCD) of two or more rational expressions is the smallest positive common multiple, called the least common multiple (LCM), of the denominators of the rational expressions. (Page 433)

Like radicals Radicals with the same radicands are *like radicals*. (Page 510)

Like terms *Like terms* have the same variables. In like terms, corresponding variables have the same exponents. (Page 64)

Linear equation An equation that can be written in the form $Ax + By = C$, where A, B and C are real numbers and A and B are not both zero, is a *linear equation* in two variables. (Page 187)

Linear function A function whose ordered pairs satisfy a linear equation is a *linear function*. (Page 187)

Mean   See arithmetic mean.

Median   The *median* of a set of data that contains an odd number of values is the middle measure. When the number of elements in the set of data is an even number, the median is the mean of the two middle measures. (Page 74)

Mode   In a listing of data, the measure that occurs most often. (Page 74)

Monomial   A *monomial* is a term that is the product of numbers and variables with nonnegative integral exponents. (Page 329)

Numerical expression   A *numerical expression* does not contain a variable. It contains at least one of the operations of addition, subtraction, multiplication, and division. (Page 2)

Odd number   An *odd number* is a number of the form $2n + 1$, where n is an integer. (Page 604)

Open sentence   An equation that contains at least 1 variable is an *open sentence. (Page 22)*

Ordered pair   An *ordered pair* is a pair of numbers, one of which is designated as first and the other as second. (Page 175)

Ordinate   In an ordered pair, the second number, or the *y* coordinate, is the *ordinate.* (Page 175)

Origin   In the coordinate plane, the axes cross at the point (0, 0), called the *origin.* (Page 175)

Percent   Percent means per hundred or hundredths. (Page 107)

Perfect square   A rational number is a *perfect square* if it is the square of a rational number. (Page 480)

Perimeter   The *perimeter* of a geometric figure is the distance around it. To find this *perimeter,* add the lengths of the sides. (Page 145)

Perpendicular   Two lines that are *perpendicular* to each other meet at 90° angles. (Page 175)

Polynomial   A *polynomial* is a monomial or the sum of monomials. (Page 347)

Postulate   A *postulate* is a statement that is assumed to be true. (Page 494)

Prime factorization   When a composite number is written as a product of prime-number factors or of powers of prime-number factors, the number is in *prime-factorization* form. (Page 377)

Prime number   A *prime number* is an integer greater than 1 that has exactly two positive integral factors, itself and 1. (Page 377)

Prime polynomial   When a polynomial has no polynomial factors with integral coefficients except itself and 1, it is a *prime polynomial* with respect to the integers. (Page 381)

Probability   *Probability* is a ratio between 0 and 1 which tells how likely it is that a certain event will happen. (Page 111)

Proportion   A *proportion* is a statement that shows that two ratios are equal. (Page 103)

Quadrant   A *quadrant* is one of four regions formed by the axes of a coordinate plane. (Page 175)

Quadratic equation   An equation that can be written in the form $ax^2 + bx + c = 0$, where a, b, and c are real numbers and $a \neq 0$, is a *quadratic equation.* (Page 529)

Quadratic formula   For any quadratic equation $ax^2 + bx + c = 0$, the solutions are $x = \dfrac{-b \pm \sqrt{b^2 - 4ac}}{2a}$. This is called the *quadratic formula.* (Page 539)

Quadratic function   A *quadratic function* is a function defined by the equation $y = ax^2 + bx + c$, where a, b and c are real numbers and $a \neq 0$. (Page 547)

Radical symbol   In the expression $\sqrt{25}$, $\sqrt{}$ is the *radical symbol.* (Page 477)

Radicand   In the expression $\sqrt{25}$, 25 is the *radicand.* (Page 477)

Range For ordered pairs, the set of all second coordinates is the *range*. (Page 181)

Rational expression A *rational expression* is an expression of the form $\frac{P}{Q}$, where P and Q are polynomials and $Q \neq 0$. (Page 421)

Rational number A *rational number* is a number that can be expressed in the form $\frac{a}{b}$, where a is an integer and b is not equal to 0. (Page 26)

Rationalizing the denominator Eliminating the radical in the denominator of a fraction is called *rationalizing the denominator.* (Page 506)

Real numbers The union of the set of rational numbers and the set of irrational numbers together is the set of *real numbers.* (Page 30)

Reciprocals Any two numbers whose product is 1 are called *reciprocals,* or multiplicative inverses, of each other. (Page 79)

Relation A *relation* is a set of ordered pairs. (Page 180)

Replacement set The *replacement set* is the set of numbers from which replacements for the variable are chosen. (Page 22)

Scientific notation When a number is represented as the product of some power of 10 and a number from 1 to 10, it is expressed in *scientific notation.* (Page 343)

Simplest form When the numerator and denominator of a rational expression have no common factors except 1 and -1, the expression is in *simplest form.* (Page 421)

Simplified radical A radical is in simplest form when the radicand does not contain a perfect square factor. (Page 488)

Sine ratio In a right triangle, the *sine* of an acute angle is the ratio $\frac{\text{length of opposite side}}{\text{length of hypotenuse}}$. (Page 587)

Slope The *slope* of a line is the ratio of the vertical change to the horizontal change between any two points on the line. That is,
$$\text{slope} = \frac{\text{vertical change}}{\text{horizontal change}}, \text{(horizontal change} \neq 0).$$ (Page 207)

Slope-intercept form of a linear equation The equation $y = mx + b$ is called the *slope-intercept form of the linear equation.* (Page 213)

Solution set A *solution set* of an open sentence is the set of numbers that makes the sentence true. (Page 22)

System of linear equations Two or more linear equations in the same two variables from a *system of linear equations.* (Page 243)

Tangent ratio In a right triangle, the *tangent* of an acute angle is the ratio $\frac{\text{length of opposite side}}{\text{length of adjacent side}}$. (Page 582)

Term A *term* is a real number, a variable, or the product of real numbers and variables. (Page 64)

Theorem A *theorem* is a statement that can be proved from postulates and definitions. (Page 494)

Trinomial A polynomial with three terms is called a *trinomial.* (Page 347)

Variable A *variable* is a letter representing one or more numbers. (Page 1)

Whole numbers The set of *whole numbers* is the set of counting numbers and zero. (Page 26)

x intercept The *x* coordinate of a point where the line intersects the *x* axis is called an *x intercept.* (Page 547)

y intercept The *y* coordinate at which a line crosses the *y* axis is called the *y intercept.* (Page 213)

Zeros of a function The *zeros of a function* are the values for which the function equals zero. (Page 548)

ANSWERS TO SELECTED EXERCISES

The answers are provided for all of the problems in the *Review Capsules*. For all other types of exercises, the answers to the odd-numbered problems are provided.

Chapter 1: Uses of Algebra

Exercises, pages 3–4

1. t **3.** s **5.** $62p$; $62(p)$ **7.** $19 - (6 + 2)$; there are no variables involved. **9.** n **11.** n; n **13.** a; d **15.** j; k; l **17.** i **19.** q added to 5; q increased by 5 **21.** r divided by s; the quotient of r and s **23.** n divided by t; the ratio of n and t **25.** q divided by 5; the quotient of q and 5 **27.** n added to t; the total of n and t **29.** $d + i$ **31.** $180 - a$ **33.** $4.50h$ **35.** $\frac{t}{24}$ **37.** 26 **39.** 13 **41.** 16 **43.** 0 **45.** 31 **47.** 23 **49.** 3 **51.** $\frac{2}{3}$ **53.** $\frac{1}{3}$ **55.** $\frac{2}{3}$ **57.** $\frac{1}{5}$ **59.** $2\frac{5}{8}$ **61.** 2; $n + 3$ **63.** $3r$; $4r$ **65.** $\frac{1}{8}d$

Exercises, pages 7–8

1. ( ), [ ], fraction bar **3.** Those within the innermost grouping symbols **5.** A **7.** M **9.** M **11.** 69 **13.** 84 **15.** 18 **17.** 57 **19.** 23 **21.** 100 **23.** 360 **25.** 7 **27.** 19 **29.** 1620 **31.** $\frac{1}{11}$ **33.** 1 **35.** 34 **37.** 160 **39.** 24 **41.** 44 **43.** $\frac{4}{23}$ **45.** 60 **47.** 18 **49.** 1 **51.** 8 **53.** 8.48 **55.** 105 **57.** 450 **59.** 1.9 **61.** $2\frac{4}{5}$ **63.** 2.25 **65.** $3 + [(3 + 3) \cdot 3]$ **67.** $(2 \cdot 12) \div (2 + 6)$ **69.** 27 divided by b; The quotient of 27 and b; The ratio of 27 and b **71.** $h + 5$ **73.** $s - 55$ **75.** $475 - 15w$ **77.** $355 + 35z$ **79.** 46 **81.** 78

Exercises, pages 11–13

1. The fourth power of 6 **3.** 4 **5.** $5 \cdot r \cdot r \cdot r$ **7.** $10 \cdot 10$ **9.** $2 \cdot a \cdot a \cdot a \cdot a \cdot a$ **11.** $\frac{4}{5} \cdot \frac{4}{5}$ **13.** $(\frac{1}{8})^4$ **15.** $r^2 - s$ **17.** 32 **19.** 1 **21.** 2.25 **23.** 1.1 **25.** $\frac{3}{5}$ **27.** 1 **29.** 52 **31.** 192 **33.** 19 **35.** 11 **37.** 108 **39.** 225 **41.** 216 **43.** 219 **45.** 27 **47.** $\frac{12}{25}$ **49.** 3 **51.** $\frac{3}{25}$ **53.** 1.69 cm² **55.** 57.76 cm² **57.** $\frac{2}{3}$ ft² **59.** 3.84 cm² **61.** 17 cm² **63.** $1\frac{1}{2}$ in² **65.** 20 **67.** 108 **69.** $\frac{1}{2}$, 0.0625, 1; $t = 0.25$ **71.** $1\frac{1}{2}$, 1.75, 1; $t = 1$ **73.** $\frac{1}{8}$, 0.0625, $\frac{1}{4}$; $t = 0.25$ **75.** 2, 4, 1; $t = 1$ **77.** $\frac{1}{4}$, 0.0625, 1; $t = 0.25$ **79.** 28; division is done first. **81.** $6\frac{1}{9}$ **83.** 168 **85.** 12 **87.** 80 **89.** 0 **91.** 24 **93.** 144 **95.** 105 **97.** $1.07

99. $1.41 **101.** Add the measure of two paper widths (17 in). Then subtract the measure of one paper length (11 in). The difference is exactly 6 inches.

Review Capsule, page 13

1. $\frac{3}{2}$ **2.** $\frac{16}{5}$ **3.** $\frac{5}{2}$ **4.** $\frac{5}{3}$ **5.** $\frac{15}{4}$ **6.** $\frac{29}{6}$ **7.** 4 **8.** 2 **9.** $\frac{1}{2}$ **10.** $\frac{1}{2}$ **11.** 7 **12.** $13\frac{1}{2}$ **13.** $3\frac{3}{4}$ **14.** 6

Exercises, pages 15–19

1. a. P: perimeter; l: length; w: width **b.** The perimeter of a rectangle is equal to the sum of twice the length and twice the width. **3. a.** C: Circumference; r: radius **b.** The circumference of a circle is equal to twice the product of π times the radius. **5.** c **7.** 10.35 m **9. a.** 1800, 2250 **b.** 450, 450 m **11. a.** 2800, 4200 **b.** 7A **13.** $t + 9$; 28; 36 **15.** 154 lbs **17.** 9 lbs above **19.** 7560 ft³ **21.** $0.03 **23.** $0.021 **25.** $0.428125 **27.** 32 **29.** 135.2 **31.** 7 **33.** 4 **35.** 4 **37.** $A = s^2 - 1$ **39.** $A = \frac{1}{2}t^2$ **41.** 12.5% **43.** $32.75 **45.** 152 cm³

Review Capsule, page 18

1. 16 **2.** 10 **3.** 5 **4.** 52 **5.** 30.5 **6.** 2.5 **7.** 1, 9, 17, 25, 33 **8.** 3, 17, 31, 45, 59 **9.** 1, 201, 401, 601, 801 **10.** 2, $\frac{14}{11}$, $\frac{22}{19}$, $\frac{10}{9}$, $\frac{38}{35}$ **11.** 6, 14, 22, 30, 38 **12.** 1

Review, page 19

1. $4d$ **3.** $2r$ **5.** 24 **7.** 1248 **9.** 11 **11.** 86 **13.** 312 **15.** 0.042

Exercises, pages 20–21

1. $23.97 **3.** 1 gallon plus 2 quarts; 1 gallon plus 1 quart; 2 gallons plus 3 quarts **5.** $32.91 **7.** Both amounts of paint would cost more than 3 gallons.

Exercises, pages 24–25

1. a and d **3.** variable **5.** The replacements for the variable that make the open sentence true **7.** T **9.** T **11.** T **13.** T **15.** T **17.** T **19.** {2, 4, 6} **21.** {2, 4, 6, 10} **23.** {2, 4} **25.** {4, 6, 8, 10} **27.** {0, 1, 2, 3, 4, 5} **29.** {3} **31.** ϕ **33.** {4, 5} **35.** ϕ **37.** {20} **39.** {5, 10, 15, 20} **41.** {0, 10, 15, 20} **43.** ϕ **45.** none **47.** some **49.** all **51.** some **53.** all **55.** $r - 7 **57.** 100 **59.** 11 **61.** 6 **63.** 128 **65.** T **67.** T **69.** T

Review Capsule, page 25

1. 2 **2.** 6 **3.** 15 **4.** 70 **5.** 15 **6.** 43 **7.** 76
8. 47

Exercises, pages 28–29

1. F; fractions are not natural numbers. **3.** T **5.** T
7. T **9.** You cannot have a zero in the denominator.
11. $\frac{4}{10}$ **13.** $\frac{37}{100}$ **15.** $\frac{-19}{3}$ **17.** $\frac{15}{4}$ **19.** $\frac{6725}{100}$ **21.** $\frac{0}{1}$
23. $\frac{1}{1000}$ **25.** $\frac{195}{100}$ **27.** $\frac{18}{1}$ **29.** 6 **31.** $^-462$
33. 76.20 **35.** $2\frac{1}{2}$ **37.** $^-3.15$ **39.** 5.7 **41.** 750
43. 2.50 **45.** 0.1$\overline{6}$ **47.** 5.$\overline{3}$ **49.** 7.1875 **51.** 1.375
53. $^-0.15$ **55.** $^-0.\overline{27}$ **57.** {0} **59.** {4} **61.** $\{\frac{1}{2}\}$
63. a. 1, 2 **b.** 2 **65. a.** 12 **b.** 12 **67.** $\frac{1}{100}$

Exercises, pages 32–33

1. Identity Property for Mult.; $5 \cdot 1 = 1 \cdot 5 = 5$
3. Associative Property for Mult.; $(8 \cdot \frac{1}{2}) \cdot 3 =$
$8 \cdot (\frac{1}{2} \cdot 3)$ **5.** Comm. Prop. for Mult. **7.** Identity
Prop. for Mult. **9.** Comm. Prop. for Add.
11. Comm. Prop. for Mult. **13.** 6; Comm. Prop. for
Mult. **15.** 1; Identity Prop. for Mult. **17.** 4; Assoc.
and Comm. Prop. for Add. **19.** 0.9; Identity Prop.
for Mult. **21.** $\frac{1}{4}$; Assoc. and Comm. Prop. for Add.
23. 950 **25.** 4500 **27.** 1300 **29.** 662 **31.** 0.6
33. 4.5 **35.** -0.46875 **37.** {1. 3, 5, 7, 9, 11} **39.** ϕ
41. {1, 3, 5, 7, 9, 11} **43.** No; $15 - (9 - 5) \neq$
$(15 - 9) - 5$ **45.** No; possible example:
$25 \div 5 \neq 5 \div 25$ **47.** 972
49. 72 **51.** 25 **53.**

Review Capsule, page 33

1. 48 **2.** 376 **3.** 363 **4.** 26 **5.** 160 **6.** 1.2

Exercises, pages 35–37

1. Transitive Prop. **3.** = **5.** Dist. Prop.
7. Reflexive Prop. **9.** Dist. Prop. **11.** Dist. Prop.
13. Symm. Prop. **15.** Trans. Prop. **17.** 48 **19.** $\frac{9}{8}$,
or $1\frac{1}{8}$ **21.** 522 **23.** 517 **25.** 3546 **27.** 27
29. 18,432 **31.** 430 **33.** $25\frac{1}{2}$ **35.** $5x$ **37.** $24 + 6x$
39. 2; Refl. Prop. **41.** 15; Dist. Prop. **43.** 6; Trans.
Prop. **45.** $\frac{1}{4}(24 + 88)$ **47.** $10(4 + 6)$ **49.** $86(97 - 3)$
51. $2(x + y)$ **53.** $xy(3 + 7)$ **55.** Comm. Prop. for
Add. **57.** Identity Prop. for Mult. **59.** Assoc. Prop.
for Mult. **61.** $^-5$ **63.** $^-1500$ **65.** 5 **67.** F **69.** F
71. T **73.** No **75.** No

Focus on College Entrance Tests, page 38

1. a 3. a 5. c 7. d

Chapter Review, page 40

1. $3p$ **3.** $\frac{a}{4}$ **5.** 56 **7.** $\frac{1}{2}$ **9.** 60 **11.** 3 **13.** 45
15. $\frac{15}{16}$ **17. a.** 3.15, 3.95 **b.** 0.4 **19.** {3, 5} **21.** {5, 7,
9} **23.** {5, 7, 9} **25.** $^-5$ **27.** 30 **29.** 7.$\overline{3}$
31. 3.$\overline{384615}$ **33.** $-0.\overline{54}$ **35.** Identity Prop. for
Mult. **37.** Comm. Prop. for Mult. **39.** Assoc. Prop.
for Mult. **41.** 2277 **43.** $\frac{7}{3}$, or $2\frac{1}{3}$ **45.** 18,054
47. Refl. Prop. **49.** Symm. Prop.

Chapter Test, page 42

1. $b - v$ **3.** 7.55y **5.** 12 **7.** 4 **9.** 11.6 **11.** {2}
13. {1, 2} **15.** F; decimals are not natural numbers.
17. T **19.** 0.$\overline{4}$ **21.** 4.5$\overline{3}$ **23.** 4; Assoc. and Comm.
Prop. for Add. **25.** 12; Symm. Prop.

Additional Practice, page 43

1. 10 **3.** 6 **5.** $\frac{2}{21}$ **7.** $\frac{1}{3}$ **9.** 11; 14; 17 **11.** 19; 28;
39 **13.** {9} **15.** {5, 7, 9} **17.** $\frac{3}{10}$ **19.** $\frac{7}{3}$ **21.** $\frac{-38}{1}$
23. Identity Prop. for Add. **25.** Comm. Prop. for Add.
27. 630 **29.** 1.15t **31.** 12 cubic meters

Chapter 2: Operations with Real Numbers

Exercises, pages 46–48

1. distance; opposite **3.** The opposite of negative
9 **5.** 0 **7.** Negative **9.** -6 **11.** 9 **13.** $6\frac{1}{2}$
15. -9.02 **17.** $\frac{2}{3}$ **19.** 9.001 **21.** $27 = -(-27)$
23. $2\frac{1}{2} = -(-2\frac{1}{2})$ **25.** $-(-200) = 200$ **27.** -5
29. -3.14 **31.** $\frac{5}{6}$ **33.** -9 **35.** -0.9 **37.** -1.2
39. 0 **41.** -3 **43.** t **45.** m **47.** $x = -9$
49. $x = 0$ **51.** $y = -3.25$ **53.** $a = \frac{3}{4}$ **55.** <
57. < **59.** > **61.** > **63.** > **65.** > **67.** >
69. < **71.** Symm. Prop. **73.** Dist. Prop.
75. Identity Prop. for Add. **77.** Trans. Prop.
79. $a - 3$ **81.** $5d$ **83.** $e - s$ **85.** Negative
87. Positive **89.** Negative **91.** Answers may vary.
Alvin had one 50-cent piece, 1 quarter, 4 dimes, and
4 pennies.

Review Capsule, page 48

1. L **2.** R **3.** R **4.** L **5.** R **6.** R **7.** L **8.** R
9. L **10.** R **11.** R **12.** R

Exercises, pages 50–52

1. right **3.** $4 + (-5) = -1$ **5.** $-4 + 4 = 0$ **7.** 2
$+ (-5) = -3$ **9.** 1 **11.** 7 **13.** 9 **15.** -4
17. -1 **19.** -1 **21.** -3 **23.** -10 **25.** Negative

27. 0 **29.** equal to zero **31.** −1 **33.** 1 **35.** The negative number **37.** The positive number **39.** −700 + (−150) = −850, or −850m **41.** −5 + 12 = 7, or 7°C **43.** −4.9 **45.** 9 **47.** > **49.** < **51.** 15; Trans. Prop. **53.** 0; Refl. Prop. **55.** 124 **57.** 25 **59.** 3 **61.** −8 **63.** −1 **65.** The amount in each stack: $1, $2, $4, $8, $16, $32, $64, $128, $256, $489

Review Capsule, page 52

1. −3 **2.** 0.5 **3.** same **4.** $\frac{3}{8}$ **5.** same **6.** 1.1 **7.** $\frac{2}{3}$ **8.** −6

Exercises, pages 55–57

1. 6 **3.** $-3\frac{1}{2}$ **5.** 15 **7.** P **9.** P **11.** N **13.** P **15.** P **17.** N **19.** 12 **21.** 50 **23.** 251 **25.** $1\frac{1}{8}$ **27.** > **29.** = **31.** = **33.** 3 **35.** −3 **37.** −3 **39.** −13 **41.** 9 **43.** −1 **45.** 1 **47.** −158 **49.** 4.9 **51.** −7.6 **53.** $1\frac{1}{4}$ **55.** $-\frac{1}{2}$ **57.** 21 + (−8) + 4; 17th floor **59.** 3 + 7 + (−6); 4°C **61.** 12,000 + (−3,000) + 780; 9780 m **63.** −40 + (−15) + 18; −37 meters **65.** −2 + 7 = 5 **67.** 6 + (−5) = 1 **69.** 7 **71.** 0 **73.** > **75.** < **77.** 59 **79.** 25 **81.** 9 **83.** 135 **85.** F; the absolute value of a negative number is a positive number. **87.** F; if x is −3 and y is 1, $|x| > |y|$. **89.** Assoc. Prop. for Add.; Add. of opposites; Identity Prop. for Add.

Review Capsule, page 57

1. 5.4 **2.** 3.8 **3.** 6.83 **4.** 3.3 **5.** $\frac{7}{10}$ **6.** $14\frac{3}{8}$ **7.** $\frac{0}{12}$, or 0 **8.** $\frac{1}{10}$ **9.** $2\frac{1}{2}$ **10.** $2\frac{5}{8}$ **11.** $\frac{7}{24}$ **12.** $6\frac{17}{24}$

Exercises, pages 60–61

1. additive inverse **3.** 6 + (−3) **5.** −10 + (−5) **7.** −5 + 2 **9.** 8 + 4 **11.** 0 + 6 **13.** −5.4 + 2.1 **15.** −6 **17.** −9 **19.** −8 **21.** 10 **23.** −10 **25.** −12 **27.** 31 **29.** 0 **31.** −19 **33.** −11.8 **35.** −7.8 **37.** 1 **39.** −40 **41.** 5.6 **43.** 19.0 **45.** −5.6 **47.** 4 **49.** 7 **51.** −28 **53.** −31 **55.** −25 **57.** 15 **59.** −10.18 − 3.9 **61.** −9.9 − (−10.58) **68.** 12° **65.** 26° **67.** 17 **69.** 0 **71.** −15 **73.** −29 **75.** 130 **77.** 9 **79.** 2754 **81.** 96 **83.** F; −8 ≠ 4 **85.** F; −2 ≠ 6 **87.** F; 16 ≠ 0 **89.** T **91.** F; 6 ≠ −6 **93.** T

Review Capsule, page 61

1. a. 18 **b.** 18 **2. a.** 15 **b.** 15 **3. a.** 14 **b.** 14 **4. a.** 24 **b.** 24 **5. a.** 24 **b.** 24 **6. a.** 15 **b.** 15 **7.** 14 **8.** 15, 75 **9.** 7, 28 **10.** 6, −54 **11.** 11, 11x **12.** 3, 3m

Exercises, page 63

1. WILL ARRIVE NEW YORK FRIDAY **3.** DEPOSIT $250,000 IN ACCOUNT 10043

Exercises, pages 65–68

1. Like terms; same variable and exponent **3.** Unlike terms; different exponents **5.** Like terms; same variables and exponents **7.** 2 **9.** −0.05 **11.** 1 **13.** 20 **15.** 10x **17.** 21.2m **19.** 14mn **21.** 10x **23.** 5m^2 **25.** 20m **27.** −8y **29.** −6.4y **31.** −17t **33.** m **35.** 3x **37.** 3x **39.** −7a **41.** 3m **43.** −5r **45.** 5a + 4 **47.** 21y + 3 **49.** 6x + 6 **51.** 12x − 6y **53.** 4x − 15 **55.** m **57.** 6x + 3y + 57 **59.** 6xy + x **61.** $14\frac{1}{12}xy$ **63.** 7.37r **65.** 7.52q + 4.87 **67.** 8h **69.** w^2 + 5w + 25 **71.** $A = 9h - \frac{1}{2}(4h)$; $A = 7h$ **73.** $A = \frac{1}{2}(13h) - \frac{1}{2}(8h)$; $A = \frac{5}{2}h$ **75.** 50 **77.** 0.8 **79.** −2 **81.** −0.69 **83.** 342 + (−58) + 32; 316 yards **85.** 86 + (−59) + 38 + (−158); 93 miles **87.** −13 **89.** 4 **91.** 49 **93.** 17x + 119y **95.** 38x + 152y **97.** 4x^2 + 4y^2 **99.** a, b **101.** c, d **103.** a, b **105.** Solutions may vary. One solution is given at the right.

Review Capsule, page 68

1. 0.56 **2.** 45.92 **3.** 4059 **4.** 1.9544 **5.** $\frac{1}{5}$ **6.** $\frac{4}{15}$ **7.** $2\frac{5}{8}$ **8.** $35\frac{119}{160}$

Review, page 69

1. 1.5 **3.** −37 **5.** < **7.** < **9.** 1 **11.** −9 **13.** $\sqrt{13}$ **15.** 0 **17.** −11 **19.** −5 **21.** −2.51 **23.** 2.8x

Exercises, pages 72–73

1. positive **3.** positive **5.** 6 · 4 **7.** 4 · (−45) **9.** N **11.** P **13.** −18 **15.** −10 **17.** 10 **19.** −12 **21.** $-\frac{1}{2}$ **23.** −28 **25.** 25 **27.** −18 **29.** 72 **31.** −5 **33.** −8 **35.** −12.0 **37.** 1 **39.** 6.0 **41.** 40 **43.** −20 **45.** −0.001 **47.** 0 **49.** $\frac{8}{27}$ **51.** −5 **53.** 40 **55.** −8 **57.** 16 **59.** 1 **61.** = **63.** > **65.** = **67.** = **69.** = **71.** −6 **73.** 6 **75.** 0 **77.** −4 **79.** 30,552 **81.** 24,320 **83.** 7x + 6 **85.** −3y − 2 **87.** 3x^2 + 5x **89.** −22 **91.** −22 **93.** 11 **95.** −11 **97.** all **99.** all **101.** negative **103.** zero **105.** positive **107.** positive **109.** zero **111.** positive

Exercises, pages 75–77

1. 40; 41; 40 and 42 **3.** measure of central tendency
5. median **7.** mean **9.** 1:00–6:00 **11.** The greatest number of customers are in the store at this time.
13. No. It doesn't indicate when the most help is needed. **15.** greater than **17.** median yearly salary
19. 1 cm **21.** 0.5 cm **23.** The mode; it indicates the most popular color. **25.** The mean; it is higher than the median or mode. **27.** -300 **29.** 84
31. -72 **33.** $-6.4xy + 3$ **35.** 23 **37.** $-7\frac{1}{3}$
39. 16 **41.** 192 **43.** They will also be multiplied by 5.

Review Capsule, page 77

1. 1.6 **2.** 0.4 **3.** 0.0 **4.** 21.4 **5.** 157.1 **6.** 7.0
7. 14.9 **8.** 76.1 **9.** 1.0 **10.** 0.0

Exercises, pages 80–82

1. Negative **3.** Negative **5.** 108 **7.** -63 **9.** -17
11. 399 **13.** 4 **15.** 0 **17.** -50 **19.** 1 **21.** -6
23. -36 **25.** $-\frac{5}{12}$ **27.** 3.2 **29.** -18 **31.** 0.0032
33. -5 **35.** -1.5 **37.** -0.0002 **39.** $+\$7,600$
41. $+0.4\%$ **43.** 5 **45.** $\frac{1}{3}$ **47.** $\frac{2}{11}$ **49.** -1 **51.** -5
53. -17 **55.** 0 **57.** 9; 9; 9 **59.** $<$ **61.** $<$
63. 102 points **65.** $x = 60$ **67.** $x = 0.03$
69. $x = 51$

Review Capsule, page 82

1. $\frac{13}{2}$ **2.** $\frac{31}{4}$ **3.** $-\frac{25}{4}$ **4.** $-\frac{39}{4}$ **5.** $\frac{11}{10}$ **6.** $-\frac{29}{8}$

Exercises, pages 84–85

1. 1 **3.** t **5.** t **7.** $-t$ **9.** t **11.** -25 **13.** -30
15. 150 **17.** 225 **19.** 325 **21.** 0 **23.** 0 **25.** 5
27. -5 **29.** $\frac{2}{3}$ **31.** y **33.** $-y$ **35.** y **37.** $-y$
39. $-3a$ **41.** $-2y$ **43.** $-\frac{4}{5}c$ **45.** $15p$ **47.** $\frac{7}{9}$
49. $-\frac{1}{8}$ **51.** $-\frac{3}{2}$ **53.** $-\frac{10}{9}$ **55.** -1 **57.** 1
59. $-\frac{4}{29}$ **61.** 2 **63.** -1 **65.** 9 **67.** 4 **69.** 12
71. -21 **73.** 6 **75.** 4 **77.** 5 **79.** Add 15.
81. Add 23. **83.** Add $\frac{1}{5}$. **85.** Add -2. **87.** -30
89. -43 **91.** 59 **93.** 20,000 **95.** 89 **97.** -1
99. 1 **101.** -21 **103.** 4; 4; 4 **105.** 49

Focus on College Entrance Tests, page 86

1. 21, 25, 29, 33 **3.** $7\frac{1}{8}$, 7, $6\frac{7}{8}$, $6\frac{3}{4}$ **5.** -64, -128,
-256, -512 **7.** 4.52, 5.02, 5.52, 6.02 **9.** 20, 26, 33,
41 **11.** 36, 36, 45, 45 **13.** 25, 16, 9, 4 **15.** $\frac{1}{36}$, $\frac{1}{49}$,
$\frac{1}{64}$, $\frac{1}{81}$

Chapter Review, pages 88–89

1. -4 **3.** -16.4 **5.** π **7.** -16.7 **9.** t **11.** $>$
13. $<$ **15.** 4 **17.** -9 **19.** 1.88 **21.** 276 **23.** 15
25. $-1\frac{3}{4}$ **27.** $5 + (-7)$; $-2°C$ **29.** -10 **31.** $\frac{8}{9}$
33. 35° colder **35.** $13g$ **37.** $11ac$ **39.** $11m - 4$
41. $114x - 36$ **43.** -24 **45.** 1 **47.** greater than
49. 230 pounds **51.** -13 **53.** $1\frac{1}{3}$ **55.** -2 **57.** 8
59. 72 **61.** $-\frac{4}{3}c$ **63.** $-7x^2$ **65.** $\frac{1}{14}$ **67.** $\frac{4}{13}$
69. -11 **71.** 7 **73.** -12

Chapter Test, page 90

1. 526.36 **3.** $-\pi$ **5.** $>$ **7.** $<$ **9.** -13.7 **11.** 9
13. 2 **15.** 15° **17.** $3\frac{2}{3}gt - \frac{1}{3}g - 2$ **19.** 20; 20; 21
21. 26 **23.** $98r$ **25.** 21

Additional Practice, page 91

1. $x = -5$ **3.** $a = \frac{1}{3}$ **5.** $t = -3.72$ **7.** 8.2 **9.** 5
11. 126 **13.** -2 **15.** $25x$ **17.** $21x + y$ **19.** 0
21. 90 **23.** 0 **25.** $3x$ **27.** $3g$ **29.** 8; 8.5; 10
31. 35° colder

Cumulative Maintenance, pages 92–93

1. c **3.** d **5.** b **7.** c **9.** c **11.** d **13.** a **15.** b
17. a **19.** b **21.** a **23.** 9°C **25.** 1 yard gained
27. 32nd floor **29.** 1.2 m³

Chapter 3: Solving Equations

Exercises, pages 97–98

1. D **3.** A **5.** F **7.** C **9.** D **11.** -2 **13.** 6
15. -9 **17.** $x = 6$ **19.** $n = -3$ **21.** $x = 18\frac{3}{4}$
23. $n = -6$ **25.** $y = -9$ **27.** $x = -3$
29. $z = 38$ **31.** $m = -2$ **33.** $z = 13$ **35.** $r = 3.5$
37. $z = 3.6$ **39.** $x = 1.65$ **41.** $z = 2$ **43.** $c = -\frac{1}{2}$
45. $q = \frac{1}{2}$ **47.** 14 **49.** 6 **51.** 9 **53.** 0.1 **55.** $\frac{1}{7}$
57. $\frac{4}{3}$ **59.** $-\frac{4}{3}$ **61.** -28 **63.** 17 **65.** $q = 13.8$
67. $m = 0$ **69.** $125 + 160 = d$; $d = 285$ miles
71. Add d. **73.** $5 + 2 \cdot 8$; $5 + 3 \cdot 8$; $5 + 4 \cdot 8$

Review Capsule, page 98

1. $\frac{25}{3}$ **2.** $-\frac{32}{5}$ **3.** $\frac{26}{9}$ **4.** $\frac{15}{4}$ **5.** $-\frac{3}{2}$ **6.** $-\frac{3}{2}$ **7.** $\frac{1}{5}$
8. $\frac{8}{57}$ **9.** $-\frac{2}{5}$ **10.** -1

Exercises, pages 101–102

1. $\frac{1}{3}$ **3.** $-\frac{5}{4}$ **5.** 5 **7.** -1 **9.** 3 **11.** 5 **13.** $x = 7$
15. $z = -4$ **17.** $b = -2$ **19.** $z = 60$ **21.** $n = 18$
23. $v = -7\frac{1}{5}$ **25.** $y = -2$ **27.** $y = 4$ **29.** $y = -6$

31. $t = -32$ **33.** $m = -\frac{1}{4}$ **35.** $n = -\frac{1}{32}$

37. $n = -\frac{3}{2}$ **39.** $t = -6$ **41.** $17x = 102$;

$x = 6$ **43.** $12n = 84$; $n = 7$ **45.** -4 **47.** -13

49. $a = 26$ **51.** $q = -4.3$ **53.** $y = -5.1$

55. $-(-120) = 120$ **57.** 12 **59.** 4 **61.** 20

Exercises, pages 105–106

1. ratio **3.** 3 **5.** $5(10) = 8x$ **7.** $15x = 5(8)$

9. $\frac{3}{20}$; 0.15; 15% **11.** $\frac{16}{20}$ or $\frac{4}{5}$; 0.8; 80% **13.** $\frac{8}{80}$ or

$\frac{1}{10}$; 0.1; 10% **15.** $x = 1$ **17.** $x = 4$ **19.** $x = 14$

21. $x = 2$ **23.** $x = 10.5$ **25.** $x = 1$ **27.** $x =$ weight

of 325 feet; $\frac{50}{2} = \frac{325}{x}$ **29.** $b =$ bags of cement;

$\frac{1}{4} = \frac{100}{b}$ **31.** 76 beats **33.** $183\frac{1}{3}$ km **35.** $96

37. about 5.5 hours **39.** $x = -32$ **41.** $m = -12$

43. $q = -4$ **45.** $n = -9$ **47.** -4 **49.** -26

51. 1:3 **53.** 3:5 **55.** Write and solve an equation.

$6x = x + 6, 5x = 6, x = \frac{6}{5}$. The number is $1\frac{1}{5}$, or 1.2.

Review Capsule, page 107

1. 10% **2.** 75% **3.** $66\frac{2}{3}$% **4.** 45% **5.** $83\frac{1}{3}$%

6. 105%

Exercises, pages 108–110

1. $\frac{8}{100}$; 0.08 **3.** $\frac{8.5}{100}$; 0.085 **5.** $\frac{800}{100}$; 8 **7.** a **9.** b

11. 9.8 **13.** 75% **15.** 75 **17.** 36 **19.** 900

21. 80% **23.** $975 **25.** $66\frac{2}{3}$ grams **27.** 1 kilogram

29. 24% **31.** 26% **33.** $1.50 **35.** 8% **37.** 625 km

39. 592 km **41.** They are both $99.

Exercises, pages 112–114

1. $\dfrac{\text{Number of successful ways}}{\text{Number of possible ways}}$ **3.** $\frac{1}{2}$, or 50% **5.** 1

7. 6 **9.** $\frac{1}{6}$ **11.** $\frac{2}{6}$, or $\frac{1}{3}$ **13.** $\frac{1}{6}$ **15.** $\frac{4}{6}$, or $\frac{2}{3}$ **17.** $\frac{5}{42}$,

or 12% **19.** $\frac{7}{42}$, or 17% **21.** $\frac{7}{42}$, or 17% **23.** $\frac{1}{8}$

25. $\frac{4}{8}$, or $\frac{1}{2}$ **27.** 0 **29.** 1800 **31.** 28.8% **33.** 15

35. $n = 12$ **37.** $n = 40$ **39.** TT, TH, HT, HH

41. $\frac{1}{4}$ **43.** See the table below. **45.** $\frac{1}{36}$ **47.** 0

49. 12 dimes

43.

	1	2	3	4	5	6
1	2	3	4	5	6	7
2	3	4	5	6	7	8
3	4	5	6	7	8	9
4	5	6	7	8	9	10
5	6	7	8	9	10	11
6	7	8	9	10	11	12

Review, page 115

1. $x = 7$ **3.** $t = -6.9$ **5.** $x = 2$ **7.** $t = 4$

9. $x = 2\frac{2}{3}$ **11.** $x = 21$ **13.** 550 pounds

15. 75% **17.** $\frac{1}{6}$ **16.** $\frac{3}{6}$, or $\frac{1}{2}$

Exercises, page 117

1.

1	Warm-up:	12% →	43°
2	Team Drills:	15% →	54°
3	Special Drills:	23% →	83°
4	Scrimmage:	40% →	144°
5	Team Meeting:	10% →	36°

3. About 33% **5.** About 30%

Review Capsule, page 118

1. $s = -1$ **2.** $d = 4$ **3.** $x = -4$ **4.** $q = 23$

5. $t = -18$ **6.** $y = -45$

Exercises, pages 119–121

1. -7 **3.** 5 **5.** 12 **7.** -10 **9.** $3t + 2 + (-2) =$

$5 + (-2)$ **11.** $1 + 15 = 7b - 1 + 1$ **13.** $-9 + 5 =$

$-\frac{1}{3}y + 9 + (-9)$ **15.** $n = 6$ **17.** $n = 4$

19. $a = 9$ **21.** $n = 7$ **23.** $a = -6$ **25.** $a = 9$

27. $a = -9$ **29.** $x = -2$ **31.** $b = 12\frac{1}{3}$ **33.** $a = 9$

35. $y = -12$ **37.** $t = -3\frac{2}{3}$ **39.** $w = 2$ **41.** $n = 6$

43. $n = -30$ **45.** $x = 40$ **47.** $x = 28$

49. $t = 105$ **51.** $n = 96$ **53.** $n = 100$

55. $x = -45$ **57.** $c = 12$ **59.** $x = 19$ **61.** $\frac{2}{3}$

63. 1 **65.** $58.00 **67.** 120% **69.** mean: 7;

median: 8; mode: 9 **71.** mean: 2.25; median: 2.5;

mode: 3 **73.** mean: 38.2; median: 37; mode: 37

75. Additive Inverse Property; Commutative Prop-

erty for Addition; Additive Inverse Property; Additive

Inverse Property **77.**

79. $\frac{1}{4}$ inch

Review Capsule, page 121

1. $44xy$ **2.** $2y^2$ **3.** $7a + 10b$ **4.** $9x^2 + 8x$ **5.** $13t$

6. $6t^2$

Exercises, pages 122–125

1. 47° **3.** 65° **5.** 180° **7.** 360° **9.** 42.5°; 52.5°; 85°

11. 75°; 15° **13.** 60°; 60°; 60° **15.** 90°; 90°; 90°

17. 66°; 66°; 114°; 114° **19.** 60°; 65°; 115°; 120°

21. 35°; 45°; 100° **23.** 50°; 65°; 65° **25.** 31°; 59°

27. 72°; 108° **29.** 45°; 45°; 135°; 135° **31.** 22.5°;

67.5°

33. $t = 6$ **35.** $x = 28$ **37.** $r = -\frac{1}{2}$ **39.** $\frac{1}{11}$
41. 0   **43.** $\frac{2}{11}$ **45.** $-9x$ **47.** y **49.** $-\frac{1}{2}a$ **51.** $8ab$
53. $-\frac{3}{10}bc$ **55.** 30°   **57.** $90° - 5t$ **59.** 85°
61. $180° - 3y$ **63. a.** circle **b.** star

Review Capsule, page 125
1. $b + t$ **2.** $g - d$ **3.** $365 - p$ **4.** $1.65t$

Exercises, pages 127–129
1. $-6y$ **3.** $y - 6$ **5.** $6y$ **7.** $6 - y$ **9.** $y - 6$
11. $25 - n$ **13.** $y - 19.3$ **15.** $-18\frac{2}{3} - (-r)$
17. $x + (-x)$ **19.** $m - (-2)$ **21.** $12 - |y|$
23. $(2q + 3) + q$ **25.** $r - (-0.5)$ **27.** $7(q + 7)$
29. $2p$ **31.** $9(z^2 - 4x)$ **33.** $r(\frac{1}{12})$ or $\frac{r}{12}$ **35.** $w =$
width of rectangle; $w + 5$ **37.** $p =$ perimeter of
base; $\frac{1}{3}p$ **39.** $c =$ cost of new car; $c - 1200$
41. $a =$ air distance; $2a$ **43.** $t =$ round trip fare;
$1200 \div 5t$ or $\frac{1200}{5t}$ **45.** $n =$ number of pages;
$\frac{n}{9} - 500$ **47.** $6k$ **49.** $\frac{1200}{m}$, or $1200 \div m$
51. $\frac{3500}{m}$, or $3500 \div m$ **53.** 30°; 60°; 90°   **55.** 30°;
30°; 120°   **57.** $n = 4$ **59.** $t = 24$ **61.** $p = -4$
63. $5x + 20$ **65.** $15r + 10$ **67.** $27\frac{1}{2}y$

Review Capsule, page 129
1. $d = 4$ **2.** $x = 6$ **3.** $x = -9$ **4.** $r = 5.4$
5. $t = 8$ **6.** $y = -7$

Exercises, pages 132–135
1. d **3.** e **5.** c **7.** Nat's and Nora's salaries
9. Together they earn $375 per week.   **11.** 12; 60
13. 12; 8   **15.** 30; 20   **17.** 33; 43   **19.** 18; 21; 25
21. Dan: $13; Bob: $39   **23.** Dress: $62.90; Coat:
$98.40   **25.** First day: 560; next day: 325   **27.** Local:
$10.92; long-distance: $52.88   **29.** List price: $660;
discount: $66   **31.** List price: $6.80; discount: $1.70
33. List price: $600; discount: $240   **35.** $d - 125$
37. $y - 29$ **39.** $z + 1\frac{2}{3}$ **41.** $6.5r$ **43.** 15°; 45°; 120°
45. $9a + 7$ **47.** $-t^2 - 4t$ **49.** $19y^2 + 7xy$ **51.** 8
53. $41

Focus On College Entrance Tests, pages 135–136
1. a. Possible. "$15 at most" means he spent $15
or less. **b.** False. "$15 at most" means the largest
possible amount was $15. **c.** Possible. See conclu-
sion **a. d.** Can't tell. No information is given about
how much Alice spent. **3. a.** Possible. "Between
30 and 40" means 31, 32, 33, 34, 35, 36, 37, 38, or 39
students belong to the club. **b.** Possible. See conclusion **a. c.** Can't tell. No information is given

about last year's membership. **d.** True. All of the
possible numbers given in conclusion **a** are below
45. **5. a.** False. "Exactly 5 out of every 7 students"
means exactly 350 of the 490 students. **b.** True. If
"exactly 5 out of every 7 students" received a grade
of C or better, then the remaining 2 out of every 7
students received a grade lower than C. **c.** True.
See conclusion **b.** "Exactly 2 out of every 7 students"
means exactly 140 of the 490 students. **d.** True. See
conclusion **a.** 350 is "more than 349 and fewer than
351."

Chapter Review, pages 138–139
1. $x = 3$ **3.** $r = -19$ **5.** $t = 35$ **7.** $y = -8\frac{1}{2}$
9. $x = 0.2$ **11.** $x = 28.8$ **13.** $x = 11\frac{1}{3}$ **15.** 1.6 meters
17. 17   **19.** 2%   **21.** 24   **23.** 18%   **25.** $\frac{2}{10}$, or $\frac{1}{5}$
27. $\frac{9}{10}$ **29.** $m = 10$ **31.** $t = 4$ **33.** $t = 42\frac{2}{3}$
35. 20°; 70°; 90°   **37.** 32°; 35°; 113°   **39.** 32°; 48°;
100°   **41.** $6.4 - w$ **43.** $\frac{1}{3}(-c)$ **45.** $\frac{-x}{2}$
47. $(6a + c) + (-7)$ **49.** $x + (3x + 7) = 75$;
smaller: 17; larger: 58

Chapter Test, page 140
1. $x = 13$ **3.** $k = -8$ **5.** $w = \frac{1}{2}$ **7.** $c = 3$
9. $b = 4$ **11.** $x = 50.4$ **13.** 2880 jars   **15.** $\frac{2}{8}$, or
$\frac{1}{4}$ **17.** 35°; 55°; 90°   **19.** $y - 1.5$

Additional Practice, page 141
1. $t = 14$ **3.** $m = -4$ **5.** $u = 33$ **7.** $409\frac{1}{2}$
9. $3\frac{2}{3}$ **11.** $37\frac{1}{2}$%   **13.** 100   **15.** $\frac{6}{9}$, or $\frac{2}{3}$ **17.** $45\frac{1}{2}$°;
$45\frac{1}{2}$°; 89°   **19.** Emily: 45; Jean: 65

Cumulative Maintenance, pages 142–143
1. b   **3.** c   **5.** a   **7.** a   **9.** c   **11.** d   **13.** c   **15.** d
17. a   **19.** a   **21.** b   **23.** $7.70   **25.** 50
27. 11,520   **29.** 6%   **31.** 7; 32

Chapter 4 : More on Solving Equations

Exercises, pages 146–148
1. $s = 9$ m   **3.** $a = 119$ m; $2a = 238$ m; $a + 147 =$
266 m   **5.** $w =$ width; $w + 10 =$ length;
$2w + 2(w + 10) = 120$ **7.** $w = 16$ in; $l = 40$ in
9. $w = 654$ ft; $l = 474$ ft   **11.** $w = 50$ cm; $l = 75$ cm
13. 6 cm; 6 cm; 15 cm   **15.** 146 mi   **17.** $AC =$
$BC = 536$ m; $AB = 857.6$ m   **19.** $m\angle A = m\angle B =$
80°; $m\angle C = 20$°   **21.** $142.50   **23.** $=$ **25.** $=$
27. $<$ **29.** $w = 32$ in; $l = 64$ in   **31.** Two possible
answers are shown: $\frac{5 \cdot 7 \cdot 3 \cdot 8}{2 \cdot 4 \cdot 6}$ or $\frac{5 \cdot 7 \cdot 4 \cdot 6}{2 \cdot 3 \cdot 8}$

1. $-x$ 3. $9y$ 5. $-3a$ 7. $2t$ 9. $9d$ 11. $5m$
13. $x = 4$ 15. $y = 4$ 17. $a = 3$ 19. $x = -3$
21. ϕ 23. $a = 6$ 25. $r = 10$ 27. $t = -10\frac{1}{2}$
29. $a = 4$ 31. $x = -8$ 33. $x = 5$ 35. $x = 11$
37. ϕ 39. $c = -50$ 41. $n = -17$ 43. 12; 12; 7
45. $270 47. -9 49. -30 51. 2 53. odd
55. even

Review Capsule, page 151
1. $y + 9$ 2. $s - 12$ 3. $p - 5$ 4. $n + 3$
5. $a + 3$ 6. $g - 15$

Exercises, pages 152–153
1. 35 3. 21 5. 15

Exercises, pages 156–157
1. 14; 16; 18; 20 3. -10; -8; -6; -4 5. $q + 2$;
$q + 4$; $q + 6$; $q + 8$ 7. 11; 13; 15; 17 9. -19;
-17; -15; -13 11. $k + 2$; $k + 4$; $k + 6$; $k + 8$
13. $x + 9$ 15. $5t - 12$ 17. -14; -12 19. -37;
-35; -33 21. Skip: 15; Paul: 5 23. 15; 17
25. 64; 65; 66; 67 27. 12 yr 29. even 31. $q = 3$
33. $z = 19$ 35. $f = 14$ 37. 16 39. $-5x$
41. $-50y$ 43. $-14.3b$ 45. less than 47. 58 years
49. 9 coins: 4 pennies, 1 nickel, 2 dimes, 1 quarter,
and 1 half-dollar

Exercises, pages 160–162
1. $x = 144$; $x = ab$ 3. $x = \frac{10}{3}$; $x = \frac{bc}{a}$ 5. $x = \frac{6}{5}$;
$x = \frac{b - a}{5}$ 7. $x = -\frac{4}{3}$; $x = \frac{b}{3} - a$ 9. $x = 3$;
$x = \frac{-b - a}{2}$ 11. $d = \frac{C}{\pi}$ 13. $h = \frac{2A}{b}$ 15. $r = \frac{d}{t}$
17. $r = \frac{i}{pt}$ 19. $F = \frac{9}{5}C + 32$ 21. $d = \frac{C}{\pi}$; $d = 7.19$
23. $l = \frac{P - 2w}{2}$; $l = 22$ 25. $w = \frac{A}{l}$; $w = 2.8$
27. $9500 29. 230 m^2 31. $n = \frac{b - a}{2}$
33. $n = 3a + b$
35. $n = 5b - 3a$ 37. $n = b + c - a$ 39. $n = 4b$
41. $n = \frac{b + c}{a}$ 43. -34; -33; -32; -31
45. Ramon: 2 yr; Anna: 8 yr 47. $t = -9$
49. $d = -7$ 51. -50 53. $-5\frac{5}{27}$ 55. $-\frac{1}{20}$
57. $-22\frac{1}{2}$ 59. $b = \frac{c}{a} - n$ 61. $a = \frac{c}{n} - b$
63. $b = \frac{2A}{h} - b'$ 65. 20 ways

Review Capsule, page 162
1. d 2. b

Exercises, pages 164–166
1. $r = \frac{d}{t}$ 3. Hiker A: r, 6, $6r$; Hiker B: $2r$, 6, $12r$
5. Passenger: $2r$, 3, $6r$; Freight: r, $3r$ 7. About 3
hours 9. 9 hours 11. 2 P.M. 13. 2 hours

15. 64 km/h 17. 8 km 19. $b = \frac{2A}{h}$ 21. $p = s + d$
23. 12 yr

Focus on College Entrance Tests, page 167
1. b 3. c 5. c 7. d 9. d

Chapter Review, pages 168–169
1. $w = 30$ m; $l = 50$ m 3. $w = 10$ ft; $l = 25$ ft
5. ϕ 7. $n = -2$ 9. $x = 7$ 11. -9; -7 13. Joe:
18 yr; Greg: 6 yr 15. $n = st$ 17. $n = r - 3p$
19. $n = \frac{4 - c - 2b}{a}$ 21. $w = \frac{V}{lh}$ 23. $4500
25. 3 hours

Chapter Test, page 170
1. $x = \frac{21}{10}$ 3. $d = -1$ 5. $a = 0$ 7. $c = \frac{b + a}{2}$
9. $c = 3x + y$ 11. 39; 41; 43 13. 55; 57; 59
15. $2\frac{1}{2}$ hours

Additional Practice, page 171
1. $a = 1$ 3. $x = 3$ 5. $y = 2$ 7. $x = 5$
9. $n = \frac{a}{b}$ 11. $n = \frac{d - c}{3}$ 13. $n = \frac{y + b}{a}$ 15. $h = \frac{A}{b}$
17. $A = 20°$; $B = 60°$; $C = 100°$ 19. 24; 25
21. 7:30 P.M. 23. 7

Cumulative Maintenance, pages 172–173
1. b 3. c 5. a 7. b 9. c 11. b 13. b 15. c
17. d 19. d 21. a 23. c 25. 42; 43; 44 27. 3
years 29. 72 miles

Chapter 5: Relations and Functions

Exercises, pages 176–179
1. I and IV 3. II and III 5. I 7. y axis 9. The
origin 11. A: II; B: I; C: IV; D: III; F: x axis; G: y
axis; H: y axis; I: III 13. 0 15. III 17. II 19. x
axis 21. origin 23. I 25. IV 27. The picture is
an elephant. 29. The graph is a horizontal line 4
units below the x axis. 31. The graph is a vertical
line coinciding with the y axis. 33. The graph is a
diagonal line passing through the origin at a 45°
angle; the line is in Quadrants II and IV. 35. A horizontal line parallel to the x axis 37. A half-plane
with the y axis as its right-hand boundary 39. $(-4,$
$5)$ 41. $(0, -4)$ 43. $(-3, -3)$ 45. 66.67 miles
47. $t = \frac{i}{pr}$ 49. $c = -4$ 51. $x = -36$
53. $(-10, 5)$, $(-4, 5)$, $(-4, 1)$ 55. $(2, 10)$, $(2, 4)$,
$(4, 4)$ 57. $(-13, 7)$, $(1, 9)$, $(-3, 3)$

Review Capsule, page 179
1. 6 2. 1.06 g

Exercises, pages 182–185

1. ordered pairs **3.** first element **5.** domain
7. D = {0, 2, 4, 6}; R = {1, 3, 5, 7} **9.** D = {0, 1, 2,3};
R = {−2} **11.** {(−4, −2), (−2, −3), (−1, 1), (1, −2),
(1, 3), (2, 1), (4, 2)} **13.** D = {−4, −2, −1, 1, 2, 4};
R = {−3, −2, 1, 2, 3} **15.** {(−3, −3), (−2, −3),
(−1, −3), (1, −3), (2, −3), (3, −3)}; D = {−3, −2,
−1, 1, 2, 3}; R = {−3} **17.** {(1, 4), (2, 4), (3, 4)}
19. {(−6, −2), (−6, 0), (−6, 5)} **21.** Yes **23.** No
25. No **27.** No; all ordered pairs have the same first
element. **29.** Yes **31.** {(8, 4), (9, 8), (10, 8), (11, 10),
(12, 11)}; D = {8, 9, 10, 11, 12}; R = {4, 8, 10, 11}
33. {(150, 5), (180, 6), (210, 7)}; D = {150, 180, 210};
R = {5, 6, 7} **35.** {(5, 150), (10, 600), (15, 1350),
(20, 2400)}; D = {5, 10, 15, 20}; R = {150, 600, 1350,
2400} **37.** All are functions. **39.** z = 5 **41.** z = 105
43. c = −4 **45.** m = −9 **47.** Car: 60 mph;
train: 40 mph **49. a.** 0, $2.50; $3.75; $5.00;
$6.25; $7.50; $8.75; $10,00; $11.25; **b.** less than
or equal to $7.50; **c.** See the Solution Key.
51. F

Review Capsule, page 185

1. 30 **2.** 25 **3.** 15.5 **4.** 17

Exercises, pages 188–190

1. 8, 12 **3.** −6, −9 **5.** 4, 6 **7.** No **9.** Yes
11. No **13.** Yes **15.** Yes **17.** No **19.** Yes
21. Yes **23.** Yes **25.** No **27.** Yes For Ex. 28–45,
each graph is a straight line containing the given
points. **29.** (1, −3), (0, 0) **31.** (0, −5), (5, 0)
33. (0, 10), (10, 0) **35.** (0, 0), (3, 1) **37.** (0, 4), (2, 0)
39. (0, 2), (3, 0) **41.** (0, 0), (2, 3) **43.** (0, −9),
(9, −9) **45.** (6$\frac{1}{2}$, 0), (6$\frac{1}{2}$, 6) **47.** −5, −5, −5
49. $\frac{3}{2}$, $\frac{3}{2}$, $\frac{3}{2}$ **51.** The set of real numbers.
In Exercises 53–56, the graph is a line prallel to the
y axis. It contains the given points. **53.** (3, −3),
(3, 0), (3, 4) **55.** (0, −5), (0, 0), (0, 5) **57.** y
59. relation **61.** D = {−1, 0, 1, 2}; R = {6} **63.** Yes
65. y **67.** 30 m **69.** (0, −6), (3, 0) **71.** (0, 2),
(3, 0) **73.** (0, 0), (0, 0)
75.

Not a linear function.
D = {real numbers}
R = {−1, 0, 1}

77.

Not a linear function.
D = {real numbers}
R = {all real numbers
greater than or
equal to zero}

79.

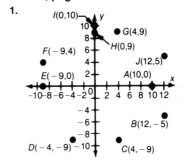

Not a linear function.
D = {real numbers}
R = {all real numbers
less than or equal
to zero}

Review, page 191

1.

I(0,10) y
G(4,9)
H(0,9)
F(−9,4)
J(12,5)
E(−9,0)   A(10,0)
D(−4, −9)   B(12, −5)
C(4, −9)

3.

	a.	b.	c.	d.	e.
abscissa	10	12	4	−4	−9
ordinate	0	−5	−9	−9	0

	f.	g.	h.	i.	j.
abscissa	−9	4	0	0	12
ordinate	4	9	9	10	5

5. D = {1, 2, 3, 4, 5, 6}; R = {10, 15, 25, 40, 60, 85}
7. 4: Yes; 5: Yes; 6: No For Exercises 8–11, each
graph is a straight line containing the given points.
9. (−2, −1), (−1, −4) **11.** (2, 0), (2, 2)

Exercises, pages 192–193

1. b. The median points are (20, 8) and (110, 58).
d. About 36 hours **3. b.** The median points are (64,
115) and (72, 180). **d.** About 148 pounds

Exercises, pages 195–197

1. $10 **3.** $7.50 **5.** $125 **7.** (0, 0), (4, 6), (6, 9)
9. About 0.75 km **11.** Almost 3 seconds **13.** To
draw the graph, use multiplies of 3 for the d axis and
multiples of 16 for the r axis. **15.** About 13 m
17. $10, $15, $20 **19.** About $12.50 **21.** About
$16.25 **23.** C = 2.50h + 5 **25.** See page 650.

25.

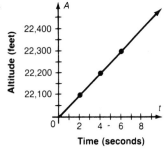

Time (seconds)

27. About 22,250 **29.** About 22,400; For Exercises 31–34, the graph is a straight line containing the given points. **31.** (0, 1), (3, 7) **33.** (−5, 0), (−5, 5) **35.** Yes **37.** No, because ordered pairs (0, −2) and (0, 2) have the same first element. **39.** 120 **41.** 15% **43.** 45¢, 65¢, $1.25

45.

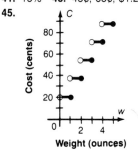

Weight (ounces)

Exercises, page 199
1. −2, −2 **3.** 4, 2, 0, 2, 4 **5.** Two vertical lines, one through (−2, 0) and the other through (2, 0) **7.** Two horizontal lines, one through (−3, 0), and the other through (3, 0) Each graph in Exercises 9–24 consists of two rays. Their initial point and the coordinates of another point on each ray is given. **9.** Initial point: (0, 0); one ray: (−1, 2); other ray: (1, 2) **11.** Initial point: (0, 0); one ray: (−2, −2); other ray: (2, −2) **13.** Initial point: (0, −4); one ray: (−2, −2); other ray: (2, −2) **15.** Initial point: (0, 7); one ray: (−1, 10); other ray: (1, 10) **17.** Initial point: (0, 0); one ray: (1, 1); other ray: (1, −1) **19.** Initial point: (−6, 0); one ray: (−8, 1); other ray: (−8, −1) **21.** Initial point: (0, 0); one ray: (−3, 1); other ray: (−3, −1) **23.** Initial point: (6, 0); one ray: (7, 1); other ray: (7, −1) **25.** (5, 1), (15, 3), (25, 5) **27.** 2 ft **29.** Patricia earned $60; Donna earned $12. **31.** See the Solution Key. **33.** See the Solution Key. **35.** See the Solution Key. **37.** See the Solution Key.

650 *Answers to Selected Exercises*

Focus on College Entrance Tests, page 200
1. B **3.** A **5.** B

Chapter Review, pages 201–202
Start at the origin and make the moves given for each point. **1. a.** Right 3, down 7 **b.** Left 3, up 7 **c.** Down 2 **d.** Right 6, down 5 **e.** Left 6, down 6 **f.** Right 7, up 5 **g.** Right $6\frac{1}{2}$ **h.** Left 2, down 5 **i.** Left 1, up 4 **j.** Right $3\frac{1}{2}$, down 5 **3.** (−5, 3) **5.** D: {−2, −1, 0, 1, 2}; R: {−1, −$\frac{1}{2}$, 0, $\frac{1}{2}$, 1} **7.** 4. No; 5. Yes; 6. Yes For Exercises 8–11, the graph is a straight line containing the given points **9.** (0, 0), (1, −4) **11.** (−3, 0), (−3, 3) **13.** To draw the graph, use multiples of $400 for the t axis and multiples of $10,000 for the p axis. **15.** The graph consists of two parallel lines, one 6 units above the x axis, and the other 6 units below the x axis. **17.** The graph consists of two rays, one in Quadrant I and one in Quadrant II, with their initial point at (0, 2). The ray in Quadrant I also passes through (1, 4), and the ray in Quadrant II also passes through (−1, 4).

Chapter Test, page 202
1.

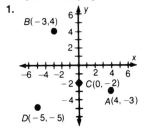

3. D = {−5, −3, 0, 5}; R = {−5, −4, 0, 4, 5}; No For Exercises 4–6 each graph is a straight line containing the given points. **5.** (0, 4), (−2, 2) **7.** (4, 5), (8, 7), (12, 9) **9.** The graph consists of two rays, one in Quadrant I and one in Quadrant II, with their initial point at (0, 0). The ray in Quadrant I also passes through (2, 6), and the ray in Quadrant II also passes through (−2, 6).

Additional Practice, page 203
For Exercises 1–5, start at the origin and make the moves given for each point. **1.** Right 3, down 5 **3.** Left 1, down 1 **5.** Left 2, up 2 **7.** x axis **9.** I

11. x axis **13.** y axis **15.** IV **17.** D = {−2, −1, 0, 1, 2}; R = {−3, −2, 0, 2, 3}; function **19.** D = {−2, 0, 4}; R = {1, 3, 9}; not a function For Exercises 20 −23, each graph is a straight line containing the given points. **21.** (−2, 0), (0, −6) **23.** (0, 4), (−2, 0) **25.** The graph consists of two parallel lines, one unit above the x axis, the other, 2 units below the x axis.

27.

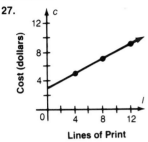

Cost (dollars)

Lines of Print

29.

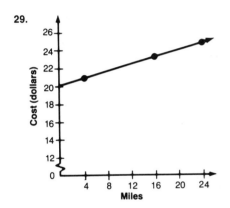

Cost (dollars)

Miles

Cumulative Maintenance, pages 204–205

1. b **3.** b **5.** b **7.** a **9.** a **11.** b **13.** a **15.** d **17.** a **19.** d **21.** b **23.** 12 mph; 18 mph
25. Number of

Square feet	1800	2300	2900
Charge	$630	$805	$1,015

Chapter 6: Lines: Slopes and Equations

Exercises, pages 209–211

1. Slope **3.** m **5.** Rise **7.** Positive **9.** ND **11.** 1 **13.** $\frac{1}{2}$ **15.** $-\frac{1}{3}$ **17.** 0 **19.** 2 **21.** $-\frac{3}{4}$ **23.** −2 **25.** AB = 1; BC = −4; AC = $-\frac{2}{3}$ **27.** PQ = $\frac{3}{7}$; SR = $\frac{3}{7}$; PS = 4; QR = 4 **29.** No **31.** No **33.** −2

35. $-\frac{1}{2}$ **37.** $y_1 = y_2$ **39.** 50; 100; 150; 200 **41.** 175 miles **43.** Width; 15 yards; length: 35 yards

45.

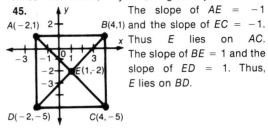

The slope of AE = −1 and the slope of EC = −1. Thus E lies on AC. The slope of BE = 1 and the slope of ED = 1. Thus, E lies on BD.

Review Capsule, page 212

1. y = 3x − 4 **2.** y = $\frac{5}{2}$(x + 1) **3.** y = $\frac{4}{3}$x **4.** y = $\frac{7 − 2x}{3}$ **5.** y = $\frac{1}{2}$x − $\frac{7}{2}$ **6.** y = 4x + 3 **7.** y = $-\frac{3}{2}$x + 3 **8.** y = −2x + 12

Exercises, pages 214–215

1. slope **3.** y intercept **5.** slope-intercept **7.** 2; 5 **9.** 3; 2 **11.** $\frac{2}{3}$; $\frac{1}{2}$ **13.** 0; 3 **15.** y = −2x + 4; −2; 4 **17.** y = −5x − 3; −5; −3 **19.** y = 2x − 4; 2; −4 **21.** y = −2x − $\frac{5}{2}$; −2; $-\frac{5}{2}$ **23.** y = −x + 3; −1; 3 **25.** y = −4; 0; −4 For Exercises 27–44, each graph is a straight line containing the given points. **27.** (−1, −3), (0, 6) **29.** (0, 1), (1, 4) **31.** (0, 0), (3, −2) **33.** (0, −2), (1, −2) **35.** (−5, 1), (0, −1) **37.** (−1, 6), (0, 0) **39.** (0, 4), (1, 6) **41.** (0, −6), (1, −3) **43.** (0, 3), (4, 8) **45.** Yes **47.** Yes **49.** No **51.** $-\frac{3}{4}$ **53.** y = $-\frac{1}{3}$x + 5 **55.** $\frac{4}{3}$ **57.** $\frac{1}{2}$ **59.** The graph consists of 2 rays. The initial point of the rays is (0, −5). One ray also contains (5, 0) and the other ray also contains (−5, 0). **61.** The graph consists of 2 rays. The initial point of the rays is (0, 12). One ray also contains (−2, 10) and the other ray also contains (2, 10). **63.** a = 2 **65.** y = −4 **67.** c = 4 **69.** m = $-\frac{A}{B}$

Exercises, pages 217–219

1. slope **3.** −5 **5.** 16 **7.** − 4 **9.** y = 3x + 4 **11.** y = $\frac{1}{2}$x − 3 **13.** y = −4x + $\frac{2}{3}$ **15.** y = 4x + 2 **17.** y = $\frac{1}{2}$x + 4 **19.** y = $-\frac{1}{4}$x − 3 **21.** y = 2x − 1 **23.** y = −3x + 17 **25.** y = x + 3 **27.** y = $\frac{1}{2}$x + 1$\frac{1}{2}$ **29.** y = $-\frac{1}{3}$x + 3 **31.** y = $\frac{2}{3}$x

33. $x = 3$　　**35.** $y = -x$　　**37.** $y = 3x + 3$
39. $y = 2x - 3$　**41.** $y = -4x + 5$　**43.** $y = -5x - 10$
45. $y = \frac{1}{2}x - 3$　For Exercises 46–49, each graph
is a straight line containing the given points.
47. $(0, 0)$, $(1, -4)$　**49.** $(1, 1)$, $(4, -5)$　**51.** $m = -\frac{1}{2}$
53. 18 yr and 6 yr　　　　**55.** $y = -\frac{1}{2}x + 4$
57. $y = -\frac{3}{2}x + 2\frac{1}{2}$　　**59.** Use the sample points,
$(a, 0)$ and $(0, b)$ to find the slope : $m = \frac{0 - b}{a - 0} =$
$-\frac{b}{a}$. Then write the line's equation in slope-intercept form: $y = \frac{b}{a}x + b$; $\frac{b}{a}x + y = b$;
$\frac{1}{b}(\frac{b}{a}x + y) = b \cdot \frac{1}{b}$; $\frac{x}{a} + \frac{y}{b} = 1$　**61.** The two hands of
the clock coincide 24 times a day.

Review Capsule, page 221
1. Yes　**2.** No　**3.** Yes　**4.** Yes　**5.** No　**6.** No

Exercises, page 221
1. a.

Interval	Midpoint	Tally	Frequency
1	1	||	2
2	2	|	1
3	3	||||	4
4	4	|||	3
5	5	|||| |	6
6	6	||||	5
7	7	||	2
8	8	||||	4
9	9	||	2
10	10	|	1

b.

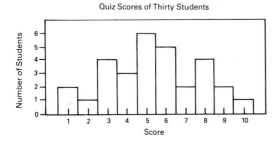

Quiz Scores of Thirty Students

3. $\bar{x} \approx 18$　**5.** $\bar{x} = 76$

Exercises, pages 224–225
1. $y = -4x + 3$　　**3.** $y = \frac{2}{3}x$　　**5.** $2x - y = 10$
7. $4x - 3y = -7$　**9.** $3x - \frac{1}{3}y = 2$　**11.** $y = 2x - 1$
13. $y = 1$　　**15.** $y = -\frac{1}{5}x + 4\frac{3}{5}$　　**17.** $y = x - 1$
19. $y = \frac{3}{2}x - 9$　　　　　**21.** $y = -x - 3$

23. $5x - 2y = -3$　　　　　　**25.** $2x - 3y = -3$
27. $\frac{6}{5}x - y = 7\frac{1}{5}$　　　　　　　**29.** $2x + 3y = 27$
31. $11x - 4y = -12$　　　　**33.** $y = \frac{1}{2}x$; Yes
35. $y = -4x + 14$; No　　　**37.** $y = -3x - 4$; No
39. 172　**41.** 201°F　**43.** $y = -x$　**45.** $y = \frac{2}{3}x - 1$
For Exercises 46–49 each graph is a straight line
containing the given points.　　　**47.** $(0, 0)$, $(1, -5)$
49. $(1, -1)$, $(0, 1)$　　**51.** $r = \frac{d - c}{m}$　　**53.** $AB =$
$\frac{1}{2}x + y = 5$; $BC = x - y = 4$; $AC = 5x + y = 14$
55. $FG = \frac{1}{5}x + y = 2\frac{3}{5}$; $GH = \frac{5}{3}x + y = -\frac{1}{3}$; $FH =$
$2x - y = 4$　　　**57.** $y = 4x - 2$; $m = 4$; $P(x_1, y_1)$,
$Q(x_2, y_2)$; $\frac{y_2 - y_1}{x_2 - x_1} = m = 4$; $\frac{y_2 - y_1}{x_2 - x_1} = 4$

Review, page 226
1. 1　**3.** $-\frac{15}{11}$　**5.** $y = -3x + 5$; -3; 5　**7.** $y = -8$;
0; -8
9.

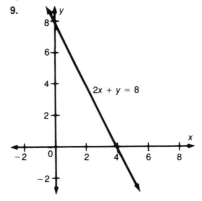

$2x + y = 8$

11. $y = -2x - 1$　**13.** $y = x$　**15.** $y = \frac{1}{5}x + \frac{3}{5}$
17. $3x + y = 4$

Review Capsule, page 227
1. $x = 5$　**2.** $x = -\frac{1}{2}$　　**3.** $x = -4$　　**4.** $y = -6$
5. $y = 3$　**6.** $x = 5$

Exercises, pages 229–231
1. direct　**3.** k　**5.** Yes　**7.** Yes　**9.** Yes　**11.** $\frac{2}{3}$
13. $-\frac{2}{5}$　**15.** $P = 4s$; Yes, this is an example of direct
variation. As s varies, p varies.　**17.** Yes; yes; y is
always $\frac{5}{2}$ times x.　**19.** 20; yes; doubled.　**21.** Yes
23. Yes　**25.** Yes　**27.** No　**29.** $p = kq$　**31.** $s = kt$
33. $\frac{2}{5}$　**35.** -4　**37.** 4　**39** 5, -10　**41.** 10　**43.** 0

45. The slope of the line increases. **47.** Yes; C is always π times d. **49.** $\frac{5}{2}x - y = 0$ **51.** $\frac{7}{4}x - y = \frac{5}{4}$ **53.** $y = 3x$ **55.** 555 mph and 645 mph **57.** increases **59.** Multiplied by n **61.** There are 30 ways to enter and leave the building.

Exercises, pages 232–234
1. $k = 29$ **3.** $522 **5.** 70 **7.** 420 mi **9.** $4.50 **11.** 9 minutes **13.** 240 lb **15.** 40 **17.** $y = 4x + 1$ **19.** $y = -2x$ **21.** $y = \frac{2}{3}x + 6$ **23.** 46, 47, 48 **25.** $y_1 = Kx_1$; $K = \frac{y_1}{x_1}$; $y_2 = Kx_2$; $K = \frac{y_2}{x_2}$; $\frac{y_1}{x_1} = K = \frac{y_2}{x_2}$

Focus on College Entrance Tests, page 235
1. 3. 5.

7. 9. 11.

Chapter Review, pages 236–237
1. -2 **3.** 0 **5.** $y = -x$; -1; 0 For Exercises 7–12, the graph is a straight line through the given points. **7.** $(0, 2), (-2, 0)$ **9.** $(0, -2), (-4, 0)$ **11.** $(0, 6), (-1, 2)$ **13.** $y = -3x + 4$ **15.** $y = -\frac{1}{2}x - \frac{3}{4}$ **17.** $y = 2x + 2$ **19.** $y = -x - 8$ **21.** $y = \frac{3}{2}x - 7\frac{1}{2}$ **23.** $y = 3x + 2$ **25.** $y = -5x$ **27.** $y = -2x + 1$ **29.** $x + y = 8$ **31.** $2x + 5y = 3$ **33.** No **35.** No **37.** 150 m **39.** 4.3 m

Chapter Test, page 238
1. 0 **3.** $-\frac{9}{7}$ **5.** $y = -\frac{3}{4}x + 1$; $-\frac{3}{4}$; 1
7.

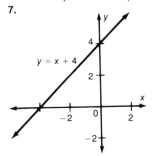

$y = x + 4$

9. $y = -x + 3$ **11.** $y = 3x + 23$ **13.** $y = 2x - 4$ **15.** Yes **17.** No **19.** 35 km

Additional Practice, page 239
1. 2 $\frac{1}{2}$ **3.** – **5.** $y = -2x + 5$; -2; 5 **7.** $y = 4x - 8$ **9.** $y = x - 2$ **11.** $y = -\frac{3}{2}x$ **13.** $5x + 6y = 18$ **15.** $x - 4y = 12$ **17.** $y = 12$ **19.** 35 km

Cumulative Maintenance, pages 240–241
1. a **3.** c **5.** a **7.** c **9.** d **11.** c **13.** b **15.** d **17.** b **19.** c **21.** a **23.** $2700 **25.** $281.25 **27.** $50,000

Chapter 7: Systems of Sentences

Exercises, pages 245–248
1. an infinite number **3.** parallel **5.** $x + y = 5$: 5, 4, 3, 2, 1; $x - y = 3$: $-3, -2, -1, 0, 1$; $(4, 1)$ **7.** No **9.** No **11.** an infinite number **13.** one solution **15.** an infinite number of solutions **17.** $(2, 1)$ **19.** $(2, -1)$ **21.** $(-3, 2)$ **23.** $(6, 1)$ **25.** $(5, -4)$ **27.** $(2, 0)$ **29.** $(1, 0)$ **31.** $(2, -1)$ **33.** $(-1, -1)$ **35.** one **37.** none **39.** none **41.** none **43.** none **45.** infinitely many **47.** none **49.** none **51.** infinitely many **53.** all equal **55.**

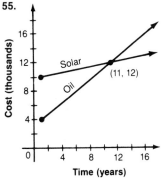

57. 10 years **59.** 105 meters **61.** $(-3, 1)$, $(-2, -1)$, $(-1, 3)$, $(2, 2)$, $(2, -2)$, $(4, 1)$; $D = \{-3, -2, -1, 2, 4\}$; $R = \{-2, -1, 1, 2, 3\}$ **63.** $\{(-4, 2),$ $(-1, 2), (1, 2), (2, 2)\}$; $D = \{-4, -1, 1, 2\}$; $R = \{2\}$ **65.** 2 hours **67.** more than 2 hours **69.** none **71.** one **73.** The number is 9996.

Review Capsule, page 249
1. $x = -2y + 3$ **2.** $x = 3y - 7$ **3.** $x = -\frac{5}{3}y + 3$ **4.** $x = 2y - 1$ **5.** $x = -y + 3$ **6.** $x = 3y$ **7.** $x = y + 3$ **8.** $x = -\frac{7}{12}y$

Exercises, pages 250–251

1. Substitute the resulting expression in the other equation. **3.** $-3y - 4$ **5.** $5d + 1$ **7.** (1, 2) **9.** $(-1, -4)$ **11.** $(5, -3)$ **13.** (6, 2) **15.** (24, 3) **17.** $(-\frac{5}{49}, -\frac{25}{49})$ **19.** (2, 1) **21.** (2, 1) **23.** (12, 4) **25.** (3, 5) **27.** $(3, \frac{1}{2})$ **29.** $(2\frac{1}{2}, 3\frac{1}{2})$ **31.** $(3, -4)$ **33.** an infinite number of solutions **35.** \$750 **37.** Yes **39.** No; ordered pairs (1, 1) and $(1, -1)$ have the same first elements, and ordered pairs $(-1, 1)$ and $(-1, -1)$ have the same first elements. **41.** $(-h, -4h)$ **43.** $(-c, -2c)$ **45.** $(\frac{3a}{2}, 4a)$

Exercises, pages 253–255

1. x **3.** x **5.** $x + y = 1$ **7.** $2q = -1$ **9.** $(3, -1)$ **11.** $(-1, 4)$ **13.** $(-1, 3)$ **15.** $(1\frac{2}{3}, 2)$ **17.** $(1\frac{3}{4}, -\frac{1}{2})$ **19.** (15, 7) **21.** $(2\frac{3}{4}, \frac{1}{8})$ **23.** $(3, -\frac{2}{3})$ **25.** $(-3\frac{5}{6}, -6)$ **27.** $(7\frac{1}{5}, 5\frac{2}{5})$ **29.** $(6\frac{1}{2}, 1\frac{3}{4})$ **31.** $(1, -2\frac{1}{2})$ **33.** (0, 1) **35.** $(6, -50)$ **37.** (1, 1) **39.** $(-1\frac{2}{3}, -4\frac{2}{3})$ **41.** $(5, -5)$ **43.** $(-1, 1)$

45.

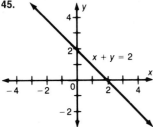

47.

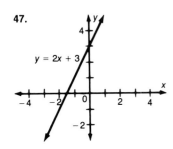

49. (c, d) **51.** $(\frac{a + 2}{3}, a - 1)$ **53.** The result is $0 = 0$. x and y can be any number. **55.** 1 pile

Review Capsule, page 255

1. $6x - 4y$ **2.** $-18a - 3b$ **3.** $-2w + 2s$ **4.** $-r - 3t$ **5.** $v - 7q$ **6.** $-7q + 9$ **7.** $-2r + 3p$ **8.** $-s + 9t$

Exercises, pages 257–259

1. Equation 2: 2 **3.** Equation 2: -9 **5.** Equation 1: 5; Equation 2: -2 **7.** Equation 1: 5; Equation 2: 3 **9.** (3, 1) **11.** $(2, -3)$ **13.** (5, 3) **15.** (1, 2) **17.** (3, 0) **19.** $(3, -4)$ **21.** (2, 2) **23.** $(-9, -5)$ **25.** $(-2, 5)$ **27.** (3, 2) **29.** $(\frac{1}{2}, 1)$ **31.** $(\frac{3}{4}, \frac{2}{3})$ **33.** (15.8, 7.4) **35.** $(6\frac{1}{10}, \frac{3}{5})$ **37.** (2, 7) For Ex. 38–41, answers will vary. **39.** $r = 5, s = 3$ **41.** $r = 3; s = -2$ or $r = -3, s = 2$ **43.** (.444445, 3.22222) **45.** (14, 10) **47.** $(2, -3)$

49.

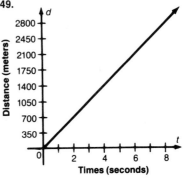

51. 2450 m **53.** 2800 m **55.** (1.3, 0.2) **57.** $(\frac{1}{2}, \frac{3}{10})$ **59.** $(\frac{1}{6}, \frac{11}{30})$ **61.** $f(-3x - y + 10\frac{1}{2}) + g(6x - 2y - 7) = 0; f[-3(\frac{7}{3}) - \frac{7}{2} + 10\frac{1}{2}] + g[6(\frac{7}{3}) - 2(\frac{7}{2}) - 7] = 0; f(-7 - \frac{7}{2} + 10\frac{1}{2}) + g(14 - 7 - 7) = 0; f(-10\frac{1}{2} + 10\frac{1}{2}) + g(14 - 14) = 0; f(0) + g(0) = 0; 0 + 0 = 0; 0 = 0$

Review Capsule, page 259

1. $x =$ amount Hal invested; $x + 2100$ **2.** $x =$ Roger's age; $\frac{1}{2}x$ **3.** $x =$ no. of Jim's pants; $3x$ **4.** $x =$ Joe's money; $x + 4$ **5.** $x =$ width of bookcase; $2x$ **6.** $x =$ no. of Cindy's mother's shoes; $x - 3$ **7.** $x =$ number of games Rick won; $2x + 1$ **8.** $l =$ length of pool; $\frac{2}{3}l$

Exercises, pages 260–261

1. 2 | 5, 7, 7, 8
  3 | 1, 1, 2, 2, 3, 5, 5, 6
  4 | 0, 0, 0
3. 72 **5. a.** Answers will vary. **b.** Reasons will vary. **7.** Median: 188; mode: 196 **9.** Theater A; Theater A

Review, page 262

1. (4, 0) **3.** $(3, -4)$ **5.** infinitely many **7.** (5, 5)

9. $(5, 2)$ **11.** $(2, -3)$ **13.** $(-2, -1)$ **15.** $(0.5, -0.6)$
17. $(1, -2)$

Exercises, pages 264–265
1. $x + y = 16$ **3.** $x - y = 4$ **5.** $x = y + 105$
7. $l = 2w$ **9.** 16, 36 **11.** length: 21 in;
width: 15 in **13.** 404 miles **15.** $13\frac{1}{3}$ in; $13\frac{1}{3}$ in;
$8\frac{1}{3}$ in **17.** 50°, 130° **19.** first: 8; second: -4
21. $76

Exercises, pages 267–269
1. 7; 2 **3.** $t + u = 8$ **5.** $10t + u = t + u + 9$
7. $10t + u = 2u$ **9.** $t = u - 5$ **11.** $t + u = 12$;
$10t + u = 12t$ **13.** $u = 2t$; $10t + u = 5u + 6$
15. $t + u = 12$; $10t + u = 12t$; 48 **17.** $u = 2t$;
$u - t = 4$; 48 **19.** $u = 2t - 11$; $10t + u = $
$7(t + u) - 6$; 85 **21.** $t + u = 9$; $10t + u = $
$10u + t + 27$; 63 **23.** $t + u = 11$; $10t + u + 45 = $
$10u + t$; 38 **25.** $10t + u = 5(t + u)$; $u = t + 1$;
45 **27.** Sean: 20; Keith: 12
29–32.

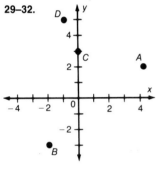

33. $9t - 9u$ **35.** $9t - 9u = 9(t - u)$; therefore, 9 is
always a factor. **37.** $100h + 10t + u - $
$(100u + 10t + h) = 100h + 10t + u - 100u - $
$10t - h = 99h - 99u = 99(h - u)$. Therefore, 99 is
always a factor. **39.** The number is 13425.

Review Capsule, page 269
1. $5k$ **2.** $25t$ **3.** $\frac{1}{2}b$ **4.** $5k$ **5.** $25q + 10d$
6. $10d + 5n$ **7.** $2.5r + 5t$ **8.** $100b + 1000q$

Exercises, pages 272–274
1. Value of each quarter: $0.25; total value of quarters: $0.25y; total number of coins: 12; total value: $1.95; $x + y = 12$; $0.10x + 0.25y = 1.95$ **3.** Amount of salt in Solution A: 0.12x; percent of salt in Solution B: 20%; amount of salt in Solution B: 0.2y percent of salt in mixture: 15%; amount of salt in mixture: 0.15 (24) **5.** 21 quarters; 24 dimes **7.** $900 invested at 9%; $4100 invested at 7% **9.** $16.50 full-fare **11.** 21 25¢ stamps; 16 15¢ stamps **13.** 15 dictionaries; 21 almanacs **15.** $16\frac{2}{3}$ kg of cashews

17. 7 g of 55% silver alloy; 23 g of 25% silver alloy
19. 200 g of Solution B; 120 g of Solution A **21.** 30
kg pecans; 10 kg almonds **23.** 60 L **25.** 12%:
$3300; 10%: $4500 **27.** Karl: 16 yr; brother: 7 yr
29.

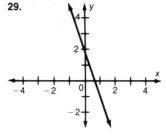

31.

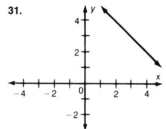

Focus on College Entrance Tests, page 275
1. 74 **3.** 7 **5.** 4.8 **7.** 72 **9.** 20 **11.** 2 **13.** 0

Chapter Review, page 277
1.

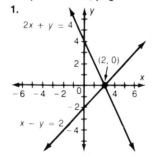

3.

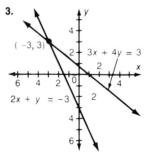

5. none **7.** $(1, 5)$ **9.** $(1, \frac{1}{3})$ **11.** $(-1, 0)$
13. $(-2, 4)$ **15.** $(2, -5)$ **17.** adult: 129; student:
214 **19.** Solution A: 4 liters; Solution B: 6 liters

Chapter Test, page 278

1.

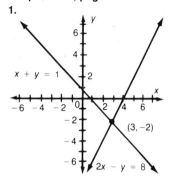

3. $(-1\frac{2}{3}, -7\frac{1}{3})$ **5.** $(3, -2)$ **7.** Carl: 26 hours; Tony: 32 hours **9.** small: 16; large: 8

Additional Practice, page 279

1.   **3.**

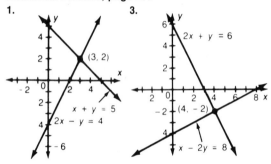

5. $(3, 7)$ **7.** $(5, -9)$ **9.** $(\frac{1}{2}, \frac{5}{8})$ **11.** $(1\frac{1}{2}, \frac{1}{2})$

13.

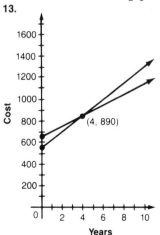

15. length: 21 cm; width: 13 cm **17.** quarters: 16; dimes: 40

Cumulative Maintenance, pages 280–281

1. a **3.** b **5.** c **7.** b **9.** b **11.** b **13.** a **15.** b
17. 7.75 hours **19.** $46,875; $703,125 **21.** 48
23. width: 12 cm; length: 32 m

Chapter 8: Inequalities

Exercises, pages 284–286

1. > **3.** > **5.** >; > **7.** >; > **9.** -5 **11.** 7
13. 1.5 **15.** $2\frac{1}{2}$ **17.** $t > -3$; all points to the right of and not including, -3 **19.** $y > 12$; all points to the right of, and not including, 12 **21.** $r < 7$; all points to the left of, and not incuding, 7 **23.** $r < 5$; all points to the left of, and not including, 5 **25.** $c < -7$; all points to the left of, and not including, -7
27. $z > 16$; all points to the right of, and not including, 16 **29.** $x < 6$; all points to the left of, and not including, 6 **31.** $x \geq 8$; all points to the right of, and including, 8 **33.** $r \geq 19$; all points to the right of, and including, 19 **35.** $n \geq -2$; all points to the right of, and including, -2 **37.** $z < -5$; all points to the left of, and not including, -5 **39.** $-1 \geq y$; all points to the left of, and including, -1 **41.** $q \leq -18$; all points to the left of, and including, -18
43. $x > -31$; all points to the right of, and not including, -31 **45.** $x \leq 0$; all points to the left of, and including, 0 **47.** $6.50 tickets: 1200; $8.00 tickets: 3300 **49.** 45 **51.** 2 **53.** 2 **55.** 0 **57.** > **59.** z
61. 3 **63.** $b + 3$ **65.** No **67.** The first palindrome is 15951, so the next palindrome is 16061. The car traveled 110 miles.

Review Capsule, page 286

1. $\{-2, -1, 0, 1\}$ **2.** $\{1, 2\}$ **3.** $\{-2, -1, 0, 1, 2\}$
4. $\{2\}$ **5.** $\{1, 2\}$ **6.** $\{-2, -1, 0, 1\}$

Exercises, pages 288–290

1. > **3.** < **5.** > **7.** >; > **9.** >; > **11.** $z > 9$; all points to the right of, and not incuding, 9 **13.** $z < -2$; all points to the left of, and not including, -2 **15.** $n < -3$; all points to the left of, and not including, -3 **17.** $y \leq 0$; all points to the left of, and including, 0 **19.** $w \leq 2$; all points to the left of, and including, 2 **21.** $r < -9$; all points to the left of, and not including, -9 **23.** $c \geq 7\frac{1}{2}$; all points to the right of, and including, $7\frac{1}{2}$ **25.** $x > 4$; all points to the right of, and not including, 4 **27.** $p < 6$; all points to the left of, and not including, 6
29. $y > -\frac{11}{3}$ **31.** $a < 3$ **33.** $x \geq -2$ **35.** $t \geq -10$
37. $z > \frac{3}{2}$ **39.** $p \leq -3$

41. $x < -\frac{4}{3}$　　**43.** $x < -\frac{1}{2}$　　**45.** $x \geq -\frac{8}{5}$
47. $m > -\frac{1}{2}$ **49.** $n > -22$ **51.** $s \geq -2$ **53.** $t \leq -\frac{13}{8}$
55. $r \leq -6$ **57.** $k > -1$ **59.** $x > 5.45833$ **61.** $y = -3x + 8$; $m = -3$; $b = 8$ **63.** $y = -2x - 3$; $m = -2$; $b = -3$ **65.** $y = 3x - 5$; $m = 3$; $b = -5$
67. 8.5%: $500; 9.2%: $1500 **69.** $>$ **71** $<$ **73.** T **75.** F; if $y = 0$, then $0^2 \not> 0$ **77.** F; if $x = 2$ and $y = -2$, then $2(-2) \not> 0$ **79.** F; if $x = 10$ and $y = 3$, then $3^2 \not> 10$ **81.** F; if $x = -3$ and $y = -4$, then $(-3)(-4) \not< (-3)^2$ **83.** Use the guess and check strategy. Solutions may vary. Two solutions are 1, 4, 8, and 9; 2, 3, 6, and 7.

Review Capsule, page 290
1. 90. **2.** 26 **3.** 139 **4.** 4.3

Exercises, pages 292–294
1. Let c = cost of bicycle; $c > 100$ **3.** Let c = cost of ticket; $c + 2.75 < 20$ **5.** $\frac{48 + 52 + 71 + x}{4} < 60$
7. $\frac{120 + 132 + 160 + 118 + b}{5} > 130$ **9.** $50 **11.** 89
13. $620.01 **15.** 101 **17.** 24 and 25 **19.** 48 and 50 **21.** 138 lb **23.** {all real numbers less than 3} **25.** 4 For Exercises 26–31, each graph is a straight line containing the given points. **27.** (0, 0), (1, −3) **29.** (0, 4), (1, 5) **31.** (0, 3), (1, −2) **33.** 11, 12, and 13

Exercises, pages 296–298
1. disjunction **3.** 0, 1, 2, 3, and 4 **5.** c **7.** d
9. b **11.** $3x - 1 = 11$ or $3x - 1 < 11$ **13.** $3 < y$ and $y < 8$ **15.** $t - \frac{1}{2} = 3\frac{1}{2}$ or $t - \frac{1}{2} > 3\frac{1}{2}$
17. $-3 < x + 2$ and $x + 2 < -1$ **19.** $-9 < 3k$ and $3k < 15$
21.
23.
25.
27.
29. $x \geq 7$ **31.** $-2\frac{1}{2} < x < 5$ **33.** $-2 \leq x < 4$
35. $-3 < t \leq 6$ **37.** $y \leq 3$ **39.** $c \geq 2\frac{1}{2}$
41. $x \leq -1$ **43.** $-3 \leq m < 0$ **45.** $1 \leq m \leq 6$
47. 130, 205 **49.** $76 < y \leq 81$ **51.** $58 < y \leq 60$
53. $\{51\frac{1}{4}, 51\frac{3}{8}, 51\frac{1}{2}, 51\frac{5}{8}, 51\frac{3}{4}, 51\frac{7}{8}, 52, 52\frac{1}{8}, 52\frac{1}{4}, 52\frac{3}{8},$ $52\frac{1}{2}, 52\frac{5}{8}\}$ **55.** $y < -3$ or $y \geq 3$ **57.** $2 < n < 3$
59. $-5 > x \geq -8$ **61.** $n < 7$ **63.** $19.99
65. $y = x + 9$ **67.** $y = -2x$ **69.** $y = \frac{1}{4}x + 1$

Review, page 299
1. $n < 3$; all points to the left of, and not including, 3 **3.** $g \leq -5$; all points to the left of, and including, −5 **5.** $c > -4$; all points to the right of, and not including, −4 **7.** $h < -3$; all points to the left of, and not including, −3 **9.** $s < 1$; all points to the left of, and not including, 1 **11.** $t > -1$ **13.** 14 and 56 **15.** $-3 < x < 2$

Exercises, page 300
1. Five 22¢-stamps; two 17¢-stamps **3.** Seven-point touchdowns: 4; three-point field goals: 3 **5.** Ten-pound weights: 4; three-pound weights: 6 **7.** $5.50 per hour job: 6 hours; $4.00 per hour job: 5 hours **9.** The following combinations are possible: 10 two-point goals and 0 three-point goals, 7 two-point goals and 2 three-point goals, 4 two-point goals and 4 three-point goals, or 1 two-point goal and 6 three-point goals.

Exercises, pages 303–305
1. $x = 5$ or $x = -5$ **3.** $m = 2$ or $m = -2$
5. $s > -3$ and $s < 3$ **7.** $n < -4$ or $n > 4$ **9.** c
11. f **13.** b **15.** $a = -5$ or $a = -1$ **17.** $y = -2$ or $y = 2$ **19.** $y = -3$ **21.** $k = -13$ or $k = 17$
23. $t = -10$ or $t = 8$ **25.** $d = \frac{1}{2}$ or $d = \frac{5}{6}$
27. $w = -17$ or $w = 13$ **29.** ϕ **31.** $m = -4\frac{2}{3}$ or $m = 4\frac{2}{3}$ **33.** $x > -5$ and $x < 5$; all points between, and not including, −5 and 5 **35.** $n > -1$ and $n < 5$; all points between, and not including, −1 and 5 **37.** $m < -7$ or $m > 1$; all points to the left of, and not including, −7or all points to the right of, and not including, 1 **39.** $x > -4$ and $x < 5$; all points between, and not including, −4 and 5 **41.** $n > 1$ and $n < 5$; all points between, and not including, 1 and 5 **43.** $t < -4$ or $t > 4$; all points to the left of, and not including, −4 or, all the points to the right of, and not including, 4 **45.** $c \leq \frac{5}{3}$ or $c \geq 3$; all points to the left of, and including, $\frac{5}{3}$, or all points to the right of, and including, 3 **47.** $n \geq -2$ and $n \leq 2$; all points to the right of, and including, −2, and all points to the left of, and including, 2 **49.** −6 or 4 **51.** 8 or −14 **53.** $y = -\frac{2}{3}x + 3\frac{1}{3}$
55. $y = x$ **57.** $y = 2x - 6$ **59.** 93 **61.** ϕ
63. $x \leq 0$ **65.** $5 < x < 8$ or $-8 < x < -5$ **67.** For 10% profit, cost = $90; $99 − $90 = $9 (profit); For 10% loss, cost = $110; $110 − $99 = $11 (loss); The shop owner had a net loss of $2.

Answers to Selected Exercises **657**

Review Capsule, page 305

1. $(4, -1)$ **2.** $(3, 6)$ **3.** $(1, -5)$ **4.** $(-1\frac{1}{2}, -3)$
5. Yes **6.** Yes **7.** No

Exercises, pages 307–308

1. half-plane; line **3.** $\geq$; $\leq$ **5.** none **7.** none
9. Above the line that contains $(0, -3)$ and $(1, -2)$
11. To the left of the line that contains $(0, -4)$ and
$(1, -1)$ **13.** To the right of the line that contains
$(0, 0)$ and $(1, -3)$ **15.** To the left of the line that contains $(0, -4)$ and $(1, -6)$ **17.** Above the line that
contains $(0, 4)$ and $(1, 3)$ **19.** Above the line that
contains $(0, 2)$ and $(3, 0)$ **21.** Above the line that
contains $(0, 4)$ and $(2, 4)$ **23.** Below the line that
contains $(0, -4)$ and $(2, -4)$ **25.** To the left of the
line that contains $(8, 0)$ and $(8, 2)$ **27.** To the left of
the line that contains $(-4, 0)$ and $(-4, 2)$ **29.** The
closed half-plane above the line that contains $(0, -4)$
and $(2, -4)$ **31.** The closed half-plane to the right
of the line that contains $(1, -6)$ and $(0, 9)$ **33.** The
closed half-plane below the line that contains $(0, -5)$
and $(2, -5)$ **35.** The closed half-plane to the left of
the line that contains $(0, 6)$ and $(1, 8)$ **37.** $x > 2$
39. $y < x$ **41.** $x = 4$ or $x = -4$ **43.** $t = -3$ or
$t = 4$ **45.** $n > -5$ and $n < 7$ **47.** $t > -3$ and
$t < 3$ **49.** $t > -3$ and $t < 2$ **51.** $a < -5$ or $a = 5$
53. $m > -3$ and $m \leq 3$ **55.** 5 **57.** Closed half-
plane **59.** Closed half-plane **61.** Straight line
63. Closed half-plane

Exercises, pages 310–311

1. c **3.** a
5.

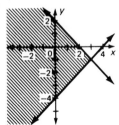

7.

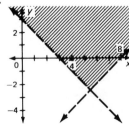

9.

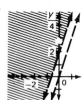

11.

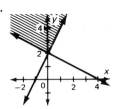

13.

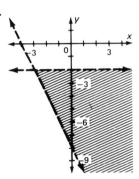

15.

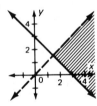

17.

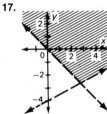

19.

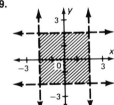

21.

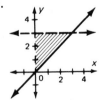

23.

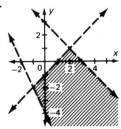

25. 120 km   **27.** $x < -6$ or $x > 6$; all points to the left of, and not including, -6 or all points to the right of, and not including, 6

29. $-11 < a < 7$; all points between, and not including, -11 and 7   **31.** zero   **33.** $\frac{5}{3}$

35. 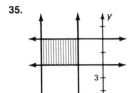   **37.**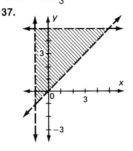

Exercises, pages 313–314

1. $24; 0$ **3.** $\frac{2}{3}; -2$ **5.** $40; 0$ **7.** $60; 0$ **9. a.** $(0, 0)$, $(0, 4)$, $(4, 0)$ **b.** 0   **11. a.** $(0, 0)$, $(0, 5)$, $(4, 1)$, $(4, 0)$; **b.** 0   **13.** $15x + 18y$

15.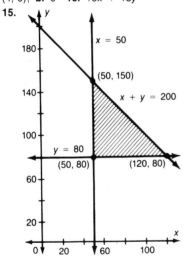

17. \$3450   **19.** $x + y \le 4$; $x \ge 0$; $y \ge 0$ **21.** $(0, 4)$, $(0, 0)$, $(4, 0)$

Focus on College Entrance Tests, page 316

1. Ann: banana; Beth: apple; Carol: orange

3.

	Teacher	Detective	Mayor
Jim	✔	×	×
Sarah	×	×	✔
Jane	×	✔	×

Jim: teacher; Sarah: mayor;
Jane: detective

Chapter Review, pages 318–319

1. $y > 4$; all points to the right of, and not including, 4   **3.** $b \le 5$; all points to the left of, and including, 5   **5.** $n > -1$; all points to the right of, and not including, -1 **7.** $r < -2$; all points to the left of, and not including, -2 **9.** $x \le 11$ **11.** $t \le 7$ **13.** 12   **15.** $x > -3$ or $x = -3$ **17.** $t > -5$ and $t < 1$ **19.** $s > 2$ or $s = 2$ **21.** $x > -3$ and $x < 4$; all points between, and not including, -3 and 4   **23.** $m > -2$ and $m \le 16$; all points between -2 and 16, including 16 but not including -2 **25.** $y = -2$ or $y = 2$ **27.** $p = 1$ or $p = 11$ **29.** $a = -11$ or $a = -1$ **31.** $-2 < n < 6$; all points between, and not including, -2 and 6   **33.** $c < -\frac{3}{7}$ or $c > -1$; {all real numbers}   **35.** The closed half-plane to the right of the line that contains $(0, -1)$ and $(1, 0)$ **37.** The closed half-plane to the left of the line that contains $(-5, 0)$ and $(0, 5)$ **39.** a   **41.** c

43.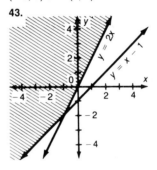

45.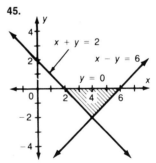

47. maximum: 24; minimum: 0   **49.** maximum: 16; minimum: -4 **51.** maximum: 8; minimum: -20 **53.** $x \le 3$; $y \le 4$; $x + y \le 5$; $x \ge 0$; $y \ge 0$ **55.** $(0, 0)$, $(3, 0)$, $(3, 2)$, $(1, 4)$, $(0, 4)$

Chapter Test, page 320

1. $x < 3$; all points to the left of, and not incuding, 3   **3.** $r \le 1$; all points to the left of, and including, 1   **5.** 94, 95   **7.** $3x + 2 = 10$ or $3x + 2 < 10$ **9.** $x \le 3$; all numbers to the left of, and including, 3

11. $n < -1$ <u>or</u> $n > 5$; all numbers to the left of, and not including, -1, <u>or</u> all numbers to the right of, and not including, 5 **13.** $t = -2$ <u>or</u> $t = 6$

15.

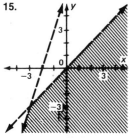

17. $x \geq 110$; $y \geq 60$; $x + y \leq 300$ **19.** (240, 60), (110, 60), (110, 190)

Additional Practice, page 321

1. $a \leq -7$ **3.** $n > \frac{1}{2}$ **5.** $2y = 5$ <u>or</u> $2y > 5$
7. $-6 < 4a + 6$ <u>and</u> $4a + 6 < -2$
9. $-4 < p \leq 0$; all points between -4 and 0, including 0 and not including -4 **11.** The open half-plane above the line that contains $(0, -1)$ and $(2, 1)$
13. The open half-plane below the line that contains $(0, -4)$ and $(-4, 0)$

15. **17.**

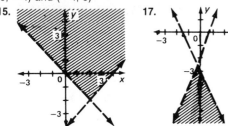

19. $15 \leq s \leq 100$ **21.** $200x + 140y$ **23.** (2, 6), (4, 3), (4, 6); $1220

Cumulative Maintenance, pages 322–323

1. d **3.** a **5.** c **7.** a **9.** c **11.** d **13.** a **15.** b
17. a **19.** $14,375 **21.** 8 hours **23.** $13,750 at 8% and $11,250 at 10% **25.** 4 ft; 16 ft; 20 ft

Chapter 9: Exponents and Polynomials

Exercises, pages 327–328

1. 17. **3.** 7 **5.** 5; 6; $5 \cdot 5 \cdot 5 \cdot 5 \cdot 5$ **7.** 2; 6; $2 \cdot 2 \cdot 2 \cdot 2 \cdot 2 \cdot 2$ **9.** 10^5; $10 \cdot 10 \cdot 10 \cdot 10 \cdot 10$
11. 10^4; 10; 4 **13.** x^1; x; 1 **15.** 10,000 **17.** 100,000
19. 10,000,000,000 **21.** a **23.** -1 **25.** -1
27. -1 **29.** 1 **31.** 1 **33.** 1 **35.** 10^5 **37.** 10^6
39. 10^3 **41.** 10^9 **43.** 10^{12} **45.** 2^7 **47.** 10^5 **49.** 2^6
51. 2^{17} **53.** a^6 **55.** m^8 **57.** 4 **59.** 2 **61.** 9
63. -6 **65.** 18 **67.** -24 **69.** See the Solution Key. **71.** See the Solution Key. **73.** $57

Review Capsule, page 328

1. 200 **2.** -378 **3.** -54 **4.** 1 **5.** 0 **6.** 3600
7. -280 **8.** -1

Exercises, pages 330–331

1. Yes **3.** Yes **5.** Yes **7.** No **9.** Yes **11.** No
13. Yes **15.** No **17.** x^7 **19.** $-y^3$ **21.** x^6 **23.** n^7
25. a^2 **27.** b^2 **29.** $-x^3$ **31.** y^3 **33.** x^3 **35.** $2^8 =$
256 **37.** $5^5(-5^2) = -5^7 = -78,125$ **39.** $6a^4b^3$
41. $-36x^8$ **43.** x^4 **45.** 10^{14} **47.** 6×10^6 **49.** 3×10^9 **51.** $2.8a \times 10^{11}$ **53.** N **55.** N **57.** N
59. 10,000 **61.** 1,000,000 **63.** -1 **65. a.** (0, 0), (6, 0), (0, 6) **b.** 0 **67. a.** (0, 0), (6, 0), (6, 4), (0, 1)
b. 0 **69.** $(-2, -5)$ **71.** (3, 1) **73.** y^{2+b} **75.** a^{x+3}
77. x^{2a+7} **79.** 2^{7a} **81.** $(x + 2)^6$ **83.** $(x + 2)^{a+b}$

Exercises, pages 333–334

1. F; because $(y^2)^3$ means $y^2 \cdot y^2 \cdot y^2$. The expression equals y^6. **3.** F; because $(-4a)^3$ means $(-4a)(-4a)(-4a)$. The expression $(-4a)(-4a)(-4a)$ $= -64a^3$. **5.** T **7.** F; because $(-x^4)^2$ means $(-x^4)(-x^4)$. The expression equals x^8y^4. **9.** x^6 **11.** x^8
13. x^{15} **15.** x^{10} **17.** y^9 **19.** b^{24} **21.** a^3b^3 **23.** $4x^2$
25. $x^4y^4z^4$ **27.** 36. **29.** $-x^5$ **31.** $16x^2$ **33.** $9a^4b^2$
35. $-27b^3$ **37.** $81a^4b^8$ **39.** $16m^{12}n^8$ **41.** $64a^{12}c^6d^9$
43. $64x^{18}y^{12}$ **45.** x^8y^6 **47.** 4×10^6 **49.** $\frac{8}{27}$
51. $\frac{c^7}{d^7}$ **53.** $\frac{x^4}{y^6}$ **55.** $\frac{c^6}{d^3}$ **57.** $\frac{a^{18}}{b^5}$ **59.** i **61.** a **63.** f
65. d **67.** x^{10} **69.** $-8a^2b^4$ **71.** 10^2 **73.** 10^7
75. $(7, -1)$ **77.** $(-4, -1\frac{3}{4})$ **79.** $(1, 1)$ **81.** $\frac{a^8}{b^4c^{12}}$
83. $\frac{a^9b^6}{c^{12}}$ **85.** $-6a^7b^8$ **87.** $\frac{-27x^6}{64y^6}$ **89.** x^{n^2} **91.** $\frac{m^k}{n^k}$
93. $\frac{3^cx^{cn}}{5^cy^{cm}}$ **95.** $\frac{3^ka^{km}b^{kn}}{2^kx^ky^k}$

Review Capsule, page 334

1. $-\frac{1}{4}$ **2.** $-z$ **3.** $-8x$ **4.** 1

Exercises, pages 336–337

1. x^6 **3.** $-xy^2$ **5.** $8^2 = 64$ **7.** 2^2 or 4 **9.** 5^3 or 125
11. a^5 **13.** x **15.** ay^2 **17.** a^2b^3 **19.** k^2m **21.** $5x^5y$
23. $9r^2s^2$ **25.** 4 **27.** P **29.** P **31.** N **33.** P
35. $-2b$ **37.** $\frac{3ab^3}{2}$ **39.** $-125a^3$ **41.** 25×10^4
43. x^8 **45.** -64 **47.** 16×10^{16} **49.** 42×10^5
51. 4.35×10^6 **53.** $ac \times 10^{x+y}$ **55.** $(-\frac{6}{7}, -3)$
57. $(-2, 2)$ **59.** $(6, -1)$ **61.** $a^{x-y}b^4$ **63.** $x^{2u-v-2r}y^{-z}$
65. a^x **67.** b^2cd^{2-2k} **69.** y^{16a-50} **71.** $1.69^{a-1} \times 10^a$

Review Capsule, page 337

1. a^{10} **2.** $-c^4$ **3.** 4^7 **4.** x^3 **5.** x^3y^2 **6.** $3c^7d$
7. 10^{10} **8.** 10^8 **9.** 6×10^6 **10.** 10.5×10^5
11. 6.732×10^8

Review, page 338

1. -9 3. -48 5. 36 7. $-x^5$ 9. $6c^3d^4$ 11. a^8b^4
13. $\dfrac{r^6}{s^3t^3}$ 15. y 17. $-4b^2$

Exercises, page 339

1. $212.27 3. $637.01 5. $315.28

Exercises, pages 341–342

1. positive 3. $\dfrac{1}{3^2}$ 5. $\dfrac{1}{5^4}$ 7. $\dfrac{1}{(-7)^5}$ 9. $\dfrac{1}{30^2}$ 11. $\dfrac{1}{16}$
13. $\dfrac{1}{r^7}$ 15. $\dfrac{1}{-8}$ 17. 16 19. $\dfrac{3}{x^5}$ 21. $\dfrac{b^2}{a^3}$ 23. $\dfrac{1}{4x^2}$
25. $\dfrac{a}{b^3}$ 27. 4 29. a^2 31. $\dfrac{1}{x^5}$ 33. $\dfrac{1}{n}$ 35. r^3
37. $\dfrac{1}{p^{15}}$ 39. c^4 41. 1 43. 2^3 or 8 45. x 47. 3×10^{10} or 30,000,000,000 49. a^{20} 51. $16c^4d^2$
53. Let $x =$ one number; Let $y =$ another number; $x = y + 8$; $x + y = 22$; 15, 7 55. Let $x =$ the large number; Let $y =$ the small number; $x - y = 9$; $2x = 4y + 2$; 8, 17 57. $\dfrac{1}{a^8}$ 59. $\dfrac{a^{21}}{b^9}$ 61. $\dfrac{b}{a}$
63. $\dfrac{1}{w^9}$ 65. $\dfrac{7x^2z^2}{y^2}$ 67. $\dfrac{s^5}{4fr^3t^{11}}$

Exercises, pages 345–346

1. scientific notation 3. negative 5. 4.6×10^3
7. 6.7×10^7 9. 2.4×10^{13} 11. 5.7×10^{-4}
13. 2×10^{-5} 15. 8×10^{-4} 17. 2×10^{-4}
19. 6×10^6 21. 3×10^3 23. 4×10^7
25. 5×10^{-3} 27. 1×10^{13} km 29. 1×10^{10} yr
31. 1.5×10^8 km 33. 1×10^{-8} g 35. 1.23×10^7
37. 4×10^{-12} 39. 5×10^{-6} 41. 1.98×10^{30}
43. 1.35×10^{34} 45. 6000 47. 0.000000022
49. $\dfrac{1}{16}$ 51. $\dfrac{3}{x^7}$ 53. $\dfrac{1}{49}$ 55. $\dfrac{1}{n^{10}}$ 57. x^5
59. $-3r^2s^4t$ 61. 45 pairs

Exercises, pages 348–350

1. binomial 3. trinomial 5. trinomial 7. $12a + 2b$ 9. $-2a^2 + 5ab - 12b^2$ 11. $12a + 2b - 4c$
13. $-p + 4t + 7x$ 15. $14x + y - 4z$ 17. $-5a^2 - 2ab - 4b^2$ 19. $7ab - 3ac$ 21. $4x^2 + 15x - 7$
23. $5a + 5b - 5$ 25. $10m + 12x - 5$ 27. $4a + 10b - 2$ 29. $a - 5$ 31. $13s$ 33. $-2b + 2c$
35. $a + b$ 37. $-x^2 + 2x + 8$ 39. $x^2 - 6x - 7$
41. $3x + 2y$ 43. $x^2 - 9y^2$ 45. $2x^2 - 2xy - 4y^2$
47. $-9a + 3b - 6c + 3d$ 49. $2x^2 + 8xy - 2y^2$
51. 4.8×10^7 53. 1.0×10^{-6} 55. 2.3×10^2
57. 3.96×10^{-2} 59. 24 61. $-3x + 3y$ 63. $a + 2b + c + 1$ 65. The perimeter of the square is 2 meters larger.

Review Capsule, page 350

1. $6a + 15b - 12$ 2. $-14x + 7y - 35$ 3. $-2a + 6b - 1$ 4. $20k - 15s + 10$ 5. $-21 + 5t + 3r$

6. $6u - 10w + 11z$ 7. a^9 8. q^3 9. $-t^7$ 10. a^{10}
11. $-27x^3y^6$ 12. $a - b + 3$ 13. $8b + 3c + 2$
14. $9n - 2$

Exercises, pages 352–354

1. x; 9 3. $-2n^3$; $5n$ 5. a; 9 7. $2x^2 + 10x$
9. $3t^4 + 6t^2$ 11. $3x^3 + 4x^2$ 13. $6y^2 - 8y$
15. $-3x^2 - 27x$ 17. $r^3 - 9r$ 19. $6x^3 - 18x^2$
21. $35m^2n - 10mn^2$ 23. $-3x^3 - 15x^2 - 6x$
25. $-12a^3b + 8a^2b^2 - 10ab^3$ 27. $-3a^3 + 2a^2 + 9a$ 29. $x^2 + 14x + 45$ 31. $7x^2 + 10x + 3$
33. $2a^2 + ab - 3b^2$ 35. $a^2 + 5a + 6$ 37. $2a^2 - 3ab - 9b^2$ 39. $ac + ad - bc - bd$ 41. $ac - ad + bc - bd$ 43. $6bc + 9bd - 8c^2 - 12cd$
45. $49n^2 - 9$ 47. $2a^2 - 11ab + 12b^2$ 49. $a^2 - b^2$
51. $\dfrac{1}{9}t^2 + \dfrac{1}{3}t - 30$ 53. $a^4 - a^2b - 2b^2$ 55. $m^4 - 4m^2n^2 + 4n^4$ 57. $3a^6 + 4a^3b^3 + b^6$ 59. $x^2 - 6x + 9$ 61. $x^2 + 12x + 35$ 63. $-11y - 48$
65. $2x + 8xy - 4y^2$ 67. $21x^2 - 55x + 36$
69. $-16x - 1$ 71. $x^2 - 49$
73. $(x^2 - 18x + 81)(1 + \dfrac{1}{8}\pi)$ 75. $x^3 + 3x^2 + 3x + 1$ 77. Square; 4 units larger 79. Square; $4x + 1$ square units larger 81. 14 dimes and 46 quarters 83. $x^3 + x^2 - x - 1$ 85. $x^3 + y^3$
87. $-3a^3 + 2a^2 + 3a - 2$ 89. $x^4 + 2x^3 - x^2 - 3x + 1$

Review, page 354

1. $\dfrac{1}{64}$ 3. $-\dfrac{1}{125}$ 5. $\dfrac{1}{x^{10}}$ 7. $\dfrac{1}{s^7}$ 9. 4.3×10^{-6}
11. 2.0×10^6 13. 3.5×10^4 15. 3.0×10^{-3}
17. $4x^2y + 7xy^2$ 19. $x^3 - 4x$ 21. $4y^3 + 8y^2$
23. $4c^2 + 12c + 9$ 25. $b + 3$

Exercises, pges 355–357

1. x^2; $3x$; $5x$; 15; $x^2 + 2x - 15$ 3. $32x^2$; $40x^2$; $12x$; 15; $32x^2 + 28x - 15$ 5. $6x^2$; $15xy$; $4xy$; $10y^2$; $6x^2 + 11xy - 10y^2$ 7. $x^2 + 8x + 15$ 9. $x^2 - 4$ 11. $a^2 + a - 6$ 13. $b^2 - 4b - 21$ 15. $p^2 + 20p + 99$
17. $d^2 + d - 20$ 19. $12y^2 + 17y + 6$ 21. $2x^2 + 13x + 21$ 23. $9x^2 - 16$ 25. $b^2 + 8b + 16$
27. $m^2 - 4m - 77$ 29. $a^2 - 4c^2$ 31. $3x^2 - x - 2$
33. $y^4 + 6y^2 + 9$ 35. $16y^2 - 24y + 9$
37. $4a^2 + 16a + 15$ 39. $5x^2 + 8x + 3$
41. $35b^2 + 3b - 2$ 43. $24x^2 - 23x - 12$
45. $6c^2 - 43c + 72$ 47. $x^4 - 16$
49. $7a^2 + 54a - 16$ 51. $6x^2 - xy - 15y^2$
53. $\dfrac{7}{2}x^2 - 17x - 24$ 55. $\dfrac{1}{12}t^2 + 4t + 48$
57. $\dfrac{1}{35}x^2 - 2x + 35$ 59. $0.36w^2 + 0.42w - 1.2$
61. $x^2 + 4x - 21$ 63. $x^2 + 10x + 25$

65. Rectangle with length $(2a + 1)$ units and width $(a - 5)$ units; 13 square units larger   **67.** $-2y^3 + 8y^2 - 14y$ **69.** $2a + 3$ **71.** $8x$ **73.** $-6b + 4c$ **75.** $8e^2 + 2e + 4$ **77.** 9 kilograms   **79.** $8x^3 + 36x^2 + 54x + 27$ **81.** $27x^3 - 27x^2 + 9x - 1$ **83.** $x^3 - 3x^2y + 3xy^2 - y^3$ **85.** $8x^3 - 84x^2y + 294xy^2 - 343y^3$

Exercises, pages 359–360

1. product   **3.** x^2 **5.** 25   **7.** m^4 **9.** $a^2 + 6a + 9$ **11.** $a^2 + 10a + 25$ **13.** $a^2 - 10a + 25$ **15.** $x^2 - 2xy + y^2$ **17.** $4a^2 + 4a + 1$ **19.** $25m^2 - 10m + 1$ **21.** $n^2 + 6n + 9$ **23.** $9x^2 - 6xy + y^2$ **25.** $4x^2 - 12x + 9$ **27.** $4x^2 + 4xy + y^2$ **29.** $4x^2 - 12xy + 9y^2$ **31.** $100a^2 + 40a + 4$ **33.** $4x^4 + 12x^2y^2 + 9y^4$ **35.** $a^4 - 6a^2b^2 + 9b^4$ **37.** $a^4 - 6a^2 + 9$ **39.** $121a^4 + 22a^2c^2 + c^4$ **41.** 361   **43.** 2,704   **45.** 441   **47.** 998,001   **49.** 10,201   **51.** $x^2 + 18x + 81$ **53.** $x^2 - 8x + 16$ **55.** $x^2 + x + \frac{1}{4}$ **57.** $x^2 - \frac{1}{3}x + \frac{1}{36}$ **59.** $36b^2 + 6b + \frac{1}{4}$ **61.** $x^2 - ax + \frac{a^2}{4}$ **63.** $x^2 + xy + \frac{y^2}{4}$ **65.** $x^2 + 9x + 18$ **67.** $x^2 - 5x + 6$ **69.** $8x^2 - 18xy + 7y^2$ **71.** $a^2 + 4a$ **73.** $2y^2 - 5y$ **75.** $-s^3 + 3s^2 - 5s$ **77.** (6, 1)   **79.** (2, 2)

Exercises, pages 362–363

1. $x^2 - 1$ **3.** $4r^2 - 25$ **5.** $9h^2 - 16s^2$ **7.** $(30 + 2)(30 - 2)$ **9.** $(30 - 3)(30 + 3)$ **11.** $(90 + 11)(90 - 11)$ **13.** $(40 + 1)(40 - 1)$ **15.** $p^2 - 49$ **17.** $p^2 - 64$ **19.** $b^2 - c^2$ **21.** $4p^2 - 9$ **23.** $R^2 - r^2$ **25.** $25x^2 - 16y^2$ **27.** $36x^4 - 49y^2$ **29.** $a^2b^2 - c^2$ **31.** $\frac{1}{4} - 4x^2$ **33.** $4c^2 - d^2$ **35.** $25y^2 - 16$ **37.** $x^6 - y^6$ **39.** 399   **41.** 9996   **43.** 75   **45.** 396   **47.** 2499   **49.** $\frac{1}{2}x^2 + (\frac{1}{2})x - 3$ **51.** Square; 16 square units greater   **53.** $a^2 - 6a + 9$ **55.** $9x^2 - 30x + 25$ **57.** $a^4 + 4a^2b^2 + 4b^4$ **59.** $49c^4 - 42c^2d + 9d^2$ **61.** $6x^2 - 37x + 56$ **63.** $y^4 + 2y^2 + 1$ **65.** $\frac{3}{2}t^2 + 19t - 28$ **67.** 35   **69.** $1 - y^{4a}$ **71.** $a^4b^{16} - 25$ **73.** $b^{2n} - c^{4n}$ **75.** $x^{4n} - 4y^{2n}$ **77.** It is cheaper to take two friends at the same time since you would need only one ticket for yourself.

Exercises, pages 365–366

1. $0t$ **3.** $0a$ **5.** $0x^3 + 0x^2 + 0x$ **7.** $2r^3 - 9r^2 + 10r + 5$ **9.** $6z^2 - 13z + 2$ **11.** $y + 11$ **13.** $p - 6 + \frac{62}{p + 5}$ **15.** $2a - 7$ **17.** $3c - 15 - \frac{36}{c - 3}$ **19.** $3a - 2 + \frac{1}{2a - 3}$ **21.** $5n + 2 + \frac{6}{3n + 2}$

23. $a^2 - 3a - 4$ **25.** $3x^2 + 5x - 2$ **27.** $a^2 + 2ab + \frac{3ab^2}{3a + 2b}$ **29.** $x - 5 + \frac{50}{x + 5}$ **31.** $a^2 + 2ab + 4b^2$ **33.** $x^2 + 3x + 7$ **35.** $x^2 - 3x + 9$ **37.** $p^2 - 64$ **39.** $x^2 - 9y^2$ **41.** $4c^2 - 25d^2$ **43.** (1, 2)   **45.** $k = -8$ **47.** $14x - 10y$ units

1. c   **3.** b   **5.** a

Chapter Review, pages 369–370

1. -8 **3.** 1   **5.** -1 **7.** 128   **9.** -128 **11.** a^8 **13.** p^5 **15.** 10^6, or 1,000,000   **17.** $3m^3n$ **19.** x^{15} **21.** $27y^3$ **23.** $27c^3d^{12}$ **25.** $\frac{m^6}{p^3n^9}$ **27.** 3   **29.** $3ab^3$ **31.** $3x^3y$ **33.** $s^{2x-1}t^{3y-2}$ **35.** $\frac{1}{3^4} = \frac{1}{81}$ **37.** $\frac{1}{y^6}$ **39.** $\frac{3}{n^2}$ **41.** 2.9×10^{10} **43.** 8.68×10^{-5} **45.** 6×10^4 **47.** $-2a^2b$ **49.** $3cd + c - d + 11$ **51.** $-18a^3 + 12a$ **53.** $x^2 - 4$ **55.** $2c^4 + 5c^2d + 2d^2$ **57.** $3y^2 - 10y + 8$ **59.** $2x^4 + 9x^2 + 4$ **61.** $0.7r^2 + 0.9rs - s^2$ **63.** $36p^2 - 12p + 1$ **65.** $16a^2 - 24ab + 9b^2$ **67.** $64 - a^2$ **69.** $16w^2 - 25$ **71.** $4b^4 - 49$ **73.** $a - 3$ **75.** $x - 2$ **77.** $n^2 + n + 1$ **79.** $2a^2 + a - 6 + \frac{-17}{2a - 3}$

Chapter Test, page 371

1. 2   **3.** -32 **5.** $-5ac^2$ **7.** $\frac{1}{8}$ **9.** $\frac{1}{y^5}$ **11.** $\frac{3}{x^4}$ **13.** 3.0×10^{-5} **15.** 1.52×10^2 **17.** 2×10^{-16} **19.** $4x - 5$ **21.** $x^2 - 8x + 16$ **23.** $-w^7$ **25.** $6b^2 - 3b$ **27.** $3y^2 - 7xy - 6x^2$ **29.** $y^2 - 16$ **31.** $x + 2$ **33.** $y + 3$

Additional Practice, page 372

1. -2 **3.** -10 **5.** 400   **7.** $-12x^2$ **9.** $18mn^4$ **11.** a^3b^{12} **13.** $\frac{a^5b^{15}}{c^{20}}$ **15.** ab^2 **17.** p^{2k+3} **19.** $\frac{1}{r^2}$ **21.** $\frac{1}{(ax)^4}$ **23.** 3.2×10^8 **25.** 6.52×10^{-5} **27.** $a^2 - 4a - 5$ **29.** $4y^2 - 81$ **31.** $36s^2 - \frac{1}{4}$ **33.** $y^2 - 4y$ **35.** Square; 1 square unit greater

Cumulative Maintenance, pages 373–375

1. c   **3.** b   **5.** b   **7.** c   **9.** c   **11.** d   **13.** a   **15.** c   **17.** c   **19.** c   **21.** c   **23.** a   **25.** b   **27.** d   **29.** Width: 5 ft; length: 7 ft   **31.** 375 pounds   **33.** 6 hours   **35.** 4%: $2000; 5%: $4000   **37.** 3000-pound cars: 15; 5000-pound cars: 3

Exercises, pages 378–379

1. prime **3.** Yes **5.** No **7.** Yes **9.** Yes **11.** No **13.** C **15.** P **17.** C **19.** C **21.** P **23.** P **25.** C **27.** P **29.** P **31.** $2^2 \cdot 3^2$ **33.** $3 \cdot 5$ **35.** 2^5 **37.** 7^2 **39.** $2^2 \cdot 7$ **41.** $2^2 \cdot 11$ **43.** 5^4 **45.** $2^3 \cdot 5^3$ **47.** $2^3 \cdot 3^2$ **49.** $2 \cdot 3$ **51.** $2 \cdot 5$ **53.** $3 \cdot 3$ **55.** $1 \cdot 11$ **57.** $\frac{1}{4} \cdot \frac{1}{4}$ **59.** $1 \cdot \frac{1}{2}$ **61.** 5 by 20; 10 by 10 **63.** No; $2^2 \cdot 3^3 \cdot 5^2 \cdot 7$ **65.** $3x + 4$ **67.** $x^2 - 9$ **69.** $4t^2 - 16$ **71.** $a < -1$

Review Capsule, page 380 See page 676.

Exercises, pages 382–383

1. 8 **3.** $3x$ **5.** $a + b^2$ **7.** $ab - 4bc + 2ac$ **9.** $x - y$ **11.** x **13.** b **15.** $x, 2y$ **17.** 3 **19.** 1, $3y$ **21.** 5 **23.** x **25.** $4a, 1$ **27.** 5 **29.** 1, $7y$ **31.** a, b **33.** $2, s$ **35.** $7(x + y)$ **37.** $4(2x - y)$ **39.** $x(3 - aw)$ **41.** $c(4 + a + b)$ **43.** $d(d + 2 + a)$ **45.** $5(x - 2y + 3z^2)$ **47.** $2\pi r(r + h)$ **49.** $cdh(h^2 + c + c^2dh)$ **51.** $(a + d)(b - c)$ **53.** $(a - s)(q - r)$ **55.** $(k + r)(p - n)$ **57.** $(x + y)(x - y)(2a + b)$ **59.** $7ab(a - 1)$ **61.** prime **63.** prime **65.** prime **67.** $7(2x^2 + xy + 3y^2)$ **69.** prime **71.** $3x(9x^3 + x^2 + 3a)$ **73.** $25x(y - 2z + 4)$ **75.** $x(3x + 6y - 2x^2)$ **77.** $21(1 - 2p)$ **79.** $4x(2x - 3y - 4z)$ **81.** $3x(x^2 - 5x - 2)$ **83.** $a^2(3 + 4a - 5a^2b)$ **85.** 2^4 **87.** $2^3 \cdot 5$ **89.** $2^2 \cdot 5^2$ **91.** $2x - 5 + \frac{3}{x + 4}$ **93.** $3x^2 + x - 4 + \frac{1}{x - 1}$ **95.** $n \geq 3$ **97.** $t \geq -2$ **99.** $y + 2$ **101.** $3z^n$

Review Capsule, page 383

1. $b^2 - 25$ **2.** $4a^2 - 1$ **3.** $9x^2 - 4$

Exercises, pages 385–386

1. Yes **3.** Yes **5.** No **7.** Yes **9.** $(y + 3)(y - 3)$ **11.** $(x + 5)(x - 5)$ **13.** $(2x + 3)(2x - 3)$ **15.** $4(2y + 3)(2y - 3)$ **17.** $(xy - a)(xy + a)$ **19.** $(3x^2y + b)(3x^2y - b)$ **21.** $(xy + z)(xy - z)$ **23.** prime **25.** $4(x^2 + 4y^2)$ **27.** $(5x + 7)(5x - 7)$ **29.** $a^2; 9; a^2 - 9; (a - 3)(a + 3)$ **31.** $\pi R^2 - 4\pi r^2; \pi(R + 2r)(R - 2r)$ **33.** $6(a - 2b)$ **35.** $c(a + b)$ **37.** $5(2 + t + t^2)$ **39.** C **41.** C **43.** C **45.** 40; 42 **47.** $(c + (a + b))(c - (a + b))$ **49.** $((r + s) + (t + u))((r + s) - (t + u))$ **51.** $(2(x - a) + 3(y + b))(2(x - a) - 3(y + b))$ **53.** He will have to buy 6 tires.

Review Capsule, page 386

1. $a^2 - 6a + 9$ **2.** $x^2 + 8x + 16$ **3.** $4x^2 - 20x + 25$ **4.** $81 + 18b + b^2$ **5.** $4a^2 + 20at + 25t^2$

6. $9p^4 - 12p^2 + 4$ **7.** $0.01 + 0.2z + z^2$ **8.** $\frac{1}{4} - bc + b^2c^2$

Exercises, pages 388–389

1. monomials **3.** Yes **5.** Yes **7.** Yes **9.** $2b$ **11.** 1 **13.** $3t$ **15.** 5 **17.** 5 **19.** $-$ **21.** $-$ **23.** $(x + 3)^2$ **25.** $(n + 7)^2$ **27.** $(2x + 3y)^2$ **29.** $(1 + 4x)^2$ **31.** $(a + 4)^2$ **33.** $(2x + 1)^2$ **35.** $(3y + 2)^2$ **37.** $(b - 3)^2$ **39.** $(3a - 2)^2$ **41.** $(7a - 6)^2$ **43.** $(x - 9)^2$ **45.** $(c + a + b)(c - a - b)$ **47.** $(4 + x - y)(4 - x + y)$ **49.** $(x - y + 4)(x - y - 4)$ **51.** 95 **53.** $4x + 12$

Exercises, page 391

1. 64 hybrid tall; 64 pure short **3.** 64 pure tall; 64 hybrid tall **5.** 14 pure rough coats; 28 hybrid rough coats; 14 pure smooth coats **7.** 28 pure rough coats; 28 hybrid rough coats

Review Capsule, page 392 See page 676.

Exercises, pages 393–395

1. 4, 3 **3.** 8, -3 **5.** $-3, -3$ **7.** $-6, -3$ **9.** $-8, 4$ **11.** 9, -8 **13.** $(x + 4)(x + 3)$ **15.** $(y + 5)(y + 3)$ **17.** $(a + 4)(a - 1)$ **19.** $(y + 8)(y - 1)$ **23.** $(x - 9)(x - 4)$ **27.** $(x - 9)(x + 8)$ **31.** $(x + 8)(x - 4)$ **33.** $(x - 7)(x - 3)$ **35.** $(x + 8)(x + 6)$ **37.** $(x + 8)(x + 1)$ **39.** $(x + 4)(x - 2)$ **41.** $(y - 11)(y - 6)$ **43.** $(y - 13)(y + 12)$ **45.** $(y + 12)(y - 6)$ **47.** $(10 + v)(2 + v)$ **49.** $(17 - k)(3 - k)$ **51.** $(r - 4t)(r - 2t)$ **53.** $(a - 12b)(a - 2b)$ **55.** $x + 3$ **57.** $(x + 13)(x - 13)$ **59.** $(x - 2)(x - 2)$ **61.** $(b - 12)^2$ **63.** $(3b - 7)(3b + 7)$ **65.** $(6 - 2y)(6 + 2y)$ **67.** $y > -2$ and $y < 4$ **69.** $a < 5$ or $a = 5$ **71.** $x > \frac{1}{2}$ and $x < 3$ **73.** -7 **75.** $((x + y) + 2)((x + y) + 3)$ **77.** $(x^2 + 5y^2)(x^2 + 2y^2)$

Review Capsule, page 395

1. $6x^2 + 17x + 12$ **2.** $3b^2 - 8b - 35$ **3.** $5y^2 - 2y - 16$ **4.** $25a^2 + 50ab + 21b^2$ **5.** $6a^2 - 7ab - 3b^2$ **6.** $7c^2 + 33cd - 10d^2$

Review, page 396

1. C **3.** C **5.** P **7.** $3^2 \cdot 5$ **9.** $2^3 \cdot 7$ **11.** $2 \cdot 5^3$ **13.** $5(a + 2b)$ **15.** $pr(r - p)$ **17.** Prime **19.** $(a - 2)(b + c)$ **21.** $(x + 2)(y + 2)$ **23.** $(a + 3)(a - 3)$ **25.** Prime **27.** $(xy - 3)(xy + 3)$ **29.** $(8 - a)^2$ **31.** $(x + 3)(x + 1)$ **33.** $(r - 6)(r + 2)$

1. x, $3x$ **3.** y, $6y$ or $2y$, $3y$ **5.** t, $9t$ or $3t$, $3t$
7. $(1, 2)$ **9.** $(1, -35)$, $(-1, 35)$ or $(5, -7)$, $(-5, 7)$
11. $(1, 10)$ or $(2, 5)$ **13.** d **15.** e **17.** c **19.** 7 **21.** 3
23. $8n$, $5n$ **25.** 7, 1 **27.** 1, 2 **29.** $(2x + 1)(x + 2)$
31. $(3y + 2)(3y - 1)$ **33.** $(3y - 4)(2y - 3)$
35. $(3x + 4)(2x - 1)$ **37.** $(5x - 1)(x - 3)$
39. $(3y + 7)(y - 1)$ **41.** $(2y + 5)(y + 1)$
43. $(3x - 2)(x - 3)$ **45.** $(3a + 5)(a - 5)$
47. $(4x - 3y)(2x - y)$ **49.** $(6 + 7y)(3 - 5y)$
51. $(2x + 3)(x + 2)$ **53.** $(4x - 7y)(3x - 2y)$
55. $(4a + 7b)^2$ **57.** $(8a + 7b)^2$ **59.** All
points to the right of 3 and to the left of -3, not
including 3 and -3 **61.** All points between, and not
including, -2 and 3 **63.** All points to the right, and
including, -2 **65.** $a(3a - 1)$ **67.** $(3x + 4)(2x - 1)$
69. $2(3y - 7)(y - 5)$ In Exercises 71–73 use the
pattern: $(1000 - 1) \times n = n$ thousand minus n.
71. $999 \times 6 = 6000 - 6$; $= 5994$ **73.** $6993 \div 999$
$= (7000 - 7) \div 999 = 7$ **75.** The wheels that are
turning clockwise are those on which the belt at the
top travels to the right. Three wheels are turning
clockwise.

Review Capsule, page 400

1. s **2.** 3 **3.** r **4.** $5x$ **5.** 9 **6.** $7a^2b$ **7.** 2 **8.** t

Exercises, pages 402–403

1. $3x$ **3.** $2a - 3b - 4c$ **5.** N **7.** P **9.** D **11.** P
13. $5(b + 6)(b - 2)$ **15.** $3(2x + 1)(x - 4)$
17. $2(3x + 2)(2x - 3)$ **19.** $3(x + y)(x - y)$
21. $3b(b - 1)$ **23.** $2m(m - 9)(m - 1)$
25. $2a(a + 1)(a - 1)$ **27.** $3(4m - 1)(m + 3)$
29. $3(x + 4)(x - 2)$ **31.** $2(x + 10)(x - 4)$
33. $2(t - 7)^2$ **35.** $x^2(x + 3)(x - 3)$
37. $2(a + 4)(a + 3)$ **39.** $s(t - 5)(t + 4)$
41. $3(x^2 + 4x + 15)$ **43.** $3t^2(2 - 5t)$
45. $a(b - 9)(b + 8)$ **47.** $(3a - 2)(a + 1)$
49. prime   **51.** $2(x - 4)(x - 3)$ **53.** $(7c + 5)^2$
55. $x(x + 1)(x - 1)$ **57.** $(1 + 2y)(1 - 2y)$
59. $(x + z)(2y + z - x)$ **61.** $(x + 4)(x - 4)(a + b)$
63. $[5r(r + 1) + 8](r - 6)$ **65.** $(x - y - 3)(x - y)$
67. $a = 4$ or $a = -2$ **69.** $y = 5$ or $y = -5$
71. $w = -10$ or $w = 2$
73. $(z + 2)(z - 2)(z + 9q)(z - 9q)$
75. $(x - 5)^2(x + 4)(x + 6)$ **77.** $4xy$
79. $(k + 1)(k + 1)(k - 1)$
81. $(t^2 + 2)(t + 1)(t - 1)$
83. $(h + a - 3)(h - a + 3)$ **85.** $(3a + 2)(a + 4)$
87. $(x + y + 3)(x + y - 3)[(x + y^2) - 7]$

89. Number the bags from 1 to 5. Since bags 1 and
2 contain 48 bulbs and bags 4 and 5 contain 41
bulbs, bag 3 contains 11 bulbs. Then bag 2 contains
$32 - 11$, or 21 bulbs, bag 1 contains $48 - 21$, or 27
bulbs, bag 4 contains $27 - 11$, or 16 bulbs, and bag
5 contains $41 - 16$, or 25 bulbs.

Review Capsule, page 404

1. $x = 4$ **2.** $y = -6$ **3.** $x = \frac{3}{2}$ **4.** $x = -\frac{5}{3}$ **5.** $3x^3$
6. $5y^5$ **7.** $2a^4$ **8.** $3t^2$

Exercises, pages 405–406

1. $x^2 + 3x - 4 = 0$ **3.** $x^2 - 4x - 32 = 0$
5. $9x^2 + 6x - 8 = 0$ **7.** $b = 0$ or $b = 1$
9. $q = 3$ or $q = 7$ **11.** $x = 2$ or $x = 3$
13. $x = -10$ or $x = 10$ **15.** $y = -7$ or $y = 0$
17. $a = -6$ or $a = 6$ **19.** $x = -5$ or $x = 5$
21. $y = -5$ or $y = -2$ **23.** $a = -\frac{2}{3}$ or $a = 4$
25. $x = 0$ or $x = 4$ **27.** $y = 0$ or $y = 8$
29. $a = -\frac{4}{5}$ or or $a = 1\frac{2}{3}$ **31.** $x = -2$ or $x = 2$
33. $x = -\frac{3}{5}$ or $x = 1$ **35.** $p = -6$ or $p = \frac{1}{4}$
37. $p = 0$ or $p = 4$ or $p = 9$ **39.** $z = -1$ or $z = 0$
or $z = \frac{1}{3}$ **41.** $a = -2$ or $a = -1$ or $a = 2$
43. $b = -4$ or $b = 3$ **45.** $x = -1$ or $x = 4$
47. $t = 1$ or $t = 6$ **49.** $x = 1$ or $x = 9$
51. $a = -2\frac{1}{2}$ or $a = 6\frac{1}{2}$ **53.** See the Solution Key.
55. $a = 3$ or $a = 4$ **57.** $z = 1$ or $z = 2$
59. $a = -2\frac{2}{3}$ or $a = 2$
61. $\dfrac{(6x + 5)(5x - 10)}{5x - 10} = \dfrac{30x^2 - 35x - 50}{5x - 10}$

Review Capsule, page 406

1. $12 - n$ **2.** $x + 15$ **3.** $3 + p$ **4.** $4m$ **5.** $\frac{y}{5}$
6. $q - 12.5$ **7.** $14a$ **8.** $\frac{b}{50}$

Exercises, pages 409–411

1. width: 6 m; length 24 m **3.** 13;14 **5.** 7, 5 **7.** 15,
14 or -14, -15 **9.** -8, -7 **11.** 9 or -8
13. width: 12 m; length: 16 m **15.** -5, -3 **17.** 11
19. 4   **21.** 100 square meters   **23.** 2 meters
25. width: 12 cm; length: 16 cm **27.** width: 60 ft;
length: 80 ft or width: 40 ft; length: 120 ft **29.** Mean:
7; Median: 4; Mode: 4 **31.** $m = 10$ **33.** $x = -6$
35. Since the number of buses used must transport
at least 250 people, $50x + 25y \geq 250$. Since only
four 50-passenger buses and six 25-passenger buses
are available, $x \leq 4$ and $y \leq 6$. Since neither x nor y
can be negative, $x \geq 0$ and $y \geq 0$. See the Solution
Key for the graph.

37. 20 ft; 50 ft　**39.** Solutions may vary. Use the guess and check method to use the clues. Clue 1: 21,340; Clue 2: 21,340; Clue 3: 23,410; Clue 4: 24,310

Focus on College Entrance Tests, page 412

1. a　**3.** a　**5.** b　**7.** d　**9.** a

Chapter Review, pages 413–415

1. 3^3　**3.** $2 \cdot 47$　**5.** $2^3 \cdot 3^2 \cdot 5$　**7.** 3, 5, 9, 15, 45
9. 2, 7, 14, 49, 98　**11.** $3(a - 2b)$　**13.** prime
15. $n(4 + m - n)$　**17.** $(3 + x)(3 - x)$
19. $(n - 1)(n + 1)$　**21.** $4(5 - 2x)(5 + 2x)$
23. $(mn - c)(mn + c)$　**25.** $(y - 5)(y - 5)$, or
$(y - 5)^2$　**27.** $(4x - 3)(4x - 3)$ or $(4x - 3)^2$
29. $(2m - n)(2m - n)$, or $(2m - n)^2$
31. $(a + 2)(a + 4)$　**33.** $(s - 5)(s + 2)$
35. $(y - 2)(y + 8)$　**37.** $(n + 9)(n - 4)$
39. $(t + 5s)(t - 3s)$　**41.** $(y - 2)(5y - 3)$
43. $(8x - 1)(x - 3)$　**45.** $(8n + 3)(2n - 1)$
47. $(8t - 5)(3t + 2)$　**49.** $2(h + 1)(h + 1)$, or
$2(h + 1)^2$　**51.** $4(p - 2)(p - 2)$, or $4(p - 2)^2$
53. $5(c - 5)(c + 5)$　**55.** $y(y + 4)(y - 2)$
57. $n^2(4n - 3)(2n + 3)$　**59.** $y = -4$ or $y = 0$
61. $b = -3$ or $b = 3$　**63.** $t = -12$ or $t = 2$
65. $y = -6$ or $y = 0$ or $y = 6$　**67.** 3, 4, 5　**69.** 22
71. 14

Chapter Test, page 415

1. $2^5 \cdot 3$　**3.** 13　**5.** $2^2 \cdot 5 \cdot 11$　**7.** $(3b - 1)(3b + 1)$
9. $(y + 3)(y + 8)$　**11.** $a^2b(b^2 - a)$
13. $(n + 8)(n - 7)$　**15.** $2(3b - 1)(b + 1)$
17. $(ab - 4c)(ab + 4c)$　**19.** $a(a - 3)(a + 2)$
21. $x = -5$ or $x = 3$　**23.** $p = -3$ or $p = 1$
25. width: 4 cm; length: 12 cm

Additional Practice, page 416

1. $3^2 \cdot 7$　**3.** $2^2 \cdot 3 \cdot 5$　**5.** $3 \cdot 5^3$　**7.** $3a(5 - 4a)$
9. $9a^2(1 - 2a)$　**11.** $(4m - 7n)(4m + 7n)$
13. $(x^5 - y)(x^5 + y)$　**15.** $(2x + 3)(2x + 3)$, or
$(2x + 3)^2$　**17.** $(x - 7)(x + 2)$　**19.** $(a + 4b)(a - 3b)$
21. $2(2x + 5)(x - 1)$　**23.** $5(x - 3)(x + 3)$
25. $2n(3n - 2)(3n + 1)$　**27.** $n = -4$ or $n = 6$
29. 10 rows, 24 chairs; 12 rows, 20 chairs; 15 rows, 16 chairs; 16 rows, 15 chairs; 20 rows, 12 chairs; 24 rows, 10 chairs　**31.** $(x - 9)$ units; $(x + 4)$ units

Cumulative Maintenance, pages 417–419

1. c　**3.** c　**5.** b　**7.** a　**9.** b　**11.** a　**13.** c　**15.** d
17. c　**19.** a　**21.** c　**23.** c　**25.** c　**27.** 36; 38
29. -8 and 7　**31.** 80　**33.** 18 pants; 4 jackets
35. 367.5 volts

Chapter 11: Rational Expressions

Exercises, pages 422–424

1. 5　**3.** 4　**5.** ab　**7.** $x + y$　**9.** $\frac{5}{4}$　**11.** xy　**13.** $\frac{2}{3}$
15. $\frac{a}{b}$　**17.** $\frac{4}{5y}$　**19.** $\frac{3x}{4}$　**21.** $\frac{4}{7}$　**23.** $\frac{1}{2}$　**25.** $\frac{8}{5(x + y)}$
27. $3(x - y)$　**29.** $\frac{(x - 6y)^2}{x}$　**31.** $\frac{5(a + b)}{2(2a + b)}$
33. $\frac{x - 2y}{3x + 4y}$　**35.** $\frac{b(2a + b)}{(a + b)(a - b)}$　**37.** 1　**39.** $\frac{1}{a + b}$
41. $\frac{1}{x + 1}$　**43.** $a + 1$　**45.** -1　**47.** $\frac{1}{9 - b}$
49. $-\frac{t - 1}{t + 1}$　**51.** $-\frac{1}{(n - k)^2}$　**53.** $2x$　**55.** $\frac{x + 2}{2(x - 4)}$
57. $\frac{6}{x - 3}$　**59.** $-3(a + 1)$　**61.** $\frac{R - r}{3}$　**63.** prime
65. $\frac{3(x + 3)}{x - 8}$　**67.** 3; 5　**69.** width: 12 m; length: 32 m
71. $a = 4$ or $a = -4$　**73.** $x = 0$ or $x = 7$
75. $a = 2$ or $a = 2\frac{1}{3}$　**77.** 5^{11}　**79.** 2^{13}　**81.** a^9
83. 2^5　**85.** $x + y - 1$　**87.** $a + b - 5$
89. $c + d - r - s$　**91.** The jar as half full after 59 minutes.

Review Capsule, page 424

1. $12n^2$　**2.** $2a^4b^4$　**3.** $-2c^{10}$　**4.** $-12x^3y^3z^8$　**5.** x^{10}
6. $\frac{1}{4b^2}$　**7.** $\frac{2rt^2}{5s}$　**8.** $\frac{x^3}{36}$　**9.** $\frac{9b^2}{2a^3}$　**10.** $\frac{36a}{7b^6}$　**11.** $6y$
12. $\frac{9x^2y^3}{4a^6b^6}$　**13.** $x^2y^2(3x - 2y)$
14. $(10z + 1)(10z - 1)$　**15.** $4x(2x + 1)(2x - 1)$
16. $9(t + 1)^2$　**17.** $(z - 9)(z + 2)$
18. $(4q - 1)(q + 3)$

Exercises, pages 426–428

1. $\frac{15}{28}$　**3.** $\frac{2}{5}$　**5.** $\frac{5}{9}$　**7.** $6a$　**9.** $\frac{m}{n}$　**11.** $\frac{c}{d}$　**13.** $\frac{1}{a^2by}$
15. $\frac{2z}{7y}$　**17.** 3　**19.** $\frac{4x^2 + 16x + 15}{2x - 5}$　**21.** 1
23. $\frac{n^2 + 6n + 9}{n + 5}$　**25.** $\frac{4xy}{1 + y}$　**27.** $\frac{n}{m}$　**29.** $\frac{a^2}{a^2 - a - 20}$
31. $\frac{x + 4}{x + 3}$　**33.** x　**35.** $x - 1$　**37.** $\frac{1}{x - 4}$
39. $\frac{x^2 - 2x}{x^2 - 3xy + 2y^2}$　**41.** $\frac{3}{4x^2 - y^2}$　**43.** $\frac{3x - 18}{x^2 - 7x + 10}$
45. $\frac{3(a + 3)(2a - 1)}{(a - 1)(2a^2 + 3a - 18)}$　**47.** $\frac{(x + 2)^2}{x^2 + 4x + 14}$
49. $\frac{(x - b)(b - 4)}{x + b}$　**51.** Width: 13 cm; length: 20 cm
53. c^4　**55.** 3^7　**57.** $8x^3$　**59.** 10^{13}　**61.** $\frac{2a + 3}{2a - 1}$
63. $\frac{1}{b}$　**65.** $-\frac{x}{2x + 7}$　**67.** There are three majorettes marching.

Review Capsule, page 428

1. 2　**2.** -25　**3.** $-\frac{1}{30}$　**4.** 3　**5.** 1　**6.** -32
7. -27　**8.** $\frac{7}{20}$

Exercises, pages 430–432

1. multiplicative inverse or reciprocal   3. $\dfrac{d}{c}$

5. $\dfrac{15b^2}{21a^2}$ 7. $\dfrac{1}{6x-3}$ 9. $\dfrac{5}{x}\cdot\dfrac{1}{y}$ 11. $\dfrac{abc^2}{xy}\cdot\dfrac{x}{a}$

13. $\dfrac{6a-7}{4}\cdot\dfrac{1}{3a-9}$ 15. 2   17. $\dfrac{1}{2}$ 19. $\dfrac{x}{3}$

21. $\dfrac{ad}{bc}$ 23. $\dfrac{b}{a^2}$ 25. $\dfrac{g}{f}$ 27. $\dfrac{1}{6a}$ 29. 1   31. $\dfrac{4}{9a}$

33. $\dfrac{x+1}{ax}$ 35. $\dfrac{a-b}{x+y}$ 37. $\dfrac{x+y}{2(x-y)}$ 39. $\dfrac{x+1}{3x}$

41. $\dfrac{a}{(a+b)^2}$ 43. $\dfrac{2}{3}$ 45. $\dfrac{b^2}{a}$ 47. $\dfrac{a^2b^3}{x^3}$ 49. x 51. $\dfrac{r^3}{t^3}$

53. x^{20} 55. $16b^{10}$ 57. $\dfrac{x^{27}}{y^{36}}$ 59. $\dfrac{a}{b}$

61. $\dfrac{yz^2(y-z-x)}{x^2(y-z)}$ 63. k 65. 9.875   67. 0.2

Exercises, pages 434–436

1. denominator   3. divisible   5. 3   7. a; a^2
9. x^2y; 2^2; y; 2; 5; y^3 11. 12   13. 30   15. 24
17. ab^2 19. $6a$ 21. $6xy$ 23. 24   25. 20   27. x^2y^2
29. $(x+y)(x-y)$ 31. $12a(a-2b)$ 33. $2(x+y)$
35. $(x-1)9x-2)(x-3)$ 37. $(x+2)(x-2)(x-4)$
39. $2(2x+3y)(2x-3y)$ 41. $(2b-3)(b+1)(3b+2)$ 43. y^3 45. $\dfrac{2}{(x+y)^2}$ 47. $\dfrac{rt}{4s}$ 49. x 51. $\dfrac{x}{(a+x)}$

53. $5x+4$ 55. $\dfrac{12a^2b^2}{a-b}$ 57. x 59. x^4 61. $\dfrac{c}{3}$
63. $-3s^3t^2$ 65. $(a+3)(a-2)(a-5)$ 67. $12(m-n)(m+n)$ 69. $(a-2)(2a+3)(2a-3)$ 71. 3 or 6

Review Capsule, page 436

1. $6r+4$ 2. $16xy+15$ 3. $3t-2$ 4. $5-5x^2y$
5. $14r-5m$ 6. $-3a-16b$

Exercises, pages 439–441

1. x; x 3. $3xy$; $3xy$ 5. $9x$ 7. $7x^2y^2$ 9. $\dfrac{16}{b}$ 11. $\dfrac{49}{q}$
13. $\dfrac{2a+17b-6}{3}$ 15. $\dfrac{10m+2}{3}$ 17. $\dfrac{15}{4}$
19. $\dfrac{-4a-13b}{12}$ 21. $\dfrac{m+n}{x-y}$ 23. $\dfrac{m}{2y+5}$ 25. $\dfrac{4x+15y}{6}$
27. $\dfrac{14ab-15a}{20}$ 29. $\dfrac{29x-27}{12}$ 31. $\dfrac{3a+2b}{ab}$
33. $\dfrac{4y-5x}{xy}$ 35. $\dfrac{13}{6c}$ 37. $\dfrac{7a-4b}{10p}$ 39. $\dfrac{3x+5}{x^2}$
41. $\dfrac{3x^2+2x+5}{x^3}$ 43. $\dfrac{8y+3}{xy}$ 45. $\dfrac{11}{6b}$ 47. $\dfrac{x+5}{2x}$
49. $\dfrac{2x-40}{(x+5)(x-5)}$ 51. $\dfrac{2x^2-xy+3y^2}{(x+y)(x-y)}$ 53. $\dfrac{2a+b}{3a-b}$
55. $\dfrac{5xy}{(2y-3)(3y-2)}$ 57. $\dfrac{17}{12}$ 59. $\dfrac{58}{35}$ 61. $\dfrac{c}{a}$ 63. $\dfrac{9y}{35z^2}$
65. 100,000   67. $\dfrac{4}{a^3}$ 69. 4.65×10^4 71. 2.005×10^5
73. 1.69×10^8 75. $\dfrac{a+1}{a+3}$ 77. $\dfrac{-2(2x^2-x-50)}{(x+5)(x-5)}$
79. $\dfrac{2x-2}{2x+3}$ 81. The train can pass through the tunnel in two minutes.

Review, page 442

1. $\dfrac{4}{7d}$ 3. $\dfrac{3}{x+y}$ 5. $\dfrac{a}{4}$ 7. $\dfrac{x^2+x-2}{x^2+5x}$ 9. $\dfrac{bx}{2a}$ 11. 33
13. $(x-4)(x+1)(x+2)$ 15. $\dfrac{3x+2y}{x^2y^2}$
17. $\dfrac{s-r^2-2rs-s^2}{r^2-s^2}$ 19. $\dfrac{2x-27}{x^2+x-12}$

Review Capsule, page 443

1. $-t^2+2t+4$ 2. b^2+2b+2 3. a^2-a-1
4. $4c+4d$ 5. $13a-22$ 6. $x^2-3x-15$
7. $9y+7z$ 8. $5r-2r^2+8$ 9. $t^2+5t-15$

Exercises, pages 444–446

1. mixed numbers   3. d; $4d$; $4d+1$ 5. $\dfrac{3a+1}{a}$
7. $\dfrac{3b+a}{b}$ 9. $\dfrac{7a-7b-4}{a-b}$ 11. $\dfrac{a^2+a+1}{a+1}$
13. $\dfrac{7r+9s}{r+s}$ 15. $\dfrac{11c-28}{c-3}$ 17. $\dfrac{ax^2+b}{x}$ 19. $\dfrac{ac-b}{c}$
21. $\dfrac{a^3+1}{a}$ 23. $\dfrac{3r-2r^2+18}{r^2-9}$ 25. $\dfrac{a^2+2a+2}{a+1}$
27. $\dfrac{14-18x}{3x-1}$ 29. $\dfrac{x^2-3x-15}{x+3}$ 31. $\dfrac{2t^2+7t-6}{t+6}$
33. $\dfrac{t^2+5t-15}{t-4}$ 35. $\dfrac{a^2+1}{a-2}$ 37. $\dfrac{x^2+4}{(x+2)(x-2)}$
39. $\dfrac{-4a-7c}{9}$ 41. $\dfrac{7m}{5y+3}$ 43. $\dfrac{d-c}{cd}$ 45. $\dfrac{11x^2y}{28d}$
47. 60   49. 24   51. m^2-n^2 53. $(a-2)(a+2)^2$
55. $-2n+2b$ 57. $20y-2$ 59. $14x^2-11$
61. $\dfrac{x^3-3x^2-13x+22}{x-5}$ 63. $\dfrac{x^4+11x-10}{(x+2)(x-2)}$ 65. $\dfrac{23}{7}$
67. $\dfrac{x-3}{x^2}$ 69. $\dfrac{6a}{3a-2}$ 71. $\dfrac{r^2+2r+1}{r^2-2r-1}$

Review Capsule, page 446

1. 6   2. -4 3. 1   4. 3   5. 7, 8   6. 4   7. 3, -9
8. $\dfrac{3}{2}$, $-\dfrac{3}{2}$ 9. 1, -3

Exercises, pages 449–451

1. LCD   3. $2n$ 5. $x-1$ 7. $2x$ 9. $a=24$
11. $a=15$ 13. $t=4$ 15. $x=\dfrac{2}{3}$ 17. $x=6$
19. $x=-\dfrac{1}{9}$ 21. $n=2$ 23. $n=2$ 25. $x=-\dfrac{1}{5}$
27. $x=-6$ 29. $x=10$ 31. $a=4$ 33. $x=-5$
35. $b=3$ 37. $x=-1$ 39. $x=23$
41. $x=-2\dfrac{1}{2}$ 43. $x=1$ 45. $x=-10$
47. $x=24$ 49. $x=13$ 51. $\dfrac{3x^2-x+y}{x}$
53. $\dfrac{13a+81}{a+7}$ 55. $\dfrac{m^2+2m+2}{m+1}$ 57. $-\dfrac{5m+14b}{15}$
59. $\dfrac{x-y}{3}$ 61. $-24x^2y+8xy^2$ 63. $y^2-2y-63$
65. $x=-6\dfrac{2}{3}$ 67. $a=-3$ 69. $k=6$
71. The correct numbers are 363 and 462.

Exercises, page 453

1. 1,660,032 in   3. 3456 in²   5. $\dfrac{1}{60}$ mi/s   7. 176 ft/s
9. $16.80

1. $<$ **3.** $<$ **5.** $>$ **7. a.** Let $x=$ number added; **b.** $\frac{3+x}{7+x}=\frac{3}{5}$ **9. a.** Let $x=$ smaller number, then $4x=$ larger number; **b.** $\frac{1}{x}-\frac{1}{4x}=\frac{3}{8}$ **11.** 4
13. 2, 10   **15.** 4   **17.** $\frac{1}{4}$ **19.** $2\frac{2}{3}$, $6\frac{2}{3}$ **21.** $\frac{3}{8}$, $\frac{5}{16}$
23. 3, 4   **25.** 5, 6   **27.** $\frac{5}{4}$ or $\frac{4}{5}$ **29.** $a^2-14a+49$
31. $4c^2-4cd+d^2$ **33.** $x^4-2x^2y^2+y^4$
35. $x^2y^4-18xy^2+81$ **37.** r^2-16
39. $9x^2-4b^2$ **41.** $\frac{1}{9}-9x^2$ **43.** $\frac{3}{4}$ or $-\frac{4}{3}$

Review Capsule, page 458
1. $d=1$ **2.** $d=\frac{2}{5}$ **3.** $t=2$ **4.** $x=7$
5. $x=-\frac{1}{8}$ **6.** $x=220$ **7.** $x=5$ **8.** $c=2$
9. $x=20$

Exercises, pages 460–462
1. $x-64$; 3; $2x$; $3(x-64)$ **3.** 435.2 km/h   **5.** 60 km   **7.** Rate going; 45 km/h; rate returning: 90 km/h   **9.** 30 km   **11.** 2 km/h   **13.** 420 km/h
15. 225 mi   **17.** 18 km/h   **19.** 3; 15   **21.** $\frac{12}{7}$; $\frac{8}{7}$
23. 30%   **25.** $x-4$ **27.** 2 km/h

Exercises, pages 466–467
1. $\frac{1}{5}$ **3.** $\frac{1}{3}$ **5.** $\frac{1}{5}+\frac{1}{3}$ or $\frac{8}{15}$ **7.** $\frac{x}{5}+\frac{x}{3}=1$ **9.** $1\frac{1}{3}$ days
11. $1\frac{41}{79}$ days   **13.** $2\frac{26}{47}$ days   **15.** $1\frac{3}{7}$ hours   **17.** $1\frac{1}{8}$ hours   **19.** $2\frac{1}{2}$ hours   **21.** $1\frac{1}{5}$ days   **23.** 4 mi/h
25. $\frac{5}{9}$; $\frac{10}{27}$ **27.** $-4x^2+5y^2$ **29.** 12 hours

Focus on College Entrance Tests, page 468
1. a **3.** d **5.** a

Chapter Review, pages 470–471
1. $\frac{3}{5}$ **3.** $\frac{x+y}{3(x-y)}$ **5.** $\frac{x}{x+2}$ **7.** -2 **9.** $\frac{x}{2}$ **11.** $\frac{3}{4}$
13. $\frac{x^2+3x}{x+1}$ **15.** $\frac{b}{2a}$ **17.** $\frac{2ab^2}{c^2}$ **19.** $\frac{x(a-b)}{a+b}$ **21.** 63
23. $9x^2y^2$ **25.** a^2-b^2 **27.** 1   **29.** $\frac{2a-b}{2ab}$
31. $\frac{a-5}{a^2+2a-3}$ **33.** $\frac{-x+y}{6x+6y}$ **35.** $\frac{3y+x}{y}$
37. $\frac{3x^2-2y}{3}$ **39.** $\frac{a^2}{a+b}$ **41.** $\frac{3x}{x-1}$ **43.** $n=18$
45. $x=2$ **47.** $a=-6$ or $a=2$ **49.** $x=5$
51. $a=-1$ or $a=2$ **53.** $y=-7$ or $y=4$
55. $\frac{1}{4},\frac{2}{3}$ **57.** Ruth: 60 km/h; Miriam: 75 km/h
59. 3 hours

Chapter Test, page 472
1. $\frac{4x}{3}$ **3.** $\frac{3x}{10}$ **5.** $\frac{1}{1+b}$ **7.** $\frac{2x+2y}{xy-y^2}$ **9.** $\frac{x-3y}{2(x+y)(x-y)}$

11. $\frac{a+4}{a+1}$ **13.** $\frac{2a^2-a+1}{4a^2}$ **15.** $y=1\frac{1}{8}$ or $y=3$
17. 8   **19.** Jan: 80 km/h; Karen: 75 km/h

Additional Practice, page 473
1. $\frac{3ab}{7}$ **3.** $\frac{1}{a-b}$ **5.** $\frac{x+y}{4x}$ **7.** $\frac{a+b}{2a+b}$ **9.** $\frac{12x+8y}{x}$
11. 2   **13.** $\frac{x^2-x-2}{x^3-x^2-6x}$ **15.** $\frac{x^2+x-1}{x+1}$ **17.** $y=18$
19. $n=31$ **21.** Kim: 60 km/h; Sue: 66 km/h   **23.** 9 days

Cumulative Maintenance, pages 474–475
1. c **3.** d **5.** c **7.** d **9.** a **11.** d **13.** a **15.** d
17. b   **19.** 7   **21.** Speed of boat in still water: 26 mph; speed of current: 6 mph   **23.** $4\frac{4}{11}$ hours

Chapter 12: Radicals

Exercises, pages 478–479
1. square root   **3.** principal square root   **5.** ± 8
7. $\pm\frac{5}{6}$ **9.** ± 100 **11.** 4   **13.** 7   **15.** ± 10 **17.** 100
19. -4 **21.** ± 100 **23.** $\frac{3}{7}$ **25.** $\pm\frac{5}{6}$ **27.** $-\frac{8}{5}$
29. $\frac{81}{100}$ **31.** 17   **33.** 25   **35.** $|b|$ **37.** $\pm|t^5|$
39. $c^2|d^3|$ **41.** $-h^4s^6$ **43.** $3|c|$ **45.** $-8|c^3|$
47. $\pm 5d^2$ **49.** $2|xy|$ **51.** 0.7   **53.** -1.5 **55.** $0.8|b|$
57. $\pm 2.5t^2$ **59.** $5r^4s^8t^6$ **61.** $-9a^6b^4d^8$
63. $\pm\frac{7t^2}{5|b^3|}$ **65.** $\frac{7a^2|b|}{3}$ **67.** $13|c^3|$ **69.** $4a^4$
71. $1\frac{7}{8}$ hours   **73.** Yes   **75.** No   **77.** P   **79.** C
81. P   **83.** 5   **85.** 5   **87.** d^2t^3 **89.** r^3st^2
91. $23d^4$ **93.** $21|t^3|$

Review Capsule, page 480
1. $0.\overline{5}$ **2.** $0.\overline{81}$ **3.** $0.\overline{39}$ **4.** $1.\overline{6}$ **5.** $4.1\overline{6}$ **6.** $0.\overline{3}$
7. 225   **8.** 2.25   **9.** 16   **10.** 0.16   **11.** $\frac{4}{9}$ **12.** $\frac{9}{16}$

Exercises, pages 482–483
1. rational   **3.** real numbers   **5.** no repeating pattern   **7.** rat.   **9.** rat.   **11.** irr.   **13.** rat.   **15.** rat.
17. irr.   **19.** rat.   **21.** irr.   **23.** irr.   **25.** rat.   **27.** irr.
29. rat.   **31.** rat.   **33.** irr.   **35.** irr. For Ex. 37–42, answers may vary.   **37.** $\frac{3}{8}$; $\frac{5}{16}$; $\frac{7}{16}$ **39.** $\frac{8}{6}$; $\frac{15}{12}$; $\frac{17}{12}$
41. 0.521; 0.5155; 0.5265   **43.** $\pm 3r^4s^3$ **45.** 25
47. $1\frac{1}{2}$ hours   **49.** $x(7-rs)$ **51.** $m(m+3+c)$
53. $x(8m-m+3)$ or $x(7m+3)$ **55.** $\frac{-5a}{6}$
57. $\frac{-7r}{40}$ **59.** $-12-2m$ **61.** 49 years

Review Capsule, page 483
1. $\frac{3}{10}$ **2.** $\frac{25}{100}$ or $\frac{1}{4}$ **3.** $\frac{-8}{1}$ **4.** $\frac{-35}{10}$ or $\frac{-7}{2}$ **5.** $\frac{10}{3}$
6. $-\frac{6}{5}$

Exercises, pages 485–487

1. terminating **3.** 1000 **5.** $8 < \sqrt{67} < 9$
7. $5 < \sqrt{27} < 6$ **9.** $11 < \sqrt{123} < 12$
11. $11 < \sqrt{136} < 12$ **13.** $7 < \sqrt{56} < 8$
15. $16 < \sqrt{260} < 17$ **17.** $100 < \sqrt{10{,}001} < 101$
19. $90 < \sqrt{8101} < 91$ **21.** $\frac{8}{9}$ **23.** $\frac{9}{11}$ **25.** $\frac{23}{99}$
27. $\frac{8}{27}$ **29.** $\frac{262}{999}$ **31.** $\frac{31}{9}$ **33.** $\frac{617}{99}$ **35.** $\frac{628}{99}$
37. $\frac{234}{55}$ **39.** $\frac{283}{100}$ **41.** 4.6 **43.** 5.1 **45.** 7.7 **47.** 9.2
49. 11.2 **51.** 11.5 **53.** 25.1 cm **55.** 3.0 m
57. width: 6.4 in; length: 32 in   For Ex. 59–65, the answers may vary depending on the computer used.
59. 2.23607 **61.** 5.09902 **63.** 6.48074 **65.** 3
67. rat. **69.** rat. **71.** irr. **73.** $-8t$ **75.** $-7|c^5|$
77. $(r - s^2)(r + s^2)$ **79.** Prime **81.** 29.6 **83.** 37.3
85. 16.4 **87.** 1.7 **89.** You might see 3 different things. **a.** A box with a cube in the rear corner; **b.** A box with a cube cut out of the front corner; **c.** A box with a cube attached outside the front corner

Review Capsule, page 488

1. $3c^2$ **2.** $-11y^5$ **3.** $-9r^4$ **4.** $-5x^3$ **5.** $7r^2$

Exercises, pages 489–490

1. perfect square **3.** 9 **5.** 100 **7.** 144×2
9. 49×2 **11.** 64×5 **13.** $2\sqrt{10}$ **15.** $2\sqrt{6}$
17. $7\sqrt{2}$ **19.** 4 **21.** 8 **23.** $2\sqrt{7}$ **25.** $4\sqrt{5}$
27. 28 **29.** $9\sqrt{2}$ **31.** $36\sqrt{2}$ **33.** -18
35. $-8\sqrt{2}$ **37.** $40\sqrt{2}$ **39.** 1,000 **41.** 1,000,000
43. 400,000 **45.** 100 **47.** $3t^3\sqrt{t}$ **49.** $5m^4\sqrt{m}$
51. $2c^3\sqrt{6c}$ **53.** $2r^2s^3\sqrt{3rs}$ **55.** $6c^4d^6\sqrt{2cd}$
57. 3.46 **59.** 6.71 **61.** 12.12 **63.** 13.86
65. 18.97 **67.** $\frac{1}{9}$ **69.** $\frac{8}{33}$ **71.** $\frac{407}{999}$ **73.** $\frac{17}{12}; \frac{31}{24}, \frac{37}{24}$
75. $(x - 2)^2$ **77.** $(4a + 5)^2$ **79.** $(-3 + 5x)^2$
81. $(x + y)\sqrt{3}$ **83.** $2(c^2 + d^2)\sqrt{7(c^2 + d^2)}$
85. $x + y$ **87.** He has 56 apples.

Review Capsule, page 490

1. 100 **2.** 225 **3.** 49 **4.** $a^2 - 2a + 1$
5. $a^2 + 2a + 1$ **6.** $4t^2 + 20t + 25$ **7.** 2 **8.** 5
9. 9 **10.** 16 **11.** 7 **12.** 25 **13.** 119
14. 207 **15.** 57 **16.** 148 **17.** ± 9 **18.** ± 6
19. ± 12 **20.** ± 11

Review, page 491

1. 8 **3.** $10|x|$ **5.** irr. **7.** rat. **9.** irr. **11.** 23.9
13. $1\frac{41}{72}$ **15.** width: 10.4 m; length: 20.8 m
17. $4\sqrt{5}$ **19.** $12d\sqrt{d}$

Exercises, page 493

1. 75 **3.** 20 miles per hour **5.** $-16°C$

Exercises, pages 496–498

1. right **3.** 5 inches **5.** 10 **7.** 15.7 **9.** 15.6
11. 12.0 **13.** 19.2 **15.** 6.1 **17.** 8.5 **19.** Yes
21. No **23.** Yes **25.** No **27.** No **29.** Yes
31. 9.9 km **33.** 36.7 ft **35.** 7.1 cm **37.** 60.7 ft
39. $2\sqrt{11}$ **41.** $4\sqrt{3}$ **43.** $4\sqrt{7}$ **45.** 9.1 **47.** 11.1
49. $(x + 9)(x + 7)$ **51.** $(a - 3)(a - 6)$
53. $(c + 9)(c - 4)$ **55.** 192 cm² **57.** A whole is equal to the sum of its parts. **59.** Substitution Property; $[2ab = 4(\frac{1}{2}ab)]$ **61.** $h = \sqrt{3}(\frac{s}{2})$
63. Use the theorem on page 495 that states if $a^2 + b^2 = c^2$, then the triangle is a right triangle.
$(2pq)^2 + (p^2 - q^2)^2 \overset{?}{=} (p^2 + a^2)^2$
$4p^2q^2 + p^4 - 2p^2q^2 + q^4 \overset{?}{=}$
$p^4 + 2p^2q^2 + q^4$
$p^4 + 2p^2q^2 + q^4 = p^4 + 2p^2q^2 + q^4$

Review Capsule, page 498

1. 8 **2.** 3 **3.** 2 **4.** 1 **5.** 10 **6.** 256 **7.** 169
8. 4 **9.** 144 **10.** 4 **11.** 17 **12.** 9 **13.** 13 **14.** 53

Exercises, pages 500–501

1. No. Robert used $\sqrt{(x_1 - y_1)^2 + (x_2 - y_2)^2}$ instead of $\sqrt{(x_2 - x_1)^2 + (y_2 - y_1)^2}$ **3.** 5 **5.** 10 **7.** 5
9. $5\sqrt{2}$ **11.** $\sqrt{41}$ **13.** 14 **15.** 13 **17.** 2 **19.** 25
21. $5 + \sqrt{37} + 3\sqrt{2}$ **23.** $6\sqrt{2}$ **25.** $8\sqrt{7}$
27. $4d^2\sqrt{2d}$ **29.** $(5y - 2)(y + 7)$
31.

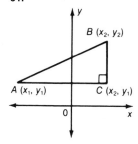

Triangle ABC is a right triangle, since AC is parallel to the x axis and BC is parallel to the y axis.
$[d(AB)]^2 = [d(AC)]^2 + [d(BC)]^2 =$
$|x_2 - x_1|^2 + |y_2 - y_1|^2 = (x_2 - x_1)^2 +$
$(y_2 - y_1)^2; d(AB) = \sqrt{(x_2 - x_1)^2 + (y_2 - y_1)^2}$

Review Capsule, page 502

1. $3\sqrt{2}$ **2.** $10\sqrt{3}$ **3.** $5\sqrt{2}$ **4.** $2\sqrt{2}$ **5.** $4\sqrt{2}$
6. $2\sqrt{3}$ **7.** $2\sqrt{6}$ **8.** $10\sqrt{10}$ **9.** 7 **10.** 3 **11.** 6
12. 2

Exercises, pages 503–504

1. 4; 4 **3.** 6; 48 **5.** $\sqrt{10}$ **7.** $\sqrt{14}$ **9.** $3\sqrt{2}$
11. $5\sqrt{2}$ **13.** 6 **15.** 6 **17.** $5\sqrt{3}$ **19.** 7 **21.** $2\sqrt{6}$
23. $4\sqrt{10}$ **25.** $15\sqrt{10}$ **27.** $28\sqrt{3}$ **29.** -168
31. $24\sqrt{15}$ **33.** $24\sqrt{42}$ **35.** $-63\sqrt{30}$ **37.** 46.5
39. 69.7 **41.** -32.9 **43.** 19.6 **45.** $a\sqrt{b}$
47. $4bc\sqrt{2}$ **49.** $3m^2n\sqrt{2m}$ **51.** $abc\sqrt{ac}$ **53.** 2
55. 4 **57.** 10 **59.** $2\sqrt[3]{3}$ **61.** 5 **63.** $\sqrt{97}$ **65.** 106
67. 40 feet **69.** $5(x-1)(x+4)$
71. $d(d+1)(d-1)$ **73.** $6(2y-1)(y-3)$
75. $-6a^3b$ **77.** $2xy^3\sqrt{x}$ **79.** $10k^2t^3$ **81.** The areas
are the same.

Review Capsule, page 504

1. $\frac{2}{5}$ **2.** $\frac{3}{4}$ **3.** $\frac{5}{7}$ **4.** $\frac{4}{9}$ **5.** $\frac{7}{10}$ **6.** $\frac{11}{5}$

Exercises, pages 507–509

1. radical **3.** Yes **5.** No **7.** No **9.** $\frac{\sqrt{3}}{7}$ **11.** $\frac{\sqrt{10}}{9}$
13. $\frac{\sqrt{7}}{5}$ **15.** $\frac{3\sqrt{6}}{10}$ **17.** $\frac{3\sqrt{3}}{4}$ **19.** $3\sqrt{2}$ **21.** $\frac{27\sqrt{3}}{13}$
23. $\frac{3\sqrt{5}}{5}$ **25.** $\frac{5\sqrt{2}}{2}$ **27.** $\frac{\sqrt{6}}{2}$ **29.** $\frac{2\sqrt{6}}{3}$ **31.** $\sqrt{6}$
33. $\frac{4\sqrt{10}}{5}$ **35.** $\frac{10\sqrt{14}}{7}$ **37.** $\frac{4\sqrt{3}}{3}$ **39.** $\frac{3\sqrt{3}}{2}$ **41.** $\frac{5\sqrt{6}}{6}$
43. $\frac{4\sqrt{a}}{a}$ **45.** $\frac{21\sqrt{2b}}{2b}$ **47.** $\frac{4\sqrt{2d}}{d}$ **49.** $\frac{2\sqrt{c}}{c^3}$ **51.** $\frac{\sqrt{7x}}{2x^3}$
53. $\sqrt{x}$ **55.** $2b$ **57.** $\frac{\sqrt{6}}{5}$ **59.** $\frac{\sqrt{21}}{8}$ **61.** $\frac{\sqrt{65}}{13}$
63. $\frac{3}{5}$ **65.** $\frac{\sqrt{31}}{2}$ **67.** $\frac{\sqrt{255}}{4}$ **69.** 6 **71.** $4\sqrt{3}$
73. 108 **75.** $-8\sqrt{15}$ **77.** 7 **79.** $\sqrt{5}$
81. $5a(a-1)$ **83.** $2(t+6)(t-6)$
85. $2(b^2+3b+1)$ **87.** $\sqrt{x+1}$ **89.** $\frac{\sqrt{y-2}}{y-2}$
91. The wire was missing 16 inches. **93.** Sally's
grandfather is 84 years old.

Review, page 509

1. 15 **3.** 3 **5.** 6 **7.** $x\sqrt{y}$ **9.** $\frac{2}{3}$ **11.** $\frac{\sqrt{10}}{5}$

Exercises, pages 511–513

1. $\sqrt{2}$, $2\sqrt{2}$ **3.** $7\sqrt{5}$, $5\sqrt{5}$ **5.** $\sqrt{2}$ **7.** $-9\sqrt{3}$
9. $14\sqrt{5}+9\sqrt{3}$ **11.** $5\sqrt{3}$ **13.** $-\sqrt{5}$ **15.** $35\sqrt{2}$
17. $10\sqrt{6}$ **19.** $\sqrt{6}+3\sqrt{2}$ **21.** $3+2\sqrt{3}$
23. $4\sqrt{6}-10\sqrt{2}$ **25.** 57 **27.** -75 **29.** $-\frac{2\sqrt{6}}{3}$
31. $-\frac{307\sqrt{2}}{210}$ **33.** $\frac{2\sqrt{3}-2\sqrt{19}+\sqrt{6}}{4}$ **35.** $6a\sqrt{ab}$
37. $9r\sqrt{3}$ **39.** $3xy\sqrt{xy}$ **41.** $1-\sqrt{2}$ **43.** $2\sqrt{3}-$
$5\sqrt{7}$ **45.** $-2+2\sqrt{2}$ **47.** $\frac{35+7\sqrt{3}}{22}$ **49.** $\frac{\sqrt{3}}{5}$
51. $\frac{2\sqrt{5}}{5}$ **53.** $\frac{3\sqrt{35}}{25}$ **55.** $3\sqrt{2}$ **57.** $-40\sqrt{2}$
59. width: 4 m; length: 6 m **61.** $\frac{23+7\sqrt{10}}{39}$

63. $\frac{3x-4\sqrt{x}+1}{x-1}$ **65.** $(a+\sqrt{10})(a-\sqrt{10})$
67. $5(x+\sqrt{5})(x-\sqrt{5})$ **69.** $(1+x\sqrt{2})(1-x\sqrt{2})$
71. $(a-\sqrt{5})^2$ **73.** When they meet, both planes
are the same distance from St. Louis.

Review Capsule, page 513

1. 5 **2.** 15 **3.** 11 **4.** 565 **5.** x **6.** $a-1$
7. $2b-1$ **8.** $9x$ **9.** $32b$ **10.** $25a-25$
11. Yes **12.** No **13.** No **14.** Yes **15.** No
16. Yes

Exercises, pages 515–517

1. variable **3.** Multiply both sides by $\frac{1}{3}$. **5.** Add -4
to both sides. **7.** $x=36$ **9.** $n=20$ **11.** $\frac{63}{5}$ or
$12\frac{3}{5}$ **13.** $x=5$ **15.** $x=14$ **17.** ϕ **19.** $x=\frac{4}{25}$
21. ϕ **23.** $y=81$ **25.** ϕ **27.** ϕ **29.** ϕ
31. $y=2$ **33.** $x=\frac{3}{4}$ **35.** 64 **37.** 22 **39.** $\frac{225}{16}$,
or $14\frac{1}{16}$ **41.** 2.2 m **43.** $s=625$ ft **45.** ϕ
47. $b\pm\sqrt{42}$ **49.** $a=2$ or $a=9$ **51.** $7\sqrt{3}-2\sqrt{2}$
53. 0 **55.** $(r+9)(r-6)$ **57.** $(x+10)^2$
59. $(7-a)(3-a)$ **61.** $b=7$ **63.** $q=2$ **65.** Yes;
squaring both sides of the second equation produces the first.

Review Capsule, page 517

1. x^7 **2.** a^7 **3.** c^3 **4.** 5^5 **5.** 10^7 **6.** x^4 **7.** x^6
8. x^6 **9.** x^9 **10.** $16b^6$ **11.** z^{12} **12.** $\frac{1}{4}z^2$ **13.** $64t^3$
14. $-64c^6$ **15.** $0.25d^2$

Exercises, pages 519–520

1. $7^{\frac{1}{2}}$ **3.** $5^{\frac{3}{2}}$ **5.** $9^{\frac{3}{4}}$ **7.** $\sqrt[3]{10}$ **9.** $\sqrt[3]{8^5}$ **11.** 3 **13.** 2
15. 3 **17.** 11 **19.** -6 **21.** $-\frac{1}{2}$ **23.** $-\frac{1}{3}$ **25.** 3
27. $\frac{2}{5}$ **29.** $-\frac{2}{5}$ **31.** 8 **33.** -3 **35.** 5 **37.** 2 **39.** 2
41. 8 **43.** -7 **45.** -5 **47.** $\frac{2}{5}$ **49.** $-\frac{1}{2}$ **51.** 81
53. 8 **55.** 343 **57.** $\sqrt[3]{-8}$ **59.** $\sqrt[6]{93}$ **61.** $\sqrt[3]{y}$
63. $\sqrt[3]{x^2}$ **65.** $\sqrt[3]{ab}$ **67.** -1 **69.** -2 **71.** 32
73. -27 **75.** -1 **77.** 25 **79.** 28 **81.** ϕ
83. $5\sqrt{5}$ **85.** 31 **87.** $(4-y)(4+y)$
89. $(9-5x)(9+5x)$ **91.** Use a simpler problem.
A 4-inch strip makes 4 squares with 3 cuts. Thus, a
48-inch strip makes 48 squares with $48-1$, or 47
cuts. Since each cut takes 1 second, it will take 47
seconds to make all the cuts.

Focus on College Entrance Tests, page 521

1. d **3.** d **5.** d

Chapter Review, pages 522–524

1. 11 **3.** $3|xy^3|$ **5.** rat. **7.** rat. **9.** irr. **11.** 0.4525
13. $7\frac{19}{20}$ **15.** $\frac{2}{11}$ **17.** $\frac{11}{27}$ **19.** 1.4 cm **21.** $24\sqrt{2}$
23. $-4ab^2\sqrt{ab}$ **25.** 7.1 **27.** 2.1 m **29.** 7
31. $2\sqrt{3}$ **33.** $2ab$ **35.** $\pm\frac{6}{5}$ **37.** $\frac{\sqrt{6y}}{2y^3}$ **39.** $\sqrt{7}$
41. $2x\sqrt{6}$ **43.** $\frac{12+3\sqrt{3}}{13}$ **45.** $-\frac{\sqrt{2}+2}{2}$ **47.** ϕ
49. 25 **51.** 10 **53.** 12 **55.** -100

Chapter Test, page 524

1. ± 10 **3.** $-6\sqrt{3}$ **5.** 9 **7.** rat. **9.** rat. **11.** 25
13. 5 **15.** $2\sqrt{10}$ **17.** $12\sqrt{2}$ **19.** $2n\sqrt{3}$
21. $x = 11$ **23.** 26 m

Additional Practice, page 525

1. -12 **3.** ± 19 **5.** $\frac{8}{9}$ **7.** $\frac{9}{11}$ **9.** $\frac{11}{37}$ **11.** $3\sqrt{6}$
13. $-12x\sqrt{5x}$ **15.** $30a^2b^2\sqrt{5b}$ **17.** 10 **19.** $6\sqrt{3}$
21. $2a\sqrt{7}$ **23.** $\frac{\sqrt{3}}{4}$ **25.** $\frac{\sqrt{3}}{2}$ **27.** $2x$ **29.** $-\sqrt{5}$
31. width: 5.5 m; length: 11 m **33.** 8.5 cm

Cumulative Maintenance, pages 526–527

1. d **3.** c **5.** b **7.** b **9.** d **11.** c **13.** a **15.** c
17. d **19.** 2.7 hours **21.** 10% sugar: 50 grams;
60% sugar: 200 grams **23.** 46 miles

Chapter 13: Quadratic Functions and Equations

Exercises, pages 530–531

1. -5 **3.** $x + \sqrt{5}$ **5.** $\{-\sqrt{5}, \sqrt{5}\}$ **7.** $x = \pm 4$
9. $x = \sqrt{11}$ **11.** $m = \pm 1$ **13.** $x = \pm 3$
15. $r = \pm 10$ **17.** $z = \pm 4\sqrt{2}$ **19.** $x = \pm\frac{1}{2}$
21. $b = \pm 11$ **23.** $m = \pm\sqrt{3}$ **25.** $z = \pm\frac{2}{3}$
27. $x = 2$ **29.** $x = -2$ or $x = 8$ **31.** $b = -3$ or
$b = 7$ **33.** $b = 3\frac{1}{4}$ or $b = -4\frac{3}{4}$ **35.** $x = \frac{1}{2}$ or
$x = 0$ **37.** $m = -\frac{3}{2}$ or $m = -\frac{5}{2}$ **39.** $y = \frac{5}{2}$ or
$y = -\frac{3}{2}$ **41.** $v = -2$ or $v = -5$ **43.** -2 **45.** $\frac{1}{7}$
47. 81 **49.** 34 **51.** $\frac{2a}{3}$ **53.** $\frac{a(r-s)}{b}$ **55.** 4
57. $x = -\sqrt{a+b}$ or $x = \sqrt{a+b}$
59. $x = -\sqrt{ab}$ or $x = \sqrt{ab}$ **61.** $x = -a - \sqrt{b}$
or $x = -a + \sqrt{b}$ **63.** $x = \frac{-a - \sqrt{b}}{2}$ or
$x = \frac{-a + \sqrt{b}}{2}$ **65.** The time required is 9 minutes.

Review Capsule, page 532

1. $(m - 2)^2$ **2.** NP **3.** NP **4.** $(t + 0.1)^2$
5. $(q - 0.3)^2$ **6.** $(p^3 - 6)^2$ **7.** $(r + \frac{1}{3})^2$ **8.** NP
9. $(b - \frac{7}{4})^2$ **10.** $(t - \frac{1}{6})^2$ **11.** $(a + \frac{3}{5})^2$ **12.** $(c + \frac{3}{8})^2$

Exercises, pages 534–535

1. 4 **3.** 16 **5.** $\frac{1}{4}$ **7.** $\frac{1}{16}$ **9.** $\frac{b^2}{4a^2}$ **11.** 16; $(y - 4)^2$
13. $\frac{1}{4}$; $(r - \frac{1}{2})^2$ **15.** 100; $(r - 10)^2$ **17.** $\frac{121}{4}$;
$(x - \frac{11}{2})^2$ **19.** $x = -6$ or $x = 2$ **21.** $n = -2$ or
$n = 4$ **23.** $a = -5$ or $a = 1$ **25.** $x = 5$ or $x = 7$
27. $x = 6$ or $x = 10$ **29.** $x = 2$ or $x = 5$
31. $n = -3$ or $n = -2$ **33.** $x = -3$ or $x = 2$
35. $y = -1$ or $y = 2$ **37.** $n = -\frac{1}{3}$ or $n = 1$
39. $x = -1\frac{1}{3}$ or $x = 2$ **41.** $p = -1\frac{1}{2}$ or $p = 3$
43. $a = -1\frac{1}{2}$ or $a = 4$ **45.** $a = \frac{-3 - \sqrt{145}}{4}$ or
$a = \frac{-3 + \sqrt{145}}{4}$ **47.** $x = 5$ or $x = -5$ **49.** $a = \sqrt{7}$
or $a = -\sqrt{7}$ **51.** $r = \frac{1}{3}$ or $r = -\frac{1}{3}$ **53.** $y = 10$
or $y = -4$ **55.** 10 **57.** -2 **59.** $\sqrt[5]{y}$ **61.** $\sqrt[3]{c^2}$
63. $\frac{7y^2}{3}$ **65.** 1 **67.** $x = 3 - \sqrt{13}$ or $x = 3 + \sqrt{13}$
69. $x = \frac{-b - \sqrt{b^2 - 4}}{2}$ or $x = \frac{-b + \sqrt{b^2 - 4}}{2}$
71. $x = -1$ or $x = 3$ **73.** $a = 1\frac{1}{3}$ or $a = 4$
75. $x = 4$ or $x = -2$

Exercises, page 537

1. ① $\frac{3}{2}$; ③ $\frac{5}{4}x$; $x^2 + \frac{5}{2}x$; $\frac{3}{2}$; ④ $\frac{25}{16}$; $\frac{3}{2} + \frac{25}{16} = \frac{49}{16}$; ⑤ $\frac{7}{4}$;
$\frac{2}{4}$, or $\frac{1}{2}$ **3.** $x = 1$ **5.** $x = 2$ **7.** $x = \frac{3}{2}$

Review Capsule, page 538

1. $3\sqrt{6}$ **2.** $-2\sqrt{6}$ **3.** $36\sqrt{3}$ **4.** $15\sqrt{2}$ **5.** $-8\sqrt{2}$
6. $35\sqrt{2}$ **7.** $-2\sqrt{2}$ **8.** $-6\sqrt{10}$ **9.** $-20\sqrt{2}$
10. $10\sqrt{11}$

Exercises, pages 540–541

1. $a = 1$; $b = -4$; $c = -5$ **3.** $a = 4$; $b = 12$;
$c = -7$ **5.** $a = 1$; $b = 3$; $c = -7$ **7.** $a = 3$;
$b = 0$; $c = -45$ **9.** $a = 5$; $b = -2$; $c = -1$
11. $x = -8$ or $x = 2$ **13.** $x = 0$ or $x = 3$
15. $n = -2$ or $n = 4$ **17.** $a = -1\frac{1}{2}$ or $a = -\frac{2}{3}$
19. $y = 1$ or $y = 1\frac{1}{2}$ **21.** $y = -4$ or $y = 1$
23. $b = -1\frac{1}{2}$ or $b = \frac{4}{5}$ **25.** $x = 1 - \sqrt{5}$ or
$x = 1 + \sqrt{5}$ **27.** $x = -2 - \sqrt{2}$ or $x = -2 + \sqrt{2}$
29. $x = \frac{1 - \sqrt{5}}{2}$ or $x = \frac{1 + \sqrt{5}}{2}$ **31.** $x = 1 - \frac{\sqrt{10}}{2}$
or $x = 1 + \frac{\sqrt{10}}{2}$ **33.** $x = -\frac{1}{3}$ or $x = 1$

35. $x = \frac{1}{4} - \frac{\sqrt{105}}{12}$ or $x = \frac{1}{4} + \frac{\sqrt{105}}{12}$

37. $x = \frac{7 - \sqrt{33}}{4}$ or $x = \frac{7 + \sqrt{33}}{4}$ **39.** $x = \frac{1 - \sqrt{22}}{3}$

or $x = \frac{1 + \sqrt{22}}{3}$ **41.** $n = \frac{1 - \sqrt{65}}{8}$ or $n = \frac{1 + \sqrt{65}}{8}$

43. $n = -\frac{2}{3}$ or $n = -\frac{1}{3}$ **45.** $a = \frac{3 - \sqrt{89}}{8}$ or

$a = \frac{3 + \sqrt{89}}{8}$ **47.** $d = \frac{-5 - \sqrt{7}}{6}$ or $d = \frac{-5 + \sqrt{7}}{6}$

49. $n = -0.5$ or $n = 1.2$ **51.** $a = -0.2$ or $a = 2.7$

53. $n = 0.3$ or $n = 1.9$ **55.** $x^2 + 5x - 7 = 0$;

1.14006; -6.14006 **57.** $4x^2 - 12x + 9 = 0$;

1.50049; 1.49951 **59.** $a = 3$ or $a = -15$

61. $n = \frac{2 - \sqrt{10}}{3}$ or $n = \frac{2 + \sqrt{10}}{3}$ **63.** $x = \frac{1 + \sqrt{181}}{10}$ or

$x = \frac{1 - \sqrt{181}}{10}$ **65.** $z = 2\sqrt{2} + 12$ or

$z = -2\sqrt{2} + 12$ **67.** $\frac{1}{28bc}$ **69.** $\frac{s - t}{x + y}$

71. $\left(\frac{-b + \sqrt{b^2 - 4ac}}{2a}\right)\left(\frac{-b - \sqrt{b^2 - 4ac}}{2a}\right)$ $=$

$\frac{b^2 - (\sqrt{b^2 - 4ac})^2}{4a^2}$ $=$ $\frac{b^2 - b^2 + 4ac}{4a^2}$ $=$ $\frac{4ac}{4a^2}$ $=$ $\frac{c}{a}$

73. Answers will vary. $x^2 + 4x - 1 = 0$; $2x^2 + 8x - 2 = 0$ **75.** They arrive at the same time.

Exercises, pages 544–545

1. a. Let w = width, then $w + 3$ = length;
b. $w(w + 3) = 40$ **3. a.** Let n = first integer,
then $n + 2$ = second integer; **b.** $n(n + 2) = 35$
5. a. Let n = number, then n^2 = square of number
b. $n^2 = 3n + 10$ **7.** 27 seats **9.** width: 5 cm;
length: 8 cm **11.** 8, or -7 **13.** length: 9 m;
width: 6 m **15.** $\frac{2}{3}$, or $\frac{1}{3}$ **17.** 10 cm
19. numerator: 3; denominator: 4; or numerator:
$-\frac{8}{5}$; denominator: $-\frac{3}{5}$ **21.** 3.39 meters
23. $x = \frac{-7 + \sqrt{69}}{2}$ or $x = \frac{-7 - \sqrt{69}}{2}$ **25.** $c = 0$
or $c = 4$ **27.** $y = -11 + \sqrt{122}$ or $y = -11 - \sqrt{122}$
29. $6ay$ **31.** $30abc$ **33.** 42 mi/h

Review, page 546

1. $x = -8$ or $x = 8$ **3.** $x = -2\sqrt{3}$ or $x = 2\sqrt{3}$
5. $x = 4$ **7.** $x = -3$ or $x = 5$ **9.** $n = -2$ or
$n = 4$ **11.** $t = -2$ or $t = 1\frac{1}{2}$ **13.** $a = -3$ or
$a = 7$ **15.** $y = -2$ or $y = 4$
17. $x = \frac{-2 - \sqrt{6}}{2}$ or $x = \frac{-2 + \sqrt{6}}{2}$ **19.** 12

Review Capsule, page 547

1. 12; 8; 6; 6; 8; 12 **2.** 79; 37; 11; 1; 7; 29

Exercises, pages 548–550

1. No **3.** Yes **5.** Yes **7.** No **9.** parabola For Exercises 11–22, the coordinates of seven points are
given. **11.** $(-8, 12), (-7, 5), (-6, 0), (-4, -4),$
$(-2, 0), (-1, 5), (0, 12)$ **13.** $(0, 8), (1, 3), (2, 0),$
$(3, -1), (4, 0), (5, 3), (6, 8)$ **15.** $(-3, 7), (-2, 0),$
$(0, -8), (1, -9), (2, -8), (4, 0), (5, 7)$ **17.** $(-5, 9),$
$(-4, 0), (-2, -12), (0, -16), (2, -12), (4, 0), (5, 9)$
19. $(-3, 6), (-2, 0), (0, -6), (\frac{1}{2}, -6\frac{1}{4}), (1, -6), (3, 0),$
$(4, 6)$ **21.** $(0, 8), (1, 3), (2, 0), (3, -1), (4, 0), (5, 3),$
$(6, 8)$ **23. a.** -4; **b.** -4 **25. a.** none;
b. none **27. a.** $-1\frac{1}{2}$ and 2; **b.** $-1\frac{1}{2}$ and 2
For Exercises 29–37, the zeros and the coordinates
of several points are given.
29. Zeros: -3 and 2; $(-4, 6), (-2, -4), (-\frac{1}{2}, -6\frac{1}{4}),$
$(1, -4), (3, 6)$ **31.** Zeros: -3 and 3; $(-4, 7),$
$(-1, -8), (0, -9), (1, -8), (4, 7)$ **33.** Zero: -1;
$(-4, 9), (-2, 1), (-1, 0), (0, 1), (2, 9)$ **35.** Zeros: -1
and 13; $(-2, -15), (3, 40), (6, 49), (9, 40), (14, -15)$
37. Zeros: -5 and 1; $(-6, -7), (-4, 5), (-2, 9),$
$(0, 5), (2, -7)$ **39.** 38 seats **41.** $n = \frac{-1 + \sqrt{51}}{10}$ or
$n = \frac{-1 - \sqrt{51}}{10}$ **43.** $a = \frac{5 + \sqrt{39}}{7}$ or $a = \frac{5 - \sqrt{39}}{7}$
45. $x = \frac{4 + \sqrt{37}}{3}$ or $x = \frac{4 - \sqrt{37}}{3}$ **47.** $\frac{-14x - 43}{20}$
49. $\frac{11s - 5}{3}$ **51.** $\frac{14y - 3m}{-2x^2}$ **53.** Zeros: $-\frac{2}{3}$ and 1;
$(-2, 12), (\frac{1}{6}, -2\frac{1}{12}), (2, 8)$ **55.** Zeros: $-\frac{3}{4}$ and $\frac{1}{2}$;
$(-2, 3\frac{1}{8}), (-\frac{1}{8}, -\frac{25}{64}), (2, 4\frac{1}{8})$ **57.** Zeros: $-2\frac{1}{2}$ and $1\frac{1}{2}$;
highest point: $(-\frac{1}{2}, 16)$

Review Capsule, page 550

1. rat. **2.** irr. **3.** rat. **4.** rat. **5.** irr. **6.** irr.
7. $a = -11$ or $a = 11$ **8.** $x = -\frac{3}{4}$ or $x = \frac{3}{4}$
9. $y = -\frac{2}{3}$ or $y = -\frac{1}{4}$ **10.** $b = \frac{1}{3}$ or $b = 3$
11. $d = -7$ or $d = -\frac{1}{4}$ **12.** $t = 2\frac{1}{2}$ **13.** $x = 5$
14. $b = 3 - 3\sqrt{2}$ or b $= 3 + 3\sqrt{2}$ **15.** $r = -\sqrt{5}$
or $r = \sqrt{5}$ **16.** $z = \frac{3 - \sqrt{29}}{10}$ or $z = \frac{3 + \sqrt{29}}{10}$
17. $q = \frac{3 - \sqrt{17}}{4}$ or $q = \frac{3 + \sqrt{17}}{4}$
18. $d = \frac{-7 - \sqrt{249}}{10}$ or $d = \frac{-7 + \sqrt{249}}{10}$

Exercises, pages 552–553

1. discriminant **3.** 1 **5.** 61 **7.** 0 **9.** -47 **11.** 36
13. -56 **15.** two real solutions **17.** two real
solutions **19.** one real solution **21.** one real solution

23. 10, −10   **25.** $k > -2\sqrt{3}$ or $k < -2\sqrt{3}$ **27.** 24,
16·   **29.** $\frac{7ab - 10}{7b}$ **31.** $\frac{b - bc + c}{c}$ **33.** one real solution   **35.** two real solutions

Exercises, pages 556–558
1. y **3.** maximum   **5.** minimum   **7.** maximum
9. maximum   **11. a.** $x = 0$; **b.** (0, 0)
13. a. $x = 0$; **b.** (0, 4)   **15. a.** $x = -4$;
b. $(-4, -9)$ **17. a.** $x = 1\frac{1}{2}$; **b.** $(1\frac{1}{2}, -2\frac{1}{4})$
19. a. $x = 1$; **b.** $(1, -1)$ **21. a.** $x = 0$;
b. (0, 1)   **23. a.** $x = -1$; **b.** $(-1, 9)$
25. a. $x = 1\frac{1}{2}$ **b.** $(1\frac{1}{2}, \frac{1}{4})$ The vertex is a minumum
in Exercises 11–19, and a maximum in Exercises
20–25.   **27.** 5   **29.** −25   **31.** 625 ft^2 **33.** second
width: x; length: $60 - 2x$ **35.** 450 ft^2 **37.** two
distinct, real solutions   **39.** one distinct, real
solution   **41.** two distinct, real solutions   **43.** −2
and 3   **45.** 4 and 5   **47.** −2 and 2   **49.** $x = 15$
51. $x = -8$ **53.** $x = 14$ **55.** maximum, or
minimum, $= [-\frac{b}{2a}, f(-\frac{b}{2a})]$ See the Solution Key for
the graphs for Exercises 56–57.   **57.** The parabola
moves down.   **59.** P represents 9, K represents 1,
and N represents 0.

Review Capsule, page 559
1. Above the line that contains (0, 2) and (−2, 0)
2. The closed half-plane above the line that contains
(0,5) and (5,0)   **3.** The closed half-plane below the
line that contains (0, −5) and (3,1)   **4.** Below the
line that contains (0, −3) and (−3, 0)   **5.** Above the
line that contains (0,−4) and (−1,−7)   **6.** Above the
line that contains (0,3) and (−2,11)

Exercises, pages 560–561
1. a. D; **b.** inside   **3. a.** S; **b.** outside   **5. a.** S;
b. outside   **7. a.** D; **b.** outside   For Exercises 9–24,
the coordinates of several points are given. D represents a dashed curve and S represents a solid
curve. The terms inside and outside indicate whether
the graph includes the region inside or outside the
curve.   **9.** (−2,4), (−1,1), (0,0), (1,1), (2,4); S; outside
11. (−2,8), (−1,5), (0,4), (1,5), (2,8); S; inside
13. (−2, −8), (−1, −2), (0,0), (1, −2), (2, −8); D; out-
side   **15.** (−1,4), (0,0), (1$\frac{1}{2}$, −2$\frac{1}{4}$), (3,0), (4,4); S; outside   **17.** (0,4), (1,1), (2,0), (3,1), (4,4); S; outside
19. (−2, −2), (−$\sqrt{2}$,0), (0,2), ($\sqrt{2}$,0), (2, −2); D; inside   **21.** (−4,0), (−3, −5), (−1, −9), (1, −5), (2,0);
D; inside   **23.** (−3, −3), (−$\sqrt{6}$,0), (3, −3), (0,6),
($\sqrt{6}$,0); S; outside

672   *Answers to Selected Exercises*

25.
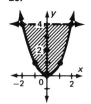

27.
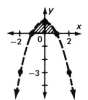

29.
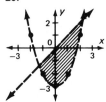

31.
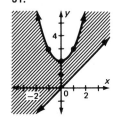

33.
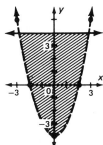

35.
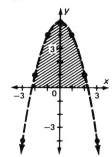

37. a. $x = 0$; **b.** (0,0); minimum
39. a. $x = 2$; **b.** (2, −9); minimum   **41.** 1 distinct,
real solution   **43.** 4
45. (0,0) is the
solution.

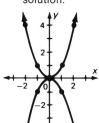

47.
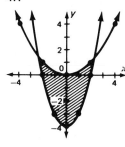

49. 3, 5 and 7, 8

Review Capsule, page 561
1. $P = 3r$ **2.** $r = kh$ **3.** $T = kh$ **4.** $d = kt$
5. $s = 210$ **6.** $p = 25$

1. Yes **3.** No **5.** No **7.** Yes **9.** decreases
11. y is halved **13.** Yes; corresponds to $xy = k$
15. No; does not correspond to $xy = k$ or $x = \frac{k}{y}$
17. No; does not correspond to $xy = k$ or $x = \frac{k}{y}$
19. Yes; corresponds to $x = \frac{k}{y}$ **21.** No; does not
correspond to $xy = k$ or $x = \frac{k}{y}$ **23.** No; does not
correspond to $xy = k$ or $x = \frac{k}{y}$ **25.** $xy = 42$
27. $xy = \frac{1}{2}$ **29.** $xy = 40$ **31.** $x = 4$ **33.** $r = 10$
35. $b = 1\frac{1}{2}$ **37.** 12 amps **39.** 6 people **41.** $2\frac{2}{5}$
hours **43.** 36 plants **45.** 192 tiles **47.** 24;
$yx^2 = 24$ **49.** 128; $yx^2 = 128$ **51.** -80;
$yx^2 = -80$ For Exercises 53–56, the coordinates
of several points are given. D represents a dashed
curve and S represents a solid curve. The terms
inside and outside indicate whether the graph
includes the region inside or outside the curve.
53. $(-1, -3)$, $(0,0)$, $(1,1)$, $(2,0)$, $(3,-3)$; D; outside
55. $(-2,-11)$, $(-1,-5)$, $(-\frac{3}{4}, -4\frac{1}{8})$, $(1, -5)$,
$(2, -11)$; S; inside **57. a.** $x = 0$; **b.** $(0,0)$;
maximum **59. a.** $x = -2$; **b.** $(-2, -4)$;
minimum **61.** $1\frac{1}{2}$ hours **63.** 1 meter **65.** $\frac{67}{176}$

Exercises, pages 568–569

1. $a = kbc$ **3.** $m = \frac{kn}{p}$ **5.** $s = \frac{kn}{r^2}$ **7.** $t = 216$
9. $x = 70$ **11.** $q = 8\frac{1}{6}$ **13.** $A = 20$ **15.** $m = 10$
17. 14 in^2 **19.** 28 cm^3 **21.** $R = 2.5$ **23.** 54 ohms
For Exercises 25–27, the coordinates of several
points are given. D represents a dashed curve and
S represents a solid curve. The terms inside and
outside indicate whether the graph includes the
region inside or outside the curve. **25.** $(-3,5)$,
$(-2,2)$, $(-1,1)$, $(0,2)$, $(1,5)$; D; inside **27.** $(-5,-5)$,
$(-4,-8)$, $(-3,-9)$, $(-2,-8)$, $(-1,-5)$; S; outside
29. $\frac{5}{xy}$

Focus on College Entrance Tests, page 570
1. b **3.** a **5.** a **7.** b

Chapter Review, pages 571–573
1. $x = -11$ or $x = 11$ **3.** $y = -3$ or $y = 3$
5. $t = -5$ or $t = -1$ **7.** $y = -\frac{2}{3}$ or $y = -\frac{1}{3}$
9. $x = 2\frac{3}{5}$ or $x = 3\frac{2}{5}$ **11.** $a = -1$ or $a = 7$
13. $x = -5$ or $x = 6$ **15.** $b = -2$ or $b = 5$

17. $x = 0$ or $x = 3$ **19.** $c = -\frac{1}{3}$ or $c = -\frac{2}{3}$
21. $y = \frac{7 - \sqrt{17}}{4}$ or $y = \frac{7 + \sqrt{17}}{4}$
23. 6 and 7 **25.** Width: 2.9 m; length: 3.9 m
27. The graph is a parabola, opening upward, with
vertex at $(1.5, -2.25)$ and y intercept at the origin;
zeros: 0,3 **29.** The graph is a parabola, opening
upward, with vertex at $(2.5, -2.25)$ and y intercept at
$(0,4)$; zeros: 1,4 **31.** The graph is a parabola,
opening downward, with vertex at $(3,0)$ and y
intercept at $(0, -9)$; zero: 3 **33.** two distinct, real
solutions **35.** two distinct, real solutions
37. no real solutions **39.** no real solutions
41. $xy = -108$ **43.** $xy = 96$ **45.** $xy = -7\frac{1}{2}$
47. 5 meters **49.** $c = 18$ **51.** $b = 480$

Chapter Test, page 573
1. $x = -2$ or $x = 2$ **3.** $x = -8$ or $x = 0$
5. $x = 3$ or $x = 6$ **7.** $y = -4$ or $y = 1$
9. $c = 2 - \sqrt{2}$ or $c = 2 + \sqrt{2}$ **11.** 2 **13.** no real
solution **15.** one distinct, real solution **17.** 10 m
19. $p = 2$

Additional Practice, page 574
1. $y = -9$ or $y = 9$ **3.** $x = -5\sqrt{3}$ or $x = 5\sqrt{3}$
5. $x = 0$ or $x = 6$ **7.** $x = -5$ or $x = 8$ **9.** $a = -1$
or $a = 1\frac{1}{2}$ **11.** Parabola opens upward; vertex:
$(-1,0)$; y intercept: $(0,1)$; zero: -1 **13.** two distinct,
real solutions. **15.** two distinct, real solutions
17. length: 12.7 m; width: 2.7 m **19.** hypotenuse:
65 m; legs: 25 m; 60 m

Cumulative Maintenance, pages 575–577
1. b **3.** b **5.** d **7.** c **9.** c **11.** d **13.** a **15.** d
17. b **19.** b **21.** d **23.** c **25.** b **27.** 15 miles
29. 3 miles per hour **31.** 87.5 ohms **33.** 30 seats

Chapter 14: Other Applications of Algebra

Exercises, pages 580–581
1. proportional **3.** $\frac{8}{4}$ **5.** $\frac{9}{n} = \frac{12}{8}$ **7.** 30 m **9.** 6.4
m **11.** 3.8 m **13.** 180

Review Capsule, page 582
1. 0.4286 **2.** 0.375 **3.** 0.4444 **4.** 0.7143 **5.** 1.1111
6. $x = 15.3999$ **7.** $w = 201.384$ **8.** $x = 21.4524$
9. $x = 4.6577$

Exercises, pages 584–586
1. adjacent **3.** tan $A = .7500$; tan $B = 1.3333$
5. tan $A = \frac{y}{x}$; tan $B = \frac{x}{y}$ **7.** .8391 **9.** 1.0000
11. 2.7475 **13.** .4663 **15.** 5.6713 **17.** 57.2900

19. 60° **21.** 31° **23.** 66° **25.** 1120 m **27.** 4.3
29. 482 ft **31.** 35 ft **33.** Find the length of $\overline{AC}$ and
the measure of $\angle A$. Then $\frac{BC}{AC}$ = tan A. **35.** Draw a
diagram. They are arranged as follows: Maria, Carol,
Luise, Glenn; or Glenn, Luise, Maria, Carol

Exercises, pages 589–590
1. RS **3.** T **5.** sin A = .3846; cos A = .9231
7. sin A = $\frac{y}{z}$; cos A = $\frac{x}{z}$ **9.** sin: .6691; cos: .7431
11. sin: .9925; cos: .1219 **13.** sin: .8746; cos: .4848
15. 23° **17.** 49° **19.** 85° **21.** 21° **23.** 58°
25. 89° **27.** decrease **29.** 8.8 m **31.** 10.6 m
33. 94.4 m **35.** 2.47485

Review, page 591
1. $6\frac{3}{4}$ **3.** .6249 **5.** 14.3007 **7.** 65° **9.** 52 m
11. .4540 **13.** 18° **15.** 74°

Exercises, pages 593–594
1. tan **3.** sin **5.** cos **7.** about 14 m high
9. about 19 cm **11.** about 3883 m **13.** Answers
will vary. **15.** Answers will vary. One answer is
shown below.

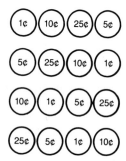

Exercises, pages 598–599
1. finite set **3.** 1 + 1 = 2; 1 + 2 = 3; 1 + 3 = 0;
2 + 2 = 0; 2 + 3 = 1; 3 + 1 = 0; 3 + 2 = 1 **5.** No;
each element does not have a multiplicative inverse;
there is no number by which to multiply 0 or 2 to get
the identity number, 1. **7.** 1 × 1 = 1; 1 × 3 = 3;
1 × 4 = 4; 1 × 5 = 5; 2 × 1 = 2; 2 × 2 = 4;
2 × 3 = 0; 2 × 4 = 2; 2 × 5 = 4; 3 × 1 = 3;
3 × 2 = 0; 3 × 3 = 3; 3 × 5 = 3; 4 × 2 = 2;
4 × 3 = 0; 4 × 4 = 4; 5 × 1 = 5; 5 × 3 = 3;
5 × 4 = 2 **9.** Yes; a "two-hour clock" is a field
11. 1 × 1 = 1; 1 × 2 = 2; 2 × 1 = 2; 2 × 2 = 1
13. Yes **15.** The total cost was $8.70.

Exercises, pages 602–603
1. conditional **3.** compound **5.** If you have no
more than 2 errors, then you do not get an A. **7.** If
I drive over the speed limit, then I do not break the
law. **9.** False **11.** True **13.** True **15.** If 15 is not
a real number, then 15 is not a rational number; if
15 is not a real number, then 15 is a rational number;
If 15 is a real number, then 15 is a rational number.
17. If I get tired, then I work hard. **19.** If Q has
exactly 3 sides and 3 angles, then Q is a triangle.
21. Conditional: If a number is an irrational number,
then it cannot be expressed as the ratio of an integer
and a natural number. Converse: If a number cannot
be expressed as the ratio of an integer and a natural
number, then it is an irrational number.
23. Conditional: If an angle is an obtuse angle, then
its measure is greater than 90° and less than 180°.
Converse: If the measure of an angle is greater than
90° and less than 180°, then the angle is an obtuse
angle. **25.** Conditional: If two equations are eqival-
ent, then they have the same solution set. Converse:
If two equations have the same solution set, then
they are equivalent. **27.** Conditional: If a polynomial is a binomial, then it has two terms. Converse:
If a polynomial has two terms, then it is a binomial.
29. If Paula is in Atlanta, then Ralph is in school.
31. If Ralph is in school, then Sue is at home. **33.** If
Paula is not in Atlanta, then Ralph is not in school.
35. Make a list. There are a total of 24 ways.

Exercises, pages 605–606
1. hypothesis; conclusion For Exercises 3–28, the
Reason appears in parentheses following each
Statement. **3.** Hypothesis: x is any number. Conclusion: $2x + 3x = 5x$ Proof: 1. x is any number. (Given)
2. $2x + 3x = (2 + 3)x$ (Dist. post.) 3. $(2 + 3)x = 5x$
(Addition) 4. $2x + 3x = 5x$ (Substitution)
5. Hypothesis: x and y are any numbers. Conclusion:
$3x + (5y + 7x) = 10x + 5y$ Proof: 1. x and y are any
numbers. (Given) 2. $3x + (5y + 7x) = 3x +$
$(7x + 5y)$ (Comm. post. for add.) 3. $3x +$
$(7x + 5y) = (3x + 7x) + 5y$ (Assoc. post. for add.)
4. $(3x + 7x) + 5y = 10x + 5y$ (Add. of like terms)
5. $3x + (5y + 7x) = 10x + 5y$ (Substitution)
7. Hypothesis: a is any number. Conclusion:
$(-2a)(-3a) = 6a^2$ Proof: 1. a is any number.
(Given) 2. $(-2a)(-3a) = (-2 \cdot -3)(a \cdot a)$ (Assoc. and
comm. post. for mult.) 3. $(-2 \cdot -3)(a \cdot a) = 6(a \cdot a)$
(mult. of like signs) 4. $6(a \cdot a) = 6a^2$ (Def. of
exponents) 5. $(-2a)(-3a) = 6a^2$ (Substitution)

674 *Answers to Selected Exercises*

9. Hypothesis: x is any number. Conclusion: $(x + 3)(x + 4) = x^2 + 7x + 12$ Proof: 1. x is any number. (Given) 2. $(x + 3)(x + 4) = (x + 3)x + (x + 3)4$ (Dist. post.) 3. $(x + 3)x + (x + 3)4 = x(x) + 3(x) + x(4) + 3(4)$ (Dist. post.) 4. $x(x) + 3(x) + x(4) + 3(4) = x^2 + 3(x) + x(4) + 3(4)$ (Def. of exponents) 5. $x^2 + 3(x) + x(4) + 3(4) = x^2 + (3x + 4x) + 3(4)$ (Comm. and assoc. post. for mult.) 6. $x^2 + (3x + 4x) + 3(4) = x^2 + 7x + 3(4)$ (Add. of like terms) 7. $x^2 + 7x + 3(4) = x^2 + 7x + 12$ (Multiplication) 8. $(x + 3)(x + 4) = x^2 + 7x + 12$ (Substitution)

11. Hypothesis: x is an even number. Conclusion: x^2 is an even number. Proof: 1. x is an even number. (Given) 2. Let $x = 2n$. Then $x^2 = (2n)^2$ where n is an integer. (Def. of an even number.) 3. $(2n)^2 = (2n)(2n)$ (Def. of exponents) 4. $(2n)(2n) = 2(n \cdot 2n)$ (Assoc. post. for mult.) 5. $2(n \cdot 2n) = 2(2n^2)$ (Comm. post. for mult.; Def. of exp.) 6. $2n^2$ is an integer (Closure post. for mult.) 7. $2(2n^2)$ is even (Def. of even numbers) 8. x^2 is even (Substitution)

13. Hypothesis: a and b are even numbers. Conclusion: $a + b$ is an even number. Proof: 1. a and b are even. (Given) 2. Let $a = 2n$, $b = 2k$. Then $a + b = 2n + 2k$ (n and k are integers) (Def. of even number) 3. $2n + 2k = 2(n + k)$ (Dist. post.) 4. $n + k$ is an integer (Closure post. for add.) 5. $2(n + k)$ is an even number (Def. of even number) 6. $a + b$ is an even number (Substitution)

15. Hypothesis: a and b are any odd numbers. Conclusion: ab is odd Proof: 1. a and b are odd (Given) 2. Let $a = 2k + 1$, $b = 2p + 1$ (k and p are integers.) Then $a \cdot b = (2k + 1)(2p + 1)$ (Def. of odd number) 3. $(2k + 1)(2p + 1) = 4kp + 2k + 2p + 1$ (Mult. of binomials) 4. $4kp + 2k + 2p + 1 = 2(2kp + k + p) + 1$ (Dist. post.) 5. $2kp + k + p$ is an integer (Closure post. for add. and mult.) 6. $2(2kp + k + p) + 1$ is an odd number (Def. of odd number) 7. ab is odd (Substitution)

17. Hypothesis: a is any odd number. b is any even number. Conclusion: ab is even Proof: 1. a is odd, b is even (Given) 2. Let $a = 2k + 1$, $b = 2p$. Then $ab = 2p(2k + 1)$. (k and p are integers) (Def. of even and odd numbers) 3. $2p(2k + 1) = 2[p(2k + 1)]$ (Assoc. post. for mult.) 4. $2[p(2k + 1)] = 2(2kp + p)$ (Dist. post.) 5. $2kp + p$ is an integer (Closure post. for add. and mult.) 6. $2(kp + p)$ is an even number (Def. of even number) 7. ab is an even number (Substitution)

19. Hypothesis: a and b are multiples of 3. Conclusion: ab is a multiple of 3 Proof: 1. a and b are mult.

of 3 (Given) 2. Let $a = 3n$, $b = 3k$, where n and k are integers. Then $ab = (3n)(3k)$. (Def. of mult. of 3) 3. $(3n)(3k) = 3(n \cdot 3k)$ (Assoc. post. for mult.) 4. $3(n \cdot 3k) = 3(3kn)$ (Comm. post.) 5. $3kn$ is an integer (Closure post. for mult.) 6. $3(3kn)$ is a mult. of 3 (Def. of mult. of 3) 7. ab is a mult. of 3 (Substitution)

21. Hypothesis: a is divisible by 6. Conclusion: a is divisible by 2 Proof: 1. a is divisible by 6. (Given) 2. Let $a = 6k$, where k is an integer (If a is divisible by 6, then 6 is a factor of a.) 3. $6k = (2 \cdot 3)k$ (Factors of 6) 4. $(2 \cdot 3)k = 2(3 \cdot k)$ (Assoc. post. for mult.) 5. $3k$ is an integer (Closure post. for mult.) 6. $2(3k)$ is divisible by 2 (Even numbers are divisible by 2) 7. a is divisible by 2 (Substitution)

23. Hypothesis: a and b are any multiples of 5. Conclusion: ab is a multiple of 5 Proof: 1 a and b are mult. of 5 (Given) 2. Let $a = 5n$, $b = 5k$, where n and k are integers. Then $ab = (5n)(5k)$ (Def. of mult. of 5) 3. $(5n)(5k) = 5(n \cdot 5k)$ (Assoc. post. for mult.) 4. $5(n \cdot 5k) = 5(5nk)$ (Comm. post.) 5. $5nk$ is an integer (Closure post. for mult.) 6. $5(5nk)$ is a mult. of 5 (Def. of mult. of 5) 7. ab is a mult. of 5 (Substitution)

25. Hypothesis: a is an odd number. Conclusion: a^3 is an odd number. Proof: 1. a is an odd number (Given) 2. Let $a = 2n + 1$, where n is an integer. Then $a^3 = (2n + 1)^3$ (Def. of odd number) 3. $(2n + 1)^3 = (2n + 1)^2 (2n + 1)$ (Factoring) 4. $(2n + 1)^2$ is an odd number (See Exercise 12.) 5. $(2n + 1)^2 (2n + 1)$ is an odd number (See Exercise 15.) 6. a^3 is an odd number (Substitution principle)

27. Hypothesis: x is any even number; y is any odd number. Conclusion: $(x + y)^2 + y$ is an even number Proof: 1. x is an even number; y is an odd number (Given) 2. $x + y$ is an odd number (See Exercise 14.) 3. $(x + y)^2$ is an odd number (See Exercise 12.) 4. $(x + y)^2 + y$ is an even number (See Example 2, p. 605.) **29.** Mike should pick 3 socks.

Chapter Review, pages 607–608
1. $HS = 18$; $QS = 21$ **3.** $\frac{5}{12}$ **5.** $\frac{5}{13}$ **7.** $\frac{12}{13}$ **9.** $x = 7.3$; $y = 6.8$ **11.** 60° **13.** 46° **15.** No; 2 has no multiplicative inverse. **17.** If I use an umbrella, then it is not raining **19.** If 6 is a factor of 24, then 6 is a factor of 12; If 6 is a factor of 24, then 6 is not a factor of 12. **21.** Hypothesis: x is any number. Conclusion: $(3x^2)(-7x^3) = -21x^5$ Proof: 1. x is any number (Given) 2. $(3x^2)(-7x^3) = (3 \cdot -7)(x^2 \cdot x^3)$ (Assoc. and Comm. Post.)

3. $(3 \cdot -7)$ $(x^2 \cdot x^3)$ = $-21(x^2 \cdot x^3)$ (Multiplication: unlike signs) 4. $-21(x^2 \cdot x^3)$ = $-21x^5$ (Product Prop. of Powers) 5. $(3x^2)$ $(-7x^3)$ = $-21x^5$ (Substitution)

Chapter Test, p. 609
1. 12   3. $\frac{3}{5}$ 5. $\frac{4}{5}$ 7. $\frac{4}{5}$ 9. 52.2 m   11. If today is Saturday, then Saturday is the last day of the week. 13. 10. If 5 is a rational number, then 5 is a whole number; True 11. If Saturday is the last day of the week, then today is Saturday; False 12. If a figure is a rectangle, then the figure is a square; False 15. Hypothesis: x is any number. Conclusion: $5(x + 2) = 10x + 5x$ Proof: 1. $5(x + 2)$ (Given) 2. $5(x + 2) = 5(2 + x)$ (Comm. post.) 3. $5(2 + x) = 10 + 5x$ (Dist. post.) 4. $5(x + 2) = 10 + 5x$ (Substitution)

Review Capsule, page 380
1. $3x + 12$ 2. $-2a - 2b$ 3. $-10s - 5t$ 4. $24 + 6y$ 5. $ab + ac$ 6. $yw - yz$ 7. $3ab - abc$ 8. $cdp + cdr$

Review Capsule, page 392
1. $a^2 + 3a + 2$ 2. $x^2 - 5x + 6$ 3. $y^2 + y - 12$ 4. $10 - 3t - t^2$ 5. $y^2 - 3yz - 10z^2$ 6. $d^2 + 3dg - 88g^2$

INDEX

Boldfaced *numerals indicate the pages that contain formal or informal definitions.*

Property
  addition, for equations, 95-96
  addition, for inequalities, 283-84
  additive inverse, 58
  associative, 30-31
  completeness, 30
  commutative, 30-31
  density, 482
  distributive, 34-35
  division, for square roots, 505
  fundamental, of arithmetic, 378
  identity, 31
  multiplication, for equations, 99-100
  multiplication, for inequalities, 287-88
  of the power of a power, 332-33
  of the power of a product, 332-33
  of proportions, 104
  product, of radicals, 488
  product, of powers, 329-30
  quotient, of powers, 335
  reflexive, 35
  substitution, 65
  symmetric, 35
  transitive, 35
  unique factorization, 378
Proportions(s), **103**-04
  applications, 103-04
  extremes, 104
  means, 104
  property of, 104
  terms of, 104
Pyramid, 17
Pythagorean Theorem, **494**-96
  applications, 497

Quadrant, 175-76
Quadratic equations, **529**-30
  applications, 542-43
  calculator applications, 539
  computer applications, 541, 621, 632-35
  decimal approximation, 539
  nature of solutions, 552
  solving by completing the square, 532-34, 536
  solving by factoring, 529
  solving by the quadratic formula, 538-40
  solving by using square roots, 529-30
Quadratic formula, **538**-40
  calculator application, 539
  computer application, 541, 621
  discriminant, 551-52
  nature of solutions, 552

Quadratic functions, **547**-48
  graph of, 547-48
    computer applications, 632, 633, 634
  zeros of, 548
    calculator applications, 548
Quadratic inequalities, 559-60

Radical(s), 477
  addition of, 510-11
  conjugates, 511
  division of, 505-07
  equations, **514**-15
  like, 510
  multiplication of, 502-03
    calculator applications, 503
  product property, **488**
  rationalizing the denominator, 506
  simplifying, **488**
  simplest form, **488**, 505
  subtraction of, 510-11
  symbol, 477
Radicand, **477**
Range, **181**
Ratio, **103**-04, 207
  trigonometric, 583
Rational exponent, **329**, 518-19
  calculator applications, 519
Rational expressions, **421**-22
  addition of, 437-39
  calculator applications, 503, 519
  computer applications, 441, 619
  division of, 429-30
  equations with, 447-49
  least common denominator, 433-34
  mixed expressions, 443-44
  multiplication of, 425-26
  simplest form, 421
  subtraction of, 437-39
Rational numbers, 26-27
Rationalizing the denominator, **506**
Real number(s), **30**-31, 480-82
Reciprocal, **79**, 455
Reflexive property, **35**
Regular price, **133**
Relation(s), **180**-82
Replacement set, **22**-23
Right angle, **494**
Right triangle, 494
Root (see Solution)

Sale price, 133
Scatter plot, 192, 623
Scientific notation, **343**-44

  applications, 345-46
Sentence
  compound, 295-96
  mathematical, 22
  open, 22-23, 302-03
Set
  empty, 23, 150
  finite, 595
  intersection of, 296
  of counting numbers, 26
  of integers, 26
  of rational numbers, 26-27
  of real numbers, 30-31, 480-82
  of whole numbers, 26
  replacement, 22-23
  solution, 22-23
  union of, 295
Similar triangles, **579**-80
  applications, 581
Simplest form (of a rational expression), **421**
Simultaneous linear equations (see System of equations)
Sine, **587**-89
  applications, 590, 592-93
Slope, **207**-08
  used to write linear equations, 216-17
Slope-intercept form of a linear equation, **212**-13
  computer applications, 628
Solution(s)
  apparent, 448, 515
  of an equation, 95
  of an inequality, 23
  of a quadratic equation, 538-40
    calculator applications, 539
  of a system of linear equations, 243
  of a system of inequalities, 309-10
  set, **22**-23
Solve a simpler problem, 130, 152-53, 538
Solving equations, 95
  addition property, 95-96
  multiplication property, 99-100
  ratio and proportion, 103-04
  for a variable, 159
  more than one step, 118-19
  variable on both sides, 149-50
Solving linear equations, 243
  by addition method, 252-53
  by multiplication/addition method, 256-57
  by substitution method, 249-50

682 *Index*